THE CAMBRIDGE HISTORY OF
STRATEGY

*

VOLUME II

From the Napoleonic Wars to the Present

Volume II of *The Cambridge History of Strategy* focuses on the practice of strategy from 1800 to the present day. A team of eminent scholars examine how leaders of states, empires and non-state groups (such as guerrilla forces, rebel groups and terrorists) have attempted to practise strategy in the modern period. With a focus on the actual 'doing' of strategy, the volume aims to understand real-world experiences when ideas about conflict are carried out against a responding and proactive opponent. The case studies and material presented in the volume form an invitation to rethink dominant perspectives in the field of strategic studies. As the case studies demonstrate, strategy is most often not a stylised, premeditated and wilful phenomenon. Rather, it is a product of circumstance and opportunity, both structural and agential, leading to a view of strategy as an ad hoc, if not chaotic, enterprise.

ISABELLE DUYVESTEYN is Professor of International Studies/ Global History at the Institute of History at Leiden University. Between 2012 and 2017 she held the Special Chair in Strategic Studies at the Political Science Institute of Leiden University. Between 2008 and 2020 she was a member of the national Advisory Council on International Affairs assigned to advise the Netherlands government on issues of peace and security, and between 2012 and 2021 she was a member of the Scientific Advisory Board of the Netherlands Defence Academy.

BEATRICE HEUSER holds the Chair of International Relations at the University of Glasgow, and is seconded to the General Staff College of the Bundeswehr in Hamburg as Section Chief for Strategy. She has worked at NATO Headquarters as a consultant. She has served on academic advisory boards of the Royal United Services Institute, the French Institute of International Affairs (IFRI) and the French government's strategic studies think tank IRSEM. She has previously taught at universities in the UK, Germany and France.

THE CAMBRIDGE HISTORY OF
STRATEGY

The Cambridge History of Strategy presents a global history exploring how leaders of social groups, civilisations, empires and states have practised strategy over the course of the past three millennia. With contributions from leading experts in each subject, these volumes analyse a series of notable case studies to reflect on the formulation and application of strategy rather than on theory. Transcending the traditional Western focus and modern-state-based framework of strategic studies, this Cambridge History offers the inclusion of a wider range of political actors and cases from parts of the world hitherto largely excluded from the literature. This leads to a discussion of whether central claims in the field of strategic studies that the practice of strategy exhibits universal features which apply always hold up against empirical evidence from different centuries and cases beyond the West.

VOLUME I
From Antiquity to the American War of Independence
EDITED BY ISABELLE DUYVESTEYN AND BEATRICE HEUSER

VOLUME II
From the Napoleonic Wars to the Present
EDITED BY ISABELLE DUYVESTEYN AND BEATRICE HEUSER

THE CAMBRIDGE HISTORY OF STRATEGY

VOLUME II
From the Napoleonic Wars to the Present

Edited by
ISABELLE DUYVESTEYN
Leiden University

BEATRICE HEUSER
University of Glasgow

Shaftesbury Road, Cambridge CB2 8EA, United Kingdom

One Liberty Plaza, 20th Floor, New York, NY 10006, USA

477 Williamstown Road, Port Melbourne, VIC 3207, Australia

314–321, 3rd Floor, Plot 3, Splendor Forum, Jasola District Centre,
New Delhi – 110025, India

103 Penang Road, #05–06/07, Visioncrest Commercial, Singapore 238467

Cambridge University Press is part of Cambridge University Press & Assessment,
a department of the University of Cambridge.

We share the University's mission to contribute to society through the pursuit of
education, learning and research at the highest international levels of excellence.

www.cambridge.org
Information on this title: www.cambridge.org/9781108479929

DOI: 10.1017/9781108801546

© Cambridge University Press & Assessment 2025

This publication is in copyright. Subject to statutory exception and to the provisions
of relevant collective licensing agreements, no reproduction of any part may take
place without the written permission of Cambridge University Press & Assessment.

First published 2025

Printed in the United Kingdom by CPI Group Ltd, Croydon CR0 4YY

A catalogue record for this publication is available from the British Library.

A Cataloging-in-Publication data record for this book is available from the Library of Congress

Two Volume Set ISBN 978-1-009-41763-1 Hardback
Volume I ISBN 978-1-108-47995-0 Hardback
Volume II ISBN 978-1-108-47992-9 Hardback

Cambridge University Press & Assessment has no responsibility for the persistence
or accuracy of URLs for external or third-party internet websites referred to in this
publication and does not guarantee that any content on such websites is, or will remain,
accurate or appropriate.

This book is dedicated to the past and present victims of war

Contents

List of Maps *page xii*
List of Contributors to Volume II *xiii*
Preface and Acknowledgements *xix*

Introduction to Volume II: The Practice of Strategy *1*
ISABELLE DUYVESTEYN AND BEATRICE HEUSER

1 · The Strategies of the Napoleonic Wars *18*
ALAN FORREST

2 · Guerrilla and Nineteenth-Century Strategies of Insurgency *38*
IAN BECKETT

3 · Russia, 1877–1917 *55*
ANDREY PAVLOV

4 · The American Civil War *79*
DONALD STOKER

5 · The Use of Naval Power *99*
ANDREW LAMBERT

6 · The Russo-Japanese War *122*
ROTEM KOWNER

7 · Chinese Strategy, 1926–1949 *142*
CHRISTOPHER YUNG

8 · First World War *156*
ROBERT FOLEY

Contents

9 · Soviet Strategy, 1917–1945 *181*
NIKITA LOMAGIN

10 · Air Power *204*
FRANS OSINGA

11 · The Second World War in Europe *226*
GUILLAUME PIKETTY

12 · The Second World War in the Asia–Pacific *247*
DAVID HORNER

13 · Soviet Strategy, 1945–1989 *270*
LAURIEN CRUMP

14 · People's War and Wars of Decolonisation *292*
MATHILDE VON BÜLOW

15 · Nuclear Strategies *310*
JEFFREY H. MICHAELS

16 · America's Way of War *329*
ANTULIO J. ECHEVARRIA II

17 · The Korean War *347*
XIAOBING LI

18 · Israel's Wars *366*
EITAN SHAMIR AND EADO HECHT

19 · The India–Pakistan Confrontations *387*
ŠUMIT GANGULY

20 · The Yugoslav War, 1991–1999 *411*
JAMES GOW

21 · Terrorism and Insurgency *435*
COLIN P. CLARKE

22 · The Forty-Year War in Afghanistan *457*
JAN ANGSTROM

Contents

23 · The Three Gulf Wars and Iraq   479
AHMED S. HASHIM

24 · China's Wars, 1950–2021   503
CHRISTOPHER YUNG

Conclusion   524
ISABELLE DUYVESTEYN AND SAMUEL ZILINCIK

Further Reading   547
Index   559

Maps

1.1	Europe in 1812	*page* 19
3.1	The Russian Empire	56
4.1	Plan of General Ulysses S. Grant, Spring 1864	80
6.1	The Russo-Japanese War	130
7.1	Chinese Civil War (1941)	143
8.1	Alliances of the First World War	158
9.1	The Soviet Union in the Second World War (1941–1945)	182
9.2	The Second World War, Mongolia and Manchuria	202
11.1	The Second World War in Europe (1940–1945)	227
12.1	Asia–Pacific War (1941–1945)	248
13.1	The Deployment of Warsaw Pact Ground Forces	271
17.1	The Korean War	348
18.1	Israel: the strategic importance of territorial dimensions	377
19.1	India and Pakistan	388
20.1	The Former Yugoslavia	412
22.1	Afghanistan	460
23.1	Iraq and Iran	480
24.1	China	506

Contributors to Volume II

JAN ANGSTROM is professor of War Studies at the Swedish Defence University. He holds a PhD from King's College, London and has published mainly on the use of force in modern war for the past two decades.

IAN BECKETT retired as Professor of Military History from the University of Kent in 2015. A Fellow of the Royal Historical Society and the Society for Army Historical Research, he held chairs in both the US and UK, and was Chairman of the Council of the UK Army Records Society from 2000 to 2014. His publications include *A British Profession of Arms: The Politics of Command in the Late Victorian Army* (2018) and, most recently, *The British Army: A Short History* (2023).

COLIN P. CLARKE is the Director of Research at The Soufan Group and a Senior Research Fellow at The Soufan Center. He was previously a professor at Carnegie Mellon University in Pittsburgh, PA, and a senior political scientist at The RAND Corporation.

LAURIEN CRUMP is an affiliated researcher in the History of International Relations at the History Department of Utrecht University in the Netherlands. She specialises in multilateral diplomacy and European security during and after the Cold War. She is a recipient of a VENI-grant by the Netherlands Organization for Scientific Research (NWO) for her project 'The Multilateralization of European Security: Conducting the Cold War through the Conference on Security and Cooperation in Europe (CSCE), 1972–1990'. Her publications include *The Warsaw Pact Reconsidered. International Relations in Eastern Europe, 1955–1969* (2015), which was awarded the international 'George Blazyca Prize' as it was considered to 'transform our understanding of the functioning of the Soviet bloc, certainly from the security perspective'.

ISABELLE DUYVESTEYN is Professor of International Studies/Global History at the Institute of History at Leiden University. She completed her PhD at the Department of War Studies at King's College in London. Previously she has worked at the Royal Military Academy in the Netherlands, the Netherlands Institute for International Relations and the Department of History of International Relations at Utrecht University. Between 2012 and 2017 she held the Special Chair in Strategic Studies at the Political Science Institute of Leiden University. Between 2008 and 2020 she was a member of the national Advisory Council on International Affairs assigned to advise the Netherlands government on issues of peace and security, and between 2012 and 2021 she was a member of the Scientific Advisory Board of the Netherlands Defence Academy.

ANTULIO J. ECHEVARRIA II is the Editor-in-Chief of the US Army War College Press, which includes *Parameters*. He is a graduate of the US Military Academy, the US Army Command and General Staff College, and the US Army War College. He holds a doctorate in modern history from Princeton University. He completed a NATO Fulbright Fellowship in 2000–2001, and a Visiting Research Fellowship at Oxford University in 2011–2012. He is a Senior Research Fellow at the Foreign Policy Research Institute, and an Adjunct Fellow at the Modern War Institute. His most recent book is *War's Logic: Strategic Thought and the American Way of War* (2021).

ROBERT FOLEY is a reader in Defence Studies at King's College London based at the Joint Services Command and Staff College at the Defence Academy of the United Kingdom. He has published extensively on the First World War, and has taught strategy and military operations for more than twenty years at staff colleges in Europe, the United States and Australia.

ALAN FORREST is Emeritus Professor of History at the University of York, where he taught from 1989 to 2012. Recent works include *The Legacy of the French Revolutionary Wars* (2009), *Great Battles: Waterloo* (2015) and *The Death of the French Atlantic: Trade, War and Slavery in the Age of Revolution* (2020), as well as a biography of Napoleon in 2012. He is general editor of the three-volume *Cambridge History of the Napoleonic Wars*, published in 2022–2023.

ŠUMIT GANGULY is a Distinguished Professor of Political Science and holds the Rabindranath Tagore Chair in Indian Cultures and Civilizations at Indiana University, Bloomington. He is also a Visiting Fellow at the Hoover Institution at Stanford University. His research focus is on contemporary politics of south Asia. His most recent edited book (with Dinshaw Mistry) is *Enduring and Emerging Issues in South Security* (2022).

JAMES GOW is Professor of International Peace and Security in the Department of War Studies of King's College London. His research interests include international peace and security, war crimes and the Yugoslav War. Between 1994 and 1998, he served as an expert adviser and expert witness for the Office of the Prosecutor at the UN International Criminal Tribunal for the former Yugoslavia. He is a permanent non-resident scholar with the Liechtenstein Institute, Princeton University. He has held visiting positions at the University of Sheffield, the Woodrow Wilson International Center for Scholars in Washington, DC, the Institute of War and Peace Studies, Columbia University and the Centre of International Studies, Princeton University.

AHMED S. HASHIM is Associate Professor of War Studies at Deakin University, School of Humanities and Social Sciences. He is a member of the Centre for Future Defence and National Security (CFDNS) at the Australian Defence College in Canberra, where he teaches on future war, insurgency and counterinsurgency operations. He also specialises in military history, conventional warfare and the evolution of military forces in the global

South. New publications *Iranian Ways of War: From Cyrus the Great to Qasem Soleimani* and *Small Wars in the Middle East and Central Asia: From Ancient Times to the Present* are forthcoming.

EADO HECHT is a military analyst and historian. His area of interest and research is the relationship between theory, doctrine and actual practice. Dr Hecht has been a senior academic instructor at the IDF Staff and Command College and the IDF Tactical Command College since 2021, teaching courses on military theory and military history. Dr Hecht is also a senior Research Fellow at the Begin Sadat Center for Strategic Studies. Prior to his teaching position he served as a career officer in the IDF. Dr Hecht's publications have appeared in *Ma'archot* (in Hebrew, IDF's main professional publication), *Survival, Parameters, Infinity,* the *Journal of Military Operations, The Strategy Bridge,* and various publications and reports by the BESA Center of Strategic Studies. In Hebrew he has published *The Operational Level Breakthrough in German Military Thinking 1870–1945* (1999) and *The Tactics of Employing Supporting Fire in Battle – Evolution and Lessons* (2013).

BEATRICE HEUSER holds the Chair of International Relations at the University of Glasgow, and is seconded to the General Staff College of the Bundeswehr in Hamburg as Section Chief for Strategy. She holds her BA and MA from the University of London (Bedford College and LSE) and her DPhil from Oxford (St Antony's College and St John's College). She also holds a higher doctorate (*Habilitation*) from the University of Marburg. Previously she taught at King's College London at the Department of War Studies and at the University of Reading, and as Visiting Professor at several Parisian universities, the universities of Reims and Potsdam, and at Sciences Po' Paris and Reims. She has worked at NATO Headquarters as a consultant, and in various positions for the Bundeswehr. She has served on academic advisory boards of several museums and research institutes, currently including the Royal United Services Institute, the French Institute of International Affairs (IFRI), and the French government's strategic studies think tank IRSEM.

DAVID HORNER, AM, FASSA, is an emeritus professor in the Strategic and Defence Studies Centre, Australian National University, Canberra, where he was Professor of Australia Defence History for fifteen years. A graduate of the Royal Military College, Duntroon, he served as an infantry platoon commander in the Vietnam War and later, as a colonel, was head of the Australian Army's Land Warfare Studies Centre. He is the author or editor of thirty-seven books on Australian military history, defence and intelligence. As the Official Historian of Australian Peacekeeping, Humanitarian and Post-Cold War Operations, he was General Editor of the six-volume series. He was also the Official Historian of the Australian Security Intelligence Organisation, the first volume of which was joint winner of the Prime Minister's Literary Award for history, and the UK Intelligence Book of the Year.

ROTEM KOWNER is Professor of Japanese Studies and Naval History at the University of Haifa and a leading expert on the Russo-Japanese War. A founder and first chair of the Department of Asian Studies at the University of Haifa, his research interests include wartime behaviour in modern Japan, race and racism in east Asia, and modern naval history. During the last two decades he has written extensively and led joint research projects on the Russo-Japanese War. His books include *Tsushima* (2022), *Historical Dictionary of the Russo-Japanese War* (2017); and the edited volumes *The Impact of the Russo-Japanese War* (2007) and *Rethinking the Russo-Japanese War* (2007).

ANDREW LAMBERT is Laughton Professor of Naval History in the Department of War Studies at King's College, London, and Director of the Laughton Naval History Unit. His work focuses on the naval, strategic and cultural history of the British Empire between the Napoleonic Wars and the First World War, the evolution of naval historical writing and the history of technology. He has lectured on aspects of his work around the world, and has made several television documentaries. His recent books include: *Crusoe's Island: A Rich and Curious History of Pirates, Castaways and Madness* (2016); *Seapower States: Maritime Culture, Continental Empires, and the Conflict that Made the Modern World* (2018), which won the 2018 Gilder Lehrman Book Prize in Military History. His latest book is *The British Way of War: Julian Corbett and the Battle for a National Strategy* (2021).

XIAOBING LI is a professor of history and Don Betz Endowed Chair in International Studies at the University of Central Oklahoma. His research focuses on the history of the Cold War and modern Chinese military history. He is the editor of *The Chinese Historical Review*. His recent books include *China's New Navy* (2023), *Sino-US Relations: A New Cold War* (2022), *The Dragon in the Jungle: The Chinese Army in the Vietnam War* (2021), *Attack at Chosin* (2020), *China's War in Korea* (2019), *Building Ho's Army* (2019), *The History of Taiwan* (2018) and *China's Battle for Korea* (2015). He served in the PLA in China.

NIKITA LOMAGIN is a professor at European University of St Petersburg and director of Institute of History of Leningrad Blockade at the State Memorial Museum of Defense and Blockade of Leningrad. He earned his doctorate at St Petersburg Institute of History of the Russian Academy of Sciences and holds a diploma in law from St Petersburg State University. He was a postdoctoral fellow at the Davis Center for Russian Studies at Harvard and researcher at the Kennan Institute, University of Michigan Law School, and Finnish Institute for International Affairs. He is the author of several monographs and numerous articles and book chapters on the history of the Second World War and Russian foreign policy. His most recent books include contributions to *The Russian Challenge to the European Security Environment* (2017); *Routledge Handbook of Russian Security* (2019); *Russian Trade Policy: Achievements, Challenges and Prospects* (2019); *Distrust, Animosity, and Solidarity: Jews and Non-Jews during the Holocaust in the USSR* (2022).

JEFFREY H. MICHAELS is the IEN Senior Fellow at the Institut Barcelona d'Estudis Internacionals (IBEI). He also holds visiting fellowships at the Oxford Changing Character of War Centre at Pembroke College and the Department of War Studies at King's College London. Earlier experience included working as a Senior Lecturer in Defence Studies at King's, as well as serving as an official with NATO and the US Defense Department. He is the co-author, with Sir Lawrence Freedman, of *The Evolution of Nuclear Strategy*, 4th ed. (2019).

List of Contributors to Volume II

FRANS OSINGA (Air Commodore (RTD)), a former F-16 pilot, is professor in War Studies at Leiden University. From 2010 to 2023 he was the Chair of the War Studies Department of the Netherlands Defence Academy. His research focuses on contemporary security, defence policy and warfare. He is member of the Netherlands Advisory Council on International Affairs.

ANDREY PAVLOV holds a PhD in history. He is a professor at St Petersburg State University and the chair of the Strategic and Arms Control Studies Master Program at the School of International Relations. His research focuses on the history of the First World War and contemporary strategy. He has also authored numerous books, book chapters and articles on the same subjects.

GUILLAUME PIKETTY is Full Professor of History at Sciences Po (Paris). He was a Visiting Research Scholar at Yale University (2010–2012), then a Visiting Fellow at Worcester College and an Associate member of the Faculty of History at Oxford University (2012–2018). His research focuses on the social and cultural history of the Second World War in France and in Europe, and, more broadly, on war and resistance. His latest book addresses the political–military relationships in France during the Second World War and the Fourth Republic. His next projects focus on the day-to-day experience of European exiles between 1939 and 1945, and on the relations between war, sensitivities and emotions throughout the nineteenth and twentieth centuries.

EITAN SHAMIR is an associate professor at the Political Science Department Bar Ilan University and a senior researcher at the BESA Center for Strategic Studies. Prior to his academic position he was in charge of the National Security Doctrine Unit at the Ministry of Strategic Affairs, Prime Minister's Office. His research focuses on topics such as national security, military command and culture. He is the author of *Transforming Command: The Pursuit of Mission Command in the US, UK and Israeli Armies* (2011), as well as numerous articles in leading journals and book chapters.

DONALD STOKER is Professor of National Security and Resource Strategy at the Dwight D. Eisenhower School of the National Defense University in Washington, DC, and a senior adviser with Atlas Organization. From 1999 to 2017, he was Professor of Strategy and Policy for the Naval War College at the Naval Postgraduate School in Monterey, California. He has published more than seventy works in strategic studies and history, including thirteen books. His book, *The Grand Design: Strategy and the US Civil War, 1861–1865* (2010), won the prestigious Fletcher Pratt award for the best non-fiction civil war book of 2010, was a Main Selection of the History Book Club, is on the US Army Chief of Staff's reading list and is a common text in history and strategic studies courses. His *Carl von Clausewitz: His Life and Work* (2014), is on the British Army professional reading list and is being translated into Chinese. The second edition of his *Why America Loses Wars: Limited War and US Strategy from the Korean War to the Present* (2019) was published in 2022. His most recent book, *Purpose and Power: American Grand Strategy from the Revolutionary Era to the Present*, was published in 2024.

List of Contributors to Volume II

MATHILDE VON BÜLOW is a lecturer in the School of International Relations at the University of St Andrews and a co-editor of the journal *War in History*. She is a historian specialising in decolonisation and the global Cold War, with a particular focus on France, Germany and North Africa. Her first book, *West Germany, Cold War Europe and the Algerian War* was published in 2016. Her interests are wide-ranging and include questions of strategy, diplomacy and intelligence, as well as non-state activism and internationalism. She is working on a number of projects, including a new monograph on the Battle of Algiers.

CHRISTOPHER YUNG is the Dean of the US Marine Corps War College, the USMC's Top Level School for senior military officers and government officials. He remains an active scholar on Asian defence and Chinese military issues. He was previously the Donald Bren Chair of Non-Western Strategic Thought and the Director of East Asian Studies at Marine Corps University. In this capacity he taught at the associated schools within the Marine Corps University umbrella (such as the Marine Corps War College, the School of Advanced Warfighting, the Command and Staff College, and the Expeditionary Warfare School). Dr Yung specialises in Chinese strategy, foreign policy, the People's Liberation Army, and China's naval and expeditionary capabilities. Previously he was the Senior Research Fellow at the Center for the Study of Chinese Military Affairs (CSCMA), Institute for National Strategic Studies, National Defense University, and he provided research, analysis and policy recommendations for the Office of Secretary of Defense, the Joint Staff and the Intelligence Community. Dr Yung also previously served as Senior Research Analyst at the Center for Naval Analyses (CNA).

SAMUEL ZILINCIK is a doctoral student of security and strategic studies at Masaryk and Leiden Universities and a lecturer at the University of Defence in the Czech Republic. His research interests include military strategy in general and its emotional aspects in particular. His work has appeared in the *Journal of Strategic Studies*, *Texas National Security Review*, the *RUSI Journal* and *Military Strategy Magazine*. He was awarded the 2022 Amos Perlmutter Prize, the 2020 'Under 30s' Trench Gascoigne Essay Prize and second place in the 2018 Strategy Bridge writing contest.

Preface and Acknowledgements

The ambition of this two-part series, *The Cambridge History of Strategy*, has been to focus on the practice of strategy across time and place. In Volume I we looked at a diversity of civilisations, empires and states which engaged in strategy. The picture that emerged was one of a messy practice, with luck and opportunity playing a major role. This is in contrast to the highly stylised representation in much of the strategic studies literature. While the theorisation to date has been mostly based on Western and recent historical case material, our main ambition has been to broaden this scope and press the question of the universality claims made in strategic studies. In the Conclusion to this volume we tackle this question directly.

In this second volume the focus will be on the modern period, and we will continue with our global history of strategy by discussing an array of cases from around the world, ranging from the Americas to southern Africa, the Russian Empire and China, and lots in between. This volume had the benefit of looking at strategy while the word gained widespread recognition, although its use was not consistent in either meaning or practice. The justification for our choices in this volume will be presented in the opening chapter.

The premise of the series of offering overviews for non-specialists, based on the state of the art, is continued here in this volume. This allows us to compare these cases. These comparisons will help us to consider further both the specific and the general aspects of doing strategy in practice. Only by emphasising what is generalisable can we benefit from history to help make sense of today and hopefully of what lies ahead.

As with the first volume, our primary indebtedness is to the authors of the individual chapters. Without their inspired contributions, this series would not have seen the light of day. Editing a series of this size is a challenging task. What kept us going, during the difficult times of a global pandemic, were the thought-provoking chapters and the many moments we felt we learned something new. Simply by asking the same set of questions of different case material, from different parts of the world and in distant times, we hoped to achieve our ambition of a consistent overview of the history of strategy. We look back on a very enriching experience.

A word of thanks also needs to be extended to Cambridge University Press's Michael Watson, who saw great merit in our original idea of a global approach to the history of strategy. Moreover, we would like to thank the team at Cambridge University Press, Emily Plater and Lisa Carter, and the copy-editors, John Gaunt and Llinos Edwards, as well as Preethika Ramalingam at Integra.

Furthermore, a special word of thanks to Samuel Zilincik, our editorial assistant, as well as our language and reference editors, Carmel Dowling and Vani Dhaka. The input from our international advisory board, consisting of Professors Jeremy Black, Martin van Creveld, Isabelle Deflers, Antulio J. Echevarria II, Lawrence Freedman, Kimberley Kagan, Joe Maiolo, Assaf Moghaddam, Michael Rainsborough, Monica Toft, Erwin Schmidl and Matthew Strickland has been much appreciated.

Introduction to Volume II
The Practice of Strategy

ISABELLE DUYVESTEYN AND BEATRICE HEUSER

How does strategy occur in the real world, in situations of antagonistic encounters, under pressure, with incomplete information and complexity being rife? As the chapters in this second volume demonstrate, the practice of strategy substantially deviates from our textbook conceptualisations. In our Introduction to Volume I, we summed up the many definitions of strategy to arrive at a succinct version of: 'a comprehensive way to try to pursue political ends, including the threat or actual use of force, in a dialectic of wills'.[1] As in Volume I, we find evidence in the nineteenth and twentieth centuries for conscious and deliberate attempts to prioritise objectives, aligning them with resources and finding ways to apply them. Nevertheless, there are many other factors that come into play in practising strategy, such as opportunities, precipitous circumstances, path dependencies, expectations, emotions and influences of geography. They form part of the crucial metaphysical influences of historic experiences, constituting part of collective mentalities and culture. The reality of the practice of strategy is thus more complex than the simple model of ends, ways and means would suggest.[2] In Volume I, we have seen the prevalence of raiding and opportunistic practices, as well as religious, dynastic and ideological motivation, influencing the practising of strategy.

In this second volume, we continue with more recent examples of strategic practices around the globe. Our aim is, again, to investigate the practising of strategy in a diversity of places across time. This is in contrast to the dominance of strategy as being about ideas and theories of how to engage in them. The practical definition we have adopted is that strategy involves

---

[1] For a comprehensive list, see Beatrice Heuser, *The Evolution of Strategy: Thinking War from Antiquity to the Present* (Cambridge: Cambridge University Press, 2020), chapter 1.
[2] See for example, Colonel Dale C. Eikmeier, 'A logical method for centre of gravity analysis', *Military Review* (September/October 2007), 62–6.

'the setting of a state's objectives and of priorities among those objectives for the allocation of resources and the establishment of priorities in the conduct of a war'.[3] Before offering the reader some of our ideas regarding the practice of strategy in the modern period, we first need to justify our choices.

Why Start Around 1800?

Where the story left off in the first volume, we noted a fundamental change in strategy making around the time of the age of revolutions. The Enlightenment and the Industrial Revolution are generally seen as the starting points of a new epoch. There is an unmistakable influence of these developments on the practice of strategy that can be observed in our case material. While Volume I covered a rich diversity of polities, the emergence of compact territorial states with defined borders led jurists and political philosophers as well as statesmen, historians and later political scientists to conceptualise warfare and its rules, increasingly in relation to states. Since antiquity, European and then Western political thought had cast states or state-like polities as the only legitimate actors in warfare, but in the nineteenth century this became formally enshrined in instruments of international law: treaties were signed and ratified by states, committing themselves thereby to uphold certain rules and norms. This categorisation of the legitimate actor is by no means unproblematic.[4] We will return to this issue in our Conclusion.

Around 1800, we note in particular two significant changes in practices: the first change is the mobilisation of larger numbers of people for the conduct of war; the second is the industrialisation of war. We address these briefly in turn.

This was not the very first time that common people had been mobilised in large numbers for the conduct of war. Religion had also mobilised people, especially in the first wave of the Muslim Wars of Conquest, the early crusades, or the confessional wars in Europe. In the French Wars of 1792–1815, however, the motivation was a new form of collective thought: while God or a king or emperor was occasionally still invoked, in Europe it was henceforth 'the nation' that would be the rallying point of wars. This ushered in a new era of mass warfare in which whole nations were seen as enemies, simply because they were 'other', not even for any creed or deed. It became

---

3 K. Kagan, 'Redefining Roman grand strategy', *Journal of Military History*, 70:2 (2006), 333–64.
4 Beatrice Heuser, *War: A Genealogy of Western Ideas and Practices* (Oxford: Oxford University Press, 2022), 81–106.

a more or less explicitly articulated strategic aim to compete with and defeat the 'other': old family or clan rivalries translated into those among entire millions-strong nations, landgrabs justified no longer by inheritance quarrels.

Apart from the *levée en masse*, a second practical development is the advance in technology. The quantity and quality of developments relating to the shift from agricultural societies to machine-based production took shape in this period, in turn leading to the industrialised mass production of goods in general, but also war materials in particular and a step-change in the speed of technological innovations. Moreover, as a result of the industrialisation of society, war changed fundamentally in appearance. Technological progress acted as a facilitator for war, with trains running on rails transporting increasing numbers of soldiers and equipment over growing distances. Also, the development of advanced weaponry caused ever more devastating effects on their targets, with the role of nuclear weapons as the most extreme. Thus industrialisation had a fundamentally important impact in reshaping the practice of strategy from this point onwards. This does not negate other continuities, which can be found especially in asymmetric warfare where at least one party did not have access to complex weapons systems.

Let us now briefly summarise commonalties and differences of sources, actors, adversaries, causes and objectives, means and prioritisation that emerge from our chapters, with an emphasis on variations around the globe.

Sources

Our contributors in the first volume drew upon a great diversity of sources, ranging from archaeology, excavation, inscription, architecture, clay and papyrus tablets, paper sources to oral history. Many of these posed considerable challenges of understanding and interpretation. As we get closer to the present, at least in the Western democracies with their emphasis on accountability and thus on record-keeping, the sources become more abundant, more easily accessible and also closer to the phenomenon we are interested in. Written sources, as the main type of source, shift from dynastic chronicles and religious tracts to official histories and ego-documents of direct participants. Still, challenges of interpretation remain. Not only do we need to do justice to meaning within its own context, but also the overall social and political contexts in which the events occurred deserve careful attention.

Despite the wealth of sources for more recent cases of practising strategy, important shortcomings and challenges need to be noted. There is still much that we do not know. We come up against language barriers as well as problems of sources, not only where these have been destroyed or never existed but also where they do not tell us what we are interested in – the reasoning and debates behind strategic decisions. Very few sources tell us about this with regard to non-state actors, such as guerrilleros, insurgents and terrorists. Only the state, international organisations or other long-standing resource-rich institutions had and continue to have the resources to record and then preserve the records over long periods of time. We find this in particular in the chapters below on the non-state actors, such as guerrilla movements in the nineteenth century (Chapter 2), the rebel groups practising revolutionary people's war (Chapter 14) or the terrorist groups conducting national or global campaigns (Chapter 21). As will be argued in more detail below, there is clear evidence that these actors practise strategy, but our source base is mostly meagre. Furthermore, the dominance of scholarly literature in English and the abundance of sources in the USA, Britain, Canada and a handful of other Anglophone countries has led to an abundance of writing about their experiences; closed, disorganised or non-existent archives have led to an under-representation of the corresponding histories of other nations. Moreover, many parts of the world, notably sub-Saharan Africa, provide us with a challenge by the scarcity or even complete absence of written sources. We continue to rely on the sources produced by visitors from other countries, in the absence of written sources detailing their own experiences; nor can oral traditions substitute, if the comparison between European oral traditions and historical or archaeological records are anything to go by. Language barriers exacerbate this imbalance, as in the case of the Boer War and the exclusion of sources in Afrikaans. Also, in the case of the Arab–Israeli wars, there is very little in regards to source material or even secondary literature concerning the Palestine Liberation Organization (PLO), Hamas and Hezbollah to offer a comprehensive picture.

We invite readers to take these limitations into consideration. Apart from continuing awareness of source limitations, the case material and historiography have also been subject to diverging levels of historiographical debate. While this is lively in some areas, testifying that the discipline is still bearing rich fruit, it is not evenly spread, as some cases have been debated far more than others, and much research is yet to be done.[5]

---

5 Max Hastings, 'American universities declare war on military history', Bloomberg (31 January 2021), www.bloomberg.com/opinion/articles/2021-01-31/max-hastings-u-s-universities-declare-war-on-military-history. And the ensuing debate: William Hitchcock and Meghan Herwig, 'There is more war in the classroom than you think', War on the Rocks (21 September 2021), https://warontherocks.com/2021/09/there-is-more-war-in-the-classroom-than-you-think/?.

Actors, Agency and Adversaries

Who had agency in setting the objectives for strategy making? In Volume I, we identified a wide variety of strategy-making agents, but most came from small elites within their respective societies. Polities ranged from being organised around individuals, tribes and ethnic groups to city states ruled by oligarchies or patricians, *mandala* polities revolving around a capital without a clearly demarcated territory, quasi-states and vast empires spanning entire continents. In Volume II we see the start of the dominance of the state-based norm and the consolidation of the international system based on the central idea of the state. In the course of the nineteenth century, a movement occurred to divide and claim the world's territory, at its apogee the Berlin Conference in 1885 carving up Africa. Initially, these territories were demarcated and claimed, notably by imperial powers. Subsequently, in Europe and later in other parts of the world, the expectation emerged and was reinforced that the state and especially the nation state would be the model for others to emulate. In Latin America this began in the nineteenth century with the decolonisation of territories from the Spanish Empire, such as Argentina, Mexico and Chile. After the dissolution of the multi-ethnic empires of the Ottomans and the Austro-Hungarians in the aftermath of the First World War, this pattern continued. In the course of the twentieth century, in often violent processes involving the British, French, Dutch and Portuguese empires, the ideal of the ethnically homogeneous or the politically sovereign nation state became the dominant paradigm.

Nevertheless, we see many cases of this state-based norm being contested and challenged, in particular by those not successful in attaining their nation state ideal, such as the case of the dissolution of Yugoslavia discussed in Chapter 20 as 'a clash of statehood projects'. Other groups actively challenged the state model by embracing alternatives and echoing patterns from the past, specifically the model of the caliphate.

Apart from the emerging dominance of a specific kind of agency via the state, we see divergences as well as important continuities. There is a strong measure of continuity in decision making when practising strategy. In Volume I, we saw that the idea of a unitary, rationally acting polity was not the dominant picture in the case material. Even in polities where there appeared to be a strong single ruler, decision making would rarely if ever be a solitary affair. Rather, power was diffused, mediated and negotiated, with groups of individuals, such as advisers and courtiers, all claiming a role. Even the Roman emperors, often seen as emblematic models of individual power, rarely decided matters alone, being surrounded by advisers and family members, including women. This picture is continued in the modern period, across time and place. One notable exception is the case of Saddam Hussein of Iraq. In Chapter 23, it will be argued that Hussein was a dictator with few to no military or political advisers who would offer him alternative options or counterarguments.

A point of divergence is the separation between political decision making and military command, which becomes increasingly visible over the course of the nineteenth and twentieth centuries. While many previous political leaders were also commanders on the field of battle, this became the exception after Napoleon's time. Moreover, from the mid-seventeenth century onwards and under the influence of the Enlightenment, leaders were increasingly measured by their performance than by their birth. Still, we do see politicians involved in the minutiae of the battlefield, and military men engaging in politics.

Finally, adversaries continued to be both internal and external to the polity. A major distinction can be made between those opponents who were considered equals and those seen as inferior, which could be based on provenance, culture or other factors. Diversity thus continues to mark the image of the adversary.

Causes and Objectives of War

Causes and objectives of war might diverge over time, but both are core elements in the development of strategy. While particular causes are unique to each war and are the product of its specific time and place, common factors and patterns can be observed. In Volume I we saw how important causes played out, such as environmental stress causing migration, opportunity for booty and conquest via raiding, but also how personal ambitions, ideological world views and dynastic succession informed strategic practices.

In this volume, many of these factors reappear. Some exceptions are the dynastic causes, which all but disappeared after the age of revolutions. First, political considerations, borrowing in no small measure from the work of Carl von Clausewitz who wrote his main treatise after experiencing the Napoleonic Wars first-hand, continue to be the dominant lens through which justifications are offered and analysed. On the one hand, politics could be broadly conceptualised and encompass all the grounds already listed above, including opportunistic raiding and power struggles within polities. On the other hand, politics could be seen as a narrower concept consisting of the power to decide on the distribution of wealth. In this last perspective, we observe a series of notable characteristics of publicly offered justifications and objectives for practising strategy.

The formulation of clear objectives continued to be a challenge. The case studies of the American Civil War, the Russo-Japanese War and, all the way up to the recent past, the engagement in Afghanistan from 2001 onwards, demonstrate the absence of clearly articulated objectives by the belligerents, apart from the broadly perceived opposition to the opponent's actions.

Second, inherited from previous centuries was the aim for imperial aggrandisement that would subject other populations to a ruling class or ethnic group. We still see this central objective in the war being waged by Russia against Ukraine at the time of writing. At the extreme end of this spectrum were the wars of conquest of Nazi Germany, fought in the name of winning living space for the Germanic 'race' but ready to subjugate or even exterminate other populations. Alternatively and increasingly, in the nineteenth and twentieth centuries objectives tended to be framed in terms of state interests, now justified in terms of interests of nations rather than of dynasties. But nations were and are constructs, especially if they are ethnically defined, and by promoting the interests of such constructed bodies of populations while ignoring those of ethnically different minorities, wars would revolve around the domination of clearly defined territories to the exclusion of other populations. We see this in Chapter 19, in the case of the emergence of India and its rivalry with Pakistan. Moreover, the search for power and recognition for the nation has been an important objective in many conflicts over the course of modern history. Napoleon sought a global empire rivalling that of Britain; a unified Germany was on a similar quest in the nineteenth century.

Third, the long-standing pattern of irregular warfare was elevated conceptually to be recognised as a distinct strategy, either on the side of the irregulars (insurgents, guerrilleros, rebels etc.) or on that of the state forces attempting to suppress the former. While this was not entirely absent in previous centuries, little had been written about it.[6] In the twentieth century, groups carrying out a revolutionary people's war aimed to unleash political and economic effects rather than seeking a direct military outcome to attain political effects. A set of objectives focused on attaining indirect effects by using coercive means aimed at direct political change, often decolonisation (by the Bolsheviks in the wars of

---

6 A rare exception is that of the Welsh-Norman Gerald of Wales (Geraldus Cambrensis) with his works on how to stage a rebellion (the Welsh way of war) and how to suppress it.

the Russian Revolution, for example) or the revolutionary transformation of one's own society (such as the 'progressive' or conservative-regressive aims pursued by Franco's Fascist rebels in the Spanish Civil War).

Means

In conflictual engagement with an opponent, a series of means or instruments can be put to use. We can distinguish not only between kinetic and non-kinetic means but also a large variety of ways in which they could be used. Non-kinetic means of strategy include diplomacy and negotiation, economic pressure and sanctions, the formation of alliances and alliance politics, and the use of soft power instruments and inducements. These non-kinetic means and their use are prominently visible in the case studies in this volume. Conflictual engagements build up over a period of time, and the role of political signalling and exchange are core features of practising strategy. In the case of the Napoleonic Wars in Chapter 1, Napoleon had little time for this process of dialogue and compromise, favouring the use of arms instead. In the assessment, this preference led to his ultimate demise, winning battles but failing to win the peace.

The importance of economic pressure is another continuation from the previous period, such as that exerted on Japan by the USA in the 1930s, and the use of commercial incentives, tribute payments and sanctions. We see such instruments in many places. Alliances with like-minded actors or alliances of convenience continue to form part of the picture in the modern period. Alliances and alliance politics were based on kinship, friendship or common enemies, and eventually were not based on dynastic ties or marriage alliances: the rulers of three of the countries pitted against each other in the First World War were cousins. The Napoleonic Wars gave rise to seven coalitions which opposed French expansion, and inspired a notable balancing act after the termination of these coalitions in the Concert of Europe. Alliances of the First World War, the Entente and the Central Powers, were to some extent alliances not only of ideas but also of convenience, based on a shared perception of threat. This seriously hampered the ability to practise strategy together. During the wars of decolonisation, support for those seeking liberation was forthcoming from the Soviet Union, China and Cuba (in the case of this last state, in the very tangible form of practical advice and fighters). In the context of the Cold War, international sponsorship was informed by the ideological stance of the regime.

Changes we observe in this period include increased connections, which caused wars to have increasingly global repercussions. The Seven Years' War is now widely considered as the first truly global war, with fighting in North America, India as well as central Europe. This global interconnectedness increasingly marked the practice of strategy and war fighting. As means of communication developed, the conduct of armed conflict would spread ever more quickly to the corners of the world. At the same time, information exchange, narratives and propaganda efforts would reach larger and larger parts of the world population. Thus conduct being seen as justified and legitimate formed part of these information efforts. The use of military force without extensive efforts to curry international favour through references to legitimate causes became increasingly counterproductive, engendering opposition where there might have been neutrality or difference. Napoleon, Hitler, Mussolini and the Japanese military leadership would all learn this to their cost. But wartime appeals to populations under the enemy's control to cast off their shackles and determine their own fates would also be remembered later, and had to be followed up in practice, as Britain and France would find out after the First World War. This is linked to the exercise of soft power instruments: trying to attract support, imitation and emulation by inspiring attitudes if not via inducement than via shock and awe.

With regard to kinetic means, the raising of a primary fighting force changed significantly over the course of the last two centuries. Previously the generation of fighting agency generally occurred via the three models visible in Volume I, of the peasant-militia, the professional soldier or the conscripted recruit. Now this last model became dominant, based on the allegiance to the nation rather than to a prince (a transition still masked in monarchies by blending the two). Professional military forces fighting for states in which they were not born became the exception.

Still, generating a fighting force faced several challenges over the course of time. While fighting forces increased in size, the puzzle became where this human power should be most efficiently put to use, to attain the largest benefit for sustaining the war effort. Human power to work the lands and factories, and to fight on behalf of the nation, became contentious. Additional fighting power came from the colonies and by opening up jobs for women, with the effect of raising calls for decolonisation and the emancipation of women. The emphasis in the use of these armed forces shifted from quantity to quality and towards increasing specialisation.

The size of the armed forces, no longer subject of estimation if not fabulation, became more reliable in modern times. Before 1800 the largest number active in the field would have been in the tens of thousands, with exceptions in antiquity and central and east Asia. Soldiers fighting in the hundreds of thousands and millions would become normal in the major confrontations of modern times. Moreover, the forces became subject to increased professionalisation and specialisation. While infantry, cavalry, artillery and navy would adapt to technological change and innovation, the air force emerged as a distinct branch. Moreover, special forces, space and most recently cyber forces entered the scene. Counting forces became a major and more exact preoccupation. The reliability of quantitative instruments of measurement led to discussions of force-ratios and their ideal composition. Mass, however, discounted the importance of quality, *esprit de corps* and determination. Ideologies focused on fighting for the nation were powerful recruitment mechanisms as well as motivators for continued engagement.

From the early nineteenth century onwards, major technological innovations fundamentally changed the face of the battlefield and the kinetic aspects of warfare. Human power and animals were slowly replaced by machines: railways, battleships, tanks, aircraft, submarines. Technological innovation occurred at unprecedented speed and with unprecedented effects, with strategies lagging behind. There developed a panoply of methods and ways in which these means could be put to use. This section will take a closer look at the variety of employment and outline the most common features.

Armed force can be used to deter. Deterrence is based on a threat or threatening behaviour to ward off possible or planned actions by a rival. The agent is capable and willing, and has communicated a threat of actions in particular violence to influence an opponent's course of action. Generally two types of deterrence can be distinguished: deterrence by punishment aims at increasing the costs of further resistance by offering a prospect of pain; deterrence by denial focuses on eliminating the means by targeting the possession of these means.

Many interesting examples of deterrence can be found in the chapters of this volume. A primary observation is that deterrence is very often based on the development and possession of a specific type of means. The possession of an ocean-going fleet in the nineteenth century itself acted as a deterrent rather than a practical instrument that could attain clear and direct results. The possession of air power acted in a similar manner in the twentieth century. The ability to bomb potential enemies in concerted strategic bombing campaigns aimed at enemy strong points or interests had a deterrent effect, which will be further elaborated below. Lastly, the possession (or suspected possession) of nuclear weapons seemed to work as a deterrent even to the conventional war between two nuclear powers, until the Indo-Pakistani War of 1999 showed that even this could occur.

A second observation relates to the ubiquity of deterrence. Deterrent action was used not only against states but also rebel groups. American actions against the rebel Pancho Villa in Mexico in 1916 were aimed at deterring him and his men from further incursions on American territory. The conventional victories of the Israeli armed forces had a deterrent effect on subsequent armed confrontation by Israel's Arab neighbours. By proving that it was willing and able to defend Kashmir against Pakistani encroachments, India had hoped to deter renewed attacks. This eventually proved unsuccessful in this case. After the invasion of Kuwait, the United States placed forces in Saudi Arabia in October 1990 to deter Iraq from developing designs on this country. Violence to deter was also used in the case of Yugoslavia, where the demonstrative use of force was employed to deter the population from resisting.

Armed forces can be used to pre-empt and to surprise, although preemption is problematic as an international legal category, with the only legitimate reason for armed action being self-defence after an armed attack or action, called for and authorised by the United Nations' Security Council. An example of using self-defence to justify the pre-emptive use of force is the 1967 war by Israel against Egypt and a coalition of Arab states, which had been amassing forces close to Israel. Strategic surprise is even more difficult to legitimise. Notable examples are the Soviet Army which was taken by surprise when Germany attacked in Operation Barbarossa in June 1941, entering with its full force on Soviet territory and pushing forward with high speed, an option for which the armed forces were ill prepared. Another example from the same period is the surprise attack against Pearl Harbor on 7 December 1941, so daring that it was not at all expected but led the US to determinedly defeat Japan. The USSR learned from these strategies and passed on the lesson to its client states: masked by large-scale exercises, Soviet forces invaded Czechoslovakia in 1968; Egypt invaded Israel in the Yom Kippur War 1973; Iraq invaded Kuwait in 1990; Russia annexed Crimea in 2014, and then invaded Ukraine itself in 2022.

Armed force can be used to coerce. Coercive action can be witnessed, for example, in the mobilisation of the Russian forces in 1876 on the eve of the confrontation with the Ottoman Empire to increase the pressure on the Sultan to give in to the Russian demands regarding the rights of the Christian Slav populations in the Empire. While mobilisation in the Russian case was an arduous process, the decision to go to war had not been taken.

This mobilisation was interpreted as coercive and set a process in motion that culminated in the outbreak of war.

Coercive violence can also take the shape of changing the behaviour of opponents or their population. One example is the shelling of populated areas of Croatia and Bosnia–Hercegovina in the wars of the 1990s. This forced people to leave the area, causing large population movements and creating the envisioned ethnically pure areas for the relocation of the Serbian population. Armed resistance can also be used, in the case of independence struggles, to demonstrate political commitment and legitimacy. Attracting attention serves liberation movements by raising the profile of the struggles and commanding support and aid without attempting to defeat the colonisers in open battle. The use of forces in revolutionary people's war never attained the third phase of conventional confrontation, the most notable exception being the Indochina War and the defeat of the French forces at Điện Biên Phủ in 1954.

Armed force can be used to decapitate, to retaliate and to escalate.[7] Decapitating the political organisation or leadership, punishing perpetrators or their families and attacking valuable targets as retaliation for a prior attack can all be ways of employing the means. A notable case discussed in Chapter 18 is the Israeli policy of retaliation against artillery attacks or incursions, which were followed consistently by retaliatory actions. Escalation occurs when more actors join, heavier weapons are used, tactics change and the geographical scope of the conflict is broadened. These might be wilful actions but they often occur as a spur-of-the-moment response or unwitting effect of prior actions. The use of Spanish irregulars fighting French occupation after 1808 was seen as an escalation, demanding French attention and efforts.

Armed force can be used to oppress and to annihilate. 'Annihilate' changed its meaning over the nineteenth century. As Colmar von der Goltz commented, it originally referred to rendering an army unable to win by wounding or killing a small but significant proportion of its soldiers, but under the influence of Social Darwinism (survival of the fittest) came to mean the massacring of entire populations.[8] Attritional violence which focused on killing and maiming made the most direct link between effecting pain in order to attain ends. Examples abound in modern history. Attrition occurred in the war in China after the Japanese invasion, with the idea of sacrificing

---

7 Isabelle Duyvesteyn, *Rebels and Escalation; Explaining the Rise and Decline of Rebel Violence* (Cambridge: Cambridge University Press, 2021).
8 Colmar Freiherr von der Goltz, *Das Volk in Waffen* (Berlin: Decker, 1883), 7, 9f. 13.

soldiers 'to bleed dry' the Japanese effort. Attrition by exhausting the opponent was the approach in the American Civil War. Attrition by ways of strategic bombing during the Second World War led to the firebombing raids against Dresden and Tokyo. Attrition through the use of naval battles with destruction as the primary focus occurred in the Battle of Jutland in May 1916 and the Battle of Leyte Gulf in October 1944. Attrition is seen as the hallmark of modern industrialised warfare, where the weight of economic and human resources to outspend the opponent in these realms is seen as the path to attain desired objectives.

Armed force can be used to occupy and to control. There appear two main parameters for control, focused on controlling either territory or people. Obviously these two cannot always be separated, but it is striking that the emphasis changes. Territory can be the prime feature when land is claimed in the name of a nationalist ideal and irridentism comes to the fore. Alternatively, territory can be seen as a key factor in claiming space or resources for the occupying state. Territorial expansion, for example in the course of American history, was about controlling territory. While Napoleon invaded Russia for reasons of opportunity and vengeance, Hitler chose to invade it to gain space and resources for his empire. In the case of Japan, activities beyond their borders from the late nineteenth century onwards were informed by a quest for resources and markets for their products. Iraq wanted to conquer and control Kuwait in 1990; the United States and the Desert Storm coalition wanted to liberate it.

The desire to control populations is prominent when the focus is on the identity of the population and their ideas of belonging. Atrocity was a core element of the strategy in the Yugoslav War of the 1990s, ethnic cleansing being a means to move and remove populations. Notorious concentration camps, such as Omarska, Trnopolje and the mass killing in Srebrenica in 1995 of 8,000 Muslim men in an act of genocide, were instruments of terror. The preoccupation with the control of territory was intended to control the population.

In order to control and occupy, force can be used to isolate, defend or lay siege. In the chapters below we see many examples. Controlling a blue water naval base was a major motivation for the Russian Empire to occupy Port Arthur. The Japanese determination to control this principal Russian naval base at all costs led to one of the greatest sieges in history in August 1904. In French Algeria, the construction of the Morice Line, a fortified border defence system, cut off the connections of the rebel group seeking independence with their neighbours. It denied the insurgents access to safe havens and exit of the battle zone. We note here that sieges form an enduring instrument of war, with Ukrainian cities suffering this fate at the hands of Russian forces as we write.

Prioritisation and Practising Strategy

Paraphrasing our definition of strategy, a polity has a series of instruments, means and resources available to work towards objects which have been prioritised; what evidence do we see of this prioritising? The instruments can be used to coax or hurt in order for the opponent to change their course of action. In this introduction, we have already noted several major developments, such societal, economic and technological changes, which informed our choice for starting our discussion of modern war in this volume around 1800. The importance of these developments notwithstanding, older forms of warfare continued to exist throughout the world in the course of the nineteenth, twentieth and twenty-first centuries. There was the razzia or raid, the uprising and its suppression, the skirmish and the ambush. It is notable that in the course of the nineteenth century, strategy was practised in a highly diverse manner. As the first series of chapters in this volume will show, the idea of strategy was not visible in the writings of Napoleon (Chapter 1); the guerrilla in the nineteenth century was only focused on tactical activity (Chapter 2); and in the American Civil War, strategy was haphazard and possibly not even very conscious (Chapter 4). Also, in the early twentieth century, several contributors to this volume conclude that strategic thinking and practising strategy was haphazard and incoherent if not lacking altogether. For instance, while the Russian Empire reached it largest size in the entirety of its history, any thought devoted on how best to use the limited means at its disposal to serve the interest of this empire was absent (Chapter 3). Pressure to respond to short-term challenges and coming from different parts and neighbours were the main causes of this absence.

In the case of the First World War, not only do we observe an ever-widening (and quite confused) political agenda, but also a mobilisation of all the sources of power to fight this war. While this had surely existed in simpler forms when communities defended themselves against invading Huns or Mongols, it became articulated as a principle from the French Revolution onwards with the famous law for the *levée en masse* passed by the revolutionary Convention in 1793. Léon Daudet, inventor of the term, would later call this 'total war'.[9] The state governments involved in the First World War

---

9 Léon Daudet, *La guerre totale* (Paris: Nouvelle Librairie, 1918), 8.

calibrated and prioritised, based on their own state's direct interests, with little regard for those of the other participants. Strategy making was mostly ad hoc and reactive, driven by pressing needs, rather than an overall idea of a shared strategy or strategic vision. In short, in the process of formulating alliance strategy, formal procedures were often absent in wartime, and decisions tended to be responses to unfolding events than following a clear idea of strategy.

Also in the Second World War, Chapter 12 illustrates the lack of clear strategic directions from the Japanese Imperial General headquarters. Among the Allies, the dominance of the USA resolved clashes of interest that would not be forgotten, as in the case of France where the American supreme Allied commander Eisenhower determined that liberated territories would be temporarily evacuated again in order to straighten the front line and prevent the encirclement of American forces by the Wehrmacht.

Moreover, in the ultimate assessment, the American capability to outproduce its rivals in military hardware was the key to victory rather than any skilful application of strategy. Similarly, the Soviet regime lost the Cold War as it was outproduced and economically ruined by the arms race with the West. (It was of course to everybody's ultimate benefit that this global competition was ended peacefully with non-kinetic coercion, and not with a Third World War.) Even in cases that seem to superficially fit the ideal type of strategy making, the reality was often more nuanced, with chance and friction playing into the domain of reasoned planning.

This observation of a very nuanced reality shows there was much continuity to previous centuries. It begs the question of whether the practising of strategy is not more convincingly explained by a model of muddling through and ad hockery rather than far-sighted processes of prioritisation and linking objectives with resources. We will revisit this question in our Conclusion. Yet we do have some evidence of reasoned strategy making from the early nineteenth century onwards. A case in point is that of the Japanese military leadership in the Russo-Japanese War, while the Russians and their commander General Aleksey Kuropatkin lacked a clear strategic action plan; that Japan won should thus not come as a surprise.

The Second World War saw the development of strategic plans and practices from the outset. National-Socialist Germany had an overall vision for Europe and the world upon which its planning and actions were based. The basic idea of its strategy was to bring down one opponent after another. As detailed in Chapter 11, this approach ultimately failed, and Germany was confronted with multiple enemies and unfinished business with each one of them. Its adversaries reactively developed visions and plans that guided their practices. The eventual formulation of the 'Beat Hitler First' strategy in January 1941 and the stress on unconditional surrender are evidence of this. The prioritising of the defeat of Germany to attain the ultimate defeat of Nazism and the victory of democracy based on the principles formulated in the Atlantic Charter showcase a textbook example of strategic practice according to the ideal type. While coming close to the core principles of our definition, it emerged by trial and error. A combined Chiefs of Staff committee, combining forces of the UK and US, was only created in the winter of 1942, and contact with the other Allies occurred mostly via ad hoc arrangements.

In the Cold War, as several chapters in this volume demonstrate, the United States drew up a strategy to contain the influence of the Soviet Union by resisting and where possible rolling back Soviet expansion wherever it occurred around the globe. The Cold War turned hot in Korea, Vietnam and in intestine wars in other parts of Asia, Latin America and Africa. On the Communist side, Stalin and Mao initially shared the vision and strategy to promote communist takeovers. They agreed to a division of labour, where Mao would focus on Asia in particular.

The Inter-Glacial Period that set in with the dissolution of the Warsaw Pact and then the end of the USSR produced further examples of complex strategy making. In the Gulf War of 1990/1991, the United States and its coalition partners were successful in liberating and restoring the territorial integrity of Kuwait. The legal reasons for invading Iraq were to redress an infringement of international law, the territorial sovereignty of an independent state. Breaking international law by forcefully changing the regime in Iraq would have undermined the claims to the moral high ground. The self-imposed limitations of this war that aimed only to restore the status quo ante but not to effect regime change in Iraq left unfinished business, a frustrated and humiliated dictator (Saddam Hussein) who would present new challenges, and, it was thought, the development of weapons of mass destruction in the form of chemical weapons. The subsequent Gulf War that began in 2003 was meant to remedy this, this time leading to prolonged coalition engagement in (occupation of) Iraq. Whether this was a case of a limited strategic vision, a mismatch between ends, ways and means, or poor strategy making in Baghdad's Green zone, in Washington, London and other capitals where innumerable vested interests collided, remains an open question.

We also find evidence of the application of strategic thinking among non-state actors. In the case of rebel movements and terrorist groups, the linking of desired ends to ways and means is visible, as will be argued in more detail in the pages that follow, especially Chapter 14. The independence movements practised strategy in the context of revolutionary people's war. Even though they borrowed heavily from the templates put to paper by revolutionary thinkers, their practices differed substantially from these theories, yet another reason why the focus on practices rather than thinking is so important. Another example is that of Al-Qaeda's struggle against the West and against secular regimes. Its leaders devised a two-pronged approach. First, they would focus on the enemy nearby, those regimes in the Middle East that were co-opted by the West and, from Al-Qaeda's point of view, needed to be purged. The attacks affected the eventual withdrawal of US forces from Saudi Arabia, which had acted as a US base after the 1991 Gulf War. The second focus would be on the faraway enemy itself, the US, which was attacked on 11 September 2001 by civilian airplanes flying into the World Trade Center in New York and into the Pentagon in Washington. Provoked by this, the US went to wage a 'War on Terror', very much against planning and expectations in Washington, and found itself in quagmires in Afghanistan and Iraq for longer than it had been involved in Vietnam; neither did interventions in Libya and Syria turn out according to Western strategic plans.

In the chapters that follow, these and many more features of the application of strategy will be further discussed and dissected.

I
The Strategies of the Napoleonic Wars

ALAN FORREST

'Strategy' was not a term that was widely used during the Napoleonic Wars. Napoleon seldom employed it during his long years of campaigning, and when he did, on Saint Helena, he used it in a very particular sense, 'referring to the manoeuvres of armies outside an engagement but leading to it'.[1] He attached great weight to the planning of manoeuvres that could outflank the enemy, gain an advantage in terrain or cut off his adversary from vital supply lines. He insisted that every army commander focus on the country's overall war aims and on the part they should play to achieve them. 'It is essential', he noted, 'when one has fourteen armies, that each wages a kind of war relative to the overall plan for the war, and to the strength and circumstances – whether topographical or political – of the opposing state.'[2] It is important, in other words, to think strategically at all times.

When others spoke of his 'military genius', it was less to describe any global strategy than to praise his control of battlefield operations and his ability to make incisive tactical decisions. Future generations were impressed by his command of detail, by the hours he devoted to studying the lie of the land and assessing the strength and likely deployment of enemy forces, as he and Berthier did, with stunning results, on the eve of the Battle of Ulm in 1805.[3] If the courses on military history offered to officer cadets at Saint-Cyr in the Third Republic gave considerable prominence to Napoleon's campaigns, they contained far less on wider strategic goals than on more immediate tactical

---

[1] B. Colson, *Napoleon on War* (Oxford: Oxford University Press, 2015), 122.
[2] N. Bonaparte, 'Note on the Political and Military Position of our Armies in Piedmont and Spain, June 1794', quoted in J. Luvaas (ed.), *Napoleon on the Art of War* (New York: The Free Press, 1999), 80.
[3] The casket which Napoleon and Berthier used to plot the movements of the Austrian Army is illustrated in the exhibition catalogue edited by É. Robbe and F. Lagrange, *Napoléon Stratège* (Paris: Liénart/Musée de l'Armée, 2018), 116.

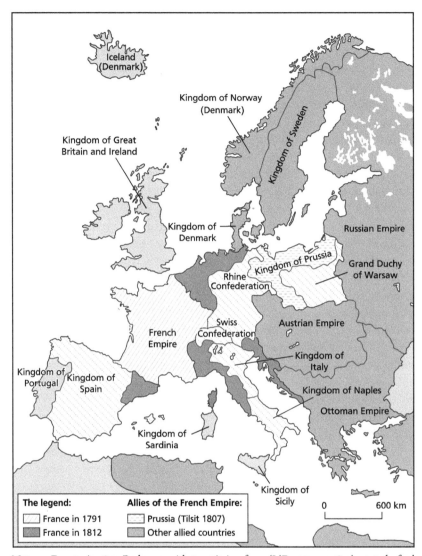

Map 1.1 Europe in 1812. Redrawn with permission from 'L'Europe en 1812', map drafted by Aurélie Boissière (Fondation Napoléon, 2019), www.napoleon.org/histoire-des-2-empires/cartes/carte-de-leurope-en-1812/.

decisions that were key to victory.[4] Yet fighting a decisive battle that forced the enemy to accept an imposed peace settlement – as he did with Prussia after

---

4 Archives de la Guerre, Vincennes, X016, *École Spéciale Militaire de Saint-Cyr, programmes des cours*, 1905–1914.

Jena – was for Napoleon a strategy in itself. Even in 1814, when he was offered a diplomatic settlement by the other powers, he insisted on fighting on, gambling on total victory to drive his enemies to the negotiating table.

Where we today might use the term 'strategy', Napoleon preferred to talk of 'grand tactics', *la grande tactique*, though this does not mean he lacked strategic sense. During the *ancien régime* French military reformers had repeatedly raised strategic issues when they discussed how France might win future wars.[5] Each successive defeat from the War of the Austrian Succession to that of American Independence had produced a plethora of reform proposals, while the operational innovations of Frederick the Great in Prussia, not least his resort to conscription to swell his ranks, had encouraged fundamental strategic rethinking.[6] Their reform proposals produced a 'military Enlightenment' that unleashed new ideas of 'heroism, citizenship, and martial agency' and applied principles of mathematics, science and engineering to the study of war.[7] From the writings of Guibert, Gribeauval and de Saxe there emerged concepts of strategy that helped shape the Revolutionary and Napoleonic campaigns and mould Napoleon's own strategic ideas.[8]

Grand strategy, as we understand it today, requires the mobilisation of all the state's resources in pursuit of its objectives in war. Michael Howard notes how, in the first half of the twentieth century, it 'consisted basically in the mobilisation and development of national resources of wealth, manpower and industrial capacity, together with the enlistment of those of allied and, when feasible, of neutral powers, for the purpose of achieving the goals of national policy in wartime'.[9] Napoleon needed to do more than win battles. He had to gear the economy to support the war effort, impose and collect taxes in France and the territories he conquered, maintain supply lines, raise loans and forge alliances. And he had to create in France and across his empire a culture that valued military ideals such as courage and sacrifice, rewarded them with civic dignities such as the Légion d'Honneur, and celebrated military triumphs in parades and civic architecture.[10] These things

---

5 J. Black, *Military Strategy. A Global History* (New Haven: Yale University Press, 2020), 23.
6 C. Telp, *The Evolution of Operational Art, 1740–1813* (Abingdon: Frank Cass, 2005), 5–34.
7 C. Pichichero, *The Military Enlightenment. War and Culture in the French Empire from Louis XIV to Napoleon* (Ithaca: Cornell University Press, 2017), 15–18.
8 H. A. Guizar, *The École Royale Militaire. Noble Education, Institutional Innovation, and Royal Charity, 1750–1788* (Basingstoke: Palgrave Macmillan, 2020), esp. 79–120.
9 M. Howard, *Grand Strategy* (London: HMSO, 1972), vol. 4, quoted in H. Strachan, 'Michael Howard and the dimensions of military history', *War in History*, 27 (2020), 541.
10 M. J. Hughes, *Forging Napoleon's Grande Armée: Motivation, Military Culture and Masculinity in the French Army, 1800–1808* (New York: New York University Press, 2012), 1–15.

he unquestionably achieved. The question for us must be whether he distanced himself sufficiently from operational matters to develop a clear strategic purpose.

Sources

If Napoleon did not write a treatise on grand strategy, or indeed any theoretical work on the nature of war, he left abundant evidence in his speeches, letters and exhortations to his men of his strategic objectives. In part, of course, his purpose was to inspire others, or, in his days as a revolutionary general, to get himself noticed in Paris. The *Bulletins de la Grande Armée* must certainly be read through a propagandist lens, along with the reports which he had sent from the army in Italy praising his speed of manoeuvre and his use of surprise tactics to outwit the enemy. Throughout every campaign, he wrote letter after letter to his military commanders, outlining campaign tactics, talking of general strategic goals or seeking to ensure that his soldiers and horses were adequately supplied. The publication over the past two decades by the Fondation Napoléon of his *Correspondance générale* has been a major landmark in Napoleonic scholarship, which has opened a window on both his often fastidious management of detail and his wider strategic concerns.[11] Because many of the letters were written while he was on campaign, there is an immediacy about them that is lacking in the thoughts he dictated to Las Cases on Saint Helena, or that he shared with his companions on the island, Generals Bertrand, Montholon and Gourgaud. These were recorded by Las Cases in the *Mémorial de Sainte-Hélène*, published in 1823,[12] and would form the basis of his own *Mémoires*, which are especially rich on the Italian and Egyptian campaigns.[13]

Napoleon's strategic reputation continued to expand in the decades following his death, with the most prominent military theorists of the day, notably the Frenchman Antoine-Henri Jomini and the Prussian Carl von Clausewitz, among his greatest admirers. Jomini first made his name with analyses of Napoleon's campaigns, and only later developed his more theoretical work, his *Précis de l'art de la guerre*, published in 1838. Here his debt to Napoleon is clear, as he praised the emperor's careful preparations for battle,

---

[11] N. Bonaparte, *Correspondance générale, publiée par la Fondation Napoléon*, 15 vols. (Paris: Fayard, 2004–2018).
[12] Comte de Las Cases, *Le Mémorial de Sainte-Hélène*, M. Dunan (ed.), 2 vols. (Paris: Flammarion, 1951).
[13] T. Lentz, *Mémoires de Napoléon*, 3 vols. (Paris: Tallandier, 2010–2011).

his reading of the enemy's strengths and weaknesses, and his appreciation of the value of topography and mapwork. Clausewitz might write generically about war and about the nature of warfare, but he also drew extensively on his own experiences as an officer in the Napoleonic Wars, who, though his outlook was Prussian, was nonetheless dazzled by Napoleon's mastery of the battle and emphasis on moral values in warfare. He had, indeed, two heroes, Frederick the Great and Napoleon, and his analysis in his master-work, *Vom Kriege*, which did much to define strategic thinking throughout the nineteenth century, helped to ensure that Napoleon's aura of genius lived on in the succeeding generation. Modern specialists including Hew Strachan, Peter Paret and Bruno Colson have shown how important Clausewitz's influence has been in gilding Napoleon's military legend.[14]

Actors

Though the Empire was a highly centralised and authoritarian regime, that should not imply that Napoleon was indifferent to the views of others. He might consider himself above politics – his parliamentary institutions were notoriously weak and persistently undermined – yet he depended on them to give his regime a veneer of legitimacy and could not afford to ignore them entirely. Rules governed the membership of the Senate and the Tribunate, and his control was never absolute. In 1807, fearful of opposition, he increased the minimum age for membership of the Legislative Body from thirty to forty; and of the 1100 members who sat between 1800 and 1814, 203 were rewarded with titles and honours.[15] Even when he was absent on campaign, he would return regularly to Paris to push through legislation or demand further funding. Among Legislative Body members were men on whose skills and judgement he came to depend, who became ministers or entered his inner circle of advisers – men such as Talleyrand, the former Bishop of Autun, who was Napoleon's chief diplomat during the years when French military victories brought one European state after another under French hegemony; Joseph Fouché, the former terrorist who served as his minister of police and was responsible for much of the repression of the imperial years; or Armand de Caulaincourt, who after a successful diplomatic posting to St Petersburg was appointed as Napoleon's aide-de-camp and would become his foreign minister during the Hundred Days. No one exercised more influence on the

---

14 See, for instance, B. Colson, *Clausewitz* (Paris: Perrin, 2016).
15 I. Collins, *Napoleon and his Parliaments, 1800–1815* (London: Edward Arnold, 1979), 143.

emperor than Jean-Jacques-Régis de Cambacérès, who was responsible for drawing up the Napoleonic Code and served as Archchancellor of the Empire from 1804 to 1815. Such men did not only hold high office in the Empire, they also exercised considerable influence over Napoleonic policy making. Cambacérès, indeed, was entrusted with managing much of France's internal policy during the emperor's long absences on campaign.[16]

On military matters, Napoleon's key advisers included his most senior marshals, foremost among them his chief-of-staff, Louis-Alexandre Berthier, Prince of Wagram.[17] And as Napoleon's project became increasingly dynastic, the influence of his family over policy matters increased. His brothers all played some part in his rise to power or in the governance of the Empire as it expanded across the continent. His elder brother, Joseph, who was often a calming influence on the more irascible Napoleon, he appointed in turn to be King of Naples, then King of Spain; Louis would be given the Kingdom of Holland; Jérome the Kingdom of Westphalia; while Murat, Napoleon's son-in-law, took over the throne of Naples after Joseph moved to Madrid. Only Lucien of the Bonaparte brothers did not wear a crown: though he had been a key ally at Brumaire and became minister of the interior after the coup, he was too loyal to his republican roots to win Napoleon's trust. Indeed, in Napoleon's eyes, all his brothers were found wanting, Louis for showing too much sympathy with the Dutch people, Joseph for his failure to impose his rule on Spain, Jérome for his inclination to offer amnesty and forgiveness to opponents.[18] Yet they had all played an important part in empire building, alongside those members of the European elites, in the Netherlands, along the Rhine, in northern Italy and across central Germany, who had provided the administrative and judicial leadership needed to rule Napoleon's satellite republics and kingdoms.

Adversaries

Napoleon's policy across the European continent was unrelentingly expansionist, creating adversaries wherever his armies threatened. Even though he came with promises of efficient governance and a law code available to all, local people could not be expected to welcome reforms imposed by a foreign invader. Nor could their rulers, who routinely turned to diplomatic alliances

---

16 L. Chatel de Brancion, *Cambacérès : Maître d'œuvre de Napoléon* (Paris: Perrin, 2001).
17 F. Favier, *Berthier: L'ombre de Napoléon* (Paris: Perrin, 2015).
18 W. H. C. Smith, *The Bonapartes: The History of a Dynasty* (London: Hambledon and London, 2005).

and military coalitions to orchestrate their resistance. In all, France faced seven coalitions of European powers during the Revolutionary and Napoleonic Wars, six of them after 1799.

Each country had its own reasons for joining one or more coalitions against Napoleon. Austria had to fight on multiple fronts if it was to prevent Russia from taking control of Poland, while the deeply conservative Austrian monarchy fought to repress revolutionary and democratic impulses that might undermine international stability. The Habsburgs suffered a number of humiliations at Napoleon's hands, not least the abolition of the Holy Roman Empire in 1806. To rebut French advances they were dependent on alliance diplomacy, which had an important place in their strategic planning.[19] Prussia, too, relied heavily on diplomatic treaties, though here the instincts of Frederick William III were generally to avoid conflict and seek safety in neutrality. Napoleon's ruthlessness, however, made that difficult to sustain: he first established the Confederation of the Rhine, then shattered Prussian resistance at Jena-Auerstedt, before driving home his advantage at Tilsit, depriving the Hohenzollerns of almost half of their territory. Tilsit ended all hope of Prussian diplomatic autonomy. The Prussian government increasingly appealed to German nationalism, with patriots leading a call to exact vengeance and expel the French from German soil. 'Our chief idea', wrote Baron von Stein, 'was to rouse a moral, religious, patriotic spirit in the nation, to inspire it anew with courage, self-confidence, a readiness to make any sacrifice for independence from foreigners and national honour.'[20] But it is easy to exaggerate the importance of German nationalism; the Hohenzollerns were more concerned with maintaining monarchical power and dynastic authority.

Spain and Portugal had altogether different priorities. Portugal, of course, was historically a close ally of Britain.[21] The Portuguese monarchy had done much to anger Napoleon: defaulting on debt after the War of the Oranges in 1801, allowing British warships to dock to take on victuals and supplies, and refusing to enforce the Continental System as the Portuguese economy was heavily reliant on British markets, especially for its wines. Spain had begun the war as an ally of France, but relations soured once Napoleon tried to force Spaniards to observe the continental blockade, leading to Spanish fears that

---

19 C. Ingrao, *The Habsburg Monarchy, 1618–1815* (Cambridge: Cambridge University Press, 1994), 234–41.
20 K. Hagemann, *Revisiting Prussia's Wars against Napoleon: History, Culture and Memory* (Cambridge: Cambridge University Press, 2015), 47.
21 For a detailed analysis see M. Robson, *Britain, Portugal and South America in the Napoleonic Wars: Alliances and Diplomacy in Economic Maritime Conflict* (London: I. B. Tauris, 2011).

France intended to send an army to invade Spain and dethrone the Bourbons. Because of his often contradictory statements, we cannot be sure when Napoleon finally decided to remove the Spanish king and replace him with his brother, Joseph. But Napoleon's intransigence had turned Spain from an ally into the most determined of enemies, and from 1807 to 1814 French troops were condemned to fight a campaign in the Peninsula that they could not win, against the regular Spanish Army, Wellington's forces and their Portuguese allies, and irregulars in the form of *guerrilleros* in Spain and *ordenanças* in Portugal.[22] Before the launch of the Russian Campaign in 1812, indeed, the Peninsula must be counted Napoleon's greatest strategic disaster.

Not all foreign rulers viewed the approach of the Grande Armée with dismay. For some German princes, Napoleon offered an opportunity to pursue their traditional ambitions or to be rewarded with their own kingdoms. In the case of the short-lived Kingdom of Westphalia (1807–1813), Napoleon simply summoned a number of German dignitaries to Paris and presented them with the draft constitution he had prepared.[23] For others, it was a chance to avenge earlier humiliations. For Poles, in particular, the French emperor was a beacon of hope, offering the possibility that they might regain the autonomy that they had lost with partition in 1795; Polish nationalists could not but be encouraged by Napoleon's project for a Grand Duchy of Warsaw.[24] But their response, and their apparent willingness to serve in Napoleon's armies across Europe and beyond – Poles would make an exceptional sacrifice in the failed bid to retake Saint-Domingue in 1802 – had more to do with their desire for liberation from Austrian, Prussian and Russian rule. So in Scandinavia, each country had its own ambitions and war aims. Finns would turn to Russia in a bid to free themselves from the Swedish crown; Norway–Denmark tried to adhere to a policy of neutrality that would allow their commercial shipping to continue trading; Sweden, after also staying neutral in the war until 1805, found itself drawn by Britain and Russia into a coalition against France.[25] In part this was a response to the threat from the Royal Navy, which had been demonstrated in the bombardment of Copenhagen in 1801. But what really attracted Gustav IV was the

22 C. Esdaile, *The Peninsular War. A New History* (London: Allen Lane, 2002), 1–37.
23 S. A. Mustafa, *Napoleon's Paper Kingdom: The Life and Death of Westphalia, 1807–1813* (Lanham: Rowman and Littlefield, 2017), 30.
24 J. Czubaty, *The Duchy of Warsaw, 1807–1815. A Napoleonic Outpost in Central Europe* (London: Bloomsbury, 2016), passim.
25 For a detailed analysis of strategy in Norway–Denmark see R. Glentøj and M. N. Ottosen, *Experiences of War and Nationality in Denmark and Norway, 1807–1815* (Basingstoke: Palgrave Macmillan, 2014), passim.

more traditional goal of conquering Norway and creating a large and powerful Nordic state that could defend itself in the Baltic. The prospect of gaining Norwegian territory was sufficiently tantalising to compensate for the loss of Finland to Russia in the Finnish War of 1808–1809.[26]

The powers which emerged as the clearest winners in the peace that followed, Russia and Britain, also had clear objectives. Alexander I was concerned to consolidate an empire in eastern Europe that had been patiently constructed over the centuries in wars with other imperial powers, notably Sweden and Turkey, and to acquire previously unconquered lands to the east, such as Novgorod and Kazan. Russia had annexed land to the west in three partitions of Poland between 1772 and 1795, and to the south, where she had sought access to the Black Sea, annexing Crimea in 1783 and Georgia in 1801. Consolidating this expansion remained a consistent Russian aim throughout the war, largely at the expense of Poland and the Turkish Empire. Until Tilsit an accommodation with Napoleon seemed possible, since, to gain Russian support in a putative campaign against India, Napoleon was prepared to make concessions in the east. But Alexander's demands proved too high: if Turkey were defeated, Alexander demanded the right to annex Constantinople and the three European provinces of Bessarabia, Moldova and Walachia, and insisted that the Straits be placed under Russian control.[27] He also made clear that he wished to maintain Russian control of Poland, whereas Napoleon saw the Duchy of Warsaw as an essential French sphere of influence. At Tilsit he tried to push Alexander eastwards, leaving German Central Europe under French control. But the Tsar would not be manipulated in this way; rather than concede, he prepared himself for war, maintaining his own strategy while Napoleon pursued increasingly unrealistic dreams. In 1809 he took Finland from Sweden, in 1812 Bessarabia from Turkey. By 1814 Russia had achieved its principal war aims.

Britain had different priorities. In Europe, it sought to remove Napoleon's forces from the Low Countries and to prevent him from opening up a deepwater port on the Scheldt from where he could mount an invasion. To this end the British government paid subsidies to other countries to persuade them to join coalitions against France and in 1808 opened up a new front against Napoleon in the Peninsula, a move that ensured Britain's role in the peace process that followed. These were not insignificant achievements,

---

26 M. Hårdstedt, 'Decline and consolidation: Sweden, the Napoleonic Wars and geopolitical restructuring in northern Europe', in U. Planert (ed.), *Napoleon's Europe. European Politics in Global Perspective* (Basingstoke: Palgrave Macmillan, 2016), 213–26.

27 M.-P. Rey, *Alexander I, The Tsar who Defeated Napoleon* (Dekalb: Northern Illinois University Press, 2012), 192.

demanding strategic decisions on the use of troops and supply.[28] But it was naval power that was crucial, both to the country's defence against possible invasion and to the blockade of the European coastline which provided supply lines to the army in Portugal. Outside Europe, too, it was critical to the defence of Britain's colonies, especially those in the Caribbean and the Indian Ocean, which remained vulnerable as long as other navies – whether of France, Spain or the Netherlands – commanded the sea lanes from Europe. French and Spanish losses in the Americas helped to strengthen Britain's colonial position, as did some strategic acquisitions elsewhere – Malta in the Mediterranean, Mauritius and Ceylon in the Indian Ocean, and the Cape of Good Hope on the southern tip of Africa.

Causes of the Wars

There can be little doubt that the principal cause of the Wars lay in Napoleon's imperial ambitions and his desire to create a modern empire to rival those of antiquity. He had no interest in maintaining the peace, or in supporting the existing balance of power on the continent, and with few exceptions he was the aggressor, the ruler intent on disrupting the existing order. The conquered lands became resources to be used, a reservoir of soldiers for future military campaigns, a source of horses, fodder, food for his armies and of taxes for his treasury, and a market for French industrial production. His adversaries sought to prevent further expansion and to defend what they saw as their own vital interests; this was the case, for instance, in the Low Countries, which Britain saw as vital to its national security since it was from there, with its deep-water ports, that Napoleon might launch a successful invasion of the south coast of England. Outside Europe, France, like Britain, sought to defend its colonial possessions against its rivals, and the Wars in the Caribbean and the Indian Ocean should be seen as simple extensions of a century-long rivalry between the Great Powers.

Ideology played a diminishing role among the causes of European warfare in the Napoleonic years, after the claims and counterclaims of leaders during the revolutionary era, when the purpose and legitimate use of war had been widely debated. The National Assembly rejected the conventional rationale of monarchies for making war, be they the annexation of disputed territories, the acquisition of overseas colonies, the seizure of vital resources or the fulfilment

---

28 C. D. Hall, *British Strategy in the Napoleonic War, 1803–1815* (Manchester: Manchester University Press, 1992), 74–101.

of dynastic ambitions, arguing that France should only make war to defend the nation's frontiers from attack or to prevent the revolution from being overthrown by its enemies. It would not, it declared, 'deploy its forces against the liberty of any people'.[29] But when the revolutionaries went on to declare a republic and execute their king and queen, they unleashed an ideological war against monarchical Europe, in which the very existence of the state was at stake – what David Bell has suggested amounted to 'total war', affecting all classes of society and requiring the mobilisation of huge material and cultural resources.[30] The possibility of compromise receded as states organised themselves to resist revolution, recruiting mass armies, accepting high casualties and showing a new openness to operational innovation. Many turned to conscription to fill their ranks; even Britain, which had resisted all calls for conscription during this period, raised over 225,000 men for the Peninsular War by a mixture of voluntary enlistment, recruitment into the militia and militia ballots.[31]

However, the ideological language used was often deceptive. The wars that engulfed Europe between 1792 and 1815 were not just wars between a disruptive, revolutionary force and the crowned heads of Europe; indeed, while France's enemies might describe them as 'the French Wars', most of Europe's Great Powers were implicated, forming seven coalitions of differing strengths, while France was aided by its own allies and the states it occupied in the Rhineland and across German central Europe.[32] Napoleon may, in Lawrence Freedman's words, have 'embodied a new way of fighting wars: a combination of individual genius and mass organisation, and objectives far more ambitious than those of his predecessors'.[33] But in other ways the wars had changed little from the wars of the eighteenth century, and when Napoleon was finally defeated, it was at the hands of *ancien régime* armies that had adjusted to the requirements of the age. They were as much cabinet wars as peoples' wars (a concept that was largely the product of nineteenth-century nationalist propaganda), and ideology was quickly forgotten both by Napoleon and by those fighting against him.[34] War had reverted to more traditional aims.

29 *Archives Parlementaires de 1787 à 1860. Recueil complet des débats législatifs et politiques des Chambres Françaises, série 1, 1787 à 1799*, Jérôme Mavidal and Émile Laurent (eds) (Paris: 1862–), vol. 15, 662, https://gallica.bnf.fr/ark:/12148/bpt6k495339.texteImage.
30 D. A. Bell, *The First Total War: Napoleon's Europe and the Birth of Modern Warfare* (London: Bloomsbury, 2007), passim.
31 K. Linch, *Britain and Wellington's Army. Recruitment, Society and Tradition, 1807–15* (Basingstoke: Palgrave Macmillan, 2011), 57.
32 For a concise discussion of the seven coalitions that formed against the French, see C. Esdaile, *The French Wars, 1792–1815* (London: Routledge, 2001).
33 L. Freedman, *Strategy. A History* (Oxford: Oxford University Press, 2013), 70–1.
34 B. Simms, *The Struggle for Mastery in Germany* (London: Macmillan, 1998), 102–3.

Objectives

Napoleon's objectives on the European continent seemed relatively consistent, at least until his treaty with Alexander at Tilsit. At first, he sought to provide France with defensible frontiers, the Rhine to the east, the Alps to the south-east, the Pyrenees in the south-west. This should not be equated with political reaction; it had been revolutionary policy, too, and had its roots in Enlightenment republicanism.[35] And, like the revolutionaries, he soon turned to empire building, to extending the territories he controlled into central Europe and northern Italy. But not everything was exploitative: there was a positive side to the Empire, too, through which he sought to win public support in the very countries he was exploiting. He brought justice and administration on the French model to the lands he conquered, offering the people the benefits of good governance, access to justice and better education. Wherever possible – essentially in what Michael Broers encapsulates in the 'inner empire', where resistance to French rule was limited and there was more of a shared political culture – he called on the authority of local elites to entrench his rule. Where this proved impossible, he did not hesitate to impose French administrators, or to remove recalcitrant rulers and replace them with his own brothers.[36] But offering good governance and winning over local people was also a weapon of war. The lands he conquered or annexed became important sources of wealth, tax revenue, requisitions and conscripts. In later years, however, Napoleon lost sight of this objective and sought to punish other European rulers who defied him or refused to do his bidding, notably when he took the foolhardy decision to invade Russia in 1812. His purpose here was purely punitive: he had no intention of adding Russian territory to his empire. But the responsibility for the campaign was surely his, since, when he imposed the Continental System on Russia as part of the peace terms at Tilsit, Alexander understood that another war was inevitable. As the Russian general Levin Bennigsen noted, 'if Napoleon was allowed to strangle Russia's foreign trade, then the economy would no longer be able to sustain Russia's armed forces or the European culture of its elites'.[37]

Napoleon also, almost obsessionally, dreamed of mounting an invasion of Britain, the country he saw as his and France's most persistent enemy. During

---

35 J. R. Hayworth, *Revolutionary France's War of Conquest in the Rhineland. Conquering the Natural Frontier, 1792–97* (Cambridge: Cambridge University Press, 2019), xiii.
36 M. Broers, 'A Turner thesis for Europe? The frontier in Napoleonic Europe', *Napoleonica. La Revue*, 2 (2009), 157–69.
37 D. Lieven, *Russia against Napoleon: The Battle for Europe, 1807–1814* (London: Allen Lane, 2009), 64; A. M. Martin, *Constructing Imperial Moscow, 1762–1855* (Oxford: Oxford University Press, 2013), 182.

the truce that followed the Peace of Amiens in 1801, he amassed a huge army along the Channel coast, training and drilling them at the Camp de Boulogne and seemingly posing a direct threat to the south of England. In the event, when hostilities resumed, the Grande Armée marched eastwards into Germany and central Europe, but Napoleon had made his intention clear, and he would not be dissuaded from it. Indeed, Nicola Todorov suggests that even after the destruction of his navy at Trafalgar the idea of invading England remained uppermost in his mind, giving coherence to the decisions he took up to and including his fateful attack on Russia. In the Baltic and along the North Sea coast he sought to establish the major ports and naval bases that would be needed if he were to embark for England. In Spain, he extended the war in order to tie down British forces and strip Britain of the troops needed for its defence. And all the while he systematically exploited Europe's forests for high-quality timber and recruited seamen to strengthen his navy, all with the goal of invading England. Even the continental blockade was tweaked to help advance the invasion: by opening up commercial shipping by a system of licences in 1810, he encouraged the recruitment of seamen among whom he could find recruits for his navy. From every perspective, observes Todorov, 'the great affair of his reign was the invasion of England'.[38]

In the colonial sphere, it is more difficult to follow a consistent line of policy. Napoleon's desire for colonies was, from the start, reflected in their value to the mother-country as an economic resource; he had little interest in free trade and stood by a traditional mercantilist view of their worth. At the heart of this vision was his desire to regain and exploit France's richest Caribbean colony, Saint-Domingue, whose plantation economy had been destroyed by war and slave insurgency, and which by the late 1790s lay at the mercy of British and Spanish forces. In the rebel leader, Toussaint-Louverture, he faced a formidable opponent, a man with the political and military gifts to wrest control of the island. In the meantime, Louisiana, which Napoleon saw primarily as a granary to supply the island with provisions, cattle and wood, had been ceded to Spain in 1795, and though he regained it in 1800, he was soon forced to send an army of 3,000 men to occupy New Orleans and the Mississippi delta, and a much bigger force, led by his brother-in-law Charles Leclerc, to reconquer Saint-Domingue for France. By 1802, however, this strategy lay in ruins, as Leclerc's army was

---

38 N. Todorov, *La Grande Armée à la conquête de l'Angleterre* (Paris: Vendémiaire, 2016), 226–9.

destroyed by a combination of Toussaint's tactics and yellow fever, and as the United States pressed to expand into French territory on the mainland. Napoleon quickly changed tack, seemingly abandoning all interest in the region and authorising the sale of Louisiana to the Americans. Louisiana had become dispensable. And when it did, the last vestige of a consistent strategy for the Americas was abandoned.

Like French governments across the eighteenth century, Napoleon still dreamed of ruling over a global empire, though he found opportunities for colonisation limited. In both Central and South America his ambitions were blocked by the maritime empires of Spain and Portugal, and in the Levant and the Indian Ocean by the Royal Navy. His 1799 campaign in Egypt was in large measure inspired by his desire to undermine the British Empire in India. Again in 1803, an expedition from Mauritius was sent to India to reoccupy Pondicherry, only to be held at bay by British forces. And in 1805 Napoleon sent a military mission to Teheran to forge a military alliance with Persia, which resulted in the Treaty of Finkenstein in 1807. But again his strategy was flawed, since, as Jeremy Black explains, his vision for the region was quite different from Persia's: 'The Persians wanted help in driving the Russians out of Georgia, while Napoleon wished to see Persia exclude British influence and hoped that it could be a base against British India.'[39] After Tilsit, the strategic importance of the region to the French declined and Napoleon's interest dramatically lessened.

Available Means

France needed a strong army to fend off attacks on the Continent, and had to invest heavily in the navy to challenge Britain in the colonial sphere. It was a difficult balance to maintain, and a very costly one for a country without Britain's fiscal strength or the strong banking traditions of Holland. Years of war had strained royal finances long before 1789; the costs of the American War, indeed, had caused the virtual bankruptcy of the monarchy. The Napoleonic Wars, too, would place huge strains on the treasury, requiring both massive loans from banks and huge indemnities from the countries Napoleon invaded. The strength of Britain's public finances and its higher tax base were major contributors to its success.

---

39 J. Black, *From Louis XIV to Napoleon. The Fate of a Great Power* (London: UCL Press, 1999), 214.

As an artillery officer, Napoleon placed greater store by the army than the navy, and though for long periods he invested in both, a mass army was his principal weapon in war. The Revolution had dramatically reformed recruitment, and by 1799 France was exacting annual conscriptions which continued throughout the Napoleonic years. And as his empire expanded, the annexed territories were in turn expected to provide recruits, as well as horses and logistical support, for the army. Relations between government and governed were often tense, as the fiscal and manpower demands of the state seemed ever-more oppressive and increasing numbers of their sons were exposed to military service, while the army and gendarmerie were deployed to impose order on rural villages and recalcitrant peasant communities. Conscription was especially resented. By 1813 public support for the war was visibly dwindling, as levy after levy drained the country of its young men and Napoleon turned to boys who had barely reached adolescence in a desperate bid to fill his ranks. Across the country, the annual conscription pitted more and more young men against the authorities: if some still marched obediently to their units, others opted to lie low in woods or in shepherds' huts, provided with food and protection by their families, village mayors and local farmers. Napoleon not only lost his former allies. He risked losing his home front too.[40]

The navy which he inherited had been weakened by the flight in the first years of the Revolution of nearly half of its officer corps, who were much more deeply royalist than their army counterparts; by chronic underinvestment in the years that followed; and by the loss of seven ships of the line when Toulon surrendered to the British and Spanish fleets in 1793. Yet, if he was to pursue his goals beyond Europe – controlling the Atlantic sea lanes, for instance, recapturing Saint-Domingue or cutting off Britain's supply routes to India – Napoleon required a navy capable of defeating the British in a battle at sea. And while he could take some comfort from the mutinies in the 1790s at Spithead and the Nore, these did not permanently undermine British naval morale. Britain maintained a vital superiority in both the quality of its ships and the number of seamen it could muster, and France was unable to achieve numerical parity.[41] Nelson inflicted a serious defeat on the French at the Nile in 1798 which led to the loss of thirteen ships and effectively destroyed Napoleon's strategy in the Levant and Egypt, while the destruction of France's Atlantic fleet in 1805 at Trafalgar guaranteed British naval superiority for the remainder

---

40 A. Forrest, *Conscripts and Deserters. The Army and French Society during the Revolution and Empire* (New York: Oxford University Press, 1989), 236–7.
41 J. Meyer, 'The Second Hundred Years' War, 1689–1815', in D. Johnson, F. Bédarida and F. Crouzet (eds), *Britain and France: Ten Centuries* (Folkestone: Dawson, 1980), 139–63.

of the war. When he invaded Spain in 1808, Napoleon lost the support of the Spanish Navy, another blow to any hopes he still entertained of maintaining an effective blockade of the coastline and protecting the Atlantic sea lanes.

Process of Prioritisation

Napoleon's first concern was the security and stability of his European empire. This was not only a military question: governing the Empire, providing its component parts with administration and justice, using the countries he conquered as granaries and as sources of much-needed troops and supplies, and preventing any outbreaks of revolt or rebellion were all interlocking parts of his imperial policy, and they were prioritised over colonial and extra-European objectives. They were also critical to providing for and servicing his armies for future conquests. The fact that his armies lived off the land allowed him to travel without encumbering baggage trains – a policy that had begun under the Revolution, which had persistently instructed its agents to *'nourrir la guerre par la guerre, faire vivre l'armée sur le pays'* ['feed war with war, and make the army live off the land'].[42] The people of central Europe might with justification feel that not only were they subjected to the rule of a foreign invader, they were also treated as milch-cows for an ever more gluttonous military machine.

Prioritising the army meant raising unprecedented sums in tax and requisitions, and directing agricultural and industrial output to the needs of the military. Napoleon understood the full importance of military logistics and reliable sources of supply. He also appreciated the value of a clear command structure. The planning of military operations passed to the army high command, whose role and composition he had reformed while on campaign with the Italian Army. The army was now answerable to his newly appointed chief of staff, Louis-Alexandre Berthier, whose *Mémoire sur l'organisation du service d'état-major* he had read and assimilated.[43] Military administration was organised around three governing principles: all officers were answerable to the high command, which was responsible for taking initiatives and ordering manoeuvres; they were committed to carrying out policy quickly and efficiently without being distracted by other priorities; and each army was

---

42 J. Godechot, 'Les variations de la politique française à l'égard des pays occupés, 1792–1815', in Centre d'histoire économique et sociale (Bruxelles), *Occupants, occupés, 1792–1815: Colloque de Bruxelles, 1968* (Brussels: Université Libre de Bruxelles, 1969), 22–5.

43 G. P. Cox, *The Halt in the Mud. French Strategic Planning from Waterloo to Sedan* (London: Routledge, 2019), 12.

assigned four adjutants-general, each responsible for a discrete part of the service. The high command divided its activities between three main areas: troop movements; materiel and logistics; and planning and intelligence. As the war progressed, it was given further responsibilities, for the management of prisoners of war and military justice, fodder supplies, field hospitals and reconnaissance. Napoleon's insistence on careful staff work and attention to detail became legendary and would be reflected in all his campaigns.

The sublimation of economic policy to his wider war aims was never clearer than when Napoleon tried to impose his continental blockade on the whole of occupied Europe, with little concern for the economic damage it wreaked. At one level, this policy was unashamedly mercantilist, aiming to protect French markets while threatening to destroy British maritime trade with northern Europe and the Baltic. At another, it was an act of war, a strategic move which would, he hoped, compensate for French naval weakness by attacking Britain's financial stability, turn British public opinion against the war, and deny Britain the financial capacity to wage it.[44] Napoleon knew that he could hurt Britain by focusing on its trade: between 1802 and 1804 the resumption of war had reduced the value of Britain's trade with France from around £2 million to a mere £20,000. If his policy failed, it was because it underestimated Britain's commercial and fiscal strength, and undermined the prosperity of much of the rest of Europe.

Execution of Strategy

Napoleon spent much of the war in the field, and his reputation as a strategist focuses heavily on his leadership on the battlefield. He took care to assess the enemy's strengths and to pick off his adversaries one by one to prevent them from combining against him. He consistently favoured offence over defence, organising his armies for aggressive campaigns and launching surprise attacks to encircle enemy units and cut them off from the main body of their army – his famous *manoeuvre de derrière* which forced the enemy to turn and face him when they were least prepared. A good example of this was at Ulm in 1805, where after an exhausting march from the Channel ports, he encircled Mack's army before attacking it from behind and taking control of the centre of the battlefield.[45] Speed of movement was paramount, whether in lines or in

---

44 K. B. Aaslestad and J. Joor (eds), *Revisiting Napoleon's Continental System. Local, Regional and European Experiences* (Basingstoke: Palgrave Macmillan, 2015), 5.
45 J. Garnier, 'À la recherche d'une typologie des batailles napoléoniennes', in Robbe and Lagrange (eds), *Napoléon stratège*, 86–9.

columns. On Saint Helena he would claim that he altered his tactics in accordance with the strengths of the enemy. 'A general never knows if he must attack in lines or columns', he explained. 'If he attacks in lines, he is weak against a cavalry attack that takes him in the flank. Faced with the Russians, for example, who employ their cavalry marvellously, that is very dangerous.' But overall he preferred to attack in columns. 'In war', he wrote, 'you have to be utterly simple. The attacking column suffices; it is formed promptly and by simple procedure.'[46] Napoleon understood the need to deploy each arm in battle, and by bringing them together into a corps system, he sought to gain the greatest manoeuvrability. He used field guns that were one-third lighter than his opponents', to allow him to concentrate artillery fire in battle; and he understood the use that should be made of cavalry in giving increased mobility, always keeping some in reserve for the later stages of a battle. 'Without cavalry', he reflected after Jena, 'battles are inconclusive.'[47] And throughout his career he insisted that he would be content with nothing less than a conclusive victory.

The Empire, as we know, ended in failure, twice – in 1814 after the *Campagne de France* (French Campaign) and again in 1815 following the misguided adventure that was the Hundred Days. By then Napoleon had lost any sense of strategic purpose; everything was geared to salvaging what remained of his empire. Indeed, after Wagram in 1809 the era of empire building was effectively over. The invasion of Russia in 1812 – surely his greatest strategic blunder – was a rash and ill-advised act of vengeance undertaken at huge cost and against the advice of his ministers, a vainglorious moment of folly that ignored the inevitable diplomatic fallout. There had been no thought of incorporating Russia into his empire; rather, this was an act of pure opportunism whose one aim was to punish Russia and compel Alexander to adhere to the terms of the Treaty of Berlin. Napoleon's retreat from Moscow was followed by the collapse of his fragile alliance system, the desertion of a majority of his allies and the construction of a sixth coalition for the 1813 campaign. Again Napoleon had shown that he was intent on total victory, and that negotiation and compromise had little place in his strategic world. Yet diplomacy is an essential part of strategy; for Napoleon to ignore it was to limit his strategic options at a time when every European power was nurturing its own ambitions and pursuing its own goals. Almost all were intent on curbing French expansion, if only to impose some form of stability on the international system.

---

46 Colson, *Napoleon on War*, 315.   47 Colson, *Napoleon on War*, 215.

In the short term Napoleon's strategy brought rapid results that shocked and impressed in equal measure. He fought over sixty battles, winning the vast majority of them. But his strategy for European dominance was flawed, his success worn away by years of attrition. And, crucially, he did not win the peace. 1815 brought a seismic change in the international order that left Britain and Russia enjoying unprecedented power on the world stage and opened the way to the rise of Prussia in German central Europe. In Paul Schroeder's view, the international system that would go on to shape diplomacy until the First World War was composed of 'two world powers, more invulnerable than ever; three major Continental powers, distinctly weaker and more vulnerable; and a host of smaller intermediary bodies'.[48] It placed new emphasis on co-operation for the maintenance of peace, as the Great Powers embarked on what Beatrice de Graaf has termed 'a unique experiment', 'the implementation of a collective security system', united against what they saw as the necessary disruption brought about by revolutionary change.[49] The alliance systems that had done so much to ensure the downfall of the Empire would live on through the return to a multipolar Europe and the creation of a consensual management system for international politics that would help to keep the peace in Europe until the Crimean War in the 1850s.

Conclusion

To his admirers, Napoleon remains the complete strategist, blessed with a vision that combined immediate military operations and wider foreign policy goals.[50] But others have questioned this, asking whether he really had an overall strategy at all. Or was he simply, in Owen Connelly's words, 'blundering to glory'?[51] Charles Esdaile suggests that too many military historians of the period have been content to advance from campaign to campaign, emphasising the tactical brilliance of his operational manoeuvres, with little discussion of what these manoeuvres were supposed to achieve. They say little about Napoleon's vision of international relations, and assume 'that his goal was the construction of a pan-European coalition directed from

---

48 P. Schroeder, *The Transformation of European Politics, 1763–1848* (Oxford: Clarendon Press, 1994), 516.
49 B. de Graaf, *Fighting Terror after Napoleon. How Europe Became Secure after 1815* (Cambridge: Cambridge University Press, 2020), 9.
50 J.-P. Bois, 'Napoléon, chef d'État, chef de guerre, chef d'armée', in Robbe and Lagrange (eds), *Napoléon stratège*, 20–5.
51 O. Connelly, *Blundering to Glory: Napoleon's Military Campaigns* (Wilmington: Scholarly Resources, 1987).

Paris that could force Britain into submission by means of the exclusion of her trade from the entire length of Europe's coastline'.[52] It is too easy, he implies, to allow Napoleon to control his own narrative, often retrospectively, and to assume that behind each campaign and each incisive battle lay a coherent strategy that may or may not have existed.

52 C. Esdaile, 'Deconstructing the French wars: Napoleon as anti-strategist', *Journal of Strategic Studies*, 31 (2008), 516.

2

Guerrilla and Nineteenth-Century Strategies of Insurgency

IAN BECKETT

There has always been a confusion of definition relating to such terms as guerrilla war, partisan war, small war, people's war, revolutionary war and insurgency. Precise meanings have changed over time, and did so particularly during the nineteenth century when distinctions made by contemporaries could be imprecise and interchangeable.

It has been suggested that guerrilla conflicts are best defined as 'wars fought between parties that are fundamentally unequal, one side possessing authority, a recognised claim to a monopoly of power and a state apparatus in some form, often including armed forces'.[1] This does not entirely answer for the nineteenth century, which presents significant problems of analysis in strategic terms. In the twentieth century, various theories of guerrilla warfare and insurgency became well known, particularly where the theorists and practitioners were associated with revolutionary ideology as in the cases of Mao Zedong and Che Guevara. These, as well as other twentieth-century theorists and practitioners such as T. E. Lawrence and George Grivas, elevated traditional tactical concepts of irregular warfare to strategic purpose.

By contrast in the nineteenth century, it is difficult to discern anything in an age-old form of warfare that was not almost instinctive reaction on the part of those opposing conquest, occupation or, in an internal context, the legitimacy of authority. Nineteenth-century guerrilla warfare was highly diverse but always the resort of the weak in face of the strong. There could be little expectation that a guerrilla strategy of itself could result in victory in such circumstances unless guerrillas could transform themselves to meet regular forces conventionally or, alternatively, co-operate with regular forces

---

[1] B. Heuser, *The Evolution of Strategy: Thinking War from Antiquity to the Present* (Cambridge: Cambridge University Press, 2020), 387.

in a partisan role. In terms of the latter, soldiers' experience of warfare in difficult terrain in the eighteenth century (in North America and on the fringes of Europe) had generated its own literature in terms of promoting specialised military forces that could be employed on the flanks or in the rear of a regular opponent. Theorists of partisan war did not express it in strategic terms and, in any case, it was seen as distinctly separate from guerrilla warfare.

In most cases, a purely guerrilla strategy amounted to no more than survival by means of evasion and the 'hit and run' tactics familiar in history since antiquity. It was easiest to take to the hills, mountains, forests, jungles or desert wastes in order to prosecute guerrilla resistance where guerrillas' local knowledge facilitated survival and the acquisition of supplies from a potentially supportive population. An opponent's lines of communication or isolated posts would be obvious targets, and decision making might be merely a question of where, when and whom to attack.

The environmental factor was always likely to be significant. At the same time, many examples of guerrilla resistance in the nineteenth century – particularly to colonial powers – emanated from indigenous cultures with oral rather than written traditions. Thus, with certain exceptions, the evidence for decision making on the part of guerrillas in the nineteenth century has most often to be discerned from what their opponents wrote and recorded rather than the guerrillas themselves. In some areas of the world, there were traditions of banditry that not only formed some part in the generation of guerrilla resistance but also largely shaped it.

There are relatively few examples where setting objectives and priorities and allocating resources can be readily identified among those who led guerrillas in the nineteenth century. In so far as some attempted to do so, the very nature of dispersed guerrilla warfare militated against central direction. Historians of guerrilla warfare have arguably imposed more pattern on guerrilla campaigns than was apparent at the time.

It was widely recognised by Western soldiers that guerrilla warfare represented a specific challenge to regulars, with the result that there was an increasing corpus of work on combatting guerrillas by the end of the nineteenth century, not least how it might be avoided. Such theoretical work, and the way in which it was applied in practice, was strategic as well as operational and tactical. Counterguerrilla warfare, therefore, might involve the kind of significant choices and resource allocation that the guerrillas themselves were not required to make. Partisan warfare had its successes in the nineteenth century but there were no examples of guerrillas overcoming their opponents through their own efforts. Guerrillas had no realistic expectation of achieving wider political objectives.

Notwithstanding the difficulty in applying strategic principles to decision making on the part of guerrillas, it is perhaps best to begin by establishing the extent of guerrilla conflict – as opposed to partisan warfare – in the nineteenth century. An obvious starting point is the very conflict that gave rise to the word guerrilla ('small war'), namely the Spanish resistance to Napoleon (1808–1814), already mentioned in Chapter 1. French revolutionary policies had already resulted in internal revolt in both the Vendée and also Brittany – the Chouannerie – between 1793 and 1796. Apart from Spain, the expansion of the Napoleonic Empire also engendered guerrilla resistance in Calabria and the Tyrol. Spain offers some strategic aspects but the guerrilla struggle was a complex one in which intended central direction largely failed to influence regional and local events. The French retreat from Moscow in 1812 saw significant examples of partisan warfare on the part of the Russians, which again added to its theory by the likes of Denis Davidov.

The struggle of the Spanish Latin American colonies for their independence and that of the Greeks for their independence from the Ottoman Empire involved some guerrilla action but linked to wider military operations. Just as there was intermittent irregular warfare in the newly independent Latin American republics, the First Carlist War in Spain at least evoked some echoes of the earlier struggle against Napoleon. Polish resistance to Russian occupation resulted in contributions to the theory rather than the practice of guerrilla and partisan warfare by theorists such as Wojciech Chrzanowski, Karol Bogumil Stolzman, Henryk Kamienski and Józef Bem. Urban insurrection was also a feature of Europe as in 1830 and 1848, and equally generated theoretical work by writers such as Carlo Bianco. Giuseppe Garibaldi also undertook limited guerrilla campaigns against Austria in the Franco-Austrian War and Austro-Prussian War. The *francs-tireurs* brought into the field alongside the *Garde Mobile* after the defeat of the main French armies in the Franco-Prussian War did suggest strategic intent, but these forces were widely fluctuating in organisation, strength and purpose, and did not achieve any significant result.

Beyond Europe, the American Civil War had many instances of guerrilla activity, but it was entirely peripheral to the main operations and without any impact on the outcome of the war. Indeed, the war provides one of the best examples of a political and, especially, military leadership specifically rejecting guerrilla warfare. There was incipient guerrilla opposition to the Qing dynasty in China during the nineteenth century while the expansion of western colonial empires offered more examples of resistance. The doyen of theorists of 'small wars', Charles Callwell, was careful to classify indigenous opponents into European-trained armies; 'semi-organised' troops; disciplined but primitive armies; fanatics; and true guerrillas. Callwell identified as true guerrillas the Maori encountered by the British during the New Zealand Wars, the Xhosa in the seventh and eighth Cape Frontier Wars, and the *dacoits* (bandits) during the pacification of Burma. Similarly, by implication in describing the measures taken against them, he identified as guerrillas Abd el-Kader fought by the French in Algeria, and Shamil (or Shamyl) who resisted the Russians in the Caucasus. Callwell also identified a sixth category, which differed from all other guerrillas in being both white and mounted, namely the Boers. The Boers, indeed, provide perhaps the best example of a conscious decision to undertake guerrilla warfare following the defeat of the main Boer field army during the South African War.

It is proposed to offer four case studies, namely the attempt to control Spanish resistance to Napoleon after 1808, the decision of the Southern Confederacy not to pursue a guerrilla strategy in 1865, Burmese resistance to British annexation between 1885 and 1895, and the decision of the Boer leadership to undertake guerrilla warfare in 1900. It will be apparent that these are examples where some documentation exists on the part of those engaged in guerrilla conflict. Most guerrillas did not have the luxury of strategic choice, access to resources or a centralised leadership, and the cases studies illustrate contrasting circumstances pertaining to how far strategic analysis can be applied to nineteenth-century guerrilla warfare.

Spain

Napoleon sent troops into Spain in October 1807 with the agreement of the Spanish king, Charles IV, en route to force Portugal into the so-called Continental System. Facing opposition, Charles abdicated in favour of his son, Ferdinand VII in March 1808. There was a rising against the French in Madrid on 2 May 1808 and, taking advantage of deep internal divisions in Spanish politics, Napoleon forced Ferdinand to abdicate in turn on 6 May, declaring his own brother, Joseph, King of Spain. The Spanish Army was soon routed and a British army sent to help was driven into the sea at Corunna in January 1809. Guerrillas began to appear first in Galicia and then Aragon, mostly it would appear spontaneously among the lowest elements of society. They were led by men of humble origin such as the Castillian, Juan Martín Diaz; Juan Palarea around Toledo; Juan Diaz Porlier in the Asturias; Jean de

Mendietta in Zamora; and Francisco Espoz y Mina, a farmer's son from Navarre. There was a highly complex mix of personal, local, political, social and religious factors involved in stimulating resistance.

The guerrilla war in Spain attracted interest from the start. Participants at all levels recorded their experiences. Those of the French ranged from Marshal Louis Suchet to General Joseph Léopold Hugo, Captain Elzéar Blaze and Sub-Lieutenant Albert de Rocca. Several future military theorists also served with the French in Spain: Henri, Baron de Jomini, Jean Le Mière de Corvey, Thomas Robert Bugeaud, and the Prussian, Heinrich von Brandt with the Polish Legion. Probably the best known memoir by a guerrilla is that of Espoz y Mina, but others include Gregorio González Arranz as well as Spanish regular army critics. Similarly, many British soldiers from Wellington downwards who encountered the guerrillas recorded their observations. There is abundant contemporary documentation available in Spanish, French and British archives. The traditional popular image of a heroic guerrilla achievement was subjected to manipulation by those mid-twentieth-century historians seeking to find a progressive political message in irregular resistance. More usefully, there have been sophisticated local studies such as that on Navarre by John Tone, but the principal revisionist challenging the traditional image and pointing to the considerable overlap with banditry has been Charles Esdaile.

Those groups which emerged in Navarre resulted more from a perception that the French threatened traditional autonomy, including a degree of tax exemption, than from any conscious identification with Spanish nationalism. There was undoubtedly a considerable attachment to the Church, which came under particular attack from the French. Most resistance in Navarre came from the more prosperous Basque areas of the north, where the population was typically from dispersed and independently minded small peasant land holdings. The more urbanised Castillian areas of the south had experienced greater social tensions before the war and there was less to lose through French occupation.

In the case of Valencia, existing peasant hostility to the Spanish government's attempt to widen conscription in 1801 and continuing resentment against seigniorial rights contributed to resistance when many prominent Spanish *afrancesados* (collaborators) were drawn from the ranks of the semi-feudal seigniors. This does not mean that guerrilla war in Valencia can be solely explained in terms of a social conflict. Nonetheless, Spain was in a state of considerable socio-economic unrest at the time of French intervention, and in southern and eastern Spain in particular there was often an underlying opposition to noble and ecclesiastical authority, which was just as significant as the presence of the French in fuelling the guerrilla war. Previous regional traditions of banditry and smuggling also contributed to resistance, notably in Andalusia. So too did the existence of local *ordenança* (home guards) such as the Catalan *somatenes* and Basque *miqueletes*, while the link between Catholic fanaticism and violent counterrevolution was just as pronounced as in the Vendée, Calabria or the Tyrol.

With central governance breaking down, local juntas (assemblies) emerged alongside a Supreme Central Junta established on 25 September 1808 to act in the name of Ferdinand VII. On 28 December 1808 the Supreme Central Junta legitimised the guerrillas, placing them on the same footing as regular troops. It called for more to oppose the French in a decree establishing *partidas* (partisans) and outlining their organisation and objectives in twenty-four articles. Articles 22–23 laid down their objectives as attacking French communications, preventing French collection of supplies and combining to attack convoys and stage fake night assaults to prevent the French from resting. Article 24 placed the *partidas* under the overall direction of regular army divisional commanders. However, the decree had effectively legalised banditry by authorising the retention of any property or goods seized from the French or their sympathisers. An ordinance issued on 17 April 1809 to further regulate what were now termed *corsa terrestre* (land corsairs) authorised the population as a whole to 'attack and loot, on all favourable occasions, the French, either individually or in groups, to take the food and the supplies intended for their use: in a word, to cause them as much harm and damage as possible'.[2] Additional local edicts were issued by local juntas including those in Galicia and the Asturias.

The Supreme Central Junta envisaged the guerrillas as operating in conjunction with the Spanish regular forces. The junta's resources were few and, in practice, its writ did not run much beyond Seville. Its authority was contested by provincial juntas and by generals who sought to replace it, which occurred in January 1810. The Council of Regency, in turn, was succeeded in September 1810 by the Cortes of Cadiz. Spanish Army officers helped raise the revolt in some areas such as Galicia and sometimes led guerrilla bands. Local rivalries, however, certainly hampered co-operation against the French as in Aragon, eastern Castille and Navarre, where Espoz y Mina waged a ruthless campaign against his rivals. Ezpoz y Mina supposedly presided over about 7,000 men by 1813, while the overall total of guerrillas may have been some 30,000.

2 R. Chartrand, 'The guerrillas: how Oman underestimated the role of irregular forces', in P. Griffith (ed.), *A History of the Peninsular War, Volume IX: Modern Studies of the War in Spain and Portugal, 1808–14* (London: Greenhill Books, 1999), 161–80.

Such expansion of guerrilla numbers did coincide with some greater regularisation in at least some cases. Several of the provincial juntas were able to impose regular-style organisation and discipline as a means of reasserting social control over the more unruly elements unleashed by the initial uprising against the French. Some leaders were prepared to accept regular commissions to give themselves status among the *partidas* as a whole when rivals might be portrayed still as mere bandits. The performance of the Spanish Army, however, was seriously undermined by the constant desertion of its rank and file to the guerrillas, who were perceived to be less disciplined and to offer greater rewards.

Whether the result of regularisation or not, however, growth came at the price of separating the guerrillas from the population to some extent and rendering them vulnerable to the French through the need to establish more permanent bases. That vulnerability, in turn, forced the guerrillas to live off rather than among their own people. They became as great a burden to the Spanish as to the French. The often random and wanton plundering of the people by the former was conceivably worse than the more systematic and regulated contributions imposed by the latter. In some areas, guerrilla intimidation of an apathetic population undoubtedly occurred. Consequently, there were cases in which the population appealed to the French for protection and the French successfully raised local anti-guerrilla units or *juramentados*. French reprisals, however, rather than the guerrillas' own depredations appear to have had the greater impact on the loyalties of the population as a whole. For many *partidas*, attacking the French was secondary to banditry.

The French were forced to disperse large numbers of men through the countryside, and their memoirs testify to the ubiquity of guerrilla attacks and the escalating violence that resulted. Guerrilla activity did prevent the French from securing easy access to Spanish economic resources. Stripping the French Army of the North's garrisons in Cantabria, the Basque country and Navarre to oppose Wellington's offensive in 1812 weakened the French hold there. The major French effort to reassert control in the face of guerrilla opposition in early 1813 then severely reduced their effort to prevent Wellington's new offensive, with his victory at Vitoria in June marking the beginning of the end of French occupation. Nonetheless, the guerrillas were largely ineffective in terms of turning the French out of their fortified posts and the French remained firmly in control of most of Spain from August 1809 until January 1812.

Thus, while the guerrillas certainly helped to weaken French morale and provided the British Army with invaluable intelligence, it must also be said that the guerrillas could not have survived without British logistical support and the pressure exerted on the French by the British Army. Ultimately, it was the latter, with its allied Portuguese and Spanish regular contingents, that liberated Spain, albeit only once Napoleon had committed himself to the invasion of Russia with all its implications for reinforcing his armies in Spain.

The real importance of the guerrillas was that they enabled Spaniards to claim a part in their own deliverance. This had a significant psychological effect on the people and one that was ultimately to contribute to a struggle between liberals and absolutists in Spain after 1814. Ironically, in that struggle a number of the prominent wartime guerrilla leaders were executed, including Diaz, Porlier and Mendietta. The prominent role accorded the guerrillas in popular memory also fuelled resentment on the part of Spanish regulars, which contributed to increasing military intervention in Spanish politics through the remainder of the nineteenth century.

The Confederacy

On 4 April 1865, the president of the Southern Confederacy, Jefferson Davis, addressed a message to his people. Davis had been forced to flee Richmond two days earlier when the defensive lines of Robert E. Lee's Army of Northern Virginia were finally broken by the Union Army after eleven months of stalemate in the eastern theatre of operations.[3] Davis urged a new strategy of guerrilla resistance.

> Relieved from the necessity of guarding cities and particular points, important but not vital to our defence, with an army free to move from point to point and strike in detail the detachments and garrisons of the enemy, operating on the interior of our own country, where supplies are more accessible, and where the foe will be far removed from his base and cut off from all succour in case of retreat, nothing is now needed to render our triumph certain but the exhibition of our own unquenchable resolve. Let us but will it, and we are free.[4]

There had already been a bitter guerrilla struggle in the border states of Missouri and Kansas, which was a continuation of the pre-war conflict between competing pro- and anti-slavery factions. In all, perhaps 10,000 people died in Missouri and 300,000 fled their homes in an escalating cycle of violence, which destroyed any sense of security and left few refuges for neutrals.

---

3 See also Chapters 4 and 16.
4 E. Thomas, *The Confederate Nation, 1861–65* (New York: Harper Torchbooks, 1979), 301.

Guerrilla activity had also been a feature of those in up-country or back-country areas of states such as North Carolina, Georgia, Alabama, Tennessee and Kentucky, in which there were significant internal divisions in terms of sympathy for Confederacy or Union. Union-occupied Louisiana and Arkansas too saw conflict between Confederate guerrillas and Union sympathisers. Guerrilla conflict was the only direct face of war experienced by many in Tennessee and Kentucky as the movements of the main armies remained distant from them throughout. Unionist guerrillas, for example, controlled many counties in eastern Tennessee, while Confederate guerrillas disputed Union control of western Kentucky and middle Tennessee.

A distinction needs to be drawn between cavalry raiding undertaken by Confederacy and Union forces in support of conventional strategy and guerrilla warfare waged on an unorganised basis between rival groups in locally contested areas. In many cases, guerrillas identifying with the Confederacy operated well outside Confederate lines and Confederate control, leading to ambiguity in official attitudes since they did have their uses. Major-General Sterling Price, for example, attempted to co-ordinate with guerrillas during his unsuccessful large-scale cavalry raid into Missouri in the autumn of 1864. The Partisan Ranger Act of 21 April 1862, which authorised Confederate partisan units operating under the same regulations as regulars, itself made little attempt at definition, other than prohibiting guerrilla action by other than authorised units.

As in the case of Spain, guerrilla warfare during the Civil War has attracted a great deal of interest. Alongside the many memoirs by participants, there is abundant documentation in US national, state, regional and local archives. Detailed local studies include those by Michael Fellman on Missouri, Noel Fisher on East Tennessee, Sean Michael O'Brien on the southern Appalachians, William Trotter on North Carolina, Robert MacKey on the Upper South, as well as the essay collection edited by Joseph Beilein and Matthew Hulbert. Daniel Sutherland has argued for guerrilla war being a decisive factor in weakening internal support for the Confederacy, but all such conflict was peripheral to the main military campaigns in the west and east, and had no impact upon the military outcome of the war.

Those on both sides still shared a common racial, ethnic, linguistic, religious and cultural heritage as well as similar socio-economic interests and aspirations. In eastern Tennessee, guerrillas on both sides coalesced around locally prominent figures and tended to be young, married and propertied, although Confederates tended to be wealthier than their Union counterparts. In Missouri, where the war had impacted upon a society already in transition from agricultural subsistence to a market-orientated economy, guerrillas were again predominantly young men. Despite reciprocal atrocities, there were some generally observed limitations or perhaps inhibitions, particularly with respect to the treatment of women and children. While their menfolk were routinely slaughtered, German and other immigrant women were invariably spared rape or murder. Such limitations did not apply to black or Indian women. Even the guerrilla war between whites in Missouri remained within the accepted barriers, however perversely men defined them.

Elsewhere, guerrilla violence within the Confederacy was far from random and, whether directed against Confederate or Unionist sympathisers, often intended to maintain law and order as a means of safeguarding the home, family and community. What has been described as an epidemic of often violent crime in eastern Tennessee persisted from 1862 until at least 1867; here, women were occasionally victims. Yet, at the same time, Union and Confederate commanders attempted (albeit unsuccessfully) to reach a local agreement to end hostage taking on several occasions.

Five days after Davis's appeal, he continued to argue for prolonging the war. Lee surrendered his army at Appomattox. Some of his subordinates also argued for guerrilla war but Lee refused to contemplate it. The Partisan Ranger Act had been repealed on 17 February 1864 after pressure from Lee. He had feared the excesses that had already resulted from the lack of discipline among rival guerrilla groups on the Kansas and Missouri borders; only two small units operating in northern Virginia (one led by John Singleton Mosby) were exempted from the repeal of the legislation. Mosby operated in the classic manner, raiding Union lines of communication and supplies.

As Lee now remarked to his artillery specialist, Edward Alexander:

> We must consider its effect on the country as a whole. Already it is demoralised by the four years of war. If I took your advice, the men would be without rations and under no control of officers. They would be compelled to rob and steal in order to live. They would become mere bands of marauders, and the enemy's cavalry would pursue them and overrun many sections they may never have occasion to visit. We would bring on a state of affairs it would take the country years to recover from.[5]

Thus, there was no continuation of the war through any guerrilla strategy.

---

5 E. P. Alexander, *The American Civil War: A Critical Narrative* (London: Siegle, Hill & Co, 1908), 605.

Burma

Having previously annexed parts of Burma in 1826 and 1853 as a result of earlier Anglo-Burmese wars, the British were concerned about instability within the Burmese polity. Modernisation was attempted by King Mindon (r. 1853–1878) but under the pliable and indolent Thibaw (who succeeded to the throne in 1878) declining revenues, increasing economic difficulties and poor harvests exacerbated the breakdown of royal administration. A trading dispute gave the British the excuse to act as they were alarmed by a Franco-Burmese treaty in January 1885. From the new capital of Mandalay, Thibaw imposed a £2.3 million fine on the Bombay–Burma Trading Corporation for allegedly exporting more teak than they had bought. Commercial interests in Rangoon were calling for annexation. An ultimatum was despatched on 22 October 1885 demanding Thibaw to: accept British control over Burma's foreign policy; appoint a British envoy with direct access to the King; agree on arbitration of the fine; and facilitate British trade with China through Burma. Thibaw rejected the ultimatum on 5 November 1885 and British occupation followed. It took just three weeks to take an area of 140,000 square miles and a population of 4 million, with the Burmese government paralysed by the speed of the British advance.

The alternative of a protectorate and indirect rule foundered on the lack of any acceptable successor to Thibaw, who was deported into exile. Neither the *Hluttaw* (Council of State) nor local administration seemed able to function effectively as a guarantor of British interests, given the rapid breakdown of any pretence of law and order following occupation. In any case, Burmese kings had little control over ethnic minorities such as the Chins, Karens, Kachins, Mons and Shans, while there were many traditional *dacoits* (bandits). At the time of the British occupation, real royal authority did not extend much beyond Mandalay. Faced with the additional difficulties of climate and terrain, the British did not succeed in bringing central Burma under control until 1891, and also had to undertake major expeditions against the hill tribes of the Chins, Kachins, Lushais and Shans between 1889 and 1895.

Despite being the longest campaign fought by the Victorian army, the pacification of Burma has received little scholarly attention. Even at the time, it was dismissed as merely 'police work'. There are relatively few published memoirs, although the Chief Commissioner, Sir Charles Crosthwaite, published a study of the pacification campaign as a whole in 1912. The government of India also produced an invaluable internal six-volume history compiled by the Intelligence Branch of the Quartermaster General's Department between 1887 and 1891. However, British official and semi-official documentation and correspondence is abundant. Burmese language sources, including the records of the *Hluttaw*, have been used by one English language monograph with a distinctly nationalist slant by Ni Mi Myint. Burmese sources have also been utilised in scholarly articles by historians such as Michael Aung-Thwin and Michael Charney.

The structures of Burmese national and local political power and of social organisation were all dismantled by February 1886, with an entirely new colonial administration supplanting some 300 years of traditional authority. Burma's disbanded army disappeared into the jungle. The regular Burmese Army was estimated at 15,650 men but volunteers responding to a proclamation on 7 November 1885 by the *Hluttaw* had swelled its numbers to about 24–28,000. As the British Official History put it, the expulsion of the king and the breaking up of the army 'completely undermined the power of the *Hlutdaw* [sic]; so that what actually occurred was a complete collapse of all central authority, and this could not be re-asserted till an executive was re-established throughout the country'.[6]

Far from welcoming the British as expected, the Burmese resented the removal of a King who if weak was still semi-divine in their eyes. Opposition was also fuelled by unwittingly symbolic evidence of disrespectful British attitudes to traditional authority such as the use of parts of the royal palace as an Anglican chapel, a British club and the Chief Commissioner's office; and rumours of wanton destruction of property, ill-treatment of monks and women, and summary executions. The increasing spread of resistance has been characterised as deriving from a combination of Burmese patriotism, millenarianism and continuing banditry.

A number of royal or claimed royal princes had evaded capture and deportation. Some such as the Myinzaing Prince, who died of fever in August 1886, proved a magnet for initial resistance. So did monks such as U Ottama, who was only captured in July 1889. Monks (*pongyi*) lost status and influence through the removal of the monarchy, and the *Hluttaw*'s proclamation in November 1885 invoked the supposed threat to the Buddhist faith, portraying the British as heretics. Some historians see Buddhist participation, like that of the princes, as attempts to restore the traditional order that had all but disintegrated during Thibaw's reign. Although they had also lost status and authority, many of the nobility and gentry did not contest British rule. They were supplanted, however, by Burmese with local influence such as

---

6 H. E. Stanton, *The Third Burmese War, 1885, 1886 and 1887: History of the War prior to the Annexation of the Country* (Calcutta: Superintendent of Government Printing, 1887), 52.

Boh Swe, hereditary *thugyi* (headman) of Mindat. Boh Swe was eventually killed in October 1887. There were also the pure *dacoits* such as Bo Hla U, an active bandit on the Lower Chindwin since 1883, who simply turned into a resistance leader; he was killed in an internecine quarrel in April 1887. Revolt spread to Lower Burma in 1886, but here it was attributed to the influence of events in Upper Burma rather than being simple banditry.

Some of those aspiring to leadership issued their own proclamations rather as that of the *Hluttaw* had called for volunteers to join the royal army. The Myinzaing Prince proclaimed that he had raised four armies to march simultaneously on Mandalay, and that those loyal to him should wear a white thread when the army arrived. Those who had sided with the British would be pardoned 'though it may be politic to kill them so as to produce a deterrent effect on their descendants'. Another royal claimant, Saw Yan Paing, instructed his followers not to harm the Burmese people or property 'but only attack and expel those who fight on the side of the British'.[7] These hardly amount to a strategy and there is no suggestion that anyone else articulated one.

The developing conflict reflected traditional Burmese rural warfare culture. Resistance was not so much to the British – and thereby indicative of national or proto-national loyalties – as to any centralising authority. Alongside royal princes, monks or bandit leaders, village communities themselves could take up arms, with internal conflict between villages where some backed the British. In this respect, there was a separate civil war running alongside the overall pacification campaign.

It was convenient for the British authorities to refer to all as *dacoits* since this suggested that they were the enemy of the British and the Burmese population alike. Whatever the source of leadership or motivation, *dacoit* bands led by those characterised as *bohs* could range from a handful to as many as 4,000 men. Invariably the British distinguished between *bohs* and their followers, suggesting the significance of local leadership. It is impossible to gauge the numerical strength of opposition to the British or the losses inflicted on the Burmese by the British.

Intimidation was applied by the *dacoits* to the local population in order to ensure their assistance although, in many cases, banditry was so long established that coercion was not required. Troops disarmed villagers, which left them more at the mercy of *dacoits*. It was exceptionally difficult to gain any

---

7 N. M. Myint, *Burma's Struggle against British Imperialism, 1885–95* (Rangoon: Universities Press, 1983), 194–7.

information and equally hard to distinguish between *dacoits* and peaceful villagers. The hill tribes were a different matter and fought much more as classic guerrillas between 1889 and 1895, but this was very much a traditional response to attempted occupation rather than a reasoned strategy. Ultimately, a combination of military and political measures brought about a sufficient degree of control in British Burma.

South Africa

A different decision was reached by Afrikaner Boer leaders at a *krijgsraad* (war council) at Kroonstad on 17 March 1900, thirty-five years after Lee's rejection of guerrilla war. The capital of the Orange Free State (OFS), Bloemfontein, had fallen to the British four days earlier. The British then advanced towards the capital of the Transvaal at Pretoria. The war, which had begun in October 1899, was in part unfinished business. The Transvaal had been annexed by Britain in 1877 but had won renewed independence as a result of the Anglo-Transvaal War of 1881. Discovery of gold in 1886 had transformed the Transvaal's economy. Afrikaner resistance to granting civil rights to the large number of *Uitlanders* (foreigners) attracted to the gold fields and their mostly British-owned mining companies coincided with the 'scramble for Africa', and provided the British with the means to orchestrate conflict in pursuit of wider strategic, political and economic imperatives. The Boers struck first, invading Natal and Cape Colony, bottling up British garrisons at Ladysmith, Kimberley and Mafeking, and inflicting a series of defeats on the relieving forces in December 1899 and January 1900. Assisted by reinforcements, the new British commander-in-chief, Field Marshal Lord Roberts, concentrated on the drive to the Boer capitals, defeating and forcing the surrender of the main Boer field army at Paardeburg in February 1900.

British counterguerrilla measures have attracted most attention in the past, and there is a great deal of literature on the British side. Afrikaner sources have remained largely inaccessible to English-speakers. This has included the major six-volume history of the war by J. H. Breytenbach, which has the most detailed account of the Kroonstad meeting based on the official record, but which has not been translated. Christian de Wet was one guerrilla whose memoirs were translated into English in 1903. Another well-known account in English is that by Deneys Reitz, published in 1929. Others remain only available in Afrikaans. Fortunately, the work of Afrikaner-speaking historians such as André Wessels and, especially, Fransjohan Pretorius have become available in English, the latter's major work on Boer commando appearing in English in 1999.

A total of twenty-five men were present at Kroonstad, including Presidents Martinus Steyn of the OFS and Paul Kruger of the Transvaal. Steyn, who took the chair, believed that prolonging the struggle might lead Britain to seek terms (Steyn reckoned only in a matter of six weeks) due to Russian machinations in Afghanistan and Persia, the state of the stock market and the possible political backlash in Britain. The fall of the capitals did not matter. Only by 'fierce fighting' could the Boers secure independence and avoid being enslaved. Rather than the futility of trying to hold positions against superior forces, the Boers should separate into smaller units and use their mobility to strike at British lines of communication. There would be no more wagon laagers of the kind in which Piet Cronje's field army had been trapped and forced to surrender at Paardeburg.[8]

Here then was a considered strategy to prolong the war by guerrilla action in order to compel the British to negotiate. It recognised, as the opening Boer offensives had not, that the commando system was ideally suited to guerrilla warfare. Mounted mobility would enable them to surprise their opponents and to withdraw quickly in order to minimise the risk of taking casualties. The Boers could live off the veld as well as captured supplies, and make use of their field skills and local knowledge to outwit the British. Decisions were also reached on the allocation of the commandos to various areas.

Steyn's formal resolution to initiate guerrilla struggle was seconded by de Wet. While Steyn initiated the discussion at Kroonstad, another soon to be prominent among the guerrilla leaders, Koos de la Rey, had argued a month earlier that the British could not be stopped through positional warfare. The war council marked the eclipse of the older generation of military leaders who were seen to have failed to adapt to new conditions and who remained opposed to offensive and mobile warfare. Apparently only one Boer general at the war's outset, Barry Hertzog, educated at the Cape and in the Netherlands, had any theoretical military knowledge, and that derived from studying Carlyle's biography of Frederick the Great. The new leadership was younger on average by twenty-one years, better educated and had had some exposure to French and German instructors.

One issue unresolved at Kroonstad was whether or not to hold the natural fortress of the Brandwater Basin in the eastern OFS as the republic's last unoccupied area. Confusion and conflicting opinions led to the surrender of over 4,000 Boers in July 1900, but de Wet escaped to continue the war. Not

---

8 J. H. Breytenbach, *Die Geskiedenis van die Tweede Vryheidsoorlog in Suid-Afrika, 1899–1902*, 6 vols. (Pretoria: Government Printer, 1978–1996), vol. V, 159–67.

only did the commandos operate in the OFS and the Transvaal but they also launched a number of forays into Cape Colony as, for example, in December 1900, February 1901 and September 1901, in the hope of stirring up rebellion among Cape Afrikaners. Effectively, once the strategic decision was made at Kroonstad, individual Boer leaders operated individually at an operational and tactical level thereafter.

Interestingly, de Wet, whose memoirs have little insight on his thinking, subsequently rejected the word guerrilla altogether to define the Boer resistance: 'The only case in which one can use this word, is when one civilised nation has so completely vanquished another, that not only is the capital taken. But also the country from border to border is so completely conquered that any resistance is out of the question.'[9] He saw guerrilla war as a legitimate continuation of hostilities by representatives of a legal government, not accepting that British annexation of the OFS in May 1900 was legal.

The war continued as a guerrilla struggle until May 1902 when the Boers recognised that they could not continue without yet more serious consequences. As with the *krijgsraad*, there was discussion among the leadership of the *bittereinders* ('the irreconcilables') who assembled at Vereeniging to negotiate with the British. British scorched-earth policies had increasingly deprived the Boers of supplies, and blockhouse lines linked by barbed wire had eroded mobility. There was, too, the fear that Africans, many of whom the British had armed, posed a significant threat; one commando was destroyed by Zulu at Holkrans on 5 May 1902. A third consideration was the Afrikaner civilian population. An estimated 116,000 civilians were held in internment camps and 31,000 Boers held as prisoners of war, but around 12,000 women and children remained on the veld. There was no prospect of foreign intervention, and most commandos had been reduced to fleeing British columns and searching for food rather than fighting. The peace terms were not wholly unfavourable to the Boers, although they lost their independence until self-government was instituted in 1910. But, prolonging the war cost the lives of an estimated 28,000 of the civilians held in internment camps and between 16,000 and 20,000 African civilians also held in camps.

Consideration of the case studies supports the notion that tactics rather than strategy characterised guerrilla warfare in the nineteenth century. Even where a conscious strategic choice was made to resort to guerrilla warfare as by the Boers in the South African War, there was little prospect of success. As the Confederacy's military leadership understood and the Boers experienced,

---

9 C. de Wet, *Three Years' War* (New York: Charles Scribner's Sons, 1903), 228.

guerrilla warfare was likely to be as damaging to guerrillas as to their opponents. That was true, also, of those opposing conquest, occupation or oppression through guerrilla warfare without conscious decision and where, as in Spain and Burma, little central direction was achieved. Guerrillas could only survive and achieve military or political objectives, as in Spain, with the assistance of others.

3
Russia, 1877–1917

ANDREY PAVLOV

The Background: Russian Strategy from Ivan III to the Nineteenth Century

The path from the independent Grand Duchy (or Principality) of Moscow to the Russian Empire – a Great Power – was quite long. The Russian state, which united many of the north-eastern Russian principalities around Moscow, finally freed itself from dependence on the Golden Horde only at the end of the fifteenth century. The following two centuries were a period of rather unstable dynamic equilibrium. Attempts to expand the territory were successful only in the eastern direction, where relatively weak khanates were formed following the collapse of the Golden Horde. The most important successes were the conquests of Kazan (1552) and Astrakhan (1558) khanates, making it possible to control the Volga River and creating opportunities for further expansion in the eastern and south-eastern directions, which actively developed over the following centuries. In other directions, Russia had to face strong opponents. In the north-west, the kingdom of Sweden cut Russia off from the Baltic Sea in the early seventeenth century. In the west, Russia was opposed by the strong Polish-Lithuanian Union (the Polish-Lithuanian Commonwealth since 1569), the confrontation with which developed with varying success in the sixteenth and seventeenth centuries. In the south, Russia's access to the Black Sea was blocked by the Crimean khanate, which also posed a constant threat of invasion. From the middle of the fifteenth century, the Ottoman Empire actively expanded its power in the northern shores of the Black Sea and around the Sea of Azov, gradually turning into Russia's main adversary in the south.

Until the beginning of the eighteenth century, Russia remained a European periphery, and the primary goal of Tsar Peter I (r. 1689–1725, and as emperor from 1721) was to change this situation. First, he tried to solve

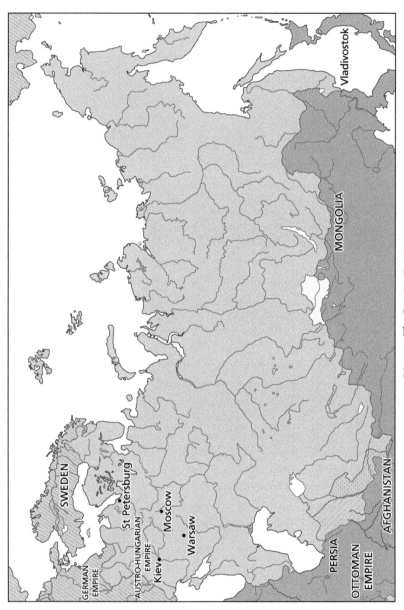

Map 3.1 The Russian Empire.

the main geostrategic problem – to gain access to the Baltic and Black Seas. The radical reforms he was carrying out coincided with the initial weakening of Russia's main external opponents, while successes in the war against Sweden (1700–1721) made it possible to gain a foothold in the Baltic Sea. In the eighteenth century, the Russian Empire continued its offensive strategy with overall success. By taking an active part in the pan-European Seven Years' War, Russia demonstrated the growing strength of a new great European power. By the beginning of the nineteenth century, Russia's position improved significantly. After a series of successful wars against Turkey and the annexation of Crimea (1783), it became possible to gain a foothold on the Black Sea coast. Sweden's attempts to at least partially return the territories lost in the Baltic were unsuccessful, and Russia even managed to expand its territory in this region. In 1770–1795, the world saw a gradual liquidation of the Polish state, with its lands divided between Russia, Austria and Prussia.

Resulting from its participation in the Napoleonic Wars, the influence of the Russian Empire grew even stronger, especially since it was the defeat of Napoleon in Russia in 1812 that marked the beginning of the collapse of his empire. In the north and west, the Russian Empire achieved the maximum number of set goals and strove to maintain the existing state of affairs through the Concert of Europe. The main strategic direction at this point became the south-east. Emperor Nicholas I (r. 1825–1855) thought it was possible to realise the geostrategic idea that had arisen at the end of the eighteenth century: after gaining a foothold in the Black Sea, to find some way to secure guaranteed access through it to the Mediterranean. The continued decline of the Ottoman Empire seemed to provide such an opportunity, but the Russian emperor underestimated the willingness of Great Britain and France to provide Turkey with assistance to prevent Russia from becoming a Mediterranean power as well. As a result of the defeat in the Crimean War (1853–1856), Russia had to abandon its offensive strategy in this direction for some time.

However, the Asian territories of the Empire continued to expand into the second half of the nineteenth century. Expansion in central Asia gradually brought the possessions of the Russian Empire closer to the northern borders of British India. Between the years of 1877 and 1917, Russia fought three drastically different wars. The Russo-Turkish War (1877–1878) was a conflict against a traditional well-known enemy in a familiar theatre of operations. During the war of 1904–1905, the Russian Empire not only faced a new enemy – Japan – but also fought in a brand new theatre of operations.

These military conflicts were a manifestation of two regional strategic plans unfolding in opposite directions. Russia's strategy in the First World War differed from them in almost all respects.

Sources and Historiography

The study of Russian strategy in the late nineteenth and early twentieth centuries reflects the volatility and the fragmentation of strategy itself. The case-by-case approach to strategy formation also determined how historians have been able to study it. The most in-depth analysis of the wars took place right after they ended; however, this type of study was of an applied nature, with the main purpose of drawing practical lessons from the recent experience. The majority of these publications consist of fairly large survey studies and collections of documents.

After the end of the Russo-Turkish War, the Russian Main Staff created a special Military-Historical Commission to analyse the experience of the war, and over the next thirty years it produced the largest publication of research and documents in the history of the Russian Empire. Dedicated to the war in the Balkan theatre alone were nine volumes containing a description of military operations and the publication of ninety-seven volumes of documents. On top of that, separate publications were devoted to the Caucasian theatre, as well as regularly published additional volumes of supplements and appendices. Some editions and individual volumes among these were not intended to be available for the general public.[1] Soon after the end of the Russo-Japanese War, a special Russian Military Historical Commission was created to study the war experience. Members of the Commission received full access to all archives. The result of its work was a nine-volume publication in 1910 containing a detailed description of all military operations.[2]

The tradition of studying the practical experience of the First World War continued in Soviet Russia. In August 1918, even before the First World War ended, the Main Staff of the Red Army had already created a special Military History Commission in order to study the experience of the war. The commission existed until 1924 and was transformed into the military history

---

[1] V. A. Zolotarev, 'Russko-turetskaya voina 1877–1878 gg. v otechestvennoi istoriografii', *Vestnik obshchestvennykh nauk AN Armianskoy SSR*, 3 (1987), 60–2.

[2] *Russko-iaponskaia voina 1904–1905 gg.: Rabota Voenno-istoricheskoy komissii po opisanijy Russko – iaponskoy vojny*, 9 vols. (St Petersburg: Izdanie Voenno-istoricheskoy komissii, 1910).

department of the Red Army Staff. Its main work was *A Strategic Sketch of the War of 1914–1918*, eight volumes completed between 1920 and 1923.[3] The authors of individual volumes were former generals of the Russian Imperial Army, among whom a special place was occupied by A. M. Zayonchkovsky, who later published the two-volume history of the First World War, as well as some other works. Among other publications were collections of documents on individual operations and battles of the First World War.

Later Soviet historiography was characterised by its isolation from more global historiographic trends and by Soviet ideological attitudes when analysing the 'imperialist' war. At the same time, foreign researchers had very limited access to primary sources in the USSR. This situation changed only after the collapse of the USSR. Archives became more accessible, while Russian historiography ceased to be isolated from the rest of the world. Special attention was given to the study of Russia's participation in the First World War, with many issues having to be investigated practically from scratch. The centenary of the First World War and the revolutions of 1917 boosted research development. The connection between the war and the revolutions was evident, but it was necessary to identify and understand the mechanisms and consequences of their mutual influence. For modern Russian society, this was not only a question of history and memory but also served as an element of modern self-awareness.

In modern historiography, the wars that Russia waged in the late nineteenth and early twentieth centuries are viewed as mostly separate from each other and not as elements of a single narrative. I. S. Rybachenok, who attempted a comprehensive analysis of Russia's foreign policy during this period, concluded that the Russian Empire lacked not only a common grand strategy but also coherent strategies in each of several main directions.[4] Thus, the fragmentation of the research on Russian strategy in 1877–1917 is not least due to the fragmentary nature of the strategy itself.

Primary sources of information on the development of Russian strategy in the last period of the existence of the Russian Empire can be found in three state archives containing materials from the three central ministries responsible for the formation and implementation of the strategy: Russian State Archive of Military History (RGVIA), Archive of Foreign Policy of the Russian Empire (AVPRI) and Russian State Naval Archive (RGAVMF).

---

3 *Strategycheskiy ocherk vojny 1914–1918 gg.*, 8 vols. (Moscow: Voennoye izdatelstvo, 1920–1923).

4 I. S. Rybachionok, *Zakat velikoy derzhavy. Vneshnyaja politika Rossii na rubezhe XIX–XX vv.: tsely, zadachi i metody* (Moscow: Rosspen, 2012), 566.

Actors

During the last half-century of its existence, the Russian Empire underwent multiple political, economic and social transformations. The armed forces of the Empire also went through some significant changes. While in flux, Russia remained an absolute monarchy. The governments were forced to formulate a strategy within the framework of a state system, in which the Tsar always had the last word. Like their predecessors, the last three Russian emperors, Alexander II (r. 1855–1881), Alexander III (r. 1881–1894) and Nicholas II (r. 1894–1917) paid particular attention to military affairs. Simultaneously, the formation of general strategies resulted from tightknit interactions between the War Ministry, the Naval Ministry, the Ministry of Foreign Affairs and the Ministry of Finances, and the intense struggles among them. High-level military officers and politicians continually struggled to influence the tsars' decisions. Created in 1865, the Main Staff was part of the War Ministry and performed functions characteristic of a general staff of that time. An independent general staff called the 'Main Directorate of the General Staff' only existed during 1905–1908, which later became part of the War Ministry once more. This body was tasked with the development of strategic plans, management of the army and preparations for mobilisation. Any major strategic decisions were ultimately made or approved by the Tsar.

Adversaries and Allies

The structure of relations between the Russian Empire and the outside world has always been characterised by perennial change, and radical change at times. The most stable element was Russia's relationship with the Ottoman Empire, which consistently remained an adversary for more than 300 years. The confrontation intensified from the mid-eighteenth century onwards, when Russia began to pursue a consistent and successful offensive strategy. Russia's desire to gain direct access to the southern seas was based on the ideas widespread at that time about the importance of geopolitics for national economic development. Following the Crimean War, Great Britain was perceived as the most significant adversary. Up to the beginning of the twentieth century, the Russian–British confrontation developed over a vast area from the Bosphorus and the Dardanelles to northern China. The geopolitical confrontation between the two empires was complicated by the gradually developed strong mutual perceptions of a grave threat to vital interests emanating from the adversary.[5] At the end of the nineteenth century, Russia's desire to consolidate its position in the Far East led to the emergence of a new adversary – Japan, whose strength was initially seriously underestimated in Russia.

In the second half of the nineteenth century, as the Ottoman Empire weakened, its place as Russia's geopolitical adversary in the struggle for influence in the Balkans began to be occupied by Austria–Hungary instead. The growing tensions with Austria–Hungary were close to provoking an armed conflict. At the same time, Russia was wary of Germany's increasing power. By the 1870s, Russia had already realised the need to contain the growing power of Germany. Formation of the anti-Russian alliance of Germany and Austria–Hungary in 1879 and the increasing ambitions of the German Empire to dominate in Europe finally turned Germany into an adversary. Added to this were the economic contradictions that led to the 'Tariff War' in 1893–1894. The alliance between Austria–Hungary and Germany increased the likelihood of war against a coalition of these powers. Russia's response to these events was the formation of a Franco-Russian military-political alliance, which significantly adjusted the Russian Empire's strategy. The Russian–French military convention, which became the basis of this alliance, was signed in 1892 and approved by Alexander III in 1893. Chief of the Main Staff (since 1881) General Nikolai Nikolayevich Obruchev personally negotiated and signed this convention on behalf of the Russian Empire.

Although the Russian–French alliance was primarily anti-German, it was also viewed by the two countries as a means of helping each other in the event of a conflict with Great Britain, although the text of the military convention did not provide for this. Developing in the second half of the nineteenth century, the Great Game also threatened to evolve into a fully fledged military clash. The Russian Main Staff constantly planned offensive operations from Russian Turkestan towards North India, through Afghanistan in case of war against Great Britain. Russian military leaders believed this to be the most effective way to strike the British Empire at its most vulnerable point. This plan was completed in 1903 on the eve of the Russo-Japanese War.[6] The situation changed only after the early stages of formation of the Franco-British alliance and the defeat of Russia in the war against Japan. The British–Russian

---

5 E. Sergeev, *The Great Game, 1856–1907: Russo-British Relations in Central and East Asia* (Washington, DC: Woodrow Wilson Center Press, 2013).
6 O. E. Alpeev, 'Planirovanie russkim General'nym shtabom voiny s Velikobritanijey v kontekste anglo-russkih otnoshenij (1885–1914 gg.)', *Istoricheskije issledovanija*, 15 (2020), 158.

agreements concluded in 1907 regarding the division of spheres of interest in Afghanistan, Persia and Tibet completed the formation of the Triple Entente of France, Great Britain and Russia.

Causes and Objectives of Wars

Each of the three wars had its own unique set of causes. For the Russo-Turkish and Russo-Japanese wars, the main reasons were similar in nature: the specific geopolitical interests of Russia were incompatible with the interests of Turkey and Japan. Along with geopolitical considerations, there were also some differences. An important aspect of the Russo-Turkish War were the pan-Slavist ideas about Russia's special mission to save Orthodox Slavic brothers from Ottoman oppression. These ideas were quite popular in Russian society and were actively used by the government to justify the need for violent action against Turkey. During the First World War, the situation turned out to be somewhat more complicated. In the cases of the Ottoman Empire and Austria–Hungary, identifying the specific reasons and goals proved to be a fairly simple process. The contradictions between Russia and Germany were much more general in nature, being primarily about the growth of German influence in Europe as a whole.

Available Means

The defeat of the Russian Empire in the Crimean War became the pivotal moment in Russian strategy of the nineteenth century. In the first half of the century after the victory over the Napoleonic Empire, the major factor in determining Russia's strategy was confidence in its own power. Consequently, the risky policy put into effect by Tsar Nicholas I in the Eastern Question led to a confrontation not only with the Ottoman Empire, but also with two of Europe's Great Powers (Great Britain and France) in the Crimean War 1853–1856. Humiliating defeat in this war forced the key decision-making figures to seriously reconsider the foundations of Russia's strategy and proceed with extra caution. This outcome also demonstrated not only the weakness of its army and navy, but also the underdevelopment of its economy, transport infrastructure and entire sociopolitical system. The outdated political and social systems hindered full-scale economic transformation, preventing Russia from embarking on the path of industrialisation until the end of the reforms. At the same time, the territorial expansion of the Russian Empire, which began in the nineteenth century, gradually accelerated and by the end of that century, the Empire reached its maximum size. The expansion of territories was accompanied by population growth and provided the military with an increase in human resources. On the other hand, a huge territory with relatively underdeveloped communications created strategic problems even for a fairly large peacetime army.

Even though Russia had considerable human reserves (overall more than 125 million inhabitants by the end of the nineteenth century), it could not fully use them. The existing system of manning for the armed forces was based on conscription from the beginning of the eighteenth century, levied only from certain classes of the population who had to furnish specific numbers of men to serve for twenty-five years. This system did not allow for the formation of permanent trained reserves, which made it impossible to increase the army's combat strength significantly in case of war.

Attempts to improve the situation were made since the early 1860s. In parallel with the social reforms in Russia, several military reforms were carried out primarily under the leadership of General Dmitry Alekseyevich Milyutin, who served as war minister from 1861 to 1881. The reorganisation concerned the military forces' system of command in peacetime and wartime, military education and troops' structure. Additionally, the army was re-equipped with upgraded types of weapons. The most critical decision was the introduction of universal conscription in 1874, which created the basis for the formation of a truly massive army.

Simultaneously with the reform of the armed forces, strategic plans were regularly reviewed. This work was carried out by the Main Staff. In early 1873, General Obruchev prepared a memorandum 'Considerations for the Defence of Russia' on behalf of Milyutin, which described the armed forces' state and their capabilities in case of war.[7] The Russian Empire's strategic environment, according to the memorandum, was one where an armed conflict could be expected from nearly any direction. In Obruchev's view, the biggest threats were posed by Germany and Austria–Hungary, thus making Russian Poland the region most vulnerable to attack, as it was surrounded on three sides by the territories of these states. To mitigate this vulnerability, it was necessary to form a system of fortresses, which would allow for a temporary defence in the event of an attack by Germany or Austria–Hungary, or both powers at the same time. The time gained in the process would then be used to mobilise and concentrate troops for the subsequent transition to offensive operations. Although Obruchev considered a military conflict along Russia's western borders as the

---

7 P. A. Zaionchkovsky, *Voennye reformy 1860–1870 godov v Rossii* (Moscow: Izdatelstvo Moskovskogo universiteta, 1952), 287–8.

primary threat, the danger of repeating the Crimean War's painful experience necessitated strengthening the defence in the Black Sea region.[8] In the event of a conflict in the Caucasian theatre of operations, it was wiser to assume an offensive strategy, since here Russia would have to deal solely with Turkey.

From the 1860s until the outbreak of the First World War, one of the essential tasks on the agenda of the War Ministry was the reduction of the time it took to mobilise and concentrate troops. In 1873 Obruchev estimated the time required for mobilisation and concentration in the event of a war with Germany at twenty to twenty-three days, and with Austria–Hungary at sixty-three to seventy days, while their opponents could mobilise twice as fast and use the gap in time for offensive operations.[9] The poorly developed railways network in the Russian Empire did not allow for rapid transport of large numbers of troops over long distances. To solve this problem, the Russian government actively stimulated the development of railway construction in 1860–1870. Nevertheless, while planning future operations against Turkey in April of 1876, Milyutin assessed the state of the railways as a crisis. In the event of war, the railways could not fully provide the army's deployment and supply.[10]

In preparing the army and navy for the war in the west, the Russian military leadership and government operated under the assumption that the war would last from three to six months, and the supplies necessary to maintain the armies would come from the stocks of weapons and ammunition accumulated before the war. During the war, the production of war materials was supposed to play a supporting role, replenishing supplies. The experience gained during the war against Japan, as well as the wars waged by other countries, forced the Russian command to raise its standards when determining the required amount of supplies and demonstrated the need to strengthen the army and navy. Unfortunately for the army, the revolution of 1905–1907 and the subsequent economic crisis did not give the government the ability to allocate necessary funds. It became possible only after the start of the economic recovery in 1909. In 1911, the government began to work on strengthening the naval forces in the Baltic and Black Seas, and in July 1913, Tsar Nicholas II approved the 'Small Programme for strengthening the army'. Following the 'Small Programme', in October 1913 came the 'Big Programme', which included the former. Within the framework of these

---

8 O. R. Airapetov, *Zabytaia karyera 'russkogo Moltke'. Nikolai Nikolaevich Obruchev (1830–1904)* (St Petersburg: Aleteya, 1998), 127.
9 Zaionchkovsky, *Voennye reformy*, 283.
10 O. N. Yeliutin, '"Zolotoi vek" zheleznodorozhnogo stroitelstva v Rossii i ego posledstviya', *Voprosy Istorii*, 2 (2004), 51.

programmes, Russia was set to complete the significant reinforcement of its military in 1917. Therefore, at the beginning of the First World War, the two programmes were only in the initial stages of their implementation.

Process of Prioritisation

In deciding how to utilise its very limited resources at the turn of the nineteenth and twentieth centuries, the Russian government always had to choose between the western and eastern directions. The diversion of resources for building a fleet, strengthening troops and building a railway system in the Far East was considered by some representatives of the War Ministry, including Kuropatkin himself, to be the wrong strategic choice because these actions simultaneously weakened Russia's position in the west in the eventual confrontation with Germany and Austria–Hungary.[11] But the war against Japan (1904–1905), as will be discussed in Chapter 6, only temporarily distracted Russian strategists' attention from their primary focus: the West.

The Franco-Russian Military Convention assumed that if France were to be attacked by Germany or Italy supported by Germany, Russia would attack Germany. If Russia were to be attacked by Germany or Austria–Hungary with the support of Germany, France would attack Germany. Both allies pledged to use their military to force Germany to wage war in the east and west simultaneously. Thus, Russia could not assume an entirely defensive strategy and prepare only to repel Germany and Austria–Hungary's attacks in a future war's initial stage. It had to be prepared for an immediate offensive assault as well. Under the Convention terms, Russia pledged to send an army of 700,000–800,000 men against Germany; France promised to mobilise 1,300,000. Events in the Far East raised doubts of whether Russia would be able to fulfil its obligations. An additional concern among the French was caused by the large amount of time it took to mobilise the Russian troops, since it determined how quickly the Russian Army could attack Germany if France was chosen as the enemy's first target. Discussion of the timing of the start of the Russian offensive became the central issue at the regular meetings of the chiefs of the general staffs of Russia and France. Of particular importance for forming the initial strategic plans were the last three pre-war

---

11 B. W. Menning, 'Neither Mahan nor Moltke: strategy in the war', in J. W. Steinberg, B. W. Menning, D. Schimmelpenninck van der Oye, D. Wolff and S. Yokote (eds), *The Russo-Japanese War in Global Perspective: World War Zero* (Leyden and Boston: Brill, 2005), 140–2.

meetings held in Russia in 1911 and 1913, and in France in 1912. The decisions of all three meetings concluded that under any circumstances, the main task of the Allied armies would be to defeat the German Army by means of a speedy offensive. In 1911, the chief of the general staff of Russia, General Yakov Grigoryevich Zhilinsky, promised that the Russian armies would launch an offensive on the eighteenth day from the beginning of mobilisation, without waiting for its completion. At the last meeting before the war in 1913, Zhilinsky adjusted his plans to launch an offensive on the fifteenth day and promised to reduce this period by two more days by the end of 1914. Another important topic on the agenda was the direction of Russian's primary offensive. Until 1912, the plan for the Russian armies already deployed against Germany was to strike at the German forces in East Prussia in order to bind them as soon as the war began, with the goal of preventing the German command from transferring forces from east to west. However, in the minutes of the conferences of 1912 and 1913, it was decided that the Russian forces should be deployed in a way that allowed operations to be conducted not only in East Prussia but also directly west towards Berlin, in order to account for the possibility of the German forces being concentrated in this direction.[12]

In 1912, Russia approved a general strategic plan that consisted of two possible courses of action.[13] Plan 'A' ('Austria') came into effect if Germany were to send its main forces against France, leaving only a few corps in the east to cover the border with Russia. In this scenario, Russia would consider Austria–Hungary the main enemy and send three of the five vanguard armies against it, while the two remaining would be left against Germany. If Germany were to send its main forces against Russia, then plan 'G' ('Germany') would be put into effect, according to which the five vanguard armies would be distributed in the inverse proportion. The Russian armies' primary aim on the German front in both plans was formulated in the same way: to defeat the German forces in East Prussia and create conditions for a further offensive. The only deviation was the strategic aim of the Austrian front armies: in the first scenario, they were supposed to inflict a decisive defeat on the armies of Austria–Hungary, and in the second, only to prevent

---

12 *Procès-verbal* of the Russo-French conferences in 1911, 1912 and 1913, in *Materialy po istorii franko-russkih otnoshenij za 1910–1914 gg. Sbornik sekretnyh diplomaticheskih dokumentov byvshego imperatorskogo ministerstva inostrannyh del* (Moscow: Komissariat inostrannyh del, 1922), 695–716.

13 'Vysochajshiye ukazaniya komandujushim vojskamy na sluchaj vojny s derzhavami Trojstvennogo sojuza', in *Vostochno-prusskaya operatsija. Sbornik dokumentov* (Moscow: Gosudarstvennoe Voennoe Izdatelstvo, 1939), 27–9.

them from entering the rear of the Russian troops operating on the German front. As it became more clear that Germany was planning to attack France first, Plan 'A' moved to the foreground as the primary strategy.

Execution/Application of Strategy

The Russo-Turkish War 1877–1878

The Russian and Ottoman empires had come to blows many times; in the nineteenth century alone, and prior to 1877, there had been three Russo-Turkish wars. As Russia grew stronger and the Ottoman Empire weaker, Russian strategic goals became more and more ambitious – from the desire to secure the southern border and gain access to the Black Sea to the desire to establish control over the Bosphorus and the passage from the Black Sea to the Mediterranean. Defeat in the Crimean War forced Russia to temporarily cease its offensive strategy. The onset of the Eastern Crisis in 1875 led to a major flux in the overall situation. The economic crisis in the Ottoman Empire forced the Sultan's government to increase taxation and default on the repayment of its foreign debts. The uprisings in Bosnia and Hercegovina, in Bulgaria and the ensuing war with Serbia and Montenegro (also formally parts of the Ottoman Empire) further undermined Turkey's power. The need to protect the Christian population of the Balkans served as a justification for Russia's new offensive strategy in this direction. Unlike in the Crimean War, it would have been much harder for the European Great Powers to support Turkey in the war against Russia. Furthermore, Russia was making sure to carry out future plans much more cautiously, attempting not to engage in open confrontation with the Great Powers. Besides, the idea of helping the Slavic brothers was trendy among Russian society.

As early as 1876, the development of the Eastern Crisis forced the Russian government to consider direct military intervention, despite the recognition that the state was not ready for war. Not all planned military reforms had as yet been fully implemented. The recently introduced universal conscription could not yet yield sufficiently large trained reserves. The reorganisation of the armed forces was practically complete, but the rearmament of infantry and artillery with modern types of weapons was still ongoing. Many outdated models of rifles and artillery pieces remained in service. Russia's economic situation was also far from ideal, and the minister of finance, Michael Graf von Reitern actively opposed war. Chancellor Prince Alexander Mikhailovich Gorchakov, who had long worked to undo the consequences of Russia's defeat in the Crimean War, feared a new clash with a coalition of European powers and tried to solve the problem peacefully. He did his best to help the Great Powers apply pressure on the Sultan in their demands for reforms.[14]

In November 1876, Alexander II ordered a partial mobilisation of the army even though the decision regarding the war had not yet been made, and mobilisation was considered, among other things, as a way to reinforce diplomatic pressure on the Sultan. Mobilisation made it possible to double the number of troops that were planned to be used in a potential war and increase it to over 546,000 men. Of this number, about 193,000 men entered the field army intended for operations in the European theatre, and about 69,000 men entered the corps, which was to operate in the Caucasian theatre. The rest of the troops were to defend the Black Sea coast, provide logistics and form reinforcements for the active armies.[15]

Milyutin shared the opinion that Russia was not ready for war, but considering that Turkey constantly evaded the demands, he gradually came to the conclusion that a military solution to this problem was inevitable. A memorandum presented to the government by Milyutin and drawn up by Obruchev in March 1877 stated that without Turkey's compliance with presented demands, the army could not be disbanded: 'Such a dissolution of the army without any achieved results would nearly equal a second lost Crimean campaign and could have the most serious consequences in our external relations.'[16] Back in October 1876, Obruchev had drawn up a memorandum on behalf of Milyutin, which contained the main strategic principles that Russia was to adhere to in the coming war. First of all, it was vital to act quickly: swiftly cross the Danube River and, without wasting time on the siege of fortresses, cross the Balkan Mountains as quickly as possible to occupy Bulgarian territory. This would prevent Turkey from concentrating additional forces, and it would not leave time for the formation of a possible anti-Russian coalition of European powers. Obruchev believed that a clash with Great Britain was unavoidable, 'but it is better to meet her [Great Britain] in Constantinople than to fight her off our shores'.[17] It was necessary

14 V. N. Vinogradov, *Balkanskaya epopeya kniazia A. M. Gorchiakova* (Moscow: Nauka, 2005), 210.
15 *Mobilizatsiya Russkoy armii i sosredotocheniye v Bessarabii: sbornik materialov po Russko – turetskoy vojne 1877–1888 gg. na Balkanskom poluostrove* (St Petersburg: Izdanie voenno-istoricheskoy komissii, 1898), vol. II, 69–71.
16 Miliutin's Memorandum, 7 February 1877, in M. Gazenkampf, *Moi dnevnik*, Prilozheniye 2 (St Petersburg: Izdatelstvo Berezovskogo, 1908).
17 Obruchev's Memorandum, 1 October 1876, in Gazenkampf, *Moi dnevnik*, Prilozheniye 1.

to move in some distance from the Black Sea coast of Bulgaria because of the presence of strong Turkish fortresses in the coastal regions and also a practically non-existent Russian Navy force in the Black Sea. A new memorandum drawn up in the spring reported a strengthening of the Turkish troops in the Balkans and therefore provided for a significant increase in the Russian troops. There was one more consequence: if in October 1876 Obruchev only hypothesised that Russia might have to occupy Constantinople at some point during the war, the new version of the strategic plan considered this action an absolute necessity. However, Alexander II did not plan to make Constantinople part of the Russian Empire, while the question of naval passage through the Bosphorus and the Dardanelles was to be decided in the negotiations following the war and along with the participation of the Great Powers. The war's strategic goal was defined as 'the absolute end of Turkish rule in the Balkan Peninsula'.[18]

War against Turkey was declared by Russia on 24 April 1877. On the main European front, the Russian Danube Army crossed the Danube River and launched an offensive under the command of Grand Duke Nikolai Nikolaevich (senior) operating from the territory of Romania. Three detachments of this army had to act independently. One of them covered the left flank of the advancing troops. The largest detachment had to move to the Balkan ridge immediately and quickly cross it. Lastly, the Western detachment was instructed to capture the fortresses of Nikopol and Plevna and then proceed to support the offensive of the second detachment. Russia was also joined by Romania, which was still formally part of the Ottoman Empire and sought full independence. On the Caucasus front, Russia's strategic goal was to secure its territories, but a limited offensive was recognised as the best way to achieve this goal.

Full implementation of the strategic plans drawn up before the war proved impossible for Russia. The main detachment was able to cross the Balkan ridge but did not receive the expected support from other detachments. Facing heavy resistance from the Turks, the detachment was forced to withdraw, nevertheless retaining control over the Balkan passes. The Western detachment could not occupy Plevna and was forced to stop to organise a siege of the fortress. The siege of Plevna, which lasted for six months, slowed down the development of operations. During this period, the Turks tried to seize the strategic initiative and organise counterattacks from three sides; however, they failed. Only after the Turkish troops

18 Obruchev's Memorandum, in Gazenkampf, *Moi dnevnik*, Prilozheniye 4.

defending Plevna surrendered in December 1877 did the Russian Army resume the offensive. The main contingent of forces crossed the Balkan ridge and, after a series of victories against the Turks, occupied Adrianople (Edirne). In January 1878, Russian troops were moved towards Constantinople in order to put pressure on the Sultan, causing disagreements among the Russian leadership regarding the need to occupy the city. Fears of direct military intervention by Great Britain and possibly Austria–Hungary in this conflict forced the Russians to start developing a plan for war with these powers.[19]

As a result, the Russian and Ottoman empires signed a peace treaty on 3 March 1878 in the village of San Stefano near Constantinople. Although Russia managed to achieve victory, it proved to be more difficult than expected. The war confirmed that the ongoing military transformations had not yet yielded the desired result and forced Russia to agree to revise the peace treaty's terms, as demanded primarily by Great Britain and Austria–Hungary.

Strategic Plans for the Far East, the Russo-Japanese War 1904–1905

In the last decades of the nineteenth century Russia became actively involved in the political and economic struggles of the Great Powers in the Far East.[20] The territories of the Russian Empire that bordered China were separated from the European territories by large open stretches of land, so connecting them to the all-Russian system of communications was the first necessary task at hand. The overall scope of Russian interests was not limited only to the territory of the Empire itself and the Empire's economic pursuits presupposed setting specific military-strategic goals. The resulting large-scale programme to strengthen Russia's position in the region began with the construction of the Trans-Siberian Railway in 1891. In 1897, Russia negotiated with China the permission to build the Chinese Eastern (North Manchuria) Railway on its territory, which significantly shortened the route to Vladivostok. Japan perceived all these actions as a growing threat to its own plans to dominate China, so when in 1898 China leased the Leizhou Peninsula to Russia to create a naval base at Port Arthur, the Russo-Japanese War became inevitable.[21] Port Arthur's strategic value for the Russians was

---

19 O. E. Alpeev, 'Planirovaniye Rossiyej vojny s koalitsiyej Velikobritanii, Avstro-Vengrii i Turtsii v 1878 g.', in K. V. Nikiforov (ed.), *Slaviane i Rossia: Rossia, Bolgaria, Balkany. Problemy vojny i mira XVIII – XXI vv. (Mify i realnost)* (Moscow: Institut Slavjanovedeniya RAN, 2019), 120–36.
20 See also Chapter 6.   21 Rybachionok, *Zakat velikoy derzhavy*, 490.

primarily determined by the fact that it was the first non-freezing port that allowed access to the open ocean and could at the same time be connected with Russia by a railroad.

In 1881, given that Russia's primary weakness in the Far East was its navy, the government approved construction of twenty-four battleships and fifteen cruisers within the span of the next twenty years. All of these ships had the capability to operate in separate theatres but were built for permanent deployment only in the Baltic and Black Seas. In the event of war in the Far East, the plan was to send naval forces there from the Baltic and the Black Sea fleets. In connection with the decision to create a permanent fleet in the Pacific Ocean in 1898, another special construction programme was adopted to implement this decision, leading Russia to enter into a short but very intense arms race with Japan in the Far Eastern theatre. Even though the programme had not been completed by the time war with Japan broke out,[22] the Russian fleet was far superior compared to the Japanese fleet. But the forces concentrated in Port Arthur were slightly inferior to the Japanese in terms of the total number of capital ships, and considerably inferior in terms of quality.

Strategic planning for a potential war against Japan had begun in 1895 and was stepped up after Russia acquired Port Arthur. An extensive programme to fortify Port Arthur from land had been launched, but by the beginning of the war, its overall fortifications were only half ready.[23] The basic principles of waging war against Japan were drawn up in 1901. Considering the significant superiority of the Japanese Army, which could be transferred to the continent quickly, Russia deemed it best to adhere to a defensive strategy to gain time before the arrival of reinforcements at the initial stage of the war. To ensure victory, a significant contingent of forces would have to be transported from the European part of Russia, which could take up to seven months counting from the moment mobilisation began.[24] The inability to predict the strategic intentions and the directions of Japanese attacks with any accuracy forced the Russian command to split up their limited forces in order to defend Vladivostok, Port Arthur and Manchuria. Thus, it was assumed that Russia would have to wage war against Japan under inferior

---

22 V. A. Zolotarev and I. A. Kozlov, *Russko-iaponskaia voina 1904–1905 g.g.: Borba na more* (Moscow: Nauka, 1990), 16.
23 O. R. Airapetov, *Na puti k krahu. Russko-iaponskaya voyna 1904–1905 gg. Voenno-politicheskaya istoriya* (Moscow: Torgovy Dom Algoritm, 2014), 207.
24 *Russko–iaponskaya voyna 1904–1905 gg.* (St Petersburg: Tipografiya Suvorina, 1910), vol. 1, 193–4.

conditions for a fairly long time. All these provisions formed the basis for the specific action plans developed in 1901–1903. The action plan at sea was developed separately and was also defensive in nature. The first stage of this plan tasked both the Port Arthur squadron and the cruiser detachment based in Vladivostok with interfering Japanese naval operations for transport and disembarkation of troops.

In 1903, the Russian Empire appointed Admiral Yevgeni Ivanovich Alekseyev to the newly created position of viceroy for the Far East. With the commencement of the war in 1904, he was appointed commander-in-chief of the land and naval forces of the Russian Empire in the Far East. The command of the ground forces was entrusted to General Aleksey Nikolayevich Kuropatkin, who previously served as war minister. Even before the war, Alekseyev and Kuropatkin had different views on military strategy, which in turn had a negative impact on the initial proceeding operations. Each of them periodically appealed for support to the Tsar, but the incoming instructions from St Petersburg brought even greater discord in the adoption and implementation of strategic decisions.[25] Only in October 1904, when it became clear that the war was going to last and events were not developing in favour of the Russians, did Nicholas II decide to remove Alekseyev from his post and completely transfer control over the conduct of operations to Kuropatkin.

Kuropatkin did not have a clear strategic plan of action. The plan he presented to the Tsar before leaving St Petersburg in February was of the most general nature: at the initial stage it would consist of conducting defensive operations on land and establishing superiority at sea. Next, it would be necessary to go on the offensive and defeat the Japanese in Manchuria, Korea and even on Japan's territory.[26] As expected in the initial phase of the plan, the Russian Army began by engaging in defensive battles. While waiting for reinforcements, separate units of the Manchurian Army were dispersed over large areas of the region in an attempt to slow down the Japanese offensive. By August, the Russian forces numbered nearly 150,000 troops, against about 110,000 Japanese. Despite this fact, the few and relatively weak attempts to seize the initiative usually ended in failure. In January and February 1905, the Russian Manchurian Army's attempt to take the offensive ended in a severe defeat during the Mukden operation. In addition to the defeats on the military front, the Empire was also facing internal

---

25 O. A. Belozerova, 'General A. N. Kuropatkin vo glave Manchzhurskoy armii v Russko–iaponskuyu vojny 1904–1905 gg.', *Mir politiki i sotsiologii*, 11 (2018), 69–71.
26 Menning, 'Neither Mahan nor Moltke', 149.

turmoil – the revolutionary events that began in January 1905 in St Petersburg were gradually spreading throughout Russia.

A similar situation was also taking place at sea. The Japanese seized the initiative from the start and managed to inflict serious losses on the Russian squadron in Port Arthur. Preparations for sending additional forces to the Pacific Ocean were made and a squadron was formed from a group of ships from the Baltic and Black Sea fleets. Some vessels were fairly new and modern, but the fleet also included more outdated vessels that were technically suitable for blue-water operations, but in practice were not fully adapted to long ocean crossings.[27] The squadron under the command of Admiral Zinovy Petrovich Rozhestvensky set out in October of 1904. After defeats suffered by the Russian ground forces, as well as the destruction of the Russian squadron in Port Arthur following its capture, all hopes were pinned on the actions of Rozhestvensky's squadron, which it was hoped would make it possible to at least end the war with a compromise between the two powers. In May 1905 these hopes dissolved after a catastrophic defeat of the Russian squadron near the island of Tsushima.

Russia in the First World War

The July 1914 crisis came at a time when Russia was not ready for war.[28] Two programmes for strengthening the army had just been put into action and could not yet provide results. In addition, the stockpiled ammunition accumulated thus far was not sufficient enough to match the newly increased standards. However, even in light of these circumstances, Russia could not leave Serbia without help. Aside from the moral obligations important mostly to the Russian elites, the strategic aspects of the situation also played an important role. A possible Serbian defeat threatened to radically strengthen the position of the Central Powers, not only in the Balkans but in Europe as a whole.

The outbreak of the war confirmed predictions of the Russian command regarding Germany's intentions to limit itself to defence in the east and strike at France. As outlined in the strategic plan 'A', the Russian Army almost simultaneously launched offensives in two diverging directions – East Prussia and Galicia (in Austro-Hungary) – but none of the goals set for either front was achieved. Russia was drawn into a long war, and was forced to carry out a large-scale mobilisation of all available resources throughout the entire period of the war.

27 Zolotarev and Kozlov, *Russko-iaponskaia voina 1904–1905*, 156.   28 See also Chapter 8.

First on the agenda was a full mobilisation of human resources. A large population and a reasonably well-functioning mobilisation system made it possible to increase the army's size rapidly and keep building it up throughout the war. In total, more than 15 million men were drafted into the ranks of the army and navy during the war.[29]

Several factors complicated the use of such an impressive mass of men. In August 1914, the length of the Russian front stretching from the Baltic Sea to the border with Romania was about 900 km. It was initially divided into two parts, each of which was held by a separate army group. Each army group was also called a 'front': the Northwestern (since August 1915, divided into the Northern and Western) and the Southwestern Fronts. Turkey's entry into the war forced the opening of another front in the Caucasus. Romania's entry into the war in 1916 on the Entente side and the subsequent defeat of the Romanian Army led to the lengthening of the Russian front at the end of 1916 by almost 500 km up to the Black Sea. The immense length of the fronts and the relatively poorly developed system of communications forced the use of a significant number of officers and soldiers to ensure supplies and communication, so that for each soldier at the front there were three or four men in the rear.

Another major problem was that no equally successful mobilisation of industry accompanied the relatively successful mobilisation of men. At the beginning of the twentieth century, the backbone of the Russian military industry was comprised primarily of state factories. These factories produced weapons and a significant portion of the ammunition. State military orders were also carried out by a number of private factories that produced ammunition, as well as certain elements of weapons and equipment. The battles of the first months of the war demonstrated that weapons and ammunition consumption exceeded all pre-war calculations. By the end of 1914, the pre-war stocks of artillery shells were completely depleted. Russian industry could not increase the production of shells fast enough. By January 1915, the existing state and private factories were operating at full capacity and increased shell production threefold, but even this only partially covered the army's needs. Any further increase in production proved to be increasingly difficult. State military factories and some private ones were generally well equipped and could produce military materials of sufficient quality; however, most of the private factories did not have high-tech equipment to create products with the required precision. It turned out to be very difficult to

---

29 *Rossia v mirovoi vojne 1914–1918 (v tsifrah)* (Moscow: Voennoe izdatelstvo, 1925), 17.

obtain this equipment, since before the war began, Russia received most of the machines from abroad.

The shortage of rifles was no less acute. Immediately before the war, arms factories had cut their production of rifles because the War Ministry believed that there were enough weapons. The pre-war calculations proved inaccurate once again. In the first months of the war, the loss of rifles turned out to be higher than expected, while the accumulated stocks were not enough to arm all the mobilised soldiers and make up for the losses. At the beginning of 1915, the army corps created reserves of unarmed soldiers waiting to receive rifles. The government's emergency measures to attract private contractors, create new production facilities and place orders abroad began to yield results only in 1916. By 1917, the ability to supply the army had increased significantly, but this could no longer save the overall situation. General economic problems were exacerbated by the transport infrastructure crisis, followed by a severe deterioration in the morale of the army and society at large. The crisis of morale began in 1916[30] and became the main reason for the rapid disintegration of the army after the February Revolution of 1917, and ultimately the most important reason for Russia's withdrawal from the war under the Bolshevik government.

The formation of strategic plans for the Russian Army during the war required the high command to make a difficult choice regarding the main focus of the war efforts. There were two options: the south-western direction where Russia was opposed by Austria–Hungary and the western direction where Germany was the main enemy. Decision making was influenced by two of the most important and closely related factors. First, there was no unity regarding this issue among the command of the Russian Army. Second, Russia had to consider the opinions of the Allies, especially in 1916 and 1917, when the Entente countries made attempts to form and implement common strategic plans.

Before the war, some Russian military leaders criticised the offensive plan that included launching offensives in two divergent directions simultaneously, believing that Russia should concentrate its main efforts against Austria–Hungary and temporarily limit itself to defence against Germany. Appointed at the beginning of the war as the supreme commander, Grand Duke Nikolai Nikolaevich (junior) considered it essential to fulfil Russia's obligations to its allies and launch an offensive against Germany as soon as

---

30 A. B. Astashov, *Russkiy front v 1914 – nachale 1917 goda: voennyi opyt i sovremennost* (Moscow: Novy Khronograph, 2014), 717–19.

possible. When developing plans for a new campaign, the Russian command fully took into account the coalitionary nature of the war and the interdependence of the Russian and French fronts. At the beginning of 1915, Quartermaster General of the Headquarters General Yuri Nikiforovich Danilov drew up a note analysing the possible directions of the offensive, the provisions of which later formed the basis of the initial strategic plan of the Headquarters.[31] Danilov argued that the Russian Army was not able to attack in both directions at once and, therefore, it was necessary to choose one of them – either Vienna or Berlin. After evaluating both options, Danilov recommended making a choice in favour of the western direction. Despite the promising prospects of a strategic offensive on the Austro-Hungarian territory, he called Austria–Hungary a 'secondary' enemy, arguing that the interests of the alliance required the main forces to be concentrated against Germany. Accounting for this new turn in strategy, the plan was revised in March 1915, and the Northwestern Front became the new primary focus. Soon thereafter, it became clear that this plan too would fail as Germany seized the initiative and launched a major offensive in May 1915. The Russian Army was forced to retreat, leaving significant territories to the enemy until the front finally stabilised by the autumn of 1915.

In August 1915, Nicholas II himself took up the post of supreme commander and appointed General Mikhail Vasilyevich Alekseyev as chief of his staff. Since the Tsar himself did not actively intervene in strategic decision making, Alekseyev played the leading role in determining the priorities of Russia's military strategy from that day until November 1916. Before the war, he actively advocated prioritising the south-western direction, and continued to push that line of thought while occupying the post of chief of staff of the Southwestern Front at the beginning of the war. In the autumn of 1915, when the threat of Serbia's total defeat was imminent, Alekseyev suggested that the allies concentrate the military efforts of the entire coalition on the south. His large-scale plan envisaged simultaneous attacks by the allies from both sides against Austria–Hungary and Bulgaria. For that to happen, the Western Allies had to stop their offensive operations in France and transfer large forces to the Balkans. This plan was meant not only to save Serbia but also to defeat Austria–Hungary followed by a joint offensive against Germany.[32] The allies considered Alekseyev's proposal as unrealisable, which was indeed true.

31 M. Bonch-Bruevitch, *Poterya nami Galitsii v 1915 g.*, Volume I (Moscow: Trudy Voenno-istoricheskoy komissii, 1921), vol. 1, 21–7.
32 Rossiiskii Gosudarstvennyi Voenno-Istoricheskii Arkhiv (Russian State Military-Historical Archive), f. 2003, op. 1, d. 1165, 5.

While planning the 1916 campaign with the allies, General Alekseyev no longer insisted on prioritising the south-west. When it became clear that the French and British commanders were preparing the main attack on the Western Front, Alekseyev decided that joint actions in the west and east were to be built along a single line. In January 1916 Alekseyev wrote: 'The decision regarding the fate of this war will depend mainly on the course of events in the European theatre, that is, in the French–Belgian and our Western theatres.'[33] The same conclusion followed from his assessment of the state of the Russian armies on different fronts. Alekseyev believed the Russian Northern and Western Fronts' armies were the only ones that could attack as they were nearly double their opponents' forces in size. By contrast, the armies of the Southwestern Front, which only slightly outnumbered the enemy, had to prepare to repel potential enemy attacks.

Thus, the most successful offensive of the Southwestern Front during the entire war, which developed during the summer of 1916, was not initially included in the Russian command plans at all. Only the persistence of the newly appointed commander-in-chief of the Southwestern Front, General Aleksey Alekseyevich Brusilov, and his confidence in his own success led to the inclusion of his front in the general plan of offensive actions. Brusilov affirmed that his troops were ready and he was able to convince Alekseyev to adjust the original plan. General Alekseyev allowed Brusilov to attack but set a limited number of goals, aiming mainly to assist the offensive of his neighbours. Meanwhile, the planned offensives on the Russian Northern and Western Fronts proved to be unsuccessful.

Considering the success of the Russian offensive in 1916 and the general improvement in the ability to supply the army in the common strategic plan of the Entente for 1917, many of its Allies placed high hopes on the Russian Empire. The Russian Army was supposed to support the Allied offensive on the French front, drawing as many enemy forces as possible. The February Revolution, which resulted in the monarchy's overthrow, forced the Russian command to abandon these plans. Attempts by the new government to restore the army's combat capability and launch an independent offensive in July 1917 were unsuccessful. The morale of the large and well-armed army of new Russia continued to deteriorate, and most soldiers did not want to continue the war. The Bolsheviks, who seized power in November 1917, began by signing an armistice with their opponents and negotiated for peace, thus taking Russia out of the war.

---

33 Alekseyev to Ebergard, 16 (29) January 1916, Rossiiskii Gosudarstvennyi Arkhiv Voenno-Morskogo Flota (Russian State Naval Archive), f. 609, op. 1, d. 884, 60.

Conclusion

Over the last forty years of existence of the Russian Empire, Russia's strategy as a whole was quite contradictory. During this time, the Empire reached its largest in terms of size in the entire history of its existence. The need to constantly respond to new challenges arising from different directions forced the state to divide its limited resources and in turn prevented it from being able to form a single long-term strategy that could be consistently implemented over longer periods of time.

4
The American Civil War

DONALD STOKER

Introduction

Few works examine strategic issues in the US Civil War. Much of this is due to the field's focus on battles. This is understandable. Battle is at the heart of war. But it is critical to understand not only *how* the battles were fought but *why*, which moves us to the realms of politics and strategy. In the Civil War, as in many conflicts predating the First World War, a method of differentiating the levels of war – tactical, operational and strategic – did not exist in the manner in which we understand them today. Most military and civilian leaders looked only at prospective battles (tactical issues), not at how engagements fit into a campaign (the operational level of war), and how this related to the nation's military strategy (the method of prosecuting it). The education of Civil War officers had not prepared them to think strategically.[1]

Sources

The literature on the US Civil War is overwhelming: over 60,000 books for a start. The most important source for examining strategy and its development is *The War of the Rebellion: A Compilation of the Official Records of the Union and Confederate Armies*.[2] Also indispensable are the letters of key figures, particularly the correspondence of Abraham Lincoln and Jefferson Davis.[3]

---

1 R. F. Weigley, *A Great Civil War: A Military and Political History, 1861–1865* (Bloomington: Indiana University Press, 2000), xx–xxi; T. Ropp, 'Anacondas anyone?', *Military Affairs*, 27 (1963), 72–3.

2 R. Scott (ed.), *The War of the Rebellion: A Compilation of the Official Records of the Union and Confederate Armies* (Washington, DC: GPO, 1880–1901), P. Oliver (ed.), *The Civil War CD-ROM* (Zionsville: Guild Press of Indiana, 1996–2000) [hereafter *OR*], series 1 (all *OR* notes are from series 1 unless otherwise noted).

3 R. P. Basler (ed.), *The Collected Works of Abraham Lincoln* [hereafter *CWL*], 9 vols. (New Brunswick: Rutgers University Press, 1953); L. Lasswell Crist, M. Seaton Dix and

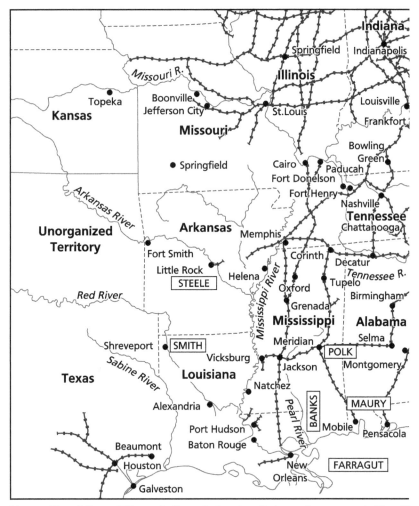

Map 4.1 Plan of General Ulysses S. Grant, Spring 1864. Redrawn from map 16 in Donald Stoker, *The Grand Design: Strategy and the US Civil War* (Oxford: Oxford University Press, 2010), 350, with permission of the Licensor through PLSclear.

The most comprehensive secondary source, one using a modern theoretical lens, is Donald Stoker's *The Grand Design: Strategy and the US Civil War*.[4] Also key are Herman Hattaway and Archer Jones, *How the North Won: A Military*

> K. H. Williams (eds), *The Papers of Jefferson Davis* [hereafter *Davis Papers*], 14 vols. (Baton Rouge: LSU Press, 1971–2015).
> 4 D. Stoker, *The Grand Design: Strategy and the U.S. Civil War* (Oxford: Oxford University Press, 2010).

The American Civil War

Map 4.1 (cont.)

History of the Civil War, and Mark Grimsley, *The Hard Hand of War: Union Military Policy Toward Southern Civilians, 1861–1865*.[5]

A ubiquitous error in Civil War strategy literature is that the South pursued an offensive-defensive strategy. This myth is largely the result of errors by

---

5 H. Hattaway and A. Jones, *How the North Won: A Military History of the Civil War* (Urbana: University of Illinois Press, 1991); M. Grimsley, *The Hard Hand of War: Union Military Policy Toward Southern Civilians, 1861–1865* (Cambridge: Cambridge University Press, 2008).

historian Frank E. Vandiver, who misunderstood the sources he used and the theoretical ideas of the Swiss-French military theorist Baron Antoine-Henri Jomini. It has been decisively refuted.[6] Related is the question of the influence of much of Jomini's ideas. No one has delivered a definitive answer here; the challenge of tracing ideas makes this difficult.[7] Davis, by using the term 'offensive-defensive' (or its inverse) followed a common *tactical* usage of the day of one of Jomini's terms that appears in the correspondence of prominent generals on both sides. There is clear awareness of Jomini's ideas (if not understanding) in the writing of individuals such as Union Major General Henry Wager Halleck, who made a name for himself before the war as a military intellectual by writing *Elements of Military Art and Science* (in many respects a poor translation of Jomini's *Art of War*).[8] One arguably sees Jomini's influence in military operations because of the emphasis on securing bases.

One of the most important purveyors of the 'offensive-defensive strategy' myth, and of historically and theoretically inaccurate ideas on strategy in the Civil War, was Russell Weigley's *The American Way of War*. Widely used as a text since the 1970s, others have illuminated some of the flaws in its representation of America's military past.[9] Weigley missed the core elements of Union strategy such as George McClellan's strategic plans, the few key strategic ideas of Confederates such as Braxton Bragg and other issues too innumerable to detail here, while focusing largely on tactical and sometimes operational matters and branding them strategy.[10]

---

6 D. Stoker, 'There was no offensive-defensive Confederate strategy', *Journal of Military History*, 73 (2009), 177–208; D. Stoker, 'Jomini meant "grand tactics", not "operational art"', *Journal of Military History*, 73 (2009), 1278–85; D. Stoker, 'The myth of the Confederate "offensive-defensive" strategy', *North and South*, 13 (2011), 48–54.

7 A. Jones, 'Jomini and the strategy of the American Civil War: a reinterpretation', *Military Affairs*, 34 (1970), 127–31; C. Reardon, *With a Sword in One Hand and Jomini in the Other: The Problem of Military Thought in the Civil War North* (Chapel Hill: UNC Press, 2012); T. H. Williams, 'The return of Jomini – some thoughts on recent Civil War writing', *Military Affairs*, 39 (1975), 204–6.

8 *Supplement to the Official Records of the Union and Confederate Armies* [hereafter ORS] (Wilmington: Broadfoot, 1994–1999), vol. 94, 194–7; *OR*, vol. 10/2, 458–9, vol. 16/1, 1088–94, 1109–12, vol. 22/1, 24–6, vol. 32/3, 536, vol. 34/1, 30, vol. 43/1, 448–52; Stoker, *Grand Design*, 65.

9 B. M. Linn and R. F. Weigley, '*The American Way of War* revisited', *Journal of Military History*, 66 (2002), 501–33; A. J. Echevarria II, *Reconsidering the American Way of War: US Military Practice from the Revolution to Afghanistan* (Washington, DC: Georgetown University Press, 2014), 9–13; T. Bruscino, 'Reflections on military strategy: killing annihilation vs. attrition', The War Room (14 August 2020), https://warroom.armywarcollege.edu/articles/annihilation-attrition/.

10 R. F. Weigley, *The American Way of War: A History of United States Military Strategy and Policy* (Bloomington: University of Indiana Press, 1973, 1977), 92–163.

Actors

The political aims, and at times the direction of the war, were set by the respective presidents of the adversaries. Lawyer and former congressman Abraham Lincoln was president of the United States, and led the force generally referred to as the Union. Jefferson Davis, former soldier, congressman, senator and secretary of war, was the president of the Confederacy. Important here for the North were those who eventually served as the Union general-in-chief: Winfield Scott, George McClellan, Henry W. Halleck and Ulysses S. Grant. Key Confederate counterparts included Braxton Bragg, Joseph Johnston and Robert E. Lee.

Adversaries

This Civil War was fought by two democratic republics governed by elected legislatures and nearly identical constitutions. Slavery existed in both in at least some measure, but dominated the Confederacy economically and socially. The North faced the monumental task of imposing its will upon an area roughly the size of western Europe – 750,000 square miles – with a population largely dedicated to keeping out Union forces. But the South, as Alfred Thayer Mahan pointed out, had an extensive and accessible coastline – 3,500 miles – with a population too small to protect it.[11] Though in many measures inferior to the North, something made clear below, the Confederacy possessed a solid strategic position: it had clear control over nearly all of the territories of the secessionist states, a defined government, and a significant and growing army. Its position was a historical anomaly as rebels usually have to fight to establish control over territory and governmental structures.[12]

Causes of the War

The American Civil War was rooted in long-running tensions over slavery and its expansion. Southerners, particularly the leaders, identified slavery and its perpetuation as fundamental to the South's way of life. Indeed, to them its end would mean the destruction of Southern life, culture and civilisation,

---

[11] Hattaway and Jones, *How the North Won*, 18; A. T. Mahan, *The Influence of Sea Power upon History, 1660–1783* (New York: Dover Publications, 1987), 42–4.

[12] J. M. McPherson and W. J. Cooper Jr, 'Introduction', in J. M. McPherson and W. J. Cooper Jr (eds), *Writing the Civil War: The Quest to Understand* (Columbia: University of South Carolina Press, 1998), 5.

thus producing barbarism. This made the value of the object for which many Southerners fought quite high. Many in the North, including the new Republican Party, resisted the expansion of slavery that the South desired. Abolitionists fought actively against it, while others were content to let it remain in the South but resisted its expansion into the new lands continuously acquired by the United States in the West.[13]

Lincoln's election as president encapsulated the worst Southern fears regarding slavery and brought the simmering dispute to a head. This was unwarranted paranoia. Lincoln had no intention of attacking slavery and made this clear to rebel leaders after his election. But South Carolina's legislature responded to Lincoln's election by calling a convention. It voted unanimously for secession on 20 December 1860. President James Buchanan pointed out to Southerners that slavery was in no danger from Lincoln's election as the president executed laws enacted by Congress, which would not pass legislation obstructing the right to own slaves. He insisted upon secession's unconstitutionality, that the Union was perpetual. He also promised that troops holding government posts would act defensively against efforts to seize them. Buchanan mentioned nothing that had not already been publicly discussed, and seven other states followed South Carolina out of the Union by 1 February 1861.[14]

Political Objectives or Aims

Strategy is a piece of the puzzle that is war – the most confusing and complex of human endeavours – and cannot be studied apart from critical accompanying factors, the most important being the political aims or objectives sought by those in arms. Understanding the aims provides a basis for analysis and determines why, where and how the war will be fought. Ideally, strategy is created to achieve the desired political aims. Lincoln determined and controlled the Union's aims. Its initial political objective was preservation of the Union. Later, emancipation of the slaves became another aim. The Confederacy's primary political aim was independence. Davis made this clear.[15] But as we will see, Davis sometimes allowed his generals to establish political aims.

13 Weigley, *Civil War*, 6–7; Hattaway and Jones, *How the North Won*, 1.
14 Hattaway and Jones, *How the North Won*, 1–2; Stoker, *Grand Design*, 15; E. B. Smith, *The Presidency of James Buchanan* (Lawrence: University of Kansas Press, 1975), 129, 138, 143, 148–51.
15 Stoker, *Grand Design*, 18–21.

Means

The South faced an unequal contest. The 1860 census put the inhabitants of the eleven Confederate states at 9,103,332, including 3,521,110 slaves. In the struggle's early stages, slavery enabled the South to mobilise a large percentage of its White manpower as slaves kept the economy going. The Union retained a population of 22,339,991, including inhabitants of the critical border states of Delaware, Kentucky, Maryland and Missouri, as well as the District of Columbia and New Mexico Territory, whose combined population was 3,305,557, including 432,586 slaves. The 525,660 people in the Rocky Mountain and Pacific Coast areas contributed little to Union military strength.[16]

In 1860, America was the world's second largest industrial power, surpassed only by Great Britain. Of the nation's 128,300 industrial firms, the eleven states of the Confederacy had only 18,206, and these generally small. The value of the South's industrial output was but 7.5 per cent of America's total. Northern agricultural production outstripped the South's. The Union had 22,085 miles of rails, the South 8,541. Railroads – their locations as well as carrying capacity – heavily influenced the war's prosecution. General William Tecumseh Sherman compared the value of rail and wagon transportation in his 1864 Atlanta campaign, using as a measure a single-track railroad running 160 cars of supplies a day for 100,000 men and their 35,000 animals. He concluded his campaign could not have been mounted without the railroad because to supply the aforementioned force would have required 36,000 wagons pulled by 220,800 mules hauling two tons per day for 20 miles. The area's roads would have made this impossible. About 1,000 steamboats worked western waterways when the war began. The Confederates took a few; the Union built hundreds. One 500-ton steamboat could carry enough material per trip to provide nearly two days' supplies for 40,000 men and their 18,000 animals.[17]

One Southern strength was military tradition. They were, Davis insisted, 'a military people'. Perhaps 'the only people in the world where gentlemen go to a military academy who do not intend to follow the profession of arms'. Almost 80 per cent of the adult, White, male population of the Confederacy aged between fifteen and forty took up arms. This unprecedented mobilisation

---

16 Weigley, *Civil War*, 31–2.
17 Weigley, *Civil War*, 35; R. N. Current, 'God and the strongest battalions', in D. H. Donald (ed.), *Why the North Won the Civil War* (New York: Harper, 1996), 33; J. Davis, *The Rise and Fall of Confederate Government* (New York: Thomas Yosseloff, 1958), vol. 1, 315–16; Hattaway and Jones, *How the North Won*, 58–9; R. E. Beringer, H. Hattaway, A. Jones and W. N. Still Jr, *Why the South Lost the Civil War* (Athens: University of Georgia Press, 1986), 118–19.

percentage translated into nearly 900,000 of 1,140,000 men. But the North had 4,010,000 men aged between 15 and 40. A smaller percentage served, perhaps 2.8 million.[18] The US Army at the beginning of the war, though, was minuscule – just over 16,000. Volunteers and militia, almost always raised at the state level, produced both armies initially. Conscription came later but was more important to the South. Neither combatant possessed a foreign ally.

Both North and South had to finance their respective struggles. The Confederate dollar held its value during the war's first two years but not thereafter. And its officials refused to tax the population. The Confederacy raised a smaller percentage of its income via taxation than any other modern wartime government. The solution: print money backed only by faith in a government in existence little longer than its currency. This helped fuel rampant inflation that destroyed the economy. Up to October 1864, paper money provided 60% of Confederate income. The Union performed better economically. By the same month of 1864, it had derived only 13% of its income from paper money; bonds generated 62%, taxes 21% and 4% came from other sources.[19]

Process of Prioritisation

Rarely did strategy in the Civil War emerge through a formal process. Its formation was usually ad hoc and arose – sometimes simultaneously – from multiple sources. President Abraham Lincoln is often hailed as a brilliant and active strategist, but his ideas generally failed to produce results. His real genius was political. Lincoln often drove or controlled the creation of military strategy in the Union, but it usually came from his generals. The Union benefited from the interaction between Lincoln and his commanders, though they carried the weight. The Confederacy lacked a coherent military strategy and adopted a series of expedients, often forced upon them by events. Neither side ever possessed a modern procedure for crafting strategy, though the North had a short-lived Blockade Board in 1861 that exercised beneficial influence. Confederate president Davis viewed himself not only as commander-in-chief as the Confederate constitution dictated, but also general-in-chief. The result

---

18 *Davis Papers*, vol. 7, 153–4; C. L. Symonds, 'Lincoln and the strategy of union', *Naval War College Review*, 27 (1975), 63–4; Hattaway and Jones, *How the North Won*, 114; T. L. Livermore, *Numbers and Losses in the Civil War, 1861–65* (Boston: Houghton Mifflin, 1900), 63.

19 D. M. Potter, 'Jefferson Davis and the political factors in Confederate defeat', in Donald (ed.), *Why the North Won*, 96–7; Current, 'Strongest battalions', 27; M. Gideonse, 'Foreign trade and commercial policy', in H. F. Williamson (ed.), *The Growth of the American Economy*, 2nd ed. (New York: Prentice-Hall, 1951), 535–6.

was micromanagement on his part, an unwillingness to delegate authority by naming an actual general-in-chief until 1865 and the South's failure to generate a clear strategy designed to deliver the political aim.[20]

Practice and Execution of Strategy

The Confederacy launched the war by bombarding Fort Sumter, South Carolina, on 12 April 1861. Fearing a lack of action would 'revive Southern Unionism', Davis, after consulting his cabinet, decided the Union presence had to go. Major Robert Anderson, Sumter's Union commander, refused the surrender demand, but told Confederate negotiators he had food for only a few days. This sparked a request for the date of Anderson's surrender. He declined to give one but committed to departure by noon on 15 April – if he received no new orders or supplies. This did not satisfy the rebels, who fretted over this very thing. They chose instead to launch the war.[21]

This was the South's first strategic mistake. Deciding *when* to begin a war is crucial. The South went to war too soon. The Confederacy should have suffered the indignity of the Yankees holding a small piece of South Carolina, exported their cotton through blockade-free ports (the South instead embargoed its own cotton in a forlorn attempt to compel foreign involvement) and used the money to import needed weapons and supplies. Davis acted impetuously by launching a war for which the Confederacy was unprepared while emboldening a reluctant foe. Moreover, the South probably did as Lincoln hoped by firing the first shots and making itself the aggressor. This did not make the Confederacy's defeat inevitable. But it could have waited and grown stronger.

The Confederacy initially implemented a cordon strategy or 'cordon defense', meaning it tried to defend the entire Confederacy and soon had troops scattered from Virginia to Texas. Politically, Davis had little choice but to do this. Governors worried about Union descents, and Southerners expected to see the new government's military strength. Davis also feared that any Union penetrations, even if the captured lands were recovered, would completely destroy the slave system in the area, making it irredeemable.[22] This, in a manner typical of the Confederacy, was ad hoc and reactive.

---

20 Stoker, *Grand Design*, 22–3, 27, 94–5, 407–8, 410–11; K. J. Weddle, 'The blockade board of 1861 and Union naval strategy', *Civil War History*, 48 (2002), 123–42.
21 E. C. Fishel, *Secret War for the Union* (Boston: Houghton Mifflin, 1996), 16; *CWL*, vol. 4, 323–4 and n. 1; Weigley, *Civil War*, 20–1.
22 *Davis Papers*, vol. 8, 58–62; A. Jones, *Confederate Strategy from Shiloh to Vicksburg* (Baton Rouge: LSU Press, 1991), 20–1; R. G. Tanner, *Retreat to Victory? Confederate Strategy Reconsidered* (Washington, DC: Scholarly Resources, 2002), 3.

The Union's most important initial strategy came from Winfield Scott. The septuagenarian general-in-chief proposed what became derisively known as the Anaconda plan. Scott foresaw a Union column pushing down the Mississippi River, severing the Confederacy in twain while the Union Navy instituted a blockade to suffocate the South. Underlying Scott's strategy was the belief common among Union leaders that most Southerners were pro-Union and simply suppressed by a troublesome minority. This meant that a slow approach to waging the war would allow time for latent Union sentiment to reclaim control. Scott's scheme overestimated Southern Unionism and underestimated Southern support for secession. Lincoln also insisted upon a quick war. He instituted a blockade, which became a foundational and successful element of Union strategy, but did not support Scott's slow squeeze. Believing it militarily feasible, he ordered an offensive in Virginia that culminated in Union defeat on the banks of Bull Run Creek in July 1861.[23] The Southern cordon held – for now.

In August 1861, Lincoln brought to Washington the successful commander of Union forces in what became West Virginia, George B. McClellan. Though not yet general-in-chief, McClellan immediately proposed one of the earliest and far-reaching American strategic plans. It called for offensive action against a variety of points of the Confederacy simultaneously and even urged the consideration of assistance from Mexico. McClellan hoped to end the war in one campaign – after properly preparing. The key components of his plan were clearing Missouri with the troops there; sending a force of 20,000 men, plus those raised in eastern Tennessee and Kentucky (once it abandoned its neutrality) down the Mississippi River; the seizure of Nashville as well as eastern Tennessee and the state's rail lines; offensives into Kansas, Nebraska and up the Red River into Texas to take advantage of supposed Union and Free State sentiment; and consideration of an advance from California via New Mexico. Most importantly, a force of 273,000 would be raised for an advance into Virginia, which McClellan viewed as the main theatre, and then further into the South in conjunction with the forces in the West. The navy was to support these moves and seize key Confederate ports. What modern military parlance defines as 'jointness', meaning joint

---

23 *OR*, vol. 2, 718–21, vol. 51/1, 369–70, 386–7; E. D. Townsend, *Anecdotes of the Civil War in the United States* (New York: D. Appleton, 1884), 55–6; D. H. Donald, *Lincoln* (New York: Simon & Schuster, 1996), 260; C. W. Eliot, *Winfield Scott: The Soldier and the Man* (New York: Macmillan, 1937), 696–7, 727; T. C. Pease (ed.), *The Diary of Orville Hickman Browning* (Springfield: Illinois State Historical Library, 1925), vol. 1, 447–8; *CWL*, vol. 4, 338–9, 346–7, 432–3, 487–9; *Report of the Joint Committee on the Conduct of the War, 1863* (Washington, DC: GPO, 1863), vol. 2, 35–6; R. U. Johnson and C. C. Buell (eds), *Battles and Leaders of the Civil War* (Edison: Castle, 1995), vol. 2, 144.

army–navy operations, was a consistent characteristic of McClellan's planning. This became the cornerstone of McClellan's strategic thinking and the fact that the administration never gave him *exactly* what he wanted, or allowed him to act *exactly* when and where he wanted, and under the conditions *he* desired, became an excuse for inaction on McClellan's part. Moreover, this plan, and its subsequent manifestations, were weakened by the fact that McClellan intended for the army under his command to deliver the decisive punch. Other Union movements were subservient to his advance.[24]

In his initial grand plan, McClellan insisted that to win the war the North had to defeat the Confederacy's armed forces, take its strong points and demonstrate the futility of resistance (while protecting private property). He also urged the reassertion of government authority through 'overwhelming physical force'. The North, though, could not hope to fully protect people and property while using 'overwhelming physical force'. 'The contest began with a class; now it is with a people', he wrote. But it had always been with 'a people'. McClellan did not understand the nature of the war. The only masses in thrall were the slaves. McClellan, like many Union leaders, chased the mirage of suppressed Southern Unionism. This also foreshadowed a later conflict between McClellan and Lincoln: a disagreement on the level of violence that should be used to conduct the war. McClellan argued for light measures against civilians and their property. Initially, Lincoln did not disagree, but as the war dragged on, McClellan's peers and superiors came to prefer something else.[25]

Would McClellan's plan have worked? His proposal had weaknesses, the biggest being the small numbers of troops in the western prongs. But, executed by someone with the talent for implementation, McClellan's plan stood an excellent chance of success. However, McClellan, for all his many gifts, lacked sufficient ability to use the army tactically or operationally. The obvious problem was raising and provisioning his 273,000-man force. This, though difficult, was not beyond Union means. The greatest weakness was that if McClellan failed to move, strategic paralysis would grip the Union, and as McClellan acquired greater influence this occurred. McClellan also did not sufficiently consider the political elements of the war, particularly the demands of Union public opinion for action, and the administration's necessity of demonstrating progress in the war to satisfy its political supporters and quiet its detractors.

When the war began, Kentucky declared its neutrality. Lincoln believed that if the Union failed to secure Kentucky, the balance of strength between the two

---

24 *OR*, vol. 5, 7–10; S. W. Sears (ed.), *The Civil War Papers of George B. McClellan: Selected Correspondence, 1860–1865* (New York: Ticknor and Fields, 1989), 95–7, 114–18, 147–8.
25 *OR*, vol. 5, 6.

combatants might shift irretrievably to the South's favour. He banked on restraint allowing Unionist spirit to arise in a 'border' state with mixed loyalties. Lincoln's patience was rewarded when in June 1861 the state's congressional elections produced Unionists 'in nine of Kentucky's ten districts'.[26]

On 28 August 1861, Davis assured Kentucky's governor that the South would also respect its neutrality. The same day, Confederate Brigadier General Gideon J. Pillow insisted that the time had come to occupy Columbus, Kentucky, on the Mississippi River. Pillow branded this 'a *paramount military necessity*'. His superior, Leonidas K. Polk, an old friend of Davis's, agreed. On the night of 3 September, Pillow's troops landed at Hickman, Kentucky, south of Columbus. Acting under Davis's direction, the Confederate secretary of war ordered Polk's withdrawal on 4 September. Argument between the soldiers and the politicians ensued. Davis sided with Polk, writing: 'we cannot permit the indeterminate quantities, the political elements, to control our action in cases of military necessity'.[27]

Invading Kentucky proved a strategic blunder. Davis put the military cart before the political horse, ignoring that 'political elements' are a part of war and that a conflict, effectively waged, is governed by political necessities. The result: rebel impetuosity and lack of firm direction from the top broadened the war to a theatre the South could not adequately defend. Kentucky's continued neutrality had made it a useful Confederate buffer, securing Tennessee against any Union moves except those launched down the Mississippi or through the inhospitable regions of Missouri. The South undermined its strategic position by opening numerous pathways for Union invasion by easing strikes down the Mississippi or overland and opening the Tennessee and Cumberland Rivers, waterways into the southern interior. Moreover, Lincoln had no immediate intention of invading Kentucky, something requiring a political decision, and Lincoln always retained political control.

When McClellan assumed the mantle of general-in-chief in November 1861, he reorganised the western theatre, establishing two commands under Henry Halleck and Don Carlos Buell, respectively. McClellan had clear ideas about what he wanted done in the West: 'political and strategical considerations' necessitated an immediate advance into eastern Tennessee. McClellan also had clear operational objectives: severing 'communication between the Mississippi Valley and Eastern Virginia', protecting Tennessee Unionists and re-establishing Union government in East Tennessee. He wanted Buell to

26 Weigley, *Civil War*, 45–7; *ORS*, vol. 93, 377–8.
27 *OR*, vol. 3, 685–7, vol. 4, 179–81, 189, 396–7, 539; *Davis Papers*, vol. 7, 325; M. M. Boatner III, *The Civil War Dictionary* (New York: David McKay, 1959), 885.

advance on Knoxville, Tennessee, 'if it is possible to effect it'. But McClellan suffered from a problem with which Lincoln became intimately familiar: subordinates who refused to act. McClellan attempted to co-ordinate the movements of his western subordinates with his own. The Union departmental commanders invariably insisted nothing could be done.[28]

Lincoln, frustrated and besieged politically, began pushing his commanders to act. This produced his famous 13 January 1862 letter showing his absorption of the ideas of his military-related reading and of his military chiefs – then taking them further:

> I state my general idea of this war to be that we have the *greater* numbers, and the enemy has the *greater* facility of concentrating forces upon points of collision; that we must fail, unless we can find some way of making *our* advantage an overmatch for *his*; and that this can only be done by menacing him with superior forces at *different* points, at the *same* time; so that we can safely attack, one, or both, if he makes no change; and if he *weakens* one to *strengthen* the other, forbear to attack the strengthened one, but seize, and hold the weakened one, gaining so much.[29]

The North's railroad capacity actually gave it the greater ability to concentrate forces, but Lincoln's larger points were true. Two other important presidential notes followed. Lincoln's Order No. 1 of 27 January 1862 designated 22 February as 'the day for a general movement of all the land and naval forces of the United States against the insurgent forces'.[30] More importantly, none of this made the Union generals advance.

The Confederacy expanded its cordon into Kentucky after Polk destroyed its neutrality. Davis's old friend, Albert Sidney Johnston, assumed command of the bulk of the South's western forces. Joseph E. Johnston controlled the most important Confederate troops in the eastern theatre. Strategically, the defence held sway. The Union war machine finally began to uncoil itself on 2 February 1862 when Grant and Flag Officer Andrew H. Foote moved to take Fort Henry, then Fort Donelson, opening the Tennessee and Cumberland Rivers, and shattering the Confederate *cordon*. The impetus for this came not from Lincoln's order to move, or from Halleck, the departmental commander, but from Halleck's subordinate, Grant. Halleck only approved the advance after receipt of an intelligence report (later proved false) indicating the arrival of Confederate reinforcements, and Grant's third

---

28 T. H. Williams, *Lincoln and His Generals* (New York: Knopf, 1952), 47–8; *OR*, vol. 7, 447–8, 450–2, vol. 8, 382, 408.
29 *CWL*, vol. 5, 98–9.   30 *CWL*, vol. 5, 111–12; *OR*, vol. 7, 928–9.

request.[31] This push, combined with Buell's drive into Kentucky and central Tennessee, destroyed the South's strategic position in the West.

This disaster struck a great Confederate nerve. The South responded by adopting what is best called a strategy of concentration. The much reviled general, Braxton Bragg, recommended abandoning all their posts on the Gulf of Mexico (except Pensacola, Mobile and New Orleans) as well as all of Texas and Florida, 'and our means there made available for other service'. 'A small loss of property would result from their occupation by the enemy', he continued, 'but our military strength would not be lessened thereby, while the enemy would be weakened by dispersion. We could then beat him in detail, instead of the reverse.' The same month, in the East, both Davis and Joseph Johnston began worrying over the exposed position of Johnston's forces in northern Virginia. When McClellan launched his Virginia Peninsula campaign in March 1862, Johnston pushed for the concentration of the Confederate forces in his department.[32] But concentration left the Confederates weak in many areas.

In the East, Confederate forces had no choice but to concentrate against McClellan. But in the West, the question of where was more difficult. Albert Sidney Johnston, with Davis's advice and assistance, eventually gathered an army at Corinth, Mississippi, to protect the Mississippi River valley. Davis urged a counteroffensive, hoping to recoup the South's losses.[33] Concentration was certainly the correct Confederate response, but choosing Corinth was a strategic error. This left the vital centre of the Confederacy unprotected. Now, the only thing that could save the South from destruction was failure on the part of the Union high command. It proved obliging.

McClellan, as general-in-chief, decided what the Union should do. He emphasised that it was 'doubly important' to hold Nashville and to take Decatur, Alabama, thereby isolating Memphis and Columbus, and making them ripe to fall. Critically, he noted that 'Chattanooga is also a point of great importance for us'. It was virtually undefended and Union forces under Ormsby Mitchel were within striking distance in mid-April, but Mitchel's pleas for reinforcements to help him take the city went unheeded. This situation dragged on through the spring and into the summer. But McClellan was no longer Union general-in-chief. Lincoln relieved him of this post on

31 U. S. Grant, *Memoirs and Selected Letters: Personal Memoirs of U. S. Grant. Selected Letters, 1839–1865* (New York: Literary Classics, 1990), 189–90; J. Y. Simon (ed.), *The Papers of Ulysses S. Grant* (Carbondale: Southern Illinois University Press, 1967–2005), vol. 4, 99, nn. 99–100; *McClellan Papers*, 160, n. 1; S. E. Ambrose, 'The Union command system and the Donelson campaign', *Military Affairs*, 24 (1960), 81; *OR*, vol. 7, 571, 577, 586–7.
32 *OR*, vol. 6, 826–7, vol. 11/3, 405–6, 408; *Davis Papers*, vol. 8, 67–9, n. 69.
33 *OR*, vol. 7, 257–61; *Davis Papers*, vol. 8, 92–4.

11 March 1862.[34] Halleck now commanded in the West. He had charge of Buell, and Buell had charge of Mitchel. But neither Halleck nor Buell possessed the vision to grasp what was important, and they let an astounding opportunity slip through their fingers by failing to take the strategic city of Chattanooga. The Union's western focus shifted to opening the Mississippi River, returning to Chattanooga and its environs in October 1863.

Meanwhile, McClellan, having received permission to try to destroy the Confederate threat via his Virginia Peninsula Campaign, set his own army in motion. McClellan saw his Peninsula Campaign as one element of a larger offensive strategy that included multiple tentacles striking the Confederacy at various points at the same time. He was still thinking in terms of destroying the South in a single, multi-pronged offensive. But when McClellan went to the Peninsula, Lincoln relieved McClellan from the post of general-in-chief and put no one else in the job. With the help of Secretary of War Edwin Stanton, Lincoln tried to do it himself.[35] The result was that Union strategy spun out of control. McClellan, despite his sloth in regard to using the forces under his direct command, was doing a solid job of directing the Union tentacles crushing the South. He realised the importance of Chattanooga and its rail net, and that it was the gateway into the core of the Confederacy. He also understood the need for supporting operations and clear operational objectives. But now Union forces no longer had a guiding hand. Moreover, this happened when the Union had a chance to secure an early victory.

When he removed McClellan as general-in-chief, Lincoln reorganised the Union's departmental structures. One mistake was placing Halleck in command of the West. Halleck possessed little talent as a strategist. When he took command of the West in March 1862, he had two primary options: he could drive on Corinth and the Confederate Army under Beauregard, or he could follow McClellan's plan, take Chattanooga and push deeper into the Confederacy. He probably had the strength to do both.

Doing either would again crack the South's strategic position in the West and lay the groundwork for the capture of the Deep South and, more importantly, Union victory. Halleck did neither. At the end of May 1862, the Confederates stole a march on Halleck, evacuating their army to Tupelo, Mississippi. They did it again at the end of July when Bragg shifted this force to central Tennessee. Halleck compounded his failure in the

---

34 *OR*, vol. 7, 671, 678, 668–9; vol. 10/1, 920–1, vol. 10/2, 111, 115, 124–6, 619–20, vol. 16/2, 679; S. E. Woodworth, *Jefferson Davis and His Generals: The Failure of Confederate Command in the West* (Lawrence: University Press of Kansas, 1990), 126–8; *CWL*, vol. 5, 155.
35 *McClellan Papers*, 167–70; *CWL*, vol. 5, 155.

summer by refusing to send some of his more than 100,000 men to help Union Flag Officer David Farragut capture nearly undefended Vicksburg.[36]

None of this prevented Lincoln from appointing Halleck general-in-chief in July 1862, the appointment that proved disastrous for Union strategy. Halleck pulled McClellan's army from the Peninsula in Virginia, giving Confederate general Robert E. Lee complete freedom to manoeuvre, and then failed to exercise his command over the various Union forces in Virginia opposite Lee, directly contributing to the Union debacle that was the Battle of Second Manassas at the end of August 1862. In the West, things completely broke down. Buell refused to move. Grant's army was left rudderless.[37] The Confederacy was given time to breathe, to plan and to counterattack.

By July 1862, Davis's military thoughts had turned to the offensive. Moreover, he now had generals – Bragg and Lee – particularly willing and eager to give life to Davis's intentions. This took the form of a three-pronged, multi-army offensive that stretched from Mississippi to Maryland. Davis delineated the South's objectives for this campaign: regaining Tennessee, and bringing Kentucky and Maryland into the Confederate fold. Nothing went as planned. The Confederates headed north, labouring under the false impression that the residents of Kentucky and Maryland eagerly awaited freedom from repressive Union bondage. Moreover, particularly in the western theatre, the offensive was plagued by poor operational planning, an unclear command structure and fuzzy operational objectives. Sterling Price was defeated at Iuka, Mississippi, on 17 September. Earl Van Dorn was repulsed at nearby Corinth a few days later. Bragg and Kirby Smith forced the Union to surrender some of its gains in Alabama and eastern Tennessee at heavy cost to their forces, and failed to regain Kentucky, partially because of poor co-ordination. Lee accomplished even less. He went north and nearly had his army destroyed at Antietam in Maryland in September 1862. Only McClellan's failure to act in the battle's aftermath kept Lee's defeat from becoming a disaster.[38]

36 J. F. Marszalek, *Commander of All Lincoln's Armies: A Life of General Henry Wager Halleck* (Cambridge, MA: Belknap, 2004), 123–5; *OR*, vol. 10/1, 902–3, vol. 10/2, 98–9, 117, 618, vol. 52/2, 330; *Official Records of the Union and Confederate Navies in the War of the Rebellion* (Washington, DC: GPO, 1894–1922), series 1, vol. 18, 593, 636, vol. 23, 121.
37 Stoker, *Grand Design*, 161–7.
38 *OR*, vol. 16/1, 1087–8, vol. 17/1, 376–82, vol. 19/2, 590–1; W. J. Cooper Jr (ed.), *Jefferson Davis: The Essential Writings* (New York: Modern Library, 2003), 260–2; C. Dowdey and L. H. Manarin (eds), *The Wartime Papers of R. E. Lee* [hereafter *Wartime Papers*] (Boston: Little Brown, 1961), 292–3; S. Foote, *The Civil War: A Narrative* (New York: Random House, 1958–1974), vol. 1, 717–20; Boatner, *Dictionary*, 176–7, 428–9; G. McWhiney, *Braxton Bragg and Confederate Defeat* (Tuscaloosa: University of Alabama Press, 1969, 1991), 335; Stoker, *Grand Design*, 189–91.

The Confederates needed to regain lost territory in the West for supply and recruiting reasons. And a 'cordon defense' had not served the Confederates well, especially in the vast reaches of the Confederacy's west, but offensive warfare badly planned and badly executed proved no better. Indeed, under concerted Union pressure the South failed even to hold its original territory in the West and struggled to do so in the East. The offensives wasted human and material resources, and demonstrated the Confederacy's inability to project power in a sustained manner. This was the only time the Confederacy launched such a series of simultaneous offensive operations.

The 1862 Confederate offensives corresponded to a hardening of the Union response. Lee's defeat at Antietam proved what Lincoln was awaiting to issue, the Preliminary Emancipation Proclamation announcing his intention to free the slaves in areas in rebellion on 1 January 1863. This was an effort to take one of the enemy's strengths and make it work for the Union. It was also part of a general attack on Southern-owned property, that is, slaves. McClellan had tried to wage war without enraging the Southern people or destroying their property. But after the failure of the Peninsula Campaign, Union leaders concluded it was acceptable, even desirable, for the rebels to feel what William Tecumseh Sherman called 'the hard hand of war'.[39] Union armies began taking any useful Southern food, supplies and animals, and burning any facilities of military value. The tempo of destruction would continually increase to destroy or erode the South's material and psychological ability to resist.

After the failure of the Confederate combined offensive, Davis sought the establishment of better command and control over the West. He disliked doing so but put Joseph Johnston in charge.[40] Such a vast area necessitated a leader with vision and decisiveness. Johnston possessed neither. In Johnston's defence, the situation he faced was nearly impossible. Grant's troops bore down on Vicksburg; Nathanial Banks pressed the other Confederate position blocking the Mississippi River, Port Hudson, Louisiana, as the Union tried to open the Mississippi River; William S. Rosecrans threatened Chattanooga and thus the gateway into Georgia (though not nearly as much as he should have). Johnston lacked the forces to counter these dangers.

Johnston's most immediate problem in spring 1863 was trying to save Vicksburg. But what mattered most? Vicksburg, or the army defending it? To Johnston the army was more important. Vicksburg mattered little. Its fall

---

39 J. G. Nicolay and J. Hay (eds), *Abraham Lincoln: Complete Works* (New York: Century, 1907), vol. 2, 479; A. C. Guelzo, *Lincoln's Emancipation Proclamation: The End of Slavery in America* (New York: Simon & Schuster, 2004), 151–3; OR, vol. 44, 798–800.
40 *Davis Papers*, vol. 8, 178–9, 449, n. 3; OR, vol. 17/2, 757–8.

would not dramatically impact the Confederacy's ability to resist. Losing its defending army would. But Davis wanted Vicksburg held. On 17 May 1863, Johnston sent a note to John Pemberton telling him to abandon Vicksburg and save his army if nearby Haines Bluff became untenable. Pemberton elected to stay.[41] This cumulative failure of Confederate leaders not only cost the South Vicksburg when it surrendered unconditionally to Grant in July 1863, but also Pemberton's army (though some fought again because of the parole system practised for part of the war).

As Grant's forces sought Vicksburg, Lee struck north. Strategically, Lee believed the only way the Confederacy could win the war was to convince the North to stop fighting. In other words, the South had to break Union public opinion, thus convincing the Northern people to stop supporting the war. Lee believed this could be done through defeating Union armies, particularly in the North, perhaps even destroying a Union force in the field. This was probably what Lee hoped to do when he crossed the Potomac. It was also a misreading of the best way for the South to achieve this, as the Confederacy consistently proved it lacked the power to inflict defeats on the necessary scale. A defensive, protracted war probably provided a better route. Operationally, Lee's objectives were much clearer. He wanted to upset the Union's plans, throw their forces north of the Potomac, clear the Shenandoah and feed his army on the enemy for the summer to save Southern resources. He temporarily added Harrisburg, Pennsylvania, and its key railroad bridge over the Potomac to his list when marching north.[42]

As Lee's campaign unwound, Lincoln appointed a tough Pennsylvanian named George Gordon Meade head of the Army of the Potomac. In a three-day battle in early July 1863, Meade defeated Lee. Strategically, what was perhaps most important happened after Gettysburg. In typical Union fashion, Meade let a great opportunity slip through his fingers. Union cavalry destroyed the Confederate bridges over the Potomac and the high waters prevented Lee's army from crossing. Meade would not attack Lee's mangled force, missing

---

41 *Davis Papers*, vol. 9, 189; C. L. Symonds, *Joseph E. Johnston: A Civil War Biography* (New York: Norton, 1992), 207–8; *OR*, vol. 24/1, 216–17, 220–3, vol. 24/3, 888–90.
42 *Wartime Papers*, 507–10, 569–70; Davis, *Rise and Fall*, vol. 2, 437–8; W. Allan, 'Memoranda of Conversations with Robert E. Lee', 15 April 1868, in G. W. Gallagher (ed.), *Lee the Soldier* (Lincoln: University of Nebraska Press, 1996), 13–14; *ORS*, vol. 27, 432–5; W. H. Taylor, *General Lee: His Campaigns in Virginia, 1861–1865, with Personal Reminiscences* (Norfolk, VA: Nussbaum, 1906), 180; W. Allan, 'Campaigns in Virginia, Maryland, and Pennsylvania, 1862–1863', paper read 9 May 1887, in *Papers of the Military Historical Society of Massachusetts* (Boston: Military Historical Society of Massachusetts, 1903), vol. 3, 446–7; *Davis Papers*, vol. 9, 261, n. 3; J. M. McPherson, *This Mighty Scourge: Perspectives on the Civil War* (Oxford: Oxford University Press, 2009), 85.

a chance to destroy Lee's army, a clear element of Confederate strength. Lincoln believed that such a blow landed against the South, combined with Grant's capture of Vicksburg, would have ensured a Union victory.[43]

After the twin Union victories of Vicksburg and Gettysburg, the Union gave the Confederacy the most important strategic gift it could bequeath: *time*. The Confederacy was beginning to succumb to the effects of simultaneous pressure from Union forces. Instead of continuing the strain, the Union flailed at the edges. Two things drove this: Lincoln's insistence upon countering French political influence deriving from Napoleon III's Mexican adventure, and Halleck's insistence upon 'cleaning up' the Confederacy's peripheral areas. This led to Union moves against Arkansas, Texas, and other areas. Grant and Sherman also embarked upon what became a Union raiding strategy that aimed at destroying Southern resources and transportation.[44]

Meanwhile, the South strengthened itself as best it could, and Confederate leaders looked to recoup their territorial losses in the West, particularly in Tennessee. What emerged was an enormously convoluted and often irrational discussion over just how this should be done that revolved around unrealistic operational plans.[45] This debate, typical of the Confederates, failed to address the key issue: how could the South win the war? This was a question the Confederacy's leaders never seriously addressed. Strategically, the North gave the Confederates a breather when it did not have to, and the South failed to use this to improve its position.

The strands of Union strategy came together when Ulysses S. Grant became general in chief in February 1864. He composed a strategic plan for ending the war by the November presidential election, including multiple, simultaneous attacks against the main Confederate armies in Georgia and Virginia, as well as strikes against key areas and cities. The plan was a good one, based upon a clear understanding of the political, strategic and operational realities facing any Union offensive, and comprised of mutually supporting operations. Grant also was willing to destroy Confederate armies using attrition if his primary plan did not yield victory. An adjunct element was the use of raids against Confederate

---

43 OR, vol. 27/1, 82–3, vol. 27/3, 605; CWL, vol. 6, 319.
44 OR, vol. 24/3, 513, 528, 546–7, vol. 26/1, 659, series 3, vol. 3, 735; CWL, vol. 6, 354–5, 355, n. 1; Grant, *Memoirs*, 389; Foote, *Civil War*, vol. 2, 769–70; Grimsley, *Hard Hand of War*, 159, 162–3; Hattaway and Jones, *How the North Won*, 489–90.
45 OR, vol. 32/2, 652–4, 667, 762, 790–2, 818, vol. 32/3, 590–1, 598–9, vol. 52/2, 634–5; D. S. Freeman, *R. E. Lee: A Biography* (New York: Charles Scribner's Sons, 1935), vol. 3, 260; D. S. Freeman, *Lee's Lieutenants: A Study in Command* (New York: Charles Scribner's Sons, 1944), vol. 3, 307–8.

supply and industrial points.⁴⁶ But there was a flaw: these various operational prongs needed good commanders; not all had them. As a result, Grant's great plan fell apart almost immediately. The opportunity to win by November passed, and Grant and the Union were forced to rely upon attrition of Confederate armies and exhaustion of the enemy's resources.

Grant's plan, and its modifications, laid the groundwork for victory. Sherman took Atlanta, Georgia, securing Lincoln's 1864 re-election and thus continuance of the war. The Confederate defence of Atlanta half-destroyed the Army of Tennessee, while that in Virginia eventually killed Lee's army. After Atlanta's fall, Sherman attacked Southern resources, armies and will in his march through Georgia and the Carolinas. Simultaneous advances; destroying Confederate armies and resources; attacking the people's will – this delivered Union success.⁴⁷ Confederate forces surrendered in spring 1865.

Conclusion

The practice of strategy during the US Civil War was plagued by poor co-ordination among various forces and commanders, and too often ad hoc implementation. Personality sometimes played a role here, particularly in the South where Davis micromanaged, and his generals, particularly in the western theatre, consistently failed to work together. Strategy creation and execution here provide more examples of what not to do than of best practice. The lack of any organised system for creating strategy was detrimental to both sides and too often produced improvisation rather than strategies intended to deliver the political aim. But there are positive lessons. From the beginning of the conflict Lincoln sought a method for winning the war, pushed his generals to construct one when they would not do so, and gave them ideas if they failed to generate their own. Davis never tried to develop a strategy to enable the South to achieve its political aim of independence. The decisive element in Union victory was its eventual construction and implementation of a coherent strategy that addressed the nature of the war, one the North implemented for as long as necessary to deliver its political aims.⁴⁸

---

46 See *OR*, vol. 32/2, 40–3, vol. 34/1, 8–9, vol. 34/2, 610–11; Foote, *Civil War*, vol. 2, 871–2.
47 Stoker, *Grand Design*, 374–94, 409–12.
48 Chapter 16 looks at the American Civil War again in the context of the American wars in modern history.

5

The Use of Naval Power

ANDREW LAMBERT

This chapter examines the strategic history of the last Great Power to rely on naval power as its primary strategic instrument, and contrasts that strategy with the uses of naval power by Great Power rivals in peace and war. The British sea power state, a consciously created polity, emphasised insularity and oceanic links over more conventional identities based on territory and land borders. Sea power states have always been relatively small, and militarily weak. They secured Great Power status through asymmetric strategies based on naval/economic power, reflecting their reliance on oceanic commerce and connections. Navies, the primary means of securing those priorities, necessarily become central elements of national identity.[1]

Maritime strategies reflect the reality that sea power states need to control maritime communications for security and prosperity: that control allows them to attack the shipping, overseas possessions and, critically, the economies of their rivals as an alternative to a land invasion. This choice reflects their inability to operate as military Great Powers. Military Great Powers have responded to the maritime threat by building military navies to secure command of the sea, to facilitate the invasion and overthrow of a sea power rival. If that option fails, they use naval resources to attack floating trade of a sea power adversary. The Anglo-French wars between 1688 and 1815 are the obvious modern example of these strategies, while the Punic Wars of antiquity explored the same dynamic, with different results. In both cases the belligerents were separated by sea and needed to dominate maritime communications to move and support armies. Roman naval dominance

---

[1] A. Lambert, *Seapower States: Maritime Culture, Continental Empires, and the Conflict that Made the Modern World* (London: Yale University Press, 2018).

proved decisive: isolating Carthaginian armies in Sicily and Italy, and preventing Macedonian armies from joining Hannibal in Italy. Rome, like the United States, had the resources to build a dominant military navy as well as a great army: France did not.

In conflicts between continental powers, navies may be useful strategic assets, but they are not, of themselves, critical. Continental powers facing sustained economic attack from the sea, who are thus unable to use their armies, have attempted to weaken or distract sea power rivals by attacking their commercial shipping. This was especially effective when the sea power in question depended on imported resources. While this strategy maximised the impact of limited naval resources it was primarily a distraction, unable to defeat a sea power that has command of the sea.

Maritime strategy begins with the Peloponnesian War; Pericles relied on naval power and fortifications to protect Athens, attack the Spartan economy, build alliances and promote the spread of democratic politics.[2] Carthage and Venice, sea power empires of trade and resource extraction, emphasised naval over military power, thus fighting for maritime communications and ports, not territory. In the seventeenth century the Dutch Republic created maritime empires in Asia and the Americas in order to sustain a dynamic maritime economy (as was also illustrated in Chapter 22 of Volume I by Adri van Vliet). When French invasions obliged the Republic to focus on continental security, England's insularity and relatively larger resource base enabled it to become the leading sea power. Exhausted by the cost of long wars with France, the Republic ceased to be a first-rank power in the eighteenth century.

Naval power dominated English/British strategy from the sixteenth century, when large cannon-armed sailing ships enabled the state to rely on naval defence. In 1545 and 1588 English fleets defeated French and Spanish invasions, asserting dominion over the adjacent seas and shifting England's economic horizons beyond Europe, where mercantilism restricted market access. Naval power became critical to economic expansion, securing sea routes against pirates, corsairs and hostile states. Naval power, money and allies enabled Britain to secure essentially negative aims in Europe, despite its lack of conventional military power.

---

2 Thomas Hobbes's translation of Thucydides was a key resource and reflected English strategic priorities; Lambert, *Seapower States*, 53.

Sources

The records of British strategic decision making are rich. After the death of King William III in 1702, the constitutional monarchy debated strategy in the Cabinet Council, under royal authority. The Council included statesmen responsible for the armed forces, diplomacy, law and finance, and senior officers from both services. Strategic decisions were taken collectively and recorded. Official orders to senior officers and diplomats were backed by unofficial letters explaining their purpose. These communications inform all serious analysis of British strategic decision making, as Sir Julian Corbett, Britain's leading strategist, demonstrated.[3] Strategic choices could be challenged in parliament and, from the late 1690s, the media. Ministers that failed lost office. Beyond the decision-making elite, strategic choices were debated by a public that considered command of the sea a birthright and naval victory inevitable. The anthem 'Rule Britannia – Britannia Rule the Waves' of 1740 supported an opposition party demanding war to secure commercial access to the Spanish Empire.

The debate about the nature of a 'British way of war' has drawn contributions from strategists and historians for more than a century. While many realised British strategy was distinct from Continental models, Corbett made the case for a limited, maritime strategy. After the Great War, Basil Liddell Hart popularised this model, relying on Corbett's friend Admiral Sir Herbert Richmond.[4] Sir Michael Howard's counterargument in the 1960s and 1970s assumed that Continental methods were universally applicable.[5] This has been linked to the argument that Europe has always been central to British policy.[6] Britain supported European stability and balance as prerequisites for economic and imperial expansion in the wider world. The latter represented Britain's ambition, the former the principal barrier to its achievement. For a relatively weak offshore power, Europe was a problem to be managed, not a strategic opportunity.

---

3 For an example: A. Lambert, *The Crimean War: British Grand Strategy against Russia, 1854–1856* (Manchester: Manchester University Press, 1990).
4 B. Liddell Hart, 'Economic pressure or Continental victories', *Journal of the Royal United Services Institution*, 76 (1931), 496–503.
5 Key texts are M. Howard, *The Continental Commitment: the Dilemma of British Defence Policy in the Era of the Two World Wars* (London: Temple Smith, 1972) and 'The British way of war: a reappraisal' in *The Causes of War and other Essays* (London: Temple Smith, 1983), reflecting an eminent former soldier's view of the contemporary strategic situation, not the reality of the past. D. French's *The British Way in Warfare 1688–2000* (London: Unwin Hyman, 1999) remains focused on the Continent.
6 B. Simms, *Three Victories and a Defeat: The Rise and Fall of the First British Empire 1714–1783* (London: Allen Lane, 2007) is representative of this approach, and references Howard.

Actors

From 1702 British ministers shaped strategy and directed conflicts. Their expertise varied, combining classical leaning with political or diplomatic service. While decisions were subject to royal oversight, the Crown rarely challenged decisions. Occasionally individual ministers or senior officers dominated strategy, but the system had an inbuilt balance. Marlborough was removed from office when his political opponents changed strategy. William Pitt the Elder controlled the middle years of the Seven Years' War (1756–1763), but resigned when colleagues rejected plans to pre-empt a Spanish declaration of war, fearing neutrals would object to such high-handed action.

This collective leadership created critical partnerships between senior officers and civilians; Pitt the Elder relied on Admiral Lord Anson and General Lord Ligonier at the operational level, while Lord Chancellor Hardwicke advised on the legal basis of economic warfare. Anson was Hardwicke's son-in-law. Frequent wars between 1688 and 1815 provided continuity. Critically, British decision makers were aware of past experience, referenced previous conflicts and emphasised long-term advantages and strategic continuity.

The Cabinet understood that the Empire was dominated by maritime communications, not territorial exploitation. India, the obvious exception, was run by a Chartered Company until the mid-nineteenth century, expanding inland to secure trade before the tax revenues of Bengal and command of the sea enabled it to become the dominant regional power. Becoming a continental power in Asia changed Britain and provided a powerful base for operations east of Suez, using Indian troops, ships and revenues. Britain's other 'continental' empire, in North America, failed when the settlers rejected the Roman model of rule from the centre. Without Roman levels of military power, Britain was unable to restore Crown authority as its imperial rivals (France, Spain and Holland) backed the rebels. The loss of America, but not Canada or the West Indies, prompted a strategic shift to the Asia–Pacific region, and ended attempts to hold colonies of settlement by force. Local self-government turned disgruntled subjects into willing allies, as the war effort in the two world wars would demonstrate. In return for an overarching security guarantee, the self-governing dominions provided manpower and resources for imperial conflicts.[7] The survival of the Empire as

---

7 D. Delaney, *The Imperial Army Project: Britain and the Land Forces of the Dominions and India, 1902–1945* (Oxford: Oxford University Press, 2018).

a Commonwealth of nations linked by democratic values and shared culture reflects the success of the post-1782 maritime imperial model.

Adversaries

Britain was an unusual Great Power with a unique world view: it had no interest in the acquisition of continental European territory. Furthermore, it had no peer competitor. Its most dangerous enemies were continental regimes that sought to dominate Europe by military force, restrict economic activity and occupy the Scheldt Estuary, the obvious base for an invasion of England. Britain used limited maritime strategy, based on economic endurance and sea control, to support anti-hegemonic coalitions. The only way to defeat Britain was by invasion, but Spain, France and then Germany were unable to challenge Britain's dominant battle fleet. All three adopted indecisive alternative strategies, attacking commerce, and then aerial bombardment.

Unable to match British naval power, Continental powers developed strategies to limit the impact of naval power on their security. The most obvious, coast defence, used fixed and floating assets, forts, minefields, defensive warships and latterly aircraft. To counterattack they targeted British maritime trade with warships and privateers: state licensed predators. Continental battle fleets rarely sought battle unless they had a terrestrial strategic aim (usually moving armies). Instead they remained in harbour as 'fleets in being', tying down British forces.[8] Preserving the fleet took priority over achieving strategic effect. While France and Spain used fleets to defend their colonial empires, Russia simply abandoned the sea, focusing on coast defence. Down to the 1890s the United States defended the coast with forts, leaving the navy to attack British commerce. In the 1890s America adopted the 'Sea Power' naval strategy advocated by Captain Alfred Thayer Mahan USN as the basis of hemispheric security and imperial expansion in the Pacific. Mahan demanded a large battle fleet to secure command of the sea, citing Rome as a successful prototype. Mahan was not writing for a sea power audience. He used the failure of Continental France to defeat sea power Britain to explain America's options; British success was not relevant to American needs because, as he recognised, America was not a sea power.[9] Imperial Germany followed a similar model, but lacked access to the open

---

8 For these strategies, see A. T. Mahan, *Naval Strategy* (Boston: Little, Brown, 1911). Mahan was the strategist of a continental naval power, not a seapower state.
9 A. T. Mahan, *The Influence of Sea Power upon History 1660–1782* (Boston: Little, Brown, 1890).

oceans, restricting the High Seas Fleet to the North Sea–Baltic region. By contrast Corbett's *Some Principles of Maritime Strategy* of 1911, the doctrine primer of a global maritime empire, was irrelevant to Continental powers.

Continental military powers built large battle fleets to deter British intervention in Europe: the policy of the 'Tirpitz Plan'. Britain responded with arms races to preserve the naval dominance that secured diplomatic freedom. The strategic irrelevance of large navies to France and Germany can be measured in the paucity of their use. In 1814 and 1918 massive fleets that had failed to achieve any strategic impact simply surrendered. Attacking floating trade by French and American privateers and German submarines proved ineffective. Commerce destroying has never defeated a sea power dominating the surface of the ocean. Effective trade defence systems, convoying, intelligence and insurance protected merchant shipping because this was a national priority. These attacks were difficult to stop, but inflicting heavy losses on raiders, imprisoning French privateer crews and the death of 75 per cent of Second World War U-boat personnel broke their morale.

Fixed coast defences were a poor investment: easily ignored, bypassed or overwhelmed. Lacking any offensive capability, they were a confession of naval/strategic weakness; the larger the fort, the more the country feared maritime attack. Although France, Russia and the United States spent heavily on coastal forts in the nineteenth century, all three were defeated and deterred by British naval power. Britain closely monitored the battle fleets of potential rivals in peacetime since it provided critical information that informed strategic choices, choices that began with deterrence, not war.

Causes of Wars

Britain fought for vital interests, translating success in war into diplomatic power and economic leverage. Most British wars with other Great Powers were responses to aggression that threatened vital interests; strategic, economic and legal, rather than dynastic ambition, personal vanity, religion, sympathy or pride. Decision makers focused on the critical role of the Low Countries in national security, the importance of sea control for prosperity and food security, the strategic importance of Lisbon, dependence on Baltic naval stores and West Indian trade, and after 1815 the importance of the Ottoman Empire as a buffer against Russian aggression. The preferred mechanism was a European Balance of Power, secured by treaties that held out the prospect of assembling coalitions to restrain future challengers, backed by carefully targeted deterrence. Both the Treaty of Utrecht of 1713 and the 1815 Congress of Vienna provided guarantees that secured decades of stability. For Britain, European wars were a defensive reflex.

Outside Europe, Britain was more aggressive, fighting for trade and becoming the dominant power in India. In all cases military action was based on (and secured by) naval dominance. Colonies of settlement, from America to Australia, took a more conventionally 'imperial' interest in land than London decision makers, who looked to secure economic interests at the lowest cost.

Critically Britain wanted peace: war was a last resort, not a preferred option. The cost of using British strategy, in wars of seven, nine or even eleven years gave statesmen reason to pause, and the Cabinet system provided a forum for debate. In 1914 four ministers resigned over the decision to defend Belgium, a binding Treaty commitment. Had the *casus belli* been assisting France, for which there was no binding commitment, half the cabinet would have resigned.

Objectives

As a Great Power, Britain fought for a stable peace that would enable the state to manage the growing national debt, the residual cost of previous wars, and reduce the interest payments on that debt, which were, for much of the period, the single largest annual expenditure in peacetime. In the nineteenth century the national debt dominated British peacetime politics as ministers tried to balance debt repayments against defence spending and social reform.[10] The obvious method of servicing the debt was to increase trade, an agenda that helped start two Anglo-Chinese conflicts and shaped British policy towards other states. Britain was far more likely to fight a closed economy than an open one. In the mid-nineteenth century, powers that restricted trade (Russia, Imperial China and the United States) were considered hostile. British attitudes in the American Civil War were dominated by economics: the South favoured free trade; the North imposed high tariff barriers.

Britain had no desire for continental European territory. It did not want any part of France but wanted the nation to remain within the boundaries set in 1713, without Belgium. This aim was secured in the Treaty of Paris in 1814,

---

10 For the national debt as a strategic asset, see: M. Slater, *The National Debt: A Short History* (London: Hurst, 2018); J. Brewer, *The Sinews of Power* (London: Allen & Unwin, 1989); P. K. O'Brien and P. A. Hunt, 'The rise of the fiscal state in England, 1485–1815', *Historical Research*, 66 (1993), 129–76.

before the final settlement of Europe at Vienna in 1815. The same logic brought Britain into the war in 1914. It fought to remove Germany from Belgium, not from France. Similarly, Britain fought to keep Portugal independent because a hostile fleet based at Lisbon could destroy the oceanic economy, cutting links with the Americas, the Caribbean and Asia. Access to Portuguese imperial trade, including Brazilian gold, was a useful bonus. Britain fought to retain physical and legal access to the Baltic sea, to block Russian expansion, access critical resources and deter Russian aggression in other parts of the world.

The combination of an asymmetric maritime-economic strategy and asymmetric responses to regional aggression enabled Britain to function as a Great Power without a substantial army, once potential opponents recognised how effective that strategy could be. Maritime strategy lacked the rapid, decisive quality of a land campaign. It could not defeat armies or seize capital cities (unless we include Copenhagen in 1807 and Washington, DC in 1814), but it could bankrupt Great Powers and fracture grand alliances.

The basis of this strategy was the right of a belligerent to stop and search neutral merchant ships in wartime and seize those attempting to break a legally enforced blockade, or carrying contraband, warlike stores, to the enemy. Britain fought to maintain these rights. The presence of senior lawyers in the Cabinet reflected the central place the law occupied in British strategy. This strategy was challenged in British Law Courts where every seizure of a neutral ship could be reviewed. Britain made minor concessions on this issue in the 1856 Declaration of Paris, and at the Hague Conferences of 1899 and 1907, but preserved the tools of economic warfare by outlawing privateering and regulating cruiser warfare.

This legal regime, not the fleet that imposed it, was the basis of Britain's Great Power status.[11] Without economic blockade, naval warfare would be impotent, reducing Britain to strategic irrelevance. It would still need a fleet for homeland defence, but that fleet would have no offensive capacity. Consequently France, Russia, the United States and Imperial Germany all attempted to restrict those rights. In 1814, Britain refused to discuss peace with the United States until it accepted Britain's legal regime. It also refused to attend the Vienna Congress if Russia and France tabled the subject. The defeat of such attempts to undermine British strategy emphasised the integration of the law into national policy; Corbett was a lawyer. In 1918–1919 his

---

11 J. Corbett, 'The capture of private property at sea', *The Nineteenth Century and After* (New York: Leonard Scott Publication Co., 1907), vol. 61, 824–39.

work rebuffed President Wilson's demand for absolute 'Freedom of the Seas' in peace and war (the second of the 'Fourteen Points') enabling Britain to maintain Great Power status for another two decades.[12]

Available Means

The basis of British power after 1688 was a stable fiscal-military system developed from Dutch methods. Ultimate authority in the state lay with parliament.[13] A national bank, the Bank of England, and a national debt replaced royal funding, enabling the state to borrow larger sums over longer periods at lower rates of interest than rival powers. The landed elite invested, committing themselves to the new constitutional monarchy; investors stood to lose everything if the Stuarts were restored. State debt became an important element in a dynamic capitalist economy.[14] British taxation levels were adjusted to fund wars. For the total wars with Revolutionary and Napoleonic France, Prime Minister Pitt the Younger imposed an income or 'war' tax which raised taxation levels to their highest point in British history. Although abolished in 1816, income tax was reintroduced in 1842 to fund key defence upgrades, and remains the basis of national finance.

British security depended on naval power: the Navy, the 'Senior Service', had priority in resource allocation. The foundations of naval dominance were laid in the 1540s, but economic weakness limited the impact of sea power strategy to short conflicts. This changed after 1688. With improved funding, the Royal Navy became the world's largest, supported by a network of bases at home and abroad, and other resources. The dockyards at Chatham, Portsmouth and Plymouth built the biggest ships, maintained the fleet, stored the reserve ships and mustered crews. While the size of the active fleet rose and fell in war and peace, there were always enough battleships to defeat the nearest rival, and normally the next two combined, along with an adequate force of cruisers and smaller craft to defend trade, relying on the domestic industrial base to reinforce the cruising fleet in wartime.

In Anglo-French conflicts, the main war stations were the Western Approaches, where global trade funnelled into the English Channel, the

---

12 A. Lambert, *The British Way of War: Sir Julian Corbett and the Battle for National Strategy* (London: Yale University Press, 2021).
13 B. R. Mitchell and D. Phyllis, *Abstract of British Historical Statistics* (Cambridge: Cambridge University Press, 1962), for long-term defence spending: 369–91, 396–400 and 401–3 for the National Debt.
14 N. A. M. Rodger, *The Command of the Ocean: A Naval History of Britain, 1649–1815* (London: Allen Lane, 2004), 199.

Grand Fleet or Western Squadron operating from Plymouth blockading the main French fleet based at Brest. The Mediterranean Fleet dominated French and Spanish fleets, supported British diplomacy and protected trade. A fleet in the North or Baltic Seas secured naval supplies, while cutting French and Spanish access to masts, timber, tar, hemp and flax. The West Indies required two fleets to defend islands and trade, the East Indies became an important station from the 1780s and China followed in the 1840s.[15] The balance of effort was reactive and fluid. In 1854 the main fleets were deployed in the Baltic and the Black Sea, the enemy being Russia, with smaller squadrons in the White Sea and east Asia. The risk of American intervention saw forces deployed to the western hemisphere.[16] Strategic movement was relatively easy: Britain invested in bases across the globe, while wooden sailing ships possessed unrivalled strategic mobility. The introduction of industrial technologies prompted major upgrades of base facilities, especially the dry docks needed to repair large warships. By 1890 Britain possessed a global network of docks, linked by the submarine telegraph cable network that dominated global trade and directed naval movements. These unique assets were a critical force multiplier. In 1914 Britain cleared the outer oceans of German warships and merchant shipping within a few months, allowing the navy to concentrate efforts on fleets in the North Sea and the Mediterranean.[17]

Before 1860 naval manpower relied on market forces. As skilled seafarers were critical to the maritime economy, few were raised in peacetime. In war the navy relied on the statutory right of the crown to the services of its sailors to impress men. By 1812 around 112,000 men were afloat, dwarfing the efforts of other fleets. In peacetime 20–30,000 was adequate. By 1914 large reserves had been created because naval ratings were no longer interchangeable with merchant mariners. The navy's manpower demands were small by the standards of contemporary Great Power armies, balancing the higher costs of naval hardware and infrastructure.

The British Army only reached the scale of contemporary Great Power armies in 1916 when conscription was introduced. This experience proved counterproductive; skilled men were removed from industrial work, often war-related, weakening the economic base that had been critical to British strategy in every war since 1688. Ministers recognised Britain could not afford naval dominance and a mass army but took the risk in 1916, hoping to win the war quickly.

15 G. Graham, *The China Station: War and Diplomacy 1830–1860* (Oxford: Clarendon Press, 1978).
16 Lambert, *Crimean War*.
17 J. Corbett, *Naval Operations, Vol. I To the Falkland Islands December 1914* (London: Longmans Green, 1920) is the best account of this process.

Hitherto Britain had relied on local and volunteer forces for home defence; primarily a naval concern, they were not liable for service overseas and released regular troops for offensive roles, attacking hostile naval bases and overseas territories, rather than campaigning inland.[18] Between 1688 and 1815, Britain's European allies had significant human resources but lacked the fiscal resources to sustain large armies. Britain provided loans or subsidies and raised mercenaries from minor powers, including the Hessian troops deployed to America in the 1770s. Mercenaries were easier to acquire than domestic manpower, given relatively high domestic wages and employment, which restricted recruiting to the margins of the kingdom. The army was unpopular, associated with absolutism and unwelcome billeting. British monarchs impressed visiting rulers by reviewing the fleet usually at Spithead, the fleet anchorage outside Portsmouth.

British fortifications focused on securing the Royal Dockyards, the Thames Estuary and major harbours against attack from the sea. London was not fortified. Imperial fortresses were maritime, protecting naval bases and trade; they existed to support the fleet. Gibraltar became a national icon.

British strategy was dominated by money, not manpower: funding the navy, supporting grand alliances and attacking hostile economies. In seven Anglo-French wars between 1688 and 1815, the cost of war and the impact of blockade crippled French strategy. The critical role of naval power in British strategy ensured that the response to naval technological change was consistent and effective. New or improved technologies were adopted as soon as they proved effective and economic: from the 1830s technology became a force multiplier in naval arms races.

The primarily deterrent role of the navy was reinforced by making British warships into mobile symbols of power. The largest ships were named for the monarch, the state, great victories, naval heroes, captured enemy flagships and famous warships from the past. The fleet at Jutland reused famous names from the Armada and Trafalgar. Yet these totems of power had been built to be used. Where Continental powers tended to keep their ships secure, treating them as major investments and diplomatic counters, the Royal Navy was highly aggressive, using battle to secure strategic and moral ascendancy, notably in Nelson's victories at the Nile in 1798 and Trafalgar in 1805. Inconclusive battle prompted public outrage.

---

18 I. Beckett, *The Amateur Military Tradition, 1558–1945* (Manchester: Manchester University Press, 1991) is the standard assessment.

Process of Prioritisation

British strategic priorities reflected the overriding importance of a stable balanced European system, the prerequisite for maritime economic expansion. These were wars of choice: none of the European conflicts between 1688 and 1945 opened with an invasion of Britain, and few with a hostile declaration of war. Insularity gave Britain the luxury of choosing if, when and how to intervene. The first desideratum was an alliance with a major Continental power or preferably powers; the more allies the greater the legitimacy of the cause, and the more obvious the hegemonic ambitions of the enemy. The British contribution to such alliances would be asymmetric: a large navy, financial assistance (including the supply of munitions), loans and a small army, often composed of mercenaries. Britain leveraged that support to secure British aims, normally agreed in writing when an alliance was created. When France joined the American War of Independence (1776–1782), Britain was unable to secure allies, despite offering cash, because France was not threatening the European balance of power. This left France and Spain free to concentrate their efforts against Britain.[19] The Indian Mutiny posed a similar risk, prompting a dynamic strategic response based on the rapid movement of troops by sea, and deploying naval forces ashore.

British aims were never restricted to Europe: strategic priorities had to be balanced between European stability and imperial expansion. In 1756–1763 the neutrality of Belgium and Holland and the survival of Prussia and Hanover enabled Britain to focus on the extra-European war, seizing the French Empire and breaking the French economy.[20] This situation was unique, and not of Britain's making. Between 1805 and 1807 Napoleon's strategy reversed that situation, forcing Britain onto the defensive. Amphibious strikes at Copenhagen, Lisbon and Walcheren secured sea control with the minimum military commitment, relying on tightening the blockade as the offensive element. Policy and strategy shifted when allies appeared, because they were offered the best hope of victory on land. After 1711 the British did not command major allied armies, as William III and Marlborough had. British politicians were unwilling to provide those resources to Hanoverian Kings with military experience.

Britain created a mass Continental army during the First World War, at enormous expense to life, treasure and culture, only to dismantle it as soon as

---

19 P. Mackesy, *The War for America, 1775–1783* (Cambridge, MA: Harvard University Press, 1964).
20 D. Baugh, *The Global Seven Years' War, 1754–1763* (London: Longman, 2011).

the war ended. After 1919 Britain returned to a strategic system that based imperial security on naval power, with local military support. In the 1920s Britain's naval budgets exceeded those of the USA and Japan combined.[21] In the Second World War Britain did not engage the main enemy army in Europe alone; defeating Italy and Germany in North Africa echoed eighteenth-century strategy. Basing British troops and aircraft in Europe after 1945 reflected a new strategic context, and Britain's reduced circumstances. The deployment had diplomatic value, supporting NATO, encouraging European allies and keeping the United States engaged. While Britain joined the United Nations effort in Korea in 1950–1953, it refused to join the American war in Vietnam.

Britain had no interest in naval allies after 1713 when Dutch naval power faded. The Royal Navy functioned at a higher level and on a larger scale than any other navy, and allied operations invariably exposed the inadequacies of foreign forces. Allies were deployed to secondary theatres and tertiary tasks. Even in the Crimean War, with the French service at a peak of efficiency, British superiority remained and was obvious. Parading professional skill in peacetime supported the vital strategic role of deterrence. The Americans were the first allies to be treated as equals, in the Second World War. The Commonwealth and Dominion Navies, led by British officers and trained to British standards, remained part of the operational Royal Navy.

Execution/Application of Strategy

English strategic concerns were shaped by the universal 'Roman' ambitions, economic leverage and strategic threat posed by Habsburg Emperor Charles V and his son Philip II, King of Spain. Both men ruled the Low Countries, and the rationale for intervening in Europe was to prevent Antwerp and the River Scheldt falling under the control of a pan-European hegemon. In 1585 England occupied key fortresses controlling the Scheldt, as security for loans to the Dutch rebels. This prompted Philip II to declare war on England as a barrier to the recovery of his provinces. The defeat of Philip's Armada in 1588 became the foundation myth of English identity, and the baseline for national strategy.

Down to 1688 England maintained one of the three great European navies, but policy was shaped by rulers: Cromwell, Charles II and James II followed

---

21 J. O. R. Ferris, *Men, Money and Diplomacy: The Evolution of British Strategic Foreign Policy, 1919–1926* (Ithaca: Cornell University Press, 1989).

personal, religious and dynastic agendas, without the long-term funding to sustain an effective maritime strategy. The Anglo-Dutch wars (1652–1674) were inconclusive because England, which won most of the naval battles, ran out of money after two campaigns. Naval power provided insular security and trade defence, but it had no influence on the Continent, at least not in the short term.

The 1688 Revolution Settlement resolved that dilemma and changed English policy. Choosing the Dutch Stadtholder as their King committed the country to resisting the hegemonic ambitions of Louis XIV's France as part of a Grand Alliance alongside the Republic, Spain and Austria. William III provided strategic leadership. William secured control of Ireland, a strategic imperative, at the Battle of the Boyne, in part by taking risks at sea. Having divided the fleet to support the Irish campaign, a weakened Anglo-Dutch fleet was defeated at Beachy Head in 1690, sent into battle by a nervous ministry against the advice of the commander-in-chief. The resulting invasion panic eased the creation of a constitutional monarchy: a partnership between the Crown and Parliament, with the latter constituting a legislature with an elected and a hereditary chamber dominated by the landed elite and the rising commercial class. A new fiscal-military system mobilised national resources for a long war. Fighting a purely naval war in 1672–1674 broke the Crown's finances, while fighting on land and sea between 1688 and 1697, and subsidising allies merely piled up debt.

Fortunately, the French were in no position to attempt an invasion of England in 1690, or support ex-King James II in Ireland. French priorities lay elsewhere, as William understood. By campaigning in Belgium he drew French attention away from the sea. English troops fought in north-west Europe, but the fleet did far more. The new national debt funded the reconstruction of the navy, which secured command of the Channel at Barfleur–La Hougue in 1692, preventing an invasion and protecting trade. From 1693 the Royal Navy also dominated the Mediterranean, overturning French control and defeating a French invasion of Spain. The economic benefits of naval power within the Straits appealed to the City of London. The classic account of this process, Corbett's *England in the Mediterranean* of 1904, was part of an attempt to record and analyse British strategic practice that stressed the essentially maritime/economic nature of a national practice.[22]

---

22 J. Corbett, *England in the Mediterranean: A Study of the Rise and Influence of British Power within the Straits, 1603–1713* (London: Longman, 1904), vol. II.

The Nine Years' War secured the English state, but diplomatic efforts to maintain peace by resolving the future of the Spanish Empire failed. When Louis XIV accepted the entire Empire, England, the Dutch Republic and the Austrian Habsburg emperor formed a grand alliance to restore the European balance. William III died, leaving the strategic direction of the war to Marlborough who shared his strategic vision. During the war, British leaders (Scotland joined the Union in 1707) advanced radically different strategies in Cabinet and in public. The Whig party demanded victory on the Continent, to remove a French prince from the Spanish throne; the Tories sought commercial expansion and an accommodation with France.[23] These two schools of thought, Continental and maritime, have polarised discussions of national strategy ever since. Despite heavy defeats and mounting debts France endured for eleven years, until a change of government in Britain led to a compromise peace, a process complicated by the impending change of dynasty. The War of the Spanish Succession emphasised the limits of British strategy. It alone could not overthrow the French state or occupy Paris, and had no interest in doing so. The Treaty of Utrecht of 1713 allowed the Republic to build and garrison a chain of forts along the Franco-Belgian border – Belgium having become an Austrian province, a tripwire to signal French aggression, and a rallying point for a Grand Alliance to restrain such aggression. Post-war Britain cut the army, and spread it around the expanding empire to secure key naval bases and commercial access points. In 1713 Britain acquired two European bases, Gibraltar and Minorca, including the great harbour at Port Mahon. These enabled the Royal Navy to separate the main French fleets, support the Balance of Power in southern Europe and secure Mediterranean commerce against corsairs, pirates and state actors. The bases, the fleet they supported and growing wealth made Britain a European Great Power. For the next twenty-five years, Britain and France stabilised western Europe, but Britain stood aside when the Polish Succession was contested: it had no reason to fight.

Between 1744 and 1815, Britain and France fought five more major wars. In all five, invasions of England were planned. In four of these wars, French power on the Continent was restrained by coalitions, largely funded by Britain, while the British fleet and army destroyed France's economy, overseas empire and commercial shipping. All five wars ended with exchanges of territory. In 1748 Britain returned French possessions in Canada, the West

---

23 For a modern analysis: J. Hattendorf, *England in the War of the Spanish Succession: A Study of the English View and Conduct of Grand Strategy, 1702–1713* (New York: Garland, 1987).

Indies and India while France restored Belgium to the Austrians. By 1758 Britain had seized the bulk of France's overseas empire; the only strategy that could recover the colonies was a knock-out blow, an invasion of Britain. In 1759 the French fleets attempted to unite, but were annihilated at Lagos and Quiberon. Bankrupt and impotent France accepted moderate British terms, and planned a war of revenge.[24] In the American War of Independence, France was not engaged on the continent, but the cost of switching strategic priorities from land to sea, and of naval power more generally, still resulted in bankruptcy. This prompted the downfall of the Bourbon monarchy. Revolutionary and Imperial France demanded the destruction of the British, a 'Carthaginian Peace', but despite mobilising far larger armies and conquering most of west and central Europe, these regimes failed. The French Navy, even when allied to Spain, lost every significant battle, even at the height of Napoleon's Imperial regime. The British quickly realised French invasion plans were a bluff, to distract them from France's continental projects, while the artist of British identity, J. M. W. Turner, used the 'Carthaginian' parallel to celebrate Napoleon's downfall.

After the defeat of Austria, Russia and Prussia between 1805 and 1807, Napoleon created a 'Continental System' to close European markets against British trade, hoping to break the 'nation of shopkeepers'. Britain did not create a mass army but instead focused on sea control and economic warfare. With command of sea ensured by Trafalgar, the British 'Orders in Council' cut Europe off from the rest of the world, with devastating consequences. British and French economic warfare forced Tsar Alexander to abandon the French alliance and face Napoleon on the battlefield. The largely bloodless Anglo-Russian war (1807–1812) emphasised the impact of economic warfare.[25] Russian success in 1812–13 generated new coalitions, which Britain supported with money, arms and diplomacy.

In 1812 Napoleon's reduction of his forces in Spain for the Russian campaign prompted the British to change their strategic aims from securing Lisbon and Cadiz, the key naval bases on the Atlantic coast, to liberating Spain. In April 1814 Britain ensured France was removed from Belgium (and Holland), Genoa and Venice, and restrained within a five-power treaty system that guaranteed the status quo. In 1815 Britain helped build

24 J. Corbett, *England in the Seven Years' War: A Study in Combined Strategy* (London: Longman, 1907).
25 J. Davey, *The Transformation of British Naval Strategy: Seapower and Supply in Northern Europe, 1807–1812* (Woodbridge: Boydell, 2012), 187–93 for the impact of the blockade on Russia.

a balanced European system, retaining Malta, Heligoland and the Ionian Islands – strategic naval bases, not wealthy provinces. Belligerent Rights, a *sine qua non*, were secured before the peace processes with Europe and America started.[26] Cape Town and Mauritius secured the route to India; later Hong Kong provided access to Chinese trade; and Aden protected the steamship route from Egypt to India. Control of global maritime communications was the vital strategic prize (access to markets being the objective) but direct rule over those markets was undesirable. The cost of direct rule was largely determined by the garrison, which accounted for 90–95 per cent of the expenditure. Britain preferred informal control through economic power and influence.

While Britain continued to see Europe as a potential strategic problem after 1815, the Vienna Settlement provided a useful security system. French attempts to resume a dominant role in European affairs were restrained by Russian objections, German anxiety and British naval power. In the Syrian Crisis of 1840, that naval power demolished the ambitions of French client Mehemet Ali, Pasha of Egypt, while mobilising a large fleet deterred France.

After that humiliation, France staged three naval arms races with Britain: in the late 1840s, mid-1850s and early 1860s. British statesmen understood that the French fleets were diplomatic levers, to exclude Britain from European affairs or reduce it to a junior partner in a French alliance. Britain won the arms races, while the Rifle Volunteers of 1859 expressed popular resolve to defend the island and avoid conscription. Naval dominance enabled Britain to work with France, notably in the Crimean and Second Anglo-Chinese Wars, without risking national security. The political instability of France simplified British decision making. The Second Bonapartist Empire, desperate for glory and status, was not a reliable ally.

In 1817 Foreign Secretary Castlereagh had stated that the only serious risk would come from a Franco-Russian alliance, and the Royal Navy should be maintained at a level equal to the combined navies of those two powers, the 'Two-Power Standard'. This naval threat was revived in 1889, when France and Russia began to rebuild their fleets. By the time the Franco-Russian Alliance was signed in 1893, Britain had already exceeded the 'Two-Power Standard': the new ships had been funded by renegotiating the National Debt, the barometer of national credit and national power. The City of London, which depended on maritime power for the security of trade and

---

26 J. Bew, *Castlereagh, Enlightenment, War and Tyranny* (London: Quercus, 2011), 339–418.

capital investments, reduced the interest rate by 0.5 per cent. The City was a key barometer: it had the power to influence governments.

Russia, which emerged as a Great Power in the early eighteenth century, did not threaten Britain directly but dominated the Baltic Sea, the critical source of timber, masts, shipbuilding supplies and grain. From 1713 Britain used the navy to restrain Russian expansion and retain access to Baltic markets. Unable to match British standards at sea, Russia's navy was an auxiliary to the army and a threat to regional powers. Russia responded to British naval power by building Kronstadt, the world's largest naval fortress, to guard St Petersburg. In Anglo-Russian wars, the Russian fleet refused to fight, allowing the British to impose a close blockade and break a fragile Russian economy that depended on the export of bulky low value produce, grain, pig iron, timber and other forest products. Before industrialisation these could only be transported by sea, usually in British ships. Exports generated Russian state revenues: war with Britain emptied the treasury, and Russia had no domestic sources of capital. After the French occupation of Holland in the 1790s, Britain dominated the European capital market, blocking access to foreign sources of capital. Britain had no need to march on Moscow, or even attack St Petersburg. Between 1807 and 1812, British naval power dominated the Baltic Sea and preserved Sweden.

In the Crimean War, the Anglo-French alliance adopted British strategic practice; the naval base at Sevastopol and the Black Sea fleet were destroyed by allied armies that were never more than a day's march from the sea. The economic blockade reduced Russia to bankruptcy by late 1855, and the Tsar was obliged to accept relatively moderate terms. Russian power in the Baltic Sea was greatly reduced, and the Black Sea was demilitarised under the 1856 Treaty of Paris. Britain used the Crimean War to push back Russia's boundaries. Having secured peace through economic blockade and a naval threat to Kronstadt/St Petersburg, Britain used the fleet created for that mission to celebrate victory in a Royal Fleet Review at Spithead on St George's Day (23 April) 1856. This was the basis of British deterrence.[27]

The Crimean War left Russia weak and vulnerable for decades, during which time the public mobilisation of a 'Baltic' fleet deterred Russian aggression against Turkey, Afghanistan and India. Russian naval strategy was dominated by coast and local defences, while a handful of cruisers were built, hoping to distract the Royal Navy. Russian continental expansion towards India and into China could not prevent a British fleet from dominating the Gulf of

27 Lambert, *Crimean War*, 338–43.

Finland. At the heart of the Anglo-Russian rivalry lay profound cultural differences that did not disappear with the fall of the Romanov Empire. To maintain the strategic balance, Britain emphasised the asymmetric leverage of naval power and avoided continental operations.

These strategic dynamics remained relevant when the European system was transformed by the aggressive actions of Imperial Germany. After 1904 Britain supported France, to maintain peace and stability. Germany, already the dominant military and economic force on the Continent, began challenging British maritime power in the 1890s, creating a battle fleet to deter Britain from intervening in Europe. Once again Britain outbuilt a potential rival, to preserve its diplomatic freedom of action, while temporarily concentrating the fleet in the North Sea. In 1905 the Channel Fleet entered the Baltic at the height of the First Moroccan Crisis, preserving peace. Britain had no wish to fight France, Germany or Russia, unless they overturned the balance of power and/or invaded Belgium. Every rational European statesman since Louis XIV had understood that reality, but several thought they could persuade the British to remain neutral by naval threats. These proved counterproductive. The Anglo-German race ensured Britain was closely aligned with France in 1914. That elements within the German leadership still thought Britain might remain neutral in return for mere promises only emphasises the delusional thinking behind the 'Tirpitz Plan'.

British deterrence was based on maritime strategy. German strategic power was geared to relatively short conflicts with neighbouring states, using mass conscript armies. Britain's asymmetric approach, sea control, economic warfare and limited use of amphibious strikes were effective in wars that lasted for seven, eight or nine years. Maritime strategy broke hostile economies, as in the case of Russia in 1807–1812, or the USA in 1812–1814. Imperial Germany was not self-sufficient in food or raw materials, while Swedish iron ore, copper and finished steel goods were essential to the war economy. From 1899 British Admiral Sir John, later Lord, Fisher, First Sea Lord 1904–1910, 1914–1915, focused strategy on blockading the Baltic sea, and signalled his intentions in peacetime by sending warships there and openly suggesting a pre-emptive attack on the German fleet and winning the naval arms race. When war broke out in August 1914, the High Seas Fleet had no strategic role in a war that was expected to be over in months. Having failed on land and feeling the impact of the blockade, Germany violated international maritime law, violations the British used to justify tightening economic warfare measures. However, the British government committed the army to France and ignored Fisher's Baltic concept, shattering the long-standing strategic model and wrecking the economy.

General Sir Frederick Maurice's *British Strategy: A Study of the Application of the Principles of War* of 1929 was created to explain British 'principles' to senior soldiers. In his introduction, chief of the Imperial general staff Sir George Milne observed: 'much as Clausewitz and Foch have to teach us ... neither mentions the sea'.[28] Well aware 'that policy and strategy must be accord', Maurice recognised that 'the chief criticism which our descendants will have to make of our conduct of the Great War will be that we did not make the best use of our amphibious power, and in fact we first turned ourselves voluntarily into a land power, and began to think of our amphibious power afterwards'. He blamed this intellectual failure on the army's unnatural reliance on Continental theorists, 'little, if at all concerned with sea power'. Britain entered the war having separated naval and military strategy.[29]

The cost of the war left Britain exposed to American aggression. America had invaded Canada in 1812, seeking to profit from a Napoleonic victory over Russia. However, Britain had secured Canada, and broke the American economy by blockade. By the summer of 1814 the USA was bankrupt, and humiliated by the destruction of the capital city. It made peace at Ghent without securing any of its declared war aims. After the war, American defence spending was dominated by coast defence programmes.[30] By contrast, Britain developed naval bases at Halifax Nova Scotia and Bermuda to support the blockade of American's eastern seaboard. The primary point of friction between the two powers was economic. As American manufacturing and trade joined the global economy, they found the British in possession of communication networks, formal and informal connections, dominated by London capital and limiting market access. The exposure of American coasts and overseas interests acted as a deterrent. Making the world a safer place for American business became a key driver of American foreign policy, leading to a significant naval rivalry. The naval parity established at Washington in 1922 avoided a costly arms race, but the assumption that the United States would have won such a race is misplaced. Britain accepted this temporary arrangement, but it had planned to build 180,000 tons of advanced capital ships per year, a far larger programme than at the height of the Anglo-German race a decade earlier, to preserve the naval dominance required to operate an effective maritime strategy. British strategists were well aware

---

28 M. Maj. Gen. Sir Fredrick Maurice, *British Strategy: A Study of the Application of the Principles of War* (London: Constable, 1929), G. Milne's introduction, xv–xvi.
29 Maurice, *British Strategy*, 55 and 127.
30 A. Lambert, *The Challenge: Britain against America in the Naval War of 1812* (London: Faber & Faber, 2012), 429–30.

that even temporary inferiority risked exposure to diplomatic bullying at the very least. In the interwar period, Britain outbuilt all other powers in those warship types that were permitted, including aircraft carriers and cruisers, the critical tools of sea control.

In the 1920s, American naval planners recognised that British economic warfare posed a serious threat, one that would persist after a successful invasion of Canada. The risk passed when Anglo-American relations improved, largely in response to third-party aggressors, Germany, Italy, Japan and then the Soviet Union. The first American attempt to supplant Britain as the global economic hegemon was defeated at the Paris Peace Conference in 1919, but the American government made sure that British Great Power status would not survive a second global conflict. The conditional support America provided to Britain during the Second World War under the 'Lend–Lease' programme was designed to wipe out British finances. When the war ended Britain was literally bankrupt, unable to sustain either the Royal Navy or the Empire (formal and informal) that it had secured. The United States became the global naval hegemon.

Between 1688 and 1945 Britain developed and used a unique maritime strategic model that linked strategic decision making to policy aims, political structures and economic realities. This strategy enabled Britain, a small offshore island, to act as a Great Power in the European and later global systems, but it was a fragile asset. Naval power had limited strategic impact: even the purely naval Anglo-Dutch wars of the seventeenth century were settled by economics, not sea battles. The combination of insularity and powerful financial instruments enabled Britain to wage long wars of limited mobilisation, but the country needed allies to defeat Great Power rivals. Securing such allies cost money and restricted war aims. The key strategic concerns were naval dominance, the security of the Low Countries and the legal basis of economic warfare. Whenever possible, the navy was used to maintain peace through deterrence and suasion; war with other Great Powers was always unwelcome because it would be long, costly and bad for business. There was no short-war strategic option. In war the army supported maritime strategy. It was not a 'Continental' force, and was never committed to that role in peace while Britain remained a Great Power. The 'British way of war' had to be at and from the sea. Britain's rivals used a variety of naval strategies to counter or limit the impact of maritime strategy: an invasion of Britain, arms racing, fleets in being, coastal defences and commerce raiding. The only method that succeeded, however, was the direct attack that broke the British economy between 1939 and 1945, backed by the construction of an immense fleet. Although no longer a Great Power post-1945, Britain persisted with maritime strategies because global maritime interests and insular location remained critical aspects of security.[31] Today the 'West' – a liberal collective under American leadership – owns maritime strategy, because it, like ancient Athens, cares about democracy, the rule of law, global trade and maritime security. British strategy remains maritime.

Historiographic Debates

Assessments of the grand strategy of the British Empire have tended to focus on specific conflicts, stressing naval and military alternatives in ways that reflect service loyalties or other cultural assumptions, such as the twentieth-century assumption that Europe was central to British concerns, and strategic models linked to the assumption that total war was inevitable.[32] These binary arguments were imposed on the past during the Cold War, and later Britain's membership of the European Union. They were never anything more than present-minded glosses on a complex process. Insular Britain cannot be invaded or blockaded while it has command of the sea. Between the seventeenth and twenty-first centuries, Britain never had the luxury of choice; it has had to prioritise the use of limited resources between Europe and the wider world in total and limited conflicts. The reality of a 'British way of war' has always been, as Corbett demonstrated a century ago, to integrate all aspects of state power, naval, military, economic, diplomatic, industrial and legal, around a maritime core that ensures the security of the home islands and the floating trade upon which it depends, the legal regime that enables economic warfare. The assumptions that shape the resulting strategic choices were and remain maritime because the loss of sea control would be fatal.

Modern Britain has never possessed the strategic power to dominate Europe. It can only support stability and balance since its strategic power is limited to the maritime peripheries. Between 1898 and 1922, Corbett produced a sequence of studies that explored the evolution of British practice from the 1570s to 1916. He used classic strategic theory, primarily that of

---

31 Admiral R. Hill, *Maritime Strategy for Medium Powers* (London: Croom Helm, 1986) reflects the weakness of post-war strategic decision making and the critical role of importance of maritime strategy in 1982, and signposts what would be required in the changed circumstance of the 1990s.
32 For these linked approaches see Howard, *Continental Commitment*; and Simms, *Three Victories*.

Clausewitz, to explain why Britain did not follow continental European strategic models. In 1911 he published an officially sanctioned doctrine primer that explained present thinking through theory and history. Large-scale military commitments to Europe in 1916–1918, 1939–1940 and 1944–1945 were entirely conditional on one or more major Continental allies being engaged in a war to maintain the balance of power. When France collapsed in 1940, Britain shifted to a maritime strategy until reinforced by American and Soviet armies. The same scenario had unfolded in the Revolutionary and Napoleonic conflicts.

6
The Russo-Japanese War

ROTEM KOWNER

The Russo-Japanese War stood as the most substantial and momentous conflict of the initial decade of the twentieth century. This clash unfolded between two ascending empires – Tsarist Russia and Imperial Japan – over dominion of Manchuria and the Korean Peninsula. Spanning nineteen months, the campaign was characterised by intense bloodshed and encompassed some of the most significant land and naval confrontations of that era. Backed by France and Germany, Russia stood as an expansionist absolute monarchy, embodying the essence of traditional European power. Conversely, with the support of Great Britain, Japan emerged as the pioneering non-Western nation to achieve effective modernisation. The conflict not only directly impacted the expansion of both belligerents, but it also shifted the balance of power in Europe on the eve of the Great War. Moreover, the war propelled the United States into a cold war with Japan and exerted considerable influence on military and naval advancements.

Sources

There is an abundance of Russian and Japanese archival sources regarding the Russo-Japanese War.[1] Both belligerents also published detailed official histories of the war which were translated into several other languages.[2] The war attracted an exceptional number of military and naval observers from all the

---

1 See also Chapter 3.
2 Japanese sources: Kaigun Gunreibu, *Meiji 37–8 nen kaisen-shi* (History of the Naval Battles of 1904–5), 4 vols. (Tokyo: Shun'yōdō, 1909–10); Rikugunshō, *Meiji gunjishi* (Military History of the Meiji Era), 2 vols. (Tokyo: Hara Shobō, 1966). Russian sources: Voenno-istoricheskaia Komissiia po opisaniiu, *Russko–iaponskaia voina 1904–1905 gg.* (The Russo-Japanese War, 1904–1905), 9 vols. (St Petersburg: A.S. Suvorina, 1910–1913); Morskoi Generalniĭ Shtab, Voenno–Istoricheskaia kommissiia po opisaniiu deistviĭ flota v voinu 1904–05, *Russko–iaponskaia voina 1904–05 gg.* (The Russo-Japanese War, 1904–1905), 7 vols. (St Petersburg: Tip. V.D. Smirnova, 1912–1918).

major powers who also published their own volumes on the war, mostly within the decade after it ended.[3] Legions of military correspondents reported on the war and many soldiers left diaries. The first peak in interest in the war ended in 1914, a second peak occurring at the time of its centennial anniversary, including international research projects and the publication of numerous monographs.[4]

The war sparked several major debates among scholars. Tsarist Russia did experience a brief period of public debate about the causes of its defeat, which, a few years after the war, culminated in the trailing of commanders who had surrendered to the enemy when their entire force was still capable of fighting. At present, no general consensus exists over several themes associated with the origins and consequences of the war. For example, it is not clear which role Manchuria played in Japanese plans on the eve of the war, nor for how long Tokyo maintained its initial plan to exchange this region for the domination of the Korean Peninsula. As for the consequences of the war, certain scholars have suggested recently that the war ought to be seen as a global conflict ('World War zero'), or at least as a dress rehearsal for the First World War, whereas others still regard it as a regional conflict with certain global repercussions.[5]

Adversaries and Actors

On the eve of the war, Russia appeared to be the stronger power in all respects. The Russian Empire stretched from the borders of Germany and Sweden in the west to Kamchatka on the edge of Siberia in the east. Covering 22,419,700 square kilometres, it was larger than the Soviet Union at its height, and its population of 146 million was comparable to that of Russia's a century later. It had three times the population, five times the gross national product and a much greater military expenditure than Japan.[6] It was thus significantly more powerful both on land

---

3 See, e.g., Great Britain Committee of Imperial Defence, *Official History (Naval and Military) of the Russo-Japanese War*, 6 vols. (London: HMSO, 1910–1920).
4 See, e.g., J. W. Steinberg, B. W. Menning, D. Schimmelpenninck van der Oye et al. (eds), *The Russo-Japanese War in Global Perspective: World War Zero* (Leiden and Boston: Brill, 2005), vol. 2; R. Kowner, J. W. M. Chapman and C. Inaba (eds), *Rethinking the Russo–Japanese War, 1904–05*, 2 vols. (Folkestone: Global Oriental, 2007); R. Kowner (ed.), *The Impact of the Russo-Japanese War* (London: Routledge, 2007); S. Ericson and A. Hockley (eds), *The Treaty of Portsmouth and Its Legacies* (Hanover, NH: Dartmouth College, 2008); M. H. Sprotte, W. Seifert and H. Löwe (eds), *Der Russisch–Japanische Krieg, 1904/05: Anbruch einer neuen Zeit?* (Wiesbaden: Otto Harrassowitz Verlag, 2007).
5 See, e.g., J. W. Steinberg, 'Was the Russo-Japanese War World War Zero?', *Russian Review*, 67 (2008), 1–7; G. Krebs, 'World War Zero? Re-assessing the global impact of the Russo–Japanese War 1904–05', *Asia–Pacific Journal*, 10 (2012).
6 See K. Ono, 'Japan's monetary mobilization for war', in Steinberg et al. (eds), *The Russo–Japanese War*, vol. 2, 253, table 1.

and at sea.[7] Its land forces were the largest in the world, and even its naval forces were more than double the size of the entire Imperial Japanese Navy (IJN). Yet when the military balance is examined in the limited theatre where the war was ultimately fought, Japan's prospects did not appear as poor. Russia's land forces were largely stationed along its European borders, so that in east Asia they were inferior to Japan on land and roughly equal at sea. In addition, the Imperial Russian Navy (IRN) had only one main base, Port Arthur. Its secondary and only other base in the theatre was Vladivostok, some 2,430 kilometres away by sea. Russia's Pacific Fleet had seven battleships (all part of the Port Arthur Squadron) compared to Japan's six and twenty-five destroyers to Japan's twenty, but was inferior in all other categories, especially considering the geographical distance between its two bases. Russia could, however, bring reinforcements into the theatre and even build additional warships, including battleships, in the event of a protracted war, while Japan could not.[8]

The two adversaries were both ruled by an emperor, had a government and were characterised by a conservative and authoritarian regime, but they differed markedly in the number of participants involved in decision making. In early 1904, the Russian Empire was ruled by a small elite. It included Foreign Minister Vladimir Lamsdorf, Interior Minister Viacheslav Plehve and ex-Finance Minister and now chair of the Council of Ministers, Sergei Witte. In addition, there were the representatives of the military branches: Minister of the Army Aleksei Kuropatkin and Minister of the Navy Fedor Avelan. An equal or even greater role was played by the grand dukes of Russia, the Tsar's uncles, such as Aleksei Aleksandrovich Romanov and Sergei Aleksandrovich Romanov, who meddled in politics and were involved in every major decision. Above all stood the Tsar Nicholas II, who bore ultimate responsibility by virtue of his absolute power dictated by the form of the regime. 'The Emperor is an autocratic and unlimited monarch' read Article I of the Fundamental State Laws laid down by Tsar Nicholas I. His great-grandson, Nicholas II, was determined to uphold this principle, and was a dominant figure in Russian decision making during the war against Japan.[9]

---

7 For the military balance on the eve of the war, see R. Kowner, *Historical Dictionary of the Russo-Japanese War*, 2nd ed. (Lanham: Rowman & Littlefield, 2017), 325–7. For the naval balance, see Kowner, *Tsushima* (Oxford: Oxford University Press, 2022), 10–16.
8 See N. Papastratigakis, *Russian Imperialism and Naval Power: Military Strategy and the Build-up to the Russo–Japanese War* (London: I. B. Tauris, 2011), 247, 255, 259–61.
9 For Russian decision making on the Far East on the eve of the war, see D. M. McDonald, *United Government and Foreign Policy in Russia, 1900–1914* (Cambridge, MA: Harvard University Press, 1992), 58–75.

By comparison, Japan seemed less autocratic. It had a constitution, a parliament and, crucially, divided state authority among a far larger number of participants. Although the constitution of 1889 stated that the emperor was 'the head of the Empire, combining in himself the rights of sovereignty', and the supreme commander of the army and the navy, he enjoyed a fairly limited degree of authority and did not interfere in everyday politics. In practice, Emperor Meiji was head of state but the prime minister was the actual head of government, and the true holders of power were members of the Meiji Restoration oligarchy and their successors. Originally mid- and low-level samurai from the domains of Satsuma and Chōshū, they had led the revolution against the Shogunate in 1868. The oligarchy was divided thirty-six years later into several groups which kept check on one another. In military matters, the highest authority was the Supreme War Council, an advisory organ set up in 1903 for the purposes of advising Emperor Meiji which included a selected number of army and navy members.

In political matters, the government was far more powerful than parliament, and some of its members – such as Prime Minister Katsura Tarō, Foreign Minister Komura Jutarō, Finance Minister Sone Arasuke and representatives of the military: Army Minister Terauchi Masatake and Navy Minister Yamamoto Gonnohyōe – were highly involved in the decision to go to war as well as to seek peace. In the early twentieth century, crucial decisions were still left to the five *Genrō*. The official role of these retired founding fathers of the modern Japanese state was to select the prime minister, but they effectively served as informal extra-constitutional advisers and were intimately involved in matters of utmost importance. Following such a consultation, and starting in 1903, the final decision in instances of extremely grave events such as war was made by an extra-constitutional conference in which the prime minister, the ministers of the army and navy, and the chiefs of the army and navy general staff convened in the presence of the emperor. Altogether, these imperial conferences (in Japanese, *gozen kaigi*) were held four times during 1903–5: twice before the outbreak of the war and twice during it. As a rule, the emperor remained silent throughout the proceedings and never expressed disagreement, let alone veto any decision.[10]

---

10 S. Okamoto, *The Japanese Oligarchy and the Russo-Japanese War* (New York: Columbia University Press, 1970).

Causes of the War

The war broke out due, in large part, to the conflicting interests of Russia and Japan in the Korean Peninsula and in the north-eastern region of China, known then as Manchuria. With time, and as the stakes grew higher, both saw the conflict as a zero-sum game in which compromise was nothing but a temporary solution. Nonetheless, it was only shortly before violence erupted that the two belligerents, and Japan in particular, started considering the conflict unresolvable by diplomatic means. Thus, the process by which intermittent border frictions turned into an all-out war requires some elaboration. From a broad historical perspective, the Russo-Japanese War was the flashpoint of prolonged frictions between two growing powers. Both belligerents had been expansionist empires for centuries. The tsarist expansion eastward began in the late sixteenth century, and by 1697 Russian explorers arrived in Kamchatka on the coast of the Pacific Ocean. Japanese expansion was more modest in scale, but no less relentless. After a failed attempt to take over the Korean Peninsula in the late sixteenth century, the nation entered a period of semi-isolation but kept trudging northward within its archipelago and into the island of Ezo (present-day Hokkaido). During the eighteenth century, the Russians slowly moved southward, and consequently sporadic encounters with Japanese fishermen and officials became more frequent.[11]

With the forced opening of Japan in 1854, its infrequent frontier frictions with Russia terminated. The two countries soon signed the first of three pre-war treaties, which included a temporary compromise regarding their disputed territories – the Kuril Islands and Sakhalin. In 1868, a revolution known as the Meiji Restoration broke out in Japan, during which the shogunal regime was replaced by an oligarchy of young samurai from the periphery, and the country entered into an accelerated process of modernisation, national unification and renewed territorial expansion. In 1869, Japan annexed Ezo and began to look for novel sites for expansion overseas while maintaining fairly stable relations with Russia. In 1875, the two countries signed a second treaty (the 'exchange agreement') that once again set out their common borders. Russia, for one, also strengthened its hold during this period by concluding several bilateral agreements with all the sovereign

---

[11] For early Russo-Japanese relations, see G. A. Lensen, *The Russian Push toward Japan* (Princeton: Princeton University Press, 1959); S. Grishachev, 'Russo-Japanese relations in the 18th and 19th centuries', in D. V. Streltsov and N. Shimotomai (eds), *A History of Russo–Japanese Relations* (Leiden: Brill, 2019), 18–41.

states of north-east Asia. In 1860, it also founded the city of Vladivostok on the southern edge of its Pacific Coast.[12]

Korea was the first place where Japan and Russia came into conflict. In the 1870s, Japanese statesmen and strategists believed this weak kingdom could offer Japan a venue for expansion and its first significant foothold in Asia, but the first barrier to accomplishing this vision was China rather than Russia. In the summer of 1894, the question of hegemony in Korea led to the outbreak of the First Sino-Japanese War. This was the first war that Japan had fought overseas for some three centuries, and although its impressive military victories evoked tremendous enthusiasm at home, they caused grave concerns in Europe around the future ascendancy of east Asian nations (the 'Yellow Peril').[13] Russia in particular was alarmed by the prospects of a Japanese takeover of the Liaodong Peninsula – a major gateway to Manchuria and the Chinese capital. On 23 April 1895, and just a week after Japan and China had concluded a peace treaty, Russia managed to obtain the support of France and Germany in forcing Japan to return the territories it had conquered in southern Manchuria to China.

In the wake of China's defeat, Russia became Japan's main rival. Although its involvement in the Three-Power Intervention expedited the rivalry, it was the exposure of Russia's full expansionist scheme in north-east Asia that now made it such a serious menace. Japan had been aware of the threat encapsulated in the Trans-Siberian Railway project which Russia launched four years earlier from its very outset, but the focus of Russo-Japanese rivalry rested in Korea.[14] From that point on, Russia, along with the United States, objected to the plans to grant the Japanese exclusive rights in Korea for raw materials, markets, railroads and naval stations.[15] This objection induced the other powers to demand such rights too. With its position starting to deteriorate, Japan prompted its agents and troops to keep hold of Seoul. Under their pressure, King Kojong of Korea found sanctuary in the Russian legation building in February 1896, leading to an uprising against the Japanese presence in Seoul.

12 For Russian ideologies of expansion in east Asia, see D. Schimmelpenninck van der Oye, *Toward the Rising Sun* (DeKalb: Northern Illinois University Press, 2001).
13 For this war, see S. C. M. Paine, *The Sino-Japanese War of 1894–1895: Perceptions, Power, and Primacy* (Cambridge: Cambridge University Press, 2005).
14 For Russia's pre-war Far Eastern policy, see A. Malozemoff, *Russian Far Eastern Policy, 1881–1904* (Berkeley: University of California Press, 1958); McDonald, *United Government*, 9–30.
15 Exercised mostly by European powers, this 'concession imperialism', Peter Duus observed, was 'halfway between the "imperialism of free trade" and direct colonial rule'. See P. Duus, *The Abacus and the Sword: The Japanese Penetration of Korea, 1895–1910* (Berkeley: University of California Press, 1995), 11.

Three months later, Japan and Russia agreed to recognise the new pro-Russian Korean cabinet and to station the same number of troops in the country.[16]

Russia's tightening relations with China added fuel to the fire. In 1896, the two countries signed the Li–Lobanov agreement, which ostensibly offered mutual aid in the event of Japanese aggression. Its most crucial aspect, nonetheless, was the concessions China gave Russia in Manchuria, allowing it to build a significant shortcut for the Trans-Siberian Railway line across the region and to lease Port Arthur two years later. Attracted by China's huge market and political weakness, several other Western powers secured a foothold in China between 1897–1898, but Japanese fears remained focused on Russia.[17] With the memories of their evacuation still vivid, public agitation in Japan compelled the Russians to buy time and offer the Japanese free rein in Korea in return for similar freedom in Manchuria. At this juncture, the Japanese formulated the doctrine of the Manchuria–Korea exchange – namely Manchuria to Russia and Korea to Japan – which soon resulted in the Nishi–Rosen agreement signed in May 1898. With this settlement, the conflict reached a temporary stalemate. Nonetheless, and while absorbing Manchuria, Russia envisaged a continuous maritime link between Port Arthur and Vladivostok, which necessitated the control, if not the subjugation, of Korea. Hence, a clash between the two nations was only a matter of time.[18]

The outbreak of the Boxer Uprising in China in November 1899 restrained the simmering rivalry as both Japan and Russia dispatched troops to the theatre. While temporarily abandoning its immediate schemes in Korea, the Tsarist Empire used this opportunity to occupy Manchuria. With the uprising quelled, the time was ripe for the Japanese to settle the struggle over the region. Fearing that the impending completion of the Trans-Siberian Railway would bring the Russians back into Korea, Katsura Tarō's militant cabinet pushed futilely for the evacuation of Manchuria. The Japanese talks with Great Britain were more rewarding, and with the conclusion of the Anglo-Japanese Treaty in early 1902, Tokyo gained a new ally and was able to isolate Russia in case of an armed conflict.[19] With Japanese confidence on the rise,

---

16 For Japanese politics in Korea, see Duus, *The Abacus and the Sword*.
17 For the Far Eastern crisis of 1897–1898, see U. M. Zachmann, *China and Japan in the Late Meiji Period* (London: Routledge, 2009), 55–88.
18 For the unfolding struggle over Korea and Manchuria, see G. A. Lensen, *Balance of Intrigue: International Rivalry in Korea and Manchuria, 1884–1899*, 2 vols. (Tallahassee: University of Florida Press, 1982); Lensen (ed.), *Korea and Manchuria Between Russia and Japan, 1895–1904: The Observations of Sir Ernest Satow* (Tallahassee: Diplomatic Press, 1966).
19 For the alliance, see I. Nish, *The Anglo-Japanese Alliance* (London: The Athlone Press, 1966); P. O'Brien (ed.), *The Anglo-Japanese Alliance, 1902–1922* (London: Routledge, 2004).

the tension mounted again. In Russia, hardliners were now leading policy with regard to east Asia. As the Trans-Siberian Railway neared completion, an influential St Petersburg group known as the Bezobrazov Circle urged a more resolute policy and the securing of additional concessions in Korea.[20] In the spring of 1903, a Russian enterprise set up its main office on the Korean side of the Yalu delta, whereas Russia wriggled out of its earlier commitment to pull its forces in Manchuria. In June, the general staff of the Imperial Japanese Army (IJA) concluded that it should resort to military means if negotiations failed. Given the sense of emergency, an imperial conference was convened for the first time that month.

Although the bilateral negotiations resumed, the decision makers in St Petersburg were trying to buy time. The Tsar, for one, wanted to avoid war, at least for the time being, but the efforts he and his ministers made were merely meant to placate Japan. The response to the Japanese proposal included an offer to turn the northern part of Korea beyond the 39th Parallel into a neutral zone in return for removing Manchuria from Japan's sphere of interest. In December, Russia sent another offer with no significant changes. In Tokyo, a sense that there was no diplomatic solution to the crisis prevailed, and the oligarchy was seeking to build a broad consensus for war. On 12 January, a second meeting of the Imperial Conference determined that Russia had not made any significant concessions over Korea. Japan sent an ultimatum the following day, stating its readiness to accept the Russian proposals regarding Manchuria if, in return, Russia agreed to similar conditions regarding Korea. The belated and uncommitted response only reached Tokyo on 7 February, but it was too late. A day earlier, Tokyo announced the rupture of diplomatic relations and the Combined Fleet left for Port Arthur.[21]

Premises Underlying Strategic Objectives and Their Prioritisation

Many of the basic features that characterised the two belligerents were fundamentally different, as were the premises underlying their strategic objectives. On the one hand, Japan was an island nation, separated from the Asian continent by the 165-kilometre wide Korea Strait, and therefore any intervention there, let alone fighting, required the transfer of troops and equipment via

---

20 See McDonald, *United Government*, 31–57.
21 For the negotiations during the final months before the war, see, e.g., I. Nish, *The Origins of the Russo-Japanese War* (London: Longman, 1985), 179–237. Malozemoff, *Russian Far Eastern Policy*; Okamoto, *The Japanese Oligarchy*.

Map 6.1 The Russo-Japanese War. Redrawn with permission based on a map in Mark Lardas, *Tsushima 1905: Death of a Russian Fleet* © 2018 Osprey Publishing (www.ospreypublishing.com).

Map 6.1 (cont.)

the sea. In addition, Japan was inferior to Russia in almost all features that determined international power, notably its military and economic capacity to influence the actions or the conduct of others. More specifically, Japan's still underdeveloped economy and fledgling military industry could not support a total war or even a long-term conflict. On the other hand, Russia was a huge continental empire with a territory stretching all the way to the theatre's boundaries. The manpower it had at its disposal was far greater than Japan's, and this, together with its autocratic regime and larger economy, allowed it to sustain a large number of initial casualties and still win a protracted war. Although the centre of the empire and the main concentration of its population was in its European part, thousands of kilometres away from the theatre, Russia laid a network of railroads that connected it to north-east Asia during the pre-war years which was partly intended to facilitate the mobilisation of troops and equipment in the event of a war.

Based on these features, each side had a different set of premises that underlaid its strategic objectives. Japan's basic geopolitical premises were as follows:

1. *Foothold in the continent.* For an emerging empire, the nearby Asian continent was the natural destination for territorial expansion and economic exploitation. The ability to maintain a foothold in the continent, and in the nearby Korean Peninsula in particular, was key for any imperial ambition.
2. *Control of the seas.* As an island nation, the control of the seas within its vicinity and the routes to the theatre of war in the continent was vital. Put bluntly, Japan could not wage a war on the continent without controlling the seas. This meant that once a war broke out, it had to strike Russia's Pacific Fleet, and, if possible, eliminate it completely.
3. *Duration of the conflict.* Due to its general inferiority in human power and economic terms, Japan had to conduct a brief war and end it before Russia mobilised sufficient reinforcements. Fighting such a war meant only modest territorial gains and the attainment of limited objectives.
4. *Number of enemies.* Due to its inferiority in manpower and economic terms, Japan had to isolate its main foe diplomatically and thus avoid fighting a coalition.
5. *Timing.* Upon the completion of the Trans-Siberian Railway, Japan would not be able to exploit its numerical advantage in the theatre as before. Hence, 1904 provided a final window of opportunity for settling the score in the region. Moreover, waging a war in the winter could amplify the

Japanese advantage because it would be more difficult to transfer Russian troops across Siberia and the port of Vladivostok would be blocked by ice.

Russia proceeded from the near-opposite of Japan's geopolitical premises:

1. *Control of the seas.* As a continental power with direct land access to the theatre, Russia did not have to control the seas to win the war, but naval dominance might expedite its victory.
2. *Duration of the conflict.* Due to its general superiority in human power and economic terms, Russia could conduct a long war which would be concluded as more troops mobilised to the front. Fighting a protracted war implied the possibility of major territorial gains and the attainment of long-term objectives.
3. *Timing.* Russia had better prospects of winning a war once its north-east Asian transportation network had been completed. As a result, it should strive to delay the outbreak of hostilities with Japan until the moment of its completion.

With the aforementioned premises in mind, Japan pursued the following objectives:

1. *Control of Korea.* In an armed conflict with Russia, Japan sought first to remove any Russian presence in Korea, and then to impose its rule over this territory while maintaining full control of the passage between the two countries.
2. *Seizure of southern Manchuria.* Although Manchuria was not part of the demands Japan had made during its pre-war negotiations, it intended to seize Manchuria's southern part, and the naval base in Port Arthur in particular in the event of an armed conflict with Russia. These gains, in turn, would allow Japan to eliminate the Russian presence in southern Manchuria and use some of the territory as a bargaining chip.
3. *Peace agreement.* Following a brief armed conflict and the realisation of the two aforementioned objectives, Japan sought to resume negotiations with Russia and reach a peace agreement that would ensure its own long-term presence and interests in Korea and China. This settlement, in turn, would mitigate the detrimental repercussions of the Trans-Siberian Railway once operational.

Russia's objectives were the inverse of Japan's:

1. *Control of Manchuria.* Russia planned to maintain its control and interests in Manchuria to the greatest extent possible while mobilising its troops

from Europe. Upon the arrival of sufficient reinforcements, Russia intended to recapture the territories it might lose to Japan.
2. *Seizure of Korea*. Following the reoccupation of Manchuria, Russia planned to take over the Korean Peninsula and remove any Japanese presence in the Asian continent.
3. *A firmer hand in north-east Asia*. Once the two aforementioned objectives had been achieved, Russia intended to expand its political and economic sphere further and play a pivotal role in the entire region.

Operationally speaking, both belligerents had completed elaborate plans on the eve of the Russo-Japanese War. As the instigator of hostilities, Japan's plan determined the course of the war for the most part. Although the general staffs of the IJA and the IJN drew up their plans separately, they had no open dispute as they would in later decades. The army's final plan was presented by Major General Iguchi Shōgo at the Imperial General Headquarters conference in June 1903. The premises Iguchi presented were confined to military issues. The most important among these was that Japan would benefit from its short supply lines and from the ability to array its forces rapidly along the front in the event of a war against Russia in north-east Asia. The war scenario proposed an opening blow by the Japanese at the harbours of Port Arthur and Vladivostok that would put the Pacific Fleet totally out of action. The army would then defeat the relatively small Imperial Russian Army (IRA) units in Manchuria before any reinforcements could be mustered by means of the still uncompleted Trans-Siberian Railway. The conquest of Manchuria and the control of its railway network would give the IJA an advantage over any Russian regrouping in Siberia. The general staff estimated that the sparsely populated region would not allow the Russians to maintain more than a quarter of a million soldiers there during the winter, a number which the IJA could easily deal with. The plan recognised that Japan could not eliminate the Russian threat forever, but assumed that even partial success would bring the Russians to the negotiating table. In such negotiations, Japan could use Manchuria as a bargaining chip since it did not need this entire vast region (at least in 1905), while a humiliated Russia would be liable to desire a war of revenge in the future. The solution therefore lay in an open-door policy in Manchuria that would combine the interests of a number of powers and curb any future Russian ambitions.[22]

22 For the Japanese grand strategy and plans, see, e.g., S. C. M. Paine, *The Japanese Empire: Grand Strategy from the Meiji Restoration to the Pacific* (Cambridge: Cambridge University Press, 2017), 54–7.

The IJN's operational plans complemented those of the army. They were based on the need for land control of Korea and naval control of the Korea Strait to cut off the Port Arthur Squadron from the remaining Pacific Fleet units in Vladivostok. The Japanese naval command calculated that their opponents in the theatre would avoid total confrontation but would instead launch brief sorties against the Japanese lines of supply from the home islands and might even harass the populated coastal areas of western Japan. It was obvious to the Japanese naval planners that the temporal dimension of the approaching war was crucial since a protracted war would allow the union of the Baltic Fleet with the Pacific Fleet and result in a decisive quantitative advantage for Russia. In the months prior to the war, it was decided that the navy would devote its main force at the beginning of the war to assisting the deployment of land forces in Korea and southern Manchuria while keeping the Russian fleet away from the theatre. About a week before the war, Admiral Tōgō Heihachirō, commander-in-chief of the Combined Fleet, decided to take advantage of the element of surprise and open the war with a strike against the Port Arthur Squadron during the first night of the war. The attack was to be carried out by a squadron of destroyers with the use of torpedoes since Tōgō was afraid to risk his trump card, the battleships, at such an early and critical stage.[23]

The Russian military operation plan was defensive by nature, and envisaged a scenario in which the Japanese would be the aggressors and attempt an invasion of Manchuria. Subjected to constant revisions, this plan was not complete by the time the war broke out. Its first draft had been prepared in 1895 after the Japanese triumph in the First Sino-Japanese War, but was updated six years later to suit changing realities, and again in 1903. On the eve of the war, it stipulated that in the event of a Japanese attack, the IRA would protect both Port Arthur and Vladivostok, and deploy defensively across the Yalu River with a particular emphasis on the region of Mukden. With the arrival of reinforcements to the region thus attaining numerical superiority, the Russian forces were to go on the offensive. The war was supposed to conclude with an invasion of the Japanese home islands, although there was no detailed plan beyond an initial deployment of the Russian defence forces. The final version of the plan was based on Russian control of the seas and a struggle to hold out until reinforcements arrived overland.[24]

---

23 D. C. Evans and M. R. Peattie, *Kaigun: Strategy, Tactics, and Technology in the Imperial Japanese Navy, 1887–1941* (Annapolis: Naval Institute Press, 1997), 85–92.
24 For the Russian operational plans, see B. Menning, *Bayonets Before Bullets: The Imperial Russian Army, 1861–1914* (Bloomington: Indiana University Press, 1992), 152–5. For the Russian estimation of Japan's war capacity, see E. Sergeev, *Russian Military Intelligence*

Available Means

In purely military terms, pre-war Russia was unquestionably a Great Power in early 1904, and far stronger than Japan. The IRA was the largest land force in the world, with 41,000 officers, 1,067,000 soldiers in twenty-nine corps and more than 3 million men in the reserve forces. Significant reforms had been implemented in the Russian Army since the Crimean War, yet several basic problems remained. One was the advanced average age and limited training of senior officers. The cavalry did not undergo any significant transformation in modern times, and there was a certain recognisable decline in its importance towards the end of the nineteenth century. The artillery apparatus, however, underwent multiple changes towards the end of the century, and when the war broke out it was about to complete a large outfitting plan, which included a new field gun and machine guns.[25] The IJA was smaller and numbered 850,000 men including the reserve forces. Notwithstanding this huge gap between the two countries, Japan had an evident advantage – however temporary – in east Asia, as it could deploy some 257,000 well-trained and disciplined regular infantry soldiers, more than double the 95,000 Russian infantrymen who were stationed to the east of Lake Baikal. Moreover, during the war Japan was able to mobilise a greater number of soldiers than pre-war – and especially pre-war Russian – estimates concluded. By the end of April 1904, no fewer than 204,000 Japanese troops had already been transported to Korea and Manchuria, and their number rose to 442,000 by the end of the war. Altogether throughout the conflict, Japan was able to mobilise 1,185,000 troops and formed some 250 battalions.[26]

The IRN also underwent reorganisation at the end of the nineteenth century as its share in the military budget grew considerably. At the beginning of the twentieth century, it was able to take pride in numerous new and modern vessels, mostly of domestic construction, which placed it among the world's largest naval forces.[27] However, the navy retained its legacy of

---

in the War with Japan, 1904–05 (London: Routledge, 2007), 31–52. For Russia's grand strategy and war plans between 1900–1904, see W. C. Fuller Jr, *Strategy and Power in Russia, 1600–1914* (New York: Free Press, 1992), 377–93.

25 See Menning, *Bayonets Before Bullets*, 123–51.
26 See E. J. Drea, *Japan's Imperial Army: Its Rise and Fall, 1853–1945* (Lawrence: University Press of Kansas, 2009), 70–96.
27 In 1904, the IRN was the world's second largest naval power in terms of manpower (after Britain's Royal Navy), third largest in the number of capital ships and fourth largest in aggregate tonnage. See J. N. Westwood, *Witnesses of Tsushima* (Tokyo: Sophia University, 1970), 5–6, 28. For a good overview of the rise of the IRN before the war, see Papastratigakis, *Russian Imperialism*.

a defensive approach and its self-perception of occupying a minor role in the national military outlook. Above all, the Russian Navy suffered from the dispersal of its units across the Baltic Sea, the Black Sea and the north-west corner of the Pacific Ocean. The enormous distances between Russia's three fleets made each of them an independent unit in practice and rendered the IRN considerably weaker than its stated strength. The IJN, in contrast, was somewhat underrated. On the eve of the war, it had just completed its construction plan, and although it was much smaller than the IRN as a whole, it was the world's sixth largest naval force and roughly equal to Russia's Pacific Fleet. Still, at Port Arthur alone, Russia had more battleships than the entire Japanese Navy (seven as against six). The Pacific Fleet also had a greater number of destroyers (twenty-five as opposed to twenty), but it was inferior in the number of cruisers and torpedo boats.[28]

The Russians' quantitative superiority in the naval theatre is more obvious when the military balance also factors the forces at Russian disposal in the Baltic Sea. Although the Baltic Fleet warships were not available immediately, Russian naval commanders could utilise them if alerted at a relatively early stage in the war. Japan, in contrast, could not expect any reinforcements during the confrontation. In such circumstances, Russia's Pacific Fleet could take greater risks or allow itself to suffer partial defeat without fearing any fatal reversal of the war as a whole. From a qualitative viewpoint, however, the IJN enjoyed an advantage made clear in retrospect. Raised as it was in British Royal Navy tradition, it was equipped with some of the best warships of its day, organised in uniform units and well co-ordinated. In addition, and before the war, the Japanese held a series of scientifically and precisely planned rigorous exercises, battle drills and war games that made it better prepared than their rival.

In the cultural sense too, the Japanese planners believed that their soldiers were better prepared. Unlike Russia, which drew its manpower from many nationalities, some of which were hostile, Japan benefited from an ethnically homogenous population, which, since the early 1890s, had been indoctrinated in a nationalist and patriotic spirit.[29] Given Japan's intense preparations and sustained strengthening since the war against China, the pre-war

---

28 Evans and Peattie, *Kaigun*, 147.
29 For the re-emergence of the concept of *bushidō* in late Meiji-era Japan and its wartime application, see O. Benesch, *Inventing the Way of the Samurai* (Oxford: Oxford University Press, 2014), 42–110. For the rise of patriotic indoctrination, see U. Eppstein, 'School songs, the war and nationalist indoctrination in Japan', in R. Kowner (ed.), *Rethinking the Russo-Japanese War, 1904–05* (Folkestone: Global Oriental, 2007), 185–201.

international image of Japan as the decidedly weaker party was to a great extent the outcome of widespread prejudice rather than a careful analysis of the facts. In actual fact, Japan enjoyed a qualitative advantage, and at times even a quantitative advantage, in the land forces and the warships at its disposal in February 1904 and even later. Nevertheless, Japan had to exploit its advantages speedily and it could not afford to fail, since defeat at any stage of the war could tilt the local advantage in the Russians' favour. Aware of their military limitations, the Japanese planners and decision makers correctly assumed that, although Russia was incomparably superior in most aspects pertinent to the war, Japan could temporarily attain local superiority and so accomplish its limited objectives. It was a calculated gamble with an ostensibly limited risk but a high pay-off.

Application of Strategy

On the morning of 6 February 1904, the day diplomatic relations between Japan and Russia were broken off, Japan's Combined Fleet set sail. This represented the execution of the first and second Japanese premises: a foothold in the continent and control of the seas. Once it approached the port city of Chemulpo, in the vicinity of Seoul, the force split into two. Most of the warships turned towards Port Arthur, while a relatively small naval force remained on the night of 8 February to guard the army's landing. The next morning, First Army forces took control of the Korean capital, while, off the neutral port, the Japanese naval force delivered its demand that the Russian naval detachment anchored within should depart. Following a short engagement outside the harbour, the Russian cruiser *Varyag* and the gun vessel *Koreets* returned to the port, where their crews scuttled them. Strategically speaking, the naval attack off Port Arthur during the night of 8 February was far more important since it had the potential to provide Japan with control of the entire naval theatre. These high hopes were not fulfilled, however, at least not immediately. Shortly after midnight, ten Japanese destroyers attacked the Russian warships anchoring in the roadstead off the port with torpedoes but inflicted only moderate damage that was soon repaired. Consequently, the IJN had to fight another eleven months until it finally established its full control of the Yellow Sea.[30]

30 For an authoritative overview of the naval theatre during the war, see J. S. Corbett, *Maritime Operations in the Russo-Japanese War, 1904–5*, 2 vols. (Annapolis: Naval Institute Press, 1994). For a more succinct and updated summary, see Evans and Peattie, *Kaigun*, 94–132.

On 10 February, Japan declared war on Russia, and during the next two months was able to occupy the entire Korean Peninsula with virtually no opposition. But while Russia hoped that its foe would be content with these initial gains, Japan was determined to cross the Yalu River, invade southern Manchuria and engage the Russian forces stationed there. The mid-scale engagement between the two belligerents along this river during 1–5 May 1904 produced the first major defeat for the IRA. In the meantime, the IJN struggled to complete its mission and had limited success. Despite the sinking of the Russian battleship *Petropavlovsk* in April, along with the commandeering of the Port Arthur Squadron, this unit still posed a major threat to Japanese naval dominance in the theatre. Its presence, however, did not prevent the landing of the Second, Fourth, and Third Armies along the southern coast of the Liaotung Peninsula within a month of crossing the Yalu River. Such landing operations enabled the Japanese strategists to cut off Port Arthur from the rest of the Russian Manchurian Army stationed further to the north. With this goal attained at the Battle of Nanshan, the Japanese Third Army began to lay siege to Port Arthur, whereas the remaining Japanese forces turned northward en route to the city of Liaoyang. During June and July 1904, the Japanese forces engaged with the enemy three times, resulting, invariably, in a Russian retreat. Another retreat followed the battles of Liaoyang and Sha-ho in August and October respectively. In strategic terms, however, the overall Japanese achievements were not decisive, and the Russian forces were able to reform their positions just south of Mukden.[31]

Back in Port Arthur, the Japanese determination to take this principal Russian naval base at all costs paid off in one of the greatest sieges in history. In August 1904, the Port Arthur Squadron attempted to escape for Vladivostok, but was intercepted and returned beaten to its base. In the aftermath of this battle of the Yellow Sea, the squadron was no longer operational but remained a 'fleet in being' during the following months.[32] Four days later, the IJN overpowered the Vladivostok Independent Cruiser Squadron which thereon would never threaten Japanese shipping again. Still, the first major watershed in the war occurred on 2 January 1905, when Port Arthur surrendered after a seven-month siege that resulted in 100,000 casualties on both sides. Consequently, the Third Army headed north and joined

---

31 For a solid overview of the land battles, see R. M. Connaughton, *The War of the Rising Sun and Tumbling Bear: Russia's War with Japan*, rev. ed. (Leiden: Brill, 2003). For a succinct and authoritative summary of these campaigns, see Menning, *Bayonets Before Bullets*, 152–99.
32 For the battle, see Corbett, *Maritime Operations*, 370–413.

the main Japanese land forces for a decisive confrontation against the Russian Manchurian Army in the vicinity of Mukden (present-day Shenyang), the largest city in southern Manchuria. This, the largest engagement in military history up to that point, ended on 10 March 1905 with horrific casualties for both sides and another Russian retreat. By then, and as Japan accomplished most of its initial objectives and with the IJA facing difficulties replacing its losses, the government began to seek an end to the conflict through peace negotiations, to no avail. Leaving for Asia in October 1904, a Russian naval reinforcement comprising the bulk of the Baltic Fleet set sail towards the theatre. On 27–28 May 1905, the two fleets clashed in what turned out to be the most devastating defeat ever suffered by the IRN.[33] With this fiasco, the last Russian hopes of reversing the military situation in east Asia were shattered, and it was compelled to engage in peace negotiations under American mediation. The two parties signed the Treaty of Portsmouth three months later which ended the war.[34]

The outcomes of the war were as dramatic as its battles. In geopolitical terms, the war had major repercussions in east Asia. Fulfilling every bit of the Japanese pre-war plans, the war stopped Russian expansion southward and ensured a Japanese foothold in the continent for several decades. Although Russia was able to get the best possible terms at the Treaty of Portsmouth, it would not regain its position in the region before 1945. Japan, in contrast, was just beginning to leave its indelible imprint on the continent. By 1910, it annexed the Korean Peninsula, and a decade later took hold of eastern Siberia as part of the Siberian expedition of 1918–1922. In 1931, its forces occupied the entire region of Manchuria, thus seizing greater territory than any strategists could envisage on the eve of the war. In the following years, the war pitted the two emerging maritime powers of the Pacific Ocean, the United States and Japan, against each other – as hypothetical enemies at first, and, eventually, in 1941, as archenemies in a head-on titanic clash. Domestically, the war generated an enthusiasm for further expansion in Japan, and in Russia, catalysed the 1905 Revolution. While the domestic upheavals Russia experienced in 1905 prevented the regime from acting with full force against Japan, the war outside Russia made it difficult to respond resolutely to the turmoil within.[35]

33 For the battle and its consequences, see Kowner, *Witnesses of Tsushima*, 40–142.
34 For the peace negotiations, see Ericson and Hockley, *The Treaty of Portsmouth*.
35 For a comprehensive overview of the global and regional outcomes of the war, see Kowner (ed.), *Impact of the Russo-Japanese War*.

The military weakness of the Russian Empire, as exposed by the war, together with its domestic turmoil, also had significant repercussions for Europe. During the war and shortly after it, significant geopolitical changes started to crystallise in Europe, leading to a new balance of power. Critically, the defeat of Russia did much to undermine the eroding military balance in the continent even further. To face the German threat, Russia, France and Britain now overcame their colonial differences and formed the Triple Entente of 1907. The impulse towards an all-European war was not irreversible, but no new alignment was formed to avert a major conflict in Europe on the diplomatic front. Strategically, the war served as a dress rehearsal for a truly global conflict a decade later – the First World War. Although it comprised a mere two belligerents in a colonial context, the war revealed the difficulties which large units face in trench warfare, and provided invaluable insights into the merits and demerits of contemporary naval technology and the battleship in particular.[36] Above all, however, the Russo-Japanese War demonstrated that when strategic objectives are carefully defined and meticulously executed, as was the case with Japan, then the prima facie weaker party may win.

---

36 See Y. Sheffy, 'A model not to follow: the European armies and the lessons of the war', and R. Kowner, 'The impact of the war on naval warfare' in Kowner (ed.), *Impact of the Russo-Japanese War*, 253–68 and 269–89 respectively.

7

Chinese Strategy, 1926–1949

CHRISTOPHER YUNG

Introduction

Three broad historiographical trends have shaped the recent study of modern Chinese military history. The first of these is the rethinking of the historical treatment of the Nationalist government of Chiang Kai-shek, especially during the Second World War. The initial negative assessment of Chiang and the Nationalists (or *Guomindang*, GMD) by on-scene journalists and of US government officials is generally now regarded as having been inaccurate and prejudicial. Recent works like those by Rana Mitter of Oxford University have mined the historical record to portray a much more balanced view of the challenges facing Chiang, and view the Chinese Communist Party's (CCP) claim of winning over the Chinese peasantry through better programmes and land reform with an appropriate amount of scholarly scepticism.

The second of these trends has been the wave of American universities in the 1990s and 2000s hiring young Chinese historians and giving them platforms to conduct historical studies of modern twentieth-century China. These include Chen Jian, Li Xiaobing, Zhang Shuguang and Qiang Zhai, to name but a few. These scholars reshaped the way in which the field looks at the specific decisions made by China's leaders in such conflicts as the Korean War, Vietnam and the Sino-Vietnam border clash.

A third trend is the opening up of the People's Republic of China – thereby leading to greater access to China's government and party archives by the aforementioned Chinese historians. This has also meant greater access to operational and campaign historical material by Western military historians and a new generation of People's Liberation Army (PLA) experts. The period of opening up and reform also led to the release of biographies and selected written works of some of China's most notable twentieth-century military

Map 7.1 Chinese Civil War (1941). Reprinted with permission from 'Chinese Civil War 1945–1949', *Encyclopaedia Britannica*, © 2021 by Encyclopaedia Britannica, Inc. (www.britannica.com/event/Chinese-Civil-War).

leaders including Peng Dehuai, Nie Rongzhen, Ye Jianying, Zhu De, Zhang Zhen and most especially, Liu Huaqing, the vice chairman of the Central Military Commission (CMC) in the late 1980s and early 1990s. These sources have been invaluable in painting a clearer picture of the Party's military decision-making process in China in the mid to latter part of the twentieth century.

A history of modern Chinese strategy immediately confronts a number of organisational challenges. It is a combination of a story of nation-building, of repelling foreign invaders, of a large-scale civil war, of military actions around its periphery and finally, of military actions taken by the Chinese to play their part in global politics. Chinese strategy in the course of the twentieth century is laced with complexity and impacted by larger political and historical forces.

Historically, considerations for the Chinese use of force have differed, depending on whether they are to attain objectives within China or to address strategic objectives outside China. Within China itself, military strategists applied a ruthless ends-ways-means approach to accomplishing political objectives through military, economic, diplomatic and other whole of government methods. If the ends entailed national or regime survival, the ways could be as harsh as sacrificing thousands of civilian non-combatants through the breaching of dams on the Yellow River or the sacrifice of millions of troops in hopes of trading space for time; for strategies outside China, strategists also applied an ends-ways-means approach to accomplishing foreign policy objectives but were more inclined to use coercion, psychology and punitive measures to bring strategic situations back to some kind of political equilibrium defined by the leadership.

Actors and Adversaries

For the early part of the twentieth century, the main protagonists in the drama were those of Chiang Kai-shek, military and political leader of the GMD, and his warlord rivals (Wu Peifu, Zhang Zuolin and Sun Chuanfang). The former sought to unify China under an emerging nationalist philosophy, while the latter sought to dominate their particular regions of China. The former sought to accomplish objectives by building a modern nationalist army, by educating a new, modern, nationalistic military officer and core fighting force; the latter sought to maintain a system of warlord alliances by supporting local subordinate warlords and creating a wide network of these types of alliance. Ultimately Chiang sought to accomplish his objectives by launching military expeditions in the mid-1920s to attack the warlord alliances, by coaxing subordinate warlords to defect and by seizing key geographical terrain in China in order to further the momentum of the military campaign. Wu, Zhang and Sun sought to prevent Chiang from accomplishing these objectives, to remain a unified fighting force and then, if circumstances permitted (which ultimately was never the case), to launch a counterinvasion attacking Chiang's nationalist base area in Guangdong Province.

Chiang Kai-shek remains the main protagonist during China's war with Japan. His military opponents were General Toshizo Nishio, Field Marshal Shunroku Hata and General Yasuji Okamura, the respective commanders of Japan's China Expeditionary Army during the war. An initial Japanese objective at the outset of the war was to expand Japanese control over key industrial territory of China in order to secure its foothold on continental Asia. These objectives increased as the war expanded to become a total war with the Chinese Nationalists and Communists. Complicating the story of Chinese strategy in the Second World War is that the Chinese comprised four large groups; Chiang and the Nationalists in Chongqing, Sichuan; Mao Zedong and his Communist forces in Yennan; Chiang's warlord allies occupying territory in the heartland of China; and Wang Jingwei heading a collaborationist government under the thumb of the Japanese in Nanjing. Chiang's initial wartime objective was to preserve as much of China's commercial and industrial capacity as he could before the expected military blow. This instructed his initial military choices. Once Japan struck and began penetrating deeper into mainland China, Chiang attempted to trade space for time: he moved his seat of government to the western province of Sichuan out of reach of Japanese forces and threw millions of troops into large-scale pitched battles with the Japanese in the hopes of bleeding them dry. Chiang convened a Military Affairs Commission made up of his key ministers and military advisers to discuss his wartime strategy, but it was Chiang himself who ultimately made wartime strategic decisions. Interestingly, the Communists participated in those discussions as wartime allies of the Nationalists. As discussed later in this chapter, Chinese Communist strategy during the war with Japan appears to have been designed as much to preserve and expand Communist power as to defeat the Japanese.

Communist Party military strategy formulation remained remarkably consistent, from the early civil war with the Nationalists throughout the war with Japan and into the second phase of the Chinese Civil War in the late 1940s. The CMC remained a key decision-making body, setting strategy and directing operations of the PLA's field armies. Mao as supreme leader played a key role in the conceptualisation of strategy and directing the formulation and execution of military policy. Nonetheless, such notable military figures as Lin Biao, Peng Dehuai and Zhu De provided military counsel to Mao, and were effective battlefield military strategists in their own right. Initial CCP objectives at the beginning of the civil war with the Nationalists in the late 1920s/early 1930s were to expand Communist base areas, increase recruits to the Red Army, initiate basic land reform and foster socialist revolution in the rural areas of the country. Nationalist objectives were to strengthen ties with warlord allies, deprive Communist base areas of economic resources and recruits, strengthen the gentry and landlord classes in the countryside, enhance national financial and commercial strength, and ultimately to smother the Communist rebellion. In the second phase of the civil war, as the PLA increasingly won its encounters on the battlefield, CCP objectives shifted rapidly to include territorial control (initially over the industrial north-east), destruction of Nationalist armies, expansion southward and westward, and ultimately victory over the entirety of mainland China.

Chinese Military Strategy within China (1926–1949)

The Northern Expedition (1926–1928)

In 1911 the last dynasty of China collapsed after a prolonged period of moral and economic decay. This decay was brought about by the absence of innovation in the later years of the dynasty, imperial mismanagement, and relentless pressure by colonial powers who had inserted themselves into the country and carved up China into spheres of influence; and of course the mid-nineteenth century Taiping rebellion which led to the loss of millions of lives and huge levels of destruction across much of the country, and became a drain on the Imperial treasury. Following the collapse, power was seized by a former military official – Yuan Shikai – but Yuan lacked the power to unify control over the entire country and he died shortly thereafter. By the mid-1920s the military situation in China was such that a military conflict was probable. Warlords dominated some of the key regions of the country, having been the benefactors of the short-lived dictatorial rule of Yuan Shikai. However, remnants of nationalist and revolutionary power were also starting to consolidate in southern China. The GMD was the organising political power which had pressed for the end of Qing rule. By 1924 the GMD had formed an alliance with the CCP, which had developed close ties with the Soviet Union and begun building up its own military capability.[1]

By 1926, Chiang Kai-shek and several senior members of the GMD believed that a major military campaign against the warlords should be launched. The military forces of the northern warlords were as follows: (1) in Henan, Hubei, Hunan, Shanxi and Taiyuan, Wu Peifu's forces numbered 200,000 soldiers; (2) in Beijing, Manchuria and Tianjin, Zhang Zuolin's force numbered 350,000 soldiers; and (3) in Anhui, Fujian, Jiangxi and Zhejiang, Sun

---

[1] D. Jordan, *The Northern Expedition: China's National Revolution of 1926–8* (Honolulu: University Press of Hawaii, 1976), 3–27.

Chuanfang's forces numbered 200,000 soldiers.[2] Chiang's strategy involved launching a major military expedition north from Guangdong province into neighbouring Hunan. After seizing Changsha, the provincial capital, Chiang envisaged moving his forces down the Yangzi River to take the city of Wuhan known for its industrial and manufacturing base. From Wuhan, the natural objective would be to continue along the Yangzi River to seize Nanjing or Shanghai.[3]

The first phase of the Northern Expedition played out exactly as Chiang strategised. Chiang's National Revolutionary Army (NRA) entered Hunan after convincing Tang Shengzhi, one of Wu Peifu's regional military commanders, to switch sides. The NRA next attacked north to take the three city complexes of Wuhan along the Yangzi. Following a month-long siege, Wuhan fell to revolutionary forces. The NRA proceeded to defeat the combined warlord forces known as the ANGUOJUN or the Northern Pacification Army (NPA) in Jiangxi and along the coast in Fujian, and by the spring of 1927 had successfully displaced warlord forces in Shanghai and Nanjing.[4]

In the winter of 1927 the NRA was again on the offensive, attacking the warlord forces in northern Jiangsu province and Anhui. Sun Chuanfang, on the ropes from these combined attacks, withdrew to the Huai River. Together with Zhang Zongchang, another warlord from Shandong, the two sought to defend the city of Xuzhou but were expelled from that key strategic city in December 1927. Sun and Zhang retreated to Shandong to await the arrival of the NRA.[5]

On 9 February 1928, Chiang met members of his general staff on a train bound for the front near Xuzhou in Jiangsu Province. The military strategy that Chiang conceived for the next phase of the campaign closely resembled that of previous military commanders in Chinese history. The NRA and its allies concentrated forces in the Yangzi River Valley, proceeded north, and now sought to wrestle for control over the North China Plain and the Shandong Peninsula. After controlling these, the ancient capital of Beiping would be vulnerable to attack.[6]

Effective co-ordination between Chiang's forces and those of former warlords Feng Yuxiang and Yan Xishan (now known as the Collective

---

2 Y. Li, *Zhong Guo Zhan Zheng Tong Jian* [*Major Wars of China with Commentary*] (Beijing: Guoji Wenhua Chu Ban Gongsi [International Cultural Publishing Co.], 1994), 812.
3 Li, *Zhong Guo Zhan Zheng*, 814; Jordan, *Northern Expedition*, 73.
4 Jordan, *Northern Expedition*, 77–134. 5 Jordan, *Northern Expedition*, 158–68.
6 Jordan, *Northern Expedition*, 175–85.

Armies (CA)) allowed them to outflank, hem in and destroy the opposing forces of Sun Chuanfang, Zhang Zongchang and Zhang Zuolin. The CA also made effective use of telegraphy and railroads to quickly manoeuvre around large concentrations of northern warlord forces. Zhang Zuolin was forced to retreat to the north when Yan's forces emerged from the Shanxi hillsides. Yan was positioned to attack Zhang's forces on the North China Plain at the Shijiazhuang rail crossing. The city of Shijiazhuang fell shortly thereafter.[7] The GMD thereafter quickly prevailed after its forces outmanoeuvred those of the warlords, seizing Beiping when allies of the warlords turned on each other. Most notable was the defection of Zhang Xueliang, the son of the assassinated Zhang Zuolin, which effectively ended warlord resistance to the expedition and the unification of the country.[8]

The First Nationalist–Communist Civil War (1927–1937)

Following the split between the GMD and the Communists in 1927 and the failed Communist-led Nanchang uprising in August 1927, the Communists fled and regrouped in base areas in a remote area around the Jinggang Mountains in Jiangxi province. Mao Zedong led a ragtag force of peasants and workers there, and when later joined by Zhu De and his troops leaving the base area of Guangdong, formed the Fourth Army on 4 May 1928.[9] To entice peasant recruits, the Fourth Army instituted land reform in the late 1920s to early 1930s. During this time Mao and Zhu developed guerrilla tactics reminiscent of some of the strategic ideas of Sunzi, but also reflecting modern military theories espoused by Clausewitz and Jomini. Mao's later writings make reference to 'culminating points', and 'interior' and 'exterior' lines; but Maoist doctrine is best summarised by the following tactical doctrine: 'The enemy advances, we retreat; the enemy camps, we harass; the enemy tires, we attack; the enemy retreats, we pursue.'[10] In time the Red Army began to attract additional followers, and base areas emerged in the rural and border areas of Hunan, Fujian, Jiangsu and Anhui.[11]

As Communist base areas grew, Chiang and his generals became alarmed. The GMD planned and executed five major offensives – or encirclement and annihilation campaigns against these bases. Against these first four campaigns,

---

7 Jordan, *Northern Expedition*, 185.   8 Jordan, *Northern Expedition*, 193.
9 X. B. Li, *A History of the Modern Chinese Army* (Lexington: University Press of Kentucky, 2007), 45.
10 Z. D. Mao, *Selected Works of Mao Tse-Tung* (Beijing: PRC, Foreign Language Press, 1965), vol. I, 213.
11 Li, *A History*, 53.

Mao devised a military strategy to lure GMD forces deep into territory familiar to the Red Army and populated by peasantry friendly to the Communist cause; this called for fluid battle lines and the Red Army's willingness to trade space for time. Maoist doctrine called for enemy forces to reach a culminating point at which point Red Army troops would launch a devastating counterattack. These guerrilla warfare and mobile warfare tactics were successful until 1933 when Chiang instituted a 'block house' strategy to box in the Communist forces. For the Fifth Encirclement campaign, Chiang used a million troops. By October 1934, the Communists had suffered a series of devastating defeats, and their base areas were becoming increasingly untenable. In the autumn of 1934, after a number of attempts to break out of encirclement, the remaining survivors of the Red Army, then numbering approximately 36,000, embarked on a retreat towards their base areas in the north-west in what has become known as the 'Long March'.[12]

The Long March followed the pattern of previously defeated Chinese rebel armies; those rebellious forces traded space for time, and settled in marginal economic areas of China just out of imperial reach. After months of being pursued by Nationalist armies, the Communists finally found refuge at Yan'an in Shaanxi Province. Shaanxi, one of China's poorest provinces, was not an obvious redoubt. In fact, one of the major disagreements among the CCP leadership during the Long March was where the final retreat should be. Some within the leadership insisted on Sichuan, which was quite fertile and considered one of China's 'rice bowls'; others, including Mao, argued for Yan'an, whose isolation but proximity to relatively fertile parts of north-west China made it a good candidate as a base area. Mao's views prevailed.[13] The first phase of the Communist–Nationalist Civil War would prove inconclusive. The Nationalists lacked the power to defeat the Communists at Yan'an and the Communists lacked the power to overthrow the Nationalists. The external threat posed by Japan was an additional factor keeping the two sides at bay. The belligerency would continue after the Second World War. At the end of phase one of the Civil War and throughout the Chinese resistance to the Japanese invasion of China, Mao's influence over the Party, military affairs and larger Party strategy grew significantly, as he consolidated power over the CCP.

---

12 Li, *A History*, 57; Mao, *Selected Works*, vol. I, 206–13.
13 Li, *A History*, 58; Li, *Zhong Guo Zhan Zheng Tong Jian*, 1097.

The War of Resistance against Japan (1937–1945)

While the Communists and Nationalists clashed in the 1930s, the Empire of Japan had slowly consolidated its position in Manchuria, parts of which it had occupied since the Russo-Japanese War. Chiang's strategy throughout most of the 1930s was to avoid a direct confrontation with Japan. He lacked the military power to risk an open conflict. By 1936 Japanese encroachments were serious enough that Chiang's warlord allies began to agitate for a truce with the Communists and a pledge to directly confront the Japanese. In 1936 one of those allies – Zhang Xueliang, the 'Young Marshal' whose defection to the GMD in 1928 led to the victory of the Northern Expedition – took the extraordinary step of kidnapping Chiang at the city of Xi'an. This incident, known as the 'Xi'an Incident' led to an agreement by the Nationalist leader to put his conflict with the Communists on hold, formally ally with the CCP and make military preparations against Japan.[14]

The GMD was in the midst of these preparations in the summer of 1937 when Japanese troops clashed with local Chinese troops at Lugouqiao (also known as the Marco Polo Bridge) outside Beiping. Chiang now realised that he could no longer give in to Japanese demands. Japanese encroachment had been so pervasive that at this point acceding to Japanese demands had major geostrategic implications. Beiping and its surrounding areas was a significant hub for all of northern China, and it was also a nexus connecting North China with several axes of advances in all directions of the country. Since ancient times there were natural lines of communication between the northern capital and Wuhan via the Grand Canal. If the Japanese seized Wuhan, Chiang believed that he would be surrendering North China indefinitely, and that he was opening the entire country to Japanese penetration.[15]

On 26 July the *Kwantung* Army struck. Beiping and Tianjin were attacked by the forces of Imperial Japan. Chiang called together the Military Affairs Commission in August to discuss his defence plans. Zhou Enlai was dispatched to the meeting by Mao to give the CCP's point of view. The participants discussed where to draw the line of defence, with Zhou, on Mao's instructions, advocating the following locales as priority: Zhangjiakou (Hebei), Qingdao (Shandong), Datong (Shanxi) and Baoding (Hebei). In mid-August, Chiang issued the order for his armies to defend Shanghai.[16]

---

14 R. Mitter, *China's War with Japan, 1937–45: The Struggle for Survival* (London: Penguin Books, 2013), 49–59.
15 Mitter, *China's War*, 73–83.
16 Mitter, *China's War*, 83–90; Li, *Zhong Guo Zhan Zheng Tong Jian*, 1292.

Why Shanghai? Chiang's larger strategy involved taking an initial stand around the economically rich areas of coastal China. It was essential for Chiang to preserve as much industry and commercial viability in prosecuting the war against Japan. The longer the GMD could levy resources from China's economy, the longer the regime could survive a conflict with such a powerful foe as Japan. He therefore had to put up a vigorous defence in Shanghai and in the lower Yangzi River. If this failed, which it eventually did, Chiang planned for a phased withdrawal, trading space for time. He made the difficult decision to move the capital from Nanjing to Chongqing in Sichuan province. Before moving the entire seat of government out to Chongqing, Chiang moved his military headquarters to Wuhan, where he sought to defend central China against the expected Japanese onslaught into central China after they had defeated Chiang's allies in northern China.[17]

Chiang sensed that once the Japanese had conquered the North China Plain, it was only a matter of time before they moved west and south, placing themselves in a position to access China's vast railway system and giving them direct penetration capability into central China. If Shijiazhuang were taken, this would give the Japanese a foothold to attack Taiyuan, which in turn gave them a direct line of access south to Xuzhou, Zhengzhou and ultimately Wuhan. If this offence combined with another one moving west from Shanghai, Chiang's forces would be caught in a pincer movement between two powerful Japanese forces. Additionally, if Japanese forces seized Kaifeng and pushed west, they would be within striking distance of the ancient capital of Xi'an and central China. Contests over these geostrategically important locations led to large-scale battles over Taierzhuang, in which the Nationalists prevailed at a cost of tens of thousands of lives on both sides; the battles for Taiyuan, Kaifeng and Xuzhou (all of which the Nationalists lost); and the battle for Zhengzhou (in which the Nationalists held the Japanese off only by breaching the dikes in the Yellow River). In the end, by 1940 the Japanese controlled the urban centres in the north and east of the country, plus parts of central China linking these metropolitan areas and pockets of territory extending out to Nanning in South Guangxi.[18]

The Nationalists ultimately retreated to the city of Chongqing, on the upper branches of the Yangzi in Sichuan province. Chiang relied on his alliances with warlords in Hebei, Henan, Guangxi and Guangdong to hold Japanese forces from attacking deep within China. The Nationalist strategy was also to form an alliance with the United States and its allies. Chiang was

17 Mitter, *China's War*, 95–7. 18 Mitter, *China's War*, 117.

barely able to hold on against later Japanese offensives (Operation Ichigo) which seized additional territory (Changsha, Guilin and Hengyang). Recent historical scholarship strongly suggests that the GMD followed a desperate strategy of bleeding the Japanese dry by sacrificing millions of soldiers in a long list of hopeless military engagements, attempting to be the loyal ally of the United States and Great Britain, and unleashing a number of disastrous efforts to keep Japan at bay (such as the aforementioned breaching of the dikes at the Yellow River). The final casualty tally for the war numbers between 15 and 20 million dead.

Despite successful Communist participation in the 'Hundred Regiments Campaign' of August–December 1940, histories based on Nationalist archives are correct to note that the PLA engaged in very few large-scale military operations against the Japanese.[19] CCP-based histories of the Second World War highlight that the Japanese concentrated 64 per cent of their military effort in China between 1941–1942 on mopping up operations against Communist base areas. The tactic by which the Japanese hoped to neutralise Communist guerrilla tactics was to eliminate all human and economic support to the bases.[20] These CCP-based histories focus on the successful educational, economic and ideological campaigns waged by the Communists at Yan'an, who launched partial counteroffensives in 1944 which were very successful; so much so that by the spring of 1945, the CCP had liberated nineteen areas with a total population of 95 million.[21] This becomes a central historiographical debate among historians of twentieth-century China. Historians sympathetic to the GMD note that the Chinese war effort survived if not prevailed owing largely to Chiang's strategy, which involved throwing a large number of military personnel into pitched battles with the superior armed Japanese military, but whose sacrifice tied down large numbers of Japanese forces and bled the Japanese Army dry. This bought the GMD time and allowed it to ally itself with the Americans and the British whose operations in the Pacific (if not in the Burma-India Theatre), combined with Chiang's resistance on the mainland, prevailed over the Empire of Japan. This strongly suggests that the Communist war effort was designed largely to preserve the CCP and its focus on educational and ideological campaigns. The CCP's operations were not large-scale pitched battles but mostly small-scale guerrilla operations, designed to beat the Nationalists after

19 Mitter, *China's War*, 224.
20 D. Zhu, *Selected Works of Zhu De* (Beijing: PRC, Foreign Language Press, 1986), 141–90; Li, *A History*, 68.
21 Li, *A History*, 70.

the war rather than defeat the Japanese. Recent histories documenting CCP leadership admissions of these realities at the time support this argument.[22]

The Second Nationalist–Communist Civil War (1946–1949)

In the early campaigns of the second phase of the Civil War which ensued in 1946 following the failed Marshall Mission, the Communists reverted to their familiar practice of guerrilla and hit-and-run tactics. These were displayed in the Sungari River campaign (1946) and the Siping Offensive (1947). By 1948 the Chinese Communist thinking on operations and military strategy had evolved. The PLA had adjusted its war-fighting doctrine to one of conventional warfare, and was increasingly taking the initiative operationally and tactically on the battlefield. Three large campaigns in 1948–1949 determined the outcome of the Civil War: the Liao-Shen campaign for Manchuria; the Huai-Hai campaign for the North China Plain and points south to the Huai River; and the Ping-Jin campaign for the Shandong Peninsula, Tianjin and Beiping. The PLA campaign plan sought to gain control of rail and supply routes, isolate and cut off Nationalist forces, and then destroy them.[23]

The total number of forces involved on both sides was immense. For Liao-Shen, the Nationalists had 480,000 soldiers deployed in four army groups; the PLA threw in 1.1 million soldiers, 700,000 of which were allotted to 53 combat divisions. For Huai Hai, the Nationalists deployed 600,000 men and the PLA threw over a million soldiers into the battle. Finally, for Ping-Jin, Fu Zuoyi's GMD forces totalled 500,000 troops deployed in 50 divisions, pitted against 800,000 PLA troops. With these large numbers came large casualties. The Nationalists lost over a million men as a result of these three campaigns. Communist losses were also significant – hundreds of thousands for the three campaigns, but nothing like the Nationalist losses.[24]

Some additional points are worth mentioning with regard to the second civil war. The first is heavy local population involvement in the conflict. Nationalists used large numbers of labourers to erect defensive works and minefields for the final Ping-Jin battles. The CCP used their commissar system to recruit large numbers of peasants for logistical support. Second,

---

22 J. Taylor, *The Generalissimo: Chiang Kai-shek and the Struggle for Modern China* (Cambridge, MA: Harvard University Press, 2009), 168–78.
23 G. H. Wang, *Jing Dian Zhanli Pingxi* [*Analyses of Classical Battles*] (Beijing: Junshi Kexue Chubanshe [Military Science Publishing House], 2010), 526–68; see also L. Wortzel, 'The Beiping–Tianjin Campaign of 1948–9' in M. Ryan, D. Finkelstein and M. McDevitt (eds), *Chinese Warfighting: The PLA Experience Since 1949* (Armonk: M.E. Sharpe, 2003), 56–68.
24 Wortzel, 'Beiping–Tianjin Campaign', 60–1.

the PLA succeeded in remaining cohesive and co-ordinating their actions, while Nationalist generals either failed to co-operate with one another or simply refused to come to the assistance of one another; this proved decisive. Finally, the PLA ability to shift from guerrilla and mobile warfare to conventional and combined arms warfare, making significant use of armour and aircraft, proved devastating to the Nationalist military. By early 1949, Chiang recognised the dire situation he and the GMD were in, and evacuated to the island of Taiwan in order to fight what he believed to be his last battle of the Civil War.[25]

Conclusion

Given its size, China has always been a territory easier to attack than to defend when an adversary accumulates enough power along its periphery. This has historically meant that Chinese military strategists have had to be keenly aware of the impact of space and time, logistics, and the dangers of reaching culminating points across vast distances of operational areas. The Nationalists were immediately at a disadvantage in facing the security threat posed by Japan which had already established a foothold in Manchuria. Once the Japanese Army began penetrating into China, the Nationalists had great difficulty in stemming the tide of that penetration. The vast size of China historically prompted the losing side of military confrontations to resort to the strategy of trading space for time. This was true of the Nationalists in the Anti-Japanese War, it was true of the warlords during the Northern Expedition and it was true of the Communists during the Civil War.

Control over specific sites inside the country gave twentieth-century Chinese militaries access and potential to control other parts. This geostrategic reality meant that control over the North China Plain, for example, provided direct access and lines of control to the south, the west and the central part of the country. That is why the North China Plain featured in the Northern Expedition, the war against Japan and the second civil war. Control over either the lower Yangzi River (Shanghai) or the middle Yangzi River (Wuhan) gave the conqueror access to other parts of the river system. Japanese conquest of Shanghai made its capture of Wuhan likely; similarly the Northern Revolutionary Army capture of Changsha (the middle Yangzi) made both Wuhan and Shanghai vulnerable to attack.

25 Wortzel, 'Beiping–Tianjin Campaign', 61.

Inside China, the symbiotic relationship between a central, unifying power and the periphery of regions internal to China also figured prominently in Chinese strategy. China's vast size meant that a central government either had to have a strong central bureaucracy with loyal regional commanders maintaining control over economically vibrant and strategically vital parts of the country, or had to cut deals with regional warlords. Strategies devised by the actors in the cases examined in this chapter point to the significance of this factor. The Northern Expedition's history is filled with examples of subordinate warlords switching sides to join the NRA. Changing sides was also apparent in the Chinese Civil War, and Chiang relied on his good relations with regional warlords to keep Japan at bay. It is noteworthy that both the GMD and CCP used political commissars to ensure the loyalty of its military, while also enticing officers of the other side to switch loyalties.

These internal war cases also illustrate the central factor of China's vast population in determining military outcomes. The NRA used large numbers of civilians to provide logistical services. An extensive number of combatants were involved in the final years of the Chinese Civil War, resulting in a huge number of casualties. The Nationalists enlisted large numbers of labourers to construct defence works during the Tianjin–Beiping campaign, and the PLA made extensive use of its political commissars to enlist the support of thousands of peasants for logistical assistance. The tactics and doctrine developed by the Communists during the first civil war heavily relied on the peasantry in the countryside. The main challenge to Chiang and the GMD was providing governmental services to the population within 'free China' while waging total war against Japan. An argument can be made that the CCP did a better job of this than the GMD, leading to its subsequent victory in 1949.

Modern Chinese strategy has very much been shaped by China's physical characteristics and central geopolitical position. As this chapter has shown, China's vast size shaped both the security challenges confronting those having to make strategy, and the strategic options available to them. As Chapter 24 on modern Chinese strategy will illustrate, Chinese strategy outside its borders was shaped by disturbances to the security and stability around China's periphery, a perceived injustice, to deter a major threat to China's national borders or internal security and by larger geostrategic concerns.

8

First World War

ROBERT FOLEY

Between 1914 and at least 1918, the 'Great Powers' of Europe and their empires were locked in a titanic struggle that stretched far beyond the borders of the continent and drew in the emerging global powers of Japan and the United States. The war ultimately transformed the European and international systems, with centuries-old empires crumbling and newer formal or informal empires profiting. The scope and scale of this conflict dwarfed almost all previous wars, aided by the rise of the modern state structures in the years before 1914 that allowed mobilisation in ways hitherto unforeseen. All of this transformed the belligerents' conception and practices of strategy and strategy making, moving this from a narrowly military sphere to a whole-of-government approach over the course of the war. This broader practice of strategy enabled the exploitation and apportionment of national, imperial and international resources to achieve not only military and naval objectives, but also ever-broadening political goals. Indeed, the scale and scope of the conflict demanded closer integration and use of all elements of national power in ways unforeseen at the start of the conflict.

Sources

Although the origins of the First World War continue to be hotly debated by historians,[1] more than a hundred years of discussion have demonstrated several important things for those interested in strategy. First, all states went to war based on their assessments of their own interests and to achieve

---

1 A. Mombauer, *The Origins of the First World War: Controversies and Consensus* (London: Longman, 2002); G. Martel, *Origins of the First World War*, 4th ed. (London, Routledge, 2017).

First World War

their own longer-term objectives. Second, the historiography of the origins of the war demonstrates the close connection and interaction between international and national politics in the decisions of each belligerent. This, in turn, helps us understand how strategy was formulated within each state and demonstrates how this differed according to the nature of the state.

With some notable exceptions, there is no want for sources on the course of the First World War. Coinciding with a revolution in record keeping, the primary sources for the conflict are extensive. Most of the key figures in strategy making during the war, both politicians and military, published memoirs or left collections of personal papers. Of course, these memoirs, as with all such literature, portray decisions and events as the actors wanted history to see them, but when combined with the extensive archival and secondary sources, are still useful means of understanding key decisions.

The archival record of the origins and course of the war is even larger than the personal records. All belligerents kept extensive files of diplomatic, military and economic affairs at the national governmental and/or sub-national level. Some of these records were damaged during the revolutions following the war or during the Second World War. However, their loss is offset by the massive document collections published in the interwar period. The rediscovery of archives in eastern Europe since the collapse of the Soviet Union also offsets some of the gaps.

Perhaps because of the overwhelming number of sources and the number of languages required, the historiography of the strategy of the war has remained stubbornly national in its approach. Moreover, this literature focuses largely on individual levers of power, and within this, examination of the military lever predominates. Further, the cultural turn in history has shifted study away from examinations of the study of strategy makers and strategy making during the war. All of this means that we lack critical examination of the wider development of strategic approaches across belligerents and alliances over the course of the war.

Actors

Although the First World War began in Europe, the fact that the Great Powers of Europe dominated the world through their empires meant that the war was global in nature from its inception. Moreover, as the war dragged on, each side attempted to enlist neutral powers formally or informally into the conflict, and by 1918, all of Europe and substantial parts of the rest of the world were associated with one alliance or the other.

Map 8.1 Alliances of the First World War. Redrawn from *The Story of the Great War; History of the European War from Official Sources* (New York: P. F. Collier, 1916–1920), https://archive.org/details/storyofgreatwar05churuoft/page/n5/mode/2up, with permission from Project Gutenberg, www.gutenberg.org/files/29341/29341-h/images/img003.jpg.

First World War

Map 8.1 (cont.)

In 1914, the main belligerents were the French Empire, the Russian Empire and the British Empire, known collectively as the 'Entente Powers'. The Japanese Empire also entered the war on the side of the Entente thanks to its treaty with Great Britain. On the other side were the German Empire and Austria–Hungary, or the 'Central Powers'. Soon after the outbreak of war, the Ottoman Empire joined the Central Powers. Despite their best diplomatic efforts, the Central Powers were only able to gain Bulgaria as an ally in 1915. The Entente Powers, on the other hand, entered formal alliances with the Italian and Portuguese empires in 1915 and Romania in 1916. In April 1917, the United States, with its massive economy and large reserves of manpower, joined the war as an associate power to the Entente. With the United States also came a range of smaller powers, including China and Brazil. All of this tipped the balance of resources much further against the Central Powers.

Of course, each national government faced domestic pressures from different political factions. Throughout Europe on the eve of the war, there was a fear that socialist elements within the state would seek to disrupt state action in the case of war. Germany, France, Austria–Hungary and Russia each had plans for the arrest and imprisonment of leading socialist politicians and activists in case of war. Even Britain was not immune from domestic political tensions in 1914. While socialism was not a major factor in Britain, domestic issues such as Irish home rule and voting rights for women created an uneasy climate that complicated decision making in 1914. While social-inspired revolutions did not come in 1914, their grievances did not go away, and the war ultimately intensified these across all polities.

In addition to having to balance competing domestic political tensions, by 1914 various elements of the empires of the European powers were beginning to exert increasing autonomy. A prime example of this was in the multinational Austro-Hungarian Empire, in which the various nationalities competed for power and autonomy from each other and from the centralised state. In 1914, Slavs outside the Austro-Hungarian Empire in Serbia exerted pressure on Slavs within the Empire and threatened to break apart the state. While not as pressing as in Austria–Hungary, pressure for independence was also straining the British Empire, and by 1914 several colonies had achieved the status of 'dominions', which granted them a greater degree of autonomy.

European states did not go to war in 1914 expecting a prolonged attritional struggle. Almost all states had well-developed military and naval plans for the outbreak of conflict. The development of these reflected the prevailing domestic political structures of the European states. In general, the further east in Europe, the less civilian governmental oversight of the development of the military plans. In Russia, Germany and Austria–Hungary, each state was headed by a politically powerful monarch, Tsar Nicholas II, Kaiser Wilhelm II and Kaiser Franz Joseph, respectively, who retained at least nominal military command. In these states, the armed forces answered directly to their emperor. In the constitutional monarchies of Britain and

Italy and the republics of France and the United States, civilian authorities exercised greater control over the armed forces, generally with cabinets led by civilian prime ministers overseeing war planning and strategy formation.

Regardless of governmental system, in each state before 1914 the armies and the navies had their own 'general' or 'admiralty' staffs that were responsible for the development of detailed plans for war and for executing these plans on the outbreak of war. Professionalisation ensured that governments generally accepted the views of their military advisers within the area of war planning, and this deference to military and naval expertise carried on throughout most of the war, particularly in the eastern European states.[2]

In Britain, in late 1916 the new prime minister, David Lloyd George, reformed the War Cabinet, making it as close to a 'grand strategic' decision-making body as any during the war. The new War Cabinet was small, initially consisting of five permanent members, most of whom served it exclusively as 'ministers without portfolio'.

The Central Powers also attempted to reform their strategy making in late 1916. In autumn 1916, Paul von Hindenburg and Erich Ludendorff, the new leaders of the German Army, asserted their authority over the various German war bureaucracies, forming a new *'Kriegsamt'* to rationalise the German industrial war.

Both sides also created structures to co-ordinate military action better. In the first two years of the war, each side made use of ad hoc meetings and conferences among military leaders to co-ordinate military action. However, there were no formal mechanisms for commanding and controlling allied forces on either side. In effect, each national army operated independently of the others.

The failures of the military offensives of both alliances in 1916 may have spurred greater integration on national levels, but they failed to do so at the strategic level. Each alliance existed to serve the interests of the constituent states, and throughout the war, tensions within the alliances prevented efficient and sometimes effective functioning. Moreover, as most belligerents were empires, or at least federated states, even state governments could not always control their constituent parts. All of this meant that creating coherent national, let alone alliance-wide, strategy was a major challenge never fully resolved during the war.

---

2 R. F. Hamilton, 'War planning: obvious needs, not so obvious solution', in R. F. Hamilton and H. H. Herwig (eds), *War Planning 1914* (Cambridge: Cambridge University Press, 2010), 1–23.

Origins of the War and War Aims

The outbreak of the general European war in summer 1914 was not preordained, despite the growing belief in its inevitability among the governing elites of Europe. The states of Europe and their empires went to war in 1914 based on choices and strategic calculations made by the policy makers in each capital. In July 1914, each statesman believed war would achieve his national objectives. Several important factors guided these calculations. First, the decisions made by predecessors to enter formal or informal alliances dictated the choices which states could make in the crisis of 1914. For Germany and Austria–Hungary, this meant the Dual Alliance, originally signed by the two powers in 1879, with Italy added in 1882 creating the Triple Alliance. For France and Russia, the Military Convention signed in 1892 created a new Dual Alliance. Seeking to reduce the burden of imperial defence so that it could concentrate on threats from Germany closer to home, Britain signed its first peacetime alliance with Japan in 1902, followed by an *entente cordiale* with the French Empire in 1904 and a later entente with the Russian Empire in 1907.

These treaties created a range of obligations for their signatories. Each of the formal alliances committed each party to go to war to protect the other, should the necessary *casus foederis* be met. Recent research on the origins of the First World War has also highlighted dynamics within the alliances and agreements that facilitated the decision to go to war in 1914. Increasingly known as the new 'sick man of Europe', Austria–Hungary seemed unlikely to survive another major international crisis. This encouraged German support for its only firm ally.[3] On the other side, growing French and Russian fears about their alliance encouraged both states to pursue more aggressive policies in the July Crisis.[4]

The secrecy in which the alliances and agreements were kept created an ambiguity that allowed the Great Powers flexibility in times of crisis. In the various diplomatic crises that preceded the First World War, this ambiguity served states well, as opponents, and even allies, did not know the precise tipping point that would lead to war. This helped deter opponents from going too far and ultimately preserved peace. However, the alliances and agreements also ensured that when war came, it would be a general, rather than local, European conflict. Further, with colonies and dominions abroad, the

---

3 H. Afflerbach, *Der Dreibund: Europäische Großmacht- und Allianzpolitik vor dem ersten Weltkrieg* (Vienna: Böhlau, 2002).
4 S. Schmidt, *Frankreichs Außenpolitik in der Julikrise 1914: Ein Beitrag zur Geschichte des Ausbruchs des ersten Weltkrieges* (Munich: Oldenbourg, 2009); S. McMeekin, *The Russian Origins of the First World War* (Cambridge, MA: Harvard University Press, 2011).

participation of the British and French empires ensured that the war would be global in scope. Finally, Britain's alliance with Japan brought the growing Far Eastern power into the conflict against Germany in 1914.

Moreover, the increasing 'militarisation of diplomacy' in the years before 1914 had emphasised the role of force in solving international crisis, and even civilian leaders across Europe had come to view war as a viable strategic option.[5] Privately, leading soldiers may have had doubts about chances in a future war, but publicly they expressed confidence in the abilities of their armies. Across the capitals of Europe in the run-up to war in 1914, military advisers assured statesmen not only that a future war was winnable, but that any war would be short and decisive.[6]

Additionally, domestic political factors shaped decision making. War was commonly seen by European governing elites not only as having beneficial effects for nations. Often imbued with social Darwinism and a *fin de siècle* fatalism, many believed that war would 'rejuvenate' tired societies.[7] Moreover, in 1914, European political leaders hoped to use fear of external enemies as a means to unite increasingly fractured polities. This is particularly evident in Germany and Austria–Hungary, but also the case in France and Britain.[8] European decisionmakers were successful in portraying their actions as defensive and in rallying their people around their flags in the summer of 1914. Although the myth of 'war enthusiasm' has been proved to have been overstated, there is no doubt of the *Burgfrieden* or *union sacrée* that prevailed across the home fronts in the initial stages of the First World War.[9]

Of course, although part of an alliance, each state that went to war in 1914 did so to pursue its own objectives, and these objectives were also carefully expressed to appeal to the broadest possible domestic and international audiences. Moreover, these aims were founded in long-standing grand

---

5 D. Stevenson, 'Militarization and diplomacy in Europe before 1914', *International Security*, 22 (1997), 125–61.
6 A. Mombauer, *Helmuth von Moltke and the Origins of the First World War* (Cambridge: Cambridge University Press, 2002).
7 M. Eksteins, *Rites of Spring: The Great War and the Birth of the Modern Age* (Boston: Houghton Mifflin, 1989); P. Crook, *Darwinism, War and History: The Debate over the Biology of War from the 'Origin of the Species' to the First World War* (Cambridge: Cambridge University Press, 1994), 63–97.
8 A. Mayer, 'Domestic causes of the First World War', in L. Krieger and F. Stern (eds), *The Responsibility of Power: Historical Essays in Honor of Hajo Holborn* (London: Macmillan, 1968), 286–300.
9 J. Verhey, *The Spirit of 1914: Militarism, Myth and Mobilization in Germany* (Cambridge: Cambridge University Press, 2000) and C. Pennell, *A Kingdom United: Popular Responses to the Outbreak of the First World War in Britain and Ireland* (Oxford: Oxford University Press, 2012).

strategic objectives. For Austria–Hungary, the assassination of Franz Ferdinand, which triggered a series of events that led to the outbreak of the war, represented a challenge to the shaky domestic authority of its political elite by Serbia. Serbia had been pursuing the break-up of the dual monarchy for a decade. Austro-Hungarian strategists, therefore, had to react to this threat to the integrity of the state, even if this meant a general European war. Germany was intent not only in supporting its only reliable ally, but in using the crisis as an opportunity to break what its strategists perceived its 'encirclement' by enemies. Moreover, German goals in 1914 link directly to its long-term *Weltpolitik*, or desire to become a 'global power'. For Britain, the official reason for entering war was the violation of Belgian neutrality by German forces. Britain's entente with its traditional enemies France and Russia shows that Britain's real goal, however, was the management of the rise of German power to meet its long-standing goal of preventing a single power dominating the continent of Europe. For France, failure to support Russia in 1914 would probably have meant the end of the Franco-Russian alliance and would have left France isolated against its traditional enemy, Germany. Moreover, the war offered an opportunity not only to regain the lost provinces of Alsace and Lorraine, lost in 1871 during the wars of German unification, but also to re-establish France as the continent's pre-eminent military power. Russia went to war, in part, to preserve its reputation. Having backed down in the face of German threats in 1909 and 1913, Russian strategists believed they needed to act in support of Serbia and France. It also saw the war as an opportunity to open access to the Black Sea, which had been restricted to Russia since the Crimean War.[10]

Not all alliance members went to war in 1914, demonstrating again the importance of national interest in strategic decision making. Italy had been a member of the Triple Alliance since 1882. However, Italy had grown closer to the Triple Entente before the war and had increasingly found itself diplomatically at odds with Austria–Hungary. In August 1914, Italy declared itself neutral. Similarly, Romania, which had secretly agreed to support the Triple Alliance in 1883, declared its neutrality in summer 1914, citing its own interests.[11]

---

10 H. Afflerbach (ed.), *The Purpose of the First World War: War Aims and Military Strategies* (Berlin: De Gruyter Oldenbourg, 2015).
11 R. J. B. Bosworth, *Italy and the Approach of the First World War* (London: Macmillan, 1983); V. Wilcox, *The Italian Empire and the Great War* (Oxford: Oxford University Press, 2021).

Public discussion of war aims was largely supressed until the end of 1916, and even then, the governments of all states wished to keep as many options for peace open as possible. As states were forced to draw more deeply on their natural resources over the course of the conflict, governments were compelled to engage their societies more, and to begin to address some of the social and political tensions that existed within their states. The 'remobilisation' of societies that took place starting in the second half of 1916 led to a more populist approach to war aims. In return for social sacrifice, the government of each belligerent promised their societies a better world after the war.

In the Entente Powers, this expansion of war aims manifested itself as a goal of dismantling 'autocratic' enemy governments and allowing peoples to choose their own government. Although the concept of 'self-determination' is most closely remembered in relation to the US president Woodrow Wilson and his 'Fourteen Points', the governments of France and Britain used this as justification for the planned break-up of the Austro-Hungarian and Ottoman empires at the end of the war. Of course, self-determination was a double-edged sword for the empires of the Entente, as their colonies and other client states, such as China, looked to make use of the concept for their own ends.[12]

The Central Powers paid lip service to the idea of self-determination, and their actions in eastern Europe in 1915–1918 demonstrated the hollowness of their promises to other peoples. Instead, the remobilisation of their societies largely focused on territorial expansion. For countries such as Bulgaria, this was a key initial objective, as it sought to make good the losses of the Balkan wars. Expansion in the east at the expense of the Russian Empire also promised greater economic and military security for Germany and Austria–Hungary. Many in Germany also advocated annexation of large parts of Belgium and more French territory, and the creation of a *Mitteleuropa* (Central European) economic bloc under German leadership. While elements of the political elite of the Central Powers objected to the more egregious demands of the proponents of *Siegfrieden* (victorious war), many of the policies were popular with the peoples of the Central Powers, as they promised a better world on the back of the sacrifices of the war.[13]

---

12 D. French, *British Strategy and War Aims, 1914–1916* (London: Allen & Unwin, 1986); B. Millman, *Pessimism and British War Policy, 1916–1918* (London: Frank Cass, 2001); D. Stevenson, *French War Aims Against Germany, 1914–1919* (Oxford: Clarendon Press, 1982).
13 F. Fischer, *Germany's Aims in the First World War* (New York: Norton, 1967); H. C. Meyer, *Mitteleuropa in German Thought and Action, 1815–1945* (The Hague: Nijhoff, 1955).

Available Means

From the outset, the Entente Powers had distinct material and geographical advantages over the Central Powers. In 1914, the populations of the Entente states came to around 791 million, when the colonial populations are considered. The populations of the Central Powers amounted to about 151 million. A larger population would more readily produce a larger army. In 1914, France with a population of around 40 million had to conscript 85 per cent of the cohort eligible for service to produce an army roughly the same size as Germany's. With a population of around 67 million, German conscripted less than 50 per cent of its eligible manpower before 1914. The scales of population shifted against the Central Powers as the war progressed and more states joined the Entente. Italy's 38 million joined the Entente in 1915, Romania's 7.7 million in 1916, and the United States' 97 million in 1917. By 1918, the Entente powers could draw on a population of more than 1.4 billion against a pool of 156 million for the Central Powers.[14]

A larger population also allowed for a better balance between those serving in the army and those remaining behind to work in the factories and the fields. However, the issue of manpower became one of the most significant factors in the war. No country was prepared for the war's enormous casualties. The first and last stages of the war, when protective trenches were not readily available, saw the highest casualty figures. Infantry and cavalry advancing over open terrain, sometimes in close order, were extremely vulnerable to modern rapid-fire rifles, machine-guns and rapid-fire artillery. As the war progressed and protective trenches became a feature of the battlefields, attrition, the slow but steady wearing down of manpower, came to the fore. Indeed, normal 'wastage', as this was termed by the British, competed with months-long battles to produce steady casualties.[15]

At the same time, armies competed with industry and agriculture for able manpower, and tensions over where to concentrate this increasingly scarce resource caused problems for all strategy makers. The decision by the German strategic leaders, Hindenburg and Ludendorff, to concentrate on replacing 'men with machines' in the trenches in the so-called Hindenburg Programme of 1916/17 left the German Army desperately short of suitable

---

14 S. Broadberry and M. Harrison, 'The economics of World War I: an overview', in S. Broadberry and M. Harrison (eds), *The Economics of World War I* (Cambridge: Cambridge University Press, 2005), 7–10.

15 T. Travers, *The Killing Ground: The British Army, the Western Front, and the Emergence of Modern Warfare, 1900–1918* (London: Allen & Unwin, 1987); W. Philpot, *Attrition: Fighting the First World War* (London: Little, Brown, 2014).

troops in the summer of 1918 and contributed to the collapse of the German Army in France. In 1918, Lloyd George was accused of 'starving' the British Expeditionary Force (BEF) of manpower during the German offensives, as his War Cabinet had also prioritised agriculture and industry over the British infantry.[16]

To alleviate this shortage of manpower, the belligerents tried a range of options. The Entente Powers used manpower from their colonies extensively behind the lines to free European troops for fighting and for work in war industries. While much of this labour was freely given, or as freely as could be given in the circumstances, Britain and Belgium coerced locals in Africa and the Middle East into service. In the campaign against German East Africa, it is estimated that the British and Belgians forced around a million locals to serve as labour over the course of the war.[17] Lacking access to the outside world, the Central Powers used the populations of the territory they occupied. In November 1916, they established an 'independent' Poland from the territory seized from Russia in 1915, hoping to be able to draw on the manpower and other natural resources of the new state.[18] When the Polish population demanded greater independence and failed to deliver the manpower expected, Germany resorted to compelling Poles to work in Germany. The German government also forced workers from Belgium and occupied France to work in Germany and sometimes close to the front lines.[19] All states made greater use of women in the workforce.

Despite all efforts, each belligerent began to run short of suitable manpower for its army over the course of the war. The French and Austro-Hungarian armies peaked in size in summer 1916, the Russian Army in 1917, and British and German armies in 1918. The departure of the Russian Army from the war in early 1918, after the Russian Revolution, left the Entente Powers in a challenging position. The introduction of conscription in Britain

16 R. T. Foley, 'From victory to defeat: the German Army in 1918', in A. Ekins (ed.), *1918 Year of Victory: The End of the Great War and the Shaping of History* (Canberra: Exisle, 2010), 69–88; D. R. Woodward, 'Did Lloyd George starve the British Army of men prior to the German offensive of 21 March 1918?' *Historical Journal*, 21 (1984), 241–52.
17 R. Anderson, *The Forgotten Front: The East African Campaign, 1914–1918* (Stroud: Tempus, 2004).
18 J. Kauffman, *Elusive Alliance: The German Occupation of Poland in World War I* (Cambridge, MA: Harvard University Press, 2015); V. G. Liulevicius, *War Land on the Eastern Front: Culture, National Identity, and German Occupation in World War I* (Cambridge: Cambridge University Press, 2000).
19 Ch. Westerhoff, *Zwangsarbeit im ersten Weltkrieg: Deutsche Arbeitskräftepolitik im besetzen Polen und Litauen, 1914–1918* (Paderborn: Schöningh, 2012); J. Theils, 'Menschenbassin Belgien': *Anwerbung, Deportation und Zwangsarbeit im ersten Weltkrieg* (Essen: Klartext, 2007).

and some British colonies in late 1916 helped replace the declining French and Russian manpower to a certain extent, but not completely. The Entente's manpower gap was only filled by the American Expeditionary Force (AEF) beginning to arrive in late 1917 and early 1918.[20]

The competition for manpower between industry and the army is demonstrative of the industrial nature of the war. Machines dominated the First World War battlefield in ways hitherto unseen. Artillery became as, if not more, important to success than infantry, and horse-born cavalry was all but wiped from the battlefield by modern weapons and barbed wire. Artillery caused the vast percentage of casualties during the war, particularly when gas was added to the arsenal of artillery weapons. Here, the Central Powers had an initial advantage, with larger numbers of modern heavy artillery pieces. The Entente Powers were able to offset their deficiency in artillery and munitions by purchasing supplies from abroad, particularly from the United States. Ultimately, their better economies allowed them to outproduce the Central Powers.[21]

The war saw the introduction of new weapons as well. On the battlefield, poison gas was used for the first time by the Germans in April 1915, and became an important element of most battles that followed. In 1916, Britain developed tanks, which were soon used extensively by the Entente. Over the battlefield, powered aircraft were used for the first time at the start of the conflict. Over the course of the war, aircraft technology developed significantly, making planes a crucial element of warfare. By 1918, aircraft were an integral part of combined-arms battle, providing reconnaissance, spotting for artillery, ground attack, and battlefield air interdiction of enemy supplies and lines of communication. While none of these weapons alone brought the battlefield decisions hoped for by their inventors, they became central elements in tactics by late 1917.[22]

Aircraft had also taken the first steps to what would later become known as 'strategic bombing'. In January 1915, Germany used long-range Zeppelins to bomb Paris and London. The goal of these raids was to pressure the French and British governments to seek peace. However, as the war progressed, more capable aircraft were developed, such as the Gotha and Hadley-Page bombers, which offered the possibility of attacking enemy industry. In April 1918, in recognition of the significance of air power, Britain formed

---

20 D. T. Trask, *The AEF and Coalition Warmaking, 1917–1918* (Lawrence: University Press of Kansas, 1993); M. E. Grotelueschen, *The AEF Way of War: The American Army and Combat in World War I* (Cambridge: Cambridge University Press, 2007).
21 S. Marble (ed.), *King of Battle: Artillery in World War I* (Leiden: Brill, 2016).
22 L. F. Haber, *The Poisonous Cloud: Chemical Warfare in the First World War* (Oxford: Clarendon, 1986); J. P. Harris, *Men, Ideas and Tanks: British Military Thought and Armoured Forces, 1903–1939* (Manchester: Manchester University Press, 1996).

the Royal Air Force as a separate service from the army and the navy. In June 1918, the Entente Powers formed the Inter-Allied Independent Air Force to systematically attack the war industry on the German home front.[23]

Navies had seen very significant technological and organisational development before 1914. The introduction of the all-big-gun battleship in 1905 revolutionised naval ship design and reset the naval arms race. New optics for spotting, better steel for armour and guns, new gunfire techniques and the use of aircraft for reconnaissance all changed naval warfare significantly by the outbreak of the First World War. However, it was the submarine that truly changed war at sea. Capable of sailing underwater for extended periods of time and attacking surface ships without warning, the submarine posed a serious threat to the sea lines of communication on which the Entente Powers depended. Germany invested in developing this technology further, and produced submarines capable of sailing underwater for longer and sailing greater distances. By the time Germany launched unrestricted submarine warfare in early 1917, the German Navy had more than 100 modern submarines available, which it believed would be enough to counterblockade the British Isles.[24]

Although Germany was one of the world's leading industrial and trading powers in 1914, its allies were largely still agricultural states. Austria–Hungary had a limited industrial base, but Bulgaria and the Ottoman Empire were largely dependent upon German industry for supplies during the war. Moreover, Germany was the only state with borders along neutral countries through which supplies could come, and only Germany had the financial might to raise funds for the war abroad. This made the Central Powers heavily reliant on Germany for weapons, munitions, finance and often food throughout the war. The economic backwardness of most of the Central Powers also seriously limited their ability to remobilise for total war from 1916, and the alliance steadily lost ground to the Entente in its ability to wage modern war. The tightening of the Entente blockade on US entry into the war in 1917 further damaged the economies of the Central Powers.[25]

---

23 T. Biddle, 'Learning in real time: the development and implementation of air power in the First World War', in S. Cox and P. W. Gray (eds), *Air Power History: Turning Points from Kitty Hawk to Kosovo* (London: Frank Cass, 2002), 3–20; J. Morrow, *German Air Power in World War I* (Lincoln: University of Nebraska Press, 1982); A. Barros, 'Strategic bombing and restraint in total war, 1915–1918', *Historical Journal*, 52 (2009), 413–31.
24 N. Friedman, *Fighting the Great War at Sea: Strategy, Tactics, and Technology* (Annapolis: Naval Institute Press, 2014).
25 A. Offner, 'The blockade of Germany and the strategy of starvation, 1914–1918', in R. Chickering and S. Förster (eds), *Great War, Total War: Combat and Mobilization on the Western Front, 1914–1918* (Cambridge: Cambridge University Press, 2000), 169–88; C. P. Vincent, *The Politics of Hunger: The Allied Blockade of Germany, 1914–1919* (Athens: Ohio University Press, 1985).

Prioritisation

Throughout the war, the belligerents struggled to prioritise their resources at both a national and an alliance level. As we have seen, the alliances of the war were alliances of convenience, driven by external threat rather than shared purpose. The Entente was a collection of empires that had spent much of the previous century warring with each other, and this animosity did not disappear with the common threat. Moreover, the link between the more democratic Britain and France and autocratic Russia was never an easy one. The Central Powers were not much better off. Italy had become so estranged from its alliance partners that no one had expected Italy to join the war in 1914. Germany and Austria-Hungary were led by houses who had rivalled for dominance within the German states for generations. Facing overwhelming German dominance during the war, Austria-Hungary and the other members of the Central Powers did all they could to assert their independence.

In addition, each state faced internal divisions over strategic prioritisation. The little prioritisation that happened on an alliance level tended to be accomplished via ad hoc meetings and conferences. The Entente leaders met a number of times through the war in large conferences. French and British military leaders were clear that the main effort needed to be placed on the Western Front, and that this was where Germany would be defeated. Moreover, military action on the Western Front served to support Russia and Italy by diverting German military power. Civilian leaders, particularly Lloyd George and French prime minister Aristide Briand, however, pushed for actions in other areas, such as against the Ottoman Empire in the Middle East and the Dardanelles, and later Italy and the Balkans. They hoped that actions outside the Western Front would provide support to allies, avoid costly offensives against the strongly held German positions in France and win the war at a lower price.

The Central Powers faced tensions between civilians and military over strategic priorities, and also lacked the appropriate mechanisms to resolve these tensions. In each, political power culminated with an unelected head of state, who was expected to adjudicate between the civil and military authorities. The rise of Hindenburg and Ludendorff and the death of Kaiser Franz Joseph in 1916 disrupted the functioning of these systems, and allowed the military greater control of the prioritisation of national resources. Unsurprisingly, the military leaders of the Central Powers struggled to manage complex industrial economies. Their focus was on increasing military power. The diplomatic, information and economic levers of power for the Central Powers were diminished to create additional military power. While this may have kept the armies of the Central Powers in the field for longer, military power alone was never going to be enough to win the war.

Execution of Strategy

All belligerents began the war focused on swift and total victory brought about by success on the battlefield. Indeed, the pre-war concept of 'strategy' prevalent among the Great Powers in 1914 was what we would understand today as 'military or naval strategy'. In August 1914, all armies launched large-scale offensives, with millions of men spread over hundreds of kilometres, in an attempt to bring about a 'decisive battle' that would end the war quickly. Each of these offensives failed; opponents were able to withdraw and avoid complete battlefield defeat. Moreover, the size of the armies involved meant that even a major defeat would not bring the total collapse of resistance expected by pre-war military doctrine, as mass armies could absorb large losses. The result of the failed offensives of 1914 was trench lines that ran hundreds of kilometres across all fronts. As the war progressed, these defensive systems became increasingly complex, adding interlocking fields of small-arms and artillery fire in ever greater depth. Moreover, these defensive systems were manned by increasing numbers of troops.

The paradigm of decisive battle, however, was deeply embedded in military thought, and most strategists remained fixated on inflicting a battlefield defeat against their opponents large enough to have strategic effect. Early successes, such as the Battle of Tannenberg in late August 1914, suggested that under the right conditions, decisive battles could be fought and won. In addition, military leaders on all sides struggled to adapt to the new realities of the First World War battlefields. Throughout 1915, 1916 and 1917, the armies of all belligerents launched offensives that grew in size, scale and duration in attempts to break the tactical and operational deadlock and bring about a decisive defeat on the enemy: the indecisive battles of Ypres, Vimy Ridge, Champagne, the Somme, Passchendaele on the Western Front, Warsaw, the Carpathians, and Gorlice-Tarnow on the Eastern Front, Gallipoli, the Caucasus, Mesopotamia and the Suez Canal in the Middle East, and the twelve battles on the Isonzo on the Italian Front were the fruits of these plans.

While most military leaders sought a breakthrough and rapid victory, attrition, or the wearing down of the enemy, became embedded in most plans. For Entente military leaders, this attrition was designed as a phase within broader plans for a decisive battle. It was clear to most that part of the strength of enemy defensive positions came from reserve forces that could be rushed to threatened points of the front, stopping any breakthrough. The high casualties inflicted on the enemy in the indecisive battles of most of the war were later justified as wearing out the enemy's manpower reserves.[26]

The commander-in-chief of the French forces on the Western Front, Joseph Joffre, sought to deal with the problem of enemy reserves by co-ordinating the actions of France's allies on other fronts. Joffre believed that simultaneous offensives on all fronts would prevent the Central Powers from moving reserves, and would allow breakthrough somewhere. This strategy came closest to working in summer 1916, when the Central Powers were hit by large-scale offensives on the Western, Eastern and Italian Fronts. While the Western and Italian Fronts held relatively easily, the Russian offensive, led by Alexei Brusilov, came close to breaking the Austro-Hungarian defensive line on the Eastern Front. Ultimately, however, the Central Powers were able to use their reserves to contain even this threat.[27]

Two military leaders sought to make deliberate use of attrition have a strategic effect. On the Entente side, Earl Herbert Kitchener, the British minister of war from August 1914 until his death in June 1916, believed that Britain should allow the Continental powers, including Britain's allies, to exhaust themselves through fruitless offensives, while Britain built up its own military strength.[28]

On the Central Powers side, Erich von Falkenhayn, chief of the general staff from September 1914 to August 1916, also attempted to make use of attrition for strategic effect. As early as November 1914, Falkenhayn had become convinced that the old paradigm of decisive battle would not work under the conditions of the war. Instead of targeting the enemy's army, Falkenhayn shifted his sights to his enemy's political centre of gravity. In the

---

26 R. T. Foley, 'What's in a name? The development of strategies of attrition on the Western Front, 1914–1918', *Historian*, 68 (2006), 722–46.
27 W. Philpott, *Bloody Victory: The Sacrifice on the Somme and the Making of the Twentieth Century* (London: Little, Brown, 2009); T. Dowling, *The Brusilov Offensive* (Bloomington: Indiana University Press, 2008).
28 P. Simpkins, *Kitchener's Army: The Raising of the New Armies, 1914–1916* (Manchester: Manchester University Press, 1988); I. Beckett, T. Bowman and M. Connelly, *The British Army and the First World War* (Cambridge: Cambridge University Press, 2017), 86–134; H. McCartney, *Citizen Soldiers: The Liverpool Territorials in the First World War* (Cambridge: Cambridge University Press, 2005).

east, he believed this was territory, and he attempted to use the conquest of Russian Poland in 1915 to pressure the Russian government to make peace.[29]

Despite the inclusive nature of battle throughout the war, military offensives remained central to the strategic approaches of all sides. With poor understanding of the operational level, leaders on all sides used tactical action to have a strategic effect. Offensives were also seen as a means of regaining important territory, such as the French and Belgian industrial regions occupied by Germany or the railway lines connecting Austria–Hungary to the Ottoman Empire, or denying important points to the enemy, such as the capture of Russian Poland or attempts to cut the Suez Canal. Finally, offensives were used to support allies. The fruitless French attacks on the Western Front and the amphibious operation at Gallipoli in 1915 were designed, in part, to support Russia and prevent its exit from the war. Similarly, the British took over a greater share of the fighting on the Western Front as French military strength waned. Indeed, when combined with naval warfare, the large-scale battles of the war did slowly wear down the resources of all sides.

The war at sea was always going to be a longer game than that promised by the armies of Europe.[30] Before 1914, Britain and Germany spent vast sums building modern battle fleets. These were designed to dominate the sea lines of communication around Europe and to choke off the enemy's trade and access to imported raw materials. All the Great Powers relied on importing food and materials needed for industry. Not immune from the allure of decisive battle, both sides hoped a large naval battle would leave one side in control of the sea. The Royal Navy and the German Imperial Navy tried to bring about such a battle on their own terms between 1914 and 1916. When a large action did take place in the Battle of Jutland in May 1916, it did not produce the decisive results expected. Both sides suffered heavy losses, but both were able to claim victory. The bruising encounter was enough, though, to convince the German High Seas Fleet to remain in port to continue to threaten the British Grand Fleet as 'fleet in being'.[31]

---

29 R. T. Foley, *German Strategy and the Path to Verdun: Erich von Falkenhayn and the Strategy of Attrition, 1870–1916* (Cambridge: Cambridge University Press, 2004); P. Jankowski, *Verdun: The Longest Battle of the First World War* (Oxford: Oxford University Press, 2014).
30 See also Chapter 5.
31 A. Gordon, *The Rules of the Game: Jutland and British Naval Command* (London: John Murray, 1996); M. Epkenhans, J. Hillmann and F. Nägler (eds), *Jutland: World War I's Greatest Naval Battle* (Lawrence: University Press of Kansas, 2015); J. Goldrick, *After Jutland: The Naval War in Northern European Waters, June 1916 – November 1918* (Annapolis: Naval Institute Press, 2018).

Naval attention shifted to economic warfare. With the world's largest navy, Britain was well placed to exert what its strategic leaders expected would be decisive pressure on the Central Powers via a naval blockade. Submarines and coastal artillery made a close blockade of German ports impossible, so the Entente established a distant blockade that interdicted ships moving into the North Sea through the English Channel or around the north of Scotland. Through this, British strategists expected to cripple the ability of Germany and its allies to wage war.[32]

The effectiveness of the Entente blockade was closely linked to the behaviours of neutral powers. Sweden, Denmark, Norway, the Netherlands and Switzerland were important conduits of raw materials to the Central Powers. Both sides used a carrot-and-stick approach towards these neutral states, promising reward and threatening punishment if they did not do as the warring powers demanded. The most important neutral, but the hardest to influence because of its size and economic power, was the United States. Through most of the war, the United States championed the rights of the neutral states to trade freely with all sides. Needing access to US markets and finance, this made it difficult for the Entente blockade to choke off the war materials keeping the Central Powers going.[33]

The opinion of the United States was also crucial to the German decisions about introducing a counterblockade of the Entente Powers via unrestricted submarine warfare. The strength of submarines lay in their stealth. Above the surface, a submarine was ungainly and vulnerable. Thus, to warn an enemy vessel prior to sinking, as required by international law, put the submarine at risk (particularly after the Entente began arming merchant ships) and sacrificed the benefits of submarines. Sinking ships without warning, however, led to loss of civilian lives, which outraged neutral countries. Entente propaganda was able to portray these acts as an example of German 'barbarity', and this helped the growth of anti-German sentiment in neutral states.[34]

32 E. W. Osborne, *Britain's Economic Blockade of Germany, 1914–1919* (London: Frank Cass, 2004). Nicholas A. Lambert, *Planning Armageddon: British Economic Warfare and the First World War* (London, Harvard University Press, 2012). Cf. M. Seligmann, 'Naval history by conspiracy theory: the British Admiralty before the First World War and the methodology of revisionism', and J. W. Coogan, 'The short-war illusion resurrected: the myth of economic warfare as the British Schlieffen plan', *Journal of Strategic History*, 38 (2013), 966–84 and 1045–64 respectively.
33 J. W. Coogan, *The End of Neutrality: The United States, Britain, and Maritime Rights, 1899–1915* (Ithaca: Cornell University Press, 1981); J. den Hertog and S. Kruizinga (eds), *Caught in the Middle: Neutrals, Neutrality, and the First World War* (Amsterdam: Amsterdam University Press, 2011).
34 W. Jasper, *Lusitania: The Cultural History of a Catastrophe*, S. Spencer (trans.) (New Haven: Yale University Press, 2016).

Hindenburg and Ludendorff used their domestic political power to overcome civilian resistance to unrestricted submarine warfare, which Germany initiated on 1 February 1917.[35] However, the German unrestricted submarine campaign failed to push Britain to sue for peace and considerably worsened Germany's strategic situation. The campaign allowed the Entente again to portray Germany as unwilling to abide by the laws of modern warfare. Faced with this, a reluctant President Woodrow Wilson brought the United States into the war on the side of the Entente in April 1917.[36]

As the war dragged on, the importance of material factors became clear to all leaders, and each belligerent was forced to consider economic strategy in unforeseen ways. Governments reacted to shortages of raw materials for the manufacture of weapons and munitions by intervening in the running of businesses.

The remobilisation of all belligerent economies beginning in 1916 demanded an intensification of the mobilisation of societies, which brought propaganda to the home front as well. The issue of 'munitions of the mind' was taken seriously by all states as the war dragged on and weariness grew across populations suffering from its effects.[37] Having suffered poor crops, mismanagement of natural resources and the increasingly effective Entente blockade, the populations of the Central Powers called for political change. In Austria–Hungary, this expressed itself in growing separatism and unwillingness to fight. In Germany, the government faced pressure to give greater political power to the population. The populations of Germany and Austria–Hungary were also the target of allied propaganda, which attempted to delegitimise the ruling elites in the eyes of the public of both states.[38]

The entry of the United States in the war coincided with the collapse of Russia. By spring 1917, the weight of the war was too much for Russia to bear. Stung by repeated battlefield failures, extraordinary casualties and political upheaval at home, the Russian Army all but collapsed. The abject failure of

35 K. E. Birnbaum, *Peace Moves and U-Boat Warfare: A Study of Imperial Germany's Policy Towards the United States, April 18, 1916 – January 9, 1917* (Stockholm: Almquist & Wiksell, 1958).
36 H. Herwig and D. Trask, 'The failure of Imperial Germany's undersea offensive against world shipping, February 1917–October 1918', *Historian*, 33 (1971), 611–36; M. S. Neiberg, *The Path to War: How the First World War Created Modern America* (Oxford: Oxford University Press, 2016); J. Q. Olmstead, *The United States Entry into the First World War: The Role of British and German Diplomacy* (Woodbridge: Boydell Press, 2018), 66–101.
37 P. Taylor, *Munitions of the Mind: A History of Propaganda from the Ancient World to the Present Day* (Manchester: Manchester University Press, 1995).
38 M. Sanders and P. M. Taylor, *British Propaganda during the First World War, 1914–1918* (London: Macmillan, 1982); D. Welch, *Germany, Propaganda and Total War, 1914–1918: Sins of Omission* (New Brunswick: Rutgers University Press, 2000).

the Kerensky offensives in summer 1917 further weakened the morale of the Russian Army, and army and navy units defected to the growing Bolshevik cause, forming soldiers' and sailors' Soviets to assume the authority formerly reserved for officers and the state. By early 1918, the Russian Army was barely capable of holding defensive positions. Without a functioning army, the new Bolshevik government was forced to agree harsh peace terms at Brest-Litovsk.[39]

The peace of Brest-Litovsk represented a victory for those in the Central Powers advocating a *Siegfrieden*. The treaty satisfied the annexationist demands of the right wing in the Central Powers and bolstered support for their increasingly authoritarian governments. However, it undermined support from those seeking a negotiated peace and deepened the divide domestically between annexationists and those seeking a compromise end to the war. To the remaining Entente Powers, it was also a powerful message about what could be expected from a peace settlement with the Central Powers, strengthening Entente resolve to continue the war.[40]

Although Russia had been knocked from the war and the French and British armies were struggling to replace their losses, the promise of US aid was a crucial element in Entente strategy making. The US Army would take time to arrive in Europe, but Entente strategists knew reinforcements were coming. Moreover, with the US as a belligerent, the Entente was finally able to compel or convince states such as the Netherlands and Sweden to reduce trade with the Central Powers. The entry of the US to the war also encouraged other neutrals, such as China and Brazil, to join the war against the Central Powers. While the material aid these other states provided was limited, their entry made the blockade easier to enforce and helped the Entente supply situation.

Despite the victory in the east, the tightening of the Entente blockade and the growing war-weariness of their populations made it clear to the Central Powers' strategists that the war would have to be ended quickly if they were to prevail in the conflict or even survive. The manpower situation in Germany, Austria–Hungary, Bulgaria and the Ottoman Empire had reached crisis point. Each state was struggling to replace the losses of almost four years of combat while also ensuring enough workers for the factories and fields.

39 P. Gatrell, *Russia's First World War: A Social and Economic History* (London: Longman, 2005); J. A. Sanborn, *Imperial Apocalypse: The Great War and the Destruction of the Russian Empire* (Oxford: Oxford University Press, 2014).
40 B. Chernev, *Twilight of Empire: The Brest-Litovsk Conference and the Remaking of East-Central Europe, 1917–1918* (Toronto: University of Toronto Press, 2017).

In March 1918, the long-awaited German attack on the Western Front began. The German high command's objective was to split the British and French armies and force the British from the continent. Like so many offensives of the First World War, this too started well, but quickly lost momentum. A series of offensives followed the initial attacks along different sectors of the Western Front. Each achieved impressive results by Western Front standards, but these results remained tactical and limited, and cost the German Army heavy casualties.[41]

The German attacks had succeeded in uniting rather than dividing the Entente armies. On 26 March, Ferdinand Foch was appointed supreme allied commander and made responsible for co-ordinating the actions of the Entente armies. While his authority was limited by modern standards, Foch quickly moved French and US units to support the heavily hit British Army. The co-operation of the Entente armies allowed them to move resources where necessary to survive the German onslaught through the spring and summer.[42] In summer, Foch launched a number of counterattacks, which pushed the German Army back and inflicted casualties they could no longer replace. By August, the German Army in the west was about 880,000 men smaller than it should have been, and its morale began to crack.[43] The weaknesses of the German Army were brought home by the major offensive launched by Foch and the Entente armies beginning 26 September. Foch launched a 'grand offensive' across the entire Western Front, which broke through the German front in multiple locations. Although not yet completely defeated, the German Army had lost important parts of its prepared defences and was struggling to keep in the field by mid-October.[44]

The failure of the German offensives and the strength of the Entente counteroffensives convinced many that the Central Powers should seek whatever peace terms they could.[45] Bulgaria was the first to collapse, as it

---

41 M. Kitchen, *The German Offensives of 1918* (Stroud: Tempus, 2001); D. T. Zabecki, *The German 1918 Offensives: A Case Study in the Operational Level of War* (London: Routledge, 2006).
42 E. Greenhalgh, *Foch in Command: The Forging of a First World War General* (Cambridge: Cambridge University Press, 2011), 376–463; M. McCrae, *Coalition Strategy and the End of the First World War: The Supreme War Council and War Planning, 1917–1918* (Cambridge: Cambridge University Press, 2019).
43 S. Stephenson, *The Final Battle: Soldiers on the Western Front and the German Revolution of 1918* (Cambridge: Cambridge University Press, 2009).
44 D. Stevenson, *With Our Backs to the Wall: Victory and Defeat in 1918* (Cambridge, MA: Belknap Press, 2011).
45 W. Deist, 'The military collapse of the German Empire: the reality behind the stab-in-the-back myth', *War in History*, 3 (1996), 186–207; M. Rauchensteiner, *The First World War and the End of the Habsburg Monarchy, 1914–1918* (Vienna: Böhlau, 2014) 906–17.

concluded an armistice agreement with the Entente, granting Entente forces free passage through its territory on 29 September.[46] On 4 October, the Austro-Hungarians requested an armistice based on Wilson's Fourteen Points. On 24 October, Hungary broke from its union with Austria, and on 28 October, Czechoslovakia proclaimed its independence. With its army collapsing in the face of an Italian offensive and the state breaking up around it, the Austro-Hungarian high command requested an armistice on 29 October. This came into effect on 4 November, by which point Austria–Hungary had ceased to exist.[47]

With the collapse of Bulgaria, it was clear even to the optimistic German military leaders that the war was over. On 29 September, the German high command informed Kaiser Wilhelm and Chancellor Georg Graf von Hertling that the German Army was close to collapse and that Germany must seek an armistice as quickly as possible. Recognising the implications of this, Hertling refused and was replaced by Prince Maximilian of Baden. A surprised Prince Max wrote to Woodrow Wilson on 5 October, requesting negotiations based on Wilson's Fourteen Points. Wilson refused to deal with the Germans until Kaiser Wilhelm was replaced by a government that reflected the will of the German population. By the time this occurred, revolution had broken out in Germany. Faced with this, German negotiators were forced to sign an armistice on 11 November.[48]

Conclusion

While different groups fought for power and territory in the defeated states, the armistice on 11 November brought the fighting between the Entente powers and the Central Powers to an end and represents the end of the First World War.[49] The Central Powers had been able to hold out as long as they had because they were effective at generating military power. However, the longer the war lasted, the less important military power became and the more important the other levers of national power – diplomatic, information and economic: areas of Entente strength and Central Powers' weakness.

---

46 R. C. Hall, 'Bulgaria in the First World War', *Historian*, 73 (2011), 300–15.
47 Rauchensteiner, *The End of the Habsburg Monarchy*, 929–1010.
48 E. Kessel, 'Ludendorffs Waffenstillstandsforderung vom 29. September 1918', *Militärgeschichtliche Mitteilungen*, 2 (1968), 65–86; H. Rudin, *Armistice 1918* (New Haven: Yale University Press, 1944).
49 R. Gerwarth, *The Vanquished: Why the First World War Failed to End, 1917–1923* (London: Penguin, 2016).

Of course, Germany committed a major strategic error by challenging British command of the seas through unrestricted submarine warfare in early 1917. Much like the decision for war in 1914, the German high command saw the decision about submarine warfare purely in naval and military terms, and by this stage in the war, the German civilian government was too weak to impose its wider view of the risk associated with the unrestricted use of submarines. As German civilian statesmen foretold, this brought the United States openly into the war against Germany and sealed the fate of the Central Powers. The entry of the United States into the war brought home the strategic advantages of the Entente powers. Not only did the United States bring soldiers to the battlefields of Europe, but it also brought US industry and finance. Moreover, its formidable diplomatic power encouraged other neutral states to join against the Central Powers and allowed the Entente powers to seal the hitherto leaky blockade of the Central Powers.

The final defeat of the Central Powers was as much a result of Entente economic and diplomatic power as it was the military defeat of its armies. The nations of the Central Powers may have had enough resources to supply their armies with food, arms and munitions, but this came at the cost of the home fronts. The shortages of food and basic materials also fatally undermined confidence in the governments of the Central Powers. With the failure of the German offensives of spring 1918, it was clear to all that the Central Powers could not and would not win the war.

The duration and the cost, both financial and human, of the war ensured that when defeat came, the consequences were serious. The defeat of the Austro-Hungarian and Ottoman empires meant their dissolution. Similarly, Germany had gone to war, in part, to reinforce the political position of the ruling elite. Defeat in 1918 resulted in the demise of the ruling houses of the German states and the destruction of the German Empire, itself less than fifty years old.

While the cost of defeat for the Central Powers was apparent, the victory for the Entente powers is less clear. Britain had succeeded in preventing the domination of the continent of Europe by a single power, one of its prime strategic objectives. Britain also gained substantial territory from the German and Ottoman empires. Indeed, the British Empire reached its zenith in terms of territory. France regained the lost provinces of Alsace-Lorraine and, temporarily at least, occupied rich industrial regions of Germany, again achieving important war aims. Italy did not achieve all the territory that had been promised by the Treaty of London in 1915, but still emerged larger than it had started. The United States achieved its goals of self-determination for the peoples of central Europe (if not the rest of the world) and the overthrow of 'militarism' in Germany.

However, the war left almost every state worse off and profoundly dissatisfied with the outcome. While the Second World War was not preordained by the results of the First World War, the seeds of a future conflict had been sown.

9
Soviet Strategy, 1917–1945

NIKITA LOMAGIN

Sources

This period of Soviet military history covers a number of events, ranging from relatively minor conflicts with neighbouring states (mostly parts of the former Russian Empire that collapsed in 1917) in the 1920s and mid-1930s to the fully fledged participation of the Soviet Union in the Second World War. Wars with Finland in 1939–1940, Nazi Germany in 1941–1945 and Japan in 1945 are the main events that fully represent early Soviet military strategy.

Although there are hundreds of books, articles and collections of documents from various Russian archives,[1] we still lack general access to some primary sources of key actors that shaped the Soviet military strategy in 1939–1945. According to Russian historians D. A. Volkogonov and M. V. Zakharov, the Soviet planning for war against Germany began in October 1939 and continued until mid-June 1941.[2] During this period, the general staff developed five variants of a plan for the Red Army's operational use against Germany. But the following documents are still classified and thus inaccessible: maps and text appendices to these plans; the memorandum on the order of strategic deployment of forces; all other plans such as the strategic

---

1 Y. G. Perechnev, 'O nekotorykh problemakh podgotovki strany i Vooruzhennykh Sil k otrazheniu fashistskoi agressii', *Voenno-istoricheskii zhurnal*, 4 (1988), 46–7, ['On some issues of the Armed forces' war readiness to meet the Nazi aggression', *Journal of Military History*]; M. V. Zakharov, *General'nyi shtab v predvoennye gody* [*General Staff in Pre-War Years*] (Moscow: Voenizdat, 1989), 213–25; D. A. Volkogonov, *Triumf i tragediia: politicheskii portret I.V. Stalina* [*Triumph and Tragedy: Political Portrait of J. Stalin*], 2 vols. (Moscow: Izdatelstvo Agenstva Pechati Novosti, 1989), vol. 1, 132–6; Y. A. Gor'kov, 'Gotovil li Stalin preventivnyi udar protiv Gitlera v 1941 godu' ['Did Stalin get ready for a preventive attack against Hitler in 1941?'], *Novaia i noveishaia istoriia* [*New and Modern History*], 3 (1993), 29–39; V. A. Anfilov, *Doroga k tragedii 1941 goda* [*The Way to the Tragedy of 1941*] (Moscow: Akopov, 1997), 157–61.
2 Volkogonov, *Triumf i tragediia*, 133; Zakharov, *General'nyi shtab*, 213.

Map 9.1 The Soviet Union in the Second World War (1941–1945). Redrawn with permission from Willard C. Frank and Philip S. Gillette (eds), 1992, *Soviet Military Doctrine from Lenin to Gorbachev, 1915–1991* Praeger, an imprint of Bloomsbury Publishing Plc. 137.

transport plan for concentration of forces in the operational area; cover plans for strategic deployment; plans for the rear detachment and logistics, communication, air defence, etc. Therefore research of the above documents which represent Soviet military planning for combat at the beginning of war with Nazi Germany remains problematic.[3]

As a result, the most intensive debate has been over Stalin's plans before and during the Second World War. According to Viktor Suvorov/Rezun,[4] Stalin built up his army and armaments industry because he planned a war of aggression to conquer western Europe; his plans were thwarted the first time in 1941 because Hitler struck first, and a second time in 1944 when Western Allies opened a Second Front against Germany by landing in France. This view finds considerable support among Russian historians, many of whom are generally disposed to believe the worst about Stalin. A few Western scholars share this view.[5] Most other scholars disagree with this aggressive-war hypothesis.[6] They believe that Stalin's generals may have planned for the contingency of an offensive war, but Stalin did not seek to create the opportunity for one.

Another point of discussion relates to the major failure of the Red Army during the initial phase of the war with Nazi Germany. The purge of the Soviet officer corps between 1937 and 1939 is the main focus. Some argue that superior technology gave the Germans an advantage, others that the Germans' combat experience in the capture of western Europe in 1940 was initially decisive. The effect of what has been called strategic surprise is regarded in post-Stalinist Soviet historiography as the decisive element in Soviet defeats up to the Battle of Moscow (December 1941–January 1942). Others blame Joseph Stalin's tight control of the military and interference in strategic operations.[7]

3 V. P. Nelasov, A. A. Kudryavtsev, A. S. Yakushevsliy et al., *1941 god – uroki i vyvody [1941 – The Lessons and Conclusions]* (Moscow: Voenizdat, 1992), 51f.
4 V. Suvorov (Rezun), *Ice-Breaker: Who Started the Second World War?* (London: Hamish Hamilton, 1990).
5 R. C. Raack, *Stalin's Drive to the West, 1938–1941: The Origins of the Cold War* (Stanford: Stanford University Press, 1995); A. L. Weeks, *Stalin's Other War: Soviet Grand Strategy, 1939–1941* (Lanham: Rowman and Littlefield, 2002).
6 G. Gorodetsky, *Grand Delusion: Stalin and the German Invasion of Russia* (New Haven: Yale University Press, 1999); E. Mawdsley, 'Crossing the Rubicon: Soviet plans for offensive war in 1940–1941', *International History Review*, 25 (2003), 818–65; T. J. Uldricks, 'The Icebreaker Controversy: did Stalin plan to attack Hitler?', *Slavic Review*, 58 (1999), 626–43.
7 Y. I. Korablev and M. I. Loginov (eds), *KPSS i stroitel'stvo Vooruzhennykh Sil SSSR (1918-iiun 1941) [CPSU and Building of the Military Forces of USSR (1918 – June 1941)]* (Moscow: Voenizdat, 1959); S. Bailer (ed.), *Stalin and His Generals. Soviet Military Memoirs of World War II* (New York: Pegasus, 1969); V. Petrov, *'22 June 1941' – Soviet Historians and the German Invasion* (Columbia: University of South Carolina Press, 1968).

In general, the war against Nazi Germany (commonly referred to in Soviet/ Russian literature as the Great Patriotic War) was a defensive war of good against evil, as Stalin stressed in his first wartime address to the population on 3 July 1941, which was to set the tone for both wartime propaganda and the post-war cult of war. It had been 'imposed' on the Soviets by their 'bitterest and most cunning enemy – German fascism'. The Red Army fought 'with unprecedented bravery' against this enemy. And the military was not alone: 'the whole Soviet people' rose up 'in defence of our fatherland'. This 'patriotic war of liberation against the fascist enslavers' was a struggle not only for the 'life and death of the Soviet state' and all the peoples of the USSR, but also for the liberation of Europe and the world from fascism. In Russia, the narrative of the Great Patriotic War had several strong strands. Above all, the Soviet Union was a clear victim in this story. It was attacked by the most barbarian dictatorship in the twentieth century, was threatened by genocidal policies and became a key player in the anti-Hitler coalition. After the loss of some 27 million lives and an enormous ordeal, the Soviet Union managed to win this war, thereby saving Europe and perhaps the world from Nazi barbarism. As a positive story of sacrifice and bravery, the myth of the Great Patriotic War thus had the advantage of largely reflecting historical reality.[8]

Actors

After the Bolshevik Revolution in October 1917, the Soviet leadership viewed standing armies as preservers of feudal and bourgeois values and instruments of state oppression. The idealists hoped that their revolution would trigger a world revolution in which the masses everywhere would overthrow bourgeois governments, making standing armies obsolete. A particularly important element to consider in assessing Soviet military strategy is the role of the Bolshevik/Communist Party, its ideology, the Political Administration of the Workers' and Peasants' Red Army, and its impact on professional development.

At the top was the Politburo, the highest political authority of the Soviets. The Politburo had the final say on all matters of policy other than those measures taken at Party congresses and conferences. Thus, all important military decisions including strategy were either made or approved at this level.[9]

---

8 M. Edele, 'Fighting Russia's history wars: Vladimir Putin and the codification of World War II', *History and Memory*, 29 (2017), 90–124.

9 Roger R. Reese, 'Red Army professionalism and the Communist Party, 1918–1941', *Journal of Military History*, 66:1 (Jan. 2002), 79.

The ministerial branch of government, the Council of People's Commissars (*Sovnarkom*), supervised military affairs through its People's Commissariat for Military and Naval Affairs (*Narkomvoenmor*) from the 1930s and until 1945 the People's Commissariat for Defence.

The Main Military Council of the Red Army was established by a joint decision of the Council and the Central Committee of VKP(b) (All-Soviet Communist Party) Bolsheviks on 13 March 1938. The Council, in turn, created the Headquarters of the High Command, the highest collegiate body over the Red Army. The Headquarters was responsible for organisation, combat and mobilisation training, procurement and technical equipment of the army. By the beginning of the war with Finland in 1939, the Main Military Council comprised eight top military commanders and Stalin who was de facto leader of the Soviet Union.

In the late 1920s, Stalin became supreme party leader. He did not leave defence policies and spending to his subordinates and took nothing for granted. Formally, the Politburo decided how much to spend on defence, but Stalin's word was decisive on all important issues. After the purges in the army in 1937–1938, the balance of power between military and civilians shifted towards the politicians. In the Soviet system, where Stalin's powers were absolute, the general staff remained beholden to Stalin's political decisions and failed to push for a strategic defence – which would have been the best military response to the dual requirements of Stalin's policy of appeasing Hitler while preparing to counter blitzkrieg.

After the German invasion of the Soviet Union on 22 June 1941, Stalin became a supreme war leader. On 23 June 1941 he authorised the creation of a Main Headquarters (*Stavka Glavnogo Komandovaniia*), usually known as the Stavka. On 30 June Politburo members created a State Committee for Defence, an emergency cabinet to oversee the entire Soviet war effort. The planning and execution of the war effort, from operations to communications and supply, was increasingly handled by the general staff.

On 10 July, Stalin became supreme commander of the armed forces. On 19 July, Stalin replaced Marshal Timoshenko as commissar for defence. Finally, on 8 August the Stavka was converted to the Supreme High Command, with Stalin at its head. As Richard Overy noted, 'it was a remarkable political revolution. Stalin had always preferred to operate behind the scenes, while public responsibility was given to others'.[10]

---

10 Richard Overy, *Russia's War. The History of the Soviet War Effort: 1941–1945* (New York: Penguin Books, 1997), 77.

In late August 1942, Stalin appointed Zhukov deputy supreme commander. The appointment marked one of the critical turning points of the Soviet war effort, not only because Zhukov had already displayed the qualities of leadership by defending Leningrad and Moscow but also because it symbolised yet another revolution in the relationship between the political leadership and the army. The regaining of political influence after the purges against several top generals who had failed to stop the German forces in the disastrous summer of 1941, was reversed in 1942. In 1942, political commissars were abolished in all minor military units, and even at the level of fronts and armies the right of the political representatives to interfere in purely military decisions was severely curtailed. In October 1942 their countersignature on operational orders was no longer required, and in December they became assistants to the commander.

The important contribution made by Zhukov was not his strategic insight, which was more the product of collective experience of the general staff than any individual input; it was his ability to stand up to Stalin and to represent the military voice at the highest level so that those strategic ideas could be nourished.[11] Stalin still insisted on being informed about the decisions by the general staff. According to Stalin's biographer, Stephen Kotkin: 'Stalin shatters any attempt to contain him within binaries. He was by inclination a despot who, when he wanted to be, was utterly charming. He was an ideologue who was flexibly pragmatic. He bore an obsessive grudge for any insults, and he was a precocious geostrategic thinker – unique among Bolsheviks – yet prone to outstanding strategic blunders.'[12]

Adversaries

After the October revolution of 1917, Soviet Russia faced real foreign threats on the basis of the profound ideological antagonism between the ideology of Soviet Communism and that of the Western powers, especially the European imperial powers identified as enemies of the working classes by Marxism-Leninism. The separate peace with Germany in March 1918 caused Russia's former wartime allies to turn against the new Soviet government and join the anti-Bolshevik forces. Soviet Russia was attacked from all sides. During 1918 the Bolsheviks suffered a series of military setbacks and their control was reduced to the area around Moscow. The Russian Civil War was exacerbated

---

11 Overy, *Russia's War*, 100.
12 S. Kotkin, *Stalin: Paradoxes of Power, 1878–1928* (London: Penguin Random House, 2014), 736.

and prolonged by the Allied support for the White forces and the German and Turkish support for the Ukrainian, Baltic, Caucasian and Finnish breakaway states. Just as the newly formed Red Army was beginning to meet the White challenge successfully, a newly independent and assertive Polish Republic under Pilsudski invaded Ukraine, provoking a counteroffensive from the Soviet state during 1920. At the end of November, the Soviet–Ukrainian–Polish war ended with the Treaty of Riga, which divided Ukraine between Poland and the Bolsheviks. The Baltic states, Finland and Poland remained independent under the post-war peace treaties. However, the Soviets managed to recapture much of the former Russian Empire, including Ukraine, Siberia, Transcaucasia and central Asia (formerly Turkestan).

Despite eventually prevailing over the White and Allied armies, the Bolsheviks understandably remained fearful of renewed intervention in the 1920s. Russia was now surrounded by countries like Finland and Poland that were less powerful but still hostile; the hostility of the neighbours was exacerbated by the memory of actions on the Soviet side such as the failed attempt to export revolution by force to Poland in 1920. Behind the neighbours were the armies of much more powerful countries including Britain, France, the United States and Japan. Only Germany was a friend at this time, motivated primarily by convenience.

In general, Soviet leaders viewed the whole world of capitalism as natural adversaries because of their ideology. Having failed with the idea of 'permanent revolution' in Europe, the Soviet state was mainly concerned with survival and focused on defensive strategy.

The Treaty of Rapallo opened up a period of normal diplomatic relations with the capitalist world. In 1924 the Soviet Union was recognised by Great Britain, Italy, Norway, Austria, Greece, Sweden, China, Denmark and France. Until the late 1930s, the Soviet Union avoided serious military conflicts, signing non-aggression pacts with France in 1931, and one with Poland in 1932 contrary to Germany's opposition to the pact. In 1926 and 1931, as strong opponents of the Versailles system, Weimar Germany and the Soviet Union renewed and amplified the terms of the Treaty of Rapallo, and the privileged relations between the two countries included not only diplomatic and economic but above all military co-operation.[13]

After Hitler came to power in 1933, the long-term threat to the Soviet Union did not emanate from its immediate neighbours but from Germany

---

13 Mikhail Heller and Aleksandr Nekrich, *Utopia in Power: The History of the Soviet Union from 1917 to the Present*, Phyllis B. Carlos (trans.) (New York: Summit Books, 1986), 252.

(where the National-Socialist lead ideology had identified Jews and Bolsheviks as the Aryan Race's primary enemy) and expansionist and militaristic Japan. In September 1931 Japan invaded Manchuria. This was the first step on the road to the Second World War. Although strong Soviet defences eventually directed Japanese ambitions to easier spoils in the British and Dutch colonies in south-east Asia, there can be no doubt that Japan originally intended to make gains at the expense of Soviet territory. Within a year a 'Russian National Union' was formed in Manchuria with the aim of forming an independent state in Siberia allied to Japan.[14] Japan continued to eye Soviet territory with cupidity until the border war of 1939.

As for Germany, Hitler secretly began to prepare the military means to create a colonial living space for ethnic Germans in eastern Europe and European Russia. By 1935, the scale of his preparations could no longer be concealed. On 31 March of that year, the Red Army commander Tukhachevskii published an article in *Pravda*, attacking 'The War Plans of Contemporary Germany'. Stalin was warned that one of Hitler's ministers had told a French banker that Germany intended to divide Ukraine with Poland.[15] Hitler risked war with Britain and France over Austria in 1936 and over Czechoslovakia in March and October 1938; after finally drawing a red line in guaranteeing Poland, Germany's likely next victim of expansion, Britain and France fulfilled their treaty obligations to come to Poland's aid when Hitler invaded it in September 1939.[16]

In 1939–1941, the head of the general staff and the defence commissar named Germany, Italy, Finland, Hungary, Romania, Turkey and Japan (i.e. almost all neighbours of the Soviet Union) as the most probable military enemies in a coming war. Soviet strategy assumed that Germany, Finland, Hungary and Romania could deploy between 236 and 270 divisions, more than 10,000 tanks, and 12,000–15,000 warplanes on the western border of the Soviet Union.

In the autumn of 1939, Stalin and the Main Military Council looked for ways to strengthen the Soviet military position achieved over the years since the non-aggression pact with Germany. The main line of strategy, laid down by the chief of staff, Boris Shaposhnikov, was as follows. The Red Army was

---

14 R. W. Davies, *The Industrialisation of Soviet Russia, Volume 4: Crisis and Progress in the Soviet Economy, 1931–1933* (London: Macmillan, 1996), 278.
15 R. W. Davies and M. Harrison, 'The Soviet military-economic effort under the Second Five-Year Plan 1933–1937', *Europe-Asia Studies*, 49 (1997), 390.
16 Mark Harrison (ed.), 'The dictator and defense', in *Guns and Rubles: The Defense Industry in the Stalinist State*, Yale-Hoover series on Stalin, Stalinism, and the Cold War (New Haven and London: Yale University Press, 2008), 1–30, 4–5.

expected to stubbornly defend the frontier, then, in Voroshilov's terms, carry the war 'onto the enemy land' with little loss of blood.[17] It was decided to establish a new line of fortifications along the front line that cut through the middle of Poland, where German and Soviet forces had met, and to abandon the defences along the old Soviet frontier with Poland further east. The second change concerned the armoured force. In 1939 it was decided to disband the separate tank corps and divide the Soviet armour force among local infantry units. This move was intended to strengthen the defensive capabilities of the covering force and allow smaller raids to disrupt enemy mobilisation. But it meant that the Soviet armoured force was divided up into multiple groupings at the very time when the German forces were to demonstrate their massive concentrated striking power.[18]

Causes of War

The Soviet–Finnish War of the winter of 1939–1940 was one of the most critical events for Soviet military strategy in the first months of the Second World War. Any annexation of Finland was not initially part of the Soviet plan. Stalin hoped to bring Finland into his orbit through political pressure alone. Stalin also wished to block access to Leningrad from the Gulf of Finland and to guarantee the security of the railway line from Murmansk. Fearing a possible attack on Leningrad, the former capital and second largest city, from Finland, the Soviet leadership tried to coerce Finland into ceding a swathe of territory to Russia, so as to move the common border further away from Leningrad. On 5 October 1939, the Soviet government presented its demands to Finland. If Finland would cede the Karelian isthmus, the USSR would in return cede a vast area, twice the size of the isthmus, from Soviet Karelia along the Finnish border. In addition, the Soviet Union demanded the right to lease the Finnish peninsula of Hanko at the entrance to the Gulf of Finland, and the ice-free port of Petsamo on the northern coast west of Murmansk for the purpose of establishing Soviet naval and air bases there.[19]

After this attempt failed, Moscow decided to solve the problem by force, and the Red Army attacked Finland in late November 1939. Stalin justified his decision to use force against Finland on the grounds of national security.

---

17 Overy, *Russia's War*, 55.   18 Overy, *Russia's War*, 55.
19 Heller and Nekrich, *Utopia in Power*, 343.

The security of Leningrad, and the whole country was at stake. Leningrad was the main industrial centre of the Soviet Union, accounting for as much as 30–35 percent of the defence industry. Moreover, Leningrad was the second capital of the country . . . . To take Leningrad and establish, let's say, a bourgeois government, . . . means creating a serious basis for civil war in the country against the Soviet power.[20]

The timing of the Soviet attack was determined by a favourable international situation.

Execution/Application of Strategy

The Russo-Finnish War

Before this war, the Soviet leadership expected total victory within a few weeks. Stalin's expectations of a quick Soviet triumph were shared by the head of Leningrad Party organisation Andrei Zhdanov and People's Commissar of Defence Marshal Voroshilov, but other generals were more sceptical. The chief of staff of the Red Army Marshal Shaposhnikov advocated a more comprehensive build-up, extensive fire support and logistical preparations, a rational order of battle and the deployment of the army's best units. Zhdanov's military commander General Meretskov reported: 'The terrain of coming operations is divided by lakes, rivers, swamps, and is almost entirely covered by forests . . . The proper use of our forces will be difficult.'[21] These doubts were not reflected in his troop deployments. Meretskov announced publicly that the Finnish campaign would last no more than two weeks.

The war began on 28 November 1939 when the Red Army shelled the Soviet village of Mainila about 800 m from the Finnish border, and then blamed the Finns for the shelling. Stalin's hope was that Finland would accept the Soviet terms of an exchange of territory and thus avoid armed conflict. Finland rejected the Soviet ultimatum, and the Soviet Union cancelled its non-aggression pact with Finland. The artillery assault and offensive began.

The battles focused mainly on Taipale in the Karelian Isthmus, on Kollaa in Ladoga Karelia and on the Raate Road in Kainuu, but there were also battles

20 'Zimnyaya vojna': rabota nad oshibkami (aprel'–maj 1940). Materialy komissij Glavnogo voennogo soveta Krasnoj armii po oboshcheniyu opyta finskoj kampanii ['Winter War': Learning Lessons (April–May 1940). Reports by Commissions of the Main Military Council of the Red Army on Summing up the Lessons of the Finnish Campaign] (Moscow: 2004), 32.
21 William R. Trotter, *The Winter War: The Russo–Finnish War of 1939–40*, 5th ed. (New York: Workman Publishing Company, 2002), 34.

in Salla and Petsamo in Lapland. All attempts to crack the Finnish defences by a frontal assault on Finland's defensive Mannerheim Line were repelled with heavy casualties.

The first offensive by the Red Army against the Finns did not lead to the expected results. The Red Army leaders in charge of the Finnish operations proved incompetent. General Shtern had been called from the Far East, and General Meretskov, head of the Leningrad command, was replaced by Marshal Timoshenko. It was not until February 1940, after twenty-seven divisions and thousands of guns and tanks were concentrated, that the troops under Marshal Timoshenko managed to overcome Finnish defences. Hostilities ceased in March 1940 with the signing of the Moscow Peace Treaty, in which Finland ceded 11 per cent of its territory to the Soviet Union. The USSR received considerable territory along Lake Ladoga and further north. The Russian war aim was achieved: the border was moved away from Leningrad. But the losses suffered in that war were significant, and the Soviet losses far exceeded the Finnish ones.

The Politburo declared that the war with Finland had exposed serious shortcomings and backward thinking in the People's Commissariat for Defence. Soviet intelligence information on the positions of gun emplacements in the Mannerheim Line had not been plotted on the field maps of the frontline units, resulting in unnecessary high Soviet losses at the hands of the Finnish batteries. Soviet troops were not at all prepared for war in harsh winter conditions. They were not trained to fight on skis. There was a shortage of mortars and automatic weapons. Many had no winter uniforms. Cases of frostbite were numerous. Canned food was not available to the troops. There was mismanagement in the use of warplanes and tanks.

After signing the Moscow Peace Treaty, Finland retained its sovereignty and improved its international standing. The poor performance of the Red Army both encouraged Adolf Hitler to believe that an attack on the Soviet Union would be successful and confirmed negative opinions abroad of the Soviet military. Moreover, the war provided strong evidence that effective offensive strategy was beyond the Red Army's capabilities, as did the failure of the military leadership to develop a viable combined arms doctrine on paper or in practice.

The Great Patriotic War

Meanwhile, Soviet military planning developed in response to the growing German threat. It envisaged repelling an enemy attack, counterattacks and a general attack to defeat the enemy. Covering army groups were to defend the border within ten to fifteen days, so as not to allow the enemy to advance on Soviet soil, and prepare an attack along with the armies of the second strategic echelon.[22]

Fifteen months after signing a non-aggression pact between Nazi Germany and the Soviet Union, the Wehrmacht invaded the USSR, and the Finns joined the Nazis in their so-called Continuation War with the Soviet Union. Given the preparations that had been made since March 1941, the Red Army maintained the posture of a powerful and agile action in June 1941, expecting to launch rapid and powerful counteroffensives against the German invasion force.

The expansion of Soviet borders towards Western Ukraine and Belarus as well as Finland and the Baltic states in 1939 and 1940 made forward defence an inappropriate choice, as the borders of the Soviet Union covered more than 4,000 kilometres from the Gulf of Finland to the Black Sea. This opened the opportunity for the Wehrmacht to launch massive surface-to-air operations in selected areas to penetrate Soviet lines and open the gates for armoured spearheads to advance into the Russian heartland. Moreover, ethnic minorities in the border districts from Western Ukraine and Baltic republics who were unhappy about their integration into the USSR initially supported the Germans as liberators from Soviet control (until they realised that the Germans considered them, along with all Slavs, to be *Untermenschen*, second-rate human beings). Finally, westward expansion of the Soviet Union in 1939–1940 brought hostile ethnic groups into the Soviet realm while abandoning the well-prepared defensive line of the old border further east.[23] A mobile defence was not an option either, as the Red Army needed not simply strength but also speed and skill to execute it. Marshal Shaposhnikov, chief of the general staff in 1939–1940, believed that defence was more difficult to plan and train for than offence. He also argued that revolutionary armies in history have always advanced better than they defended. At the same time, he was opposed to the decision to abandon the old defensive line, insisting that only insignificant covering contingents should be placed in the new area.

---

22 Cover armies were the first echelon, and further in the rear there were armies of the second echelon that were supposed to enter combat in two weeks and to crush the enemy. See Perechnev, 'O nekotorykh problemakh podkotovki', 46f; Zakharov, *General'nyi shtab*, 213–25; Volkogonov, *Triumf i tragediia*, vol. 2, 132–6.

23 C. A. Roberts, 'Planning for war: the Red Army and the catastrophe of 1941', *Europe-Asia Studies*, 47 (1995), 1296–7.

Also, the Soviet military leadership did not draw the operational and strategic lessons of the defeat of Poland and France, especially from the initial phase of the war. Although setting strategy was the prerogative of the political leadership and Stalin himself, the underestimation of Germany's war-fighting potential was as significant as political taboo on discussing strategic concepts. There was a widespread belief that the German–Polish war illustrated that a considerable amount of preparatory work was carried out in the pre-war period, and that initial period grew directly and gradually into the period of main operations.[24]

Lacking both sound strategy and professionalism, the Red Army's only reliable asset was strength, both material and human. The army grew very quickly. Between 1928 and 1941 the regular forces of the Red Army had increased ninefold. In 1928 there were 562,000 men in the regulars, which numbered 5.7 million in June 1941.[25]

On the eve of the war, the general staff viewed Ukraine as the most probable direction of the German assault, while an attack on the Baltic republics, Belarus and Karelia was considered highly unlikely. The Western flank became the main focus of strategic deployment of the Soviet forces.[26] Apart from sound strategy and professionalism, another substantial problem was the disconnect that existed between Soviet political strategy and military operational doctrine before the outbreak of war. At least since 1940, Stalin's policy towards Germany demanded that the Soviet Union adopt a non-provocative stance towards Berlin in order to eliminate any pretext for invasion. Therefore, the Red Army could no longer count on early and secret mobilisation against a likely German attack, overturning a central and long-standing planning assumption.[27]

The military high command committed serious errors in its assessment of how the German forces were deployed and what their plans and intentions were. As Marshal Zhukov, chief of the general staff from January 1941, later admitted in his memoirs, 'The most dangerous situation strategically was in the Southwestern Direction, that is, Ukraine, and the Western Direction, that

---

24 Roberts, 'Planning for war', 1310.
25 *Velikaia Otechestvennaia voina 1941–1945* [*Great Patriotic War 1941–1945*] (Moscow: Nauka, 1998), vol. 1, 89; Y. G. Zimin, N. F. Kuzmin, A. N. Grylev et al., *50 let Vooruzhennykh Sil SSSR* [*Fifty Years of Military Forces of the Soviet Union*] (Moscow: Voenizdat, 1968), 198.
26 Nelasov et al., *1941 god*, 214–15; V. P. Naumov (ed.), *1941 god*, documents, 2 vols. (Moscow: Mezhdunarodny fond 'Demokratia', 1998), vol. 1, 185, 241, 745, vol. 2, 217, 359–60.
27 Roberts, 'Planning for war', 1293.

is, Byelorussia, for in June 1941 the Nazi command had concentrated its most important land and air forces in those areas'.[28] Zhukov had never been a general staff officer and had to rely greatly on the advice of his deputies. The time that remained before the war broke out was used to press forward the building of fortifications and the establishment of large numbers of air and tank units in the forward defence zone that were to absorb the German attack, should it come. Zhukov was among those who argued that the Stalin Line along the old Soviet frontier should not be abandoned, and was supported by Shaposhnikov. Stalin refused to accept the argument and did not authorise defence in depth, ordering the newly acquired territories to be defended at all costs. Only in June 1941, shortly before the German invasion, did Stalin concede that the old line should be manned at 30 per cent of its garrison strength.[29]

The defence plan for the western border was seriously flawed. It provided for an immediate counteroffensive as soon as the Germans struck. It did not foresee that the enemy would be able to penetrate deep into Soviet territory, yet the high command was well aware of the weakness of its border defence lines. Manoeuvres in January 1941 had clearly shown that Soviet forces would be in great danger if the enemy penetrated as far as Bialystock and Lemberg (Lviv).

Thus, on the eve of war, a large part of the best-trained and best-equipped Soviet military forces was deployed in an offensive posture along an 1800-kilometre border, dangerously exposed to German attack and encirclement. Moreover, the Red Army was not only vulnerably deployed in June 1941, it was also extremely weak. The purge of the military in 1937 had liquidated the vast majority of senior officers and depleted the ranks of experienced middle-ranking officers. This contributed not only to the Red Army's defeats in the early battles of the war, but also to the magnitude of those defeats.[30] When fighting finally did break out, the commanders of the military districts on the border were deprived of all initiative when orders were issued not to retaliate, so as to avoid giving any pretext for armed action by the Germans.[31]

The German attack was the very opposite of what Soviet military planners had expected. Instead of ten days of initial probing attacks, followed by the clash of the two fully mobilised armies, the entire German force swept forward in the first hours. The speed of the German penetration resulted in a loss of 200 out of 340 military supply depots. Without air cover, supplies and

28 Heller and Nekrich, *Utopia in Power*, 369.   29 Overy, *Russia's War*, 65.
30 Roberts, *Planning for war*, 1293; Reese, 'Red Army professionalism', 101.
31 Heller and Nekrich, *Utopia in Power*, 369.

proper intelligence, the Red Army suffered severe setbacks. In the first four weeks of Operation Barbarossa, 319 Soviet units were committed to battle. Almost all of them were destroyed or severely damaged.[32] By the end of September 1941, the Soviet air forces in the western border districts lost 8,166 combat aircraft, over 80 per cent of their pre-war strength. By December 1941, the Red Army had lost a total of 20,500 tanks, nearly 90 per cent of its pre-war tank park. Also, about 5 million Soviet soldiers were either killed, wounded or captured. Although the Red Army survived this blitzkrieg, it was not because the Soviet leadership had calculated the strength of the attack or urged Stalin to adopt a defence in depth. Instead, the Red Army was saved by space, reserves and the bravery of its soldiers.[33] Nor is it surprising that a week after the German invasion, when Stalin finally understood the gravity of the crises, he told his colleagues on the State Defence Committee: 'Lenin founded our state, and we have fucked it up.'[34]

In early September, the situation at the front continued to deteriorate. At the meeting with the British Ambassador Cripps on 7 September 1941, Stalin explained that if the Red Army had to abandon the industrial region of Donbas with its coal mines and steel production, as well as Moscow and Leningrad – the centre of the machine-building industry – the USSR would have lost two-thirds of the production capacity for the front. As a result, the Soviet Union would have to cease active combat operations and take up a defensive position, perhaps across the Volga.[35] In the meantime, Stalin sent Zhukov to Leningrad to reinforce the city's defensive efforts.

Devastating losses suffered by the Red Army during the initial period of the Nazi invasion made the Soviet leadership revise its strategy. The main slogan for the whole war period was 'Everything for the front, everything for the victory!' In case of retreat, industrial and agricultural machines and equipment, as well as strategic goods, should be either evacuated to the east or destroyed; in occupied territory, guerrilla warfare was organised; mass mobilisation took place, including creating people's militias of almost half a million in large cities such as Moscow and Leningrad. On the diplomatic front, the Soviet leadership did its best to build an anti-Hitler coalition and gain both political and material support to stop the Wehrmacht and its allies,

---

32 Overy, *Russia's War*, 77.   33 Roberts, *Planning for War*, 1307.
34 David Reynolds and Vladimir Pechatnov (eds), *The Kremlin Letters: Stalin's Wartime Correspondence with Churchill and Roosevelt* (New Haven and London: Yale University Press, 2018), 21.
35 Reynolds and Pechatnov, *The Kremlin Letters*, 44–5.

especially Finland, which became closer to Leningrad by regaining its recently lost territory. Gaining more time would allow the Soviets to regroup their vast resources and put in order the whole system of governance to build new divisions and produce military equipment in its factories. A combination of Soviet counterattacks with deep defence to weaken the enemy and the accumulation of military power in main sectors of the front, especially near Moscow, resulted in breaking the speed of advance of the German blitzkrieg.

By the end of November 1941, the force of the German attack was weakening. The number of dead and wounded increased dramatically as Soviet resistance stiffened. By the end of November, more than 25 per cent of the effective strength of the German forces had fallen. By December, the Red Army had lost 2,663,000 killed in action, and 3,350,000 had been taken prisoner.

The German high command believed that the Red Army had 'no large reserve formations'[36] and did not expect the Soviet counteroffensive. Fifty-eight new divisions, some of them from eastern Russia, were to reinforce the counterattack. The recruitment and training of entire new armies took the German leadership completely by surprise. The force Zhukov raised to defend Moscow was no larger than the German force it faced and was much weaker in tanks and warplanes. But the Soviet forces had winter equipment, while the Wehrmacht was ill-prepared for the cold: winter clothing was in short supply, and fuel for transport was totally unsuitable for harsh winter conditions. This greatly diminished German superiority in tanks and aircraft. Over 133,000 cases of frostbite weakened the German front. On 5 December 1941, when the Red Army opened the offensive, the temperature was −20° Celsius. By mid-December, the German threat to encircle Moscow was over, although strong German formations still stood outside the capital.

After a successful counteroffensive near Moscow in December 1941, Stalin returned to his old habits of command and pushed his armies beyond what they could realistically achieve. In April 1942, convinced that the Wehrmacht on the southern flank was weaker than the armies in front of Moscow and Leningrad, Stalin ordered an offensive to retake Kharkov, a vital railway junction for the German front. German forces were ready for it, and ten days after the Soviet offensive began, they encircled and captured three Soviet armies. Further south, a Soviet attempt to drive German forces out of the Crimea met a similarly tragic end. After month of systematic German air and artillery bombardment, German forces captured the heavily fortified city of Sevastopol on the Black Sea.[37]

36 Overy, *Russia's War*, 117.   37 Overy, *Russia's War*, 156.

As in 1941, initial German success was compounded by failures of Soviet intelligence. Stalin and the general staff were convinced that Hitler's main target would be Moscow, and they were slow to redeploy reserves to the south. As late as 5 July 1942, the Stavka was convinced that the new offensive was just a cover before the main thrust against Moscow. Shortly afterwards, the Wehrmacht reached the Don at Voronezh and then turned south down to Rostov at the mouth of the Don. After the city fell on 23 July 1942, Hitler divided his forces and ordered Army Group A south to take the Caucasus oilfields, while Army Group B drove east to seize Stalingrad.[38] At the time, it looked as if the Germans were going to carry everything in front of them. Shocked by the retreat of the Red Army, Stalin issued order No. 227, '*Ni shagu nazad!*' ('Not One Step Back!').[39]

The survival of Stalingrad became not just a military and economic necessity: As Richard Overy rightly commented,

> The city came to symbolize the new spirit of defiant nationalism conjured up after the disaster at Rostov. The city bore Stalin's name ... and was transformed into an industrial city, populated by giant engineering plants turning out machine tools and tractors. The rest of Russia could have continued to fight after the loss of Stalingrad and the south, but prospects of victory would have been remote. Both sides knew this. Defender and attacker came to see the struggle for Stalingrad as decisive.[40]

The defenders of Stalingrad did their best to keep their frontline as close as possible to the German one, to prevent the enemy from using their superior air and fire power. The German Army was unprepared for urban fighting. By 12 November 1942, the German offensive stalled, and both sides dug in. In October–November 1942, the general staff developed a detailed plan for the counteroffensive at Stalingrad, Operation Uranus. In all, the Red Army built up a force of over a million men. The deployment went undetected by German intelligence. Operation Uranus was kept secret from Soviet front headquarters, to ensure they continued to fight for Stalingrad. Within four days, the two Soviet pincers clashed on the Don about 90 kilometres west of Stalingrad. In all, 330,000 German soldiers were captured.

Operation Uranus was a collective effort and signalled a revolutionary development in strategic decision making as Stalin left the rescue of Stalingrad to the experts.[41] Moreover, the success was based upon the revival

---

38 Reynolds and Pechatnov, *The Kremlin Letters*, 128.
39 Reynolds and Pechatnov, *The Kremlin Letters*, 128.   40 Overy, *Russia's War*, 164–5.
41 Overy, *Russia's War*, 169.

of the Soviet economy, which began to produce larger quantities of tanks, aircraft and artillery than the Germans, who had four times as much steel. The Soviet military surge in 1942 and 1943 was linked to the recovery of the struggling industrial economy.[42]

After defeating the Sixth German Army and remnants of the Fourth Panzer Army, two new operations were on the agenda. The first, Operation Saturn, was an ambitious plan to cave in the German southern front and retake Rostov-on-Don to cut off German forces in the Caucasus. The second was an operation to destroy the encircled German armies at Stalingrad, Operation Koltso (Ring). The first had mixed results. Substantial German forces managed to avoid capture in the Caucasus by fighting their way through a narrow corridor along the Black Sea coast. Moreover, German forces stabilised the front in the south by March 1943.

During the following operations during the winter of 1942–1943, the Soviets worked hard to correct the deficiencies evident in November. Despite these improvements, the Red Army again experienced great difficulty. The attrition rate of the tanks was well over 60 per cent in each of the corps. Moreover, the corps were advancing beyond mutual support distance of one another and well beyond the range of supporting foot infantry and artillery. German reinforcements took advantage of the weakness and dispersion of Soviet mobile forces by counterattacking, and temporarily halted the advance.

The Soviets exploited these lessons in subsequent operations. When preparing for the Donbas operation (29 January–20 February 1943), which was designed to encircle all of German Army Group Don, Southwestern Front commander Vatutin placed four of his tank corps under a single headquarters subordinate to his orders. This was the first Soviet use of a front mobile group. For three months after the operations in the Donbas and Kharkov, Germans and Soviets alike planned for strategic operations in the summer. During this time, the Soviets used the lessons of their winter experiences to rebuild their mobile forces and make them larger and more powerful formations. At the same time, the Soviets refined mobile operational and tactical techniques to give both front and army commanders a solid operational manoeuvre capability. Soviet strategic plans in the summer of 1943 relied in large part on the successful employment of these refined mobile groups.

42 Overy, *Russia's War*, 170.

The most important measure in the build-up of Soviet mobile forces was the creation of new tank armies. The new armies (numbered 1 to 5) had over 500 tanks each and were soon supplemented by newly formed self-propelled artillery units. Similarly, the Soviets refined the established strength of the separate tank and mechanised corps by adding a wide range of combat and combat service support units. By July 1943 the Soviets had established twenty-four tank and mechanised corps.

By the summer of 1943, the modernisation of Soviet combat power was an essential element of strategic planning, as the gap in organisation and technology between the two sides was reduced to the point where the Red Army was prepared to confront German forces in the battle of manoeuvre and fire power. Moreover, the Soviet high command had a good idea of where the weight and direction of the German attack would lie. From the concentration of German forces around Orel to the north of the Kursk advance and around Kharkov to the south, it seemed obvious that the main blow would come there. The more difficult decision was how to respond. Ultimately, the plan represented a return to the traditions of Soviet military thinking expressed in the concept of deep defence. The defensive field was prepared with a depth of six lines inside the salient, with two further defence belts in front of the reserve armies. It was designed to maximise Soviet fire power and allow defensive forces to manoeuvre effectively to counter German attacks. Building up reserves in the rear to initiate a counteroffensive presented the general staff with difficult co-ordination and timing challenges never before met by the Soviet command.

The Red Army concentrated for the battle at Kursk comprised 1,336,000 men (40 per cent of the Red Army's manpower), 3,444 tanks (75 per cent of armoured forces), 2,900 planes and 19,000 guns. The Germans had 900,000 troops, 2,700 tanks, 2,000 planes and over 10,000 guns. They were about to fight the greatest set piece battle in history. On the morning of 12 July, the largest tank engagement of the war took place at Prokhorovka, where 850 Soviet T-34 tanks met more than 600 superior German Tiger tanks and Ferdinand self-propelled guns. On 15 July 1943, the battle finally ended with both sides more or less where they started, but losses on both sides were high. The SS divisions were devastated. Some German divisions were down to as little as seventeen operational tanks left. The Soviet Fifth Guard Army under the command of Rotmistrow also lost half of its force. The Battle of Kursk ended any realistic prospect of German victory in the Eastern Front.[43]

43 Overy, *Russia's War*, 210.

After the Kursk strategic operation, the Red Army began a general offensive along the entire Eastern Front, and the German forces began a general retreat to the line of the Dnepr River, where they hoped to find shelter behind a more defensible natural barrier. During the advance to the Dnepr River, in the southern sector of the front, the Soviets for the first time employed a cavalry-mechanised group to conduct deep operations and drive German Army Group South back towards the Dnepr River and the Crimea.

At the very end of 1943, the Red Army began a series of strategic offences which eventually led to overall victory. During the winter and spring of 1944, the Red Army concentrated large mobile forces to drive the Germans out of Ukraine. For the first time, Soviet mobile forces operated successfully during the period of spring thaw that in previous years had brought operations either to a standstill or disaster. Military superiority allowed the Soviets to undertake three simultaneous and two successive operations, each one by a single front. Eventually, multiple use of tank armies, mobile corps and cavalry-mechanised corps undermined German defence lines in Ukraine and forced the Wehrmacht to move to Poland and Romania.

Improved logistics allowed Soviet operations to take place in greater depths and over longer periods of time. Soviet success in Ukraine made the Germans believe that the next Soviet offensive would take place against the Wehrmacht in southern Poland and Romania. In fact, under the guise of this grand strategic deception plan, the Soviet high command developed four successive strategic strikes: first in Belarus, second in western Ukraine, third in the Baltic republics, and finally, in Moldova. Each operation targeted a specific German Army group for destruction, and three out of four relied on manoeuvres of mobile forces of almost strategic proportion.[44] During the summer offensive of 1944, Soviet mobile forces utilising manoeuvre and deception penetrated deep into Poland and Romania, destroying large German forces.

The January 1945 offensive operation against the Wehrmacht in East Prussia and Poland proved to be 'a textbook model of successful deep operations by large-scale mobile forces using deception and operational manoeuvre which allowed Soviet forces rapidly to sweep through Poland and to the Oder river'.[45] This offensive was to be carried out on a tighter and more heavily fortified front that included Riga, the Baltic coast and East Prussia. To achieve the objectives, deep and rapid advance of up to 300

---

44 D. M. Glantz, 'Developing offensive success: the Soviet conduct of operational maneuver', in W. C. Frank Jr and P. S. Gillette (eds), *Soviet Military Doctrine from Lenin to Gorbachev, 1915–1991* (Westport and London: Greenwood Press, 1992), 148.
45 Glantz, 'Developing offensive success', 146.

kilometres was required. A well-co-ordinated execution of deep manoeuvre alongside with deception was needed. Deception measures hid the scale of Soviet concentration for the offensive and, combined with economy of force measures elsewhere, permitted the Red Army to gain force superiority of over ten to one in manpower and six to one in armour. It was a result of significant improvement in the Soviet logistical capability to support operational manoeuvre. The Red Army in 1945 was able to carry out a coherent, well-organised, mutually supporting offensive westward. Tank armies led the advancing front by distances of up to 100 kilometres. Tank armies were themselves separated by as much as 80 kilometres with separate tank corps of advancing armies echeloned slightly to the rear of and in between the tank armies. Other formations (separate mechanised and tank corps and brigades) also operated in a well-organised way.[46]

The final blow of the mighty and experienced Red Army was against Berlin. The Soviets built up a logistic base and re-equipped their forces before an offensive on the German capital. On 16 April 1945, the Soviet forces began the Berlin operation, which was a classic double envelopment of Wehrmacht defending the eastern approaches to the city.

Two fronts under the command of Zhukov and Konev were to effect the encirclement of Berlin by an offensive across the Oder and Neisse rivers. Zhukov's advance to Berlin was extremely difficult and costly because of fierce German resistance and significant concentration of manpower and weaponry. It appeared that armoured and mechanised forces structured to conduct war in large spaces were not fully suited for combat in heavily urban terrain. Yet Konev's front successfully broke through the German defences and by using tank armies seized Berlin.

The final strategic operation that Soviet forces undertook in August 1945 was against Japanese forces in the Far East. The nature of the Manchurian operation was shaped by unique factors not experienced in the war in Europe – principally imperatives of time, geography and politics. The political conditions on which the Soviet Union was entering the war with Japan were discussed between Stalin and Roosevelt on 8 February 1945. The American president 'felt there would be no difficulty in regard to the southern half of Sakhalin and the Kurile Islands going to Russia at the end of the war'.[47] On 11 February, Stalin, Roosevelt and Churchill signed an agreement stating that within two or three months of Germany

---

46 Glantz, 'Developing offensive success', 154.
47 Reynolds and Pechatnov, *The Kremlin Letters*, 539.

surrendering, the USSR would enter the war against Japan, on conditions that in Outer Mongolia the 'status quo shall be preserved', that the 'former rights of Russia violated by the treacherous attack of Japan in 1904 shall be restored' and that the Kurile Islands 'shall be handed over to the USSR'.[48]

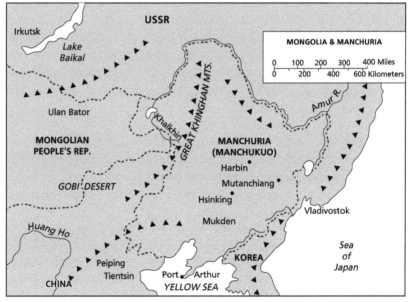

Map 9.2 The Second World War, Mongolia and Manchuria.

Stalin's promise to Truman, Roosevelt's successor, that he would help to conclude the war with Japan was kept on 9 August 1945, although preparations for the offensive into Manchuria had begun in June 1945. They were well under way by the time of the Potsdam Conference. About ninety divisions crossed Russia to fight Japan. By August there were 1.5 million Soviet troops against a little over 1 million recently recruited Japanese. The Red Army was already extremely tired of warfare, and few soldiers saw the point in waging war against Japan. Furthermore, a complicated terrain and concrete fortifications to the north and north-west created significant difficulties for the offensive in Manchuria. Shortly after the United States dropped the first atomic bomb on Hiroshima on 6 August, Stalin ordered immediate attack.

48 Reynolds and Pechatnov, *The Kremlin Letters*, 539.

Soviet Strategy, 1917–1945

The Soviet high command used its huge superiority in troops and munitions. The Red Army undertook a rapid manoeuvre on a strategic scale aimed at both pre-empting Japanese defences and paralysing Japanese command and control. The Soviets planned an envelopment operation. Two fronts were to invade Manchuria from east and west, while a third front exerted pressure from the north.

Fulfilment of this plan required extreme use of all manoeuvre techniques developed in European operations. Massively equipped and led by skilful officers, the Red Army managed to overcome Japanese resistance in just ten days. About 600,000 Japanese soldiers surrendered. After occupation of Manchuria, Soviet forces occupied the Kurile islands, southern Sakhalin and the Pacific Coast around Mukden. Mongolia remained a virtual Soviet satellite. Manchuria and North Korea came under Soviet influence. Port Arthur became a Soviet naval base. On 3 September peace came at last.[49] At the end of the Second World War, the Soviet Union had recovered much of the territory the former Russian Empire had lost in the earlier wars of the twentieth century, including in Europe a part of Finland, the Baltic states, western Belarus and Moldova. In Asia too, the Soviet Union regained what had been lost in the Russo-Japanese War.

After the Bolshevik Revolution in October 1917, particularly important elements to consider in assessing Soviet military strategy were the role of the Bolshevik/Communist Party and its ideology on professional development of the army. Especially during the war with Germany, there was a radical shift towards professionalism in strategic planning and waging of military operations. The general staff and high command became the key institutions in the military planning that was decoupled from the Communist ideology. Together with heavily increased industrial production of modern weaponry, it resulted not only in the successful ending of the Second World War but also in the emergence of the Soviet Union as one of the strongest military powers.

49 Overy, *Russia's War*, 286.

10

Air Power

FRANS OSINGA

Introduction

Air power is the defining characteristic of modern warfare. Emerging in the context of industrialised interstate warfare of the twentieth century, its capability for mass destruction redefined what power means. Today air power, attuned to contemporary societal attitudes and now with drones and precision weapons, has become the icon of the West's preferred style of warfare. While military technologies and societal attitudes concerning the use of force have changed, the theoretical foundations laid by the early air power theorists a century ago and the debates about the utility of air power still resonate. The impact of air power on the First World War itself was very limited, but the unique characteristics of air power – speed, height and reach – were immediately recognised as its attributes: ubiquity, agility and concentration. Air power can pose or counter threats simultaneously across a far wider area than surface capabilities, can quickly switch the point of application within and between operational theatres, and can create tactical or strategic effects. It allows easy adjustment to the scale and intensity of operations in response to political or strategic guidance and, compared to land and maritime power, air power enables military power to be concentrated more responsively in time and space where it is required. Its potential for future war was obvious: apart from frontline air attacks, this new instrument promised a unique and novel approach for direct attack on enemy rear zones, cities, economies and civilian populations, and thus new strategic options to influence the behaviour of actors and the course of events.

Actors: Major Powers

Air power theory development commenced early in the 1920s by scores of authors in the major powers of Great Britain, the US, Russia, Germany, Italy and France. Authors were almost invariably active duty officers with substantial operational flying experience. All focused on the question of what the primary role of air power should be in war. They were united in stressing air power's offensive potential, the crucial value of achieving and maintaining air superiority, and the inherent problems of creating effective air defences. Organisational interests often coloured their views: a conviction that the proper use of air power required independent air forces. Their theories included arguments concerning what type of air power capabilities their nation should invest in (strategic bombers, light bombers or fighter aircraft), and what the role and relevance of air forces should be relative to the other traditional military branches. These arguments – and the underlying theories – evolved due to rapid technological and scientific developments (aerodynamics, metallurgy, engines, radio, photography, electronics, for instance). Theory, while often speculative as it preceded experience and empirical validation, in turn also inspired new technology developments, interbellum defence policies and the nature of air power capabilities a country would start to develop.

The strategic and moral context of the interbellum shaped the nature of the arguments and aspirations of interbellum air power theorists. Early theorists saw in air power practice of the First World War a possibility to avoid a repetition of that war's trench warfare massacres and restore mobility and manoeuvre on the battlefield. This spawned two distinct theoretical schools: (1) the pure strategic attack school; and (2) the air–land school. The strategic attack school argued that air power should be exploited for striking strategically relevant targets, the enemy's centres of gravity, or threatening with such attacks as a deterrent. The air–land school, more or less ignoring the strategic potential of air power, argued that the optimum way to command and exploit air power's offensive capabilities was as an integral element of joint air–land operations, focused on attacking the military capabilities of an opponent, in particular its land forces, and defending one's own ground forces against air attacks.

The Strategic Attack School: Great Britain and the US

The strategic attack school was influential in particular in the maritime powers (US and Great Britain) where strategic distance was always an overriding consideration.[1] While authors such as H. G. Wells and Liddell Hart prophesied future war dominated by aerial destruction, providing a receptive audience for strategic bombing theories, the true intellectual groundwork was laid by a few theorist/practitioners such as Julio Douhet, Billy Mitchell and Hugh Trenchard. Others refined theory, experimented with it, developed doctrines based on the little empirical material they had and tried to solve practical problems of bombing highlighted by those experiments. In particular the US Air Corps Tactical School brought together a group of airmen that debated, tried and expanded air power theory and doctrine. During the Second World War, as commanders in the US Army Air Force, they put these theories into practice first by informing the decision to develop a strategic bomber force and second by laying the groundwork for the Combined Bomber Offensive (CBO) against Germany and later the strategic attacks against Japan.

Theorists differed on the questions of: (1) what type of targets should be subjected to strategic attacks (e.g. cities, the population, specific industries or critical infrastructure); (2) what effects might be achieved (physical or mainly moral); and (3) what logic informed target selection prioritisation. Pragmatists such as the RAF's John Slessor also argued that air power could and should support land operations, but all looked beyond the traditional ground-centric warfare paradigm, asserting that in a future war, air power could break or even avoid the stalemate witnessed in the First World War by attacking the capacity and will to continue war. Perhaps strategic air attacks could even be sufficient to convince an opponent to cease hostilities.

Indeed, Douhet, the commander of the first Italian aviation battalion 1912– 1915, in his influential book *Command of the Air*, asserted that war could be won through the use of air power alone through strategic bombing raids against 'vital centres' such as industry, transport infrastructure, communication centres and the government, and by eroding the will of the people. The effect on morale would be so great that it would force them to overthrow their government or demand an end to hostilities. Strikes on government buildings would weaken the state's capacity to respond and control societal upheaval, followed by attacks on infrastructure such as railroads, bridges, trains, depots, roads and industries. This would sap both the will and capacity

---

1 For outstanding discussions of air power theory development during the interbellum, see P. Meilinger (ed.), *The Paths of Heaven: The Evolution of Airpower Theory* (Maxwell AFB: Air University Press, 1997); and T. D. Biddle, *Rhetoric and Reality in Air Warfare: The Evolution of British and American Ideas about Strategic Bombing, 1914–1945* (Princeton: Princeton University Press, 2003).

to sustain a war. To accomplish this, heavily armed bombers, fighting their way through enemy air defences, would drop several types of munitions (gas, incendiary, explosive bombs). Uncertain of the direction of the next bombing raid, contemporary slow air defence fighters would be unable to mass forces in time and stop the bombers. In short, the side that could muster the largest bomber formations and execute the most devastating air attacks repeatedly, would come out victorious. However, strategic success could only be accomplished if and when the enemy's air power capabilities were destroyed and command of the air was achieved through the destruction not only of its aircraft in the air, but also on the ground and of the aviation production industries. After the enemy had surrendered, ground troops would come in to occupy enemy territory. In order to ensure maximum concentration of force, this strategy required an independent air force which should, being the most efficient military instrument for securing victory (and compared to armies and navies, also the cheapest), also receive the largest slice of the defence budget. Its coherence and readability, and its translation into various languages (English, Russian, French, German) assured an immediate following among fellow airmen.

In similar vein, the American Billy Mitchell saw great use in the strategic bombing of vital centres, including high-value military targets, such as battleships. His followers (and future commanders in the Second World War such as Hap Arnold and Ira Eaker) at the Air Corps Tactical School (ACTS) promoted attacking key economic nodes to destroy 'organic essentials' using massed formations of bombers, all equipped with defensive armament, in daylight raids (so called High Altitude Precision Daylight Bombing). Targets included electrical power generation and distribution, transportation networks, steel manufacturing and specific factories that produced generators, motors and transformers.[2] The father of the Royal Air Force (RAF), Trenchard, argued for targeting railways, airfields, communication and transportation networks and industrial centres. In similar vein, Arthur Harris would argue that a sustained offensive against German urban areas would break German civilian morale, hampering military production which eventually would lead to the collapse of the German Reich (and thus obviate the need for a cross-Channel invasion).

Societies were considered fragile, with social cohesion prone to break down quickly when fear and terror would rain down on the population.

---

2 See P. Faber, 'Interwar US Army aviation and the Air Corps tactical school, incubators of American airpower', in Meilinger (ed.), *Paths of Heaven*, 183–238.

Economic systems were regarded as fragile spider webs with their existence depending on well-functioning links between critical nodes, and modern nations as sensitive precision instruments: damage a vital part of a watch and the whole ceased to function.[3] In short, all of these theorists nurtured the belief, sometimes only implicitly, that strategic attacks would either change the behaviour of the enemy's government through the threat of civil uprising, or through social collapse, fear or economic paralysis, or that they would bring about military defeat by causing the enemy's operational paralysis.

Theory was well ahead of what was practically possible and failed to account for the non-linear interactive nature of war. A deterministic Newtonian mindset and an underdeveloped analysis of the workings of modern industrialised societies informed theoretical assumptions. Quantification and linear prediction marked theorising and arguments: if one could identify the critical industrial and infrastructural nodes in the system, one could calculate how much tonnage would suffice to destroy sufficient targets in order to paralyse the entire economic and social system. The American officer-theorists of ACTS who, on invitation, developed Air War Plans Division-1, predicted in August 1941 that an initial consignment of 6,860 bombers massed against 125 German target sets would produce victory in six months.

Table 10.1 synthesises the main authors and their air power theories, including the logic that informed their thinking: which military or political mechanism would produce the intended outcome.[4]

These notions echoed political and societal fears prevalent among European nations. Strategic considerations trumped humanitarian and ethical concerns. Although only military objectives were considered legitimate targets, in the context of total war the targeting of virtually anything supporting the war effort, including infrastructure, industry, labour and the will of a state's population, was an acceptable strategy. Creating a normative consensus against the bombing of non-combatants was almost impossible, in part precisely because of the strategic potential of the terrifying destructive power of air raids and the promise of a quick end to war. Also the growing menacing German power after 1933 precluded a ban on terror bombing: it was perhaps immoral and unlawful, but it was also the essence of the deterrent logic and role that countries such as Great Britain envisioned for

---

3 See P. Faber, 'Paradigm lost, airpower theory and its historical struggles', in John Olson (ed.), *Airpower Reborn* (Annapolis: Naval Institute Press, 2015), 19–23.
4 This table is based on Faber, 'Paradigm lost', 30.

Table 10.1 *Synthesis of interbellum air power theories: strategic attack proponents*

Theorist(s)	Political outcome	Target(s) set	Mechanism
Douhet	Change government or its behaviour	Population, cities	Revolution
Mitchell	Change government or its behaviour	Vital centres	Civil uprising
Trenchard (1920s)	Change government or its behaviour	War material, transportation, communication	Operational paralysis
ACTS	Change government or its behaviour	Key economic nodes (industrial web)	Social collapse, break popular will
Harris	Change government or its behaviour	Population, cities	Fear, lost morale

their bomber forces.[5] In an era when air defence was still woefully ineffective, bombers could bring the war to the enemy, thus avoiding another war of attrition.[6]

The Air–Land School: Continental Powers

On the Continent in contrast, the air–land school became the dominant one. First, before 1939, the technology and economic resources to develop and produce large, complex bomber aircraft simply were not available in most countries. Second, Continental analysts recognised the limited effects of the few strategic bombing efforts in the First World War and the Spanish Civil War. Third, their national defence policies revolved around territorial control by armies.[7]

Even in Italy, Douhet's thesis was not accepted uncritically. The only Italian application of his ideas was the strategic bombing raid against Barcelona during the Spanish Civil War in March 1938. The more influential voice was that of Amedeo Mecozzi, who, having the ear of Italian Air Minister Balbo, advocated the primacy of assault aviation, considering

---

5 W. Thomas, *The Ethics of Destruction* (Ithaca: Cornell University Press, 2001), 125.
6 See R. Overy, 'Strategic bombardment before 1939', in R. C. Hall (ed.), *Case Studies in Strategic Bombardment* (Washington, DC: Air Force History and Museums Program, 1998), 11–17, 72–3.
7 This draws in particular from J. Corum, 'Airpower thought in Continental Europe between the wars', in Meilinger (ed.), *Paths of Heaven*, 151–82.

interdiction and close air support the most effective use of air power. In addition to developing ideas to create effective air defences with fighter groups patrolling in different zones, he promoted the organisation of air power in three air forces: one for supporting the navy, one for attacking the opponent's army and one for strategic attack. Based on moral objections and the insights from operations in Ethiopia and Spain that suggested air support (in contrast to strategic attack) was effective, he refuted Douhet. As a consequence, Italy concentrated on producing fighters, fighter-bombers and medium bombers.

In Russia, early air power thinking emphasised the offensive role in the deep battle concept of theorists such as Marshal Tukhachevski. In essence, air power functioned as long-range artillery to assist in the breakthrough by motorised and mechanised troops, support their advance deep into enemy territory and strike at enemy reserves. He and the early Russian theorist Alexander Lapchinsky also recognised the potential of strategic attack role, and during the mid-1930s the latter influenced the creation of a large strategic bombing force. In light of Russian experiences in the Spanish Civil War and the limits of the Russian aviation industry, the strategic bombing fleet was downgraded; the air force concentrated on achieving air superiority and the operational and tactical support role to the ground campaign with a concentration of all air forces in a given time at a given front. Similarly, and influenced by Lapchinsky (who, along with 75 per cent of air force officers, was a casualty of Stalin's purge), Alexandr Novikov emphasised the concentration of all types of combat aircraft in support of combined-arms forces with air forces centralised in air armies, corps and divisions all under the control of the 'front', a concept that was to be implemented by the Russians in 1942.

In France, the leading air power nation in the First World War, interbellum thinking was initially informed by Douhet, but later repudiated by army-dominated French high command who made air power subordinate to the army strategy of static defence along the Maginot Line. During the 1930s, the visionary Air Minister Cot took several initiatives to modernise the air force by reorganising French aircraft production methods and setting up three tactical commands: a bomber command (for strategic attacks and deep interdiction), a fighter command (for air superiority) and army support command, with only the latter serving under army command. After Cot left, air defence was distributed over three different ministries, the strategic air force was disbanded, and the bombers and fighters were put under direct command of army regional commanders. Air–land co-ordination for effectuating close air support (CAS) was hardly practised.

This stands in stark contrast to Germany which conducted a comprehensive study of air power in the First World War, and turned theory through experimentation and exercises into a highly effective doctrine. The German Army command already recognised in 1916 the need to set up an air service that centralised all aviation matters which, in the interbellum, gave rise to the independent Luftwaffe. Airmen such as Helmut Wilberg deduced from lessons of the First World War that air superiority required destroying air forces on the ground. The second role was commander-in-chief of the German Army Von Seeckt, who, expecting future German land forces to envelop and destroy enemy formations by manoeuvre, saw air power also playing a major role by disrupting the enemy mobilisation and transport system, thereby paralysing it. Strategic bombing was also studied in the 1920s. In 1926 this resulted in one (notional) air force for supporting the army and another air force for conducting long-range strategic bombing missions. Douhetian aspirations were absent however in light of the limited effectiveness of German bombing raids during the First World War. Strategic bombing doctrine also did not focus on cities or morale but on military industrial targets. Following the Nazi rise to power in 1933, strategic bombing theory reached a high point under Walther Wever, resulting in the development of a prototype long-range four-engined bomber. Technological limitations of the industry resulted in disappointing aircraft performance however, and production was subsequently shifted to focus on modern medium bombers, dive bombers and fighter aircraft. While strategic bombing remained a prime task for the Luftwaffe, the death of Wever effectively halted further capability development. Moreover, the German operations in the Spanish Civil War validated doctrine and led to the perfection of CAS methods (see Table 10.2[8]).

The interbellum air-land school harboured an enduring debate that often played up during operations in the Second World War, in particular within US and British forces. Air-minded officers would often differ from the army colleagues who, first, preferred direct support at the frontline – CAS – a high-risk mission for pilots and, in the absence of precision weapons, often not effective against small targets such as tanks. It also put high demands on close co-operation, training and radio, and other co-ordination methods to avoid fratricide. Airmen instead considered air interdiction against massed armour formations, bridges, railroad facilities and command centres a more effective and efficient employment of scarce air assets. Second, ground commanders favoured direct control over air assets that should be organically assigned to

---

8 This table is based on Faber, 'Paradigm lost', 30.

Table 10.2 Synthesis of interbellum air power theories: air–land integration proponents

Theorist(s)	Political outcome	Target(s) set	Mechanism
Wilberg, Weber, Seeckt, German general staff	Military defeat	Enemy fielded army	Battlefield breakthrough, army destruction
Slessor, Coningham (GB), Quesada (US)	Military defeat	Troops, supplies, production	Interrupt or destroy equipment and supplies
Lapchinsky, Novikov (Russia)	Military defeat	Enemy fielded forces and air forces	Battlefield breakthrough, army destruction
Mecozzi (Italy)	Military defeat	Enemy fielded forces and air forces	Battlefield breakthrough, army destruction

their tactical unit akin to artillery. Airmen countered that such dispersion and 'penny-packing' of scarce air assets would be easy targets for well-co-ordinated enemy air defence fighters. Therefore centralised tactical command was called for by air officers who would assign specific air assets to specific ground units for a limited amount of time, depending on the scarcity of assets, overall demands for air support and the flow of the land battle. Centralised command at the operational and strategic level also allowed for properly set priorities, thus ensuring air defence over the theatre of operations as well as appropriate allocation of aircraft across that theatre for the variety of air support and strategic attack missions.[9] Prior to the Second World War, the army perspective by and large overruled the arguments of airmen.

Theory Meets Reality: The Air War of the Second World War

During the Second World War, strategic and tactical air power integrated in an overall joint strategy dominated air operations. The rapid German victories over Poland, the Low Countries and France suggested that the air–land school of thought was validated, and the French fragmented command of air

---

9 C. McInnes, 'Command and control', in J. Olsen (ed.), *Routledge Handbook of Air Power* (London: Routledge, 2018), 130–41.

power and air defence suggested the merits of centralised command. Air superiority and success in defensive air warfare proved pivotal for Britain's survival (due to the advanced air defence system connecting early warning radar with air operation centres and fighter squadrons) and for the defence of shipping convoys against German submarines in the Atlantic. The effective British air defence system validated having an independent air force and also strongly warned against the employment of unescorted bombers and daylight bombing. In North Africa the British Army and RAF, much like the German and Russian military, learned how to effectively integrate air operations with the tactical plans of ground forces and to support those during battles, resulting in joint planning involving dedicated air force organisational elements incorporated in the operational headquarters of ground units. The loss of air superiority severely hampered Rommel's Afrika Korps. Following tragic losses in North Africa, the US Army also adopted the RAF model, and this was carried forward into the preparation of the advance into France and Germany where skills in CAS were honed and long-range interdiction missions roamed the skies.[10] Air power also revolutionised maritime warfare. Japanese and American aircraft carriers demonstrated the vulnerability of ships to massed air attacks, and the aircraft carrier replaced the battleship as the capital vessel in naval warfare. The US's amphibious 'island hopping' operations in the Pacific also revolved around air power: the defeat of Japan depended on obtaining airbases for fighters, which would support the amphibious attack on the next island, and for strategic bombers, that could strike the Japanese homeland.

Strategic bombing certainly had a major impact on the Second World War, but not necessarily in the way envisioned by the early air power theorists. The capitulation of Holland in the wake of a destructive and demoralising bombardment of Rotterdam seemed to give credence to the pure strategic bombing school. Following such German raids against Rotterdam, Warsaw and London, morale became for the RAF the prime target of night-time strategic bombing. Cities or urban centres served that purpose: attacking workers, destroying their houses and reducing their willingness to work were designed in the long run to reduce German war production. Following logically from the British interbellum deterrence strategy, until 1942 those night raids into the heart of Germany were Winston Churchill's only viable

---

10 See B. Cooling (ed.), *Case Studies in the Development of Close Air Support* (Washington, DC: USAF History Program, 1990), chapters 4–6.

and symbolically important means of retaliation. Moreover they temporarily placated Stalin, who demanded the opening of a second front in the West.

Allied strategic attacks gained strength with the introduction of vast numbers of US bombers and the development of the CBO. The US objected to the RAF's city morale bombing, emphasising instead economic target categories to wear down Germany prior to a land invasion (the German Air Force, submarine buildings, communications, electric power, oil, aluminium and synthetic rubber production). The aim of CBO as dictated in the Casablanca Directive of January 1943 bridged both preferences: 'the progressive destruction and dislocation of the German military, industrial and economic system, and the undermining of the morale of the German people to a point where their capacity for armed resistance is fatally weakened'. Strategic bombing thus served the wider strategy of the liberation of Europe and did not aspire to independently force Germany to surrender.[11]

At the operational level, too, there were disagreements. In the Mediterranean and Pacific theatres, army commanders emphasised interdiction and CAS, navies demanded support for maritime blockades and air commanders stressed the need for air defence and strategic bombing. In preparation of Operation Overlord, CBO commanders argued for unrelenting bombing of German cities and industries, while those immediately responsible for the invasion of Normandy argued for employing strategic bombers for interdiction of the transport network and achieving air superiority.

CBO revealed the attritionist dynamics of air warfare. Against an opponent with sufficient numbers of aircraft, air superiority could only be achieved temporarily and locally. German air defences, with radar operators directing fighters towards enemy formations, inflicted massive and unsustainable attrition rates that sometimes exceeded 10 per cent of a bomber formation. Still, while incredibly costly in terms of casualties among Allied airmen, CBO played a vital role in the overall Allied victory. In Italy air raids against Turin, Rome and Milan undermined Mussolini's fragile hold on power. In Germany it forced a diversion of production capacity towards air defence capabilities and the reallocation of guns from the frontline to enhance German homeland air defence. Over time, bombing raids, increasingly escorted by long-range fighters, severely disrupted Germany's industrial output.

---

11 R. Overy, *The Bombing War, Europe 1939–1940* (London: Allen Lane, 2013), in particular chapter 6.

But considering the vast scientific, industrial and financial investments required to produce the vast fleets of strategic bombers, in hindsight, strategic bombing did not achieve the high interbellum expectations. Several (implicit) key assumptions of interbellum theorists and Allied planners were, unsurprisingly, invalidated. It was uncharted territory to consider what effect large-scale bombing was really having on an enemy economy or on enemy war-willingness and what appropriate measures of success were. German manufacturers dispersed their production facilities, enabling continuous production of military equipment (but suffering in terms of efficiency and innovation capabilities). Morale at the local level was affected, but mere survival instead of revolt marked the reaction of the population. Furthermore, bombing proved inaccurate due to navigation and target identification problems in adverse European weather and the quality of bomb-aiming devices. The many weather aborts and intense German air defences reduced the intensity of the campaign. Finally, Allied target selection was erratic, featuring continuous debates concerning targeting prioritisation (oil, synthetic rubber, transport, cities, military industry, ball-bearing factories or the Luftwaffe?), despite the establishment of dedicated target analysis organisations.[12] While in practice the British and US approaches were indistinguishable in their devastative impact, CBO consisted of two related but separate strategic campaigns and two separate bombing organisations without a unified commander with sufficient command authority to establish targeting priorities for both forces.[13]

In the end, not the political but the military strategic impact was the most significant. It created attrition-style battlefields in the skies over Europe, resulting in air superiority over the beaches of Normandy and later over Germany. More than land warfare, the fight for air superiority over Germany evolved into a technological and tactical innovation contest involving radar-jamming techniques, night-precision navigation systems and the development of long-range fighters that could escort bombing formations. High attrition rates among German fighters and attacks on German airbases ultimately eliminated the Luftwaffe; the air defence of Germany distorted German strategy, disrupted logistics and starved the

---

12 This draws from Hall (ed.), *Case Studies*, chapters 2 and 3.
13 Overy, *Bombing War*, 305–8.

frontline troops of air support.[14] Losing air control meant catastrophe. Against Japan, where horrific firebomb raids claimed hundreds of thousands of casualties, moral considerations were even less relevant than against Germany. How war and strategy had changed due to air power was underscored by the Japanese surrender following the dropping of the two atomic bombs.

The Cold War

The Cold War context dominated air power thinking in the major powers (US, Russia, the UK and France). The word 'strategic' came to be associated with nuclear attack, and a fleet of strategic bombers armed with nuclear bombs was considered the most important military capability for the future. Both sides were involved in a technological race in the air domain. Rapid advances – the introduction of jet fighters, avionics, sensors – resulted in a series of increasingly capable and complex combat aircraft capable of flying at supersonic speeds and high altitude, often specialised in single roles such as intercepting high-flying strategic bombers. During the 1960s advances in radars and missile technology (infra-red and radar-guided) increased intercept ranges. Specialised aircraft were developed for identifying enemy electronic emissions and suppressing the increasingly capable radar-guided ground-based air defence systems (the so-called SEAD role). Air-to-air refuelling aircraft (modified civilian airliners) were introduced, extending the range and endurance of bombers, transport aircraft and fighters. Strategic and theatre transport aircraft with increasing capacity ensured rapid massive reinforcement options in times of crises from the US to Europe. Maritime patrol aircraft benefited from technologies that enabled detection of submarines in the vast oceans such as the Atlantic.

But the air wars over Korea and Vietnam also demonstrated the long shadow of the air war of the Second World War in terms of air power theory, strategy and joint warfare. US strategic bombing campaigns against North Korea from 1950 involved attacks against arsenals and communications centres, hydroelectric stations and dams, and transport networks. Pyongyang and other towns were annihilated. Again the aim was to destroy the enemy's war infrastructure and to isolate the front units, but also to

14 Overy, *Bombing War*, 626–8.

shatter enemy morale.[15] And once again unity of command over air operations of the various armed services proved a persistent problem, with disagreements between the US Navy and the Air Force over ways to integrate land- and sea-based air assets into a coherent air striking force, and between the Army and the Air Force over the level of air effort appropriate for CAS for the ground forces versus air interdiction.[16] The Korean War saw the employment of several more or less separate air forces: a strategic bomber command, US Navy air assets, the US Marine Corps Air Wing and the US Fifth Air Force, each conducting its own bombing campaign independent of the ebb and flow of ground operations. Internationally the bombing of civilian targets was criticised, creating domestic political pressure in the US which resulted in targeting restrictions for US air operations in Korea. An international sensibility was emerging that bombing attacks which resulted in many civilian deaths were not a legitimate means of warfare.[17]

The Vietnam War saw two air wars: one of an operational and tactical nature that focused on the ground war within Vietnam, and a strategic one that aimed to influence the will of Hanoi.[18] Like the Korean War, inter-service disagreements emerged about command and control for the air strikes in North Vietnam and the required allocation of assets for CAS to support US ground operations in South Vietnam. Once again the default solution was to allow the various services to conduct their own air campaign in areas they were assigned. But against an opponent applying irregular warfare tactics, without massed mechanised formations that could be spotted and attacked from the air, offensive air power proved relatively ineffective. The heavily forested environment and the significant North Vietnamese air-defence capabilities presented significant operational challenges, forcing air commanders to allocate large numbers of sorties against airfields and surface-to-air missile (SAM) systems, and the employment of scarce electronic warfare (EW) and SEAD capabilities.

The two strategic coercive campaigns were designed to directly influence Hanoi's strategic decision making by increasing the costs of war, echoing aspirations of the early air power theorists. The first was Operation Rolling

15 T. C. Hone, 'Strategic bombing constrained', in Hall (ed.), *Case Studies*, 469–527.
16 J. Winnefeld and D. Johnson, *Joint Air Operations* (Annapolis: Naval Institute Press, 1993), chapter 5.
17 T. Ward, *The Ethics of Destruction: Norms and Force in International Relations* (Ithaca: Cornell University Press, 1999), 150–1.
18 Winnefeld and Johnson, *Joint Air Operations*, chapter 6.

Thunder, a gradually escalating interdiction campaign designed to destroy the emerging industrial base of North Vietnam, later to degrade North Vietnam's ability to infiltrate troops and supplies into South Vietnam and, in the third phase, to destroy the industrial and transportation infrastructure in and around Hanoi, Haiphong and buffer zones near the Chinese border. The final phase of the campaign from April to November 1968 saw a de-escalation of the bombing in order to promote negotiations.[19] The second campaign was Operation Linebacker (I and II), an eleven-day bombing campaign against military installations, rail yards, petroleum stocks, bridges, roads, electric power production facilities and steel works, that aimed to pressure the North Vietnamese to end the conflict. These strategic attacks were significantly influenced by the White House's political desire to avoid active intervention by China or the USSR, which resulted in direct political influence on the target selection process, tactical instructions and restrictions to limit the risk of civilian casualties.

Strategic thinking and air power doctrine in Europe focused primarily on the defence of the Atlantic and the Inner German Border where NATO troops faced a numerically superior opponent. Air power played an increasingly crucial role. Reflecting the wars for air superiority of the Second World War, the Vietnam War and the Israeli experiences of 1967 and 1973, the first priority was air defence for countering the massive and modern air power capability of the Warsaw Pact, requiring persistent defensive counter air operations.[20] NATO developed an integrated system of layered defence-in-depth using reactive air-to-air fighters, SAM systems and additional aircraft placed on ground or airborne alert. The second primary role for air forces in Europe was delivering air support to ground units in the Northern and Central Army Groups. The US, with F-111 long-range bombers and SEAD capabilities, preferred deep strikes for air interdiction (AI) (and offensive counter air (OCA)). European air forces, lacking the required air assets for such risky missions, instead preferred to focus on CAS and battlefield air interdiction against Warsaw Pact ground forces on or near the front line. During the 1980s deep strike assets (such as the Tornado) and new types of multi-role aircraft (such as the F-16) replaced single role systems, enhanced the flexibility of air power for a commander and enabled more offensive attack options. Only the US and the UK maintained strategic bomber forces for, primarily, nuclear strikes.

19 M. Clodfelter, *The Limits of Air Power* (New York: The Free Press, 1989).
20 T. Mason, 'The domination of confrontation', in T. Mason (ed.), *Air Power, A Centennial Appraisal* (London: Brassey's, 1994), 92–102.

Airpower in Western Interventions 1990–2000

The end of the Cold War also ended the relative stagnation of air power theory development. Following the liberation of Kuwait in the winter of 1991, air power started to redefine the new image of modern warfare. The air power-centred joint campaign resulted in a lopsided victory lasting just thirty-nine days of intensive air bombardment and a four-day ground war.[21] It benefited from a unified command of almost all air power assets under one Joint Forces Air Component commander, thereby avoiding the debates of earlier decades, as well as high training standards, an abundance of combat aircraft and recently introduced technologies – stealth, cruise missiles, night vision equipment, precision-guided munition. F-117 Stealth aircraft – with a radar reflection surface of a golf ball – conducted strikes, almost unseen, deep into Iraqi airspace against command centres and radar systems despite intense air defences. Precision guided munitions (PGMs) produced a dramatic rise of intensity, lethality and efficiency of air attacks and, combined with cruise missiles and electronic warfare, air superiority was achieved in just a number of days, not just locally but over the entire Iraqi operation. The offence had regained dominance over the defence. The resulting virtual sanctuary in the third dimension was exploited for various purposes, such as reconnaissance, surveillance, interdiction, CAS and strategic attacks. PGMs offered the ability to strike targets accurately even from high altitude.[22]

But theoretical innovation was also key. In what amounts to a rediscovery of conventional strategic attack theory of the interbellum, John Warden, the architect of the strategic part of the Desert Storm air campaign, argued well prior to Desert Storm that these new technologies enabled accurate conventional strategic attacks simultaneously against multiple target-categories of a nation state (military units, political and military leadership, 'organic essentials' and critical infrastructure). Such high-intensity precise air strikes could overwhelm and rapidly degrade the functioning of the entire 'enemy system', and could cripple the strategic command capabilities before attacking fielded forces. It suggested too that, instead of focusing on the enemy's armed forces, disproportional strategically relevant effects could be achieved by focused attacks on enemy political and military leadership, as with PGMs, such targets could be accurately bombed even if they were near civilian

---

21 E. Cohen and, T. Keaney, *A Revolution in Warfare? Air Power in the Persian Gulf* (Annapolis: Naval Institute Press, 1995).
22 F. Osinga and M. Roorda, 'In control: harnessing aerial destructive force', in R. Bartels, J. C. van den Boogaard, P. Ducheine et al. (eds), *Military Operations and the Notion of Control Under International Law* (The Hague: Asser/ Springer, 2020), 161–94.

infrastructure.[23] With bombs striking within metres of a target, planners could now also think in terms of specific first- and second-order effects that needed to be achieved, instead of merely hoping that targets would be destroyed.[24]

These ideas informed the strategic part of the air campaign which focused on Iraqi national leadership, military and civil command and control to put physical and psychological pressure on the regime, demonstrate its vulnerability to the Iraqi people and reduce its capacity to command Iraqi forces, that is, to isolate, incapacitate and paralyse it. In traditional fashion, electric power generation and oil refineries, distribution and storage were targeted, as well as transport infrastructure to isolate the Kuwaiti battle area (railroads and bridges) and military capabilities such as weapons of mass destruction (WMD), military support capabilities, scud ballistic missiles and Iraqi air defences. This became an integral and leading part of the joint air–ground campaign plan to achieve the political objectives: the liberation of Kuwait and ensuring the security and stability of Saudi Arabia and the Persian Gulf.

The coalition ground offensive was also shaped by these new air power capabilities. Prior to it, air interdiction disrupted the logistical flow into Kuwait, isolating the Iraqi forces, and air strikes destroyed almost 50 per cent of Iraqi armour and artillery equipment. PGMs enhanced the utility of air power against Iraqi Army units: one fighter could now attack several targets in one mission. At the operational level this translated into a higher pace of operations for coalition ground troops and a huge reduction of the risk involved for them.

Desert Storm suggested that modern Western interventions need not involve the traditionally high number of civilian casualties and collateral damage. A revolution in military affairs was in the offing according to many analysts. Industrial age warfare was over. Precision-age air power became the option of choice for Western politicians in the highly sensitive and constrained post-Cold War peacekeeping operations. Following Desert Storm, the US set up two no-fly zones over Iraq to pressurise the Iraqi regime to stop repressing Kurdish and Shiite enclaves and later to accept UN WMD inspections. In the ethnic war in the Balkan, defenceless peacekeepers on the ground depended on air power for protection. This context inspired a rediscovery of the interbellum ideas for deterring and compelling political

23 R. Davis, 'Strategic bombardment in the Gulf War', in Hall (ed.), *Case Studies*, 527–622; J. Warden, 'The enemy as a system', *Airpower Journal*, 9 (1995), 40–55.
24 D. Deptula, *Effects Based Operations. Change in the Nature of Warfare* (Arlington: Aerospace Education Foundation, 1996).

and military leaders of the various ethnic factions, with analysts comparing the merits of a Punishment strategy (increasing the cost of achieving a strategic aim) versus a Denial strategy (eliminating the means to carry out the strategy, thus decreasing the chances of success). Warden's theory added (virtual) Decapitation and Incapacitation (paralysing the country or its military apparatus by eliminating command nodes or disrupting command processes) as potential approaches.[25]

However, politics instead of theoretical logic informed strategy in practice. A very limited UN mandate only permitted pin-prick air strikes, if at all, and an overriding concern for avoiding civilian casualties and the risk of warring factions taking peacekeepers hostage effectively cancelled any potential coercive effect of air strikes during NATO's Operation Deny Flight. The Srebrenica massacre in summer 1995 urged the UN and NATO to finally create proper conditions for the effective use of force, which enabled the eighteen-day Operation Deliberate Force against Bosnian Serb forces (in fortuitous simultaneity with a Croat ground offensive). This coerced them to accept the Dayton Accords.[26]

Similar strategic problems affected NATO in 1998 and 1999 in its efforts to stop the ethnic drama unfolding in Kosovo. Operation Allied Force (March 24–June 27 1999) aimed to halt the Serbian human rights abuses against the citizens of the Kosovo province, by attacking Serb military and security forces in Kosovo while ensuring minimising loss of friendly aircraft and collateral damage, as well as holding NATO together and protecting allied ground forces in neighbouring Bosnia from Serb raids. Initial coercive effect was nil due to squandered credibility in 1998, the low level of intensity of the first air strikes (only 48 sorties a day, versus 1300 daily during Desert Storm) and a very limited set of only fifty targets such as Serb forces, tanks and artillery, which represented little coercive value. With NATO's credibility again in doubt, European political leaders reluctantly agreed with US preference for escalating the campaign and targeting Serbian railroad and highway bridges, ammunition storage facilities, petroleum reserves and oil refineries, command posts, military airfields, electrical and broadcast services, news media and two of Slobodan Milošević's homes. After seventy-eight days, Milošević gave in to NATO due to the sustained and escalating air campaign, combined with the political isolation of the Serb leadership, the

---

25 D. Byman and M. Waxman, *The Dynamics of Coercion* (Cambridge: Cambridge University Press, 2001).
26 R. Owen, 'Operation Deliberate Force', in J. Olson (ed.), *A History of Air Warfare* (Washington, DC: Potomac Books, 2010), 201–24.

increasing activities of the Kosovo Liberation Army and the exhaustion of possible Serb countermoves.[27] Claims that air power had finally fulfilled the interbellum promises were exaggerated, but certainly the use of precision-age air power had become the societal norm, the icon of 'humane warfare', because it had demonstrated it could generate political pressure obviating the need to put a large number of army boots on the ground, and without the risks for civilians traditionally associated with air strikes.[28]

Air Power in the Twenty-First Century: Engaging Non-State Actors

While the military success of Operation Iraqi Freedom in 2003 reconfirmed the strategic value of air dominance and proper air-land integration, what stands out post-2000 is the increased effectiveness of air power in irregular wars against violent non-state actors such as the Taliban, Hezbollah, Hamas and ISIS.[29] Traditionally air power's utility had been limited against guerrilla forces and in mountainous or forested areas air power, and during the 1990s Western air power failed to timely identify, track and engage small mobile targets such as scud launchers and SAM systems, posing persistent strategic problems. In response the US military introduced technical and organisational changes to speed up the level of responsiveness (the so-called kill chain). Sensors, headquarters and offensive systems connected through datalinks subsequently enhanced timely dissemination of target information which enabled striking 'time-sensitive-targets'.[30] This proved its tactical, operational and strategic value in subsequent counterterrorism and counter-insurgency (COIN) operations such as Operation Enduring Freedom (OEF), the International Security Assistance Force (ISAF) and Operation Inherent Resolve.

In response to the attacks of 9/11, the US had few options available to retaliate and attack Al-Qaeda. Pakistan denied a large ground invasion from its soil. With an enemy trained in guerrilla fighting in landlocked

---

27 I. Daalder and M. O'Hanlon, *Winning Ugly: NATO's War to Save Kosovo* (Washington, DC: Brookings Institution Press, 2000).
28 Ch. Coker, *Humane Warfare, the New Ethics of Postmodern War* (London: Routledge, 2002).
29 K. Shimko, *The Iraq War and America's Military Revolution* (Cambridge: Cambridge University Press, 2010); B. Lambeth, *The Unseen War, Allied Air Power and the Takedown of Saddam Hussein* (Annapolis: Naval Institute Press, 2013).
30 F. P. B. Osinga and M. P. Roorda, 'From Douhet to drones, air warfare, and the evolution of targeting', in P. A. L. Ducheine, M. N. Schmitt and F. P. B. Osinga (eds), *Targeting: The Challenges of Modern Warfare* (The Hague: Springer, 2020), 56–7.

mountainous terrain, without significant infrastructure offering strategic coercive leverage, air strikes in close co-operation with only 300–500 Special Forces (SF) physically within Afghanistan co-operating and empowering local 'proxy' forces presented the only viable alternative.[31] This 'Afghan model' resulted in the fall of the Taliban after seventy-eight days. Averaging a hundred combat sorties a day, in essence this was an air campaign conducted in conjunction with and supported by SF units and proxy forces, who spotted emerging targets and relayed time-sensitive, up-to-date, accurate target information to shooter platforms inbound or already circling in the vicinity.

Intense air–land integration was also essential during NATO Operation ISAF (2003–2014) for the protection of its limited ground forces that were spread out over a vast terrain against a growing opposition from returning Taliban elements and other militant groups. ISAF also depended on continued strategic and theatre air transport effort involving thousands of sorties for logistical supply, air mobility, timely Medevac, rapid and precise CAS for troops in contact and air reconnaissance for convoy protection, and detection and tracking of enemy movement. While also accused of causing civilian casualties, compared to other COIN operations, ISAF, like OEF, was fairly successful in limiting casualties and engaging small groups of irregular fighters due to these force protection tactics.[32]

The strategic utility of the combination of special forces, local fighters and offensive air assets was demonstrated again in Operation Unified Protector over Libya in 2011 and Operation Inherent Resolve against ISIS. As the UN Security Resolution precluded insertion of ground troops in Libya (and absent Western political appetite for such an adventure), NATO's strategy relied on a maritime blockade and a no-fly zone using offensive air power to protect the Libyan civilian population against Gadhafi's troops. The six-month air operation exploited a range of reconnaissance assets, substantial air-to-air refuelling aircraft (indispensable considering the long flying distances and air patrol times) and a new generation of small calibre precision weapons (averaging thirty-six bombs per day). As during OEF, progress took off when special forces of several nations, covertly inserted, started to assist rebel forces and facilitated air–ground co-operation.

Coalition strategy in Operation Inherent Resolve was dictated by Iraqi politics (and Western casualty sensitivity) that precluded returning to Iraq

31 B. Lambeth, *Air Power Against Terror* (Santa Monica: RAND, 2005).
32 R. Sinterniklaas, 'Information age airpower in Afghanistan', PhD thesis, University of Amsterdam (2019).

with massive ground formations. Instead, Western special forces assisted Iraqi troops, operating under an umbrella of coalition air surveillance systems and offensive air assets which, in 2016–2017, delivered several thousands of bombs monthly on ISIS targets, steadily eliminating ISIS forces, even in urban environments, and reducing their hold on Iraqi territory.[33]

The introduction of armed Unmanned Aerial Vehicles (UAVs) – 'drones' – alongside manned fighter aircraft, also greatly expanded the capability to rapidly find, identify, track and engage fleeting targets. This increased the utility of air power as a counterterrorist instrument in so-called targeted-killing operations against, for instance, key leaders and small groups of Taliban, Al-Qaeda and ISIS insurgents. The effectiveness, legality and ethics were hotly debated initially, leading to accusations of the 'dehumanisation of war' and 'dronification of foreign policy'. Later disclosed information revealed the legal and accountability framework guiding such operations, and empirical data strongly suggest that strikes (by drones or fixed wing aircraft) against key members of insurgent and terrorist groups (bomb-making experts, ideological leaders, media producers, operators caught laying road-side bombs or firing mortar tubes) reduce their lethality.[34] This is also the recent Israeli experience (Operations Cast Lead 2008, Pillar of Defence 2012 and Protective Edge 2014) where networks of multiple UAVs, fighter aircraft and artillery managed to strike targets within minutes, and support army actions in the dense urban environment of the Gaza Strip. Such operations aim not for decisive battlefield victory but for restrictive deterrence: limiting the risks and impact of terrorist attacks rather than absolutely preventing them.[35]

Conclusion

These campaigns demonstrate air power's progressive trajectory in terms of its military and political utility. Ever since the Second World War, air power has played a major role in warfare. It can be applied, at short notice, across the strategic, operational, and tactical levels of war simultaneously, significantly increasing the options available to national leadership. It can

---

33 B. Wasser, S. Pettyjohn, J. Martini et al., *The Air War Against the Islamic State* (Santa Monica: RAND, 2021).
34 Osinga and Roorda, 'From Douhet to drones'.
35 A. Wilner, 'Fencing in warfare: threats, punishment, and intra-war deterrence in counterterrorism', *Security Studies*, 22 (2013), 740–72; T. Rid, 'Deterrence beyond the state: the Israeli experience', *Contemporary Security Policy*, 33 (2012), 124–47.

potentially negate the requirement to deploy a larger force over a broader timescale by land or sea, and by minimising or removing the requirement for land forces, air power can make it easier to commit in politically ambiguous circumstances.[36] While interbellum theoretical concepts still echo, contemporary Western air warfare in no way resembles the massive destruction air attacks wreaked in the major wars of the twentieth century. Expectations sometimes exceeded what flawed strategy, political restrictions or inadequate resources allowed, yet the successes of precision-age air power – in concert with ground forces or independently in an expanding variety of operations – signify the dramatically enhanced effectiveness of modern air operations. Catering to societal sensitivity and political risk aversion, it has become a cultural and normative expression of the Western way of war.[37]

---

36 RAF, 'UK joint doctrine publication 0–30, UK air and space power', 2nd ed. (2017), www.gov.uk/mod/dcdc.
37 Coker, *Humane Warfare*; M. Shaw, *The New Western Way of War, Risk-Transfer War and its Crisis in Iraq* (London: Polity Press, 2005).

11

The Second World War in Europe

GUILLAUME PIKETTY

The Shadow of the Great War

Soon after the signing of the Treaty of Versailles, Paul Cambon, the Ambassador of France in London wrote: 'Now peace is signed. I feel it looks like a storehouse of explosives that will explode all over the world one day or another.'[1] In 1923, when the fighting was over for good,[2] two-thirds of European political geography had changed. New states had been created from imperial ruins, old frontiers had been displaced, new countries had appeared. Furthermore, by eliminating some minorities, the various peace treaties had created new ones: roughly 30 million people found themselves as minorities within larger nations.

Among the main belligerents of the First World War in Europe, the Austro-Hungarian and Ottoman empires had disappeared. For defeated Germany, the years that immediately followed the conflict were marked by the loss of its colonies and 15 per cent of its territory, by the dismantling of its military power and the acknowledgement of its responsibility in triggering the Great War. Full of humiliation, bitterness and frustration, these years saw the rise of the 'stab-in-the-back' legend. The political turmoil that accompanied the disintegration of the imperial system and the weight of reparations on the economy made an already weak Weimar Republic even more instable. In that tricky context, the National-Socialist ('Nazi') party rose slowly but steadily, significantly helped from the autumn of 1929 by the consequences

---
[1] 'Voici la paix signée. Elle me fait l'effet d'un dépôt d'explosifs qui éclateront sur tous les points du monde un jour ou l'autre'; P. Cambon, *Correspondance 1870–1924* (Paris: Grasset, 1946), vol. 3, 341.
[2] R. Gerwarth, *The Vanquished: Why the First World War Failed to End, 1917–1923* (London: Penguin, 2017).

The Second World War in Europe

Map 11.1 The Second World War in Europe (1940–1945).

of the world economic crisis and the inability of its opponents to properly unite. Adolf Hitler's assumption of power on 30 January 1933 would be decisive for world peace.

France emerged from the Great War victorious but white-bled and having suffered huge industrial, financial and economic damages. In other words, the victory of 1918 was indeed a pyrrhic one. Satisfied by the post-war territorial arrangement, France devised a restricted and defensive military policy, and signed a series of diplomatic treaties in order to receive its due reparations and uphold the new European status quo. Horrified by the human cost of the First World War and its economic consequences,

Britain entrenched itself in its islands, relied on its empire and endeavoured to make sure that the peace settlement would be respected. A member of the club of victors, Italy had gained Trentino Alto Adige and a part of Istria, but not Fiume, which was first given to Yugoslavia then declared a free city in 1920. More broadly, Italy did not obtain the other territories that had been promised by Britain and France. Playing on the idea of a 'mutilated victory', the nationalists added fuel to the ongoing social unrest of the post-war years. Benito Mussolini took advantage of the political and social instability to reach power on 30 October 1922. Three years later, the fascist regime was firmly in control.

For its part, the United States emerged stronger from the Great War both at the economic and military levels. Despite President Wilson's Fourteen Points and his commitment to the Paris Peace conference that notably led to the signing of the Treaty of Versailles, the US Senate did not ratify the latter and voted against accession to the League of Nations. Throughout the 1920s, the USA slowly but steadily reverted to isolationism, a move that was even reinforced by the consequences of the 1929 economic crisis. Born from the revolution of October 1917, the new Soviet State finally managed to vanquish counterrevolutionary forces and win the civil war, but had to sign with Poland, in 1921, the peace treaty of Riga according to which it lost a series of territories populated by Belarussians and Ukrainians. Isolated from the rest of Europe by a so-called 'sanitary cordon', weakened by years of conflict and with a military apparatus largely reformed in 1924–1926, the USSR (founded on 30 December 1922) endeavoured then to establish 'Socialism in one country' while hoping that major capitalist powers would fight one another.

All in all, despite the desire for peace born from 'the war to end war', the wisdom of many European diplomats and the best efforts of the League of Nations, European peace came under threat in the early 1930s.

Sources

The official histories of Britain and the United States, and the published diplomatic documents of Germany, Britain, France and the USA provide a good starting point.[3] They are completed by scholarly and popular books

---

3 *Akten des Auswärtigen Amtes; Documents of British Foreign Policy; Documents diplomatiques français; Foreign Relations of the US.*

that address the British, French, German, Italian, Soviet and US cases, of which most consider and discuss strategic issues. The multiple biographies of key decision makers, be they political leaders or military commanders, provide some stimulating supplements. Excellent broad syntheses, of which a few are mentioned below, provide a global and detailed overview of the strategic aspects of the Second World War.[4] As for the application of strategic decisions in the field and the consequences for combatants, during the three last decades a new harvest of excellent scholarship has provided some very stimulating insight from a bottom-up point of view.[5]

Most of the issues about Second World War strategy have been analysed thoroughly. There nevertheless remain some debates about the actual efficiency both of blitzkrieg when deprived of the surprise effect[6] and of the bombing strategy.[7] General Eisenhower's all-out strategy to enter Germany and his decision not to try to reach Berlin in spring 1945 still trigger some scholarly debates, even if the latter is very much connected to Cold War issues rather than to realistic assessments of the actual situation in the field at

---

4 See the Further Reading section on page 548.
5 See for example: T. Barkawi, *Soldiers of Empire: Indian and British Armies in World War II* (Cambridge: Cambridge University Press, 2017); J. Fennel, *Combat and Morale in the North African Campaign – The Eighth Army and the Path to El Alamein* (Cambridge: Cambridge University Press, 2014); S. Hart, *Colossal Cracks: Montgomery's 21st Army Group in Northwest Europe, 1944–45* (Mechanicsburg: Stackpole Books, 2000); I. Johnston-White, *The British Commonwealth and Victory in the Second World War* (London: Palgrave Macmillan, 2017); J.-L. Crémieux-Brilhac, *Les Français de l'an 40, Volume II, Ouvriers et soldats* (Paris: Gallimard, 1990); J. Jackson, *The Fall of France: The Nazi Invasion of 1940* (Oxford: Oxford University Press, 2003); E. R. May, *Strange Victory. Hitler's Conquest of France* (New York and London: I. B. Tauris, 2000); O. Bartov, *Hitler's Army: Soldiers, Nazis, and War in the Third Reich* (New York/Oxford: Oxford University Press, 1991); R. Citino, *Death of the Wehrmacht: The German Campaigns of 1942* (Lawrence: University Press of Kansas, 2007); S. Neitzel and H. Welszer, *Soldaten. On Fighting, Killing and Dying. The Secret Second World War Tapes of German POWs* (London and New York: Simon & Schuster, 2013); D. Stahel, *Operation Barbarossa and Germany's Defeat in the East* (Cambridge: Cambridge University Press, 2009); M. Knox, *Hitler's Italian Allies: Royal Armed Forces, Fascist Regime, and the War of 1940–1943* (Cambridge: Cambridge University Press, 2000); R. Atkinson, *The Liberation Trilogy* (New York: Henry Holt and Company, 2002, 2007 and 2013); P. Schrijvers, *The Crash of Ruins. American Combat Soldiers in Europe during World War II* (New York: New York University Press, 1998); C. Merridale, *Ivan's War: Life and Death in the Red Army, 1939–1945* (New York: Metropolitan Books, 2006).
6 See for example: K.-H. Frieser with J. T. Greenwood, *The Blitzkrieg Legend: The 1940 Campaign in the West* (Annapolis: Naval Institute Press, 2005); P. Kennedy, *Engineers of Victory: The Problem Solvers Who Turned the Tide in the Second World War* (New York: Random House, 2013).
7 See R. Overy, *The Bombing War: Europe, 1939–1945* (London: Penguin, 2015).

the time and diplomatic issues.[8] Lastly, if the importance for the post-war years of the resistance organisations' and partisan movements' activity during the conflict is well acknowledged, the reality and effectiveness of these organisations' and movements' contribution to the liberation of Europe are still debated.[9]

Adversaries

The Second World War saw the participation of multiple actors. In Europe, six main protagonists stood on the foreground. They were all 'Great Powers', with hundreds of thousands or millions of square miles of territory and vast economic resources at their disposal, able to mobilise million-strong armed forces.

From the onset, Hitler considered that Germany's destiny was to dominate the whole world, and the necessary war to meet this objective was envisioned as a means to achieve greatness and to give birth and 'living space' to the true 'master race'. To do this, he tore up the Versailles Peace Treaty, while considering France as a traditional foe to be defeated for good and communism as a direct threat to be dealt with brutally alongside the so-called 'Jewish Question'. Upon assuming power, the new chancellor strongly accelerated the secret rearmament programme that had already been launched by his country. In 1933, Germany withdrew from the League of Nations and the world disarmament conference that had opened in Geneva in February of the previous year. In March 1935, conscription was restored in the Third Reich, leading to a tripling of the size of the German Army. The same year saw the re-forming of a German Air Force. From 1937, the development and the modernisation of the German Navy were accelerated. More broadly, massive investments were made in the arms industry. In the meantime, on 25 November 1936, Nazi Germany and Imperial Japan signed the Anti-Comintern Pact directed at the USSR.

From the early 1920s, bearing in mind his country's pre-First World War and wartime objectives, and taking into account actual strategic issues, Mussolini developed an ambitious international programme for portions of the Balkans, Anatolian Turkey and the Arabian Middle East.

---

8 See the broad syntheses mentioned in the Further Reading section on page 548.
9 See for example: R. Gildea and I. Tames (eds), *Fighters Across Frontiers. Transnational Resistance in Europe, 1936–48* (Manchester: Manchester University Press, 2020); O. Wieviorka, *The Resistance in Western Europe 1940–1945* (New York: Columbia University Press, 2019).

This programme was also supposed to extend Italy's domination over a series of African territories from Tunisia to Ethiopia, and possibly extending south of the Sahara Desert. Well aware of his country's geographical situation and military weaknesses, the Duce restrained from any aggressive move against Yugoslavia and France, and participated in negotiations about disarmament and collective security. In 1935 nevertheless, he launched a victorious campaign against Ethiopia, at the end of which he proclaimed the Italian Empire on 9 May 1936. In a speech delivered in Milan on 1 November of the same year, he used the expression 'Rome–Berlin Axis' for the first time. A year later, on 6 November 1937, Italy joined the Anti-Comintern Pact. On 11 December, it, too, withdrew from the League of Nations.

In 1934 and 1935, alarmed by Germany's moves, France tried with little success to revive its alliance with Britain but managed to conclude a mutual assistance pact with the USSR. In the meantime, France slowly but steadily built up its military power. The Eastern frontier fortifications (Maginot line), the construction of which had begun in 1929, were nearly completed by 1937. From 1933 on, the French Air Force was developed. The French Navy was expanded to protect and make the most of French imperial possessions (by 1940, it was the fourth largest in the world), and the defences of the empire were strengthened as much as possible. In the meantime, rearmament progressed steadily. Nevertheless, the French Army's organisation and tactical training were not modernised, neither was resolved the essential inconsistency between France's diplomatic commitments and its defence policy.

In the mid-1930s, considering that a war against Germany had become possible again, the British general staff devised a programme to expand and modernise the small army to be able to send an expeditionary force to the Continent to fight alongside France. At first, the government made them reduce their ambitions. Then, in early 1938, firmly deciding never again to face the human and economic costs of the First World War, Prime Minister Neville Chamberlain resolutely opted for an appeasement foreign policy and a strategy of deterrence, centring on the RAF to be modernised and much enlarged and the stationing of the bulk of the Royal Navy in the Mediterranean as a warning for Italy.

Since the beginning of the 1920s, and despite their relative withdrawal into themselves, the United States of America had devised a series of military plans, of which some were named after the colour corresponding to the enemy they were supposed to take care of (black for

Germany, red for Britain, orange for Japan, etc.). Other plans were supposed to answer to a global war, and still others merely corresponded to general staff exercises. As Japanese naval power grew, War Plan Orange gained even greater precision. In the meantime, US planners devised Joint Plan Red-Orange, which envisaged a conflict against an alliance of Great Britain and Japan. Even if politically unrealistic, this hypothesis led to the consideration of the possible challenges posed by a two-ocean war. Throughout these years, attention was also devoted to mobilisation procedures, industrial mobilisation and wartime procurement.

The Soviet Union lagged behind among the to-be main Second World War protagonists for more than a decade in terms of grand strategy and the means to pursue it. That was notably due to the conditions of the Union's birth and progressive settlement. The first Soviet war plans were drawn up in the late 1920s–early 1930s, triggered by the fear that the USSR would have to fight neighbouring states backed by major capitalist powers. Having designated Poland and Romania as the most likely adversaries, they displayed a strategy in which the first stage was to be defensive while mobilising Soviet forces, then to conquer the Baltic states so that Leningrad would be secured. A powerful counteroffensive would then follow. During the first half of the 1930s, the nature of the threat changed, switching to Nazi Germany and militaristic Japan. It made the USSR join the League of Nations in September 1934, sign a mutual assistance pact with France in May 1935 and thoroughly develop its armed forces.

The Path to War

Following the method that he would systematically use during the global war to come, dealing with one front at a time, Hitler spent the second half of the 1930s addressing one international issue after the other. A series of trials of strength ensued, that saw the rest of Europe adapting as much as possible to Nazi Germany's moves while isolationist USA struggled with the consequences of the Great Depression and watched from afar. On 7 March 1936, despite the provisions of the Treaty of Versailles and the Locarno treaties notably guaranteeing the frontiers between France and Germany and between Belgium and Germany, elements of the Wehrmacht entered the previously demilitarised German-populated Rhineland. France and Britain chose not to react militarily. In mid-July of the same year, a group of nationalist generals rose up against the Spanish republican government, starting a bloody civil war that was to last almost three years during which, among other things, nationalist forces received firm and protracted support from Nazi Germany and fascist Italy. On 12 March 1938, the German Wehrmacht crossed the border into Austria; the Austrian military put up no resistance. Less than a month later, a plebiscite officially ratified the country's annexation by the Reich.

Then the German Führer turned to Czechoslovakia and more specifically the Sudetenland, the borderland areas in which numerous German-speakers lived. After months of tension and threats, British, French and Italian leaders met Hitler in Munich, Germany, on 29–30 September 1938. There, in spite of the 1924 alliance agreement and 1925 military pact between France and the Czechoslovak Republic, Britain and France accepted that the Sudetenland would be given to Germany in order to avoid a major war. In March 1939, despite his promise at Munich that he had no further territorial claim, Hitler marched his Wehrmacht into Czechoslovakia which he broke up into the Slovak Republic and a newly created 'Protectorate of Bohemia and Moravia', gaining full control of the Czechoslovakian military arsenal and showing one last time that British appeasement policy failed to stop his expansionism. In April, Italy conquered Albania after a five-day campaign. Following Mussolini's visit to Germany in September 1937 and Hitler's to Italy in May 1938, and their de facto partnership in Munich, the two leaders signed a military alliance, the Pact of Steel, in Berlin on 22 May 1939. Three months later in Moscow, a non-aggression pact was concluded between Nazi Germany and the Soviet Union. Eager to expand the USSR's influence and, even more, to buy time in order to strengthen Soviet armed forces, Stalin had decided to switch alliances. According to the 23 August agreement, each country officially pledged that it would not ally itself to or aid an enemy of the other. A secret protocol also defined the borders of the German and Soviet spheres of influence across Finland, Estonia, Latvia, Lithuania and Poland.

On 1 September 1939, the German invasion of Poland began. On 17 September, one day after concluding a ceasefire agreement with Japan following the battles of Khalkhin Gol (Eastern Mongolia), the Soviet Union invaded Poland too. In the meantime, France and the United Kingdom had declared war on Germany on 3 September, followed by Australia, Canada, New Zealand and South Africa. Apart from a small French offensive into the Saarland, these countries did not provide military support to Poland but began a naval blockade of Germany. For its part, Italy decided to wait. On 27 September, nevertheless, it signed the Tripartite pact with Germany and

Japan, also known as the Axis alliance. In November, Bulgaria, Hungary, Romania and Slovakia joined the alliance. For its part, despite its growing interest and empathy for Germany, Turkey opted for a non-belligerent status that it would maintain year in, year out until its entry into war against the Reich on 20 February 1945.

Actors, Objectives and Prioritisation

Throughout the Second World War, the grand strategy followed by Germany was essentially conceived by Adolf Hitler as supreme commander of the Wehrmacht. Major General, and from mid-July 1940, General Field Marshal Wilhelm Keitel headed the high command (*Oberkommando*) of the Wehrmacht (OKW) and dutifully followed the Führer's orders. With a mix of fear, promotions and bribes, the latter managed to obtain the support of a vast majority of the members of the German high command. The victories of 1939–1941 further reinforced this support. During the war years, Hitler generally listened to his generals and admirals, and sometimes followed their suggestions. Yet he was always the only one to take the final decision. As noted, his method was to deal with one front at a time. For each, he, and he alone, defined and prioritised the objectives. Poland was to be conquered first, then Norway. Western Europe was next on the list. The Soviet Union was to follow. In each occasion, the plan was to strike hard in a 'lightning campaign' (blitzkrieg) and to win quickly so that negotiations could be launched in the most favourable position. The rules of behaviour of the invading armies would depend on the front, being much less harsh in the north and the west of Europe than elsewhere. As for the German population, the choice was made to make every effort to spare them the consequences of the war in day-to-day life, or at least to mitigate them, and thus to exploit the resources of the vanquished foes to the maximum.[10] Eventually, when the tide of war turned, the main motto became to hold out at all costs without ceding one inch of ground.

Mussolini managed to control the Italian high command until July 1943. Alongside the general staff of the armed forces that had been created in 1925 to co-ordinate the planning of the chiefs of staff of the three services, the *Commando Supremo* (the Italian high command) was instituted on 29 May 1940 with Mussolini at its head. From then on, the Duce was able to discard the

---

10 G. Aly, *Hitler's Beneficiaries: Plunder, Racial War, and the Nazi Welfare State* (New York: Metropolitan Books, 2007).

professional strategic advice he had received if he deemed fit, and instead launch his own strategic initiatives, which were regularly specified then dutifully executed by his officers. In the spring of 1940, the Italian leader decided that his country would wage a 'parallel war' in order to carve out its own domain in North Africa and the Balkans. Having failed to secure both objectives while fighting alone, he had no other choice than to request Germany's help. Between the winter of 1941 and the summer of 1943, Italian strategy became increasingly dependent on Germany. After the armistice of 3 September between the Italian government and the Allies, Italy became a pawn in the game of both sides.

In the mid-1930s, the Soviet high command had adopted the principle of 'deep operations' developed by armies and army groups.[11] A combination of mechanised formations and aviation would break enemy defences and allow mobile forces to exploit the gaps thus created and finish off the opponent's resistance. Due to the successive purges in the military hierarchy (1937–1938) and Stalin's determination to be the main Soviet strategist, these reflections were not enacted as much as they should have been. Nevertheless, plans were devised between 1936 and 1939 that first concerned Germany and Poland. They combined covert mobilisation, surprise and pre-emption, and were to be executed by three army groups: the Northwestern, Western and Southwestern. These plans were momentarily put aside after the signing of the Soviet–German Pact and the following expansion of Soviet influence in eastern Europe, and during the Soviet–Finnish 'Winter War' (30 November 1939–13 March 1940). When a conflict with Germany became highly plausible again, Soviet planners shifted from defensive (on the flanks) / offensive (at the centre) measures to more defensive ones. All of this was reduced to a shambles by the German mechanised onslaught launched on 22 June 1941. Right after the beginning of Germany's offensive, Stalin decided to modify the chain of command inherited from the First World War and the Civil War so that he would concentrate all the State's resources in his hands. He created the Stavka (headquarters) on 23 June and the State Committee for Defence on 30 June, and quickly assumed the direction of both. On 8 August, he became supreme commander of the armed forces. In the meantime, he had taken and enforced the fateful decision not to yield an inch of territory, leading to terrible losses of Soviet military and civilian lives, as well as territory and economic and industrial resources. In the months that followed, immense pressure from Moscow to regain the initiative led commanders in the field to launch too many ill-fated offensives. For two years, the Red Army

11 See also Chapter 9.

managed to block and repel German offensives through improvisation and slowly improving organisation with two objectives in mind: to survive to fight another day, and to inflict a war of attrition on the enemy. At the end of the summer of 1943, after a resounding success at the Battle of Kursk, it regained the initiative. From then on, drawing on hard-won experience, the enormous human resources at its disposal, an industry running in full swing in the service of the war and US material help, the Soviet leadership became increasingly capable of devising complex strategic planning in multiple directions, or 'fronts', that would both vanquish Germany and secure political goals in eastern Europe.

In the spring of 1939, following the Munich crisis and the carving up of Czechoslovakia, the British Chiefs of Staff Committee began to prepare plans for a war against Germany and Italy. They envisaged a conflict in three phases. With the help of a small British expeditionary force, the French Army was supposed to check the enemies' offensive on the Continent. Then the Allies would make the most of their empires and neutral trading partners, in the first instance the USA, while weakening Germany and Italy thanks to economic blockade and propaganda. Lastly, after roughly two years, they would launch a counteroffensive and strike into Germany. Despite their industrial and economic shortcomings, these war plans were globally accepted by the French. From 9 April to 8 June 1940, British and French forces endeavoured to cut German supply in Swedish iron ore through the Norwegian port of Narvik, but the operation eventually turned into a major setback for the Allies. Then the quick and astonishing successes of the German offensive on Holland, Belgium and France forced a major change in British strategy. After briefly contemplating the possibility of a negotiated peace, the new coalition government headed by Winston Churchill decided that total victory was the only option to be considered. From then on, British war planning was taken over by a Defence Committee (created in May 1940), with Churchill at its head as minister of defence, in connection with the War Cabinet, headed by Churchill too as prime minister. Three successive strategies were devised throughout the rest of the war. From June 1940 to December 1941, Britain adopted the position of the last bulwark against totalitarianism and oppression in Europe and more broadly in the world. While slowly building up its own land forces, and relying on the Royal Navy, the RAF and the military and economic might of its Empire, it put the emphasis on economic blockade, air attacks on Germany and subversion in occupied Europe by a new secret service, the Special Operations Executive, helped by local resistance forces. After the USSR's switch of alliance following its invasion by Germany and, even more, the entry of the United States into war in December 1941, British planners considered returning to their initial strategy of 1939. But, as will be seen below, they had to take into account the rising might of their new partners and thus increasingly negotiate each step of the grand strategy. After the Tehran conference with the USA and the USSR (28 November–1 December 1943), and even though it took its full share of the war effort, Britain had to follow its great allies' strategic decisions.

Due to its crushing defeat in the spring of 1940 and later geostrategic constraints, France was the major belligerent whose fate in some respects saw the biggest upheavals throughout the Second World War. The Munich crisis and its consequences led Paris to a series of strategic updates. First, more attention was paid to imperial defence with a specific emphasis on North Africa. Furthermore, General Gamelin, chief of the national defence staff and commander-in-chief designate in case of war, was ordered to co-ordinate inter-allied negotiations on war plans. Notwithstanding a possible early action against Italy, and without considering the promises of help made to allies in central and eastern Europe, these talks eventually led to the aforementioned three-phased Franco-British strategy. As for France's north-eastern frontier where the fight on the Continent was to take place, Belgium's decision to pursue a policy of 'independence' (October 1936) led French strategists to hesitate between a forward defence on the River Scheldt and a rapid advance of the best French armies to the River Dyle that would be more risky but might bring the Dutch and Belgian armies to fight alongside France and Britain. As soon as the German 1940 offensive began, the French first and seventh armies incorporating the best trained and most modern units of the land forces dutifully executed the 'Dyle–Breda' manoeuvre, leaving France insufficiently defended against what was to be the enemy's main blow across the Belgian and Luxembourg Ardennes. Less than six weeks later, the new French government headed by Marshal Pétain asked for an armistice that was quickly signed on 24 June. After that astonishing disaster, two opposite French strategies were developed. The first consisted in withdrawing to the southern part of the metropolitan soil that remained under the Vichy regime's authority and defending the Vichy part of the Empire. The second strategy was adopted in the early summer of 1940 by General de Gaulle's Free France and briefly (January–May 1943) by French forces in North Africa under General Giraud. It consisted in rallying all military forces wherever some fighting against Axis forces was taking place. Eventually, the forces of the interior resistance were integrated into these plans. After the fusion of Gaullist and Giraudist organisations in Algiers during the summer of 1943, a French provisional government and a military high command endeavoured to build up and modernise their armed forces in order to participate as much as possible in the fighting for the liberation of the European soil and to preserve the Empire. For broad geopolitical reasons, France was eventually admitted among the concert of the five major victors of the war.

From the beginning of 1939, US Army and Navy planners had begun to think about a possible war between and alliance of Britain and France on the one hand and Nazi Germany on the other. They also had considered the hypothesis of the latter's victory leading to a German threat on the Western hemisphere. A series of war plans, named Rainbow, ensued of which some envisioned a multi-theatre coalition war. German successes against Belgium, France and Holland in May and June 1940 and Japanese moves in Asia led US political and military decision makers to a series of assessments and scenarios, the most influential of which was the memorandum produced by Admiral Stark, chief of naval operations, and approved by General Marshall, army chief of staff. That so-called 'Plan Dog' memo argued that USA and British securities were closely linked, and that eventual victory was most likely to be achieved through an offensive in the Atlantic and a defensive in the Pacific. In January 1941, the first secret 'ABC' talks gathered American, British and Canadian planners in Washington, DC. They established the principle that defeating Germany would be the first objective of the Allies. In April, the US Joint Army–Navy Board completed War Plan Rainbow 5 which confirmed that Germany and/or Italy would be the first targets of US military action, and envisaged the building up and projection of US armed forces in the eastern Atlantic and then in Europe, possibly in Africa and in the Middle East. In the months that followed, the Joint Board refined Rainbow 5 so that it would correspond to a war waged on two oceans in which Germany would remain the principal foe, and adjusted its estimations of US military needs in case of a conflict. In other words, the USA were fully committed to coalition strategic planning even if they were not at war and if a majority of the US population was reluctant to renounce isolationism and participate in a conflict. In the meantime, and with the authorisation of Congress, President Roosevelt had made his country an 'arsenal of democracy' and had had the Lend–Lease Bill passed (March 1941) to provide war material to the Allies. In August 1941, he announced with Churchill the so-called 'Atlantic Charter' that notably reasserted basic freedoms and called for the creation of a post-war international system. After the Japanese attack on Pearl Harbor on 7 December 1941 and Hitler's declaration of war on the United States on 11 December, the latter found itself involved for good in the world conflict. As commanders in chief, Roosevelt and later Truman would have supreme decision-making authority. But they would work closely with the Joint Chiefs of Staff Committee created in February 1942 in which Admiral King, commander-in-chief, US fleet, and General Marshall would play a decisive role until the end of the conflict.

In early 1942, all the main protagonists were fully and finally involved in the world war. In the European and North African theatres of operations, Hitler dominated all Axis strategical decisions. As for the Allies, a close co-operation was instituted between Britain and the United States. It revolved around Churchill, Roosevelt, the Combined Chiefs of Staff Committee (created during the winter of 1942, which included the main military decision makers of the two countries) and many ad hoc groups in which American and British planners met. Until the end of the war, the USSR (and in Asia, Chiang Kai-shek's China) was increasingly associated with this strategic planning. Even if challenged a few times in the United States, the Germany-First principle was never abandoned. In July 1942, the Anglo-Americans took the decision to land an expeditionary force in French north-west Africa to make a first move towards Europe and fulfil Roosevelt's promise to Stalin to open a second front that would ease the pressure on the Red Army which was carrying the burden of the ground war all by itself. At the Casablanca conference (14–24 January 1943), the Western Allies decided that defeating the U-boat offensive in the Atlantic was a priority, agreed on a full bomber offensive to systematically destroy Germany's industry and infrastructures, opted for an invasion of Sicily as soon as the North African campaign ended, and declared their determination to impose unconditional surrender on the Axis powers. At the Trident conference in Washington (May 1943), an agreement was reached to invade the Italian mainland after the campaign in Sicily. At the Quadrant conference in Quebec (August 1943), the Allies decided that the next step would be a cross-Channel invasion to take place in spring 1944 despite Churchill's best efforts in favour of an offensive from the south of Europe. Headed by American General Eisenhower as supreme commander, the allied landings in France (June and August 1944) and the rapid progresses that ensued were followed by a strategy of all-out invasion of Germany from the West, destined to make the most of Allied might and similar to the one used by the Red Army in the east.

Available Means

During the 1930s, as the possibility of a new European general conflict loomed larger and larger, the major powers endeavoured to prepare for it according to the strategies they had chosen. The duration of the world war and the various, often unexpected or underanalysed situations, led the powers that were still in the fight to adapt their military means and to invent and develop new ones. Volumes have been written about these adaptations, inventions and developments.[12] Only a few will be mentioned in the following paragraphs.

Adopting a strategy of extending German territory bit by bit, isolating each victim before striking, Adolf Hitler and his military advisers had begun to believe that each conflict to come, the one against the USSR included, would be won quickly. For Belgium, France and Holland, ten panzer divisions supported by Me 109 fighters and Ju 87 dive-bombers proved to be enough. But neither the Ju 88, a long-range bomber, nor the big battleships and herds of U-boats of the Kriegsmarine were able to bring Britain to its knees and, later, to sever the Atlantic supply line. In the USSR, the Wehrmacht had to face an enemy for which it was ill-prepared. The environment – a combination of formidable distances, difficult terrain and bad weather conditions – took a huge toll on German forces and literally 'demodernized' them.[13] Furthermore, the medium tank Panzer IV rather quickly found itself in difficulty when facing the Soviet T-34. From 1943, a new medium tank, the Panther, was introduced, soon followed by heavy tanks, the Tiger I and Tiger II. Nevertheless, despite the progressive mobilisation of its economy in the service of the war effort, Germany was never able to produce these tanks in sufficient numbers to face the increasing might of its enemies. In terms of propaganda and of mobilisation of its full might in the service of a 'total war', however, the 'Thousand-Year Reich' performed astonishingly until the very end of the war.

By contrast and from the onset, Italian armed forces were no real match for Allied forces, even on sea despite the initial strength of the navy. Furthermore, the fascist state was never able to fully mobilise the capacities of the country. This is why, until the summer of 1943, Italy grew more and more dependent on its powerful German ally. The situation quickly became the same for the other European members of the Axis alliance.

During the so-called 'Phoney War' (3 September 1939–10 May 1940), France endeavoured to improve the composition, organisation and the armament of its forces. On land, its materiel was roughly equivalent to Germany's in terms of artillery, motorised transport and tanks. Nevertheless, though better armoured and gunned and more numerous than most of their German

12 For a necessarily partial but stimulating perspective, see for example Kennedy, *Engineers of Victory*.
13 See for example Bartov, *Hitler's Army*, chapter 1, 'The demodernization of the front'.

counterparts (with the exception of the Panzer IV), the tanks were dispersed in small squads instead of being used in powerful armoured units. The French Air Force did not match Germany's Luftwaffe, and events moved too fast in spring 1940 for the powerful French Navy to be fully employed. France suffered a crushing defeat. Thereafter, the French armed forces under the authority of the Vichy regime were limited in number, equipment and armament. For their part, the few tens of thousands of Free French Forces were totally dependent on British supply. From the summer of 1943 to the end of the war, the progressively growing French armed forces were essentially supplied by the Anglo-American allies and, for the most modern units, organised, trained and employed according to American standards.

Like France, Britain strove to make the most of the Phoney War to develop both its army (the aim at this time was fifty-five divisions) and the Royal Air Force. Alarmed by the turn of events in France in May 1940, Churchill decided to keep back the bulk of the latter for future needs. Thanks to a last-minute evacuation and the self-sacrifice of French troops, the greatest part of the ten divisions of the British Expeditionary Force on the Continent were saved from the Dunkirk pocket in early June. But they had lost all their equipment and heavy armament. Shielded by the Royal Navy, the RAF and a dense radar network, the main British Isles escaped invasion. From the autumn of 1940 to the end of the war, thanks to investments, technical progress, the surge of personnel, increased production of equipment, and the improvement of training and doctrine of employment, the British and Imperial Army was able to contribute its fair share of the final victory. So did the Royal Navy in the Atlantic and the Mediterranean, and the RAF in European skies, especially after the provision of a Rolls-Royce Merlin engine to the P-51 Mustang fighter so that it could escort bombers very far over the Reich.

In June 1941, the Red Army had just begun to make up for the deficiencies that had appeared during the moves following the Soviet–German agreement, the Polish campaign of 1939 and the Winter War against Finland: poor training of the soldiers, disorganisation of the officer corps following the purges of 1937–1938 and obsolescence of a large part of the armament and equipment. The production of new models such as fighters Yak-1 and Mig-3 and tanks T-34 and KV-1 had been accelerated since the beginning of the year, but only 15 per cent of the air units and 20 per cent of the armoured divisions had been supplied with these weapons systems. The huge number of soldiers and their motivation to fight (and the fear instilled by the State apparatus) on the one hand, and the immensity of the Soviet territory on the other, were the assets first used by the USSR to resist the German onslaught. From the end of 1942, the Soviet industry was able to provide the Red Army with huge quantities of increasingly sophisticated materials of which some, such as the heavy JS tank and the Il-1 fighter, outperformed their German counterparts. This impressive result was completed by important deliveries of US and British supplies according to the Lend–Lease agreement. In spring 1945, the Soviet conventional armed forces were undoubtedly the most powerful in the world.

As the second giant to awaken throughout the Second World War, the USA started from a low base. In September 1939, the US Army was 190,000 personnel strong, rather well trained but poorly equipped. This was also true of the personnel of the US Army Air Corps (renamed US Army Air Forces (USAAF) in June 1941). For its part, the US Navy was organised around battleships and battlecruisers. It also had 5 aircraft-carriers and about 60 submarines (the US Marines were not employed in Europe, so their situation will not be considered here). Throughout the war, these numbers were drastically increased so that, in 1945, the army could field 90 divisions (among which 16 armoured ones and 5 airborne), the USAAF counted 16 air force divisions and the navy was notably equipped with 138 aircraft-carriers (among which 111 escort carriers), 10 battleships, 47 cruisers, more than 200 submarines and 60,000 landing crafts. As noted, American industry was also able to supply the rest of the alliance through Lend–Lease. If its production was not always of greater quality than that of Germany, it could compensate with numbers. American logistical means and organisation were rather remarkable. In the North African and then European theatres, US combatants managed to overcome their first disappointments and perform well against their formidable German opponents, notably becoming excellent in terms of infantry-artillery co-ordination and air–ground support.

Application of Strategy

Four successive phases can be distinguished in the European part of the Second World War during which respective strategies were put to the test and if necessary adapted, or even transformed where possible. From September 1939 to the autumn of 1941, the Axis managed to implement its strategic decisions and globally kept the upper hand. After the quick, ruthless and successful campaign in Poland (1 September–6 October 1939) and the sharing out of its land with its allies, and while the Red Army struggled against Finnish combatants, Germany invaded Norway on 9 April 1940. The victorious German campaign ended on 8 June with the evacuation of the last Allied units. In the meantime, as strongly suggested by Lieutenant General von Manstein, the Wehrmacht's onslaught in the West had begun on 10 May, its main forces advancing through the Belgian and Luxembourg Ardennes. The Allied forces having been unable to counterattack, Dutch forces had capitulated on 14 May followed by Belgium on 28 May. On 10 June, Italy entered the war alongside Germany. Seven days later, the French government asked for armistice, ending a six-week campaign that at the time astonished the world but that, in the bigger picture of the war, ended in a fatal victory. During the summer, Hitler seriously considered a landing in the British Isles (Operation Sea Lion), but with the Kriegsmarine being unable to compete with the Royal Navy and the Luftwaffe having failed to destroy the RAF, he renounced his plans in mid-September. At the time, he was already looking east. For his part, Mussolini was busy waging his parallel war in Egypt (from 13 September 1940) and in Greece (from 28 October 1940). Both Italian campaigns foundered, forcing Germany to intervene successfully in Libya (March 1941) and the Balkans (April 1941). In the meantime, the Italians had been finally defeated in Ethiopia (6 April) by British and imperial troops helped by a small contingent of Free French Forces. In June–July 1941, an Allied force composed of Australian, British, Free French and New-Zealander units conquered Lebanon and Syria over French Vichy troops. At this point, however, the main theatre of operations was situated in eastern Europe. Indeed, on 22 June the Wehrmacht had launched its grand offensive against the Red Army with the help of some Finnish, Italian and Romanian troops. By early August, the Axis forces had won stunning victories, made huge numbers of prisoners and penetrated deep into Soviet territory. But they had failed to break the Red Army and, in some places (mainly the southern and northern ends of the front), they had faced some strong counterattacks and suffered heavy blows. Furthermore, the Soviet government held firm. In November–December, the onslaught was stopped outside Moscow. All in all, the German strategy of bringing down one enemy at a time had failed.

From the beginning of 1942, a balance was gradually established between the two sides. Even if continental Europe was largely dominated by the Axis and its allies, the rise of interior resistance forces (supported by Britain, where possible) was beginning to be felt while groups of partisans were organising, notably in the Balkans and the portions of Soviet territory under Axis occupation, in order to harass the occupier. In the long term, these would be numbered in the hundreds of thousands. In some places, especially in

Greece, Yugoslavia and the USSR, the guerrilla forces would play a growing role throughout the war as the constant threat they represented pinned down forces that the Axis might have employed elsewhere. In France during the summer of 1944, the resistance organisations contributed to the success of the landings and then the advance of the Allies by harassing German forces. Back in late 1941 on the Eastern Front, a strong Soviet counteroffensive (December 1941–February 1942) managed to push the Germans back and alleviate the pressure on Moscow and the centre of the front. On 28 June 1942, the Wehrmacht and its Hungarian, Italian and Romanian allies launched an offensive (Operation Blau) of which the main objectives in the south-east were to capture the city of Stalingrad and then to head to the Caucasus and the Caspian Sea. In November nevertheless, a Soviet counteroffensive (Operation Uranus) began to wipe out the main results achieved by the Axis. From the very beginning, and according to Hitler's orders, the fight in the east had been conceived as a war of annihilation. Huge numbers of prisoners of war were killed outright, or left to die of starvation or exposure, or worked to death; members of the Soviet state apparatus were executed; civilian populations were terrorised and reduced to slavery; scorched-earth strategy was used against partisans; entire villages were burnt down and their populations massacred for harbouring partisans; and hundreds of thousands of Jews were hunted down and slaughtered by special units supported by the Wehrmacht. The military reverses did not change Nazi policy; quite the contrary. Violence on the Eastern Front would reach unimaginable levels, to which the Red Army would retaliate in kind.

During the summer and autumn of 1942, in Libya and in Egypt, British and imperial forces supplemented by units belonging to external European resistances managed to slow down and then stop Rommel's Italo-German units. After the second battle of El-Alamein (October–November 1942), the Axis forces began to retreat towards Tunisia. Forced to fight on two fronts, Hitler had failed on both. At the end of 1942, the situation was becoming even more dire for the Reich as its U-boats had not managed to cut the vital Atlantic lines of supply, the effects of the Allied bombing were beginning to be felt, the American military presence was growing in Britain and, last but not least, the Anglo-American landings in Algeria and Morocco (Operation Torch, 7–8 November 1942) had been a success.

In 1943 and 1944, the Axis definitely lost the initiative and was forced to fight on multiple fronts. On 2 February 1943, the last surviving Germans encircled in Stalingrad surrendered. The Wehrmacht's Sixth Army and the Fourth Romanian Army had been wiped out in the vain attempt to capture the city. Of very important consequences in the field, this Soviet victory was probably even more important on the symbolic and the psychological levels. On 13 May, after a bitter six-month campaign, and despite the initial sending of reinforcements, the last Italo-German units fighting in Tunisia surrendered to the Allies. As a consequence of this second defeat in a few months, the Axis powers were pushed out of North Africa as nearly 250,000 soldiers were taken prisoners and important quantities of military equipment were lost for good. On 10 July, the Anglo-Americans landed in Sicily. By 17 August, the island was conquered. Even if about 100,000 German and Italian soldiers and a great deal of equipment had been evacuated, the result of the operation was clear: from then on, Hitler would be forced to fight on two fronts in continental Europe. In the east in early July, the Wehrmacht had launched an offensive to suppress the Soviet Kursk Salient (Operation Citadel). After this largest tank battle of the war, the German effort was broken. Kursk was followed by the first major Soviet summer offensive (Operations Kutuzov and Rumiantsev). Thus, in the east too, the Axis had lost the initiative. During the very same summer of 1943, the Allies managed to turn the tide in the north Atlantic and secure their lines of supply. Following the Allied landing in southern Italy and the signing of the armistice of Cassibile between Italy and the Allies (3 September), Hitler assigned two German armies to the defence of the peninsula and sent German units to replace Italian occupation forces in France, Greece and Yugoslavia. Nevertheless, the Mediterranean was largely in Allied hands. The year 1944 saw the addition of another front on which the Wehrmacht had to fight. While struggling in Italy but winning the air war over Europe, the Allies managed to land in Normandy on 6 June. Despite a fierce German defence in the Norman bocage, the Allies broke through in late July. On 15–16 August, a second landing took place, this time in Provence, on the French Mediterranean coast. In September, the Allied armies reached Belgium, eastern France and Holland. After a failed attempt to bypass the Siegfried Line and conquer the Ruhr in order to end the war quickly in the West (Operation Market Garden, 17–25 September), the Allies went back to their earlier all-out strategy. In the meantime on the Eastern Front, a huge offensive launched by the Red Army on 22 June (Operation Bagration) and consisting of a sort of Soviet blitzkrieg had literally destroyed the German Central Army Group. By mid-July, the Soviets had reached the Niemen and the Vistula. Even if the Wehrmacht managed to make up for some of its losses, its presence in the USSR was over.

The first months of 1945 saw the Allies go in for the kill. As 1944 came to its end, Hitler made one last attempt to go back to his favourite strategy. He concentrated units, notably armoured ones, for an offensive in the Belgian and Luxembourg Ardennes even if they were desperately needed on the Eastern Front, in the hope of splitting his enemies' forces and forcing the Anglo-American allies to negotiate. Launched on 16 December 1944 and completed on 1 January 1945 by another offensive in the direction of Strasbourg and the Vosges mountains, the attack took the Allies by surprise. A stubborn resistance of American units in the field and the prompt sending of reinforcements by the Allied high command were followed by a proper counterattack. By the end of January, the so-called Battle of the Bulge had turned into a total Allied victory. During the same month, the Red Army broke through German defences on the Vistula. In February and March, while the Soviets were progressing everywhere, the Allies eliminated all German resistance west of the Rhine. April saw the Wehrmacht yield on all fronts. On 7 May in Reims and 8 May in Berlin, the Reich's envoys signed their country's act of unconditional surrender.

Conclusion: New Strategies for a New World

At the end of what some actors and analysts came to call a 'Thirty-Year War', an extensive reorganisation of Europe's devastated territories and traumatised populations was carried out by the victors. It eventually led to the division of the continent into two zones of influence. But, at least, the extremely violent and large-scale warfare experienced by Europe on its soil during the two world wars did not happen again. Outside Europe, in the years following the Second World War, British, French and Dutch imperial possessions rapidly transformed themselves from precious assets to burdens. Furthermore, two new superpowers emerged from the war. The conjunction of their ability to raise huge armies, their modern and very powerful conventional military means, and their capacity to develop and use atomic weapons paved the way for a new strategic era.

12

The Second World War in the Asia–Pacific

DAVID HORNER

The Asia–Pacific War was caused by the expansionist ambitions of Imperial Japan. It was Japan that decided to invade China, to conquer south-east Asia and to go to war with the United States. The last decision is the most intriguing. Considering the industrial strength of the United States and its location far distant across the Pacific Ocean, Japan could never have defeated the United States. Why then did Japan go to war against the one country, the USA, that had the power to crush it? Any discussion of the strategy of the Asia–Pacific War must, therefore, begin with an examination of Japan's decisions both to attack China in 1937 and Pearl Harbor in 1941. Further, because the Allies needed to react to Japan's attacks, Japan's decisions largely shaped Allied strategy.

Sources

The starting point is the official histories of the United States and Britain, which have volumes dealing specifically with the strategic level. Most scholarly and popular books about the whole Pacific War discuss the strategic issues. Their focus, however, is often determined by the nationality of the author – Americans are more likely to focus on the naval war and their books have titles that often refer to the 'Pacific War'. British authors give more attention to Singapore, Burma and India, with titles such as *War in the Far East*. There is also much about Pacific War strategy in the biographies of the key decision makers, from Winston Churchill and Franklin Roosevelt at the top, to strategic-level commanders such as General MacArthur and Admiral King. While books on specific campaigns continue to appear, fewer books on the entire Pacific War have been published since 2000 than in the preceding

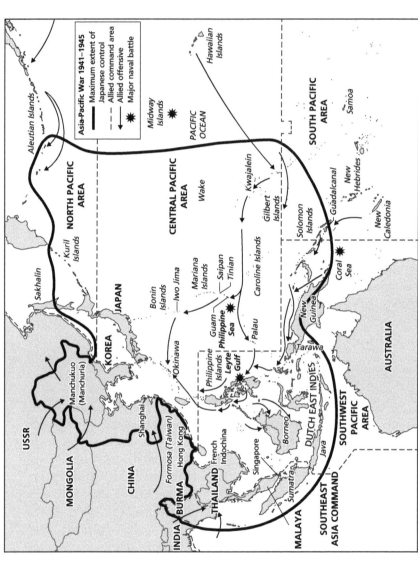

Map 12.1 Asia–Pacific War (1941–1945). Redrawn with permission from the Australian National University, creative commons licence BY SA 4.0.

two decades.[1] Except for the question of whether the atomic bombing of Japan was necessary, most of the issues about Pacific War strategy had been well analysed by 2000. Japan's National Institute of Defence Studies has made available its 102-volume official history written between 1966 and 1980 (although strategy is not covered in any depth and most volumes have not been translated), as well as encouraging contemporary scholarship on Japan's role in the war. This is most valuable, because the Pacific War was all about Japan.

Underlying Causes of the War

The causes of the war reach back to the late nineteenth century. Having emerged from their feudal isolation in the second half of that century, the Japanese were acutely conscious of their vulnerability. Over the preceding centuries European powers (Britain, France, the Netherlands and Germany) had seized colonies in the Asia–Pacific region. The Europeans and the Americans had also won concessions from a weak and disorganised China.

If Japan were to survive against this European threat, it needed to establish a powerful and modern army. Its new army drew its inspiration from Prussia, whose army had been structured for continental warfare in Europe. Japan's leaders saw the nation's destiny to be the dominant continental power in east Asia, rather than a maritime power, which its geography actually dictated. This was to prove a fatal error. Nonetheless, as an archipelagic nation off the coast of Asia, Japan still needed a capable navy. Japan's Navy derived its philosophy from the American strategist Alfred Thayer Mahan, whose 1890 book, *The Influence of Sea Power upon History*, advocated a climactic battle for 'command of the sea'.[2]

To support these forces, Japan began a rapid process of industrialisation, but lacking natural resources, it had to secure supplies of raw materials and find markets for its goods. The Japanese observed that the Europeans had gained economically by exploiting their military and diplomatic power. Taking this lead, in 1894 Japan went to war with China. But to their fury and under pressure from the Western powers, the Japanese were forced to give up some of their gains, and only secured the island of Formosa (Taiwan).

---

1 A notable exception is R. B. Frank, *Tower of Skulls, A History of the Asia–Pacific War* (New York: W. W. Norton & Company, 2020).
2 Alfred Thayer Mahan, *The Influence of Sea Power upon History* (Boston, MA: Little, Brown and Company, 1890).

Following their successful war against Russia in 1904–1905,[3] however, the Japanese gained the Liaotung peninsula in southern Manchuria, and stationed troops to protect the Manchurian railroad. The success of their army and navy was both a source of pride to the Japanese and a warning to the West that a new power had arisen in Asia.

By 1910 Japan had annexed Korea. Further, as one of the Allies in the First World War, Japan seized Germany's possessions in China and the Pacific, and after the war Japan retained the Pacific colonies under a mandate from the League of Nations. Japan's ambition was illustrated in 1918, when the Allies sent troops to Siberia to help the non-Communists during the Russian Civil War. The US president asked Japan to send 7,000 troops; Japan sent 73,000 troops and 50,000 civilian settlers, hoping to form a buffer state against Russia. They did not withdraw until 1922, two years after the other Allies had departed. Japan's willingness to use its military to seek territory or concessions on the Asian mainland set it on a course that led inexorably to war, first with China, and then with the USA.

As the Japanese Empire continued to build, Western countries became concerned. Meanwhile, Japan was feeling aggrieved at the lack of respect from the West. At the Versailles Peace Conference they failed to have racist policies overturned. At a conference in Washington in 1921–1922, the USA, Britain and Japan agreed to limit their capital ships according to a ratio of 5:5:3, which the Japanese saw as an affront. In 1923, Britain ended its alliance with Japan; the following year the USA introduced an Immigration Act, aimed at preventing migration from Japan.

By the mid-1920s, Japan's economy was coming under great strain, and it was particularly hit by the outbreak of the Great Depression in 1929, even more so when the USA 'erected the most formidable tariff barrier in a century'.[4] If the West would not trade, the Japanese felt they had no option but to pursue opportunities in China, which they saw as a weak vulnerable power, but one that was not giving Japan the respect it deserved.

Actors

A democracy in name only, Japan's principal decision makers were its high-level military officers, backed by Emperor Hirohito. By the early 1930s the Japanese government was under increasing pressure from militant

---

3 As discussed in Chapter 6.
4 C. M. L. Paine, *The Japanese Empire: Grand Strategy from the Meiji Restoration to the Pacific War* (Cambridge: Cambridge University Press, 2017), 113.

nationalistic groups, led by young army officers, who exploited the economic crisis. The Japanese had not been defeated by a foreign power in a thousand years, and their militarism was built on their belief in their national uniqueness and heaven-granted mandate to assume leadership in east Asia.

The political strength of the Japanese military was demonstrated in 1931 when the semi-autonomous Japanese *Kwantung* Army, policing the Japanese-owned Manchurian railroad, contrived an incident with the Chinese and soon took control of Manchuria and nearby Chinese provinces. Powerless, the Japanese government acquiesced, and Japan established a puppet state: Manchukuo. This so-called Manchurian Incident marked the beginning of full-scale Japanese aggression in Asia. When the League of Nations branded Japan as the aggressor, Japan withdrew from the League.

Despite its belligerent attitude, the Japanese government was actually in disarray – what commentator Hugh Byas described as 'government by assassination'.[5] Two prime ministers and several leading politicians were assassinated before young officers mounted an unsuccessful *coup d'état* in 1936. The army leaders, standing aloof from the rebels, gained even more power. Under the Japanese constitution the emperor commanded the army and the navy, and the Parliament (the Diet) had little control over them. The army and the navy ministers were serving officers, and if they resigned, they could bring down the government. In effect, the military ran the government, and they pressed to expand their activities in China. Behind them were the powerful industrial conglomerates who would reap immense profits from war production.

Japan's expansionist policy was shaped by two competing strategies: continental and maritime. The army, the advocate for a continental strategy, wanted to continue expanding into northern China, but needed to be ready to deal with the threat from Soviet Russia. In November 1936 the army negotiated the Anti-Comintern Pact with Germany and Italy. It was directed squarely against the Soviet Union, which was supporting China.

The navy saw that the army's policy would curtail plans to build more ships. Instead, the navy proposed expanding into south-east Asia, which would provide vital natural resources. Under pressure from both services, the Japanese Cabinet undertook to pursue both the continental and maritime strategies. This required the expansion of both forces, although the army still received substantially more funds. Neither service was fully happy, but the Japanese had no proper mechanism for co-ordinating national strategy. In

---

5 Hugh Byas, *Government by Assassination* (New York: Alfred A. Knopf, 1942).

1937, the army and the navy headquarters staffs came together to form Imperial General Headquarters, but as the staffs continued to prepare their own plans, it failed to provide unity of command. The one mechanism for reconciling competing views was the Imperial Liaison Conference, presided over by Emperor Hirohito, who rarely spoke and exercised little power.[6]

Adversaries

During the 1930s, Japan's principal adversary was China, with the Soviet Union a secondary adversary. In July 1937, when shots were fired between Chinese and Japanese forces near Peking (Beijing), the Nationalist Chinese leader, Chiang Kai-shek, thought the time had arrived to resist Japan. Japan quickly deployed forces into northern China and landed troops near Shanghai. To some historians, the China Incident, as the Japanese called it, marks the beginning of the Second World War. When in October President Franklin Roosevelt finally condemned Japan's aggression, a leading Japanese diplomat, Matsuoka Yosuke, soon to be foreign minister, retorted, 'Japan is expanding and what country in its expansion era has ever failed to be trying to its neighbours?'[7]

Thrusting deeper into China, by the end of 1938 Japan had captured large areas of the north, the Yangtze valley and pockets along the coast. Japan deployed about 600,000 soldiers in these campaigns.[8] The troops were well-trained and experienced. One of the strengths of the Japanese armed forces was the Bushido code of honour; the way of the warrior. All members were responsible directly to the emperor, and often conducted suicidal banzai charges with the troops shouting the battle cry, 'Long live the Emperor!'

Poorly equipped and inadequately trained, the Chinese armed forces were divided between those under the control of the Nationalist Chinese government, those organised by the Communist Party, and those under various warlords.[9] The Nationalist Army in 1937 numbered about 1.2 million, the Communist Army about 92,000. Although driven inland, the Nationalists would not give up and worked hard to win American support. Pursuing a flawed military strategy, Japan had been drawn further into China, but had

---

6 However, H. P. Bix, *Hirohito and the Making of Modern Japan* (New York: Harper Collins, 2000) argues otherwise.
7 John Toland, *The Rising Sun: The Decline and Fall of the Japanese Empire 1936–1945* (London: Cassell & Company, 1970), 48.
8 E. J. Drea, *Japan's Imperial Army: Its Rise and Fall, 1853–1945* (Lawrence: University Press of Kansas, 2009), 197.
9 Also discussed in Chapter 7.

not obtained the expected economic benefits. Eventually, in July 1939 the United States announced that it would be abrogating the 1911 Treaty of Commerce and Navigation with Japan. Economic sanctions were likely to follow.

The Japanese now faced a dilemma. They could not conquer all of China, and the war was a heavy drain on their resources, fuel and finances. Its national strategy of seeking an empire in China had proved a disaster. To conclude the war, Japan needed fuel and other resources from south-east Asia. If Western countries would not supply this fuel, and this was becoming problematic, then Japan would have to seize it.

Towards the end of 1938 the Japanese prime minister, Prince Konoe Fumimaro, spelt out Japan's plans for a 'New Order for East Asia', involving the eradication of European and American imperialism and also of communism from east Asia. Later the Japanese would declare their national objective to be the setting up of a 'Greater East Asia Co-Prosperity Sphere'. In effect, the Asian countries would be subservient to Japan, providing it with raw materials and markets.

Meanwhile, Soviet support for the Chinese precipitated several clashes between the *Kwantung* Army (about 200,000 troops) and Soviet forces (about 450,000 troops) in the region. Finally, in July 1939 the *Kwantung* Army crossed into Mongolia. A Soviet army mounted a counteroffensive near Nomonhan that killed more than 8,000 Japanese troops. In the midst of this campaign, in August, the Japanese were shocked to learn of the Nazi-Soviet Pact. Then, the following month, Germany invaded Poland, and Britain and France declared war on Germany. Japan quickly arranged a ceasefire in Manchuria.

Bogged down in China and checked by the Soviet Union, the Japanese were unsure of their next step. The German invasion of France in May 1940, however, suddenly offered Japan new opportunities to cut China's overseas supplies. The Japanese Navy now pressed the case for a strike to the south, even if this meant eventual war with the United States, and the army leaders soon supported the southern strike, hoping that it would enable them to end the war in China. The first step, in July 1940, was to demand that Britain close the road from Rangoon in Burma to Chungking, which was supplying the Nationalist government with vital supplies. Preoccupied in Europe, Britain was not strong enough to resist Japan's demands. Japan was now on a clear trajectory for war.

Other Adversaries

Although Japan's principal adversary during the 1930s was China, by its actions it was generating other, more robust, adversaries: the United States, Britain and its empire and, to a lesser extent, the Netherlands. The United States had become a Pacific power in 1898 when it annexed Hawaii, the Philippines and Guam. These actions aroused hostility in Japan, and US military planners soon began to consider how the threat from Japan was to be countered. The US Joint Army and Navy Board developed defensive plans for war with various countries, each designed by a colour. The plan for war with Japan was 'War Plan Orange'. The vital problem was how to defend the Philippines, which in time of war would need to be reinforced from the continental United States. The US Pacific Fleet, formed in 1907, would have the key role, but would need forward-operating bases. In 1908 Pearl Harbor in Hawaii was selected as a major base, with a minor base to be established near Manila in the Philippines.

After the First World War, both Britain and the United States seriously began to consider Japan as a potential enemy in the Pacific, hence the Washington Navy Conference of 1921–1922 that sought to restrict the size of the Japanese Navy. But how was Britain to defend its Pacific colonies as well as Hong Kong, Malaya, Singapore and North Borneo? The independent but thinly populated British dominions of Australia and New Zealand also needed to be defended.

Faced by the conundrum of defending these far-flung territories, in 1923 Britain decided to build a major naval base at Singapore, to which its main fleet would be deployed in time of war with Japan. But with funding scarce, the base was not completed until 1938. There were two fundamental problems with this Singapore strategy. First, it relied on Britain deploying its main fleet to Singapore in order to deter Japan from aggression in the Pacific. But as critics pointed out, Japan was unlikely to act unless Britain was preoccupied in Europe, when it would be reluctant to send its main fleet away from the European theatre. Looking ahead, this is what happened in 1941. Second, the strategy would fail if the Japanese were to capture Singapore. The fortress would be particularly vulnerable if the Japanese landed on the Malayan Peninsula and attacked it from the landward side. This is what happened in 1941–1942. Nonetheless, Australia and New Zealand went along with this faulty strategy.

Following the Washington Navy Conference, the United States dusted off Plan Orange and reshaped it as an offensive strategy following the Mahanian principle of command of the sea. By this stage, the US Pacific Fleet had been reduced to a component of the US fleet. While fighting the next war with battleships remained the dominant philosophy, some senior naval officers saw the potential of naval aviation. In 1936 the US Congress authorised the construction of the first new battleships since 1921, and two years later Congress authorised a 20 per cent increase in the size of the navy.

If the US Navy were to advance across the Pacific, as proposed by Plan Orange, it would need to seize some of the islands controlled by Japan as forward naval and air bases. It might also need to retake Luzon, the main island of the Philippines. The US Marine Corps, which was facing the possibility of disbandment, saw an opportunity and began to develop concepts for amphibious operations. The big question was what do with the Philippines. Neither the army nor the navy were large enough to defend the Philippines properly. The choice was either to try to defend the Philippines at the end of a long line of communications, or to abandon the Philippines and be prepared to fight the way back through Japanese-owned islands.

The army saw its main role as the defence of continental United States by holding a line from Alaska through Hawaii to Panama. The navy wanted to conduct offensive operations forward of this line. The 1938 Plan Orange, a reworking of the original plan, gave the edge to the navy, which would have the basic objective of defeating Japan, assisted by the army once the situation allowed. Events in Europe, however, began to raise the possibility that the United States might need to fight a war in both the Atlantic and the Pacific Oceans. Beginning in 1939, the Joint Board developed five so-called Rainbow Plans, covering a range of contingencies for war in the two hemispheres.

Proximate Causes of the War

The underlying cause of the war had been simmering for half a century, but the proximate causes only became evident after the German occupation of France in May 1940 spurred the Americans into action. The Pacific ships of the US fleet were deployed to Pearl Harbor, and the following month the United States began a large naval expansion programme so that the navy could operate in both the Atlantic and Pacific Oceans. In September the Japanese occupied bases in northern Indochina, from which its planes could attack southern China. The same month, the US Congress agreed to a peacetime draft.

The United States imposed a further trade embargo on Japan, while in September 1940, Japan, Germany and Italy signed the Tripartite Pact, which recognised Japan's leadership in establishing a new order in greater east Asia. But there would be little co-ordination of the Axis powers' strategies. In December, the United States made $100 million in credit available to the Chinese Nationalist government. The Japanese Navy reacted by ordering a full mobilisation, a process that would be completed by December 1941.

With war becoming increasingly likely, Britain, the USA (concerned for the security of the Philippines), Australia and the Dutch East Indies considered defensive plans in south-east Asia. Belatedly, Britain built up its garrison in Malaya and Singapore with British, Indian and Australian troops. But under great pressure in Europe and the Middle East, Britain did not give Malaya high priority.

In November 1940, the US chief of naval operations, Admiral Harold Stark, prepared a memorandum known as Plan Dog, in which he argued that the United States might need to fight a war in both the Atlantic and the Pacific theatres. In what an American official historian called 'perhaps the most important single document in the development of World War II strategy', Stark contended that the United States would need to remain on the defensive in the Pacific while it first won the war in the Atlantic.[10] The Joint Board approved the document on 21 December 1940.

Building on this development, between January and March 1941, senior British and American military officers conferred in Washington to consider the strategy to be employed if both countries became involved in a war with German and Japan. Their agreed strategy, known as ABC-1, was similar to Plan Dog and was later described as the 'Beat Hitler First' strategy. It became the foundation of US–British coalition strategy once war eventuated.

The importance of this strategy was emphasised when in February 1941, the US fleet was split into three fleets, the Atlantic, the Pacific and the Asiatic. By December 1941, the Pacific Fleet, based at Pearl Harbor, would include nine battleships, three carriers, twenty-one heavy and light cruisers, sixty-seven destroyers and twenty-seven submarines. The smaller Asiatic Fleet, based at Manila, would have three cruisers, thirteen destroyers, twenty-nine submarines, two seaplane tenders and sixteen gunboats.

---

10 L. Morton, *Strategy and Command: The First Two Years* (Washington, DC: Office of the Chief of Military History, 1962), 81.

For the Japanese planners, the German attack on Russia on 22 June 1941 fundamentally changed the situation. Japan could either fall on Russia's Far East empire while Russia was still fighting for its life in Europe, or it could continue its southern expansion secure in the knowledge that Russia would be too preoccupied to attack in Manchuria. In April, Japan had signed a non-aggression pact with the Soviet Union. On 2 July Japan decided to strike south by seizing bases in southern Indochina.

US cryptanalysts had broken the Japanese diplomatic ciphers and Japan's decision was known within a few days in Washington, London and Canberra. Thus, Roosevelt was well prepared when on 24 July the Japanese moved into southern Indochina. Two days later the USA, in agreement with the British and the Dutch, froze Japanese assets and applied a further trade embargo. That same day General Douglas MacArthur, a retired American officer commanding the Philippines Army, was recalled to the colours and appointed commander of the US Army in the Far East. On 1 August Roosevelt ordered an embargo on high octane gasoline and crude oil exports.

The embargoes had a devastating effect on the Japanese economy. Neither the Japanese government nor its people were willing to accept the massive loss of face that would result from withdrawing from China. There was no alternative but to seize the resources they needed from Malaya and the Dutch East Indies. The Japanese Navy planners also believed that the USA would not remain neutral, and with its forces in the Philippines, it could strike at the flanks of Japanese invasion fleets. But would the United States have actually gone to war if Japan had not attacked Pearl Harbor and the Philippines, and rather had just attacked the British and Netherlands colonies? The answer is not certain.

Japan's Objectives

The Japanese Navy had been preparing for war with the USA for many years. Imbued with Mahan's philosophy of the climactic battle, the navy planned to seize the Philippines and Guam. Then, when the US Navy deployed to recover these territories, the Japanese Navy would destroy the US fleet. By December 1941 Japan's Navy would number 391 warships, including 10 battleships and 10 aircraft carriers. It was the world's third most powerful navy, and, unlike the US and British navies, it would only operate in the Pacific. It was a well-trained force; its gunnery was good and its navigators skilful. Its strength was the naval air force, with its 1,750 fighters, torpedo bombers and bombers, operating from both aircraft carriers and island bases. By comparison with the combined Allied fleets in the Pacific, the Japanese Navy had the same number of battleships and ten against only four Allied carriers.[11]

The commander-in-chief of the Japanese fleet, Admiral Yamamoto Isoruku, had served in the USA, knew the power of the American industrial base and was opposed to war. However, he became convinced that if war was inevitable, the only hope was to abandon the passive strategy of waiting for the US Pacific Fleet, but rather to destroy it with a daring pre-emptive strike at its Pearl Harbor base. The strike was approved and Yamamoto selected the date for the attack, the morning of Sunday 7 December, when most of the US fleet including its aircraft carriers was usually in port for the weekend.

The Japanese also planned near-simultaneous attacks on Hong Kong, Malaya, British Borneo, Guam, Wake and the Philippines, with invasions of Burma and the Dutch East Indies to follow. The offensives would use only a small percentage of the Japanese Army, which numbered 1.7 million soldiers in fifty-one divisions. Most of the army, twenty-seven divisions, was stationed in China, with a further thirteen in the *Kwantung* Army.

The Japanese knew that they could not defeat the United States, but planned to seize and fortify a defensive perimeter that would stretch from the Kuriles, north of Japan, through Wake Island in the mid Pacific, include the Marshall Islands, continue through the Solomon Islands and New Guinea, and include all of the Dutch East Indies and Burma. Having smashed the Pacific Fleet, the Japanese planned to defend this perimeter until the United States grew weary of war and agreed to negotiate a favourable peace. The strategy completely misread the resolve of the American people, who would be determined to avenge the attack on Pearl Harbor.

The Japanese government tried to negotiate with the United States, but its unreasonable demands were not accepted. When the war minister, General Tojo Hideki, declared that he had lost confidence in the negotiations advocated by the prime minister, Prince Konoe, Konoe resigned, and on 17 October Tojo became prime minister, while retaining his posts as war and home ministers. Known as 'the razor', Tojo was determined to establish Japanese primacy in the Far East, defeat the Western nations that had colonies in the Far East, incorporate China into Japan and establish the East Asia Co-Prosperity Sphere in the countries of south-east Asia.

---

11 S. E. Morison, *The Rising Sun in the Pacific, 1931-April 1942* (Boston: Little, Brown and Company, 1988), 58.

On 2 November, Tojo appeared before the emperor and argued that Japan had to seize the moment. Three days later the Japanese government issued war orders and gave its diplomats until 25 November to solve the problem. This was unlikely and the Japanese leaders knew it. Germany had not been consulted or even warned of the impending attack. On 26 November the fleet to attack Pearl Harbor set sail.

Japan's Successful Military Strategy

Beginning with an amphibious landing in north-east Malaya in the early hours of 8 December 1941, over the following fourteen hours the Japanese also attacked Hawaii, Thailand, the Philippines, Guam Island, Hong Kong and Wake Island. The most dramatic of these attacks was the strike at Pearl Harbor by carrier-borne aircraft on the morning of 7 December (Hawaii time). Catching the Americans unaware, Japanese aircraft sunk six US battleships and damaged three. Three light cruisers, three destroyers and four other vessels were also sunk or damaged. On the airfields, 188 aircraft were destroyed and another 159 damaged. It was an overwhelming tactical victory, but not the strategic victory for which the Japanese had hoped. In due course, all but three US ships were repaired and returned to service. Furthermore, the carriers and heavy cruisers were at sea at the time of the attack and escaped damage.

The Pearl Harbor attack produced three important outcomes. First, the appointment of Admiral Chester Nimitz as commander-in-chief of the Pacific Fleet (after his predecessor had been sacked) brought to the theatre a commander who would prove to be an outstanding strategist. Second, the US Navy was forced to rely on its aircraft carriers rather than its battleships to take the fight to the enemy; it marked the demise of battleships as the major maritime strike weapon, although they still remained the most important ships for the exercise of sea control. Third, the attack was a tremendous blow to American pride. Before the attack, the USA had been largely isolationist; after the attack its people would not rest until Japan had been defeated.

Japan's other attacks were also outstandingly successful, revealing the high competence of its forces and the shortcomings of the defenders. The advance down the Malay Peninsula against a numerically larger British, Australian and Indian Army was a brilliant demonstration of aggression, audacity and determination.

Setting Priorities

As well as China, Japan was now at war with Britain and its empire, Australia, Canada, New Zealand, the Netherlands and USA. On the other hand, on 11 December, Nazi Germany declared war on the USA, with the potential of diverting the United States from the war in the Pacific. The British prime minister, Winston Churchill, moved quickly to consolidate support from the United States. Between 22 December 1941 and 14 January 1942, he and his military advisers conferred with President Roosevelt and his advisers in Washington to set Allied priorities. This so-called Arcadia Conference was to have a profound effect on the war's strategy. Churchill and Roosevelt agreed that they alone would determine Allied strategy.

They would be advised by a new body, the Combined Chiefs of Staff, consisting of the chiefs of staff of the two countries and based in Washington. The United States was represented by its newly formed Joint Chiefs of Staff, consisting of General George Marshall, US Army chief of staff, Lieutenant General Henry ('Hap') Arnold, chief of the US Army Air Forces, Admiral Stark, chief of naval operations, and Admiral Ernest King, newly appointed commander-in-chief of the US fleet.

Roosevelt and Churchill agreed that the Beat Hitler First strategy, decided the previous March, would remain unchanged. Admiral King, a rude, abrasive Anglophobe, never fully accepted this strategy and continued to argue for more forces for the Pacific. He would play a major role in shaping the Pacific War.

No strategy works without appropriate command structures to implement it, and the Arcadia Conference took the first step towards establishing joint allied commands. Chiang Kai-shek was appointed supreme commander of the China theatre (with a US deputy), underlining that China was part of the Allied war effort and needed to be supported.

More immediately, British General Sir Archibald Wavell was appointed to commander-in-chief of ABDA (American–British–Dutch–Australian) command, responsible for all Allied operations from Burma, through Malaya, the Dutch East Indies to the Philippines. With his headquarters on Java, Wavell had inadequate forces for his task, and co-ordination was lacking. The Japanese captured Singapore on 15 February, sending thousands of British, Australian and Indian troops into captivity. Wavell's forces could not stop the Japanese invasions of the Dutch East Indies, and by early March ABDA command had ceased to exist. By the end of March, the Japanese had seized most of Burma (cutting the land route to China), Malaya, Singapore, Borneo, the Dutch East Indies, New Britain and the north coast of Australian New Guinea.

The problem for the Americans was the defence of the Philippines. As a former chief of staff of the US Army, General MacArthur was highly influential in Washington and demanded reinforcements. Meanwhile, his underequipped Filipino and American troops had been driven into the Bataan Peninsula and the island of Corregidor, eventually being forced to surrender. The small US Asiatic Fleet had sailed to the Dutch East Indies where it was progressively destroyed. On 12 March, under orders from the president, MacArthur was withdrawn to Australia.

In an effort to reinforce the Philippines, the Americans sent a convoy carrying aircraft to Australia, hoping that the aircraft could then fly to the Philippines. This reinforcement never happened, but it led to a build-up of US forces in Australia. Further, in an ultimately unsuccessful effort to persuade the Australian government to deploy its divisions returning from the Middle East to the Far East rather than to Australia, President Roosevelt sent an infantry division to Australia. These decisions had a 'profound effect on the war in the Pacific'.[12] Basing troops in Australia had never been part of Plan Orange.

The focus on Australia also affected the Japanese, who were deciding their own priorities. Afflicted with what some historians call 'the victory disease', senior navy officers in Imperial General Headquarters advocated an invasion of Australia. The army strongly resisted the navy's plan as it could not spare the ten or perhaps twelve divisions from China and Manchuria, and the ships needed for an invasion could not be released from their prime task of transporting the newly won raw materials from south-east Asia to Japan. Instead, the army preferred an offensive in Burma and India.

In any case, the navy was not unanimous about the need to invade Australia. Admiral Yamamoto wanted to attack Midway in the central Pacific, to draw the US Pacific Fleet into battle. A compromise was reached: the invasions of Australia and India were put aside, and on 15 March Imperial General Headquarters agreed to capture Port Moresby and the southern Solomons, and 'to isolate Australia' by seizing Fiji, Samoa and New Caledonia.[13] If Australia could be isolated, it would no longer be a base for an American counteroffensive.

America's Strategy

With the British pushed out of south-east Asia, the Pacific was now an American theatre to be run by the Joint Chiefs of Staff. Admiral King had taken over from Stark as chief of naval operations while retaining his post as

---

12 Morton, *Strategy and Command*, 198.
13 Samuel Milner, *Victory in Papua* (Washington, DC: Office of the Chief of Military History, 1957), 13.

commander-in-chief of the US fleet. A little later Admiral William Leahy was brought out of retirement to become Roosevelt's chief of staff and to chair the Joint Chiefs.

Unity of command demanded that one officer command the whole Pacific theatre, but inter-service jealousies came into play. The navy did not trust MacArthur to command the navy, and the army could not envisage its forces being commanded by a naval officer. The Joint Chiefs, therefore, divided the Pacific into two theatres. Admiral Nimitz in Hawaii would command the Pacific Ocean Area, which covered most of the Pacific Ocean, and MacArthur in Australia would command the South West Pacific Area, which included Australia, New Guinea, the islands of south-east Asia and the Philippines. MacArthur would command all of Australia's combat forces in his area, as well as relatively small numbers of American ships, planes and combat troops. Admiral King would provide direction to Nimitz, on behalf of the Joint Chiefs, and General Marshall would direct MacArthur. With undoubted self-interest, MacArthur declared that 'of all the faulty decisions of the war perhaps the most unexplainable one was the failure to unify the command in the Pacific'.[14]

The other Pacific Allies – Australia, Canada, China, New Zealand and the Netherlands – were dismayed to find themselves with no voice in deciding Pacific strategy, and on 1 April the Pacific War Council was formed in Washington to control the Allied war effort. Chaired by Roosevelt, it included representatives of Britain and the other Allies. However, the Council never operated as intended, and Roosevelt merely used it as a means of passing on information.

Australia in particular felt aggrieved; it was facing the possibility of invasion, and a complete infantry division had been captured by the Japanese. Australia's prime minister John Curtin preferred to try to influence Pacific strategy by communicating directly with Churchill and Roosevelt. Australia also used MacArthur to put a case directly to Marshall. When he had arrived in Australia from the Philippines, MacArthur had vowed, 'I shall return.' Like the Australians, he opposed the Beat Hitler First strategy, and he implored Washington to send him reinforcements so that he could mount an offensive from Australia.

Allied strategy, however, continued to be shaped by the Japanese. Enraged that American aircraft, flying from an aircraft carrier, had attacked the Japanese home islands, Yamamoto decided to attack Midway. Meanwhile,

14 D. MacArthur, *Reminiscences* (New York: McGraw-Hill, 1964), 172–3.

the Japanese continued their thrust into the south-west Pacific to isolate Australia. In early May a Japanese invasion force sailing to seize Port Moresby on the south coast of New Guinea was intercepted by an Allied naval force with two carriers. In the Battle of the Coral Sea, the Japanese and the Americans each lost a carrier and had another damaged. Although the Japanese had achieved a slight tactical victory, they called off their attack on Port Moresby, and Yamamoto would have two fewer carriers for his Midway operation – a critical deficiency.

Warned by intercepts of Japanese signals, Nimitz deployed three carriers to meet the Japanese fleet with four carriers near Midway. In the crucial battle of the Pacific War, on 4 June 1942, the Americans sunk all four Japanese fleet carriers for the loss of one of their own. With these losses, Japan postponed its plans to seize New Caledonia, Fiji and Samoa; instead, it was even more urgent to capture Port Moresby. The Japanese, therefore, decided to land army troops on the north coast of Papua (New Guinea) and take Port Moresby by land.

The US Navy's success at Midway encouraged the US Joint Chiefs, and on 2 July they ordered an offensive in the New Guinea–Solomons area to recapture Rabaul, the main Japanese base on the island of New Britain. Because of inter-service jealousy, responsibility for the offensive was split. A US naval force under Vice-Admiral Robert Ghormley was ordered to seize several islands in the southern Solomons, including Guadalcanal. MacArthur planned to occupy the north coast of Papua, where airstrips would be prepared to support his advance towards Rabaul.

Unfortunately for these plans, the Japanese moved first, landing on the north coast of Papua on 21 July to advance on Port Moresby. MacArthur's forces, mainly Australians, were drawn into a protracted campaign in Papua. Meanwhile, US Marines landed on Guadalcanal. Over the next six months MacArthur's Australian and American soldiers in Papua and US Marines (later joined by army troops) at Guadalcanal fought bitter, protracted and ultimately successful campaigns against the Japanese. In naval battles around Guadalcanal, the US Navy lost twenty-nine ships including two carriers, and the Japanese lost thirty-eight ships, including two battleships and a light carrier. In the midst of the campaign, Ghormley was relieved by Vice-Admiral William Halsey, bringing to the fore another major commander of the Pacific War.

The Counteroffensive Strategies

In January 1943, as the Guadalcanal and Papua campaigns were ending, Roosevelt and Churchill, with their military advisers, met at Casablanca, Morocco, to set the strategic direction for the coming year. One key decision was to declare that they would accept nothing but unconditional surrender from the Axis powers. Although the leaders relegated the Pacific War to fifth on the list of priorities (after the Atlantic, Russia, the Mediterranean, and the United Kingdom), the directive of 2 July 1942 to capture Rabaul remained unchanged. Again, the tasks were shared. Halsey's South Pacific Area would advance through the Solomon Islands to Rabaul. Meanwhile, MacArthur's forces would advance through New Guinea to seize the western end of New Britain.

Halsey's offensive began in June 1943 with hard-grinding battles on New Georgia, and by November his forces had reached the northern Solomons island of Bougainville. The fighting in the New Guinea area was marked by fewer naval engagements but larger land operations than in the Solomons. Five Australian infantry divisions conducted a series of operations that included two amphibious landings. In December, a US Marine division landed on New Britain and in January 1944 a US Army division landed further along the New Guinea coast.

Even before these operations began, the US Joint Chiefs had begun considering the Pacific strategy to be pursued once Rabaul was taken. Plan Orange had envisioned an advance, island to island, across the central Pacific to relieve the Philippines, and Admiral King strongly advocated this long-anticipated approach. MacArthur, however, wanted to continue along the north coast of New Guinea, whence he could strike at the Philippines. Critics have argued that either approach would have been better than a dual thrust, but inter-service jealousies came into play. On 8 May 1943, the Joint Chiefs accepted the principle of a dual thrust, a strategy that was only possible because of the overwhelming strength of the Americans.

This strategy was confirmed when Churchill, Roosevelt and their advisers met in Washington later in the month. More broadly, they agreed that British forces in India would invade Burma with the aim of opening a land route to China, and that US submarines would attack the Japanese lines of communication. The Americans would start bombing Japan as bases in China and the Pacific became available, they would capture Japanese-held areas of New Guinea, and would seize the Marshall and Caroline Islands. As the year progressed, the Joint Chiefs agreed it was no longer necessary to capture Rabaul. With the green light for an advance through the central Pacific, King pressed for more ambitious operations.

To counter the Americans offensives, in September 1943 Japan's Imperial General Headquarters restructured its war strategy. Japanese forces would hold a strongly manned and fortified line running from western New Guinea to the Caroline Islands (called the absolute zone of national defence), while they regained their strength for a final decisive battle in 1944. MacArthur's forces breached this line before it could be prepared.

It was not until the latter months of 1943 that the US Navy had gathered the necessary strength to prosecute its campaign in the central Pacific. Nimitz now had ten large and medium carriers, seven escort carriers and a dozen battleships, and these formed the key elements of the Fifth Fleet under Vice-Admiral Raymond Spruance. This force began conducting raids on Japanese island bases, and these were followed in November 1943 by landings on Tarawa and Makin in the Gilbert Islands. In January 1944, US Marine and Army troops landed on Kwajalein in the Marshall Islands, followed by the seizure of Eniwetok the following month.

With the US Navy moving faster than expected in the central Pacific, MacArthur was fearful of being left behind. In a spectacular campaign beginning in April 1944, his American forces conducted a series of landings along the north coast of New Guinea, advancing 1,400 kilometres in three months.

While MacArthur was advancing, Nimitz was focusing on Saipan and Tinian in the Mariana Islands, whose airfields were within bombing range of Japan. Realising the danger, the Japanese deployed nine carriers and 450 aircraft to attack the American invasion fleet. The Japanese were totally outclassed by American aircraft and their more skilful pilots. In the 'Great Marianas Turkey Shoot' on 15 June 1944, the Japanese lost three fleet carriers and 400 aircraft; the Americans lost 130 aircraft. Onshore, US Marine and Army troops took until 9 July before they could secure Saipan. By this stage, the Americans had refined their amphibious landing techniques and had introduced innovative equipment such as tracked amphibious vehicles. Many historians consider that America's system of amphibious warfare was the Pacific War's most important contribution to military strategy. The defeat of the Japanese carrier force and the seizure of the Marianas were a severe blow to the Japanese high command. On 18 July 1944, Tojo resigned as prime minister and war minister. Lieutenant General Koiso Kuniaki succeeded him as prime minister.

Throughout the campaigns in the south-west and central Pacific, operations were also taking place in Burma. In October 1943, the Allied South East Asia Command was formed under Admiral Lord Louis Mountbatten, with its headquarters in Ceylon (Sri Lanka). Its tasks were to increase pressure on the Japanese and thus force them to transfer forces from the Pacific theatre, to maintain the airborne supply route to China and to open a land route through northern Burma to China. To pre-empt the expected Allied offensive, the Japanese commander in Burma decided to strike into India. The offensive began in Arakan near the coast in February 1944 and then moved to the Imphal area, leading to the northern Indian state of Assam. In major battles, the British–Indian Army defeated the Japanese offensive, causing disastrous Japanese losses.

The main strategic purpose of the Burma campaign was to open a resupply route to China. Since July 1942, China had been resupplied by American transport aircraft flying over the mountains from India. Chiang Kai-shek realised that the Allies were going to win the war and he wanted to preserve his armies for a future war against the Communists. But he needed to give the impression that he was fighting the Japanese in order to maintain the flow of American arms and equipment. In April 1944 the Japanese began a major offensive to overrun the Allied airfields in southern China. The Japanese were successful, but called off the offensive as they transferred troops to the Pacific, and to Manchuria to meet an increasing Russian threat. The war in China cost the lives of 1.3 million Chinese troops and tied down 1 million Japanese troops, but in reality, after 1942 it was a sideshow in a war that was won and lost in the Pacific.

In the Pacific, the American submarine campaign against Japanese merchant shipping was strangling the Japanese home economy and starving the forward areas of reinforcements, supplies and equipment. At the beginning of 1944, the Japanese had 4.8 million tons of merchant shipping; by the end of the year this was down to 2.7 million tons.[15]

Conclusive Campaigns

Despite the Allied counteroffensives, in mid-October 1944, the Japanese East Asia Co-Prosperity Sphere was still largely intact. Nonetheless, the Japanese Navy had been decimated and it had lost large numbers of irreplaceable naval

---

15 J. Ellis, *Brute Force: Allied Strategy and Tactics in the Second World War* (London: Andre Deutsch, 1990), 472.

aircraft and pilots. Military leaders in Tokyo knew that they had no hope of victory. Yet equally, there was no thought of surrender and they hoped that, somehow, they might resist their attackers, perhaps obtaining a negotiated peace. The Allies were never likely to contemplate such an outcome.

The shape of the last year of the Pacific War was set at important meetings in Quebec and Washington in mid-September and early October 1944. During the previous six months, Churchill had been engaged in a bitter dispute with his military advisers, seeking their agreement to a British-led invasion of Sumatra. The British chiefs keenly opposed Churchill's plan, but they recognised that Britain needed to play a more substantial role in the Pacific War. Roosevelt accepted Britain's offer of a major fleet to operate with the US Navy in the Pacific. The Americans, however, would conduct the remainder of the offensives, including the strategic bombing campaign against Japan and a landing at Mindanao in the southern Philippines.

In the midst of the conference came news from Admiral Halsey, whose carrier-borne aircraft had struck the central Philippines, that there would be little Japanese opposition on Leyte Island. On 15 September, the Joint Chiefs approved a landing by MacArthur's forces on Leyte, beginning on 20 October. The landing on Mindanao was abandoned. Finally, on 3 October, the Joint Chiefs agreed that after taking Leyte, MacArthur should invade Luzon, while Nimitz's Pacific command would seize Iwo Jima and move on to Okinawa on 1 March 1945.

MacArthur's forces duly landed on Leyte on 20 October, initially against light opposition. But the Japanese Navy reacted with three striking forces, initiating one of the largest and most decisive naval battles in history – the Battle of Leyte Gulf. The Japanese lost four carriers, three battleships, nine cruisers and ten destroyers, and never recovered from this defeat. The battle on land proved more difficult and protracted than expected. Nonetheless, on 9 January 1945 MacArthur's forces were able to land on the main island of Luzon, and advance quickly to Manila.

Meanwhile, once Saipan and Tinian in the Marianas were captured and airfields constructed, the new B-29 Superfortress bombers of the US Twentieth Air Force started a bombing campaign against Japan, initially without great success. Its commander, Major General Curtis Le May, reported directly to the Joint Chiefs through the chief of the US Army Air Forces, General Arnold. Le May changed tactics from high-level daylight raids against specific targets to low-level night attacks with incendiaries against area targets. The first attack on Tokyo on 9–10 March succeeded beyond expectations; more than 80,000 inhabitants were killed and 40,000 wounded, and 250,000 buildings were destroyed. Le May stepped up the offensive against other cities. The strategic bombing campaign complemented the Allied blockade of the Japanese home islands applied by the submarine campaign and the aerial mining of Japanese waters. The blockade had a devastating effect on the Japanese economy and people.

The Japanese Empire was now under attack in other areas – Burma (where the British–Indian Army had mounted a successful invasion), China and in the bypassed islands of New Guinea, the Solomons, southern Philippines and Borneo. These latter campaigns, fought by Australians and the US Eighth Army, were strategically irrelevant, as the Americans closed off Japan from the south. In February–March 1945, at great cost, US Marines captured the island of Iwo Jima. Then on 1 April, a massive American force, supported by the British Pacific Fleet, invaded Okinawa. The Japanese resisted fiercely, as they considered the Ryukyu Islands to be part of their home territory. The US naval force numbered 1,300 ships, the land force 250,000 troops. It took until 22 June to secure the island. The Japanese had launched 1,900 kamikaze (suicide) planes against the US fleet, had sunk 36 US ships and had damaged 368.

The outcome of the battle was deeply troubling to the Americans. On 25 May, MacArthur and Nimitz were ordered to prepare for an invasion of Japan, beginning with Kyushu on 1 November. On the basis of the casualties on Okinawa, the Americans could expect more than a quarter of a million casualties in Kyushu. In the home islands, the Japanese Army was rapidly forming new divisions to repel the expected American invasion. Soon it would number 2 million troops, to be supported by a National Volunteer Force with a potential strength of 28 million.

By this time, the Allied leaders were meeting in Potsdam, Germany, where on 26 July the Allies issued the Potsdam Declaration, promising utter destruction of the Japanese homeland unless there was an unconditional surrender. The Japanese rejected this demand two days later.

On 6 August an American B-29 based at Tinian dropped an atomic bomb on the city of Hiroshima, killing some 78,000 inhabitants. Again, the Americans asked for surrender, promising another attack. The Japanese hoped the Soviet Union might assist in negotiations with the Americans. They received their answer on 8 August, when the Soviet Union declared war. Next morning, Soviet forces invaded Manchuria, just ahead of news of another atomic bomb being dropped, on Nagasaki, killing 35,000.

The double shock of the atomic bombs and the Russian attack decided the issue. Late on 14 August, Japan informed the Allies that it had accepted the Allied terms. The next day, the emperor broadcast his orders to cease hostilities.

In Manchuria, however, the war continued briefly, as the Soviets sought to gain territory. The Japanese leaders formally signed the surrender document on the US battleship, USS *Missouri*, in Tokyo Bay on 2 September 1945.

Conclusion

The Asia–Pacific War was not just a clash of imperial powers, but also a clash of cultures, with both sides holding beliefs of racial superiority. Japan was driven by notions of heaven-sent destiny, national superiority and emperor worship. The United States, the 'bastion of democracy', moved from isolationism to a developing belief in a world mission. Britain sought to hold on to its crumbling empire.

In going to war in 1941, Japan had pursued a disastrous strategy. Yet many Japanese still believe that they had no alternative and had been pushed into the war by the economic embargoes. They do not take into account that the embargoes were triggered by the war in China, in turn caused by expansionist policies that went back to the late nineteenth century. The Japanese failed to reconcile their continental and maritime strategies, and most of their army remained in China and Manchuria. Imperial General Headquarters did not provide coherent strategic direction. Ironically, however, the Japanese actually achieved one of their war aims: the decolonisation of Asia. But through their harsh treatment of the native people, the Japanese forfeited any claims to being superior to the former European masters.

The Allies too had their weaknesses. Britain's Singapore strategy was a disaster; as a result, after the war Australia and New Zealand sought security in an alliance with the United States. The Americans failed to provide unity of command and employ a consistent overall war strategy. But because of America's industrial power and the size of the forces it could deploy, these shortcomings did not ultimately prove detrimental.

Industrial power and size are key ingredients in strategy. During the war, the USA constructed almost 300,000 aircraft, 88,000 landing craft, 215 submarines, 147 carriers and 952 other warships. Japan could never come close to the US rate of munitions production, for example, building only thirteen aircraft carriers of all types. Only the USA had the industrial and scientific capacity to build the atomic bombs that ended the war. Size and power, not necessarily strategic acumen, remained the hallmark of US strategy in the post-war era. Moreover, at first glance, it seemed that within an instant all the strategies of the Pacific War had become outdated, as the world faced the prospect of nuclear war.

13

Soviet Strategy, 1945–1989

LAURIEN CRUMP

Sources

Soviet strategy during the Cold War covers a wide span of events, ranging from nuclear strategy to military interventions on the global arena, such as the one in Afghanistan in December 1979 or the covert involvement in the Korean War through involving Soviet air-force pilots from 1951 onwards under Chinese or North-Korean markings. Since all of these are separately treated in this volume, I will focus on Soviet strategy within Europe in this chapter. In recent years, some war plans have become available, which form a blueprint for a Soviet invasion in western Europe, such as the 1964 Warsaw Pact war plan which envisages conquering Lyon after nine days.[1] This is, however, the *theory* of Soviet strategy, since no such plan ever materialised. Concerning Europe, the Kremlin only embarked on interventions *within* rather than *beyond* its own influence sphere in Europe in *practice*, something that ironically defied theory: according to Marxist–Leninist ideology, socialism was an inevitable end goal that would liberate the working classes rather than suppress them. I have therefore chosen to focus on the Soviet interventions *within* the Soviet bloc throughout the Cold War, namely the deployment of Soviet troops in East Germany (GDR) in 1953, in Hungary in 1956 and in Czechoslovakia in 1968.

A wealth of literature is available on Soviet strategy, but the abovementioned interventions have hardly been studied in that light, since it was never the Kremlin's *intention* to intervene within its own orbit, but rather a necessity

[1] 'Parallel history project on cooperative security: taking Lyon on the ninth day? The 1964 Warsaw Pact plan for a nuclear war in Europe and related documents', PHP Publications Series (Washington, DC and Zurich: 2000), www.files.ethz.ch/isn/108642 /warplan_dossier.pdf.

Soviet Strategy, 1945–1989

Map 13.1 The Deployment of Warsaw Pact Ground Forces. Redrawn with permission from NATO cartography section, www.nato.int/cps/en/natohq/declassified_138256.htm.

that called for improvisation and retrospective justification.[2] Similarly, the interventions in question have been studied in detail, not from the perspective of Soviet strategy but rather in the light of political developments within the

---

2 See for the *theory* of Soviet military strategy e.g. S. J. Cimbala, 'The Cold War and Soviet military strategy', *Journal of Slavic Military Studies*, 10 (1997), 25–55; the translated collection of Soviet sources in H. F. Scott and W. F. Scott, *The Soviet Art of War: Doctrine, Strategy and Tactics* (Boulder: Westview Press, 1981); J. D. Douglass Jr, *Soviet Military Strategy in Europe* (New York: Pergamon Press, 1980) and the more recent analysis by G. Snel, *From the Atlantic to the Urals: The Reorientation of Soviet Military Strategy, 1981–1990* (Amsterdam: VU University Press, 1996). In N. Friedman, *The Fifty Year War: Conflict and Strategy in the Cold War* (Annapolis: Naval Institute Press, 2000) there is more emphasis on the *practice* of Soviet strategy, but the interventions under consideration are only discussed very summarily.

Soviet bloc.[3] In order to study the *practice* of Soviet strategy, the interventions within the Soviet bloc are accordingly particularly interesting: there was *no* theory in those cases, but only practice, which reveals a fascinating process of planning for the unplanned and justifying the unjustifiable.

Moreover, since the collapse of the Berlin Wall, a wealth of primary sources from former Warsaw Pact countries has become available, and can either be consulted in the archives in former eastern European capitals or online. The situation in the former Soviet archives is a little more delicate, since accessibility has become more difficult under Russian president Vladimir Putin's regime, and the Kremlin has not allowed military records pertaining to the Warsaw Pact to be declassified. However, many of those can be found in other eastern European capitals, and other Soviet sources had already become accessible via the National Security Archive.[4] This has also formed the basis for several extensive source collections collated within volumes by Central European University Press, which I will use widely in this chapter. Many of these sources have also been published – often in collaboration with the National Security Archive – on websites such as the Parallel History Project on Cooperative Security and the Wilson Center Digital Archive.[5]

Actor(s)

Soviet strategy within the Soviet bloc was primarily reactive. Its aim was to keep the Soviet bloc intact and support friendly regimes in neighbouring countries. There was a considerable shift in decision making throughout the Cold War. The decision making initially resided with the Soviet first secretary himself, namely Joseph Stalin, and then with the collective leadership that followed in his wake. Ultimately, decision making in the Kremlin became less unilateral, and more and more other actors were involved, varying from foreign leaders in the decision making to intervene in Hungary in 1956 and most members of the Warsaw Pact in 1968.

---

3 E.g. H. M. Harrison, *Driving the Soviets up the Wall: Soviet–East German Relations, 1953–1961* (Princeton: Princeton University Press, 2003); J. Gyorkei and M. Horvath (eds), *Soviet Military Intervention in Hungary, 1956* (Budapest: Central European University Press, 1999); G. Bischof, S. Karner and P. Ruggenthaller (eds), *The Prague Spring and the Warsaw Pact Invasion of Czechoslovakia* (Lanham: Lexington Books, 2010).
4 See: https://nsarchive.gwu.edu.
5 See respectively: www.php.isn.ethz.ch and https://digitalarchive.wilsoncenter.org.

In the wake of Stalin's death on 5 March 1953, a collective leadership was established in the Kremlin, consisting of Lavrentii Beria, Georgii Malenkov and Vyacheslav Molotov and assisted by first secretary, Nikita Khrushchev, in order to break with the unilateral decision making that had characterised Stalin. The decisions were made in the so-called presidium – later the Politburo – according to the tenets of 'democratic centralism', in which the minority had to bow to the view of the majority. When workers began to protest against the East German Politburo after a 10 per cent increase in production norms in spring 1953, Vladimir Semyonov, the Soviet high commissioner in the German Democratic Republic, and Marshal Andrei Grechko, commander-in-chief of the Soviet forces in the GDR, provided the members of the presidium with the necessary information for their decision making. It was the presidium which ultimately decided *whether* or not to deploy troops, but it was the military which decided *how* to do so.[6] During the crisis in East Germany, the Soviet chief of the general staff, Vasilii Sokolovskii, was also sent to the GDR to advise the Kremlin.[7] The decision to intervene in East Germany seemed to have been made after little discussion within the presidium. Although the collective leadership marked a move away from Stalinism, the way in which the repercussions of the Berlin uprisings were dealt with echoed the Stalinist past: Lavrentii Beria, who had advocated a more liberal course in the GDR, was forced to take the blame and was executed in the wake of the uprisings. This changed the nature of the collective leadership, and paved the way for Khrushchev to claim the power as first secretary of the Communist Party, effectively abolishing the collective leadership.

In 1955 there was a considerable shift in Soviet foreign and defence policy through the foundation of the Warsaw Pact in May in reaction to the fact that West Germany entered NATO. Khrushchev founded an alliance of all communist countries in eastern and central Europe other than Yugoslavia to create a multilateral platform, which inadvertently gave them a stake in decision making. The Warsaw Treaty, which reflected the Atlantic treaty of NATO, specifically gave scope to the smaller members of the alliance, which would convene in the so-called 'Political Consultative Committee' (PCC). This raised the stakes of smaller Warsaw Pact members and decreased the Soviet scope for manoeuvre. The statute of the unified command was created as a sort of afterthought, separate from the PCC, and that was under Soviet

---

6 C. F. Ostermann (ed.), *Uprising in East Germany, 1953* (Budapest: Central European University Press, 2001), 192.
7 Sokolovskii was also the author of the famous handbook on Soviet military strategy; see V. D. Sokolovskii, *Soviet Military Strategy* (Santa Monica: RAND, 1963).

control. Political decision making took place within the PCC, although the Warsaw Pact seemed largely dormant in the second half of the 1950s, both politically and militarily.[8]

The shift away from Stalinism was further emphasised in Khrushchev's secret speech in February 1956, in which he officially broke with Stalinism and the unilateral decision making attached to it. The doctrine of peaceful coexistence replaced Stalin's tenet of the inevitability of war with the West. The speech seemed to reverberate more in the decision making surrounding the uprisings in Hungary in October 1956 than the foundation of the Warsaw Pact. There was genuine discussion in the presidium as to whether or not to intervene after a great number of workers protested against the government in October 1956. The presidium relied to a large extent on information from Yurii Andropov, the Soviet ambassador in Hungary, who emphasised that the situation was growing out of control. Khrushchev reluctantly sided with the hardliners and decided in favour of intervention in late October 1956; another motive was to consolidate his own power, which was questioned by the hardliners after his secret speech. Khrushchev was not in a position to decide by himself, although his intervention could tip the balance.[9]

When the first intervention on 24 October 1956 did not quell the uprisings as much as anticipated, there was another remarkable shift in decision making leading up to the second Soviet intervention on 4 November 1956. By that stage, the consequences of intervening in a Soviet bloc country – thus indicating that socialism could only be upheld by force – seemed to have fully dawned on Khrushchev. In order to canvass support for another intervention *within* the Soviet bloc and underscore the legitimacy of the intervention, Khrushchev travelled through eastern Europe, even consulting the Yugoslav leader, Josip Brod Tito, as well as the Chinese leadership. This was particularly remarkable, because Stalin had excommunicated Tito from the Soviet bloc in 1948, and it would have been unthinkable under Khrushchev's predecessor. Although Khrushchev clearly had the agency for the decision making, not only did he have to get the other members of the presidium on board, but he also had to canvass support outside the Soviet Union, and even outside the Warsaw Pact. He also consulted other Warsaw Pact leaders on an *individual* basis, all of whom urged him to intervene because the survival of

---

8 See L. C. Crump, *The Warsaw Pact Reconsidered: International Relations in Eastern Europe 1955–1969* (New York: Routledge, 2015), 21–4.
9 P. Kenez, 'Khrushchev and Hungary in 1956', in C. Fink, F. Hadler and T. Schramm (eds), *1956: European and Global Perspectives* (Leipzig: Leipzig University Press, 2006), 117.

a communist regime was at stake, and all other communist leaders feared a domino effect if the regime in Hungary collapsed.[10]

The Warsaw Pact as an alliance did not seem to have become an important body for decision making yet, although that changed in the period leading up to the Prague Spring in 1968. In the interceding years, the Warsaw Pact had become an increasingly important political gremium in order to collectively decide on issues which pertained to the entire Soviet bloc, such as the non-proliferation treaty, the preparation for a European security conference and the war in Vietnam. Khrushchev's successor, Leonid Brezhnev, had turned the Warsaw Pact into a priority in terms of determining Soviet bloc foreign policy, but the announced programme of liberalisations in Czechoslovakia in March 1968 under the name of the 'Prague Spring' posed Brezhnev with a new challenge. Eager to discuss in a multilateral context how the Czechoslovak reform programme could be prevented from spinning out of control, Brezhnev unilaterally convened a meeting of all Warsaw Pact leaders except the Romanian leadership in Dresden on 23 March 1968. This was *not* an official Warsaw Pact meeting, since it dealt with the internal affairs of one of its members rather than external matters, and Romania was deliberately excluded exactly for that reason: the Romanian leadership would have protested against such an intervention in internal affairs.[11]

No decisions were made during this meeting, but the dynamics were remarkable: the Polish, Bulgarian and East German leaders each put the Czechoslovak first secretary Dubcek under pressure to adopt a different and less liberal course, each fearing a spillover effect in their own country. Only Hungarian general secretary Janos Kádár defended the Czechoslovak scope for manoeuvre in managing its internal affairs. A new pattern had been set of convening multilateral meetings outside the confines of the Warsaw Pact. More meetings were to follow, for example in Moscow in May and in Warsaw in June, and in each case Brezhnev was pressurised by other Warsaw Pact leaders – most notably the Polish and East German ones – to take further decisive actions against the liberalisation in Czechoslovakia. The collective decision was made to stage military exercises on Czechoslovak soil under the guidance of Soviet Marshal Ivan Yakubovskii. Here too decisions to deploy troops were made at the political level, but once actual troops were involved,

---

10 See J. Granville, *The First Domino: International Decision Making during the Hungarian Crisis of 1956* (Texas: Texas A&M University Press, 2004), 213.
11 M. Retegan, *In the Shadow of the Prague Spring: Romanian Foreign Policy and the Crisis of Czechoslovakia, 1968* (Oxford: Oxford University Press, 2008), 85–6.

Yakubovskii was in charge as the Warsaw Pact's supreme commander, and unilaterally 'sought to prolong the exercises', thus paving the way for a potential intervention.[12]

Further meetings between the five Warsaw Pact members followed, to which Czechoslovakia was invited but which it refused to attend, such as one in Moscow in July and Bratislava on 3 August. As in the Hungarian case, the Warsaw Pact itself had to be kept out of the equation, because it concerned unrest *within* a Warsaw Pact country. While Brezhnev and Kádár continued to prefer a military to a political solution, there was mounting pressure from the Polish, Bulgarian and East German leaders to intervene at last in order to salvage socialism. The ultimate decision was, however, made in the Politburo, where Brezhnev had been under mounting pressure to invade by the hardliners, such as Minister of Defence Andrei Grechko – the former commander-in-chief in the GDR – and Politburo member Alexander Shelepin, both of whom coveted Brezhnev's position. As in Khrushchev's case, Brezhnev eventually had to side with the hardliners to save his own skin.

Adversaries

The irony of Soviet strategy in Europe is that it was in *theory* directed against the enemy outside, but in *practice* against the people within. The Kremlin accordingly had a significant problem in terms of defining its adversaries in all these cases, since they were internal ones – students, workers etc. – rather than external ones, which sat very uncomfortably with the central tenet of Marxism–Leninism, namely the socialist paradise as inevitable outcome of the laws of history. The actual adversaries needed to be continuously redefined in order to legitimise intervention within the Soviet bloc without undermining Marxist–Leninist theory.

In the 1953 Berlin uprisings, the adversaries were East German workers protesting against the higher work norms. This was particularly problematic, since communism was designed to serve the workers – the proletariat – rather than to antagonise it. The cause of the uprising was accordingly identified as a 'rather major planned provocation' in which West Berliners played a central role.[13] Shifting the responsibility to 'reactionary and fascist agents' and calling it a 'provocation ... organized and directed from Western sectors of Berlin' served to legitimise the fact that the intervention in East

---

12 J. Navrátil (ed.), *The Prague Spring 1968* (Budapest: Central European University Press, 2006), 191–2.
13 Ostermann, *Uprising in East Germany*, 170.

Germany was intended to quench the protests by East German workers.[14] The East German Politburo was not the enemy, but it needed Soviet military support to remain in power in the face of the growing protests.

In fact, anyone who challenged the Communist system was an adversary in the Kremlin's eyes. This became clear in Hungary in 1956 when student protests led to the Soviet decision to intervene. Here, too, the situation needed to be redefined as a 'counterrevolution' in order to justify interference in internal affairs.[15] The fact that the Communist leadership – contrary to the East German case – ultimately seemed to yield to the students' demands, also turned the Hungarian first secretary Imre Nagy and his comrades into adversaries. The turning point here seemed to be Nagy's establishment of a multi-party system on 31 October 1956. By relinquishing the Communist monopoly of power, Nagy had turned into an adversary, too, which ultimately led to his execution as a traitor.

The adversaries were accordingly those who either challenged or failed to uphold the Communist monopoly on power. This was also the fear in the case of the reforms that were part of the Prague Spring, where those engaging in reforms came to be defined as the 'rightist and anti-socialist forces'.[16] The redefinition of the situation in Czechoslovakia as a 'counterrevolution' by the anti-reformist faction of the Czechoslovak leadership proved the tipping point.[17] As in the case with Nagy, the Czechoslovak first secretary Alexander Dubcek was not considered an adversary from the outset. He only became one when the Kremlin no longer deemed him capable of ensuring the Communist Party ruled supreme. The definition of adversary thus shifted in accordance with the objective that needed to be legitimised.

Causes

The causes of the military interventions were in all cases unrest within the Soviet bloc due to internal protests and riots, which seemed to endanger the Communist monopoly on power, the security of the borders and the integrity of the Soviet bloc. In the case of the uprisings in Berlin, the workers' riots seemed to endanger the survival of Walter Ulbricht's regime as well as causing a record number of East Germans to flee to West Berlin. With East Germany as front line of the Iron Curtain, the East German

---

14 Ostermann, *Uprising in East Germany*, 196.
15 C. Békés, M. Byrne and J. M. Rainer (eds), *The 1956 Hungarian Revolution: A History in Documents* (Budapest: Central European University Press, 2002), 337.
16 Navrátil, *The Prague Spring*, 333.   17 Navrátil, *The Prague Spring*, 324.

uprisings seemed to pose a direct existential threat to the Soviet bloc as a whole. With West Berlin on its doorstep, the Kremlin feared that a challenge to the Communist Party in East Berlin would particularly endanger the existence of a divided country that was hardly recognised anywhere.

The student revolts in Hungary in 1956 led to similar concerns, which were perhaps even deeper since the Hungarian Communist Party seemed to give in to popular demands by announcing a multi-party system on 31 October. Thus the monopoly of Communist power was completely undermined, which could eventually lead to a capitalist regime in Hungary and in its wake the disintegration of the Soviet bloc. The Hungarian decision to withdraw from the Warsaw Pact and declare neutrality seemed secondary to the declaration of a multi-party system, since it was the latter that directly triggered the decision to invade. There was, however, a genuine concern that 'cracking the East European buffer zone would be an intolerable security threat'.[18] The cause of intervening in Hungary as in East Germany was, accordingly, a perception of insecurity, which seemed aggravated by the fact that the Communist leadership did not manage to restrain the uprisings themselves and even gave in to the people's demands.

The perceived insecurity ties in with the fear of the domino effect, namely the concern of the uprisings spilling over into other Soviet bloc countries. This was the primary reason why Khrushchev seemed to muster quite some international support among both Warsaw Pact countries and even the Yugoslav and Chinese leaderships for intervening in Hungary. This was even more the case in Czechoslovakia in 1968 when the East German, Bulgarian and Polish leadership increasingly pressurised Brezhnev to intervene in Czechoslovakia. In that case, the reform programme as part of the Prague Spring caused the fear that the Communist leadership seemed to lose control over the people, especially when freedom of the press and freedom of speech also became allowed. The increased liberalisation was considered an immediate threat to other countries where the contagion became evident, with people in Poland for example chanting 'Long Live Czechoslovakia'.[19] The fact that Dubcek failed to react decisively to the 'Two Thousand Words' manifesto on 17 June 1968, which asked for further liberties such as freedom

---

18 Békés, Byrne and Rainer (eds), *The 1956 Hungarian Revolution*, 210.
19 A. Kemp-Welch, *Poland under Communism: A Cold War History* (Cambridge: Cambridge University Press, 2008), 163.

of the press, was a tipping point. When, halfway through August, the Czechoslovak leader still did not succeed to live up to a Soviet ultimatum to take matters in his own hand, the CPSU Politburo definitively decided to intervene, since it would 'never permit the socialist gains in fraternal Czechoslovakia to be damaged'.[20]

Objectives

The objectives in each case seemed very similar and amounted to ensuring the security and integrity of the Soviet bloc and upholding the monopoly on Communist power. The issues were accordingly related to politics and security at the same time, with the assumption that the undermining of the Communist monopoly of power would also pose a threat to the security of the Soviet bloc.

In the case of East Germany, these objectives were relatively simple to achieve, since the Soviet intervention was aimed at supporting the East German leader, Walter Ulbricht, in quenching the protests and remaining in power. Ulbricht himself was not regarded as a threat to the Communist monopoly of power; on the contrary, the Kremlin was at that stage – in the wake of the New Course, developed after Stalin's death – more reform-minded than Ulbricht himself. The intervention could accordingly be relatively minor, and could easily be linked to the means at the disposal of the Kremlin, namely by using the Soviet troops already stationed in East Germany, recalling them from their summer training camps and ordering them to intervene.[21]

The objectives in the Hungarian case were much more complex, since the Kremlin wavered on whether to support Nagy or not as leader of the Hungarian Communist Party. Moreover, the Soviet leadership intervened twice, first with a small-scale intervention on 24 October to quell the public protests and then again on 4 November with a large-scale intervention to restore order. The first Soviet intervention was a miscalculation, since it increased the anti-Soviet sentiments and turned the revolution into a fully fledged anti-Soviet liberation struggle. In order to appease the protesters, Nagy was compelled to declare Hungary a multi-party system on 31 October, thus undermining the Communist monopoly on power and indirectly also the

---

20 Navrátil, *The Prague Spring*, 391.   21 Ostermann, *Uprising in East Germany*, 168–9.

security of the Soviet bloc. In the Kremlin's words it was everyone's 'chief and sacred duty' to 'guard the communist achievements of people's democratic Hungary', and when that was perceived to be at stake, the objectives changed to ousting Nagy from power through a second, large-scale intervention on 4 November and installing a new government.[22] Contrary to the East German case, this intervention was aimed at regime change. Moreover, in the case of East Germany the objective was to put an end to protests, rather than to reverse a revolution, as was the case in Hungary.

The situation in Czechoslovakia was even more volatile, since the Prague Spring was a long-term process of incremental reforms, and therefore it was less easy to define if and when an intervention was necessary. The Soviet objectives therefore evolved over time, too, starting with large-scale military manoeuvres in June 1968 with 'political objectives . . . to help the Czechoslovak people defeat the counterrevolution'.[23] Moreover, the Czechoslovak government was promised that the troops would be withdrawn from Czechoslovak territory 'as soon as the danger to the independence and security of Czechoslovakia and to the socialist future of the Czechoslovak people is eliminated'.[24] Thus, it was made explicit that the military pressure served to safeguard the Communist monopoly on power as well as the integrity of the Warsaw Pact. When both of these were called into question, preparations were made for a full-scale invasion. Both the military exercises and the invasion involved Hungarian, Bulgarian, East German and Polish Warsaw Pact members, since there was another objective at stake in the Czechoslovak case: namely to prevent contagion of liberalising ideals in other countries within the Warsaw Pact and to contain the process of liberalisation. This objective overrode the one of regime change. So long as the reforms could be stopped, Dubcek could remain in power.

Available Means

Defence was an absolute priority for the Soviet Union. According to the latest estimate, up to thirty per cent of the Gross National Product was spent on defence.[25] Between 1945 and 1948 the Red Army had succeeded in first liberating

---

22 Békés, Byrne and Rainer (eds), *The 1956 Hungarian Revolution*, 302.
23 Navrátil, *The Prague Spring*, 277.   24 Navrátil, *The Prague Spring*, 402.
25 R. W. Leonard, 'Soviet military', in R. van Dijk, W. G. Gray, S. Savranskaya, J. Suri and Q. Zhai (eds), *The Routledge Encyclopaedia of the Cold War* (New York: Routledge, 2008), vol. 2, 826.

East Germany from the Nazis and then occupying most of it, with Soviet troops permanently stationed in most countries of the Soviet bloc and from 1955 onwards the Warsaw Pact. Approximately 350,000 Soviet troops were still stationed in East Germany as part of the Soviet Occupation Forces in East Germany, with the Soviet Control Commission controlling East Germany in accordance with the four-power Potsdam agreement after the Second World War.[26]

Hungary had been under Soviet control from 1948 when the multi-party system was abolished. Under the Stalinist leadership of Mátyás Rakosí, who was backed up by the Kremlin, the Hungarian Army adopted Soviet military doctrine, and Soviet troops had unlimited access to Hungarian territory.[27] From 1955 the Warsaw Pact regulated the stationing of Soviet troops in Warsaw Pact countries, officially aimed against NATO, and it also regulated the continued stationing of five Soviet divisions on Hungarian soil. In total, 60 of the Soviet Union's 180 divisions were directed against NATO, including tens of thousands of tanks, aircraft and missile launchers. Most of the equipment was second-rate, but the troops could easily be moved from one country to the other within the Warsaw Pact.[28] Approximately 31,500 Soviet troops were redeployed to Budapest and other Hungarian cities during the first invasion on 24 October 1956.[29]

Czechoslovakia had been under Soviet control from 1948 onwards, with the establishment of a single-party state. But there was one big difference with Hungary, namely the fact that the Czechoslovak president Edvard Benes had successfully negotiated the removal of both Soviet and American troops in 1945.[30] This meant that the Kremlin had to pave the way to invading with the pretext of military exercises on Czechoslovak territory in June 1968. The so-called 'Sumava Exercises' consisted of 30–40,000 troops from the Soviet Union, Poland, Hungary and Bulgaria with East Germany added as an afterthought; exactly those Warsaw Pact countries that considered intervening in the first place.[31]

---

26 F. Slaveski, *The Soviet Occupation of Germany: Hunger, Mass Violence and the Struggle for Peace, 1945–1947* (Cambridge: Cambridge University Press, 2013), 115.
27 L. Borhi, 'Hungary', in van Dijk et al. (eds), *Routledge Encyclopaedia of the Cold War*, vol. 1, 423.
28 Leonard, 'Soviet military', 825.
29 M. Kramer, 'The Soviet Union and the 1956 crises in Hungary and Poland: reassessments and new findings', *Journal of Contemporary History*, 33:2 (1998), 163–214, 185.
30 B. Rohlik, 'Czechoslovakia', in van Dijk et al. (eds), *Routledge Encyclopaedia of the Cold War*, vol. 1, 220.
31 Navrátil, *The Prague Spring*, 199–201.

Process of Prioritisation

In all cases the Kremlin's priority was to safeguard socialism in the Soviet bloc and, accordingly, to secure the integrity of the Soviet bloc. In the first instance, the Kremlin tried to do so by pressurising the respective leaderships into gaining control over the situation, containing the protests or reforms and upholding the Communist monopoly on power. In each case, the Kremlin started from the assumption that the cause of the protests was somehow to be found *outside* the socialist system rather than within. Marxist–Leninist ideology stood in the way of a clear analysis, since it failed to explain how workers, students or other citizens could protest against the system: the socialist system was, after all, inevitably aimed at securing their well-being. Trying to find the causes of the unrest elsewhere – imperialist agents, fascists, counterrevolutionaries – was therefore more than a way to justify intervention within the Soviet bloc. It was also symptomatic of an engrained failure to acknowledge the flaws of the socialist system. At the same time, the Kremlin did have to use such rhetoric in order to explain military interventions *within* the countries that were supposed to be their allies.

The decision to intervene was therefore never easy. In the case of East Berlin, it was made most quickly and justification was not so much of an issue, since it was officially a divided country with the Eastern part under Soviet control and therefore had a somewhat different status from other countries in the Soviet bloc. Since the East German leadership was *incapable* rather than *unwilling* to control the riots, it was not a priority to oust the leadership. That priority in each case was secondary to the main goal, namely to safeguard the Communist monopoly on power. This also explains why the Soviets reacted so ambivalently in the case of intervening in Hungary twice over. In the first case the situation seemed more similar to the one in East Germany, with quelling the riots as the main priority. The priorities quickly changed when the monopoly of Communist power seemed at stake and Nagy *neither* seemed willing *nor* capable of controlling the situation. By that stage regime change became the main objective, since that was the only way to restore order, and a second larger-scale invasion was decided upon. Regime change was, however, never an end in itself, which can explain for example why the Soviet Union never intervened in Romania even though the Romanian leadership was notoriously obnoxious towards the Kremlin. Moreover, there was, as Granville puts it, 'little or no analysis of costs and risks'.[32]

---

32 Granville, *The First Domino*, xiii.

The invasion in two stages shows the wavering decision making of the Kremlin as well as the awareness that there was a problem in justifying the invasion of a 'fraternal' country. Despite the number of military interventions in the Soviet bloc, they were a last resort to uphold the Communist monopoly on power and, thereby, also secure their own regime. The Communist Party was the linchpin of the Communist bloc, and when that was being eroded the security of the Soviet regime itself was also at stake. In fact, all Soviet actions were aimed at maintaining the status quo, as was also the case in Czechoslovakia in 1968. In that case it took the Soviet Union almost six months to decide whether or not to intervene and another priority materialised, namely to keep other Warsaw Pact allies on board, some of whom had already proposed a military intervention in March 1968, attempting to legitimise interference in internal affairs 'in situations when so-called domestic affairs naturally become external affairs, thus affairs of the entire socialist camp', as the Polish leader Gomulka put it.[33] Contrary to the Kremlin, the East German, Bulgarian and Polish leaders did not have to worry about justifying the intervention, since they did not have to uphold the role of leader of the Communist world, unlike the Kremlin. For the Soviets this had become a particular concern after the Sino-Soviet schism in the early 1960s.

The Kremlin accordingly used the term 'active measures in defence of socialism in the CSSR' as a euphemism for the invasion, which it called an 'internationalist duty' in an attempt to legitimise that 'the governments of the five countries have ordered their military units to take all necessary measures on 21 August'.[34] The concept of 'internationalist duty' returned in an article called 'Sovereignty and the International Obligations of Socialist Countries'. According to this article, military interventions in the Soviet bloc were vindicated by declaring any threat to socialist rule in a Warsaw Pact country a threat to them all, thus prioritising safeguarding socialism over sovereignty.[35] This so-called 'Brezhnev Doctrine' was particularly designed to retrospectively justify the invasion by the Soviet Union and four other Warsaw Pact countries of Czechoslovakia, but with the same reasoning the invasions of East Germany and Hungary could also be legitimised. The Kremlin clearly prioritised socialism over sovereignty and deemed a military intervention a necessary means to safeguard the former.

The tension between the two was, however, evident to all Soviet leaderships, and it is noteworthy that in both cases external events also took a role in

33 Navrátil, *The Prague Spring*, 67.   34 Navrátil, *The Prague Spring*, 402.
35 Navrátil, *The Prague Spring*, 502–3.

prioritisation. In the case of the interventions in Hungary, the Kremlin was well aware of the fact that the French and British on the one hand and the Americans on the other were at loggerheads with one another over the situation in Suez, and the Suez crisis was mentioned several times in the Kremlin's decision making, with the Soviets underlining that the 'capitalists' could hardly claim the moral high ground due to the British and French involvement in Suez.[36] This calculation proved correct, in that the Americans even refused to discuss the Hungarian revolution at the United Nations, since it wanted to use all the available time to discuss the Suez crisis. In the case of the intervention in Czechoslovakia, the Vietnam war played a role in the decision making since the Kremlin estimated 'communist unity' all the more imperative at a time when 'American imperialism has not abandoned its policy of strength and open intervention against peoples fighting for freedom'.[37]

Execution of Strategy

The intervention in East Germany was relatively minor and not very complex, since sufficient Soviet troops were already stationed in East Germany as part of the Soviet Occupation Forces in Germany 'to restore order in Berlin'.[38] On 17 June 1953 two mechanised divisions were operating in Berlin with the twelfth tank division approaching its north-eastern suburbs. All roads to the government buildings were blocked by Soviet troops, tanks and artillery. The primary districts of East Berlin were controlled by Soviet forces. Fighting was particularly fierce outside the East Berlin police headquarters, where Soviet tanks fired at the protesters, resulting in executions and mass arrest.[39] Martial law was declared in East Berlin and several East German cities at 1 p.m. to facilitate the quelling of the uprisings, and the members of the East German government were evacuated to the Soviet headquarters in Karlshorst. At the same time a mechanised division had been despatched to Magdenburg, a mechanised infantry regiment to Dresden, and a mechanised regiment and a motorbike battalion to Leipzig.[40] By 9 p.m. Soviet deputy defence minister and chief of staff Marshal Vasilii Sokolovskii and Marshal Leonid Govorov had arrived in Berlin, which suggests that the Kremlin perceived this as a major military crisis. Control of East Berlin had

36 Békés, Byrne and Rainer (eds), *The 1956 Hungarian Revolution*, 349.
37 Navrátil, *The Prague Spring*, 422.   38 Ostermann, *Uprising in East Germany*, 192.
39 Ostermann, *Uprising in East Germany*, 190.
40 Ostermann, *Uprising in East Germany*, 193.

'essentially been transferred to the hands of the Soviet organs'.[41] In the western sector of Berlin, NATO troops were put on high alert, and Sokolovskii complained that the Soviet Control Commission in East Germany had not taken the situation seriously enough.[42] It took the Soviet troops until 24 June to gain full control over the situation, although the majority of the protests were already quenched on 17 June. In all, 55 people were killed, 8000–10,000 arrested and more than 15,000 sentenced, including 2 death penalties.[43]

The intervention in Hungary took place in two phases. In the first phase Hungarian first secretary Ernő Gerő actually called upon the Soviet Union to intervene via the military attaché at the Soviet embassy in Budapest, because he did not manage to control an increasingly large demonstration consisting of approximately 200,000 people in Budapest by himself.[44] The Kremlin ordered Zhukov to use Soviet troops that were already stationed in Hungary, as well as two divisions from Ukraine and one from Romania, both of which were close to the Hungarian border, in order to occupy Budapest. The total number of troops amounted to 31,500 soldiers, consisting of tanks without infantry support. The Soviets had miscalculated and were confronted with greater resistance than anticipated, mainly young rebels trying to block the progress of Soviet tanks to key objectives in Budapest, such as the railway and the radio station. Because of the curfew and the strict control of information, the uprisings initially did not spread beyond Budapest.[45]

The troops arrived in Budapest at 4.00 a.m. on 24 October 1956 and the Kremlin felt they had successfully restored order by the evening apart from some resistance on roof tops and balconies.[46] At the same time, Soviet Politburo members Anastas Mikoyan and Mikhail Suslov arrived in Budapest early on 24 October, together with General Mikhail Malinin, who was in charge of Soviet troops during this phase of the invasion, and Ivan Serov, the head of the KGB. At 4.30 a.m. a news bulletin was read over the radio which already declared, 'The counterrevolutionary gangs have largely been eliminated', followed by a statement from the Council of Ministers at 6.30 a.m., which even declared, 'The attempted counterrevolutionary coup

41 Ostermann, *Uprising in East Germany*, 169.
42 Ostermann, *Uprising in East Germany*, 209.
43 Ostermann, 'East German uprising', in van Dijk et al. (eds), *Routledge Encyclopaedia of the Cold War*, vol. I, 278.
44 Békés, Byrne and Rainer (eds), *The 1956 Hungarian Revolution*, 224.
45 Békés, Byrne and Rainer (eds), *The 1956 Hungarian Revolution*, 193–6 and 224–6.
46 Békés, Byrne and Rainer (eds), *The 1956 Hungarian Revolution*, 224–6.

has been eliminated'. At 8.30 a.m. a state of emergency was declared and a military committee was formed to co-ordinate the Soviet and Hungarian forces.[47] The Soviet embassy was protected by thirty tanks.[48]

However, the uprising was not quelled altogether and the people continued to rebel in the continuing days, with an estimated number of 15,000 combatants – mostly working class youths – putting up a fight against the Soviet occupiers, the Hungarian military and the Hungarian AVH security police with small arms and Molotov cocktails. The Soviets seemed to believe so much in their own propaganda of quenching a counterrevolution rather than a widely supported popular uprising that they had underestimated the Hungarian resistance, and had not anticipated that the use of Soviet troops would only further escalate the situation into a fully fledged anti-Soviet liberation struggle. The fighting became fiercer, with Soviet and Hungarian soldiers shooting at unarmed Hungarian civilians as well as – in the fog of war – occasionally shooting at each other, and war planes were also being deployed to target rebels – often innocent citizens – from the air.[49]

On 28 October the Kremlin agreed to pull its forces out of Budapest and support a new programme by Nagy, which gave in to some of the protesters' demands without agreeing on the Soviet withdrawal of troops or on free multi-party elections. Since the uprisings had spread to the countryside and Hungarian soldiers began to side with the rebels, the Kremlin wanted to give Nagy the chance to find a political solution. The military intervention so far had proved counterproductive. Nagy had become convinced that it was not a 'counterrevolution' but a 'democratic movement'.[50] On 30 October Hungarian prospects seemed even more hopeful, since the Kremlin composed a proclamation which underlined respect for equality, territorial integrity and non-interference, and explicitly stated that 'the Soviet Government has given its military command instructions to withdraw the Soviet military units from the city of Budapest as soon as this is considered necessary by the Hungarian Government'.[51] When the violence also turned against Communist officials and Nagy announced a multi-party system, the Kremlin decided that a military solution was needed after all. This time it operated without the collusion of the Hungarian government, even

---

47 Békés, Byrne and Rainer (eds), *The 1956 Hungarian Revolution*, 194.
48 Békés, Byrne and Rainer (eds), *The 1956 Hungarian Revolution*, 226.
49 L. Borhi, 'Hungarian uprising', in van Dijk et al. (eds), *Routledge Encyclopaedia of the Cold War*, vol. 1, 421.
50 Békés, Byrne and Rainer (eds), *The 1956 Hungarian Revolution*, 284.
51 Békés, Byrne and Rainer (eds), *The 1956 Hungarian Revolution*, 302.

indicating to Nagy that the troops entering the country served to facilitate the withdrawal from the Red Army.[52] In the meantime, Soviet troops started to seal off airfields on Hungarian territory and the Kremlin drew up a number of alternatives to replace the Nagy government. To that end Politburo members Kádár and Ferenc Münnich were flown to Moscow on 1 November, where the Soviets composed a list of ministers and a policy programme in Russian, which Kádár did not read. His hope that 'This government must not be puppet-like', accordingly seemed vain.[53]

On 3 November Soviet troops encircled larger cities, closing main roads and the Western border. The four divisions already stationed in Hungary were increased to a total of seventeen divisions, totalling approximately 60,000 Soviet troops, led by Soviet Marshal Ivan Konev. The Hungarian delegation that demanded the withdrawal of Soviet troops was arrested by KGB chief General Ivan Serov, as was, ultimately, Imre Nagy. The Soviets installed Kádár in power. It took the Soviet military until 20 November to quench the final unrest, and in the preceding month approximately 3,000 Hungarians were killed, 300 executed, 19,000 wounded, 20,000 jailed, 17,000 interned and almost 200,000 fled to the West, but the Communist monopoly on power was restored. On the Soviet side, 669 soldiers had been killed, 1540 wounded and 51 were missing.[54]

The intervention in Czechoslovakia followed a slightly different pattern. In June 1968 the Kremlin had gained Czechoslovak consent in bringing the date forward of the Sumava exercise that had already been planned for late 1968 or early 1969. According to a Hungarian report, 'the exercise was organised essentially for political reasons and with political objectives', as a 'kind of camouflage' to demonstrate 'the strength and unity of the Warsaw Pact ..., influence the Czechoslovak events, ... and shore up the authority of the Soviet Union and the Warsaw Pact'. The same report mentioned 'unacceptable shortcomings, irregularities, and inadequate provisions'.[55] Although the exercise itself was not a resounding success, Yakubovskii (the Warsaw Pact's supreme commander) refused to withdraw and the troops stayed on Czechoslovak soil.

When the actual invasion was approved, the command was at the last moment transferred from Yakubovskii to the Soviet General Ivan Pavlovskii, the Soviet deputy minister of defence. The invasion, contrary to conventional wisdom, was *not* a Warsaw Pact enterprise (and could not be, since it was

---

52 Békés, Byrne and Rainer (eds), *The 1956 Hungarian Revolution*, 211.
53 Békés, Byrne and Rainer (eds), *The 1956 Hungarian Revolution*, 357.
54 Borhi, 'Hungarian uprising', 422.   55 Navrátil, *The Prague Spring*, 199–201.

directed against a Warsaw Pact member), but rather a Soviet enterprise with support from East German, Polish, Bulgarian and Hungarian allies.[56] This was in the literal sense a coalition of the willing, since the leaders of the countries in question were eager to restore unity in the socialist camp. Thus approximately 170,000 Soviet troops were supported by Polish, Bulgarian and Hungarian combat units, and an East German liaison unit. Because East German participation was particularly painful considering the German invasion of Czechoslovakia in 1938, the Kremlin had declined the East German offer of supplying ground troops for exactly that reason.[57] The Soviet troops were strictly instructed to 'exercise maximum restraint' and to turn around as soon as any NATO troops were encountered; everything was done to ensure this would not turn into an East–West confrontation and to avoid bloodshed.[58] Under Soviet pressure the Czechoslovak president Svoboda appealed to the Czechoslovak soldiers and officers 'to stand together with the fraternal armies in the defence of socialism'.[59] The Czechoslovak defence minister General Martin Dzur ordered all Czechoslovak troops 'to remain in their barracks'.[60]

Soviet forces thus completely defeated the Czechoslovak People's Army, which also lacked an independent chain of command. They made their way to Prague without much resistance where Soviet paratroopers stormed the government building. Like Nagy, Dubcek was arrested by the KGB and flown to Moscow, but because there was no alternative government in place he was allowed to return to Prague as party leader six days later. In total, 137 Czechoslovak citizens were killed, approximately 70,000 Czechoslovak citizens emigrated in the short term and 300,000 in the long run, and the Prague Spring was put on hold. Moreover, the Kremlin persuaded the Czechoslovak leadership to keep 70,000 to 80,000 troops on Czechoslovak soil for a 'temporary stay, without any fixed time limits'. The Czechoslovak leadership had little choice, since the Soviet troops were already there, thus inadvertently agreeing to remedy a remarkable lacuna in safeguarding the security of the eastern European border with inter alia West Germany. The troops accordingly served as important 'protection against foreign enemies',

---

56 G. Bischof, S. Karner and P. Ruggenthaler, 'Introduction', in Bischof et al. (eds), *Prague Spring*, 4.
57 Crump, *Warsaw Pact Reconsidered*, 241; M. Kramer, 'The Prague Spring and the Soviet invasion of Czechoslovakia: new interpretations', in J. G. Herschberg (ed.), *From the Russian Archives*, Cold War International History Project Bulletin No. 3 (Washington, DC: Woodrow Wilson International Center for Scholars, 1993), 48.
58 Navrátil, *The Prague Spring*, 375; Friedman, *The Fifty Year War*, 346.
59 Friedman, *The Fifty Year War*, 408.   60 Friedman, *The Fifty Year War*, 412.

since 'they protect not only our country, but also the territory of other Warsaw Pact states'.[61] The Prague Spring had provided the Kremlin with a useful pretext to strengthen the Warsaw Pact's borders with western Europe through a bilateral treaty.

Czechoslovak–Soviet relations only really soured half a year later, when approximately 100,000 Czechoslovak citizens started protesting against the presence of Soviet troops after the Czechoslovak ice hockey team defeated the Soviets twice during the World Ice Hockey Championship in Sweden on 21–28 March 1969. After the Soviet Politburo had framed this as an 'open attack by Czechoslovak counterrevolutionary forces', Soviet defence minister Grechko arrived unannounced in Prague to discuss the situation with his Czechoslovak counterpart Dzur. This time an alternative regime had materialised and on 17 April 1969 Dubcek was ousted. Unlike Nagy he was, however, not executed, showing that the Kremlin had indeed distanced itself still further from Stalinist methods.[62]

Conclusion

The Soviet intervention in Czechoslovakia was the last one within Europe. Under pressure from hardliners within the Politburo, Brezhnev agreed to one more intervention to secure Soviet security and quell unrest at its borders, namely the one in Afghanistan on 24 December 1979.[63] Here, too, the aim was to establish a friendly communist regime in its neighbourhood. With Soviet forces bogged down in Afghanistan for another ten years, the intervention drained Soviet resources and was almost immediately regarded as a failure, also by the Kremlin itself. KGB chief, Iurii Andropov, and defence minister, Dmitrii Ustinov, who had been one of its engineers, established a committee to prevent more such strategic failures, and as such they were responsible for aiming to prevent a Soviet intervention in Poland, where the newly established trade union Solidarnosc threatened to become a viable alternative to the Communist Party in 1980–1981.[64]

In the Polish case, Brezhnev already seemed to have given up his own doctrine de facto. Even though socialism was at stake, the Politburo decided in December 1981 *not* to intervene, despite the request by the Polish first

---

61 Friedman, *The Fifty Year War*, 544.   62 Friedman, *The Fifty Year War*, 441.
63 Also discussed in Chapter 22 in this volume.
64 V. Mastny, *The Soviet Non-Invasion of Poland in 1980/81 and the End of the Cold War*, Cold War International History Project Working Paper, 23 (Washington, DC: Woodrow Wilson International Center for Scholars, 1998), 8–9.

secretary Wojciech Jaruzelski to do so. According to a Politburo meeting on 10 December, the Kremlin did 'not intend to introduce troops in Poland ... even if Poland comes under the authority of Solidarity', since that might cause trouble with 'the capitalist countries ... with various kinds of economic and political sanctions', which would be 'very difficult' for the Soviet Union.[65] Soviet troops at the Polish borders put Jaruzelski under pressure to solve the situation himself, which he did by establishing martial law and arresting many members of Solidarnosc on 13 December 1981. The Soviet bloc's borders were safeguarded by the 1975 Helsinki Final Act, which at the same time raised the price of intervening in another country. Without an international crisis, such as Suez or Vietnam, to divert attention, and with their own forces stuck in Afghanistan, the price for yet another Soviet intervention was deemed too high. When Soviet leader Mikhail Gorbachev officially declared the Brezhnev Doctrine dead in 1985, the way to the collapse of the Berlin Wall was paved. Without Soviet forces to uphold the Soviet Empire, East Germany collapsed in 1990, with the Warsaw Pact and the Soviet Union in its wake in 1991.

The collapse of the Soviet Union was famously regarded as the 'greatest geopolitical catastrophe of the century' by President Vladimir Putin.[66] The troops which he ordered to enter Ukraine on 24 February 2022 were, however, not only meant to 'unite' Ukraine with Russia in a new kind of Russian Empire. Many of the objectives by his predecessors in East Germany, Hungary and Czechoslovakia were shared by Putin. Like them, he wanted to protect the security of Russia by establishing a friendly regime on Russian borders. He, too, attempted to prevent Ukraine from turning further westwards in an attempt to occupy the country, as was the case in both Hungary and Czechoslovakia. And under the guise of 'denazification' he also hoped for regime change, like in Hungary in 1956. Moreover, like in Czechoslovakia in 1968, military manoeuvres were both used to pressurise the incumbent regime and to pave the way to an intervention if need be.

Like Khrushchev in Hungary, Putin miscalculated. In this case, the entrance of Russian forces on Ukrainian soil turned the Ukrainian people much more against Russia, as the Soviet forces did in Hungary. Neither the Soviet nor the Russian forces were hailed as liberators, and something that started as a desire to align with the West developed into resistance against the

---

65 A. Paczkowski and M. Byrne (eds), *From Solidarity to Martial Law: The Polish Crisis of 1980–1981* (Budapest: Central European University Press, 2007), 350.
66 'Putin: Soviet collapse a genuine tragedy', NBC News (25 April 2005), www.nbcnews.com /id/wbna7632057.

Russians. Putin like his predecessors in the Cold War seemed to have believed so much in his own propaganda of liberation that he failed to appreciate the anti-Russian sentiments within Ukraine. But Putin's overstretch was even bigger, since his objective was not to quell uprisings and reverse the situation into the Communist monopoly on power, but to replace a regime of a country that had already liberalised and turned westwards. East Germany, Hungary and Czechoslovakia had each remained in the Soviet orbit, even though their loyalty was under pressure. Ukraine had already left it in 1991, and reversing a process of more than thirty years is an altogether different issue. The people in Ukraine, unlike those in East Germany, Hungary and Czechoslovakia, were not used to repression and their resistance was accordingly a lot fiercer. The objectives followed a familiar Cold War pattern – regime change, upholding Russian power, safeguarding a buffer against NATO – but the context was altogether different.

Moreover, Putin is much more radical than Khrushchev and Brezhnev. They had distanced themselves from Stalin, but Putin seems to have reverted to Stalinist methods. His rhetoric of denazification and demilitarisation echoes that of Stalin's occupation of eastern Europe after the Second World War. His cruelty and ruthlessness are more akin to Stalin than to Khrushchev or Brezhnev, who never had causing harm as one of their objectives. In Putin's case there is a similar struggle to legitimise the illegitimate, namely intervening in a sovereign country in the name of 'liberating' it. During the Cold War the belief in communism was still such that some people both at the political and military level in the countries under occupation actually believed in this rhetoric and collaborated with the Soviet interventions. The other Warsaw Pact leaders also became increasingly supportive of such interventions to save themselves. Belarussian president Aleksandr Lukashenko might support Putin's invasion of Ukraine for similar reasons. He too probably fears a domino effect. Russian rhetoric falls, however, on completely deaf ears in Ukraine, uniting the Ukrainian people against Russia together with their political and military leaders in a way that is without precedent during the Cold War.

14

People's War and Wars of Decolonisation

MATHILDE VON BÜLOW

The international order witnessed significant transformations in the twentieth century. One of the most striking came about through decolonisation, understood here as the attainment of political independence by territories hitherto under various forms of European colonial or settler control. Decolonisation led to the emergence of many dozens of new states, mostly in the so-called global South. This change to the international order resulted from an uneven process that spanned decades. Some colonial dependencies gained their political independence precipitously while others had to wait decades; some enjoyed a relatively peaceful transfer of power while in other cases the path to independence was extraordinarily violent. As a process, decolonisation was deeply entwined with the major conflicts that marked the century – the First World War, which brought about the demise of the Ottoman, German and Austro-Hungarian empires; the Bolshevik Revolution and its global reverberations; the rise of fascism and Nazism; the ensuing Second World War and Holocaust, which, by hastening the rise of human rights discourse, helped transform the normative underpinnings of international relations; and the Cold War competition between socialist and capitalist models of modernity. Decolonisation both shaped, and was shaped by, these profound and global conflagrations.

The entanglement of global and local politics was perhaps most conspicuous in the context of the wars of decolonisation that proliferated in the decades following the end of the Second World War. Initiated by insurgent movements to end decades or more of exploitation and oppression, (re-)establish national sovereignty, and seize state power from colonial and white minority-rule governments, the wars of decolonisation involved a form of warfare that witnessed a weaker and poorer side, the colonised, take on a far more powerful adversary, the coloniser. This mode of warfare is often referred to as people's war, which, as highlighted by Ian Beckett in Chapter 2, has a long history. People's war has had many different names: guerrilla warfare; partisan warfare; revolutionary warfare; insurgency or insurrectionary warfare. In the colonial context, such conflicts were classified by Europeans as 'small wars', though colonising forces often refused to use the nomenclature of warfare at all. Instead, they spoke of rebellions, upheavals, emergencies, brigandage or terrorism.[1] What distinguishes this mode of warfare from modern European warfare is its reliance on irregular fighters organised into small, mobile groups and using unconventional military tactics (e.g. ambushes, raids or sabotage) to oppose a larger, less mobile and conventionally organised military force. The 'people's wars' of the nineteenth century, Beckett argues, represented an almost instinctive response by indigenous societies and local forces to foreign conquest and occupation. The motivations that underpinned guerrillas in the nineteenth century and insurgents during the wars of decolonisation were therefore quite similar: these were struggles for freedom and self-determination and against subjugation, oppression and tutelage. Yet there was an important difference between the two eras: whereas nineteenth-century 'people's wars' generally ended in defeat for the insurgents, those of the twentieth century frequently resulted in setbacks or concessions on the part of the colonial and settler authorities.

What accounts for this difference? Changes in context and process will have played a role, including the transformed normative framework of the post-Second World War era, which increasingly regarded colonialism as an anachronism. Yet the twentieth century also witnessed a growing theorisation of people's war as the concept was adopted – and adapted – by leftist revolutionaries around the world. This theorisation bestowed upon the concept not only novel tactics and methods but also a strong emphasis on political mobilisation and, with this mobilisation, a far greater sense of strategic purpose. By the mid-twentieth century, theories of people's war were mostly associated with the Chinese Communist leader Mao Zedong, the Vietnamese leaders Hồ Chí Minh and Võ Nguyên Giáp, and Cuban-Argentinian revolutionary Che Guevara, all of whom implemented their theories to great effect during the Chinese Civil and Second Sino-Japanese Wars (1927–1949), the First and Second Indochina Wars (1947–1975) and the

---

[1] D. Walter, *Colonial Violence. European Empires and the Use of Force*, P. Lewis (trans.) (Oxford: Oxford University Press, 2017).

1959 Cuban Revolution, respectively. The concept was developed further by leftist intellectuals such as Régis Debray or Carlos Marighella. In the post-1945 era, two types of people's war emerged, which involved mostly a rural but at times also an urban dimension: those in opposition to what can be termed outside rulers, especially colonial and settler authorities; and those in opposition to local or domestic elites. This chapter will concern itself only with the former category of conflicts, though the latter, too, frequently involved anti- and de-colonial dimensions. Moreover, the chapter will not concern itself with theories of people's war. Rather, it explores the *practice* of people's war. It will do so by focusing on the wars of decolonisation that occurred in northern and southern Africa, from the Algerian War of Independence (1954–1962) to the armed struggle of the African National Congress (ANC) against apartheid (1960–1994). The chapter will highlight some of the key means, methods and priorities adopted by African anti-colonial liberation movements. As will be shown, these rarely followed the strict schemas set out by the theorists of people's war. Indeed, when it came to the concept of people's war, as a rule, theory and practice diverged considerably.

Sources

Almost from their inception, the wars of decolonisation were the subject of intense scholarly production. The Indochina wars alone, especially the Vietnam war, have generated an entire sub-field of scholarship. The same can be said of Algeria's liberation struggle, which had a similar impact on France as the Vietnam war had on the United States of America. Yet the liberation struggles of sub-Saharan and in particular southern Africa – Angola, Mozambique, Guinea-Bissau, Zimbabwe (formerly Southern Rhodesia), South Africa or Namibia (formerly South-West Africa) – have equally generated a rich literature, increasingly so, one might argue. Not all of this scholarship focuses on military aspects. Scholars have also explored the political, diplomatic, social and cultural impact these conflicts had, as well as their manifold legacies. The continued fascination arises at least in part from the ways in which these wars continue to reverberate not just locally but globally. After all, with the exception perhaps of the so-called Kenya Emergency (1952–1960), African liberation struggles were all imbricated to varying degrees with the global Cold War. Early accounts of the wars of decolonisation in Africa, by a diverse range of writers including Arslan Humbaraci, Edgar O'Ballance, David Galula, Frank Kitson, Peter Paret, Gérard Chaliand, Basil Davidson, Thomas Henriksen, John Marcum, Brendan Jundanian, Terence Ranger and Kenneth Grundy, frequently sought to determine the extent to which African insurgent movements were revolutionary in their goals and methods, or the degree to which they were dependent on, and subservient to, the Soviet Union or conversely to the People's Republic of China (PRC). The same can be said of early works of broader comparative analysis of the era's people's wars by writers such as Walter Laqueur, Robert Asprey, Geoffrey Fairbairn, Chalmers Johnson and Bard O'Neill. While some of these studies made innovative use of oral history and other primary sources, other accounts were journalistic, and others still were written by military practitioners, or with them in mind. Much of this literature was also deeply Euro- or Western-centric, and much of it focused more on the counterinsurgencies waged by the colonial or settler authorities than on the insurgencies themselves.

More recent scholarship on Africa's wars of decolonisation has also prioritised the counterinsurgent perspective, especially recent literature on the conflicts' military dimensions.[2] In part, this is explained by the onset of the global 'War on Terror' after the terrorist attacks of 11 September 2001, which prompted renewed interest in historical examples of counterinsurgency warfare. But it is also explained by a commonly held belief that it is supposedly easier to study the counterinsurgent's perspective: there are fewer languages to learn; the languages themselves are perceived as being easier to learn; and the existing records tend to be seen as more centralised, voluminous and accessible in the archives of the former colonial powers than they are in post-colonial states, where records are sometimes scattered, fragmentary, held privately or difficult to access.[3] Finally, the tendency to focus on the counterinsurgent is reinforced by the persistent proclivity, both within and beyond academia, to privilege Western and 'white' perspectives.[4]

This notwithstanding, excellent studies do exist that shed light on the insurgent perspectives of Africa's wars of decolonisation. Raphaëlle Branche's *L'embuscade de Palestro* and Neil Macmaster's *War in the Mountains* are just

---

2 For a relatively recent literature survey, see: I. Beckett, 'The historiography of insurgency', in P. B. Rich and I. Duyvesteyn (eds), *The Routledge Handbook of Insurgency and Counterinsurgency* (London: Routledge, 2012), 23–31.
3 The exception here is South Africa, where the post-Apartheid state retains control over Apartheid-era records and has made these – for both sides – accessible to researchers. South Africa also has an outstanding digital history portal, at www.sahistory.org.za/. Also of great use is the African Activist Archive maintained by Michigan State University, available at: https://africanactivist.msu.edu/. The Université du Québec à Montréal, meanwhile, maintains a multi-language 'interdisciplinary tool' on the First Indochina War, at www.indochine.uqam.ca/en/historical-dictionary.html.
4 For a critique of Western-centric approaches to insurgency, see: S. Metz, 'Rethinking insurgency', in Rich and Duyvesteyn (eds), *Handbook of Insurgency*, 32–44.

two recent studies that have helped illuminate the origins and methods of the Algerian insurgency against France. Some of the richest scholarship currently being produced on the insurgents' perspective focuses on the wars of decolonisation of southern Africa. While it is impossible to include all who have been instrumental in producing this scholarship, Jocelyn Alexander and JoAnn McGregor, Gerald Chikozho Mazarire, Eliakim Sibanda and Blessing-Miles Tendi, for instance, have done much to illuminate the Zimbabwe war of liberation (1964–1979); Christian Williams's work, meanwhile, sheds important light on the activities of the South West Africa People's Organisation (SWAPO), as do the wide-ranging contributions to two recent edited volumes on the history of resistance and war in Namibia – Jeremy Silvester's *Re-Viewing Resistance in Namibian History*,[5] and Ian van der Waag and Albert Grundlingh's *In Different Times*;[6] Stephen Weigert has produced an important military history of modern Angola; while Thula Simpson, Hugh Macmillan, Stephen Ellis, Arianna Lissoni, Stephen Davis and Simon Stevens have focused on the ANC's armed struggle.

Memoirs and biographies, of which more and more are being published, constitute another important source of information on anti-colonial insurgencies. On the Algerian war, for instance, Chihab Editions have recently published the memoirs of Lakhdar Bentobal (edited by the Algerian historian Daho Djerbal), a founder and key military leader of the *Front de libération nationale* (FLN, National Liberation Front) who then served as interior minister in the movement's government-in-exile during the Algerian independence struggle. More sources are also being translated into English, for example the memoir of Mokhtar Mokhtefi, who rose to become head of Algerian communications during the FLN's liberation struggle, or António Tomás's important new biography of Amílcar Cabral, the charismatic leader of the *Partido Africano para a Independência da Guiné e Cabo Verde* (PAIGC, African Party for the Independence of Guinea and Cape Verde), who was assassinated in 1973. Patrick Chabal's older biography of the Guinea-Bissauan leader and anti-colonial thinker remains an equally rich source for those seeking to understand the PAIGC's successful insurgency against the Portuguese. Many of these memoirs and biographies focus on key leaders and decision makers, such as Eduardo Mondlane, president of the *Frente de Libertação de Moçambique* (FRELIMO, Mozambique Liberation Front) until his assassination in 1969; Agostinho Neto, who led the *Movimento Popular de Libertação de Angola – Partido do Trabalho* (MPLA, People's Movement

---

5 Jeremy Silvester, *Re-Viewing Resistance in Namibian History* (Windhoek: University of Namibia Press, 2015).
6 Ian van der Waag and Albert Grundlingh, *In Different Times* (Singapore: Sun Press, 2019).

People's War and Wars of Decolonisation

for the Liberation of Angola – Labour Party); Jonas Savimbi, a collaborator of Holden Roberto's *União das Populações de Angola* (UPA, National Front for the Liberation of Angola) and co-founder of its successor, the *Frente Nacional de Libertação de Angola* (FNLA, National Front for the Liberation of Angola), who in 1966 went on to found the rival *União Nacional para a Independência Total de Angola* (UNITA, National Union for the Total Independence of Angola); Robert Mugabe, who rose to become leader of the Zimbabwe African National Union (ZANU) in 1975; General Solomon Mujuru, one of Mugabe's closest collaborators; Joshua Nkomo, leader of the rival Zimbabwe African People's Union (ZAPU); or Nelson Mandela, Oliver Tambo and multiple other leaders of the ANC and its armed wing, *uMkhonto we Sizwe* (MK). Memoirs and biographies should be read alongside other published source materials produced by the insurgent movements and their leaders, though some of this documentation will have served propaganda purposes. Aquino de Bragança and Immanuel Wallerstein's three-volume *African Liberation Reader*[7] provides a useful starting point, while JSTOR's primary course collection on *Struggles for Freedom: Southern Africa* contains a rich variety of digitised pamphlets, interviews, oral histories and other documentation.[8] These sources are particularly useful for those seeking to understand the strategic practice of anti-colonial insurgent movements.

Causes and Objectives

The literature and sources on anti-colonial insurgencies are thus both rich and varied. Yet few scholars, especially more recently, have focused explicitly on questions of strategy. Western bias may, again, help to explain this omission: since military practitioners and theorists tend to view counterinsurgency warfare as involving tactics more than strategy,[9] the corollary must be that insurgency warfare, too, regardless of nomenclature, cannot be 'strategic'. Such thinking is problematic. It replicates the discourse of the colonial and settler authorities, whether French, Portuguese, British, Rhodesian or South African, which deliberately sought to delegitimise insurgent movements by portraying their activities as criminal, terrorist and depraved, thereby denying the political nature of their aims. It was for this

---

7 Immanuel Wallerstein, *African Liberation Reader* (London: Zed Press, 1982).
8 Available at: www.jstor.org/site/struggles-for-freedom/southern-africa/.
9 G. P. Gentile, 'A strategy of tactics: population-centric COIN and the army', *Parameters*, 39 (2009), 5–17, https://press.armywarcollege.edu/parameters/vol39/iss3/7; C. Gray, 'Concept failure? COIN, counterinsurgency, and strategic theory', *Prism*, 3 (2012), 17–32.

reason that colonial and settler governments generally refused to name these conflicts for what they were: wars. This colonial discourse obscured a fundamental reality. Whatever the precise character of the movements waging them, the wars of decolonisation – in Africa as much as elsewhere – had clear political goals: namely, the ending of colonialism and racialism; the seizure of state power; the attainment of political independence and sovereign statehood; as well as radical socio-economic change. People's war, especially in the Maoist tradition, provided a blueprint for achieving those goals, just as socialism offered an alternative model of modernity to that of colonial capitalism. The creation of base areas from whence to recruit, train, organise; the resort to guerrilla warfare; the willingness to engage in a protracted war; the emphasis on political mobilisation, especially of noncombatant populations, and on an integrated political and military struggle; the efforts exerted not only to control territory but to govern people through the creation of a counterstate capable of contesting the authority and legitimacy of the colonial or settler regime – all of these core elements featured prominently in African wars of decolonisation, even if none conformed strictly to the 'classic' three-phased model of Maoist people's war. Anticolonial insurgent leaders undoubtedly 'set objectives, established priorities among them, and allocated resources to them', to use Kimberly Kagan's definition of strategy, regardless of 'whether or not they develop[ed] or [kept] to long-range systematic plans'.[10]

While they may have implemented these objectives to varying degrees of success and rigour, the insurgent leaders contesting colonial and white minority rule in Africa thus did practise strategy. The question that remains is, how? To answer this question, one might start by looking at the activities and movements of insurgent leaders prior to the outbreak of hostilities. The decision to instigate armed struggle was rarely taken lightly or precipitously. For leaders of the ANC, which had previously espoused non-violence in its fight against apartheid, the decision was reached as a last resort in response to the 1960 Sharpeville massacre. For others, too, the decision to resort to armed struggle came in response to colonial atrocities – the Sétif and Guelma massacres of May 1945 in French Algeria; the Pidjiguiti massacre in Portuguese Bissau of August 1959; the brutal suppression of the Baixa de Cassanje revolt of early 1961 in Portuguese Angola. In Southern Rhodesia, meanwhile, it was white settlers' categorical refusal to accept the new British

---

10 K. Kagan, 'Redefining Roman grand strategy', *Journal of Military History*, 70:2 (2006), 333–64, 348.

policy of granting independence only to majority rule governments that prompted the start of armed resistance by both ZANU and ZAPU from July 1964. By the early 1960s, armed struggle had come to be seen as the only viable means of contesting the colonial situation, which, as the Martiniquan psychiatrist turned FLN propagandist Frantz Fanon argued, was itself predicated entirely on racist violence. Fanon's *The Wretched of the Earth*, first published in French by François Maspero in 1961, became one of the most influential texts to inspire anti-colonial and leftist insurgents of the era. But the leaders of African insurgent movements also looked elsewhere for inspiration and instruction. The founders of the FLN, for example, looked to the Bolshevik Revolution and Irish War of Independence, the global fight against fascism during the Second World War, the Chinese Civil War and the First Indochina War, which had ended in such a humiliating defeat for the French at Điện Biên Phủ.[11] Nelson Mandela, one of the founders of the MK, studied the guerrilla tactics of the Anglo-Boer War as well as those deployed by the Irgun during the Jewish insurgency in Palestine, while also reading works by and about Che Guevara, Mao Zedong and Fidel Castro.[12] Like other insurgent leaders from southern Africa, he also looked to the FLN, which was in the final stages of its successful liberation struggle just as Mandela and other African insurgent leaders were beginning to launch theirs.

Priorities, Means and Outcomes: Understanding the Strategic Practice of Liberation Movements

Once taken, the choice for armed struggle frequently involved long periods, even years, of preparation. Insurgent leaders had to recruit and indoctrinate militants, forge alliances and create united fronts, secure domestic as well as foreign backers, procure weapons and munitions, train fighters in the tactics of guerrilla warfare, plan their opening salvos, and establish base camps and safe havens. These preparations took place clandestinely and under extremely difficult circumstances. After all, colonial and settler authorities maintained a strict monopoly on the means of violence and forbade all activities that threatened, or appeared to threaten, the status quo. With the security services constantly on the alert and repression the norm, the risks

---

[11] For an early effort to apply the lessons of these conflicts to the anti-colonial struggle in Algeria, see: 'Rapport par Aït Ahmed du bureau politique du PPA au comité central élargi (décembre 1948)', in Mohammed Harbi (ed.), *Les archives de la révolution algérienne* (Paris: Jeune Afrique, 1981), 15–49.

[12] Nelson Mandela, *Long Walk to Freedom* (London: Abacus, 1994), 326.

were frequently so great that much of this planning took place abroad. Starting in the late 1940s, for instance, North African nationalist movements dispatched representatives to Cairo, where they co-ordinated activities and lobbied the newly formed Arab League. Following the revolution of 1952, the Egyptian regime under Gamal Abdel Nasser became a fervent supporter of anti-colonial nationalism. Years prior to the outbreak of the FLN's revolution on 1 November 1954, Cairo had become a haven for Algerian militants, and an important source of material, military and political assistance. Thus although the FLN was formed only in 1954 and its initial membership was small, those who launched the Algerian War of Independence drew on connections, plans and experience forged over the course of many years. To the FLN's founders, the importance of planning and preparation will have been further reinforced by the experiences of the ill-fated *Organisation Spéciale* (Special Organisation), a paramilitary organisation set up in the aftermath of the 1945 massacres and dismantled by French police in 1951, to which many of them had belonged.

The quickening pace of decolonisation in Africa, starting in the mid-1950s, made it progressively easier for insurgent movements to seek shelter and support from the many emerging newly independent states. Many of these states, moreover, fervently supported the anti-colonial cause. By the early 1960s, Morocco hosted the first seat of the 'Conference of Nationalist Organisations of the Portuguese Colonies', comprised of representatives of the nationalist movements of Angola, Guinea-Cape Verde and Mozambique. In Morocco, these nationalists sought to consult and co-ordinate not only among themselves but also with the FLN and a range of visiting officials and revolutionaries, who offered advice and instruction and who frequently pledged support. In early 1962, meanwhile, Mandela and several ANC colleagues embarked on a tour of independent African states. Their aim was 'to enlist support, money, and training' for the recently established MK, which had initiated its first sabotage campaign in December 1961.[13] Mandela attended a conference in Addis Ababa of the Pan-African Freedom Movement for East, Central and Southern Africa, a precursor to the Organisation of African Unity (OAU), before visiting a number of capitals, including Tunis, Rabat, Dakar and Conakry. That same year, Mondlane founded the FRELIMO from the safety of Dar-es-Salaam. The Tanzanian capital remained the movement's headquarters throughout the Mozambican War Of Independence, which formally began in September 1964, and the country would go on to host many other southern

---

13 Mandela, *Long Walk*, 342.

African liberation movements.[14] The PAIGC, too, opted for safety when in 1960, nearly three years before the start of its liberation struggle, it began to operate primarily from neighbouring Guinea-Conakry. Roberto's FNLA, meanwhile, set up its main base in the Republic of Congo. From there, the FNLA launched its first incursion into northern Angola in March 1961, opening the Angolan War of Independence.

Insurgent leaders thus understood the importance of preparing the ground for armed struggle and securing base areas from whence to pursue their war effort. Increasingly, the liberation movements chose to base themselves beyond the boundaries of the contested state even after the opening of hostilities, in newly independent 'front line' and otherwise friendly or 'neutral' states.[15] External 'sanctuaries' helped offset the asymmetry of power between insurgents and counterinsurgents. Based beyond the colonial and settler authorities' control, they offered insurgents increased protection against repression and extermination. They also bought insurgents the time they required to organise, recruit, train, plan and develop an 'insurgent-state-in-waiting'. From 1957, newly independent Tunisia and Morocco came to host a plethora of camps, bases and headquarters for the FLN, its armed forces, the *Armée de libération nationale* (ALN, National Liberation Army) and its government-in-exile, created in September 1958. The FNLA continued to pursue its war effort from bases in the Republic of Congo (Congo-Léopoldville, later Zaire), whereas the MPLA and UNITA operated mostly from bases in Zambia and Namibia (South-West Africa). In addition to Tanzania, the FRELIMO, too, operated from bases in Zambia. So did the ZAPU and its armed wing, the Zimbabwe People's Revolutionary Army (ZIPRA), while their competitors, the ZANU and its armed wing, the Zimbabwe African National Liberation Army (ZANLA), maintained their principal camps and bases in Tanzania and, from 1976, in independent Mozambique. Angola, which gained its independence that same year, then became a refuge for the SWAPO, which also operated from Zambia. Finally, the ANC and MK, exiled from South Africa in the early 1960s, pursued their struggle against apartheid from bases and camps located at different points in Tanzania, Zambia, Angola, Uganda, Botswana, Mozambique, Lesotho and Swaziland.

14 George Roberts, *Revolutionary State-Making in Dar es Salaam. African Liberation and the Global Cold War, 1961–1974* (Cambridge: Cambridge University Press, 2021).
15 Mathilde von Bülow, 'Exile, safe havens and rear bases: external sanctuaries and the transnational dimension of late colonial insurgencies and counter-insurgencies', in Martin Thomas and Gareth Curless (eds), *The Oxford Handbook of Colonial Insurgencies and Counter-Insurgencies* (Oxford: Oxford University Press, 2023), 653–73.

The insurgent forces that came to operate from these dispersed locations also had to be equipped, sheltered and fed. Thus, in addition to the creation of secure bases and camps, insurgent leaders prioritised the procurement of funds, war materiel and other needed resources. This would remain a constant preoccupation. Compared to the counterinsurgents, even the less wealthy ones such as Portugal or Rhodesia, African liberation movements initiated their wars of decolonisation from positions of extreme material weakness. Given the poverty in which most colonial subjects lived, remittances and other forms of support from among the populations, whether voluntary or coerced, only went so far – though they certainly did play an important role in sustaining fighters, especially those in the field. Weapons and munitions were often seized directly from the colonial and settler security forces by means of ambushes or raids. Such tactics, however, could never secure a steady and sufficient supply of materiel, especially as insurgent forces began to grow. From the start, therefore, insurgent movements sought out aid and assistance from sympathetic states and organisations further afield. Considerable support came from external host nations, which provided facilities and a plethora of other vital services, including water and electricity, transport, communications, as well as (diplomatic) passports that enabled travel.[16] The Egyptian, Libyan, Tunisian and Moroccan authorities also served as intermediaries through which the FLN, for example, purchased many of its arms and munitions. Egypt, Algeria (upon independence in 1962), Morocco and other African nations further provided specialist training to insurgents, for example in guerrilla tactics, sabotage, ordnance or radio communications. In addition to such bilateral assistance, liberation movements by the mid-1960s could also draw on multilateral aid. The OAU, founded in 1963, pledged as one of its primary objectives to eradicate all forms of colonialism from Africa. To this end, it established a Liberation Committee, tasked with the harmonisation of assistance to anti-colonial insurgent movements. Among other things, the committee co-ordinated the provision of funding, logistical support, training as well as publicity to all liberation movements formally recognised by the OAU. Perhaps the greatest source of material support, however, came from the Sino-Soviet bloc. From the late 1950s, the Soviet Union, together with its Eastern-bloc satellites and Cuba, became increasingly active in Africa, providing training and materiel, and seconding instructors, advisers as well as

---

16 This also allowed host nations to exercise a degree of supervision and control over their insurgent guests.

intelligence officers to the insurgent groups they supported. So did the PRC, which by then was a rival to the USSR. Western powers, for their part, and with the notable exception of the Scandinavian states, tended to support the counterinsurgent forces, often covertly. Of the liberation movements, only Roberto's FNLA and Savimbi's UNITA received substantial Western aid.[17]

Through a combination of diplomatic dexterity and generosity on the part of donors, some insurgent groups ended up awash in military equipment. An abundance of materiel, however, guaranteed neither improved military effectiveness nor the ability to transition to the third and final phase of people's war. Indeed, in contrast to the Việt Minh in Indochina, none of the liberation movements in Africa reached a point where they were able to wage an offensive war. The key difficulty faced by most was logistical. Almost all struggled to ensure that supplies and reinforcements arrived where and when they were needed. The ALN, for example, assembled an impressive and well-led conventional force on its military bases in Tunisia and Morocco, the so-called *armée de la frontière*, but was prevented from deploying that force by the so-called Morice and Pedron lines – heavily defended, extensive and fortified barriers through which the French military had essentially sealed off Algeria from its eastern and western neighbours. The Morice and Pedron lines effectively asphyxiated the ALN's dwindling internal forces, which were also hit hard by the French military, especially after the onset of the Challe offensive in 1959. For other liberation movements, such as the ZANU or ZAPU, FRELIMO, MPLA and especially the ANC, the problem was not so much one of impenetrable border defences, of which there were relatively few in southern Africa, as it was one of distance. The various base camps of these insurgent groups were situated in sanctuary states often far removed from the fighting fronts. To reach these fronts, insurgents had to cross vast distances, sometimes through hostile, white minority-ruled territories. At the same time, the contested states were themselves immense and underdeveloped. Accordingly, the supply and

---

17 Lena Dallywater, Chris Saunders and Helder Adegar Fonseca (eds), *Southern African Liberation Movements and the Global Cold War 'East'* (Berlin: De Gruyter Oldenbourg, 2019); Piero Gleijeses, *Conflicting Missions: Havana, Washington, and Africa, 1959–1976* (Chapel Hill: University of North Carolina Press, 2002); Elizabeth Schmidt, *Foreign Intervention in Africa: from the Cold War to the War on Terror* (Cambridge: Cambridge University Press, 2013); David Shinn and Joshua Eisenman, *China and Africa: A Century of Engagement* (Philadelphia: University of Pennsylvania Press, 2012); Vladimir Shubin, *The Hot 'Cold War': The USSR in Southern Africa* (Durban: University of KwaZulu-Natal Press, 2008); Natalia Telepneva, *Cold War Liberation: The Soviet Union and the Collapse of the Portuguese Empire in Africa, 1961–1975* (Chapel Hill: University of North Carolina Press, 2022).

transportation of equipment, very frequently on foot and across difficult terrain, posed a considerable challenge. These logistical obstacles were then compounded by the absence of stable communications. The PAIGC was perhaps the only African liberation movement for whom problems of distance and size did not pose a significant problem to its supply chains and communications. The movement's external bases in Guinea and Senegal were so close to the internal front, which was itself exceptionally small, that supplies, reinforcements and communications were easily assured. This made it easier for the insurgents to seize and hold territory, so much so that by the time of the Carnation Revolution in 1974, which effectively ended the wars of decolonisation in the Portuguese colonies, over half of Guinea-Bissau was controlled by the PAIGC.

When it came to the creation of liberated zones, few African liberation movements witnessed the success of the PAIGC. Even so, their insurgencies should not be dismissed as failures. While few liberation movements in Africa achieved the kind of sustained military successes of, say, the Vietnamese, almost none were militarily defeated either. The Challe offensive in Algeria may have severely routed the ALN's internal fighters, but, contrary to what the French military liked to claim, it never fully vanquished them. Angolan insurgents, in many respects the weakest, most divided and hence most ineffectual of the African liberation movements, were also never fully defeated by the Portuguese. The ANC struggled to sustain its internal struggle, relying more and more on exile politics. Yet the MK endured, and by the 1980s, it was able to step up its operations within South Africa. Apart from the small and isolated Kenya Land and Freedom Army (KLFA), referred to by the British as the Mau Mau, all the major anti-colonial insurgent groups in Africa managed to sustain their guerrilla activities enough to continue to harass, stretch and wear down the counterinsurgent forces, both physically and in terms of morale.

This proved important, as armed struggle in the form of protracted guerrilla warfare, sabotage or terrorism also served an important political and psychological purpose. On the internal front, it helped maintain a climate of insecurity among the contested populations, which was propitious for the insurgents. By generating fear and terror, and by provoking a response from the colonial and settler authorities that was almost always heavy-handed and disproportionate to the initial trigger, armed resistance helped drive a wedge between coloniser and colonised. In doing so, it forced those populations that had hitherto remained uncommitted to pick a side in the anti-colonial struggle.

This further highlights an important point, one that was poorly understood by counterinsurgents too wedded to the theories of people's war: insurgent movements did not have to hold liberated territories to be in de facto control of the people or the terrain. Thus, although it did little sustained fighting during the Algerian war's final years, and its internal forces grew ever weaker, the ALN still came to be seen, both within Algeria and abroad, as the spearhead of the Algerian people fighting for their liberation. Likewise, the MK's military efforts, while largely ineffective, nonetheless helped enhance the ANC's reputation, so much so that the movement came to be regarded as 'the custodian of South African liberation'.[18] The very act of armed resistance, in other words, regardless of its effectiveness, enhanced the liberation movements' political credibility and legitimacy. It served a similar purpose on the external front, where armed struggle – however performative and symbolic – helped insurgent groups garner international aid and assistance. As such, the continuation of the armed struggle, even if it was intermittent and uneven, remained a prime objective for liberation movements.

Military victory, on the other hand, was rarely a prime objective for those contesting colonial and white minority rule. Most liberation movements recognised that violence alone would not dislodge the regimes they sought to overthrow. As one FLN leader advised Mandela in early 1962: 'Guerrilla warfare ... was not designed to win a military victory so much as to unleash political and economic forces that would bring down the enemy.' It was imperative, therefore, 'not to neglect the political side of war while planning the military effort', for public opinion, including international public opinion, 'is sometimes worth more than a fleet of jet fighters'.[19] The FLN thus understood the importance of the political struggle, the twin pillar to the military struggle in people's war. Even though the movement was riven by internal rivalries, especially between its political and military factions, the FLN placed great emphasis on political organising. In September 1958, the movement created a government-in-exile that sought to challenge the legitimacy of the French colonial state in Algeria, replicating many of its functions. In this manner, the FLN arrogated for itself not only moral authority but also many of the attributes of sovereignty and statehood. Under the leadership of the charismatic Cabral, the PAIGC was even more successful at political mobilisation. Whereas the FLN created its counterstate largely in sanctuaries that bordered Algeria, the PAIGC also mobilised the population

18 Hilary Sapire, 'Liberation movements, exile, and international solidarity: an introduction', *Journal of Southern African Studies*, 35:2 (2009), 276.
19 Mandela, *Long Walk*, 355.

in the liberated zones it controlled. Cabral sought to raise political consciousness by stressing the importance of African cultures and co-opting the support of local communities and elders. To achieve this, he decentralised power to the village level and focused on enhancing daily life. This he achieved by improving farming techniques (Cabral was, after all, an agronomist), introducing a trade-and-barter system and providing healthcare and education to local populations. In this manner, the PAIGC was able to create an effective counterstate and introduce socio-economic change within Guinea-Bissau. The many exile camps established and maintained by the SWAPO, meanwhile, were instrumental in developing many of the social and political hierarchies that would continue to shape Namibian life post-independence. Other liberation movements, such as the ANC, ZAPU and FRELIMO, initially prioritised the armed struggle, hoping in this way to enforce capitulations or concessions. Military setbacks soon taught these movements to emulate the PAIGC and FLN. Political mobilising, after all, involved a slow and painstaking process that required careful planning, guidance and control. For some, this proved more difficult than for others. The ANC, for example, struggled for a long time to regain a foothold within South Africa after it was forced abroad in the early 1960s. Like the FLN, it increasingly focused on creating an effective government-in-exile. Angolan nationalists, on the other hand, were so divided that it proved impossible to establish a united front. Instead, the MPLA, FNLA and UNITA, and to some degree also the ZANU and ZAPU, continued to rely on regional and ethnic mobilisation.

The political struggle served several purposes, of course, including the recruitment of fighters and militants, and the 'encasement' (*encadrement*) of local populations, whose active and passive support was required to sustain insurgent forces in the field. Most importantly, however, the political struggle sought to bolster the insurgents' reputation and deprive the colonial and settler authorities of recognition and legitimacy. In this sense, the political struggle was aimed not just at local populations within the contested states but also at metropolitan audiences and the wider international community. While its precise objectives evolved over the course of the war, the FLN, for instance, always conceived of its struggle as having two equally important and simultaneous dimensions involving 'an internal action, both political as well as armed, as well as an external action that, with the support of our natural allies, will make of the Algerian problem a reality for the entire world'.[20] Based in their

---

20 'Proclamation du Front de Libération Nationale, 1er novembre 1954', in Harbi (ed.), *Les archives de la révolution*, 102.

respective external sanctuaries, African liberation movements, especially those that laboured most to sustain and expand the internal armed and political struggle, increasingly came to prioritise the external front. Like the FLN, the ANC assembled an impressive apparatus through which to communicate and interact with the wider world. By organising public relations campaigns, producing printed as well as audio-visual propaganda, participating in a wide range of regional and international conferences, establishing both permanent and roaming quasi-diplomatic missions, and seeking international recognition for their movements, African insurgent groups also sought victory by means of what historian Matthew Connelly, writing about the FLN, has called a 'diplomatic revolution'.[21] To achieve that end, they could draw on a growing list of allies and platforms: from other formerly colonised states and Eastern bloc states to a range of international organisations and conferences, such as the United Nations, the OAU, the Afro-Asian Non-Aligned Movement, the Non-Aligned Afro-Asian People's Solidarity Organisation and subsequent Tricontinental conference. In the context of the new and growing social movements of the 1960s, moreover, anti-colonial liberation movements also secured the support of an ever-wider range of transnational solidarity movements based predominantly in the West. Of these, the Anti-Apartheid Movement, founded initially by South African exiles in the UK as a consumer boycott organisation, would become the largest and best known.

Diplomatic and propaganda campaigns on the international stage proved to be at least as important to liberation movements as the internal armed and political struggle. 'The struggle had ceased to be strictly national', Cabral told the UN General Assembly in 1972; it 'had become international'.[22] In spite of the PAIGC's success on the internal front, even Cabral invested considerable time and energy in this external effort. 'For weapons', as Connelly wrote about the FLN, which in many ways set a precedent by its diplomatic campaigns, insurgent groups 'employed human rights reports, press conferences, and youth congresses, fighting over world opinion and international law more than conventional military objectives'.[23] The key aims of this action were threefold: first, to secure the material aid needed to sustain the armed and political struggle, as outlined above; second, to garner recognition as the

---

21 Matthew Connelly, *A Diplomatic Revolution: Algeria's Fight for Independence and the Origins of the Post-Cold War Era* (Oxford: Oxford University Press, 2002).
22 'Amílcar Cabral, second address before the UN, 16 October 1972', in Africa Information Service (ed.), *Return to the Source. Selected Speeches of Amílcar Cabral* (New York: Monthly Review, 1973), 19.
23 Connelly, *Diplomatic Revolution*, 4.

legitimate representatives of the people and states they sought to lead; and third, to delegitimise and internationally isolate the counterinsurgent forces and the colonial and white minority regimes they sought to uphold. The joint pursuit of both the internal armed and political struggle and the external diplomatic struggle ultimately sought to compel the colonial and settler authorities either to give in or to give up. While they could not be defeated outright, the aim was to wear down and isolate the entrenched regimes to such an extent, morally, politically, economically and diplomatically, so as to render their continued authority untenable. The aim was, moreover, to oblige these authorities to accept the liberation movements as the only valid interlocutors for peace talks and negotiations for a transfer of power. In this, most of the major liberation movements that contested colonial and white minority rule in Africa during the era of decolonisation proved successful, irrespective of the course of events that followed the formal transfer of power. The one that did not succeed, the KLFA, was also the movement that remained the most isolated, both internally from the Kenyan population, and externally from the international community, including other African liberation movements and post-colonial states.

Conclusion

The wars of decolonisation in Africa were contested by national liberation movements that, to varying degrees, all modelled their insurgencies on leftist notions of people's war. Whether in Algeria, Angola, Guinea-Bissau, Mozambique, Namibia, South Africa or Zimbabwe, the principal cases upon which this chapter has focused, insurgent groups took up arms against considerably stronger, conventionally organised forces with the intention of ousting colonial and white minority regimes, achieving national independence and bringing about lasting socio-economic change. Almost all African liberation movements achieved at least the first two of these prime objectives, albeit to varying degrees of success. Only the KLFA, which in any case never aimed for *national* liberation, was decisively defeated. While some may have started from a fixed notion of people's war and how to wage it, most liberation movements wound up applying the concept, and the theories upon which it was based, rather loosely. They understood that military success alone would not defeat the regimes they sought to dislodge. People's war thus represented more of a guiding principle from which to draw key lessons than a preordained and immutable blueprint for victory. Three lessons stood out in particular: the use of guerrilla warfare; the importance of base areas;

and the integration of military as well as political action, including diplomatic action. These lessons helped liberation movements plan, organise and prioritise their various objectives as well as the broad means through which to achieve them.

Theories of people's war thus certainly influenced the strategic practice of African liberation movements. Yet that practice was also informed to a considerable degree by the foresight and direction of their leaders, some of whom, like Cabral and Mondlane, proved quite exceptional, and by adaptation to local conditions. Guerrilla warfare remained the prime method of direct armed action for African liberation movements, whose insurgencies rarely passed beyond the second phase of people's war. Base areas, moreover, were increasingly located not within but beyond the confines of the contested state. Perhaps because of that circumstance, many of the liberation movements progressively came to prioritise the external front over the internal front. It was in the international arena that these insurgent groups sought to raise the funds and materiel, and gain the training they needed to sustain their war efforts. Given the difficulty for most of establishing and holding liberated areas, their efforts turned increasingly to winning the 'hearts and minds' not just of the local populations they sought to represent but of the international community. Most also focused their energies on the construction of an 'insurgent-state-in-waiting' based in their external sanctuaries. This is not to suggest that the internal armed and political struggles were abandoned; they were not, and they remained important for a range of reasons, not least to secure new recruits and delegitimise the opponent. For many of the movements, however, circumstances dictated a change of course. This ability to adapt ultimately proved vital. For one, it helped insurgent groups survive the relentless pursuit of the counterinsurgent forces. More importantly, it helped them develop and sustain the discourse and methods through which they came to be recognised, both internally and externally, as the rightful leaders of the peoples whose liberation they sought. In this manner, African liberation movements, even if they did not achieve consistent military success, were able to break the will, undermine the legitimacy of and ultimately defeat the colonial and white minority governments they sought to oust.

15
Nuclear Strategies

JEFFREY H. MICHAELS

'Nuclear strategy' as a concept defies easy definition. In one sense it is a contradiction in terms. Such is the destructive power of many nuclear weapons that to employ them would not bring any tangible political benefit, especially if an adversary can threaten nuclear retaliation. Moreover, they constitute a politically sensitive category of weapon so that even to use the less destructive types to achieve a discrete military objective or to demonstrate resolve still carries enormous political risks. Indeed, they hold so little political appeal that since 1945, nuclear weapons have not been used in conflicts and are effectively regarded as unusable weapons, a phenomenon known as the 'nuclear taboo'. The most common reason cited by states acquiring a nuclear arsenal is that nuclear weapons are deemed useful to deter attack by a nuclear-armed opponent or an adversary that maintains strong conventional forces. Though a less cited justification, nuclear weapons have often been viewed as political tools that are useful for making threats or bolstering national prestige.

Another reason nuclear strategy is a difficult concept is that the prospect of a war in which only nuclear weapons are used might exist in theory but would be a remote possibility. Instead, the practice of nuclear strategy has been dominated by ideas about nuclear use in war *alongside* conventional weapons – providing an 'umbrella' for conventional operations against a nuclear adversary, using against an enemy's armed forces to support one's own conventional military offensive, or helping to stop or defeat an adversary's conventional offensive. Hence, rather than a concept of 'nuclear strategy', a more useful analytical term would be the slightly more cumbersome 'strategy with a nuclear component', in relation to a broader political strategy, diplomatic strategy, military strategy and so forth.

Notably, despite contemplating and planning numerous ways in which nuclear weapons might be employed in potential military conflicts, and acquiring and sustaining costly nuclear arsenals, political leaders have been unwilling to use them. Nevertheless, strategists have insisted that sophisticated ways of employing nuclear weapons are still needed to ensure they would not be used in the lethal sense, especially if there was the risk of a direct attack on one's country, one's armed forces or one's allies. To this end, elaborate theories of nuclear deterrence have been developed to maintain the status quo. Different ways and means of employing nuclear weapons were conceptualised for the purpose of being able to inflict unacceptable damage on an adversary. On the other hand, by considering scenarios in which nuclear weapons were the only ones that really mattered, with the role of politics and other real-world variables crucial to understanding the broader context of war being largely unaccounted for, it was almost certain that ideas about 'nuclear strategy' constituted an intellectual bubble that remained separate from the practice of strategy in post-1945 conflicts.

The literature on nuclear strategy can be classed into three interrelated types. The first type considers how nuclear weapons might be used, usually set against the backdrop of technological developments or an adversary's evolving capability. These are the works of civilian and military theorists, and are, by their nature, speculative. They deal with ideas about how a future nuclear war might be fought or how nuclear crises might unfold in order to address questions about what sort of nuclear posture is needed to deter an enemy. Various social scientific methods such as game theory have often been employed to enhance the rigour of this speculative endeavour. The second type of literature is mainly historical. Relying heavily on declassified documents and insider accounts, historians have sought to uncover the role played by nuclear weapons in the decision making of state and non-state actors. Public statements and other contemporary open sources have also been used to gain insights into the nuclear strategies of these actors. A third type is the literature on nuclear proliferation, arms control and disarmament. While nuclear strategy is not the principal focus of this literature, it is nonetheless a topic central to any debate about maintaining the nuclear status quo, reducing nuclear arsenals or eliminating them altogether.

To provide a general overview of the practice of nuclear strategy, this chapter will begin by examining the strategic ideas underpinning the US military's use of the atomic bomb at the end of the Second World War. It will then discuss the different strategies nuclear states devised in relation to other nuclear states and nuclear aspirants. Finally, the strategies of non-nuclear states when confronted with nuclear adversaries will be analysed.

The Use of the Atomic Bomb

As the use of atomic bombs at Hiroshima and Nagasaki in August 1945[1] provides the single example of nuclear use in wartime, it is important to dwell briefly upon the strategy debates that preceded the bombings. Doing so will highlight that many key ideas relevant for nuclear strategy after 1945 had already been discussed prior to the United States dropping the first atomic bomb.

Initially, the need to acquire an atomic weapon was premised on the idea of deterrence, or as US president Franklin D. Roosevelt put it, 'to make sure that the Nazis don't blow us up'.[2] In other words, assuming that Germany developed atomic weapons, it would refrain from using them if the Allies were able to inflict retaliation in kind. This attitude was consonant with prevailing fears about chemical weapons use. Despite the 1925 Geneva Protocol banning the use of chemical weapons, many of the key participants in the Second World War had developed arsenals of these weapons but avoided using them due to fear of retaliation, rather than out of concerns that they would be violating international law.[3] As the Manhattan Project got underway, with the prospect of an atomic bomb on the horizon, some limited thought was given to how it might be employed, and against whom. In one high-level policy discussion in May 1943 it was argued that 'the best point of use would be on a Japanese fleet concentration in the Harbor of Truk'. Use against Tokyo was also suggested but it was pointed out that if the bomb failed to explode, it could be easily salvaged. Japan rather than Germany was the preferred target on the basis that if it failed to explode, the Japanese would be less able to 'secure knowledge from it' than the Germans.[4] Very few details exist about how use of the atomic bomb was conceptualised at this early stage, yet the reference to attacking the Japanese Navy suggests that it was not viewed as a 'war winning weapon' in its own right, but instead as one that would be useful to facilitate conventional

[1] See also Chapter 12.
[2] Roosevelt cited in W. Lanouette, *Genius in the Shadows: A Biography of Leo Szilard, the Man behind the Bomb* (New York: Charles Scribner's Sons, 1992), 210.
[3] J. Ellis Van Courtland Moon, 'Chemical weapons and deterrence: the World War II experience', *International Security*, 8 (1984), 3–35.
[4] 'Memorandum by L. R. Grove, "Policy meeting, 5/5/43," top secret', https://nsarchive.gwu.edu/documents/atomic-bomb-end-world-war-ii/003.pdf.

operations. This view about 'battlefield' use would also be discussed in 1945 by senior US military officials, such as General George C. Marshall, when talking about efforts to support a ground invasion of Japan. One option mentioned was to support an amphibious operation by dropping an atomic bomb on a Japanese Army headquarters in the vicinity of the landings. However, with so few atomic bombs likely to be available prior to the invasion, it was recognised they would be of limited utility as battlefield weapons.[5]

By contrast, use of the bomb on a city, as occurred in the case of Hiroshima and Nagasaki,[6] was inspired, to some extent at least, by the 'school' of strategic air power theory, with its emphasis on using bombing to undermine an adversary's war-making potential and the morale of its population without the requirement for large ground operations. Similar to the conventional bombs dropped on other Japanese cities, with the March 1945 firebombing of Tokyo representing the climax of this effort, dropping the atomic bomb on Hiroshima was largely viewed as being able to produce the same destructive effect more efficiently. Hiroshima was to be the first of potentially a string of Japanese cities that might be bombed with atomic weapons, albeit this would largely be dependent on many factors, such as how many bombs would become available and how soon, and whether the Soviet Union declared war on Japan, which, according to US intelligence would 'finally convince the Japanese of the inevitability of complete defeat'.[7]

When developing atomic strategy at this stage, four background considerations set the context for the American debate. In the first instance, the decision to use the atomic bomb reflected a deliberate choice *not* to use chemical weapons, of which the US had ample supply. By spring 1945, the US military had made plans for use of chemical weapons against Japan but never received authorisation to proceed.[8] Second, similar to chemical weapons, atomic bombs were considered a special category of weapon, with policy regarding their use discussed and sanctioned only at the highest level. Unlike other types of military action, the decision to use atomic weapons was only taken following consultation among politicians, senior military officers and scientists. A third consideration dealt with how use of

---

5 B. J. Bernstein, 'Eclipsed by Hiroshima and Nagasaki: early thinking about tactical nuclear weapons', *International Security*, 15 (1991), 149–73.
6 See also discussion in Chapter 10.
7 'Estimate of the enemy situation (as of 6 July 1945), report by the Combined Intelligence Committee (July 8, 1945)', https://nsarchive2.gwu.edu/NSAEBB/NSAEBB162/28.pdf.
8 N. Polmar and T. B. Allen, 'The most deadly plan', *Proceedings* (January 1998).

the bomb would affect American security over the longer term. Finally, there was the practical question of how to use the bomb to accelerate Japan's defeat in the short term.

Many of the scientists who developed the atomic bomb believed that to use it against Japan would jeopardise American security over the long term by undermining any effort to place international controls on the technology. Instead, it was more likely to provoke an arms race, and in any event, use of the bomb would 'prejudice the world' against any US effort to prevent others from using it. The bleak future vision these scientists presented was one of 'sudden destruction visited on our own country, of Pearl Harbor disaster, repeated in thousandfold magnification, in every one of our major cities'.[9] The scientists predicted the possibility of placing atomic bombs in enemy cities and exploding them simultaneously, of first strikes to hinder retaliation, of 'super-super bombs' delivered by a 'guided missile', making all population centres vulnerable.[10] Therefore, to avoid sliding down a slippery slope, a 'technical' demonstration of the atomic bomb was preferable to 'military' use.

A different view was held by several key policy makers who believed that use of the bomb, in addition to helping end the war, would serve as a demonstration of American power. They believed this would provide diplomatic leverage when dealing with the Soviet Union in the post-war period. This latter consideration affected not simply the decision to use or not use the atomic bomb, but also had an impact on *how* it would be used. Attacking the cities of Tokyo and Kyoto were ruled out on the basis that it would be considered 'such a wanton act' that the Japanese would prefer to 'reconcile' with the Soviet Union than the United States.[11]

Several options were discussed about the most appropriate means of using the atomic bomb to end the war. For example, instead of dropping it on a city, a technical demonstration for an audience of international participants could be arranged on a desert island. Other options included detonation in the sky over Tokyo or in less densely populated areas in Japan, such as a forest. These less lethal demonstration options were rejected on the same, somewhat questionable grounds, that the option of providing the

9 'Memorandum from A. C. Compton to Secretary of War (June 12, 1945)', https://nsarchive2.gwu.edu/NSAEBB/NSAEBB162/16.pdf.
10 'Memorandum from V. Bush and J. B. Conant, Office of Scientific Research and Development, to Secretary of War (September 30, 1944), top secret', https://nsarchive.gwu.edu/documents/atomic-bomb-end-world-war-ii/005.pdf.
11 'Stimson diary (July 24, 1945)', https://nsarchive.gwu.edu/documents/atomic-bomb-end-world-war-ii/048.pdf.

Japanese a warning was also dismissed, namely that it would have lessened the shock value, that it was unworkable and that it would have placed American military personnel in greater jeopardy. Although other reasons were discussed, the need to induce a 'psychological shock' was the primary reason Hiroshima, described as 'an important army depot and port of embarkation in the middle of an urban industrial area' that was 'largely untouched' by earlier American bombing, was chosen. A list of other Japanese cities was prepared and these were to be struck one after the next until Japan surrendered.[12]

Three days after the atomic bomb was used on Hiroshima, another one was dropped on Nagasaki, although the intended target was Kokura. A day earlier, the Soviet Union had entered the war against Japan. Truman ordered a halt to further atomic bombings on the grounds that the 'thought of wiping out another 100,000 people was too horrible' and he did not like the idea of 'killing all those kids'.[13] Nevertheless, prior to the announcement of Japan's surrender, cities continued to be attacked with conventional bombs and napalm.[14]

Thus, by the end of the Second World War, several themes that would shape the future discourse around nuclear strategy had already emerged. Though the discussion was somewhat primitive, the need for atomic weapons as a deterrent, similar to chemical weapons, was recognised, as was the idea that they constituted a special class of weapon requiring a high level of control due to the political implications of their use. Interest in tactical employment against military targets had also been explored, as had the prospect of demonstrative use and signalling. It was also well understood that atomic weapons were not war-winning weapons and could not substitute for conventional forces. At best, their value lay in the efficiency in which enormous destructive power could be delivered which might have the prospect of producing sufficient psychological shock to force an adversary to capitulate, but this was highly dependent on a wider array of factors rather than being independent of them. Finally, the normative bias against atomic weapons, similar to the one with chemical and biological weapons, became

---

12 L. Freedman, 'The strategy of Hiroshima', *Journal of Strategic Studies*, 1 (1978), 76–97; 'Memorandum from Major J. A. Derry and Dr N. F. Ramsey to General L. R. Groves, "Summary of Target Committee meetings on 10 and 11 May 1945," (May 12, 1945)', https://nsarchive2.gwu.edu/NSAEBB/NSAEBB162/6.pdf.
13 'H. Wallace diary, diary entry, Friday (August 10, 1945)', https://nsarchive.gwu.edu/documents/atomic-bomb-end-world-war-ii/078.pdf.
14 'Planes blast Jap mainland with new US secret weapon', *Washington Post* (10 August 1945), A1.

an important factor in Truman's 10 August 1945 decision not to employ them again. Even if it meant saving the lives of one's own soldiers, there was a reluctance to use them, or as Truman put it after Nagasaki, 'I can't bring myself to believe that, because they are beasts, we should ourselves act in the same manner.'[15] The normative bias against using atomic weapons was further enhanced in later years when the effects of radiation became more widely known.[16]

Strategies of Nuclear States

With the onset of the nuclear age, war between nuclear states did not become unthinkable but it did become increasingly risky and therefore unattractive. For any war to include nuclear attacks and counterattacks, most likely involving the destruction of societies, the political calculation of costs and benefits completely shifted so that the former far outweighed the latter. In a war between nuclear adversaries, the term 'victory' became synonymous with physical survival rather than reflecting more traditional political motivations for going to war, such as the acquisition of territory. Consequently, the political interactions of nuclear states had to be handled with particular care so that political crises did not escalate to all-out conflict. And if conflict was unavoidable, then it should be conducted in such a way that it was limited in scope, which meant keeping the stakes so low that nuclear use would not be viewed as a credible option. For instance, when fighting erupted along the Sino-Soviet border in 1969, or between India and Pakistan in the 1999 Kargil conflict, the territory being contested was remotely located with the military forces involved quite small. In both cases, the governments involved took deliberate efforts to keep the fighting isolated and avoid further escalation.[17] It was also the case that nuclear states had little desire to use nuclear weapons in their conflicts with non-nuclear adversaries, even when using them on the battlefield might have offered a military advantage, such as at Điện Biên Phủ in 1954 or Khe Sahn in 1968.[18]

15 Letter from H. S. Truman to R. B. Russell, 9 August 1945.
16 L. M. Blume, *Fallout: The Hiroshima Cover-Up and the Reporter who Revealed it to the World* (New York: Simon & Schuster, 2020).
17 M. S. Gerson, *The Sino-Soviet Border Conflict: Deterrence, Escalation, and the Threat of Nuclear War in 1969* (Arlington: Center for Naval Analyses, 2010); M. Krepon, R. W. Jones and Z. Haider (eds), *Escalation Control and the Nuclear Option in South Asia* (Washington, DC: Henry L. Stimson Center, 2004).
18 J. Prados, *The Sky Would Fall: Operation Vulture: The Secret US Bombing Mission to Vietnam, 1954* (New York: Dial Press, 1983); D. E. Sanger, 'U.S. General considered nuclear response in Vietnam War, cables show', *The New York Times* (6 October 2018).

To use nuclear weapons against a non-nuclear adversary was viewed as breaching an international norm, and therefore the political costs of doing so were likely to exceed any tangible battlefield gain. Moreover, a more general fear existed, at least during the Cold War, that to use nuclear weapons in this way, for instance by the Americans in Korea or Vietnam, would open a 'Pandora's box' by legitimating their use.[19] Thus, in addition to alienating international opinion, nuclear use against a non-nuclear adversary risked provoking an arms race as other states would seek nuclear weapons for their defence, or would lead other nuclear powers to use nuclear weapons against their non-nuclear adversaries which might then spiral into a war between the nuclear powers themselves.

These political realities, while providing a framework for the practice of international politics in the nuclear age, had only a marginal impact on the development of military strategy, war plans and military postures. For the most part, the 'nuclear strategy' of policy makers, or the assumptions about nuclear use they exhibited during international crises, typically bore little relation to the behaviour attributed to them in the theories and scenarios of the nuclear strategists. Policy makers were always aware of the risk of nuclear war lurking in the background and thus preferred to navigate their way carefully through crises. By contrast, for the nuclear strategists, the prospect of nuclear use was much more likely as they were mostly unconcerned with the political dynamics of crises and wars.

As Michael Howard observed, 'The object of deterrence is to persuade an adversary that the costs to him of seeking a military solution to his political problems will far outweigh the benefits'.[20] Deterrence was often at the root of the perceived need to acquire nuclear weapons and to adjust strategies, plans and postures accordingly, as the 'requirements of deterrence' evolved based on technological developments and adversary capabilities. The ultimate purpose was to ensure that 'unacceptable damage' could be inflicted on an adversary regardless of the damage that an adversary could inflict. In practice, deterrence was not simply about deterring a nuclear attack. Other, more likely types of aggression, which seemed to fall below the nuclear threshold, ranging from conventional wars to minor incursions, still needed

---

19 N. Tannenwald, *The Nuclear Taboo: The United States and the Non-Use of Nuclear Weapons Since 1945* (New York: Cambridge University Press, 2008).
20 M. Howard, 'Reassurance and deterrence: Western defense in the 1980s', *Foreign Affairs*, 61 (1982), 309–24.

to be dealt with, hence the reason for maintaining conventional forces. This then raised the question of what balance of nuclear and conventional forces was optimal given finite resources.

Countries such as the United States and the Soviet Union that could afford massive arsenals of air, land and sea-based nuclear weapons of both the high-yield and low-yield varieties, and were simultaneously able to maintain large conventional forces, had many options available to them that were unavailable to the smaller nuclear powers. But to acquire a massive arsenal was itself a deliberate choice rather than an inevitability. For instance, China, which could also afford both a massive nuclear arsenal and a large conventional military, chose instead to remain content with a minimum deterrent with which it would effectively limit nuclear attacks to enemy cities (countervalue) rather than targeting an adversary's military forces (counterforce). By contrast, with a large and diverse arsenal of nuclear weapons, the options available to the US and Soviets included attacking an adversary's means of nuclear retaliation, attacking non-nuclear forces, targeting the economic and industrial system, focusing on leadership targets, etc. Moreover, by investing in missile defences, it was considered theoretically possible to limit or eliminate an adversary's retaliatory capability. In reality, however, missile defences offered little reassurance, in large part due to questions about their inability to distinguish between incoming missiles and decoys, the prospect of an adversary building more offensive missiles to overwhelm the defence system, or simply employing other means of delivery. Thus, missile defence was not only unable to ensure complete protection for oneself, much less for one's allies, but instead was more likely to create new nuclear dangers of an uncontrolled arms race. By the late 1960s, many American strategists believed that *not* to invest in defensive capabilities was advantageous for superpower deterrence as it would not undermine the strategic stability associated with a roughly symmetrical nuclear balance.[21] This strategic logic was ignored by later advocates of missile defence such as President Ronald Reagan, with his 1983 announcement of a 'Strategic Defense Initiative', and later with President George W. Bush's 2002 decision to abandon the Anti-Ballistic Missile Treaty.[22]

---

21 'Statement of Secretary of Defense R. S. McNamara before the House Armed Services Committee on the fiscal year 1968–1972 defense program and 1968 defense budget', www.bits.de/NRANEU/others/strategy/1968_DoD_Annual_Report-Sanitized.pdf.
22 L. Matchett, 'Debating missile defense: tracking the Congressional record', *Arms Control Today* (March 2021).

Notions of a preventive war, in which a nuclear adversary would be attacked with massive numbers of nuclear weapons without provocation, were rejected by policy makers on all sides, almost as a matter of course, though from the perspective of the nuclear strategists this scenario was always discussed. This was to be expected since the strategists had to plan for the worst case of being on the receiving end of a surprise attack. Therefore, even if it made little or no sense for an adversary to conduct a massive unprovoked attack, it was believed necessary to maintain a nuclear arsenal that could still offer sufficient retaliation in a worst-case scenario. Only by being able to conduct a devastating second strike after suffering the consequences of a first strike would an adversary be deterred from attacking at all. It was the intensity of the second strike, and the diversity of targets one might need to attack, that served to justify the maximum deterrents of the US and USSR. However, these types of strategic considerations were only one of several reasons why the arsenals remained so large whereas other types of nuclear posture remained unattractive. The prestige associated with a large arsenal was an important factor. For the US to have fewer weapons than the Soviet Union or Russian Federation, or vice versa, has traditionally been considered a political impossibility. In addition, pressure from the military-industrial complex has also been a major factor. Both states' insistence upon maintaining a large arsenal remained a consistent theme despite scientists warning from the 1980s onwards that launching a large nuclear attack, even in the absence of nuclear retaliation, would still lead to unacceptable losses due to the horrific environmental consequences. 'Mutually assured destruction' based on the threat of nuclear retaliation had thus evolved to 'self-assured destruction' without the need for nuclear retaliation.[23]

Other nuclear states, such as Britain and France, remained content with a minimum deterrent. For these countries, the ability to destroy even a small number of the adversary's cities in a second strike was deemed sufficient to deter attack. For example, the 'Moscow criterion', or being able to destroy Moscow, was used to justify an 'independent' British nuclear deterrent. For the French, being able to destroy a significant part of Soviet industry was, at one point at least, believed to constitute an adequate deterrent. The minimum deterrent was predicated on the idea that following a British or French nuclear attack, the consequences of which would be awful in themselves, the

---

23 A. Robock and O. B. Toon, 'Self-assured destruction: the climate impacts of nuclear war', *Bulletin of the Atomic Scientists*, 68 (2012), 66–74.

Soviets would then be at a major strategic disadvantage relative to the United States. For the Chinese, being able to destroy a small number of American or Soviet cities was also believed enough to deter a US or Soviet nuclear attack. The key to a successful minimum deterrent strategy was survivability. So long as some nuclear weapons survived an enemy first strike and could be delivered against an adversary's population centre, then this was all that was deemed essential to deter an adversary, and therefore the numbers of weapons could be minimised.[24]

Two strategic concepts that gained prominence during the Cold War were 'massive retaliation' and 'flexible response'. Massive retaliation, which was enunciated by the Eisenhower administration in 1954, essentially referred to a strategy whereby conventional aggression by the Soviet Union would be countered with nuclear weapons. In reality, this had been NATO policy since 1949 rather than reflecting a new development. At the time of its public announcement, the key difference was that previously it had been the Alliance's intent to build a large conventional force to defend western Europe *in addition* to relying on American strategic nuclear weapons to deter a Soviet bloc attack. But with the development of battlefield nuclear weapons, combined with economic concerns about funding a large conventional military force, the decision was taken by NATO to limit the conventional role to that of a tripwire. A key problem with this strategy was that it was unclear at what point an adversary's actions would constitute sufficient provocation to warrant a nuclear response, and therefore questions were raised about its credibility, particularly as any NATO nuclear attack on the Soviet bloc would result in nuclear retaliation. As the Soviet Union acquired an intercontinental ballistic missile capability, this meant that in addition to the destruction caused in western Europe, the US itself would be at much higher risk of nuclear devastation.

The alternative strategy of flexible response emphasised building up sufficient conventional forces so that limited aggression could be countered without resort to immediate nuclear use. In the event of large-scale Soviet bloc aggression, NATO would delay a decision to initiate a nuclear response until conventional defeat was imminent. At this point, nuclear use would occur in three stages, commencing with initial use, then follow-on use, and ultimately leading to a full-scale strategic nuclear exchange, assuming that the

---

24 L. Freedman and J. Michaels, *The Evolution of Nuclear Strategy*, 4th ed. (London: Palgrave, 2019). See chapters 22, 23 and 26.

conflict had not been terminated earlier. As will be discussed, the key debate within the Alliance dealt with the timing, intensity and geographic reach of the initial and follow-on use.[25]

Variations of these strategies have been employed elsewhere. In recent years, Russian nuclear strategy has been summed up by the phrase 'escalate to de-escalate', which is effectively the same concept as flexible response. In other words, if Russia gets involved in a conflict with NATO and its forces face conventional defeat, they will escalate to nuclear use in an effort to get NATO to cease hostilities. What this nuclear use might consist of remains unclear. It may be the case that military forces are targeted. Alternatively, demonstrative use might be preferred.[26] Some US strategists have argued that to defeat Russia's strategy requires the development of its own low-yield nuclear options so that the US could match Russia's use of low-yield weapons rather than relying exclusively on higher-yield weapons. In recent years this idea has dominated American nuclear strategy debates.[27]

That post-Cold War Russian nuclear strategy largely mimics NATO strategy from the Cold War reflects a reversal of roles. Having once maintained conventional superiority over NATO that would probably have allowed Soviet bloc forces to overrun western Europe, post-Soviet Russia's conventional forces were much weaker. From the perspective of post-Cold War Russian strategists, the fear was of NATO intervention in Russia's 'near abroad' if not into Russian territory itself. In one important sense, however, there was continuity despite the changed circumstances. For the bulk of the Cold War, Soviet scenarios of war erupting with NATO were predicated on the idea that it would be NATO that *initiated* hostilities by attacking eastern Europe, most likely using nuclear weapons, with the Soviet bloc forces then conducting a counteroffensive into western Europe, also using nuclear weapons. Under Mikhail Gorbachev, Soviet strategy shifted in the late 1980s. NATO was still deemed to be the aggressor but the geographic extent of the Soviet counteroffensive was reduced to merely re-establishing the pre-war territorial status quo rather than continuing into western Europe. With this reduced mission, the size of Soviet forces in

---

25 J. M. Legge, *Theater Nuclear Weapons and the NATO Strategy of Flexible Response* (Santa Monica: RAND, 1983).
26 N. Sokov, *Russia Clarifies Its Nuclear Deterrence Policy* (Vienna: Vienna Center for Disarmament and Non-Proliferation, 2020).
27 B. Roberts, *The Case for U.S. Nuclear Weapons in the 21st Century* (Stanford: Stanford University Press, 2015).

eastern Europe could be reduced as well. This shift in strategy helped lead to an overall reduction of East–West military tensions and lowered the risk of nuclear war.[28]

In south Asia, Pakistan's nuclear strategy evolved from the late 1990s onwards from one relying exclusively on nuclear weapons targeted at Indian cities, essentially massive retaliation, to one increasingly reliant on short-range, battlefield nuclear weapons in the first instance. One key reason for this shift was India's development in the mid-2000s of a limited conventional war capability known as 'Cold Start', and Islamabad's fear that a massive retaliation capability would be of little use against it.[29] However, by acquiring a battlefield nuclear capability, an invading Indian force could still be defeated should conventional forces prove insufficient. For India, this posed a serious challenge as it relied on a doctrine of massive retaliation against Pakistan's cities if Pakistan used nuclear weapons first, either against Indian territory or against Indian forces. Despite this challenge, India has remained reluctant to develop nuclear weapons for battlefield use, nor has it been willing to abandon its policy of no first use.[30]

Interestingly, India and Pakistan only emerged as openly acknowledged nuclear states following a series of nuclear tests in 1998, though India had previously conducted a 'peaceful nuclear explosion' in 1974 and Pakistan was believed to be nuclear-capable in the 1980s. Israel, on the other hand, deliberately chose not to acknowledge the existence of a nuclear arsenal, despite the widespread assumption that it had a nuclear capability as of the late 1960s. While other countries, such as North Korea, insisted on conducting nuclear tests to demonstrate the credibility of its deterrent, as well as for reasons of national prestige, the deterrence value of Israel's nuclear arsenal would derive from merely hinting at its existence. Meanwhile, Israel relied primarily on the strength of its conventional forces to deal with non-nuclear threats. But when it came to preventing other countries from acquiring a nuclear capability, such as Iraq, Syria or Iran, it avoided overt nuclear threats, preferring diplomatic means to bring international pressure and economic sanctions to bear, as well as using its military and intelligence services to conduct airstrikes and cyberattacks on nuclear facilities and

---

28 J. H. Michaels, 'The *Barbarossa* mentality and the Russian concept of war in the 21st century', *Journal of Slavic Military Studies*, 33 (2020), 535–41.
29 J. Sankaran, 'The enduring power of bad ideas: 'Cold Start' and battlefield nuclear weapons in south Asia', *Arms Control Today*, 44 (2014), 16–21.
30 K. Sundaram and M. V. Ramana, 'India and the policy of no first use of nuclear weapons', *Journal for Peace and Nuclear Disarmament*, 1 (2018), 152–68.

assassinate nuclear scientists.[31] This type of multi-pronged counterproliferation strategy marked a sharp departure from the rest of the international community, which preferred non-violent threats and inducements to prevent nuclear proliferation.[32]

As these examples highlight, the nuclear strategies of nuclear states cannot be disentangled from the conventional conflicts and international crises in which the prospect of nuclear use remained a possibility, even if a distant one. Yet one of the major problems of attempting to understand the role of nuclear strategy in the practice of nuclear states' conduct of war and diplomacy is to distinguish between the nuclear and non-nuclear considerations and priorities that underpinned policy decisions. For some policy makers, concerns about nuclear escalation may have induced caution; for others, confidence in their nuclear arsenal may have spurred them to take more risks. But whether the policy decisions that led nuclear states to confront one another or to avoid confrontation had to do with confidence in one's own nuclear strategy or the weakness of the adversary's, or any number of other non-nuclear factors such as the substance and intensity of the political dispute, is probably impossible to discover in any meaningful way. What is certain is that no political dispute between nuclear states has reached the point where policy makers believed the stakes involved were sufficiently large to unleash nuclear devastation on an adversary, regardless of whether they were able to retaliate.

Strategies of Non-Nuclear States Confronting Nuclear States

As most countries do not possess nuclear weapons, and those that do at one time did not, what strategies have they employed when confronting a nuclear state? Is it impossible for a non-nuclear state to go to war with a nuclear state, or for a non-nuclear state to defend itself from a nuclear state aggressor? One notable case was the Soviet Union prior to its own acquisition of the atomic bomb in 1949. During the early Cold War years, in which the USSR confronted the US in multiple crises, such as the 1948–1949 Berlin blockade, Moscow was cognisant of the need to avoid the risk of war against a nuclear-armed adversary, and therefore placed important limits on its actions. More

---

31 A. Cohen and M. Miller, 'Bringing Israel's bomb out of the basement: has nuclear ambiguity outlived its shelf life?' *Foreign Affairs*, 89 (2010), 30–44.
32 N. L. Miller, 'The secret success of nonproliferation sanctions', *International Organization*, 68 (2014), 913–44.

generally, the Soviets sought to deter American nuclear use by maintaining strong conventional forces capable of overrunning western Europe, as well as to undermine Washington's will to use nuclear weapons by stressing their immorality and promoting international public opposition.[33] It is also worth remembering that during the first years of the Cold War, when atomic weapons remained scarce, they were not conceived as a sufficient deterrent in their own right to stop large-scale aggression. For the Americans, it was understood that in a war with the Soviet Union, even if the United States used atomic weapons against the Soviets, this would be insufficient to stop them from physically conquering Europe, the Middle East and Asia. Instead, the more important deterrent was a combination of atomic power *plus* the ability to mobilise sufficient conventional power to defeat the Soviet Union in a long duration war.[34] For the Chinese, a different argument was used. Less concerned about raising questions about the morality of American nuclear use, they sought to downplay it, referring to the US atomic arsenal as a 'paper tiger' while emphasising the idea that these weapons would not be decisive in a 'people's war'. In other words, at least at a rhetorical level, Chinese leaders were willing to sacrifice large segments of the country's population, confident that sufficient numbers would survive a nuclear attack to still be triumphant in a war.[35]

The downplaying of nuclear dangers has taken many forms. Among the more notable strategies to employ are a strong reliance on civil defence and guerrilla warfare. And though more of an unconscious strategy, the willingness to rely on international norms of behaviour to induce a restraining effect on nuclear use has been the longstanding practice of non-nuclear actors when faced with nuclear actors. Several examples can be used to illustrate this phenomenon. For instance, when Egypt and Syria attacked Israel in 1973, the attacking powers assumed that Israel possessed a nuclear capability but remained confident that in a conflict with limited territorial goals, the use of nuclear weapons was highly unlikely, particularly given the prevailing norm against nuclear use and the prospect of superpower intervention.[36] In

---

33 P. C. Avey, *Tempting Fate: Why Nonnuclear States Confront Nuclear Opponents* (Ithaca: Cornell University Press, 2019), 115–35.
34 J. H. Michaels, 'Visions of the next war or reliving the last one? Early alliance views of war with the Soviet bloc', *Journal of Strategic Studies* (2020).
35 J. W. Lewis and X. Litai, *China Builds the Bomb* (Stanford: Stanford University Press, 1988).
36 P. C. Avey, 'Who's afraid of the bomb? The role of nuclear non-use norms in confrontations between nuclear and non-nuclear opponents', *Security Studies*, 24 (2015), 563–96.

the case of Iraq during the 1991 Persian Gulf War, the Iraqi leadership appreciated that use of chemical weapons on US, UK or French forces, or on Israeli cities, might have risked nuclear escalation, but that otherwise the chances were slim, and in any event, the mere possession of chemical weapons would probably serve to deter nuclear use against Iraq.[37] In other words, in these types of cases there was an underlying belief among the non-nuclear actors that so long as the conflict with the nuclear states remained within limited boundaries, nuclear use would not constitute a serious risk.

Perhaps the best-known strategy for non-nuclear states has been to rely on extended nuclear deterrence. To some degree, members of the Communist bloc relied upon the Soviet Union's possession of nuclear weapons to offset the risks posed by the US nuclear arsenal, though in the case of China, relying on Moscow for protection was deemed insufficient for Beijing's political and security needs so it opted instead to develop a nuclear deterrent of its own. Similarly, many US allies sought protection under the American 'nuclear umbrella'. In the case of NATO, the non-nuclear European states were covered by formal commitments that the US would come to their defence if attacked. A similar, albeit more elastic, approach to extended nuclear deterrence was adopted by other US allies, such as Japan, South Korea and Australia.[38] For all these non-nuclear states, the major problem with relying on a foreign country to provide nuclear protection was that the foreign country might not be willing to use nuclear weapons on behalf of an ally, especially if it meant risking nuclear devastation itself if it did so. This was also a problem for the nuclear state because if its non-nuclear allies remained unconvinced they would be protected, they were likely to adopt more accommodationist policies with their common adversaries.

One option to reassure militarily exposed allies was to forward deploy nuclear weapons onto their territory. However, doing so created problems for the non-nuclear state on whose territory the weapons were located. For instance, NATO states such as Italy and Turkey that housed American nuclear-armed missiles were likely to be at greater risk of nuclear attack. West Germany, which was always considered the main target of a Soviet bloc invasion, was likely to be the victim of nuclear devastation if war erupted: either the Soviets would launch widespread nuclear attacks to destroy NATO's nuclear weapons based in West Germany, or NATO forces would

---

37 H. Brands and D. Palkki, 'Saddam, Israel, and the bomb: nuclear alarmism justified?', *International Security*, 36 (2011), 133–66.
38 J. F. Pilat, 'A reversal of fortunes? Extended deterrence and assurance in Europe and east Asia', *Journal of Strategic Studies*, 39 (2016), 580–91.

use nuclear weapons throughout the country's interior to stop a Soviet conventional attack. Therefore, West Germany preferred that any initial NATO nuclear use would be limited and occur shortly after the outbreak of hostilities close to the inner-German border so that the interior of the country would be spared. The underlying premise was that if nuclear weapons were used early on, this would convince the Soviets that they had grossly miscalculated NATO's resolve and would cease hostilities.[39]

This concept was opposed by the United States largely on the grounds that it would force Washington to make an immediate decision on nuclear use, whereas their preference, at least from the early 1960s onwards, was to delay a decision as long as possible, hence the requirement for large conventional forces to mount a strong defence to buy time. From the American side, there was also a concern that other NATO allies might follow the same path as Britain and France and develop their own 'independent' nuclear arsenals, a prospect to which they were bitterly opposed. Therefore, in addition to forward-based conventional forces the US chose to 'share' access to their nuclear weapons. Initially this was done as part of a dual-key arrangement whereby NATO allies were responsible for delivering nuclear warheads provided by the US. However, as the US physically controlled the warheads, this limited the extent to which allies were reassured. An alternative arrangement was for control of the warheads to be given to the European allies as part of a Multilateral Force (MLF). Failure to devise appropriate mechanisms for the control and disposition of nuclear forces led to the MLF's demise. Instead, rather than seek a 'hardware' solution to the problem, an alternative 'software' approach was selected, with NATO allies being given a greater input into the Alliance's nuclear policy and strategy. This led to the formation of NATO's Nuclear Planning Group.[40]

In some cases, fear of being attacked by a nuclear power, or the loss of prestige and self-confidence that would result if it did not possess a nuclear arsenal, led many countries to develop nuclear weapons or threaten to cross the nuclear threshold if necessary. The impetus behind the North Korean nuclear programme was an attempt to counter the American nuclear presence in South Korea, fear that Seoul was also seeking to develop nuclear weapons and the lack of a nuclear protector, especially after the Soviet collapse. India became a nuclear power mainly as a response to China's

39 A. Lutsch, 'Merely "docile self-deception"? German experiences with nuclear consultation in NATO', *Journal of Strategic Studies*, 39 (2016), 535–55.
40 B. Heuser, *NATO, Britain, France and the FRG: Nuclear Strategies and Forces for Europe* (London: Macmillan, 1997).

development of nuclear weapons, with Pakistan seeking to match India. Likewise, Japan has retained the option of 'going nuclear' at short notice if it feels insufficiently protected by the United States. As for Iran, it has also relied on a strategy of reaching the nuclear threshold but not crossing it, with Saudi Arabia threatening to develop a nuclear arsenal in response to Iranian acquisition.

Most countries simply rely on a policy of seeking to reduce nuclear dangers by pursuing arms control and disarmament initiatives. During the Cold War, countries such as Sweden and Switzerland, both capable of developing nuclear arsenals, chose to abandon this option, preferring instead to sign up to the Non-Proliferation Treaty. Their reason for doing so was based to a large extent on the belief that becoming a nuclear state would increase the risk of being targeted with nuclear weapons – therefore it was better to rely on a combination of international diplomacy, and strong conventional and civil defences. Similar to these other countries, Ukraine, which inherited the world's third largest nuclear arsenal following its independence from the Soviet Union, chose to give up its nuclear weapons because its leaders felt the security benefits of a nuclear arsenal were highly questionable, with the political and economic consequences an absolute certainty. In the early 1990s, South Africa also abandoned its small nuclear capability. Due to the social and political changes then underway, the leadership of the flailing Apartheid government preferred to destroy the country's nuclear capability rather than let it fall into the hands of the ascendant African National Congress.[41]

Conclusion

Whereas most military strategy consists of ideas about using violent means in war to achieve an objective, be it offensive or defensive, nuclear strategy consists of ideas that are mainly useful in peacetime and whose primary purpose is to avoid nuclear weapons being used in anger. Nuclear weapons do not eliminate the desire of states to wage war, hence the need for nuclear states to retain their conventional forces, and with them, the requirement for non-nuclear military strategies. For nuclear states fighting other nuclear states, or non-nuclear states fighting nuclear states, the fact that one or both adversaries possess nuclear weapons places structural constraints on the conflict that would not necessarily exist otherwise, such as limiting the objectives sought or the means employed to achieve them. Consequently,

---

41 Freedman and Michaels, *Evolution of Nuclear Strategy*. See chapters 24, 39, 40 and 41.

nuclear weapons have shaped non-nuclear military strategies in important ways. But if possessing nuclear weapons is mainly intended to increase a state's prestige or to be used as a means of political coercion, then the strategy for their use should be evaluated in political rather than military terms, so that success can be measured by the extent to which a state's prestige is increased, an adversary gives in to a political demand and so forth. Such a strategy would be more appropriately classed as a 'political strategy with a nuclear component' as opposed to a 'nuclear strategy'.

Although the success of nuclear strategy has typically been defined as the lack of nuclear use in a military conflict since 1945, the failure of nuclear strategy can also be described in precisely the same way. The inability to find ways of employing nuclear weapons in a conflict, as with other military capabilities, in such a way as to be sufficiently attractive for political leaders to use them, reflects the most important challenge that no strategist has yet overcome. In part, this simply reflects the international norm against using weapons of mass destruction – a norm policy makers have been careful to maintain. Perhaps just as important, policy makers refuse to make intra-class distinctions regarding nuclear weapons. To use a low-yield nuclear weapon against a purely military target is treated the same way as using a high-yield nuclear weapon against a city. This is mainly due to the belief that using even the lowest-yield nuclear weapon will produce a chain reaction ending with the use of high-yield weapons. Despite contemporary strategists seeking to make low-yield nuclear options more attractive, the prospect of using these weapons will remain unappealing to policy makers in the absence of a major shift in international norms. In the decades ahead, strategic theorists are likely to be preoccupied with the implications for nuclear deterrence of the emergence of a new generation of non-nuclear capabilities, such as drones, hypersonic missiles and cyberweapons, though as in the past, a notable chasm will remain between the conflict scenarios they design and the conflict behaviour that occurs.

16

America's Way of War

ANTULIO J. ECHEVARRIA II

Introduction

This chapter introduces readers to America's way of war and the types of military strategies it employed from the American Revolution to the conflict in Afghanistan. Much has been said, most of it critical, some of it exploratory, about America's way of war since historian Russell Weigley first took up the study of the subject in the early 1970s. His book, *The American Way of War: A History of United States Military Strategy and Policy*, an intellectual history that quickly became a classic, analysed how American strategic thinking evolved from the 1770s to the 1970s.[1] For Weigley, a 'way of war' represented habits of thought or traditions; an American way of war, therefore, amounted to those habits exhibited by Americans with respect to armed conflict over the course of US history. For three decades, Weigley's *American Way of War* reigned as the definitive source for understanding the traditions of American strategic thought.

Importantly, however, it had several failings which were highlighted at the beginning of the twenty-first century, when controversies over the emergence of a 'new' American way of war began to appear. Foremost among these shortcomings is the fact that the book does not discuss the American tradition regarding so-called small wars, which have been many times more numerous in US military history than major wars. Second, the work overlooks military strategies outside annihilation and attrition, both of which it defined idiosyncratically in any case.[2] Regrettably, it leaves underexplored

---

1 R. Weigley, *The American Way of War: A History of United States Military Strategy and Policy* (Bloomington: Indiana University Press, 1973).
2 Weigley defined annihilation as crushing an opponent's will by confronting and destroying its military power directly; he defined attrition as undermining an opponent's will indirectly, through erosion or what British military critic Sir Basil Liddell Hart called the 'indirect approach'. For a fuller discussion, see A. J. Echevarria II, *Reconsidering the*

America's active traditions of employing strategies of decapitation, strategic coercion and forms of deterrence other than nuclear.[3] In sum, Weigley's *American Way of War*, although magisterial in many respects, tells only a portion of the story of US strategic thinking. But it is to Weigley's redounding credit that his book laid the groundwork for further research. Undertaken largely at the beginning of the twenty-first century, this research explored such questions as what the word 'American' might mean, what a 'way of war' is, when an 'American way of war' can be said to have begun, and what, if anything, might distinguish it from other ways of war including those from which it likely borrowed, such as the French, British and German modes of fighting.

What follows is a brief chronological survey of the many armed conflicts America engaged in, from the Revolutionary War to the campaigns in Afghanistan and Iraq. This survey is by no means exhaustive. Nonetheless, it should acquaint readers with two facts: America has had not one way of war, but several; and it has had not one binary framework from which to choose, namely, annihilation or attrition, but a veritable smorgasbord of methods of co-opting or breaking an opponent's willingness to resist. US strategists have employed all of them at one time or another. Since this chapter covers a broad span of time, it cannot provide details regarding the strategy formulation process or the prioritisation of goals for each conflict. It will, however, identify the chief war aims and the type(s) of strategy employed by US political and military leaders. It accepts the premise that strategy is 'the setting of a state's objectives and of priorities among those objectives' for the allocation of resources and establishment of priorities in the conduct of a war.[4] While strategy itself is both more and less than allocating resources and prioritising tasks, a sober appreciation of the interdependence of ends and means is strategy's essential first step.

America's War of Independence

The Second Continental Congress convened in May 1775, after the armed clashes at Lexington and Concord between colonial militias and the British Army. The Congress's war aim was to achieve independence from the British

---

American Way of War: US Military Practice from the Revolution to Afghanistan (Washington, DC: Georgetown University Press, 2014), 9–13.

3 These and other strategies are further explicated in A. J. Echevarria II, *Military Strategy: A Very Short Introduction* (New York: Oxford University Press, 2017).

4 K. Kagan, 'Redefining Roman grand strategy', *Journal of Military History*, 70:2 (2006), 333–64, 348.

Crown by engaging it in a series of battles that it hoped would prove more costly to Britain than to the Colonies, thereby opening the way to fruitful negotiations. However, the Congress had underestimated King George's willingness to retain the Colonies, despite mounting debts. Unfortunately, at the same time, it overestimated its ability to field a force capable of inflicting appreciable losses on the British Army. The Congress repeatedly pressed its general in the field, George Washington, to deliver a decisive victory.[5] But, until late in the war, that goal remained well beyond the capabilities of the Continental Army, which was chronically underpaid, undersupplied, understrength and undertrained. Moreover, contrary to conventional wisdom, time favoured neither side. While the Crown had considerable debts and wished to bring the issue of the Colonies' rebellion to a swift conclusion, the Continental Congress also remained in arrears with mounting war debts, a grossly inflated currency and no authority to tax the former Colonies. Every month of conflict, furthermore, cost the Colonial economy dearly, taking individuals away from their farms and trades.[6] Hence, each side suffered as the war dragged on.

The Patriots needed victories to demonstrate to potential allies, namely France and Spain, that they could win and, thus, were worth the risk of investing money and other resources in support of their cause. By the second half of the war, the former Colonies had assumed the bulk of the financial burden of the conflict, but that change did not mean that a long war was welcome.[7] In fact, the Congress would not gain the major victory it needed until the battles at Saratoga (19 September–7 October 1777), even though Washington won some minor actions at Trenton (26 December 1776) and Princeton (3 January 1777) which boosted Patriot morale.[8] France entered the war in 1778 and Spain in 1779, events that gave the Patriots important advantages. Nonetheless, the Treaty of Paris (1783), which officially ended the war, would only come after devastating raids against the Iroquois Confederacy in New York (1779), the loss of British strength in South Carolina and Virginia through guerrilla actions and Cornwallis's defeat at Yorktown through a combined American-French blockade (1781).

---

5 R. Weigley, *History of the United States Army* (New York: Macmillan, 1967), 65.
6 E. P. Newman, *The Early Paper Money of America*, 3rd ed. (Iola: Krause Publications, 1990); E. J. Ferguson, *The Power of the Purse: A History of American Public Finance 1776–1790* (Chapel Hill: University of North Carolina Press, 1961).
7 Ferguson, *Power of the Purse*, 32.
8 Richard W. Stewart (ed.), *American Military History* (Washington, DC: US Center for Military History, 1989), 67–9.

Although the Continental Congress possessed little authority to direct the resources of the newly established 'United States of America', it can still be said to have pursued both a grand and a military strategy in its war for independence from Great Britain. Its actions fall within the definition of grand strategy stated above, and it certainly influenced Washington's military strategy. While victory in rebellions and insurrections is said to go to the side that can gain the support of the populace, in America's war for independence the outcome depended on obtaining financial and military support from abroad. This was a critical point that prominent Patriot ambassadors such as Benjamin Franklin, who tirelessly recruited French support, clearly understood. Presumably, one-third of the population in the former Colonies had committed to the revolution, one-third remained loyal to the Crown and one-third was uncommitted, waiting for the fortunes of war to tip conclusively one way or the other.[9] For that final third, support from abroad combined with battlefield victories provided strong indicators as to the likely outcome of the conflict. Battlefield victories are, accordingly, important; in fact, too important to squander. Nevertheless, it is also easy to place too much stock in them. Winning battles does not automatically equate to winning wars. In any event, the British Crown emerged from the war in a better financial situation than did the newly independent American states.

America's Wars of Consolidation

Although the thirteen states had achieved independence in 1783, they soon faced challenges internally and externally that threatened the sovereignty of their fledgling government. For instance, Shays' Rebellion (1786–1787), which took place in western Massachusetts but had repercussions across all the states, had to be put down by non-government militia forces financed by wealthy elites.[10] It suggested the United States needed a stronger central government with the power to enforce its decrees. Similarly, the Whiskey Rebellion (1794–1796), which was defused by the intervention of George Washington at the head of a force of federalised militia, threatened federal government's ability to collect taxes.[11] The US Constitution had only been

---

9 K. Phillips, *1775: A Good Year for Revolution* (New York: Viking Press, 2012), xix–xx; A. R. Millett, P. Maslowski and W. B. Feis, *For the Common Defense: A Military History of the United States from 1607 to 2012* (New York: Free Press, 2012), 49.
10 L. L. Richards, *Shays's Rebellion: The American Revolution's Final Battle* (Philadelphia: University of Pennsylvania Press, 2002).
11 T. P. Slaughter, *The Whiskey Rebellion: Frontier Epilogue to the American Revolution* (New York: Oxford University Press, 1986).

ratified in 1790 (and the Bill of Rights the following year) but the nature of checks and balances within the federal government, and its powers in relation to those of the states, would continue to evolve. For the four decades following the Treaty of Paris, therefore, the US government pursued mainly limited war aims both by choice and by necessity in the undeclared war with France (1798–1800) and the Barbary Wars (1801–1815). It conducted *guerre de course* operations that culminated in the Convention of 1800 which abrogated the French–American alliance of 1778 and ensured American neutrality in the Napoleonic Wars; the Barbary disputes were settled by dispatching a combination of warships and infantry to conduct raids, freedom of navigation operations, shows of force and gunboat diplomacy.[12] The US government managed to achieve its primary objectives in these conflicts, namely, stability for seaborne commerce and increased respectability, both domestically and abroad.

America's Wars of Expansion

Although the United States fought limited wars external to North America, it began to pursue wars of territorial conquest in the interior of the continent, such as the campaigns in the Northwest Territory against indigenous peoples during the 1790s.[13] The same held true for the War of 1812, in which the US government, seeking to break Britain's de facto containment of the newly established United States, invaded Canada to annex crucial portions of the St Lawrence waterways.[14] The US government finally succeeded in securing the Northwest Territory in 1795, after serious setbacks. However, its incursions into Canada in the War of 1812 failed after two major attempts. The US Navy carried out several successful operations in the Great Lakes region, but Washington City, the seat of the US government, was razed by British troops in 1814. Andrew Jackson secured a victory against British forces in the vicinity of New Orleans, though the Treaty of Ghent had already been signed. Contrary to Alfred Thayer Mahan's

---

12 F. C. Leiner, *The End of Barbary Terror, America's 1815 War Against the Pirates of North Africa* (Oxford: Oxford University Press, 2007); M. L. S. Kitzen, *Tripoli and the United States at War: A History of American Relations with the Barbary States, 1785–1805* (New York: McFarland, 1993).
13 R. Douglas Hurt, *The Ohio Frontier: Crucible of the Old Northwest, 1720–1830* (Bloomington: Indiana University Press, 1996).
14 J. Black, *The War of 1812 in the Age of Napoleon* (Norman: University of Oklahoma Press, 2009).

denigration of *guerre de course* operations nearly a century later, the War of 1812 demonstrated how useful they could be.[15] Collectively, America's early wars of expansion reveal poor strategic reckoning, including an inability to balance ends and means, on the part of US strategists. In each of these conflicts, the strategic pattern, if it can be called such, amounted to the United States engaging in armed conflicts with minimal force, then scrambling to adjust but not always successfully.

America continued to pursue expansionistic aims in its war with Mexico (1846–1848).[16] US president James K. Polk initially attempted to pressure the Mexican government into selling the territories of present-day California, Arizona and New Mexico, but his efforts were rebuffed. He then instigated an armed conflict with Mexico, which enabled him to use military force to seize California and New Mexico, thereby extending America's national borders from the Atlantic Ocean to the Pacific Ocean and fulfilling the country's 'manifest destiny'.[17] The US military strategy for the conflict was to apply force gradually in the hopes of inducing Mexico to cede the territories Polk desired. In concept, the strategy resembles Thomas C. Schelling's theory of exerting 'graduated pressure', a theory that came into vogue in the late 1960s and early 1970s as a new wave of histories of the war with Mexico were being written.[18] In due course the Mexican Army was defeated, the country's major ports were captured and its capital city was occupied by US troops on 14 September 1847. Negotiations were prolonged, however, partly because the Mexican government was divided internally, and the war became a liability for the Polk administration. Eventually, the Treaty of Guadalupe Hidalgo (2 February 1848) granted the United States the territories it wanted and recognised the annexation of Texas, but for half the sum Polk had offered the Mexican government before the war began.[19]

---

15 A. Thayer Mahan, *Sea Power in its Relations to the War of 1812* (Boston: Little, Brown, 1905), vol. 2.
16 P. Guardino, *The Dead March: A History of the Mexican–American War* (Cambridge, MA: Harvard University Press, 2017); A. Greenberg, *A Wicked War: Polk, Clay, Lincoln, and the 1846 U.S. Invasion of Mexico* (New York: Knopf, 2012).
17 O. Singletary, *The Mexican War* (Chicago: University of Chicago Press, 1962).
18 T. C. Schelling, *Arms and Influence* (New Haven: Yale University Press, 1966); see for example K. J. Bauer, *The Mexican War, 1846–1848* (Lincoln: University of Nebraska Press, 1974).
19 J. H. Schroeder, *Mr. Polk's War: American Opposition and Dissent, 1846–1848* (Madison: University of Wisconsin Press, 1973).

America's Civil War

For President Abraham Lincoln, only one war aim was acceptable for the conclusion of the American Civil War: the restoration of the Union.[20] That aim, in turn, meant the dismantling of the Confederacy as a political entity, which accordingly required defeating and disarming its military forces. As Lincoln explained to Mr Horace Greeley, editor of the *New York Tribune* on 22 January 1862, less than twelve months into the war:

> My paramount object in this struggle is to save the Union and is not either to save or to destroy slavery. If I could save the Union without freeing any slave I would do it, and if I could save it by freeing all the slaves I would do it; and if I could save it by freeing some and leaving others alone I would also do that.[21]

While some Union political leaders urged Lincoln to seek a negotiated settlement to end the killing (an argument that grew stronger as casualties mounted), the president rejected such persuasions, even though he often despaired over the casualty lists and the difficulty of finding a competent field general.

By comparison, Jefferson Davis could achieve his aim of political independence for the Confederacy if the argument for a settlement that recognised his government as legitimate would carry the day. To that end, the South endeavoured to wear down the North's willingness to fight by inflicting telling (if not decisive) defeats on Union forces and by gaining recognition and support from abroad, especially from Great Britain.

The Union essentially implemented the 'Anaconda strategy' originally proposed by Winfield Scott, the celebrated hero of the War of 1812 and the Mexican–American War. The objective was to strangle the Confederacy economically by severing its seaborne commerce and its ability to transport goods and supplies along its inland waterways.[22] Scott's plan was publicly derided when it was proposed, as it was unclear how many warships would be required, how long it would take to construct them and whether, or when, it would succeed. Many pundits believed the conflict would be short and thus that Scott's strangulation strategy would not be needed.

---

20 See also Chapter 4.
21 J. M. McPherson, *Battle Cry of Freedom: The Civil War Era* (New York: Oxford University Press, 1988), 510, 859.
22 D. Stoker, *The Grand Design: Strategy and the U.S. Civil War* (New York: Oxford University Press, 2010); H. Hattaway and A. Jones, *How the North Won: A Military History of the Civil War* (Urbana: University of Illinois Press, 2006).

Unfortunately, neither side fully understood the character of the war as it unfolded, especially the destructive power of the available weapons which had largely outpaced the tactics of the day. Both also underestimated the psychological resilience of their opponents. Consequently, the conflict dragged on for years with both sides suffering egregiously. At the time, each side subscribed more or less to Antoine Henri Jomini's definition of strategy as the art of making war on the map. Accordingly, battles and sieges were fought for critical points, such as transportation hubs and fortified cities commanding major railways and rivers, that would give one side control over the theatre of operations or war zone. The priority for each side was its opponent's field army, the defeat of which would render a belligerent's seats of power vulnerable. The initial Jominian modus operandi of capturing ports and transportation hubs provided an essential but insufficient means to accomplishing that end. Lincoln finally found a competent general in Ulysses S. Grant who, among other things, expanded this Jominian-style military strategy by permitting General William T. Sherman to capture or destroy crops and livestock in a broad path from Atlanta to Savannah in 1864. Sherman thus brought the 'hard hand of war' to the South's civilian population.[23] For Grant and Sherman, destroying armies in the field would not suffice if those forces could simply be reconstituted and returned to the fighting at a later date; one had to destroy the economic base that enabled reconstitution.

Ultimately, the military strategy that won the war for the Union was a variant of the Anaconda plan with major ground offensives. The cumulative effect of Sherman's style of economic warfare, the ongoing pressure of the Union blockade, the capture of major cities along the Mississippi River and the surrender of Robert E. Lee's Army of Northern Virginia, which started a chain of capitulations by Confederate forces, proved fatal to Jefferson Davis's regime. Lincoln's successor, US president Andrew Johnson, declared the war over on 20 August 1866. While major combat operations had indeed ended, another type of strategy, one involving stability operations in the form of Reconstruction, remained to be implemented. That strategy, unfortunately, only partially achieved its objectives of rebuilding and repatriating the South. Reconstruction partially rebuilt the South economically but also victimised it, whereas political reconstruction essentially failed, despite ten years of effort.

23 M. Grimsley, *The Hard Hand of War: Union Military Policy toward Southern Civilians, 1861–1865* (Cambridge: Cambridge University Press, 1995).

America's Wars on the Northern and Southern Plains

The US government's war aim regarding the Native American peoples of the northern and southern plains was to relocate them from their homelands to other, generally less desirable areas. Strategically, these conflicts took the form of a fierce and brutal type of coercion. Moreover, the US government accomplished its war aims with minimal resources, fielding one soldier for every 100 square miles of territory.[24] Typically, however, the US Army's tactics were inhumane, as many non-combatants were killed or wounded. As Schelling once noted, the 'power to hurt is bargaining power. To exploit it is diplomacy – vicious diplomacy, but diplomacy'.[25] These conflicts were typically more coercive than diplomatic, yet they sometimes involved considerable parlaying by both sides prior to as well as during the campaigns. Most definitions of coercive diplomacy exclude the use of force; that is, once force is used, diplomacy ends. But such definitions are too narrow. Depriving a people of the wherewithal to survive in the harsh environment of the plains, as the US Army did to Native Americans on many occasions, is nothing less than a brutal act of force. Therefore, Schelling's distinctions between 'brute force' – taking something from someone – and 'coercive force' – making someone give up something – quickly evaporate in the physical world.[26] Whether the victims die by a bullet or by starvation and exposure, the result is the same.

America's Imperial Wars

Despite years of tensions with Spain over its efforts to deal with an insurrection in Cuba, US president William McKinley's war aims remained vague at the outset of the Spanish–American War (1898). Historians continue to debate what his true aims might have been, but the weight of the evidence suggests he would have been content with Cuban autonomy (rather than independence) as well as an expansion of US markets into the Caribbean region. Autonomy was acceptable to Madrid, but not to the Cuban insurgents who continued to agitate for independence. Even though the causes were unclear at the time, the explosion and the sinking of the USS *Maine* in Havana harbour on 15 February 1898 heightened animosity towards Spain

---

24 Stewart (ed.), *American Military History*, 318; Weigley, *History of the United States Army*, 267.
25 Schelling, *Arms and Influence*, 2.   26 Schelling, *Arms and Influence*, 2–3.

and left McKinley with little choice but to ask Congress to fund a military intervention on behalf of Cuban independence. US strategy originally entailed blockading key Spanish ports in Cuba and the Philippines, putting troops ashore to defeat Spanish forces, while also strengthening America's coastal defences against possible naval raids. In fact, the US Navy essentially decided the war by quickly annihilating the largely obsolescent Spanish Navy in two major battles, thereby cutting off Madrid's ability to resupply its forces in both theatres. American troops landed in Cuba and the Philippines, and defeated or secured the surrender of Spanish forces in both locations; the major fighting had ended by 13 August 1898, well before many US volunteers had been deployed. The Treaty of Paris (signed 18 December 1898) officially ended the conflict and recognised Cuban independence. It also granted the Philippines, Guam and Puerto Rico to the United States, and required Washington to pay $20 million ($619 million in 2020) to Madrid. As a result of the Spanish–American War, the United States found itself in possession of an empire, quite to the surprise of McKinley and to the outrage of America's powerful (but unsuccessful) Anti-Imperialist League. McKinley had not aggressively sought an empire, but he had not actively avoided one either.

The United States soon had an insurrection on its hands, however, as Filipino guerrillas under Emilio Aguinaldo made their own bid for independence and contested the American occupation. McKinley had not previously considered granting independence to the Philippines as he judged the Filipinos unfit to govern themselves. Consequently, the United States began waging a counterinsurgency campaign. On 4 July 1902, McKinley's successor, Theodore Roosevelt, unilaterally announced that the insurrection had ended.[27] Nevertheless, the US Army continued to conduct counterinsurgency operations against various Filipino peoples within the archipelago well into 1913. Even in the early twentieth century, in other words, political leaders endeavoured to accord difficult or sensitive campaigns as low a profile as possible.

In the two decades following the Spanish–American War, the US government dispatched troops to several Latin American states, among them Panama (1903), Cuba (1909), Nicaragua (1909–1912), Haiti (1915–1934) and the Dominican Republic (1916–1924). This series of interventions became known as the 'Banana Wars'. America's war aims in each of these 'imperial wars' amounted to restoring, or preserving, political and economic stability. In

---

27 B. McAlister Linn, *The Philippine War, 1899–1902* (Lawrence: University Press of Kansas, 1989), 219.

most cases, US troops were able to employ strategies of decapitation by which they captured or killed the rebel leaders responsible for causing violence or otherwise threatening US interests. In other cases, the interventions became a form of gunboat diplomacy by which the United States coerced a local government into promoting American economic interests, especially those of the 'United Fruit Company'. These interventions also illustrate just how long military forces might have to remain in a weak or underdeveloped state to preserve stability.

America's Interventions in Mexico

Despite his historical reputation as an idealist who promoted 'peace without victory', US president Woodrow Wilson showed little reticence to use military force during his time in office. In April 1914, for instance, he dispatched troops to occupy Veracruz in response to an affront to American honour perpetrated by Mexican forces during the Tampico affair.[28] This incident was one example of multiple US military interventions into Mexico, the largest of which occurred in the summer and autumn of 1916, when Wilson ordered Brigadier General John J. Pershing's task force of 12,000 US troops into Mexico to capture or kill Francisco 'Pancho' Villa, whose band was believed to be responsible for a raid in Columbus, New Mexico, which killed eighteen Americans (actually, between July 1915 and June 1916, some thirty-eight cross-border raids occurred, resulting in the deaths of thirty-seven Americans). Due perhaps to Wilson's penchant for lofty rhetoric, the aim of capturing or killing Villa and dispersing his band was too ambitious as expressed, since it would have enabled Villa to draw US troops deep into Mexican territory, thereby increasing the costs of the campaign beyond the value of the objective. The War Department thus revised the mission to the 'pursuit and dispersion of the band or bands that attacked Columbus', which allowed the commander on the ground to determine when the mission had been accomplished.[29] Pershing managed to kill or capture some of Villa's men, although Villa himself escaped. US military strategy for the mission had thus shifted from decapitation to a show of force in an effort to deter further such raids into the United States.

---

28 R. E. Quirk, *A Matter of Honor: Woodrow Wilson and the Occupation of Veracruz* (New York: Norton, 1967). The affront in question referred to the Mexican refusal to fire a twenty-one gun salute in apology for having wrongfully arrested nine US sailors on 9 April 1914.
29 For details, see F. S. Calhoun, *Uses of Force in Wilsonian Foreign Policy* (Kent, OH: Kent State University Press, 1993), 36–42.

America's First World War

President Wilson desired to keep the United States from being drawn into the First World War for as long as possible, while at the same time clandestinely supporting the democracies that made up the Entente with loans and supplies to defeat the Central Powers.[30] Despite this duplicity, he attempted to persuade the war's major belligerents to accept his Fourteen Points: his idealistic plan to achieve the aim of 'peace without victory'. He announced the plan on 8 January 1918 and promoted the points until well after the Armistice of 11 November 1918. Unfortunately, for several reasons – including but not limited to: domestic and foreign opposition to the plan; the untimely arrival of the so-called Spanish Flu; Wilson's failing health; and his desire to bargain away most of the Fourteen Points to establish the League of Nations – his war aims went unrealised. Thus, while the Central Powers were defeated, the US president's war aims were not achieved.

A major US military objective, in the meantime, had been to prevent American forces from becoming mere replacements to fill the ranks of depleted French and British armies. That aim was accomplished through the creation of the American Expeditionary Force (AEF). By the Armistice of 11 November 1918, the AEF had suffered approximately 320,000 casualties (16 per cent of its strength overall), of which over 50,000 were killed in action.[31] As with most of America's allies at the time, US military strategy during the AEF's operations was to erode the material and moral strength of the German Army through a series of battles and campaigns.

Notwithstanding Wilson's failing health and diplomatic struggles at home and abroad, he committed American forces to multinational Russian and Siberian expeditions from 1917 to 1920. Part of Wilson's rationale for supporting America's French and British allies in these expeditions undoubtedly had to do with his desire to gain their acceptance of his peace plan and especially the establishment of the League of Nations.[32] The expeditions achieved some limited defensive military objectives, and conducted some successful stability, support and counterguerrilla operations, particularly near Vladivostok. Nonetheless, they did not accomplish Wilson's political objective of gaining support for his peace plan. Additionally, the United States sent troops into

---

30 See also Chapter 8.   31 Stewart (ed.), *American Military History*, 403.
32 Calhoun, *Uses of Force*, 115; C. W. Melton, *Between War and Peace: Woodrow Wilson and the American Expeditionary Force in Siberia, 1918–1921* (Macon: Mercer University, 2001); C. Richard, '"The Shadow of a Plan": the rationale behind Wilson's 1918 Siberian intervention', *Historian*, 1 (1986), 83; and J. W. Long, 'American intervention in Russia: the North Russia Expedition, 1918–19', *Diplomatic History*, 4 (1982), 45–68.

Panama (1918–1920), Nicaragua (1926–1933) and China (1912–1938). The aims of these missions varied from providing security for US citizens and property to enforcing the terms of existing treaties and deposing of hostile leaders (Nicaragua), and were generally realised. By the mid-1930s, however, the United States had withdrawn many of its troops from its overseas commitments, largely due to the financial pressures of the Great Depression.

America's Second World War

Although the voices of anti-interventionism, or isolationism, remained strong in the United States throughout the 1930s and into 1940, US president Franklin Delano Roosevelt supported Britain, France, China and later the Soviet Union with loans and war materiel against the aggression of the Axis Powers, though he avoided entering the conflict directly.[33] The attack on the US fleet at Pearl Harbor on 7 December 1941 by Imperial Japan, followed almost immediately by Nazi Germany's declaration of war on the United States, brought America into the conflict and allowed Roosevelt to call for full mobilisation. At the Casablanca Conference on 24 January 1943, Roosevelt and Churchill announced 'unconditional surrender' as the official war aim of the Allies.[34] Roosevelt had previously decided on a strategy of 'Germany first' believing, correctly, that the Wehrmacht was the greater threat to the Allied military forces at the time; should either Great Britain or the Soviet Union be defeated, overcoming Hitler's Germany would be much more difficult. Nevertheless, aside from sending large quantities of war materiel and supplies to the British and Soviet militaries, the 'Germany first' strategy was more rhetorical than reality until the final eighteen months of the war. By the end of 1943, the United States had deployed 1.87 million troops, 7,900 aircraft and 713 warships against Japan; compared to 1.81 million troops, 8,800 aircraft and 515 warships against Germany.[35] In short, halting Japan's early advances in the Pacific theatre had drawn substantial US troops and materiel away from the European theatre, and in any case various developments pushed the date for the cross-Channel invasion to 1944.

The Allied strategy was based on attrition, destroying more military power than the Axis could produce, retaking conquered territory and maintaining

---

33 See also Chapters 11 and 12.
34 G. L. Weinberg, *A World at Arms: A Global History of World War II* (Cambridge: Cambridge University Press, 2010), 433.
35 M. Matloff, *Strategic Planning for Coalition Warfare: 1943–1944, The U.S. Army in World War* (Washington, DC: Government Printing Office, 1955), 398.

relentless pressure against Berlin and Tokyo. The industrial capacity of the United States and its liberal application of fire power throughout the second half of the conflict, particularly through strategic bombing, have created the impression that the 'true' American way of war is the use of overwhelming force in an attrition-based strategy. Yet Great Britain and the Soviet Union followed the same approach in so far as their resources would permit. The Second World War was, after all, the quintessential industrial-age conflict with the application of a state's full economic and human resources its chief characteristic. While attrition strategies have been derided as unimaginative, attrition was the right choice for the Allies in the Second World War since it allowed them to take advantage of their most important strength, industrial capacity. But strategic bombing also contained elements of a strategy of terror, the goal of which was to inflict as much suffering on a state's citizenry as necessary to break its willingness to fight. Nonetheless, while the bombing of major metropolitan centres of Nazi Germany and Imperial Japan caused the deaths of an estimated 400,000 German and 500,000 Japanese civilians, it failed to induce those states to surrender.[36] Ultimately, the war aims of the Allies were achieved, though the Japanese emperor was allowed to remain the state's titular sovereign subordinate to the supreme commander of the Allied forces.

America's Cold War Conflicts

America's war aims for the Korean conflict (1950–1953) marked a radical departure from the objective of unconditional surrender as pursued in the Second World War. The United States and its allies had achieved complete military victory over the Axis forces in 1945; however, when the Korean conflict began, US president Truman merely sought to preserve the government in Seoul and the territorial integrity of South Korea by driving Communist forces north of the 38th Parallel. The message from Washington was that force would be met with force. At the time, the US government also had to balance resource commitments for two major strategic missions: operations in Korea and deterrence in western Europe. Those aims were achieved after three years of fighting, though Truman had

---

36 *United States Strategic Bombing Survey (European War) (Pacific War)* (Washington, DC: Air University Press, 1987); M. Ishikida, *Toward Peace: War Responsibility, Postwar Compensation, and Peace Movements and Education in Japan* (Bloomington: iUniverse, Inc, 2005), 30.

to relieve General Douglas MacArthur for insubordination after the general openly challenged the soundness of Washington's war aims.

With the US intervention in Guatemala in 1954, one year after the armistice that brought peace to the Korean peninsula, the American way of war shifted from relying primarily on conventional forces to a greater dependence on unconventional forces – the Central Intelligence Agency (CIA), special forces and indigenous groups – in clandestine as well as covert operations to contain Communist expansion.[37] Unconventional forces required fewer resources, offered plausible deniability, carried lower risk of escalation and fitted more appropriately into what the former US Foreign Service Officer, George Kennan, referred to as 'measures short of war' to contain Soviet influence. Measures short of war, as Kennan's 1946 lecture of the same name indicates, consisted of the tools available to diplomacy for waging political warfare, that is, below the threshold of a shooting war.[38] This shift in America's way of war succeeded in Guatemala (1954), British Guiana (1963), Brazil (1964) and Dominican Republic (1965). However, it failed in Cuba (1961) and Vietnam (1960–1975). The latter failure occurred even with a renewed emphasis on conventional forces, which included the combined weight of an unprecedented bombing campaign and a landmark escalation of ground troops.

For a time, it was unclear whether Communist expansion was being contained via what the US defence secretary Robert McNamara and other officials referred to as 'brush-fire wars' or whether Washington's hard and soft powers were being eroded by such wars. Many of America's flawed strategic assumptions, such as the foundational 'Domino theory', were exposed by the country's failure in Vietnam. That failure certainly generated serious repercussions for US prosperity and influence, but it did not result in a chain reaction marked by the fall of Thailand, Malaysia or Indonesia to communism. Similarly, the inability of American strategic thinkers to understand the critical role of Clausewitz's third (psychosocial) dimension, a dimension indispensably important to democracies but marginalised by US limited war theorists and nuclear strategists, contributed to that failure. Fortunately for the Free World, the Soviet Union undertook a strategic misadventure in 1979 when it invaded Afghanistan, only to retreat a decade later after much loss of blood and funds. The United States eventually recovered from its misadventure in Vietnam; however, the Soviet Union

---

37 Echevarria, *Reconsidering the American Way of War*, 136.
38 G. D. Harlow and G. C. Maerz (eds), *Measures Short of War: The George F. Kennan Lectures at the National War College, 1946–47* (Washington, DC: National Defense University Press, 1991).

could not recover from its debacle in Afghanistan, which contributed to its political and economic collapse in the early 1990s.

America's Post-Cold War Conflicts

The eventual disintegration of the Soviet Union raised questions about what form US grand strategy should take in the wake of containment.[39] Throughout the 1990s and into the early 2000s, myriad theories were proposed; from neo-isolationism to selective engagement to co-operative security to primacy.[40] Nonetheless, this period proved disappointing to many, as US academics and policy practitioners felt that the White House failed to settle on a legitimate strategy. While most of America's grand strategic questions – its interests, objectives, threats and appropriate responses – remained unanswered, the US Department of Defense pursued an aggressive transformation agenda designed to leverage the power of information technology. The development of US military capabilities was thus decoupled from grand strategy. It was also disconnected from the larger portion of American strategic practice in the 1980s and 1990s, which required the capacity to conduct stability operations. For instance, the post-Vietnam era saw US forces intervene in El Salvador (1979–1991), Colombia (1978–2011), Grenada (1983) and Panama (1989), even as America continued to maintain its leadership role in NATO and its deterrence posture with conventional forces in western Europe and Korea.

During the 1990s, US forces participated in Desert Shield/Desert Storm (1990–1991) largely with conventional forces. The war aim of the American-led coalition in this case was to compel the Iraqi military to withdraw from Kuwait. But that successful operation was directly followed by other interventions in Somalia (1992–1994), Bosnia (1992–1995) and Kosovo (1999). In these interventions, military force was used primarily in humanitarian relief/humanitarian assistance operations to forestall wide-scale starvation, protect refugees, stop or prevent ethnic cleansing, and restore stability to some states thought to be either 'failed' or 'failing'.[41] Transporting and distributing food

---

39 See also Chapters 21, 22 and 23.
40 B. R. Posen and A. Ross, 'Competing visions for US grand strategy', *International Security*, 3 (1996), 5–53.
41 These terms remain controversial; see Robert Longley, 'What is a failed state? Definition and examples', Thoughtco (27 July 2020), www.thoughtco.com/what-is-a-failed-state-definition-and-examples-5072546.

and medical supplies, and protecting refugees and other non-combatants sometimes resulted in clashes with militias, warlords and hostile clan leaders, such as 'General' Muhammed Farah Aideed.

Managing humanitarian assistance activities along with direct-action combat operations against such leaders and their forces required a delicate balance between restraint and aggressiveness. For the bulk of the second half of the twentieth century, America's way of war sought to provide humanitarian assistance to crisis situations while simultaneously attempting to avoid the political and cultural entanglements of nation building. But that ambivalence would put US policy makers at a disadvantage when considering the conditions and means necessary to conduct successful counterinsurgency operations in the early twenty-first century, as the real complexities of such operations were underappreciated. For better or worse, the challenges of building nations or states and defeating insurgencies often go hand in hand.

While that issue remained an important one, it was overshadowed by the attention given to the so-called information revolution and the whole-scale technological transformation of the US Defense Department that followed the Cold War. At the time, America possessed unparalleled technological capabilities, including the capacity to respond swiftly to crises almost anywhere on the globe. However, the US military itself lacked the capacity to sustain major stability operations in two theatres simultaneously. America's initial war aims in Afghanistan and Iraq resembled those it had carried out, or attempted to, in the 1980s and 1990s, namely, the protection of non-combatants, the neutralisation of nefarious militia and clan leaders, and the establishment of legitimate governance and stability for a weak or failing state. Removing nefarious actors from positions of power was difficult but far from impossible. That fact notwithstanding, the core problems associated with establishing good governance and stability were not militarily soluble, aside from the task of providing security to indigenous populations. Unfortunately, the other tools of US government and elements of national power have not received sufficient investment to meet the challenges of security in the twenty-first century.

Conclusion

America's way of war does not represent a unique approach to armed conflict. Rather, it has varied over time, from its War of Independence to its wars of consolidation, wars of expansion, civil war, imperial wars, interventions in Mexico and Latin America, First and Second World Wars, Cold

War and post-Cold War interventions, and response to the terror attacks of 9/11. It has thus adapted to and reflected the circumstances of the day, including the means at hand, as well as the skills of the political leaders and military commanders employing those means. At times, America's way of war has been characterised by overwhelming force. At other times, it has been defined by the employment of minimalist force. At still other times, it has been marked by force used in a clandestine (secret) manner and at others distinguished by violence employed in a covert (deniable) way. At all times, however, it has been imminently political – that is, it has served both domestic and foreign policy agendas, whether the interests at stake were driven by the executive branch of the US government, by one political party at the expense of another, by economic motives (promoting capitalism) or by ideological goals (promoting democracy). This was true even when America's way of war was its most destructive. It has won and lost its share of wars and borrowed freely, if sometimes injudiciously, from other ways of war, which in turn have borrowed from it. It has also leveraged a wide array of military strategies, including annihilation, attrition, exhaustion, decapitation, coercion, deterrence and terror, either individually or in combination. It has also begun to explore how to employ and defend against social manipulation strategies, such as those employed by Russia and China in the early twenty-first century. One cannot know how America's way of war will respond to the emerging challenges of competition in a world being transformed by sociocultural and ethnic tensions as well as new technologies with intriguing potential. But if the past is any guide, its response will be manifold.

17

The Korean War

XIAOBING LI

On 25 June 1950, North Korea (Democratic People's Republic of Korea, DPRK) launched a surprise attack on South Korea (Republic of Korea, ROK), commencing the Korean War. On 7 July, the UN set up a military command in Korea. Three days later, US president Harry S. Truman appointed General Douglas MacArthur to head the UN Force (UNF), since more than 90 per cent of the UNF were American troops. On 25 October, the People's Republic of China (PRC) announced it would send the Chinese People's Volunteer Force (CPVF) to Korea for the 'War to Resist the US and Aid Korea'.[1] Thereafter, the Korean War essentially became a conflict between China and the United States. When the Armistice Agreement was signed on 27 July 1953, about 3 million Chinese troops fought against the US-led UNF. Confronted by US air and naval superiority, the Chinese forces suffered 1 million casualties.[2] More than 1.8 million American soldiers were sent to Korea; 36,914 were killed, 108,000 wounded and 8,170 listed as MIA. South Korea reported 250,000 military deaths and 750,000 wounded, while North Korea counted 294,151 dead and 90,000 captured or MIA. Some scholars estimate civilian deaths at 2 million during the war.

Sources

Among the important documents for US strategic study are the Truman and Dwight D. Eisenhower Libraries' Presidential Papers, which include the records of the White House, National Security Council (NSC), Central

[1] Marshal D. Peng, 'My story of the Korean War', in X. Li, A. R. Millett and B. Yu (eds), *Mao's Generals Remember Korea* (Lawrence: University Press of Kansas, 2001), 32–3.
[2] Major General Y. Xu, 'Chinese forces and their casualties in the Korean War', X. Li (trans.), *Chinese Historians*, 6 (1993), 56–7.

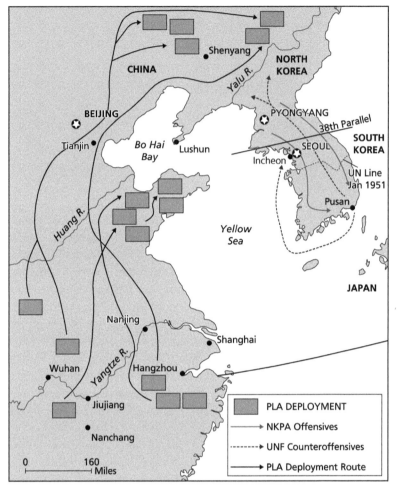

Map 17.1 The Korean War. Drafted by Brad Watkins. Redrawn with permission from Xiaobing Li, *China's War in Korea: Strategic Culture and Geopolitics* (London: Palgrave Macmillan, 2019), 85.

Intelligence Agency (CIA), secretaries of state and senior military leaders. The National Archives and Records Administration (NARA) holds official records of the Department of State (RG 59), the Department of Defense, the Far East command, the Pacific command and the Korea Military Advisory Group. Among other important collections at the NARA are the records of the Joint

Chiefs of Staff (JCS) and the Foreign Service Posts (RG 84). Individual papers, memoirs and oral history of secretaries, directors, chiefs, field generals and key senior Truman and Eisenhower administrations' officials are indispensable sources for research on the US strategy. The best source on the ROK's war strategy is the US State Department's *Foreign Relations of the United States* (*FRUS*), even though the Korean government archives are readily available in Seoul. Fifteen UN members had collective strategies under UN command (UNC) and all played a political and diplomatic role in the war.[3] William A. Taylor states: 'By late fall 1950, the UN General Assembly had replaced the UN Security Council as the centre of authority and diplomatic efforts regarding international involvement in the Korean War.'[4] Archival records from these UNC member countries such as Britain, France, Australia, Canada, New Zealand, Turkey and India are available.

Due to inaccessibility of sources in communist states, few wars in strategic history pose more difficulties than the study of the Korean War. In the 1990s, some Russian documents became available at the Archives of the President (APRF), Foreign Ministry, the Communist Party Central Committee and the general staff of the Soviet armed forces after the collapse of the Soviet Union. Although Russian sources usually focused on political and geostrategic issues, these archival documents certainly revealed new perspectives on the origin of the Korean War. Some translated Russian and North Korean documents were printed in the *Bulletin* of the Cold War International History Project (CWIHP), the Wilson International Center in Washington, DC. The *Bulletin* also included documents from former Warsaw Pact nations during the war. Even though North Korea's archives remain closed to Western researchers, some DPRK documents were seized by the UNF, translated and made available in the National Archives (RG 242).

China's renewed interest in learning from the Korean War resulted in more source availability, especially in government documents and private collections, and inspired many publications in the 2000s. Among Chinese archives are select documents from the Central Committee of the Chinese Communist Party (CCP), the Central Government of the PRC, the Central Military Commission (CMC) and the high command of the People's Liberation Army (PLA); reprinted in *Collection of Important Documents since the Founding of the PRC* (11 vols.) and *Selected Documents of the CCP Central*

---

3 T. K. Robb and D. J. Gill, *Divided Allies: Strategic Cooperation against the Communist Threat in the Asia–Pacific during the Early Cold War* (Ithaca: Cornell University Press, 2019), 57–9.
4 W. A. Taylor, 'The United Nations', in J. I. Matray and D. W. Boose Jr (eds), *The Ashgate Research Companion to the Korean War* (Farnham: Ashgate, 2014), 100.

Committee (14 vols.). In the 2000s, the PRC Ministry of Foreign Affairs declassified tens of thousands of diplomatic files (10,000 in 2004 and 60,000 in 2009) from the PRC's early years. Many documents relate to China's strategy in the Korean War. Among Chinese leaders' military manuscripts, instructions and telegrams are manuscripts of Mao Zedong (15 vols.), Zhou Enlai (4 vols.) and Liu Shaoqi (7 vols.), who were the undisputed decision makers throughout the war. Some of these documents and manuscripts are translated and available.[5]

Actors

Confronted by the increasing Soviet influence on the Asian mainland in the late 1940s, Truman faced international and domestic critiques against his 'asymmetrical containment' Cold War strategy: offensive in the west but defensive in the east. In the spring of 1950, his administration designed a new national security guideline detailed in the NSA-68, calling for symmetrically containing Communist expansion wherever it occurred. The North Korean invasion that summer helped prove the legitimacy and assumptions about Communist expansion and ensured that the new policy would be the US global security strategy for two decades. In essence, this strategy called on resistance and counterattacks wherever and whenever communist countries invaded. Truman feared that communist success in Korea would place Japan within easy striking distance of a communist army. While some scholars view the US intervention as inevitable, since it needed a war to militarise containment, others argue that the Truman administration needed the crisis to make collective defence credible.[6] From this perspective, expansion of Soviet Communism had to be contained. Truman's advisers who helped reverse his disengagement policy towards east Asia included Dean Acheson, George Marshall, Louis Johnson, Omar N. Bradley and Paul Nitze. Congress and the public supported Truman's decisions since few Americans doubted the evil communists had to be combated; McCarthyism was a major cause of this consensus on fundamentals.

---

5 For example, S. Zhang and J. Chen (trans. and eds), *Chinese Communist Foreign Policy and the Cold War in Asia: New Documentary Evidence, 1944–1950* (Chicago: Imprint, 1996).
6 M. Hogan, *Cross of Iron: Harry S. Truman and the Origins of the National Security State, 1945–1954* (New York: Cambridge University Press, 1998); among other historians is W. Stueck, *The Korean War: An International History* (Princeton: Princeton University Press, 1995).

As UNF commander, MacArthur was a Second World War hero and 'the American-approved emperor of an occupied Japan'.[7] The general warned against the communist threat, especially the Russo-Chinese coalition. He agreed with Republican members of Congress in accusing some State Department staff of communist sympathies. However, in his arrogance and indifference, MacArthur failed to quickly and effectively respond to North Korea's invasion in June 1950. Although MacArthur almost alone had successfully fought for Inchon in mid-September, he failed to accept the reports that large numbers of Chinese troops entered Korea in October. At Wake Island, MacArthur informed Truman that he did not believe in China's capability to withstand a war against the US.[8] David Halberstam argues the general 'had created a dangerously self-isolating little world, one of total social, political, and military separation from everyone and everything else, where no one dared dissent'.[9] However, MacArthur's generals such as Matthew B. Ridgway, James A. Van Fleet and Edward 'Ned' Almond ensured UNF operations success from 1951–1953, and transformed the US Army from a Second World War 'liberation force' to a Cold War 'containment force'.[10]

Winning the election in 1952, President Eisenhower naturally bore the mark of leadership accompanied by popular anti-communist beliefs. His belief in America's moral leadership in a struggle against communism placed him at the centre of the broadest consensus of twentieth-century American history. For him, the transition from World War to Cold War required only transferring what he had learned about Hitler and the Fascists to Stalin, Mao and the Communists. In 1953, he was prepared politically and militarily not to accept another victory for the international communist spectra.[11] Eisenhower was not alone in his tough-on-communism policy. Secretary of State John Foster Dulles also fully committed to the anti-communist efforts and even put forward liberation and rollback against any communist aggression. Among other extreme anti-communists of the Eisenhower administration were Richard Nixon, Arthur Radford and Allen Dulles.

---

7 D. Halberstam, *The Coldest Winter: America and the Korean War* (New York: Hyperion, 2007), 104.
8 H. Sides, *On Desperate Ground: The Marines at the Reservoir, the Korean War's Greatest Battle* (New York: Doubleday, 2018), 60.
9 Halberstam, *The Coldest Winter*, 104.
10 S. Taaffe, *MacArthur's Korean War Generals* (Lawrence: University Press of Kansas, 2016).
11 D. D. Eisenhower, *Mandate for Change, 1953–1956: The White House Years* (Garden City: Doubleday, 1963), 180–1.

After the Communist government established itself in Pyongyang, Washington abandoned its goal of a unified Korea in favour of an independent South Korea with its capital in Seoul. With US support, the South Korea National Assembly was elected in May 1948, followed by the promulgation of a new constitution. Syngman Rhee, a politician with strong American support, became the ROK president in July. After the new government was officially established in August, North Korea denounced the ROK and threatened to unify the peninsula by force. President Rhee faced serious threats from organised guerrilla activities in the South. In November, he passed the National Security Law outlawing communism. He labelled all forms of dissent as communist activities and quickly suppressed them with force, including purging thousands of officers in his military. By 1949, as Jinwung Kim states, 'South Korea was now a "national security state" under Rhee's dictatorial rule'.[12] Northern invasion in June 1950 helped Rhee complete his authoritarian leadership, and MacArthur's offensive campaign against the North provided Rhee with a good opportunity to unify the country. Although the ROK Army suffered heavy casualties, Rhee intentionally slowed the truce talks from 1951 to 1953 to keep his plan alive for a national unification with the South. Eventually, under US pressure, Rhee accepted the Korean Armistice Agreement.

Adversaries

Among the communist actors, Soviet leader Joseph Stalin played a central role in the war, despite the Soviet Union's near invisible participation in Korea. As international communist supreme leader, Stalin made final decisions on communist warfare and truce negotiations in Korea, until his death in 1953. Although Stalin approved North Korea's plan, he did not wish to risk war with the US for east Asia, as he was not ready for a Third World War. Meanwhile, he did not wish to shoulder the responsibility for anything that went wrong, such as the entry of the US into the war. In case of escalated war, he asked Kim Il-sung to attain Mao's approval of the war plan and agreement to assist North Korea.[13] American intervention would lead to an increase in hostilities between Washington and Beijing, but to the cynical Stalin this was not all bad because it would increase Mao's dependence on the Soviet Union.

12 J. Kim, 'South Korea', in Matray and Boose Jr (eds), *Ashgate Companion to the Korean War*, 28.
13 N. Khrushchev, *Memoirs of Khrushchev*, Sergei Khrushchev (ed.) (University Park: Penn State University Press, 2006), vol. 2, 91–2.

At the very least, a war in Korea would test American resolve and draw US power away from Europe. On 14 February 1950, the Sino-Soviet Treaty of Friendship, Alliance, and Mutual Assistance was signed in Moscow.[14] During Mao's visit, Stalin asked that China share responsibilities in international communist movements, especially in leadership of east Asian revolutions. Despite Mao's displeasure with Stalin's demand, he understood the Soviet leader's intention and agreed to the 'division of labor'. Thereby, at Stalin's request, whether ideologically bound to international communism's mission or simple, nationalistic self-interest, China made commitments to the Soviet Union in the Cold War.

China fought the Korean War mostly for national security purposes, partially for Stalin's Cold War policy, as well as for the North Koreans. After founding the PRC on 1 October 1949, Mao began building a new republic according to the CCP's vision. The Chinese defence strategy was rooted in three elements underlying Mao's intent: political legitimacy for the new regime, a geopolitical context in Cold War east Asia, and military and economic sources available for national defence. A failed defence would have cost the CCP's control of the new republic. According to Mao's Cold War theory, a Sino-American clash was inevitable. In 1950, the US threatened China's security through intervention in Korea, Vietnam and Taiwan. Concerned with geopolitics, regional economics and transportation capabilities within the three conflicts, the Chinese believed that America's Korean intervention was the most critical threat to the new regime. Mao described American involvements as 'three knives threatening China: America in Korea was like a knife over her head; America in Taiwan was one around her waist; and Vietnam was one on her feet'.[15] Thus, Korea, instead of Taiwan, was considered the most immediate threat. Conversely, Chinese leaders made a significant strategic shift from the liberation of Taiwan to the intervention in Korea. Mao appointed Marshal Peng Dehuai as the CPVF commander.

After Kim Il-sung proclaimed the founding of the DPRK with himself as premier in 1948, he controlled the party, state administration and the military. Kim pursued national liberation against US-supported South Korea. He started border clashes to increase Soviet aid, while he received 47,764 Korean officers and soldiers with their weapons from China, having 150,000

---

14 'The Minutes of the Meeting between Stalin and Mao on December 16, 1949', file no. 00255, *Government Documents from the Soviet Archives*, in the Research Center for the International Cold War History, East China Normal University, Shanghai.

15 Major General Y. Xu, *Mao Zedong yu kangmei yuanchao zhanzheng [Mao Zedong and the War to Resist the US and Aid Korea]*, 2nd ed. (Beijing: PLA Press, 2006), 146.

troops in total.[16] Although seasoned Korean–Chinese soldiers played an important role in the invasion, Kim failed to reach his goal of taking over South Korea in June–August 1950. Soon he found defending the North almost impossible after the UNF crossed the 38th Parallel in October. Zhihua Shen and Yafeng Xia state that '[after] China sent massive numbers of troops to North Korea, Beijing gradually came to dominate [North] Korean affairs and to have a say in war strategies and tactics. Kim Il-sung was forced to endure humiliation by deferring to Chinese decisions'.[17] They, however, criticise a controversial view of Sino-Korean relations as 'North Korea provided a "strategic shield" for China, and China served as North Korea's "great hinterland"'. The co-authors argue that 'Kim Il-sung saw Stalin as the world revolutionary leader, not Mao'.[18] Benjamin Young further explains: 'This mistrust between the two Asian neighbours undeniably affected Kim Il-sung's political thought in the post-war period and later led to his conception of the *Juche* idea (national self-reliance).'[19] The war tested the limits of military co-operation among the communist states.

Causes and Intentions

On 30 January 1950, Stalin secretly summoned Kim to Moscow for war preparation against South Korea. In April, Kim visited Stalin and discussed the North Korean People's Army (NKPA) attack plan. In early May, Kim returned to Moscow and 'reported to Stalin that he was absolutely sure of the success of this venture'. Stalin 'expressed some doubt', but approved North Korea's plan. Stalin also asked Kim to get Mao's approval of his war plan.[20] Fulfilling Stalin's request, Kim briefed Mao on 13 May regarding the North's invasion of South Korea. That spring, Beijing preferred delaying North Korea's invasion since it was preparing a massive amphibious campaign against Taiwan. But Mao agreed with Kim's plan as it fitted with China's strategy and promotion of communist revolutionary wars in east Asia. CCP leaders and PLA high command symbolically 'approved' North Korea's bid for forceful, national reunification after receiving Stalin's approval. Despite

---

16 Marshal R. Nie, 'Beijing's decision to intervene', in Li, Millett and Yu (eds), *Mao's Generals*, 47–8.
17 Z. Shen and Y. Xia, *A Misunderstood Friendship: Mao Zedong, Kim Il-sung, and Sino-North Korean Relations, 1949–1976* (New York: Columbia University Press, 2018), 75.
18 Shen and Xia, *Misunderstood Friendship*, 4.
19 B. R. Young, 'Review on Shen and Xia's book', *The Chinese Historical Review*, 27 (2020), 91.
20 Khrushchev, *Memoirs of Khrushchev*, vol. 2, 92.

Chinese concerns about foreign intervention, Mao agreed with Stalin's decision and supported Kim's military effort.[21]

Two days after North Korea's attack, the UN Assembly adopted a resolution on 27 June to use all possible means in aiding the ROK against northern Communist invasion. Truman extended US air and naval operations to include North Korea and authorised US Army troops to protect the port of Pusan. Having reached consensus between Congress and the Pentagon, Truman also sent the US Seventh Fleet to the Taiwan Strait against Chinese Communist attacks on Jiang-held Taiwan. Chinese leaders believed it best for China's security to aid North Korea. Beijing also approved Moscow's request to use Chinese railways, airspace and territorial waters in Manchuria to transport Russian military aid to North Korea. The Soviet Union involved China in the war. Stalin telegraphed Mao on 1 October, suggesting that China 'should send at once at least five to six divisions . . . so that our Korean comrades will have an opportunity to organize a defence of the area north of the 38th Parallel under the screen of your troops'. These Chinese soldiers were 'considered as volunteers' and remained under Chinese command.[22] On the same day, Kim sent his representative to Beijing. In his letter, Kim directly asked Mao and Zhou to send Chinese troops to Korea.

Mao held deep concerns for the PRC's independence. He believed that direct Western threats from the Korean peninsula did not bode well for CCP political control in China. Mao explained: 'If it [the US] destroyed North Korea, our Northeast would live under its threat every-day. Even if it did not cross the Yalu River, our daily life would be miserable and our economic construction would be very difficult.'[23] Mao misperceived the global Cold War as Western powers, and more specifically the United States, vying for control of China. To overcome 'technological gaps' between China's military and the West, Mao favoured pre-emptive action abroad rather than reactionary strategies at home. Instead of waiting for Western powers to invade China, Mao engaged foreign forces in neighbouring countries such as Korea and Vietnam. This 'proactive defense' stopped enemies outside Chinese borders and avoided any major confrontation on the mainland. Chinese generals found proactive defence

---

21 X. Li, *China's Battle for Korea: The 1951 Spring Offensive* (Bloomington: Indiana University Press, 2014), 11.
22 Stalin's telegram in the Presidential Archives of Russia, f45, 01, d337, 167, quoted in Shen and Xia, *Misunderstood Friendship*, 42.
23 Mao's conversation with Wang Jifan and Zhou Shizhao on 27 October 1950, quoted in an article from http://bbs.creaders.net/history/bbsviewer.php?trd_id=1368581.

sensible: no matter the outcome of fighting in a neighbouring country, Chinese territory was not endangered. Thereby, Mao escalated China's war preparation from a 'border defense in China' to 'a proactive defense in Korea'. Mao said, 'One successful strike [of ours] would prevent hundreds of [enemy] strikes from coming'.[24] Deterrence of possible foreign invasions motivated Mao's decision. Mao strove to eliminate any potential security threat and to defend the PRC's sovereignty and territorial integrity.

War Objectives and Changes

After North Korea launched the attack on 25 June, the invading NKPA divisions, equipped with Russian-made tanks and heavy artillery, quickly threw the South into chaotic confusion. Kim's war objective for the NKPA was quick victory to diminish any chance for international intervention to save the South. The Communist troops captured Seoul in four days, forcing Rhee's government to flee the capital city. The military situation deteriorated daily as the invasion columns encountered only token resistance. It was evident the South possessed neither manpower nor equipment to stop the invaders. By late June, the NKPA drove ROK forces into a pocket around the southernmost city of Pusan.

When the UN established the UNF on 7 July, its objective was to repel the invading troops from the North and save the ROK government in the South. The UNF halted North Korea's invasion at Pusan on 4 August. As UNF commander, MacArthur soon planned the amphibious landing at Inchon. On 15 September, MacArthur's large-scale landing campaign, behind enemy lines in central Korea, collapsed the northern invasion, cutting off the NKPA's transportation and communication lines. Soon the UNF retook Seoul in late September. When the UNF reached the 38th Parallel, MacArthur wanted to drive into North Korea and inflict a total defeat on the Communist aggressors. The UN resolution, however, provided authorisation only to repel the North Korean Army, not to invade North Korea. The Truman administration feared possible Russian or Chinese intervention if MacArthur crossed the 38th Parallel. The British especially questioned the wisdom of crossing the 38th Parallel. MacArthur believed that the Chinese would not enter the war so late and in the teeth of a victorious US Eighth Army on full offensive, supported by powerful air and naval forces.

24 Mao's words quoted in 'Dang'an' [Archives] by Beijing TV, *Great War to Resist the US and Aid Korea, 2: Decision*, series no. 771, https://bit.ly/3D63Ctv.

MacArthur's war objective extended from saving the South to freeing the North from the Communist regime when the UNF crossed the 38th Parallel and advanced into North Korea on 1 October. After the US I Corps captured Pyongyang on 19 October, MacArthur ordered the UNF's pursuit of NKPA remnants all the way to the Yalu River, in an immediate offensive and over the entirety of North Korea. Two days later, the UNF launched an all-out offence along the Pyongyang–Wonsan line towards the Korean-Chinese border.

On 5 October, Mao convinced the CCP Politburo to send troops to Korea. Chinese leaders intended to halt the UNF's northward advance and keep the North Korean state intact. Mao's primary objective for the CPVF was establishing defensive positions in the mountainous regions north of Pyongyang and Wonsan, as their first foothold in Korea.[25] However, misinformed Chinese leaders underestimated UNF command's intentions and determination as the latter moved much faster and farther than the Chinese expected. After receiving Peng Dehuai's report on the UNF advance, Mao immediately changed Chinese objectives from defence to offence on 21 October. Mao abandoned the positional defence plan and prepared an attack. The first attack, known as the Battle of Unsan, is celebrated on 25 October as China's official anniversary for the CPVF's War to Resist the US and Aid Korea. From 25 October to 7 November, the CPVF engaged in its albeit ill-prepared campaign. CPVF commanders considered it a meeting engagement or contact battle; Chinese armies ambushed three ROK divisions and the US First Cavalry Division. On 3 November, the US Eighth Army command ordered the retreat of all UNF troops on the western front from north of the Chongchon River. The first campaign convinced Mao that the CPVF's superior numbers could weaken UN forces, were capable of larger offences and could destroy more enemy troops. For the first time since the Inchon Landing, the CPVF stabilised the military situation for North Korea, providing a valuable buffer by pushing the front line south of the Chongchon.

In mid-November, three weeks after China's intervention in Korea, Mao believed the CPVF could change the unfavourable situation by destroying several UNF divisions. Therefore, Mao changed the CPVF's mission with a new objective: winning the war and driving the UNF out of Korea. The new goal far exceeded Chinese military capabilities. Mao placed his own political

---

25 Mao's telegram to Zhou Enlai at 10 p.m. on 13 October, 1950, in *Jianguo yilai Mao Zedong junshi wengao* [*Mao Zedong's Military Manuscripts since the Founding of the PRC*] (Beijing: PLA Military Science Press and CCP Central Archival and Manuscript Press, 2010), vol. 1, 252–3. Hereafter as *Mao's Military Manuscripts since 1949*.

consideration over Peng's military calculation. Meanwhile, Beijing rejected a UN Security Council peace proposal in December, drafted by thirteen non-Western countries. Although the CPVF first offensive campaign surprised MacArthur, he believed that Chinese force was merely symbolic and insufficient to halt his final campaign to unify Korea.[26] His objective was to return to the offensive: drive the Chinese back to the Yalu and complete the reunification of Korea.

Mobilisation and Available Means

When the UN adopted a resolution calling for all possible means to aid the ROK on July 7, the Truman administration announced it was sending in US forces. Meanwhile, fourteen nations contributed military assistance, and at peak strength, UNF numbered 400,000 South Korean troops, 250,000 US troops and 35,000 troops from other nations. Two British and Canadian units formed the First Commonwealth Division. Turkey provided a brigade, and there were troops from Australia, Thailand, the Philippines, Colombia, Ethiopia, France, Greece, Belgium, Luxembourg, the Netherlands and New Zealand. Other nations provided medical units.

On 7 July, the CMC held the first national defence meeting in Beijing and established the Northeast Border Defense Army (NEBDA), totalling 260,000 troops, to forestall any emergency situation that might arise along the Chinese–Korean border.[27] On 4 August, Mao chaired a Politburo meeting discussing China's possible involvement in the Korean War. The next day, he ordered NEBDA forces 'to get ready for fighting in early September' in Korea.[28] On 18 August, Mao ordered the Ninth Army Group, which totalled 150,000 men and was originally purposed for the Taiwan offensive to join and strengthen Manchurian defences.[29] In his report to Mao and Liu Shaoqi on

---

26 General W. B. Smith, 'Memorandum by the Director of the Central Intelligence Agency to the President, November 1, 1950', *FRUS 1950, Korea* (Washington, DC: U.S. Government Printing Office, 1976), vol. 7, 1025.
27 CMC, 'National defense report to Mao, July 7, 1950', in *Mao's Military Manuscripts since 1949*, vol. 1, 428.
28 CMC document, drafted by Mao, 'Telegram to Gao Gang, August 5, 1950', in X. Li, X. Wang, and J. Chen (trans. and eds), 'Mao's dispatch of Chinese troops to Korea: 46 telegrams, July–October 1950', *Chinese Historians*, 5 (Spring 1992), 64.
29 Mao, 'Korean War Situation and Our Policy', speech at the Ninth Plenary of the Central Government (5 September 1950), *Mao's Military Manuscripts since 1949*, vol. 1, 201–3.

3 September, Zhou Enlai detailed the high command's plan to increase the NEBDA to forty-two infantry divisions, totalling 700,000 troops.[30] On 8 October, Mao reorganised the NEBDA into the CPVF, which were volunteers in name only and simply the same PLA troops that were assigned to Korea.[31] CPVF command was the PLA's front command. By early December, Chinese forces in Korea totalled thirty-three divisions, nearly 450,000 men; this was only the beginning of Chinese involvement. China accomplished rapid deployments without alerting the UNF command. The Chinese high command hoped its greater numbers, coupled with the element of surprise, would offset its inferior equipment and technology. To them, it seemed rational that a larger force would be decisive for a successful defence.[32] By April 1951, nearly 950,000 Chinese troops were in Korea. By December 1952, Chinese forces in Korea totalled 1.45 million men, including fifty-nine infantry divisions and fifteen artillery divisions.

Starting in 1952, the PLA rotated Chinese troops into Korea to gain modern war-fighting experience. Through troop rotation, the PLA gained experience in fighting American forces and CPVF troops were relieved and recuperated. The Chinese Army had fought the Japanese Army and Chinese Nationalist Army in previous wars, but knew little about the American, British, Canadian and other technologically equipped Western forces. Korea was a 'combat laboratory' where Chinese officers and soldiers gained essential combat training. By the end of the war, about 73 per cent of Chinese infantry troops had been rotated (25 out of 34 armies, or 79 of 109 infantry divisions). More than 52 per cent of Chinese Air Force divisions, 55 per cent of tank units, 67 per cent of artillery divisions and 100 per cent of railroad engineering divisions had been sent to Korea. More Chinese troops were sent to Korea because of this process.[33]

---

30 Zhou's report to Mao and Liu on 3 September 1950, in *Jianguo yilai Zhou Enlai wengao, 1949–1950* [*Zhou Enlai's Manuscripts since the Founding of the PRC*] (Beijing: CCP Central Archival and Manuscript Press, 2008), vol. 2, 247–51.
31 Mao, 'CMC order to establish the CPVF', in Zhang and Chen (eds), *Chinese Communist Foreign Policy*, 164–5.
32 Peng, 'Speech at the CPVF Army and Division Commanders Meeting, October 14, 1950', in *Peng Dehuai junshi wenxuan* [*Selected Military Papers of Peng Dehuai*] (Beijing: CCP Central Archival and Manuscript Press, 1988), 324.
33 X. Li, *Attack at Chosin: The Chinese Second Offensive in Korea* (Norman: University of Oklahoma Press, 2020), 156.

Process of Prioritisation

The UNC's strategy became clear by the spring of 1951. After seizing and consolidating their new positions, they attacked swiftly, not allowing Chinese troops to resupply or reinforce. The UNF used this strategy to exhaust the CPVF of its soldiers and supplies. Although it worked, the war became prolonged. While the CPVF campaign planners based their operations on significant reinforcements in Korea, the issue of maintaining combat effectiveness and adequate supplies became top priorities for the PLA high command.

Truman had to prioritise increased defence budgets over his domestic reform programmes to fight the Korean War. Nevertheless, since his administration had previously designed and executed foreign aid programmes as containment policy in the late 1940s, the president simply continued Cold War mobilisation as NSC Paper 68 called for a massive defence build-up. Moreover, Paul G. Pierpaoli Jr notes that 'this fear of becoming [a garrison state] influenced and guided strategists' decisions and the public's reactions to these decisions'. While the Korean War as a whole 'was a watershed for American economic and military policy', it was the Chinese intervention in November 1950 that turned a 'fragmented' mobilisation into an 'institutionalized' rearmament drive.[34] The US government regarded the PRC as its main enemy in east Asia and implemented a full-scale containment policy against it.

Meanwhile, Beijing justified intervention as a retaliatory response to America's aggressive policy in east Asia. Through Communist government leadership, the People's Republic defended itself by halting American advances in Korea. CCP propaganda conjured images of two hostile nations that perceived one another as constant enemies. Mao used the 'lips-and-teeth' and 'door-and-room' rhetoric that prevailed in Chinese descriptions of PRC–DPRK relations to convince Chinese people that fighting the Korean War was defending China. From 1950 to 1953, the CCP rallied the 'Great Movement for Resisting America and Aiding Korea' for China's war against America. The PRC spent a total of $3.3 billion during the war. In terms of war materials and supplies, the Chinese government transported into Korea a total of 5.6 million tons of goods and supplies during the intervention, losing 399 airplanes, 12,916 tanks and vehicles, and 4,371 artillery pieces in the

---

34 P. G. Pierpaoli Jr, *Truman and Korea: The Political Culture of the Early Cold War* (Columbia: University of Missouri Press, 1999), 9, 40.

endeavour.[35] Between 1950 and 1953, China's military spending represented 41 per cent, 43 per cent, 33 per cent, and 34 per cent respectively of its total governmental annual budget.[36]

During the war, Beijing's priority was to improve CPVF logistics and transportation. In 1951, the CMC issued its order to establish the CPVF'S Logistics Department to improve logistics capacity at regiment and battalion levels and increase frontline troops' combat effectiveness. Chinese solutions to battlefield problems were not elegant, but they were effective. The Chinese military's performance in Korea fits this characterisation, and although they undertook a steep learning curve, very often they achieved their battlefield objectives. The next priority was to obtain large numbers of weapons and munitions from the Soviet Union. Soviet military aid was indispensable for the CPVF's war efforts on the front. During the first quarter of 1951, the CPVF needed 14,100 tons of ammunition for the Korean front. While China's own defence industry produced a mere 1,500 tons, the Soviet Union supplied the remaining 12,000 tons between January and March. In May, Mao sent Xu Xiangqian to Moscow to purchase more arms from the Russians.[37] According to the Sino-Soviet agreement, China received a $1.34 billion loan as military aid and the Soviet government agreed to deliver the arms for sixty Chinese divisions in 1951–1952. Another priority was to deploy the PLA's Air Force (PLAAF) in the Korean War. In March 1951, the CPVF–North Korean Joint Air Force command was established to conduct air operations under Soviet advisers' supervision. The Fourth Division (MiG-15 fighter division) was the first one to be deployed on the front in September. By October, the CPVF-NKPA joint command had 450 fighters and bombers for air operation and engagement in Korea. Eleven more Chinese Air Force divisions participated in the war through 1953, including 60,000 pilots and ground personnel.

Executions and Modifications of Strategy

China shocked the world when it launched the Second Offensive Campaign. On 25 November, four Chinese armies conducted an all-out attack on the US I and IX Corps against MacArthur's 'home-by-Christmas' offensive, spanning

---

35 Nie, 'Beijing's decision', 50.
36 PLA Academy of Military Science (AMS), *Zhongguo renmin zhiyuanjun kangmei yuanchao zhanshi [Combat Experience of the CPVF in the War to Resist the US and Aid Korea]* (Beijing: PLA Military Science Press, 1990), 233–4.
37 Marshal X. Xu, 'The purchase of arms from Moscow', in Li, Millett and Yu (eds), *Mao's Generals*, 139–48.

over a 100-mile-wide front on the west wing. On 29 November, UNF command issued an overall retreat in the west to allow the Eighth Army's withdrawal to South Korea. On 4 December, the UNF evacuated Pyongyang ahead of the CPVF's attack and occupation on 6 December. On the eastern front, the CPVF attacked the US X Corps, including the US First Marines and Seventh Infantry Division.[38] On 29 November, the Marines counterattacked to break the Chinese encirclement and unite their scattered units. On 1 December, the Chinese attack overran the Thirty-Second Regiment of the Seventh Division. This is the only case in the Korean War where the CPVF destroyed an entire US regiment.

From 31 December 1950 to 8 January 1951, the CPVF launched its Third Offensive Campaign along the 38th Parallel against a strong UNF defence. The CPVF and NKPA armies pushed east of Seoul and outflanked the US I and IX Corps. To avoid a disaster, Ridgway ignored the ROK's desperate pleas to save the capital and ordered a withdrawal from Seoul to the Han's south bank on 3 January. Chinese strategy and tactics in the first three offensives proved effective. Beijing was overwhelmed by the CPVF's victory in their first three campaigns. After taking over Seoul, political pressures from Mao, Stalin and Kim mounted for another attack. From 25 January until 21 April, the CPVF engaged in its Fourth Campaign. Instead of a mass offensive, it became a series of mobile, back-and-forth battles.

While the Chinese waged a large-scale war against the US/UN forces, the Truman administration decided on a limited war strategy in Korea to avoid a larger war with China and possibly the Soviet Union. Nevertheless, MacArthur suggested expanding the war into China, which contradicted Washington's strategy. Truman relieved MacArthur of command in April 1951. Allan R. Millett concludes, 'MacArthur's removal proved the right move for mixed reasons. It restored the professional dominance of the Joint Chiefs of Staff in the strategic direction of the war'.[39] Nevertheless, the general returned a hero to many Americans, but especially to the 'limited war' and Truman critics. MacArthur delivered his celebrated 'old soldier's' speech before a joint session of Congress and received a ticker-tape parade in New York City.

---

38 H. Mulhausen, 'The Chosin Reservoir; a marine's story', in R. Peters and X. Li (eds), *Voices from the Korean War: Personal Stories of American, Korean, and Chinese Soldiers* (Lexington: University Press of Kentucky, 2004), 98–116.
39 A. R. Millett, *The War for Korea, 1950–1951: They Came from the North* (Lawrence: University Press of Kansas, 2010), 425.

After MacArthur's dismissal, the UNC adopted a number of effective, preventive countermeasures against annihilation and encirclement, and used it as an opportunity to inflict more casualties on the attacking Chinese troops. UNF units reorganised their troops into strongholds protected by tanks and self-propelled artillery instead of retreating quickly, and awaited reinforcements. By that spring, the CPVF command faced a war in which the UNF command adopted a cautious strategy, slowly advancing northward to inflict more CPVF–NKPA casualties. However, Chinese commanders failed to ascertain the UNF's modified war strategy.

After April, Mao modified his war strategy from achieving swift victory and routing the UNF to a prolonged war. His goal shifted from total Chinese victory to American withdrawal from Korea. Mao believed that it would 'take several years to inflict casualties of hundreds of thousands of American troops to make them [the US] beat a retreat in the face of difficulties'.[40] To inflict more American casualties, the CPVF launched the Fifth Offensive, from 22 April to 2 June, the longest and most decisive Communist operation of the war. The CPVF–NKPA joint command deployed more than 700,000 men, including 600,000 Chinese troops, against 340,000 UNF troops. The UNF offered a strong defence. US officers were able to make good use of their experience from the Second World War as they consolidated the UNF defence line, pushed offensive campaigns into North Korea and built confidence in fighting back the Communist invasions.

When the Chinese offensive slowed, Van Fleet agreed with Ridgway that the CPVF and NKPA faced tremendous logistical difficulties, which not only stopped their attacks but also provided UNF an opportunity for a rapid advance to cut Chinese supply lines. On 20–23 May, the UNF counterattacked. The UNF's unexpected response turned the CPVF Spring Offensive Campaign into the most disastrous operation in CPVF history, as Chinese forces suffered 45,000–60,000 casualties, 'the most severe loss since our forces had entered Korea'.[41] The UNF then drove Chinese forces back north of the 38th Parallel. Chinese forces lost their Fifth Offensive Campaign and never again came close to Seoul, nor mounted another major southward incursion. Mao's failed mobile warfare forced him to reconsider both his political and military aims in June 1951. Realising China was incapable of ousting the UNF from Korea, Chinese leadership accepted a settlement without total victory.

---

40 Mao's conversation in Peng, 'My story', 35.
41 General X. Hong, *Hong Xuezhi huiyilu* [*Memoir of Hong Xuezhi*] (Beijing: PLA Press, 2007), 483.

After the truce talks began in July 1951, bloody fighting ensued, the front lines remained unchanged in stalemate, and both sides 'dug in' and prepared to stay. Peng adopted a more cautious defensive strategy. The trench warfare in Korea became the most forgotten phase of the 'forgotten war', even though 45 per cent of all US casualties tragically occurred during the peace talks. Mao was interested in using negotiations to strengthen China's security and reinstall a Sino-centric system in east Asia. Beijing focused on its geopolitical security and created an ominous commencement for the peace talks, which dragged on for more than two years. Despite increased fighting in the spring, President Eisenhower publicly stated his determination to do everything possible to end the war, including a nuclear threat. Stalin's death in March 1953 became a decisive factor in the Communist delegation's agreement on POW issues, which had blocked negotiations for more than a year.[42]

Conclusion

The Korean Conflict not only became the bloodiest war since the Second World War, but also changed the direction of Cold War politics. US Ambassador Charles Bohlen wrote, 'It was the Korean War and not World War II that made us a world military–political power'.[43] After the PRC–US confrontation in Korea, China and east Asia became a focal point of the global Cold War. China's intervention poisoned its relations with the US and much of the Western world for more than two decades. China was forced to adopt a pro-Soviet policy, further isolating itself from the world. Historians agreed that the alliance between Beijing and Moscow was the cornerstone of the international communist alliance system in the 1950s.[44] Chinese scholars generally agree that China's war in Korea restored its Great Power status in east Asia, which would play an important role in the Geneva and Bandung conferences in 1954 and 1955, respectively. Xi Jinping emphasised this in his speech at the seventieth Anniversary of China's intervention: 'The War to Resist the US and Aid Korea had created a strong fighting spirit of Chinese nation. We must carry on this spiritual strength to defend our country and

---

42 For more information on the prisoner of war issues, see D. Ch. Chang, *The Hijacked War: The Story of Chinese POWs in the Korean War* (Stanford: Stanford University Press, 2020).
43 The quote from S. F. Wells Jr, *Fearing the Worst: How Korea Transformed the Cold War* (New York: Columbia University Press, 2020), 488.
44 J. L. Gaddis, *The Cold War: A New History* (New York: Penguin, 2005); O. A. Westad, *Brothers in Arms: The Rise and Fall of the Sino-Soviet Alliance, 1945–1963* (Washington, DC: Wilson Center and Stanford University Press, 1998).

defeat the enemy.'[45] The Korean War is the only meaningful reference point for sustained PLA contingency operations beyond China's border. It is also the only real experience, no matter how outdated, that the PLA had of operating against US ground forces. Moreover, the war divided North and South Koreas along the 38th Parallel, which remains one of the hottest spots in the post-Cold War world. Strategically, the war cost China its most important goal of liberating Taiwan and concluding the Chinese Civil War. Taiwan remains as the ultimate dangerous dispute that could potentially drag China and the US into another bloody war.

---

45 'Xi Jinping's speech at the 70th anniversary celebration of the CPVF's participation in the war to resist the US and aid Korea', *Renmin ribao* [*People's Daily*] (26 October 2020), 1–2.

18

Israel's Wars*

EITAN SHAMIR AND EADO HECHT

Sources

Primary sources on the military aspects of the Arab–Israeli conflict are limited. None of the Arab states neighbouring Israel have government archives open to the public. Only Israel has a policy of opening government archives after thirty years, or on sensitive matters, after forty or fifty years, but they may be vetted; that is, defence-related information of great sensitivity may still be withheld, as is normal procedure in the archives of democracies. As a result, there is a vast discrepancy in the quantity and quality of sources, providing much more information and polemical publications on Israel than on its adversaries.

By contrast, memoirs have been published by key actors and eyewitnesses on all sides, even though here again, there is a preponderance of Israeli publications. Official accounts of various military operations have been published by Israel and its neighbours. In short, the source base favours the Israeli perspective, as it is only from this perspective that archives-based research can be conducted, even given the continuing restrictions of access to the most sensitive material.

Actors

Israel is a parliamentary democracy in which governments tend to be formed by coalitions of parties who jointly have a majority in the Israeli Knesset (parliament).[1] Major decisions, such as the initiation of a major military operation, are taken by majority vote in the government; smaller decisions, however, are made by a committee of ministers designated the 'Security

---

* This chapter was completed before the outbreak of the conflict on 7 October 2023.
1 The supreme authority over Israel's security policy and its military is in the hands of the entire government (in Israel taken to mean the collectivity of the elected ministers), not of a single person (such as the prime minister).

Cabinet' and headed by the prime minister and the defence minister. They take day-to-day decisions and directly command the chief of the general staff of the Israel Defence Forces (IDF) and the chiefs of the various intelligence organisations.

Every operational decision or action by any of these organisations requires approval by the government. As an example – during the repeated small-scale Syrian attacks in the 1960s, the prime minister and defence minister, after consulting the chief of the IDF general staff and chief of military intelligence, determined the parameters of each Israeli response down to the size of the force involved, which weapons were to be used and which targets were to be engaged. This was to ensure that the military action was always commensurate to the general political situation, internal and external, as well as to the intensity of the Syrian attack.[2] Actions above a certain strength or strategic decisions as to general guidelines for future actions required the convening of the Security Cabinet. Deciding to initiate a major operation or war required convening the entire government, which then delegated the authority of actually managing the war back to the prime minister and defence minister, with periodic updates or reconvening of the government for changes in the policy and strategy approved in the initial decision. So, for example, the decision to attack across the Suez Canal in the middle of the 1973 war required a government decision after first discussing the political and military benefits and dangers of such an operation.[3]

The chiefs of the IDF and the various intelligence agencies participate in government discussions to describe the situation and suggest possible courses of action but do not participate in the vote on the actual course of action chosen. In 1999 another advisory organisation was established – the National Security Council (NSC). The purpose of this body is to support the political echelon by improving background staff-work required to improve co-ordination and integration between Israel's many security agencies. The NSC's main job is to prepare papers on the situation and options available especially relevant to long-term decision making.

---

2 Y. Freedman, 'Together and separately – the first Eshkol government and its ministers facing Israel's security issues 1963–1966', PhD thesis, Tel-Aviv University (2021) (Hebrew).

3 S. Golan, *Decision Making of the Israeli High Command in the Yom Kippur War* (Moshav Ben-Shemen: Modan and Ma'arachot, 2013) (Hebrew), 728–36, 891–8.

Adversaries

Israel's adversaries have been and are multiple, including both state and non-state actors (the latter sometimes acting as proxies of states), often forming coalitions. Since 1920, the main adversary to Jewish statehood have been the Palestinian Arabs – organised in varying rival factions that have often fought each other no less furiously than they have fought Israel. On their own, the Palestinians have never been able to create a military force equivalent in strength to the Arab states.

From May 1948 a number of Arab states have fought Israel directly or provided financial and military support to the Palestinian Arabs in their fighting against Israel. The willingness of each state to participate in actual combat has fluctuated depending on prevailing ideological commitment to the cause of eradicating Israel or political expediency relative to other issues each of the states was grappling with – these have included internal conflicts in each state, inter-Arab conflicts and economic issues. Israel's main state adversaries have been Egypt and Jordan (until the mid-1970s), Syria, Iraq and (since the 1980s) Iran. Other Arab states have sometimes provided small expeditionary forces for armed conflicts with Israel, but more often have only provided political and financial support.

Israeli security doctrine defines state adversaries as belonging to a First Ring – Egypt, Jordan, Syria and Lebanon have direct land borders with Israel; a Second Ring – Iraq, Saudi-Arabia, Sudan and Libya are separated from Israel by one of the First Ring states; and a Third Ring – all states beyond the Second Ring. Until the advent of long-range missiles, Second and Third Ring states could fight Israel only if allowed to do so via the First Ring. The first use of missiles to attack Israel launched directly from a Second Ring state was by Iraq during the 1991 war for Kuwait.

The perceived ability of each state's military to effectively prosecute the fighting against Israel has varied over time. Since 1974, the willingness of Israel's neighbour states to fight Israel directly has waned. Some actually signed peace agreements with Israel (Egypt in 1979, Jordan in 1994 and a number of Gulf states in 2020); others, such as Syria, have preferred to cease direct confrontation and conduct only proxy wars, while still others have ceased any active participation without officially declaring it.

In addition, non-Arab states have at times participated directly or via proxies in the fighting against Israel – the two most important being the Soviet Union and Iran. From the mid-1950s the Soviet Union gradually became the main supplier of weapons to Egypt, Syria and Iraq. In 1956,

1967 and 1973, it threatened to intervene with its own troops. Soviet military advisers were embedded in Syrian units from the mid-1960s to mid-1970s and in Egypt from 1968 to 1974 while they fought Israel. From February to August 1970, Soviet air and anti-air units actively but covertly fought Israel on the Egyptian front alongside Egyptian forces. The Soviet goal was to prevent a military collapse of Egypt and acquire, in return, exterritorial basing rights in Egypt and Syria.[4]

Since its revolution in 1979, Iran's involvement is motivated by ideology. It created Hezbollah, a Shia Islamist political party and militant group, as a proxy force in Lebanon,[5] has provided funding, weapons and training to religious Palestinian organisations such as Hamas and the Palestinian Islamic Jihad, and from 2012 began to establish a military base in Syria – initially to assist the Syrian regime in defeating the rebellion against it, but gradually adding activities aimed at Israel. The Iranian regime has declared the eradication of Israel as a central objective and has even defined an official date, 2040, by which time this objective is to be achieved.[6]

Causes of Wars

The physical core of the conflict is the dispute over territory between Jews and Arabs, but overlaying this is a religious conflict between Islam and Judaism and between Arab nationalism and Israeli nationalism.

Religiously motivated Muslim violence against Jews, as a minority living under Muslim domination, began with Mohammed in the seventh century, but has generally been less intense than Christian religious and European persecutions of Jews. Political motivation was added following the inception in the late nineteenth century of a Jewish movement, Zionism, to reinstate an independent Jewish state in the Holy Land, and especially following the British/Christian conquest of the land from the Ottoman/Muslim Empire (1917–1918) when the prospect of establishing a Jewish state became imminent.

---

4 D. Adamsky, *Operation Kavkaz – the Soviet Intervention and Israeli Surprise in the War of Attrition* (Tel-Aviv: Ma'arachot, 2006) (Hebrew). Officially the Soviet Union denied participation and contemporary Russia maintains this denial.
5 S. Shapira, *Hizbullah Between Iran and Lebanon* (Bney-Brak: HaKibbutz HeMeuchad, 2000) (Hebrew).
6 'Leader says jihadi morale will leave no serenity for Zionists', Islamic Republic News Agency (9 September 2015), https://en.irna.ir/news/81753808/Leader-says-jihadi-morale-will-leave-no-serenity-for-Zionists. The date has since been regularly repeated by Iranian political and military leaders in official speeches.

From 1920 to 1948, Palestinian Arabs, Jews and the British fought each other intermittently over control of the land. On 15 May 1948, after the British withdrew and the Jews officially established a state on the territory designated by the United Nations (UN), the armies of Egypt, Jordan, Iraq, Syria and Lebanon joined the Palestinian Arabs in attempting to destroy the newly established Jewish state and the Jews fought to maintain it. The Arab invasion failed – Israel maintained its existence and that existence has been the heart of the conflict since then. Gradually, as the feasibility of destroying Israel lost credibility in their eyes, the fighting between Israel and its Arab state neighbours devolved into a struggle to determine the exact borders between them.

While the absence of a Palestinian Arab state has been seen internationally as the key reason for the continuation of the conflict, from 1948 to 1967 (when virtually all the territory designated for that state by the UN was in Arab hands) no attempt was ever made by the Palestinian leaders or the Arab states to establish one. Two recent offers by Israel (2000, 2008) to withdraw from large parts of territory captured by it in 1967 to enable the establishment of a Palestinian Arab state were both turned down by the Palestinian leaders as insufficient.[7] The Oslo Accords signed in 1993 by the Palestine Liberation Organization (PLO) and Israel required the former to annul the paragraphs in their Charter calling for the destruction of Israel. This was never carried out, however, and like the PLO Charter, the Hamas Charter also expressly calls for the destruction of Israel.[8]

As noted, third parties have sometimes exploited the local conflict for their purposes, causing escalations in the fighting. Thus, for example, the 1956 war pitting Israel against Egypt had at its origin France's and Britain's attempt with the help of Israel to recapture the Suez Canal that had been constructed by and had subsequently remained under French and British control, but was seized by Egypt that year.[9] The crisis leading directly to the 1967 war began

---

7 C. Haberman, 'Dennis Ross's exit interview', *New York Times* (25 March 2001), www.nytimes.com/2001/03/25/magazine/dennis-ross-s-exit-interview.html. Reuters Staff, 'Palestinians reject proposal by Israeli PM', Reuters World News (12 August 2008), www.reuters.com/article/us-palestinians-israel-idUSLC6231820080812. 'History of Mid-East peace talks', BBC News (29 July 2013), www.bbc.com/news/world-middle-east-11103745.
8 The Palestinian Charter (1968), articles 9, 10, 15, 19, 20, 22, https://palwatch.org/page/2. The Covenant of the Islamic Resistance Movement (1988), articles 11, 13, 15, 35, https://avalon.law.yale.edu/20th_century/hamas.asp.
9 Y. Henkin, *The 1956 Suez War and the New World Order in the Middle East: Exodus in Reverse* (New York: Lexington Books, 2015), 91–118.

with a Soviet attempt to exploit the hostility between Israel and Syria to improve the USSR's own strategic position in the Middle East vis-à-vis the West.[10]

Objectives

Israel's strategic objective was initially to establish the state of Israel, an objective realised in May 1948. Thereafter, Israel's principal strategic objective has been to maintain it, solidify its borders and protect its citizens. In late March 1948, after nearly four months of defensive fighting, the objective stated in the first-ever Israeli offensive plan was 'to take control of the territory allocated to the Hebrew state and to defend its borders and the settlements and Hebrew population beyond those borders'.[11]

Territorial questions have remained at the heart of the many conflicts since 1949, but as far as Israel is concerned, since that year, permanently gaining more territory has never been a political goal for war, though temporarily gaining territory to be used as a bargaining chip has been a goal. For example, immediately after the 1967 Six-Day War, the Israeli government decided that in return for a peace treaty, it would return all of the recently captured Sinai to Egypt and the Golan Heights to Syria and most of Judea and Samaria (aka the West Bank of the Jordan River) to Jordan with minor changes, especially in Jerusalem.[12] The Arab response was to proclaim that there could be 'no peace with Israel, no recognition of Israel and no negotiations with it'[13] and the renewal of fighting within weeks of the ceasefire set the political background for the continuation of fighting, gradually strengthening those in Israel who supported partial annexations.

Conversely, the central objective of Israel's enemies was first to prevent the establishment of the Jewish state; failing that – to eradicate it; and failing that – to reduce its territory and prosperity in order to create a situation that would enable its future eradication.

Israel's long-term political objective has been to gradually convince adversaries that Israel's existence was an unchangeable fact and that attacking it, in whatever form or strength, bears costs out of proportion to possible gains.

---

10 M. Oren, *Six Days of War: June 1967 and the Making of the Modern Middle East* (New York: Presidio Press, 2002), 54–5. I. Ginor and G. Remez, *Foxbats Over Dimona* (New Haven: Yale University Press, 2008).
11 Haganah National Headquarters, 'Plan D' (March 1948) (Hebrew).
12 Israel State Archives, 'Minutes of Government Meeting, 10 a.m. 15 June 1967', (Hebrew).
13 League of Arab States, *Khartoum Resolution* (1 September 1967), https://bit.ly/3INxLAS.

However, given the disparity in size, wealth and political power, Israel can never achieve a total defeat of its enemies. As explained by Prime Minister David Ben-Gurion:

> [A]fter every war from which we emerge victorious we shall face the same problem ... we can never assume that we are able to land such a crushing blow on the enemy that it will be the final battle .... Our neighbours are in the opposite situation, they can assume the possibility of a final battle, that they can hit Israel so powerfully that they will destroy the problem and the Israeli–Arab issue will cease to exist.[14]

Therefore, the general military objective chosen to achieve the political goal is to deter attacks on Israel's territory, and when deterrence fails, to defeat them decisively if only temporarily in order to recreate deterrence.

Though fluctuating in intensity, fighting to achieve the above long-term objectives has been continuous – there has never been a complete ceasefire between 'wars'. Within the framework of the long-term objectives, specific escalations in military operations have been aimed by each side to achieve medium-term and short-term objectives, regarded as stepping stones leading to their rival long-term objectives.

Available Means

The Israeli Defence Force (IDF) gradually evolved over a period of forty years. It grew from a small commercial security firm (1907) to a community-funded nationwide clandestine defence organisation (1920) – both focused on protecting specific villages or city neighbourhoods against criminally and politically motivated attacks by Arab irregulars. Then it evolved further into a guerrilla army (1946), rebelling against the British while defending against the Palestinian Arabs, to be transformed into an increasingly regular army (1947) that would defeat the mostly improvised Palestinian Arab fighting forces, and then employing mostly infantry reinforced with hastily acquired aircraft, tanks and artillery to defeat the invading regular Arab state armies (1948).

Israel's population and economic base are considerably smaller than the combined populations and economic bases of its adversaries. Some of the individual adversaries are by themselves bigger and richer than Israel. Israel's

---

14 D. Ben-Gurion, 'Can we consider a preventative war against Egypt? – speech in Military Commanders' Conference, 16 December 1955', *Uniqueness and Purpose – Notes on Israel's Security (Anthology of speeches and writings)* (Tel-Aviv: Ma'arachot, 1971) (Hebrew), 219.

response to this disparity has been to allocate a percentage of its budget greater than most countries to defence and creating a system of military service that includes a greater proportion of its population.

IDF human power includes three components: voluntary career personnel (the minority), compulsory short-service regulars and compulsory long-service reservists (the majority). Compulsory service includes all Israeli Jews unless exempt for religious, medical or socio-economic reasons. In addition, some of the non-Jewish minorities (Druze, non-Arab Christians, etc.) are required to serve in the IDF. Israeli Arab citizens are exempt from military service though individuals may volunteer, and some do. Short-term compulsory regular service lasts for two to three years. Since 1950 the duration has been changed several times depending on the perception of the threat-level and budgetary or social considerations.

On completion of the initial military service, citizens have to be available for reserve service for twenty to thirty years (depending on the profession), but some volunteer to serve longer. Reservists are routinely mobilised every year to train or participate in active operations for a period of days or a few weeks, depending on their profession. In crisis times or war, mobilisation may last months (in 1973 some reservists were demobilised only after six or seven months of continuous service as fighting continued on the Syrian front), or the reservist may be called up more often, with considerable consequences for the economy and society.

Most Arab states also have professional personnel and citizens doing fixed-term military service. However, whereas in the IDF the reserves are integrated into regular units or fill complete reserve units and routinely participate in active operations, in most Arab armies they generally serve only as fillers for shortfalls in the regular army units. The armed forces of the Palestinian organisations and the autonomous Palestinian Authority have always been based only on volunteers, whether long-term regulars or temporary volunteers for a particular action.

Gradually, since Egypt and Jordan in particular withdrew from the conflict, Israel has been able to achieve numerical military superiority in specific confrontations and reduce the damage to its economy by mobilising only part of its available military force; since 1974 Israel has not needed to simultaneously mobilise its entire reserves force to successfully prosecute any major operation. To make up for the numerical disparity, the IDF has emphasised quality of personnel and equipment.

In the mid-twentieth century, both Israel and its adversaries could purchase only limited amounts of second- or even third-hand equipment. Well into the 1970s, and in some items into the 1980s, the IDF and its adversaries continued to employ equipment manufactured during the Second World War. In 1955 the Soviet Union began to supply Egypt and Syria with large amounts of equipment, including some of the latest versions. In 1956 France and later Britain began to sell used and new weapons systems to Israel, followed by the Federal Republic of Germany in the 1960s which furnished used systems as part of the Reparations Agreement for the Holocaust. From the mid-1960s, the USA too began to sell weapons to Israel. Until 1973, Israel purchased most military equipment from its own funds, but could not sustain this expense during the arms race that followed the 1973 war. The USA, which had gradually become Israel's prime ally, began to provide financial assistance which continues till today (currently approximately one-sixth of Israel's defence budget). Israel's economic crisis in the early 1980s, triggered to a great extent by the increased expenditure on defence, required a change in fiscal priorities and the budget was reduced. Government funding released from defence was reorientated to economic development and together with the hi-tech revolution rebuilt the economy and created rapid growth, enabling the government to maintain the reduced budget and gradually increase it again from the mid-1990s at about 5–6 per cent of the growing Gross Domestic Product.[15]

Until the 1980s, most of the equipment used by the IDF was technologically equivalent to that of its adversaries, some items were inferior and a few were superior. To save funds and enable the acquisition of what was considered to be the minimum necessary quantity of forces, much older equipment was upgraded to be just good enough rather than purchasing more of the best equipment. Thus, upgraded Second World War vintage Sherman tanks fought against 1960s vintage T-62s in the 1973 war, and prevailed because of superior crew training.

The initial Israeli response to the 1973 war was increased fear of invasion: within eight years, the standing army and reserves were increased two and a half times their pre-1973 war numbers. This was achieved by drastically reducing medical and socio-economic exemptions from service, to enable the transfer of all able-bodied men to combat units, and stretched Israel's human power and economy beyond their limits. This was a major (some claim *the* major) cause for a severe economic crisis in the 1980s, when Israel reached the limits of its capability to create quantity of forces. Partially as a solution to this

15 Central Bureau of Statistics/Government of Israel, 'Defence expenditure in Israel 1950–2019', Publication 1820 (January 2021), 10–11, www.cbs.gov.il/he/publications/DocLib/2021/1820_defence_expenditure_2019/e_print.pdf.

problem, the IDF gradually began to emphasise the development and acquisition of technology qualitatively superior to that of its adversaries. This trend increased from the 1990s, leading to a sizeable reduction in the size of the IDF in the twenty-first century, especially of ground forces, while building up an arsenal of the latest in technological capabilities.

Prioritisation

Given the relative strengths and locations of Israel's adversaries, and the fluctuating participation of various adversaries in actually fighting Israel, Israel's priorities have often shifted. Furthermore, as fighting fluctuated from low intensity to high intensity and back, this too shifted priorities.

Most of the actual fighting from 1920 until today has been low intensity between Israel and the Palestinians, but except for a brief period in early 1948 the latter were never deemed to be an existential threat. From May 1948 till 1974 the prime adversary was Egypt. Egypt was the most powerful adversary both politically, as a possible leader of an Arab coalition against Israel, and militarily, having the largest and best-equipped army.

Until 1967 geography dictated that the most dangerous of Israel's borders was with Jordan. The location of almost two-thirds of Israel's population and economy within range of Jordanian artillery made it especially vulnerable. However, the Jordanian Army, though considered the best trained, was also considerably smaller than either Egypt's or Syria's, and the Jordanian monarchy was the least aggressive of the active adversaries, busy as it was with stabilising its own existence against internal threats. In late 1970, Israel supported Jordan in its war against the PLO, whose headquarters were based in the country, and a Syrian invasion (a period of strife referred to as Black September). From then on relations between the two states were cordial, and King Hussein actually provided Israel with intelligence about Syrian preparations to attack Israel in 1973 and maintained a peaceful border with Israel during the 1973 war. He did, however, send a tank brigade to participate in the fighting against Israel inside Syria.

Beyond Jordan was Iraq – with a larger army – which sent forces in 1948 and 1967–1970 to fight Israel through Jordan and in 1973 to reinforce Syria. These actions could drastically change the balance of military strength on the dangerous Jordanian border and, therefore, Iraqi entry into Jordan was regarded a *casus belli*. Israel's initial indecision whether to initiate war in 1967 ended when Iraqi forces entered Jordan en route to the border with Israel. The initial Israeli strategic decision was to attack only Egypt, however, in the hope that rapidly defeating the largest Arab army would cause the others to withdraw without a fight, or at least with only token participation. This strategic plan failed in practice: Jordan and Syria joined the war, but it did demonstrate Israel's strategic prioritising.

Syria was the most active of the First-Ring Arab states. However, it was weaker than Egypt and controlled a smaller section of border. From the 1980s onwards, after Egypt withdrew from the conflict, Syria doubled its military capability and became the main perceived threat. The weakening of Syria's military strength as a result of its civil war has drastically reduced its status as a threat. At the same time, however, Iran increased its efforts to turn Hezbollah into a medium-sized army, created bases in Syria and transportation routes from Iran through Iraq to the Syrian–Israeli border, and placed Iranian and proxy forces within striking distance of that border. Thus, although the Syrian state is deemed a lesser threat, Syrian territory, together with Lebanese, has become the focus of Israel's threat perception.[16]

To sum up, Israeli priorities have shifted repeatedly between the constant routine threat of terror and guerrilla attacks and the occasional but more dangerous threat of a massive high-intensity attack by a coalition of Arab states. Because the latter was deemed more dangerous, IDF capabilities were built with it as the priority and the former as secondary. From the 1990s, as the probability of the latter diminished, the focus gradually shifted to more capabilities required for counterterror and counterguerrilla. This led in 2006 to an imbalance that brought many tactical failures in the war against Hezbollah, a formerly guerrilla warfare-focused organisation that had begun to acquire conventional warfare capabilities. In Gaza the Hamas organisation followed Hezbollah's lead. Furthermore, for the first time since 1967, long-range rocket artillery enabled Israel's enemies to once again attack Israel's civilian heartland. All these developments have brought the IDF to rebalance its required capabilities, especially as Iran began to develop a base for possible future operations against Israel in Syria. Furthermore, Iran's drive to acquire not only forward bases on Israel's borders via proxies and for its own forces, but also long-range missiles and a potential future nuclear capability, declaring the destruction of Israel to be a central objective, has required Israel to create power-projection capabilities to reach Iran, a Third-Ring state.

16 IDF, 'IDF strategy 2018', 14, 16 (Hebrew), https://bit.ly/3JsAsIf.

Israel's Wars

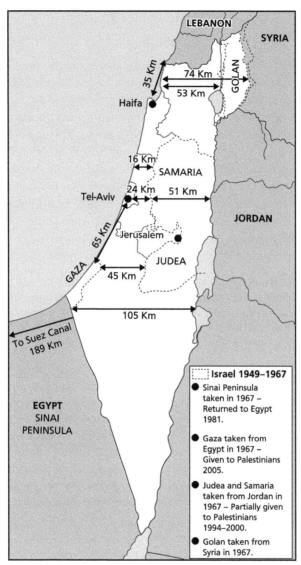

Map 18.1 Israel: the strategic importance of territorial dimensions. Redrawn from https://commons.wikimedia.org/wiki/File:Israel_location_map.svg with permission from creative commons licence Attribution Share Alike 3.0 Unported. Markings, arrows and distances added.

The Application of Strategy

Doctrine

Israel has been continuously at war for the past hundred years. Though for the sake of convenience the term 'war' has usually been applied only to the high-intensity confrontations, in fact, Israel's political and security establishments do not think of the conflict as separate 'wars', but rather as a single war fluctuating in intensity and with varying adversaries. This war is divided into long 'chapters' of low-intensity warfare, punctuated by brief 'chapters' of medium-intensity or high-intensity warfare. Although the Israeli leadership might define a specific immediate objective and strategy for each chapter, the strategy will always include references to the medium-term objectives as well as the overall long-term objectives. Thus, while conducting operations to reduce Palestinian terrorist attacks from Egyptian and Jordanian territory in the mid-1950s, chief of the general staff Moshe Dayan stated:

> Our successes and failures in the tiny battles along the border and beyond it greatly influence our routine security, the Arab assessment of Israel's strength and Israel's belief in its own strength .... Decisions not to confront Israel will be made only if the Arabs have reason to believe that they will face powerful responses and drag us into a confrontation which they will lose.[17]

So, while conducting 'between-war' operations for 'between-war' objectives, Israeli strategy has always taken into account the effect of these operations on the probability and conduct of future 'wars'. In the early 2000s, the IDF named these operations: 'The Campaign Between Wars'. The converse is true too – large operations have been initiated to quell low-intensity fighting, escalating to achieve de-escalation, the Second Lebanon War (2006) being a typical example. Likewise, almost each 'war' has been immediately followed by renewed low-intensity fighting aimed at affecting the immediate and medium-term political and military results of that 'war'. The most prominent case was the 1967–1970 War of Attrition which began merely three weeks after the official ceasefire of the Six Day War.

Despite the political and military connection between 'wars' and fighting 'between-wars' and the fuzzy boundary between them, Israeli strategists quickly understood the need for separate strategies for the conduct of each. They divided the plethora of threats into two categories: Routine Threats and Fundamental Threats.

---

[17] M. Dayan, 'Retribution operations as a means to maintain the peace', speech to IDF Commanders Conference, July 1955, published in the IDF journal, *Monthly Summary* (August 1955) (Hebrew).

Routine Threats were the continuous low-intensity attacks by individuals, small groups, organisations and states. None of these attacks of themselves were deemed an immediate threat to Israel's existence, but they did threaten the lives and livelihoods of Israeli civilians and could over time create a process of gradual exhaustion of Israel's population, causing it to abandon living near the borders and perhaps leave Israel altogether. These threats were to be handled by the regular army reinforced with a portion of reserve units in rotation.

Fundamental Threats were high-intensity attacks ('wars') by the Arab state armies, aimed to conquer Israeli territory and fully destroy Israel in one blow. These threats required maximum mobilisation of the entire IDF. The 1973 war, though regarded by many Israelis as a catastrophe, resulted in a significant reduction of the fundamental threat, as Arab leaders realised that in the best possible situation for them, the Egyptian and Syrian armies had gained only limited military success and had ultimately been defeated.

Initial attempts to meet Routine Threat attacks only defensively quickly failed and an offensive component, Retribution Actions, was added. As explained by Dayan: 'It is beyond our ability to [completely] prevent the murder of workers in an orchard or of sleeping families, but we can set a high price for our blood. A price too expensive for the Arab village, the Arab army and the Arab government to pay.'[18]

The vast majority of these attacks were conducted by Palestinians who focused on killing Israeli civilians, destroying property and plundering moveable property, but many were conducted by Arab state armies who, in addition to long-range fire and small raids, attempted to 'nibble' at the borders and gradually gain ground at Israel's expense. Israel at first separated responses to Palestinian attacks and to Arab state attacks, but after realising that finding the actual perpetrators of each Palestinian attack was beyond Israel's ability, the decision was made to focus only on attacking the army and national infrastructure of the state hosting the particular Palestinian attackers. Initially, this increased hostilities with those states and caused them to increase their support for the Palestinian groups conducting the attacks, but gradually the cumulative price inflicted did indeed prove unacceptable: Arab state hosts restricted the frequency of attacks after drastic Retribution Actions and then gradually relaxed the restrictions again till the next escalated retribution action. Lebanon was too weak to restrict Palestinian (1970–1982) and Hezbollah attacks (1991–2006), leading Israel to initiate the two Lebanon

---

18 Dayan, 'Retribution operations'.

wars (1982, 2006) directly against these adversaries. The same strategic logic was applied in response to attacks emanating from the autonomous Palestinian areas in Judea, Samaria and Gaza – thus operations temporarily recapturing Palestinian autonomy areas in Judea and Samaria from 2002 to 2005 and the series of major Israeli operations against Gaza since Israeli withdrew from it in 2005.

Fundamental Threats required a different approach. Given the small geographic size of Israel, the proximity of its population centres and economic centres to the borders and the small size of the standing army, it was physically unfeasible to prevent massive penetrations and damage to the civilian rear with a defensive strategy. Only a rapid mobilisation and a no less rapid offensive pushing the front line into enemy territory could defend the rear. Any major Arab offensive required mass mobilisation of the reserve forces to defeat it – an action requiring time and dislocating the economy, so Israel needed to know when to mobilise 'just in time', not too late and not too early. It also needed to discharge the reserves as quickly as possible back to their economically productive jobs. These requirements were met by a three-stage concept described in the slogan: Deterrence, Early-Warning, Decisive-Defeat. While this suggests a linear progression, in fact it described a cyclical approach. Though first used to describe counterterrorist operations in the early 2000s, the catchphrase, 'mowing the grass', also describes the rationale behind Israel's Fundamental Security strategy and the understanding, as quoted above from Ben-Gurion, that Israel can never achieve a military victory so decisive that its adversaries will not be able to recover from it and choose, if they wish, to threaten Israel again. The idea is that as one never completely eradicates the grass – it always grows again and must be mown again periodically, so the threat can never be completely eradicated and requires periodic action to reduce.[19]

Deterrence meant the adversaries preferred not to provoke Israel too much, thus mass mobilisation was not required. Deterrence would be achieved by the decisive results of the previous war and maintained by the actions between the wars, within the framework of the Routine Security operations. Israeli intelligence was to monitor whether deterrence was succeeding or degrading, and just before deterrence collapsed issue a warning which would lead the government to order mobilisation. Once mobilised the IDF would strike at the earliest opportunity to inflict a decisive

19 E. Inbar and E. Shamir, 'Mowing the grass: Israel's strategy for protracted intractable conflict', *Journal of Strategic Studies*, 37 (2014), 65–90.

defeat of the relevant adversary or adversaries. The military objectives of this offensive would be chosen to rapidly push the war into enemy territory, maximise damage to the adversary's military capability and political prestige thus quickly bringing them to prefer a ceasefire, and thus renew deterrence and enable demobilisation of the reserves.

Practice

We can divide Israel's military practice into roughly three periods. In the first period (1949–1982) Israel fought five wars against Arab states (1956, 1967, 1969–1970, 1973, 1982). In 1982, during the war in southern Lebanon, for the first time, the PLO conducted medium-intensity fighting. In the second period (1983–2002) only the Palestinian organisations and Hezbollah fought Israel, but they were incapable of creating a threat requiring Israel to escalate operations to a level considered to be a 'war'. During the third period which began in 2002, the Palestinians, especially Hamas, and Iran's proxy, Hezbollah, gradually augmented their military capabilities and Israel found itself occasionally engaged in medium-intensity wars against them.

Each time, the actual strategy chosen to counter these threats was hotly debated in Israel, with a variety of options discussed in government and parliament, and the following description summarises only the final decisions.

Pre-Emption or Reaction?

The principle of pre-empting enemy threats proved politically difficult to implement and in fact, except in two cases, 1956 and 1967, most escalations by Israel were a reaction to enemy escalations rather than pre-emptions – though in some cases Israel's escalation was significantly more powerful than expected by the adversaries. To quote one example – after the 2006 war with Hezbollah, sparked by one of many Hezbollah attacks on northern Israel, Hezbollah's general secretary stated in an interview:

> We did not think, even one per cent, that the capture [of two Israeli soldiers who would then be held hostage] would lead to a war at this time and of this magnitude. You ask me, if I had known on July 11 ... that the [Hezbollah] operation [a cross-border raid] would lead to such a war, would I do it? I say no, absolutely not.[20]

---

20 'Nasrallah says he did not want war', Al-Jazeera (27 August 2006), www.aljazeera.com /news/2006/8/27/nasrallah-says-he-did-not-want-war.

On the side of Israel, the 1956 war was preventative rather than pre-emptive, while France and Britain reacted to Egypt's nationalisation of the Suez Canal. Israel feared that Egyptian president Nasser was gradually uniting the Arab world under his leadership, thus creating a single superpowerful Arab military entity beyond the capabilities of the IDF. Secondary goals included reducing Palestinian attacks from Egyptian territory, breaching the Egyptian maritime blockade of the Tiran Straits which prevented Israeli commerce with Asia and eastern Africa, and delaying the Egyptian Army from absorbing a huge recent influx of Soviet weapons.[21]

The 1967 war was a pre-emptive attack against the Egyptian-led coalition of Arab armies assembling adjacent to Israel's borders. The Soviet Union initiated the crisis by providing false information that Israel was planning to invade Syria in retaliation for Syrian forces firing on Israeli villages. Though he knew that the information was false, President Nasser apparently hoped to gain political points in the Arab world and not actually start a war. Initially Israeli leadership concluded the same and only gradually mobilised the reserves as more Egyptian units approached the border. The general Arab response of supporting a war with Israel, however, the movement of Syrian and Jordanian forces to Israel's borders and finally the movement of Iraqi forces into Jordan forced Israel's hand.[22] The 1967 war was the last major pre-emptive action, although small pre-emptive raids have since been conducted against specific targets, especially in counterterror and counterguerrilla operations.

During the 1967–1970 War of Attrition, Israel responded to adversary escalations with counterescalations, conducted counterbombardments, ground raids and air strikes but did not initiate major ground manoeuvre operations.

In 1973, a complacent intelligence assessment resulting from Soviet-style Egyptian use of military exercises to create a false alert and later to mask the assembly of Egyptian forces for actual war prevented a timely Israeli countermobilisation. When the intelligence did provide the final alert, the expectation of negative international political ramifications convinced Israel not to strike first.[23] The goals set by both Egypt and Syria in this attack were limited – the Syrians planned to return to the pre-1967 border with perhaps local improvements, the Egyptians planned to capture a small strip of land and create an international crisis that would drag the superpowers into conflict and therefore, to prevent this, both the USA and USSR would pressure Israel into

---

21 M. Golani, *There Will Be War Next Summer . . . The Road to the Sinai War, 1955–1956* (Tel-Aviv: Ma'arachot, 1997), 111–63, 195–294, 317–93 (Hebrew).
22 Israel State Archives, 'Minutes of Government Meeting, Afternoon 4 June 1967'.
23 Israel State Archives, 'Minutes of Government Meeting, 12.00 6 October 1973'.

territorial concessions – hopefully all of Sinai. Only the extra territory taken in 1967 prevented the initial tactical defeats at the front from becoming a total national disaster. Despite attacking in the best possible circumstances – initially fighting only the enormously outnumbered Israeli standing army as the reserves mobilisation, requiring seventy-two hours to complete, was initiated only a few hours before the Arab offensive began – the Syrians and Egyptians were defeated after having made initial territorial gains. While the Egyptians held on to a narrow strip of Sinai, the IDF approached Damascus, surrounded nearly a quarter of Egypt's army, captured a sizeable piece of Egyptian territory and inflicted extremely heavy casualties on enemy forces. This created maximum deterrence for the surrounding Arab states.

From 1974 till 2021, every Israeli decision to escalate its offensive operations has always followed a pattern. Whenever terror or guerrilla raids on Israeli soil, or artillery bombardments against Israel, reached a level deemed unacceptable by the Israel government, and if small pre-emptive or retribution raids were no longer sufficient in reducing the trend of escalation, it authorised a major operation in retaliation.

Thus, in the summer of 1981, in response to an artillery bombardment on Israeli civilians by the PLO from Lebanon, Israel conducted a counterbombardment aimed at halting the fire. In February, April and May 1982 Israel considered but did not respond to PLO bombardments and other terrorist attacks. Finally, in June 1982, in response to yet another bombardment, the Israeli government decided to conduct a major operation in Lebanon. The same pattern of action occurred during the fighting with Hezbollah from 1991 to 2006 – major offensive operations being initiated by Israel in response to Hezbollah attacks in 1993, 1996 and finally, the biggest offensive operation, in 2006. And the same pattern can be discerned as fighting with the Palestinians escalated from 2000: Operation Defensive Shield in 2002 after Palestinian attacks; and the series of major operations against Gaza in summer 2006, December 2008, November 2012, summer 2014 and May 2021 following Palestinian raids and artillery bombardments into Israel.

Following the success of the 1967 war, the principle of pre-emption was no longer deemed militarily critical to Israel's existence nor politically viable, given Israel's need for American support.

Military Objectives and Methods

Two political factors determined the military objective designated by the Israeli government in each war: the damage deemed necessary in order to compel the adversary to request a ceasefire and recreate deterrence, and the time deemed available to achieve that damage.

From 1949 till 1982 each military operation was crafted to achieve the end result as rapidly as possible – IDF ground units concentrated on a limited number of axes, broke through enemy defences and advanced rapidly to the enemy rear. The main effort was conducted by mechanised ground formations supported by the air force.

From 1982 to 2021, as the intensity of operations deemed necessary to achieve the objective diminished, the time allocated became longer. Gradually, as advanced target acquisition and precision munitions technology developed, the main effort was transferred from the mechanised ground manoeuvre to the air force. Air strikes were complemented by infantry units operating in complex terrain that restricted the air force's capabilities because of the presence of civilians or the difficulty of discovering the enemy hidden in houses, woods, caves and tunnels. Limited manoeuvre by large mechanised formations, as in 2006 in Lebanon, or smaller formations, as in Gaza in 2009 and 2014, became a last resort employed only when stand-off fire and light-infantry actions proved insufficient.

In 1956 the military objective was to capture almost all Sinai with a minimum of fighting: 'to dislocate the Egyptian forces' deployment in Sinai to bring about their collapse' within five days by manoeuvring into positions that threatened their rear but allowed them to retreat.[24] However, in 1967 the operational objective was to 'destroy the Egyptian air force and the majority of their forces in Sinai'.[25] IDF forces were to penetrate halfway into Sinai, surround enemy forces and destroy them within four days. The 1973 war was to begin defensively, but, prior to the war, a vigorous debate on the defensive strategy was ultimately decided by the assumption that the double objectives of defeating the enemy attack and the subsequent counter-offensive to recreate deterrence must be completed within one week.[26] Counteroffensive plans aimed at destroying a maximum of enemy military forces; capturing territory was considered secondary, and only to the extent needed to achieve that destruction and perhaps gaining bargaining chips for post-war negotiations.

In 1982 Israel initially aimed at a limited goal of pushing the PLO beyond the range of its artillery – advancing approximately 40 kilometres into

---

24 Lieutenant-General Moshe Dayan, chief of the general staff, 'Instructions for the Operation Plan' (25 October 1956).
25 IDF general staff, Operations Branch, 'Operation Order Nakhshonim' (4 June 1967).
26 Summaries of the debates: C. Guy, *Bar-Lev: A Biography* (Tel-Aviv: Am Oved, 1998) (Hebrew), 174–80, 191–2; H. Bartov, *Dado – 48 Years and 20 Days* (Tel-Aviv: Dvir, 2002) (Hebrew), 188–282.

southern Lebanon within two days.[27] The government subsequently decided to attempt to completely evict the PLO from Lebanon. This required advancing another 40 kilometres to Beirut and an appropriate extension of the time available to a week. Initially the plan was to avoid contact with Syrian forces deployed in Lebanon, but this proved impossible as some Syrian units were deployed adjacent to PLO forces and 'shadow-boxing' by Israeli and Syrian forces manoeuvring to gain local tactical advantages degenerated into firefights; it was deemed necessary to push the Syrian forces aside while pursuing the anti-PLO objective.[28] International intervention then halted major operations before achievement of the final objective, and the Israelis were forced to continue their advance segmented in small bounds until finally the PLO and adjacent Syrian forces in Beirut were compelled to surrender. The PLO forces were dispersed by ships to other countries having no land border with Israel, whereas Syrian forces surrounded in Beirut were allowed to drive through Israeli-held territory to join their compatriots in eastern Lebanon.

Operation Peace for Galilee in 1982 was the last Israeli offensive to begin with a major ground manoeuvre. In all offensive operations since 1983, the military objectives have been defined in limited terms of destroying a certain proportion of enemy forces preferably by stand-off fire and specific target-focused small ground raids rather than by massed ground manoeuvre. The latter was initiated only if stand-off fire failed to achieve the strategic objective of inducing a ceasefire.

In all of the offensive operations employing large ground forces against the Palestinians (2002, 2006, 2009, 2014), objectives were limited – capture and clear a particular area in order to destroy a specific enemy unit or capability.

The Second Lebanon War (2006) began with large air strikes, and when these did not suffice to cause Hezbollah to cease fire, ground forces were inserted to locate and destroy specific Hezbollah positions and units. Only when these too failed to achieve the desired outcome, did Israel launch a large-scale, though limited objective, ground manoeuvre.

Conclusion

From an Israeli perspective, Israel has been at war ever since 1920 and today this is still a war in progress. This present war state affects the quantity and the quality of the information available and the ability to assess in retrospect

---

27 IDF general staff, Operations Branch, 'Operation Order Peace for Galilee' (6 June 1982).
28 S. Golan, *Israel's War in Lebanon 1982* (Moshav Ben-Shemen: Modan and Ma'arachot, 2017), 283–383 (Hebrew).

the quality of many of the strategic decisions made by Israel and its various adversaries. Furthermore, it is a war that has aroused great emotions, and the controversy over the rights and wrongs has also heavily affected the quality of writing on what has actually occurred and why. Accusations of war crimes, crimes against humanity and even genocide have surfaced throughout the confrontations. Also, myths created during or immediately after events remain durable 'common knowledge' even after later deeper research has disproved them. Future historians will have their work cut out for them to focus on more balanced assessments, which should include sources from other sides and angles as well.

The physical core of the conflict is the dispute over territory between Jews and Arabs, but overlaying this is a religious conflict between Islam and Judaism as well as between different national ideals, Arab and Israeli. Israel's adversaries have been and still are a loose coalition of non-state organisations and states, sometimes in dispute, even at war, with each other no less ferociously than against Israel. Apart from the Palestinian Arabs, the active participation of all the other adversaries, most of them militarily much more powerful than the Palestinians, has been intermittent, and over time some have completely withdrawn from the conflict while new ones have joined in. Fighting has been constant but its intensity has fluctuated – constant non-stop low-intensity warfare punctuated by brief episodes of medium- to high-intensity fighting, each one creating the political and military conditions for the other.

Knowing it is not presently possible to achieve a complete single military victory that would end the conflict, Israel's constant objectives have been first to ensure its survival, second to reduce the damage caused by each iteration of fighting and lastly to gradually convince its adversaries to prefer diplomacy over combat. A realistic political settlement has been close at times but warfighting without attainable political aims creates a situation of perennial crisis. On the whole, since 1920, when the Jews had no state, until 1948 when they fought to establish and maintain it, and over time as they have fought to improve its survivability and the security of its population, the security of Israel is considerably better today.

19

The India–Pakistan Confrontations

ŠUMIT GANGULY

How have the security strategies of India and Pakistan interacted over the Jammu and Kashmir dispute? What are the sources of their respective strategies? How have such strategies evolved since each nation's emergence as independent states after the collapse of the British Indian Empire? What have been the key turning points? How are they likely to evolve in the future? This chapter focuses on the violent interactions of the two major powers on the south Asian subcontinent.

Sources

The sources that we can draw from, however, remain to date rather limited. Apart from the partial opening of relevant documents in India's National Archives, not much archival material is available relating to the origins of the India–Pakistan confrontation. Pakistan's National Archives on the subject remain inaccessible to researchers. The majority that are available comprise the British Transfer of Power Documents and The United States Foreign Relations documents. These sources provide accounts, albeit partial, of two of the major, pertinent powers' perspectives of the origins of the India–Pakistan confrontation over Kashmir.

Scholarship concerning the conflict's origins is also limited and, for the most part, reasonably partisan. One of the few early Indian analyses of the conflict is that of Sisir Gupta, an Indian scholar-diplomat. His work, however, is a deft defence of the Indian position.[1] Practically all writing on the Kashmir dispute deriving from Pakistan is either in the service of the state or utterly polemical.

---

1 S. Gupta, *Kashmir: A Study in India–Pakistan Relations* (New York: Asia Publishing House, 1966).

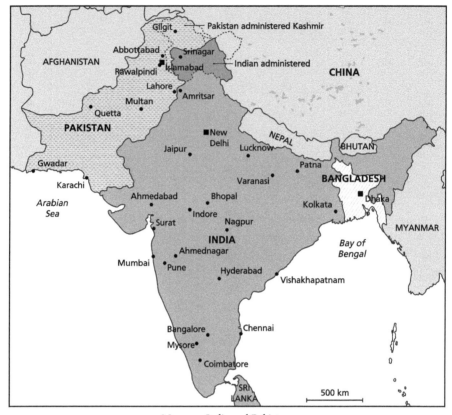

Map 19.1 India and Pakistan.

Bluntly stated, there is no real scholarship on the subject that is of Pakistani origin. In recent years, several foreign scholars have contributed to the extant literature, and a handful of these are worthy of discussion. T. V. Paul, an Indo-Canadian scholar, edited a book which adopted a theoretical perspective of the rivalry and its sources.[2] This work, while useful, is unbalanced. Beyond this collection, C. Christine Fair's book, while relevant, does not directly deal with the sources of Indo-Pakistani discord, but rather focuses on Pakistan's military strategy towards India.[3] Finally, S. Paul Kapur's work seeks to trace the ideological origins of Pakistan's military strategy towards India.[4]

---

2 T.V. Paul (ed.), *The India–Pakistan Conflict: An Enduring Rivalry* (New York: Cambridge University Press, 2005).
3 C. C. Fair, *Fighting to the End: The Pakistan Army's Way of War* (New York: Oxford University Press, 2014).
4 S. P. Kapur, *Jihad as Grand Strategy: Islamist Militancy, National Security and the Pakistani State* (New York: Oxford University Press, 2016).

Actors

India's Strategy and Practice

To a great extent, a combination of material and ideational forces shaped India's strategy in the immediate aftermath of its emergence as an independent state following the collapse of the British Indian Empire in 1947. The material circumstances concerned the partition of the British Indian Empire into the states of India and Pakistan. The partition of unified India came at a horrific human cost. According to most reliable estimates, at least a million individuals lost their lives and anywhere between 10 and 12 million were displaced.[5] This episode created an indelible legacy of implacable mutual hostility among the elites of both India and Pakistan.[6]

The second factor that shaped India's strategy had an ideational basis. It stemmed from the beliefs and world view of India's first prime minister, Jawaharlal Nehru. Nehru, as various scholars have remarked, was *primus inter pares* when it came to the formulation of India's foreign and security policies. Long before India's independence, he had taken an active interest in international affairs and had written on global politics with considerable verve and authority.[7] After India attained its independence, there was hardly anyone in his Cabinet, with the possible exception of his minister of home affairs and deputy prime minister, Sardar Vallabhai Patel, who could match his stature on matters of international politics. Consequently, Nehru had almost complete latitude in the formulation of India's foreign and security policies.

Such freedom enabled him to implement his specific foreign policy vision. To that end, for the most part, he fashioned an ideational foreign policy designed to promote decolonisation, global nuclear disarmament and support for multilateral institutions.[8] There is no questioning the sincerity of his commitment to these goals. However, there was also a significant element of pragmatism that undergirded his ideational worldview. He was acutely cognisant of the country's dire poverty and was keen on promoting economic development. Consequently, he was intent on limiting defence expenditure.[9] Furthermore, he was also acutely concerned that an inflated

---

5 Y. Khan, *The Great Partition: The Making of India and Pakistan* (New Haven: Yale University Press, 2008).
6 R. Jervis, *The Logic of Images in International Relations* (Princeton: Princeton University Press, 1970).
7 J. Nehru, 'The unity of India', *Foreign Affairs*, 16 (1938), 231–43.
8 S. Ganguly, *Indian Foreign Policy: Oxford Short Introductions* (New Delhi: Oxford University Press, 2015).
9 S. P. Cohen, *The Indian Army: Its Contribution to the Development of a Nation* (Berkeley: University of California Press, 1971).

military might encourage the state to entertain expansionist ambitions. His misgivings were understandable. The military apparatus that his nationalist government had inherited had loyally served the British Empire until India's independence. Worse still, the military coup in Pakistan that took place in 1954 reinforced his apprehensions.

These concerns, in turn, were reinforced as a consequence of the emerging dispute over the control of the contested 'princely state' of Jammu and Kashmir.[10] India wanted to amalgamate the state into the Indian Union in order to demonstrate that a Muslim-majority state could thrive in a predominantly Hindu but constitutionally secular polity. Pakistan, with equal zeal, wanted to incorporate the state on the grounds that it was created as a homeland for the Muslims of south Asia. As a consequence, when the Hindu monarch of Kashmir, Maharaja Hari Singh, acceded to India, it initiated a war to seize the territory.[11] The onset of this conflict in the latter half of 1947 was one of the two most influential factors which determined India's security strategy. India's leadership quickly concluded that this dispute would prove to be intractable because it dealt with an issue that was indivisible.[12] This assumption proved to be correct as it has continued to animate India–Pakistan relations into the following century.[13]

Nevertheless, regardless of the ideological positions of the government in office, India has remained a status quo power. Aside from a handful of intemperate statements on the part of opportunistic politicians (mostly intended for a domestic political audience), India has not undertaken any steps that would contribute to territorial aggrandisement. In this context, it should be made clear that India's absorption of the Portuguese colony of Goa in 1960 did not constitute an expansionist move. Prime Minister Nehru had negotiated in good faith with the Salazar dictatorship in Portugal, seeking a peaceful Portuguese withdrawal from its colonial enclaves. Faced with Portuguese intransigence, Nehru authorised the use of force.[14]

---

10 H.V. Hodson, *The Great Divide: Britain, India and Pakistan* (Oxford: Oxford University Press, 1986).
11 A. Whitehead, *A Mission in Kashmir* (New Delhi: Penguin Global, 2008).
12 S. E. Goddard, *Indivisible Territory and the Politics of Legitimacy: Jerusalem and Northern Ireland* (Cambridge: Cambridge University Press, 2009).
13 S. Ganguly, *Deadly Impasse: India–Pakistan Relations at the Dawn of a New Century* (New York: Cambridge University Press, 2016).
14 A. Rubinoff, *India's Use of Force in Goa* (Bombay: Popular Prakashan, 1971).

Pakistan's Strategy and Practice

Pakistan was, in the evocative words of the novelist, Salman Rushdie, 'a place insufficiently imagined'. What is the import of Rushdie's phrase? Pakistan's independence movement had mostly been fashioned around the charismatic personality of Mohammed Ali Jinnah. However, Jinnah, unlike his Indian counterparts, had done little to carefully nurture the organisational features of the political party that he had dominated, the Muslim League. The party had known no intra-party democracy, had mostly secured its electoral support with parochial ethno-religious appeals and had failed to draw up any blueprints for governing the country.[15] Consequently, it was singularly ill-prepared for the challenges of administering a complex, ethnically diverse polity.[16] To compound matters, at the time of independence and partition, India's political leadership had proven to be less than forthcoming in the division of the assets of the British colonial legacy.[17] Both these factors made conditions less than propitious for the emergence of a robust democracy in the country. Faced with the task of consolidating the Pakistani state, its post-independence political leadership proved inept. Its failure enabled a bureaucratic-military nexus to seize control over the reins of governance.[18] The military, to serve its own ends, fostered an image of India as an implacable adversary committed to the destruction of the Pakistani state.

Yet a decade before the military seized and consolidated power, Pakistan had initiated a war with India on the basis of an irredentist claim to the former princely state of Jammu and Kashmir.[19] The strategy that Pakistan employed in this war deserves comment. It involved the use of proxy forces backed up by regular Pakistani armed forces personnel in mufti.[20] To that end, Pakistan used local Pathan tribesmen to spearhead the attack, thereby granting the Pakistani state a degree of deniability. As will be discussed at length later in this chapter, it resorted to a markedly similar strategy when initiating the 1965 war with India,[21] and pursued a similar strategy when it became involved in the 1989–1990 Kashmir insurgency and thence in the 1999 Kargil War.

---

15 M. Tudor, *The Promise of Power: The Origins of Democracy in India and Autocracy in Pakistan* (Cambridge: Cambridge University Press, 2017).
16 K. B. Sayeed, *Pakistan: The Formative Phase: 1857–1948* (Karachi: Oxford University Press, 1991).
17 A. Jalal, *The State of Martial Rule: The Origins of Pakistan's Political Economy of Defence* (Cambridge: Cambridge University Press, 2007).
18 A. McGrath, *The Destruction of Pakistan's Democracy* (Karachi: Oxford University Press, 1996).
19 B. N. Ramusack, *The Indian Princes and Their States* (Cambridge: Cambridge University Press, 2008).
20 A. Khan, *Raiders in Kashmir* (Islamabad: National Book Foundation, 1975).
21 Kapur, *Jihad as Grand Strategy*.

Its use of this proxy war strategy, in considerable measure, can be attributed to Pakistan's relative weakness vis-à-vis its principal adversary, India. The religious overlay that has also imbued this strategy stems, at least in part, from the vision of the state as the homeland of south Asian Muslims. Furthermore, its leadership has also viewed the use of Islamist ideology as an important rallying cry against a predominantly Hindu state which, in their view, had little more than a patina of secular pretensions.

What has remained constant is the leadership's preoccupation with the complete and eventual absorption of the state into Pakistan. To that end, its leadership, both civilian and military, has agreed that all diplomatic and military means be deployed to accomplish that goal. The military means, in particular, involves a strategy of attrition that seeks to wear India down through the relentless use of proxy forces. Pakistani strategists have referred to it as a 'war of a thousand cuts'.[22]

Causes of the Wars

Faced with the Pakistani invasion, Nehru authorised the Indian Army to mount an effective defence in Kashmir. At best, given India's limited resources, this was a strategy of deterrence by denial.[23] In the event, Indian forces were only able to secure around two-thirds of the original territory of the state before a United Nations-sponsored ceasefire brought the hostilities to a close.[24] Nehru, with his faith in multilateral institutions and following the advice of Lord Mountbatten, the last British viceroy, had referred the dispute to the United Nations Security Council to seek a resolution. To his subsequent shock and dismay, the issue quickly became embroiled in the politics of the Cold War.[25] Furthermore, Pakistan's diplomatic delegation proved to be far more adept in swaying Great Power opinion on the subject. Instead of a focus on India's original complaint which emphasised Pakistan's breach of international peace and security, the terms of debate were deftly shifted to India's supposed maltreatment of its Muslim minority. India's largely legalistic arguments held little appeal for the Great Powers, especially the United

---

22 P. Chalk, 'Pakistan's role in the Kashmir insurgency', TheRANDBlog (1 September 2001), www.rand.org/blog/2001/09/pakistans-role-in-the-kashmir-insurgency.html.
23 G. H. Snyder, *Deterrence and Defense* (Princeton: Princeton University Press, 1961).
24 L. P. Sen, *Slender Was the Thread: Kashmir Confrontation 1947–48* (New Delhi: Sangam Books, 1994).
25 C. Dasgupta, *War and Diplomacy in Kashmir, 1947–48* (New Delhi: Sage Publications, 2001).

Kingdom and the United States. The UN process nevertheless dragged on for the better part of a decade and a half, with the desultory debates culminating in a deadlock. By the early 1960s, the Great Powers had lost interest in the dispute.

The Second Kashmir War

By the early 1960s, the UN process had reached an impasse. Neither India nor Pakistan could reach an agreement on the sequencing of the various relevant UN resolutions and neither were prepared to make any territorial concessions. The failure of the UN to promote a resolution to the dispute constituted a critical backdrop to the onset of the second war over Kashmir.

At home, owing to the failure of the UN efforts, Pakistan's decision makers remained unreconciled to the status of Kashmir.[26] Worse still, following a military coup in Pakistan in 1958, the putative threat from India took on a greater significance even though, for all practical purposes, Pakistan had secured its principal strategic goal in the 1947–1948 war. Most importantly, the headwaters of the rivers in Kashmir had come under its control.[27]

Apart from the military's willingness to exaggerate the Indian security threat, domestic politics within Pakistan also contributed to war-proneness. The military dictator of Pakistan, General Mohammed Ayub Khan, was facing a degree of domestic dissatisfaction owing to two distinct factors. At one level, Pakistan's economic development, which had been on a sound trajectory, was starting to taper off. Simultaneously, Khan's leadership was facing a challenge from his charismatic minister of foreign affairs, Zulfiquar Ali Bhutto. Under these conditions, seeking a resolution to the Kashmir issue through the use of force could provide a respite for the regime.

Events in Indian-controlled Kashmir also made conditions more favourable for initiating a war with India. Specifically, in December 1963, riots ensued in Srinagar, the summer capital of the Indian-controlled portion of the state. These riots had stemmed from the theft of a sacred relic, believed to be a hair of the Prophet Mohammed, from the Hazratbal mosque. Since the disturbances had a distinct anti-Indian element, it construed such sentiments as indicating support for Pakistan in the Kashmir Valley. After Indian intelligence authorities successfully located the relic and local clerics duly authenticated it, the riots promptly subsided.

---

26 Z. A. Bhutto, *The Myth of Independence* (New York: Oxford University Press, 1969).
27 A. M. Shah, *The Army and Democracy: Military Politics in Pakistan* (Cambridge, MA: Harvard University Press, 2014).

The riots led Pakistan's leadership to conclude that conditions were ripe for fomenting an anti-Indian rebellion in the valley. Other developments reinforced Pakistani beliefs that a suitable moment had indeed arrived to seize the valley in a short, sharp war. In 1964, Prime Minister Nehru, who had been ailing for some time, died of a heart attack. His successor, Lal Bahadur Shastri, lacked Nehru's domestic and international stature, and thus his ability to handle Nehru's mantle was uncertain. Since this area was of little strategic significance, Prime Minister Shastri accepted British mediation and referred the issue to the International Court of Justice for resolution. However, in Islamabad, his decision to seek a judicial settlement was construed as a sign of Indian pusillanimity. In turn, it encouraged Pakistan's decision makers to draw up extensive plans for Pakistani troops and paramilitary forces disguised as locals to infiltrate the Kashmir valley to create conducive conditions for an invasion.[28]

When the infiltration process was set in motion in the late summer of 1965, the operation went awry from the outset. Local Kashmiris quickly alerted Indian military and intelligence authorities about the infiltrators, and thus any hopes that the regime in Islamabad had entertained about precipitating an anti-Indian uprising failed to materialise. Nevertheless, having committed itself to this war strategy, the leadership went ahead with Operation Gibraltar – a full-scale military invasion of Kashmir. The principal objective of this strategy was to seize as much Indian territory as possible.

One of the key inferences that can be made from Pakistan's decision to launch the war is that it reflected a failure of the Indian conventional deterrence strategy. India had made clear its willingness to defend its territorial integrity, had designed a strategy of deterrence by denial and had had the requisite forces in place to implement the strategy. Nevertheless, Pakistani decision makers made a series of flawed assumptions about India's willingness and ability to thwart a Pakistani invasion, and had sought to design around India's deterrence strategy.[29]

The Creation of Bangladesh

The third Indo-Pakistani confrontation in 1971 did not involve the Kashmir issue. Instead, this crisis and the ensuing war stemmed from the exigencies of Pakistan's domestic politics. Briefly stated, its origins can be traced to Pakistan's first free and fair elections that were held in 1970. To the dismay

28 R. Brines, *The Indo-Pakistani Conflict* (New York: Pall Mall, 1968).
29 Š. Ganguly, 'Deterrence failure revisited: the Indo-Pakistani War of 1965', *Journal of Strategic Studies*, 13 (1990), 77–93.

of the country's military and its allies, most notably the West Pakistan-based Pakistan People's Party (PPP), the outcome of the elections saw the emergence of an East Pakistan-based party, the Awami League (AL), which had campaigned on a platform seeking local autonomy. More to the point, since the East was more populous, the success of the AL meant that it would have a majority in parliament. Unwilling to accept this outcome and with the tacit backing of the military, the PPP started negotiations with the AL on power-sharing arrangements. This dialogue, however, quickly reached an impasse.

Faced with this deadlock and fearing a turn to secessionism in East Pakistan, the Pakistani military went on a rampage in late March 1971, turning their guns on politicians, intellectuals and students alike. Faced with this campaign of mass repression, nearly 10 million refugees fled across the porous borders to India over the course of the next month. Pressure from this extraordinary refugee burden forced India's political leadership under Prime Minister Indira Gandhi to make a careful assessment of the country's options. Based on the advice of some of her senior advisers, she fashioned a deft politico-military strategy designed to ensure the refugees to East Pakistan's safe return and to enable it to secede from West Pakistan.[30]

Recent scholarship has demonstrated that Indira Gandhi as well as some key advisers had mixed motives in designing this plan. Obviously, breaking up Pakistan, a long-term and nettlesome adversary, was a strategic imperative. However, there is evidence that humanitarian concerns about the dire plight of the refugees were also at play in their calculations.[31] Regardless, as India sheltered the refugees, a global diplomatic effort began which alerted the major powers to the situation in East Pakistan as well as the condition of the refugees. While a number of the Great Powers expressed sympathy for the refugees and were willing to provide humanitarian assistance, the United States under President Nixon, proved to be intransigent.

American callousness towards the unfolding crisis in the region stemmed from the geopolitical considerations of both Nixon and national security adviser Henry Kissinger. In late 1970, Kissinger, relying on Pakistan as a conduit, had made a secret visit to Beijing as part of a strategy to end the diplomatic isolation of the People's Republic of China (PRC). Consequently, quite apart from their well-documented personal antipathy towards Indira

---

[30] S. Raghavan, *1971: A Global History of the Creation of Bangladesh* (Cambridge, MA: Harvard University Press, 2013).
[31] G. J. Bass, *The Blood Telegram: Nixon, Kissinger and a Forgotten Genocide* (New York: Penguin Random House, 2014).

Gandhi and India, Nixon and Kissinger felt beholden to Pakistan.[32] Acutely cognisant of American hostility and fearful of the PRC opening a second front along the Himalayan border, in August 1971 India persuaded the Soviet Union to sign a twenty-year treaty of 'peace, friendship and cooperation'. Article 9 of this treaty basically provided India with a security guarantee.[33]

Onset of War

India went ahead with its strategic plans and quickly moved to clandestinely support the anti-Pakistani guerrilla movement within East Pakistan, the 'Mukti Bahini' (literally 'liberation force'). To that end, it offered sanctuary and provided them with military training and weaponry. Simultaneously, it developed plans for a land invasion of East Pakistan. By late autumn, Indian forces were already engaged in shallow cross-border incursions into East Pakistan. Faced with growing military pressures from the Mukti Bahini as well as from across its borders, Pakistan launched Operation Chengiz Khan, a series of air raids on India's western military airfields on 3 December 1971. These air raids provided India with a formal *casus belli*, and the same night the Indian Air Force carried out retaliatory strikes on West Pakistan.[34] Shortly thereafter the Indian Army embarked on a multi-pronged land invasion of East Pakistan. Within thirteen days the war was over as East Pakistan fell to the Indian forces, creating the new nation of Bangladesh. The Indian objective of dismembering Pakistan, which its policy makers had decided on in April–May 1971, had been realised.[35]

The break-up of Pakistan led to the collapse of the military regime in West Pakistan. The new civilian leadership of President Zulfiquar Ali Bhutto, convinced of Pakistan's conventional strategic inferiority, decided to embark upon a clandestine nuclear weapons programme as a strategic bulwark against India.[36] Of course, India's first nuclear test, which came in 1974, significantly boosted the Pakistani nuclear weapons programme.

---

32 Bass, *Blood Telegram*.
33 R. Donaldson, *Soviet Policy Toward India: Ideology and Strategy* (Cambridge, MA: Harvard University Press, 1974).
34 Ganguly, *Deadly Impasse*.
35 J. F. R. Jacob, *Surrender at Dacca: Birth of a Nation* (Dhaka: The University Press Limited, 1997).
36 H. Abbas, *Pakistan's Nuclear Bomb: A Story of Defiance, Deterrence and Deviance* (London: Hurst, 2018).

The Long Peace in South Asia

The outcome of the war ensured India's strategic dominance of the subcontinent. Even though Pakistan remained unreconciled about the status of Kashmir, the military asymmetry between the two states ensured that it could do little to challenge India's pre-eminence in the region. Resultantly, a cold peace lasted for at least two decades. It was not until the Soviet invasion of Afghanistan, which delivered a significant exogenous shock to the region, that the power balance shifted. It ensued because the United States under President Ronald Reagan declared Pakistan to be a 'front-line state' in its clandestine efforts to dislodge the Soviets from Afghanistan.[37] To that end, the Reagan administration moved with considerable dispatch to provide a significant tranche of economic and military assistance to Pakistan, along with a contingent of the latest fighter aircraft, the F-16. This package of aid, especially its military component, eroded India's military advantage over Pakistan. The renewal of the US–Pakistan military nexus emboldened the new military regime of General Zia-ul-Haq in Pakistan to trouble India.

The first opportunity materialised in the mid-1980s when an indigenous, ethnoreligious insurgency erupted in the Indian border state of Punjab. General Zia lost no time in quickly entering the fray providing sanctuary, military training and weaponry to the Sikh insurgents. Faced with Pakistan's involvement in the insurgency, which had greatly increased its threat, and being unable to thwart Pakistan's activities, India's policy makers decided to use a military exercise, 'Brasstacks', to forcefully persuade Pakistan to terminate its support for the insurgents. This exercise contributed to an inadvertent spiral of hostilities, bringing the two parties perilously close to war. Swift American and Soviet intercession in this crisis led to its resolution.[38]

Yet another crisis came in its wake. Once again, this stemmed from Pakistan's decision to intervene in another domestic upheaval with India. Stemming from the exigencies of Indian domestic politics, another insurgency had erupted in the Kashmir Valley in the disputed state of Jammu and Kashmir in December 1989.[39] Confronted with this insurgency which had quickly elicited substantial Pakistani support, India adopted a particularly

---

37 G. S. Bhargava, *South Asian Security after Afghanistan* (Lanham: Lexington Books, 1983).
38 K. Bajpai, P. R. Chari, P. I. Cheema, S. P. Cohen and S. Ganguly, *Brasstacks and Beyond: Perception and the Management of Crisis in South Asia* (New Delhi: Manohar, 1995).
39 S. Ganguly, *The Crisis in Kashmir: Portents of War, Hopes of Peace* (Washington, DC: Woodrow Wilson Center Press and New York: Cambridge University Press, 1997).

ham-fisted counterinsurgency strategy designed to quell the danger. Unfortunately, this had the effect of widening the insurgency's scope and placed the control of the Kashmir Valley at risk.

The 1990 Crisis

The widening of the insurgency led India to move forces closer to the Line of Control, the de facto border, in Kashmir. Pakistan, in turn, it is widely believed, considered a resort to the use of nuclear weapons in the event of an Indian cross-border strike.[40] US intelligence sources concerned about the possible escalation alerted high-level security officials in the George H. W. Bush administration. These warnings led President Bush to dispatch the national security adviser, Robert Gates, to New Delhi and Islamabad in an attempt to dampen tensions. In New Delhi, Gates counselled restraint and in Islamabad he made clear that in every war-game scenario that the Pentagon had played out, Pakistan had emerged as the loser. Under the circumstances, he pressed the leadership to desist from its support for the insurgents in Kashmir. The crisis, which had peaked in the spring of 1990, slowly dissipated after the Gates mission to the subcontinent.[41]

Over the course of the next several years, India refined its counterinsurgency strategy to a great extent. It included superior intelligence collection, a more calibrated use of force and better efforts to seal the Line of Control in Kashmir.[42] These changes, along with the provision of free and fair elections in the state, brought a modicum of order if not law to the troubled region. Ironically, it was India's very success in containing the insurgency and the concomitant loss of global interest in Kashmir that prompted the military regime of General Pervez Musharraf to undertake a bold and risky military operation.

The Kargil War

In May 1998 both India and Pakistan had crossed the nuclear Rubicon with their nuclear weapons tests. The international community and especially the United States had expressed grave concerns about the risks of nuclear war on the subcontinent. Against this backdrop, and probably in an effort to assuage

---

40 C. U. Bhaskar, 'The forgotten India-Pakistan nuclear crisis: 25 years later', *The Diplomat* (18 May 2015), https://thediplomat.com/2015/05/the-forgotten-india-pakistan-nuclear-crisis-25-years-later/.
41 D. Hagerty, 'Nuclear deterrence and the India–Pakistan Crisis of 1990', *International Security*, 21 (1996), 176–85.
42 S. Ganguly and David P. Fidler (eds), *India and Counterinsurgency: Lessons Learned* (London: Routledge, 2009).

the misgivings of the Great Powers and the international community, Prime Minister Vajpayee of India undertook a bold gesture. To that end he decided to visit Pakistan with a message of friendship and reconciliation.[43] When in Lahore (the site of the Muslim League resolution of 1940 which had called for the creation of Pakistan), Vajpayee, in a remarkably symbolic gesture, affirmed India's commitment to the territorial integrity of Pakistan.[44]

India's foreign and security policy establishments viewed Vajpayee's visit to Pakistan as a success and hoped that it might contribute to the genesis of some form of reconciliation with Pakistan. As a consequence, they reduced the level of their military alertness along the border as well as intelligence collection on Pakistan.[45] These shifts were to prove disastrous for India.

For the most part, unbeknown to Prime Minister Nawaz Sharif, the Pakistan Army under General Pervez Musharraf once again devised a military strategy of infiltrating members of the Northern Light Infantry (paramilitary units affiliated with the Pakistan Army) across the Line of Control in Kashmir. This strategy had two goals: the first was to seize critical salients, presenting India with a fait accompli, and then force it to negotiate with Pakistan. The second was to resurrect the Kashmir question before the international community and revive Pakistan's case.[46]

The strategy, at a tactical level, proved to be a success. In April of 1999, Indian forces became aware of Pakistan's infiltration across a range of areas along the Line of Control, only after an Indian patrol disappeared during a routine operation. Confronted with this situation, India's politico-military apparatus moved with dispatch to forcibly dislodge the intruders regardless of the human and material costs. The ensuing conflict proved to be a demanding task for the Indian forces because the Pakistani military had successfully occupied heights along a number of important areas in the Kargil region. Nevertheless, with steady artillery barrages, relentless infantry assaults against well-fortified positions and deft use of air power, over the course of the next two months or so India forced the Pakistani military to retreat.[47]

---

43 N. J. Wheeler, *Trusting Enemies* (Oxford: Oxford University Press, 2018).
44 S. Sinha, *Vajpayee: The Years that Changed India* (New Delhi: Penguin Random House, 2020).
45 S. Ganguly, *Conflict Unending: Indo-Pakistani Tensions Since 1947* (New York: Columbia University Press, 2001).
46 P. R. Lavoy (ed.), *Asymmetric Conflict in South Asia: The Causes and Consequences of the Kargil Conflict* (New York: Cambridge University Press, 2009).
47 B. Lambeth, *Airpower at 18,000 Feet: The Indian Air Force in the Kargil War* (Washington, DC: Carnegie Endowment for International Peace, 2012).

Faced with imminent defeat, Prime Minister Sharif made an abrupt visit to Washington, DC in the first days of July to appeal to President Bill Clinton to intervene in the crisis. Clinton met Sharif on the Fourth of July weekend but made it abundantly clear that he saw Pakistan as the aggressor.[48] Accordingly, he expected it to promptly withdraw its forces and thereby restore the sanctity of the Line of Control. Clinton's stance marked a significant departure from previous American responses to wars and crises in south Asia, where the US had equivocated in terms of assigning blame for the conflicts. Shortly after Clinton's intervention the war drew to a close. Despite India's clear-cut victory, any prospect of rapprochement with Pakistan effectively ended.

Beyond these conventional wars, since the 1980s General Zia-ul-Haq, the military dictator of Pakistan, sought to exploit India's internal cleavages with support for domestic insurgencies. To that end, Pakistan became deeply involved in aiding the Khalistani rebels in the Indian state of Punjab in the 1980s. Zia provided them sanctuary, weaponry and training, thereby expanding the scope of the insurgency and sustaining it.[49]

Zia also applied this strategy to considerable effect against the Soviet occupation of Afghanistan. A range of Afghan guerrilla groups found sanctuary within Pakistan. The Inter-Services Intelligence Directorate (ISI-D) of the Pakistan Army along with the Central Intelligence Agency (CIA) funded, trained and armed a host of Afghan guerrilla organisations. As is well known, they played a crucial role in dislodging the Soviet military from Afghanistan.[50] As the Afghan war[51] drew to a close, Zia turned his attention to the troubles that were brewing in Indian-controlled Kashmir. To that end, the Pakistan Army started in an incipient fashion to promote anti-Indian elements within the state. After Zia's death the ISI took up his mantle, especially after an indigenous rebellion erupted in December 1989. Within months, battle-hardened condottieri from the Afghan war years became involved in the Kashmir insurgency.[52]

---

48 B. Reidel, 'July 4, 1999: Clinton, Nawaz, Vajpayee, and a N-War', *The Indian Express* (17 May 2002).
49 G. Singh, 'Punjab since 1984: disorder, order and legitimacy', *Asian Survey*, 36 (1996), 410–21.
50 M. Adkin and M. Yousaf, *Afghanistan: The Bear Trap: The Defeat of a Superpower* (Havertown: Casemate, 2008).
51 See also Chapter 22.
52 P. Swami, *India, Pakistan and the Secret Jihad: The Covert War in Kashmir, 1947–2004* (Abingdon: Routledge, 2006).

The willingness of these groups to resort to terror proved most effective in tying down significant elements of the Indian armed forces deployed in counterinsurgency operations in Kashmir. Indeed, some analysts have argued that the use of these proxy terrorist forces became a model for the ISI-D to deploy more broadly against India.[53]

That strategy has long outlived General Zia and his immediate successors. Its most dramatic manifestation, of course, was the swarming terrorist attack that took place in late November 2008 at multiple sites in the western Indian coastal megalopolis of Bombay (Mumbai). Members of the Pakistan-based terrorist organisation, the Lashkar-e-Taiba (LeT) attacked a range of targets including the iconic Taj Hotel at the Gateway of India. Over the course of the next three days, they wreaked havoc across the city and embarked on a killing spree while holding substantial numbers of guests at the hotel hostage. The Indian counterterrorist response was mostly shambolic and exposed how grossly unprepared the state was in coping with urban terrorism.[54]

Objectives

In three out of the four Indo-Pakistani conflicts, Pakistan, the revisionist state, has sought to seize the entire region of Jammu and Kashmir. This goal has been an *idée fixe* of Pakistan's civilian as well as military governments. Both Pakistan's populace in general and its elites in particular, for the most part, remain convinced that the country has a duty to change the status quo in Kashmir and, if possible, take the territory under Indian control.

The loss of East Pakistan in 1971, for all practical purposes, should have ended this irredentist claim. The reasons are fairly straightforward. A common commitment to Islam had led, in the first place to the creation of the two wings of Pakistan. However, the rise and success of Bengali linguistic sub-nationalism demonstrated that a common faith was insufficient for the maintenance of national unity. Linguistic identity for the Bengalis of East Pakistan proved to be of greater significance and resonance to them than adherence to a shared faith. If the two wings of Pakistan could not adhere on the basis of faith alone, what moral or intellectual claim did Pakistan have on

---

53 P. Chalk, 'Pakistan's role in the Kashmir insurgency', *Jane's Intelligence Review*, 13 (2001), 26–7.
54 C. Scott-Clark and A. Levy, *The Siege: 68 Hours Inside the Taj Hotel* (New York: Penguin Random House, 2013).

the Muslim-majority region of Kashmir? In effect, the separation of East Pakistan underscored the hollowness of the Pakistani irredentist claim to Kashmir.[55]

Despite this crucial development, Pakistan's leadership maintained its unyielding commitment to terminate Indian rule in Kashmir. What explains the post-1971 focus on Kashmir if the underlying basis of Pakistan's quest to control Kashmir had been undermined? The question, in the absence of publicly accessible documentary evidence, has to be answered mostly on the basis of inference and attribution. The best possible explanation for Pakistan's fixation with Kashmir can perhaps be attributed to its overweening military establishment's interest in maintaining its substantial privileges and budgets. Portraying India as an implacable enemy determined to unravel the Pakistani state is a staple of the Pakistani military's rhetoric. Furthermore, its effective penetration of every facet of Pakistan's state and society has given it considerable leeway in promoting this image of India as an unrelenting adversary. Of course, periodic jingoistic statements from particular Indian leaders, especially those of a right-wing persuasion, simply play into the hands of the country's security establishment.[56]

What have been India's objectives in Kashmir? From the outset, it has sought to maintain control of the portion of Kashmir in its possession. At various times, particular Indian politicians, though not all in positions of leadership, have made intemperate claims to the entire state including those areas under Pakistan's control. Also, in February 1994, both houses of the Indian parliament passed a resolution that asserted India's legal right to the original dimensions of the former princely state.[57] The feckless statements and the parliamentary resolution aside, few individuals in India in positions of authority genuinely believe that those territorial claims will ever be realised. In December 1963, among other matters Pakistan had ceded northern portions of the state to the People's Republic of China despite India's vigorous diplomatic objections.[58] There is little or no prospect of India resorting to war to induce the PRC to leave this segment of the state.

---

55 H. Zaheer, *The Separation of East Pakistan: The Rise and Realization of Bengali Muslim Nationalism* (Karachi: Oxford University Press, 1994).
56 H. Haqqani, 'Pakistan's endgame in Kashmir', *The India Review*, 2 (2003), 34–54.
57 'Parliamentary Resolution on Jammu and Kashmir' (22 February 1994), www.satp.org /satporgtp/countries/india/document/papers/parliament_resolution_on_Jammu_a nd_Kashmir.htm.
58 A. H. Syed, *China and Pakistan: Diplomacy of an Entente Cordiale* (Amherst: University of Massachusetts Press, 1974).

As discussed earlier, India's original claim to Kashmir was based on its commitment to a secular constitutional order. Having a predominantly Muslim state within its fold would demonstrate its commitment to the equal treatment of all citizens regardless of their religious affiliation. During the early years of the Indian Republic this commitment, for the most part, was quite robust.[59] However, since the late 1970s and despite a formal commitment to secularism, a range of governments have failed in practice to adhere to such norms.[60] There is ample evidence that Muslims, India's largest minority, face substantial institutional and societal discrimination. Consequently, India's determination to hold on to Kashmir is no longer emblematic of its staunch defence of secularism. Instead, for at least three decades its control of the state has stemmed from two sources. The first involves a territorial imperative: India does not want to concede territory that it deems to be its own to an adversary. In a similar vein, the second can also be attributed to a deep-seated fear that making such a territorial concession could have an important internal domino effect: other disaffected populations in various parts of India who have resorted to arms against the Indian state could then feel emboldened to secede from the country.

Available Means

The means available to the two warring parties have also evolved significantly over the course of the past seventy years. When Pakistan undertook its first foray into Kashmir, it was mostly in a state of disarray having just emerged from the travails of partition. Unsurprisingly, it resorted to a proxy war strategy, combining regular Pakistan Army troops with disaffected local tribesmen. As the elements of statehood were pieced together over the course of a year, it was the newly constituted Pakistan Army that sustained the fighting. Since the war ended quickly in 1948, the state did not have to devote significant amounts of blood and treasure to this endeavour.

India, which also faced significant resource constraints in the wake of partition, mostly pursued a holding action in the state. It had neither the political ambition nor the military clout to force the Pakistan Army out of those portions of the former princely state that it had come to occupy in the initial days of the campaign.

---

59 D. E. Smith, *India as a Secular State* (Princeton: Princeton University Press, 1963).
60 P. R. Brass, *The Politics of India Since Independence* (Cambridge: Cambridge University Press, 1994).

The military balance between the two states would soon change after 1954. This shift was a result of two important factors. First, Pakistan signed a major military pact with the United States in 1954 and thereby became a significant recipient of US military assistance. Second, the Indian state, which spurned President Eisenhower's offer of similar military assistance, chose not to invest significantly in its military capabilities. Prime Minister Nehru was not only acutely concerned about the significant costs of defence spending but was also fearful of expansionist ambitions within the Indian military. As a consequence, when Pakistan initiated the 1965 war, India was at a significant military disadvantage. The military modernisation programme that it had undertaken in the aftermath of the disastrous Sino-Indian border war of 1962 had yet to yield significant results. Consequently, its armed forces were still mostly reliant on Second World War vintage military equipment of vastly varying quality. Its army was reliant on American Chafee and British Centurion tanks, and its air force was reliant on British Canberra bombers, the Hawker Hunter fighters and the indigenous HF-24 fighter aircraft. Pakistan on the other hand had more sophisticated American Patton tanks and both the F-86 Sabre and F-104 Starfighter transonic fighters.

Nevertheless, India's forces, with appropriate political direction from Prime Minister Lal Bahadur Shastri, Nehru's successor, displayed a degree of boldness in the conduct of the war, resorting to horizontal escalation to relieve pressure on the Kashmir front. To that end, Indian forces breached the international border in Punjab, placing the Pakistani city of Lahore at risk. Again, UN intervention brought this war to a close.

As discussed earlier, the third Indo-Pakistani war in 1971 was not fought over Kashmir. By this time, India's forces had, in considerable measure, recovered from the military debacle of 1962. In this conflict Pakistan found itself at a significant disadvantage because in the wake of the 1965 war, the United States had imposed an arms embargo on both India and Pakistan. The effects of this embargo had had a disproportionate impact on Pakistan because of its reliance on American military assistance. India, on the other hand, in the post-1965 era, had steadily improved ties with the Soviet Union and thereby had access to Soviet weaponry. Among other items, it had, shortly after the 1962 Sino-Indian border war, reached an agreement with the Soviet Union to manufacture the MiG 21 transonic fighter.[61] Consequently, its armed forces were far better prepared than ever before to undertake a war with Pakistan.[62]

61 I. C. C. Graham, 'The Indo-Soviet MIG deal and its international repercussions', *Asian Survey*, 4 (1964), 823–32.
62 S. A. Hoffman, 'Anticipation, disaster, victory: India 1962–71', *Asian Survey*, 12 (1972), 960–79.

Finally, the Kargil War of 1999 was the world's second conflict between two nuclear-armed powers. The first had taken place in 1969 between the PRC and the Soviet Union in 1969 along the Ussuri River.[63] It is not entirely clear what role nuclear weapons played in this conflict and scholars draw vastly different views. One argument holds that the weapons had an important impact in limiting the scope and the lethality of the war.[64] The other holds that they actually emboldened Pakistan to undertake the risky foray in the first place.[65]

That debate aside, the central goal of Indian strategy had been the restoration of the status quo ante. Beyond that objective, India had no plans for territorial aggrandisement. To that end, it had effectively employed a strategy designed to wear down the intruders through frontal infantry assaults, artillery barrages and the calibrated but relentless use of air power.[66] There is little or no question that India, despite its intelligence failure, had significant military advantages and used them to very good effect in the conflict. To that end it relied on its Mirage-2000 fighter aircraft to deliver precision-guided munitions and also on the Bofors field artillery to considerable effect. Pakistan, on the other hand, made scant use of air power in this conflict.

Over the longer haul, Pakistan, even if it refuses to abandon its quest for Kashmir through either diplomatic or military means, has for all practical purposes, lost this rivalry.[67] The discrepancies between these two states are significant and growing. It is hard to visualise how Pakistan can possibly address the structural differences that have come to characterise its relationship with India. To begin with, India's economy is ten times the size of the Pakistani economy.[68] Moreover, its annual military budget is just shy of $60 billion while Pakistan's is just under $11 billion (India, of course, is confronted with a two-front problem, facing a threat from the PRC in the Himalaya). India also has 2,140,000 military personnel compared to Pakistan's 653,000. Other indicators of military strength also underscore the widening discrepancies between the two states. For example, India has 5,681 armoured

---

63 L. J. Goldstein, 'Return to Zhenbao Island: who started shooting and why it matters', *The China Quarterly*, 168 (2001), 985–97.
64 S. Ganguly, 'Nuclear stability in south Asia', *International Security*, 33 (2008), 45–70.
65 S. P. Kapur, 'Ten years of instability in a nuclear south Asia', *International Security*, 33 (2008), 71–94.
66 A. Singh, *A Ridge Too Far: War in the Kargil Heights* (New Delhi: Variety Book Depot, 2016).
67 M. MacDonald, *Defeat is an Orphan: How Pakistan Lost the Great South Asian War* (London: Hurst, 2017).
68 'Comparing India and Pakistan by economy', http://statisticstimes.com/economy/india-vs-pakistan-economy.php.

vehicles compared to 3,066 in Pakistan. India also has 323 jet fighters compared to Pakistan's 186.[69] Beyond these simple numerical comparisons, India has qualitatively superior weaponry and a growing, if uneven, defence industrial base.

The only area where Pakistan has a numerical advantage is in the realm of nuclear weapons. It has, it is believed, about 160 nuclear warheads compared to India's 150.[70] This discrepancy, however, is of little consequence in terms of maintaining nuclear deterrence. The more disturbing issue is Pakistan's growing reliance on tactical nuclear weapons. The deployment of these capabilities could lower the nuclear threshold in the event of a future conflict with India.[71] Pakistani analysts, however, argue that this strategy is a necessary response to India's resort to a strategic shift which seeks to respond swiftly to a Pakistan-based terrorist attack.[72] Indian strategic reform came about in the aftermath of a Pakistan-based terrorist attack on the Indian parliament in December 2001. In the wake of the attack, India had resorted to a lumbering strategy of coercive diplomacy. The pace of the Indian response had given Pakistan ample time to prepare against Indian military retaliation. India's policy makers quickly realised that such a long, slow mobilisation process allowed Pakistan to organise its defences. Simultaneously, it gave the international community ample opportunity to intervene in the crisis and prevent escalation.

Process of Prioritisation

Since its emergence as an independent country, Pakistan has had an India-focused military strategy. Consequently, it has consistently devoted its resources to dealing with a much larger and more militarily capable adversary. The only other security issues that it has confronted are strictly internal. Initially involving East Pakistan, political turmoil has subsequently developed in the province of Sind and with armed insurgencies in Baluchistan and

---

69 Online comparison tool; see https://armedforces.eu/compare/country_India_vs_Pakistan.
70 Centre for Arms Control and Non-Proliferation, 'India and Pakistan', https://armscontrolcenter.org/countries/india-and-pakistan/.
71 P. K. Kerr and M. B. Nikitin, *Pakistan's Nuclear Weapons* (Washington, DC: Congressional Research Service, 2016).
72 M. Ahmed, *Pakistan's Tactical Nuclear Weapons and Their Impact on Stability* (Washington, DC: Carnegie Endowment for International Peace, 2016), https://carnegieendowment.org/2016/06/30/pakistan-s-tactical-nuclear-weapons-and-their-impact-on-stability-pub-63911.

Khyber-Pakhtunkhwa. Despite such domestic challenges to political order, Pakistan has nevertheless maintained its single-minded focus on India. This fixation with India is unlikely to change in the foreseeable future due to the status of the Pakistan Army within the political apparatus of the country. The military since the early 1950s has been *primus inter pares*. The dominance of the military will ensure that India remains the principal concern of Pakistan's security calculus. The threats that the country faces from internal turmoil, in the view of the military, are deemed to be manageable. Ironically, many of the policies that the military has pursued, especially when it has been in office, have exacerbated the domestic cleavages within the country and have precipitated violence.[73] Furthermore, the military establishment has played a significant role in supporting the Taliban in Afghanistan.

India, on the other hand, since the mid-1950s, has confronted a problem on two fronts. Despite initial hopes of an amicable relationship with the PRC, India soon became embroiled in an intractable border dispute.[74] To compound matters, from the early 1960s it also had to face growing Pakistan–PRC strategic co-operation.[75] Indeed, by the 1980s the PRC had transformed Pakistan into a strategic surrogate in south Asia through arms transfers and in providing assistance to its nuclear weapons programme. Owing to Pakistan's relentless hostility, India has been forced to maintain a certain level of military vigilance along its borders. Since the early 1990s, the onset of the insurgency in Kashmir and its subsequent effects in India has also forced the country to devote significant military resources to the region simply to maintain political order.

However, within the past decade India has encountered growing and sustained military pressure on its northern borders with the PRC, despite having sought to stabilise the boundaries through a range of confidence-building measures that were agreed upon in the 1990s. Consequently, it faces a two-front threat that is unlikely to end soon. That said, India is likely to prioritise the threat from the PRC over that from Pakistan because the latter, for the most part, is deemed to be manageable. The threat from the PRC is

---

73 S. Ahmed, 'Centralization, authoritarianism and the mismanagement of ethnic relations in Pakistan', in M. E. Brown and S. Ganguly (eds), *Government Policies and Ethnic Relations in Asia and the Pacific* (Cambridge, MA: MIT Press, 1997).
74 J. W. Garver, *Protracted Contest: Sino-Indian Rivalry in the Twentieth Century* (Seattle: University of Washington Press, 2001).
75 A. Small, *The China–Pakistan Axis: Asia's New Geopolitics* (London: Hurst, 2019).

not only multi-faceted but of a wholly different order and magnitude because of the significant asymmetries in the capabilities of the two states.[76]

Execution of the Strategies

Pakistan, despite repeatedly initiating wars with India, has not succeeded in altering the territorial status quo beyond what it managed to seize in the 1947–1948 conflict. The repeated failures, however, have not deterred it from continuing its initial strategy.[77] In considerable part, Pakistan's willingness to persist with a fundamentally flawed strategy has to be attributed to the role of hyper-nationalism; a form of ethnic nationalism that sees India as an implacable adversary has come to permeate much of Pakistan's political culture. This has also been fostered through a state-sponsored process of political socialisation, including the portrayal of India in history textbooks as a country that poses an existential threat to Pakistan.[78] These processes, in turn, have contributed to what the political scientist Steven Van Evera has referred to as 'false optimism' and has repeatedly led generations of Pakistani leaders to pursue an unrelenting strategy.[79] Unless the military stranglehold on Pakistan's politics is broken, it seems unlikely that this strategy towards India, involving a war of attrition, will undergo a fundamental reappraisal even though it has yielded little or no success.

India's strategies, other than seeking to maintain the territorial status quo in Kashmir, have varied. In the 1965 war, for example, it managed to seize the strategic Haji Pir Pass.[80] However, despite the objections of the Indian military, the political leadership chose to return it to Pakistan as part of the post-war negotiations at Tashkent. Accordingly, it can be argued that until the crisis of 1971, when India acted out of an amalgam of humanitarian concerns as well as sheer political opportunity, it had grudgingly accepted the territorial integrity of Pakistan. Even when India played a critical role in breaking up Pakistan in the 1971 war, it did not attempt to seize any Pakistani territory. Instead, it was content to give genesis to the new state of Bangladesh and perform a holding action in Kashmir. In effect, its strategic practice has focused on maintaining the territorial integrity of India.

76 Online comparison tool; see https://armedforces.eu/compare/country_India_vs_China.
77 A. Gauhar, 'Four wars, one assumption', *The Nation* (5 September 1999).
78 K. K. Aziz, *The Murder of History in Pakistan: A Critique of History Textbooks Used in Pakistan* (Lahore: Sang-e-Meel, 2010).
79 S. Van Evera, *The Causes of War: Power and the Roots of Conflict* (Ithaca: Cornell University Press, 1984).
80 Brines, *Indo-Pakistani Conflict*.

Pakistan's strategic practice, however, has involved its persistent irredentist claim on Kashmir. Also, following its military defeat in 1971, it has also involved the quest for 'strategic depth' in Afghanistan in the event of a full-scale Indian military assault on its eastern border.[81]

Conclusion

Is India's strategy likely to change in the future? The question is worth raising because in 2014 the jingoistic, right-wing Hindu nationalist Bharatiya Janata Party (BJP) government assumed office in India. In 2019, it returned to power with an overwhelming majority in parliament. Since assuming office a second time, it appears intent on undermining the country's secular foundations.[82] However, this BJP government has not fundamentally changed India's security strategy towards Pakistan. The shifts that have taken place are more in the form of tone rather than substance. For example, irritated by Pakistan's repeated outreach to secessionist parties in Kashmir, the BJP broke off ongoing talks in August 2014 and has not resumed them since. It has also significantly ramped up its rhetoric against Pakistan, especially in the wake of a Pakistan-sponsored terrorist attack in Kashmir on an Indian convoy in February 2019. It also initiated a retaliatory military strike against Pakistan following this incident. Pakistan in turn responded with air strikes of its own. However, despite the heated rhetoric from both sides, the crisis did not escalate.[83]

From Pakistan's standpoint, India has undertaken a step that is seriously inimical to its interests. This has involved the abrogation of Article 370 of the Indian Constitution which had granted a substantial degree of autonomy to Jammu and Kashmir. Stripping the state of this important constitutional provision has further undermined Pakistan's legal claim to Kashmir.[84] Pakistan, quite understandably, has vigorously protested this move but has not been able to generate much support for its position within the international community. The only country, quite predictably, that has extended diplomatic support for its position is the PRC.

---

81 A. Parkes, 'Considered chaos: revisiting Pakistan's "Strategic Depth" in Afghanistan', *Strategic Analysis*, 43 (2019), 297–309.
82 S. Ganguly, 'An illiberal India?', *Journal of Democracy*, 31 (2020), 193–202.
83 T. N. Pegahi, 'From Kargil to Pulwama: how nuclear crises have changed over 20 years', *Washington Quarterly*, 2 (2019), 149–61.
84 S. Ganguly and A. Tarapore, 'Kashmir: a casualty of India's rising power status?', *The National Interest* (22 October 2019), https://nationalinterest.org/feature/kashmir-casualty-indias-rising-power-status-90311.

Despite this obvious setback, Pakistan will not abandon its claim to Kashmir. The issue has become deeply embedded in the domestic politics of the country, and abandoning it has become all but unfeasible for any political actor. This is especially the case given that the Pakistani military establishment wields disproportionate power in the country's governing structure and is intent on keeping the issue at the forefront of the country's political agenda.

Under these circumstances, particularly with the rise of a form of virulent Hindu nationalism in India, the two countries appear locked into their respective antagonistic military strategies for the foreseeable future. A conflict whose origins can be traced to the genesis of the two states shows no prospect of abating in the twenty-first century.

20

The Yugoslav War, 1991–1999

JAMES GOW

Sources

The Yugoslav War was hallmarked by atrocity and the commission of war crimes.[1] A by-product of this notoriety was the UN International Criminal Tribunal for the former Yugoslavia (ICTY), which produced an archive of material that became a valuable treasure trove for scholars of different kinds, which records were taken over by the UN International Residual Mechanism for the International Criminal Tribunals (IRMICT).[2] The material available includes transcripts of public proceedings – especially oral evidence, documentary evidence introduced publicly in trials, judgments and other court documentation. While the amount of material is vast and a substantial resource for research, it is inevitably shaped by the demands of criminal justice, as are the findings of its Trial Chambers. Consequently, the material available is selective, as extensive as it is, in addition to which, only material made public in trials is open to the public, which is problematic.[3] Because of this, there are tensions and discussions about the work of the Tribunal with regard to history, strategy and other matters and concerns among scholars about the limitations of the material – notwithstanding its extent.[4]

---

1 I have written extensively about the Yugoslav War and this contribution inevitably draws on other work, both previous, and also in development, including *The Serbian Project and Its Adversaries* (London: Hurst, 2003).
2 United Nations, 'International Residual Mechanism for Criminal Tribunals', www.irmct.org/en.
3 I. Vukušić, 'Why we should open archives from war crimes trials to the public', www.ushmm.org/genocide-prevention/blog/why-we-should-open-archives-from-war-crimes-trials.
4 R. A. Wilson, *Writing History in International Criminal Trials* (Cambridge: Cambridge University Press, 2011).

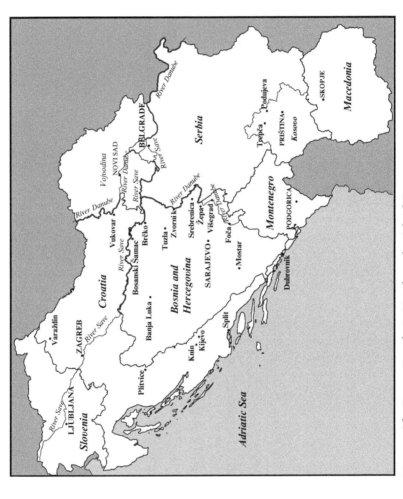

Map 20.1 The Former Yugoslavia. Map drawn by Gabriel Gow.

The war and its contexts – the dissolution of the Yugoslav federation and the establishment of successor states with independent international personality – are rife with disputes and controversies. The number of acute debates is too great to discuss here. Some of the major examples are covered in two important volumes framed around the contested character of so many issues: the Scholars' Initiative collection on controversies edited by Charles Ingrao and Thomas Emmert, and the authored review of scholarly debates by Sabrina Ramet.[5] Three of the most notable continuing debates concern the causes of conflict (see below), who started it, when and where,[6] and the character of the conflict – was it driven 'top-down' or 'bottom-up' (or, better, what was the balance in these factors)?[7]

Actor(s)

The central figure in the Yugoslav War was Slobodan Milošević, the Serbian leader. Occupying a number of different political leadership positions in Belgrade, Milošević was always leader and key decision maker there, whatever his title at a given moment. Other principal actors on the Serbian side in the war are usually considered to be Jovica Stanišić, Ratko Mladić, Radovan Karadžić, Goran Hadžić and Milan Martić. The last two were leaders of the putative Serbian state carved from Croatia, the *Republika Srpska Krajina* (RSK). Karadžić was leader of the equivalent in Bosnia and Hercegovina, the *Republika Srpska* (RS). Mladić, most importantly, was appointed commander of the Serb Bosnian Army (VRS, *Vojska Republika Srpska*) in May 1992, but had previously been deputy commander of the Yugoslav People's Army (*Jugoslovenska Narodna Armja*, JNA) 9 Corps in Croatia, playing a leading role there. Mladić was also part of a 'military line' (*'vojna linija'*) of officers in the JNA established by Milošević's head of intelligence and security, Stanišić. Stanišić was a vital figure in the Serbian strategy, as head of the Serbian Security Service (*Služba Državna Bezbednost*, SDB) from January 1992, having previously been seen as de

---

5 C. Ingrao and T. A. Emmert, *Confronting the Yugoslav Controversies: A Scholar's Initiative* (Purdue: Purdue University Press, 2006); S. P. Ramet, *Thinking About Yugoslavia: Scholarly Debates About the Yugoslav Break-up and the Wars in Croatia, Bosnia and Kosovo* (Cambridge: Cambridge University Press, 2005).
6 Different impressions on these questions emerge in almost every account. Examples include M. Glenny, *The Fall of Yugoslavia* (London: Penguin, 1992); M. Thompson, *A Paper House* (London: Random House, 1993); J. Zametica, *The Yugoslav Conflict*, Adelphi Paper No. 270 (London: IISS, 1992).
7 I. Vukušić, *Serbian Paramilitaries in the Breakup of Yugoslavia* (New York: Routledge, 2022); Andreas Møller was conducting relevant research for a PhD at King's College London on low-level perpetrators and the drivers of violence.

facto chief while officially deputy leader from March 1991. Stanišić was Milošević's closest collaborator, aside from his wife Mirjana Marković, during this period until 1998, when he was made national security adviser, after disagreements with Marković and a loss of trust by Milošević. With the exception of Mladić, these are all civilian figures. In addition, Jovica Stanišić, while less recognised, was a vital figure in the Serbian strategy.

Among the regional adversaries to the Serbian project, the most prominent were: Franjo Tudjman, president of Croatia and the single most important decision maker on the Croat side; Alija Izetbegović, president of Bosnia and Hercegovina, leader of the *Stranka Demokratska Akcija* (SDA), the main party representing ethnic Bosnian Muslims; Hashim Thaçi, an ethnic Kosovo Albanian military and political leader of the Kosovo Liberation Army, who emerged as its key political figure during and after the conflict in Kosovo; Adem Jashari, an ethnic Albanian, who spearheaded the initial insurgency against Serbian forces in Kosovo; and Milan Kučan, president of Slovenia. Each of these led a discrete strategy that countered Milošević's Serbia, while taking account of wider international engagement.

Beyond the 'Yugoslav' actors, a range of Western political figures are seen as playing important roles at times; however, none of these made a consistent contribution to the armed conflict. The most significant among these were UK Prime Minister Sir John Major, US President William J. Clinton and US Assistant Secretary of State Richard Holbrooke. The most significant international military contributions were made by then-Lieutenant General Rupert Smith, although the roles of Generals Philippe Morillon and Bernard Janvier (France), Michael Rose (UK) and Mike Ryan (US) were also important.

Adversaries

The adversaries might be characterised as 'Serbia – or Serbs – versus the rest'. While the situation was more complicated than this simple suggestion, none the less, war pivoted on Belgrade, the capital of Serbia, and also three formal federal arrangements during the years of conflict. The adversaries may be divided into three categories: neighbours to the west – Slovenia, Croatia, and Bosnia and Hercegovina; ethnic Albanians in the province of Kosovo, consolidated in the insurgent Kosovo Liberation Army (KLA), to the south; and a range of primarily Western international actors, including notably France, the UK and other European members of the EU and NATO, and the United States (US), all operating variously through international organisations such as the UN and NATO.

Causes of the War

The Yugoslav War was a clash of statehood projects. It occurred in the context of the dissolution, or collapse, of Yugoslavia. Yugoslavia – meaning the land of the South Slavs – was an attempt to give self-determination to various South Slav peoples after the First World War. Established under the Serbian monarchy, it was riven with tensions between different peoples – Serbs, Croats, Slovenes, Slav Muslims (later dubbed 'Bosniaks'), Montenegrins and Macedonians. Those tensions led to extreme violence during the Second World War period in a complex conflict. The victorious Partisans established a federation of six sovereign states under communist rule in 1945 in an attempt to address the statehood questions that had undermined Royal Yugoslavia. In its 1974 Constitution, this communist federation was called the Socialist Federative Republic of Yugoslavia (SFRY). The SFRY was a new effort to resolve the same national questions that blighted the first Yugoslavia. By 1991, that federation had ceased to function and the different actors held mutually exclusive views of the future. It dissolved in a process that began in the late 1980s, impelled by competition of those national projects and dissatisfaction with attempts to reconcile them. These mutually exclusive political positions over statehood seemingly could only be resolved by Clausewitz's famous 'other means', that is, violence.[8] Other factors that different authors regard as the most decisive cause were nationalism,[9] economic failure,[10] social change[11] and political-constitutional structure.[12]

Even though the positions of Serbia and others in the Yugoslav framework made war inevitable, it was Milošević's Belgrade that saw opportunity in Yugoslavia's disarray to redraw the map, and that prepared, planned and instigated war, and which, above all, defined the strategy of atrocity that made widespread, systematic abuse of human rights a central element of military-political purpose. It was this approach that defined the Serbian campaign and, therefore, the war as a whole. The core problem was the Serbian state project and the decision to prosecute that project using the commission of atrocities as a core element of strategy. Because of this and the centrality of Milošević to the war, the present study primarily concentrates on Serbian strategy.

---

8 C. von Clausewitz, *On War*, Colonel J. J. Graham (trans.), Colonel F. N. Maude (introduction and notes), J. W. Honig (introduction to the new edition) (New York: Barnes and Noble, 2004).
9 S. P. Ramet, *Balkan Babel* (Boulder: Westview Press, 1999).
10 J. R. Lampe, *Yugoslavia as History*, 2nd ed. (Cambridge: Cambridge University Press, 2000).
11 J. B. Allcock, *Explaining Yugoslavia* (London: Hurst, 2000).
12 J. Gow, 'Deconstructing Yugoslavia', *Survival*, 33 (1991), 291–311.

Objectives (Ends)

At its most basic, the war was a contest between a Serbian project to create new state borders and a new correlation between state borders and population groups, based on the notion that all Serbs should live in one state, on one side, and the interest of the other states involved to preserve their territorial integrity (although Croatia's policy certainly echoed Serbia's, at times, as well as opposing it).

The Serbian aim was to establish the new borders of a set of territories linked to Serbia that would be 'for' the Serbs – for the most part, ethnically pure – and also control strategic assets and communication routes. The term 'ethnic cleansing' (in Serbo-Croat, *etničko čišćenje*) became widely used to describe the practice of creating ethnically pure territories. Ethnic cleansing is the strategic use of excessive violence against civilian population centres, demonstrative atrocity and mass murder in order to remove that population. While it involves some murder, the intention is not physically to eliminate every member of an ethnic group. Rather, murder and mutilation are demonstrative violence intended to induce all members of a group to flee. The complete destruction of property further to inhibit return is a further aspect of the strategy – although, often, 'new' families are moved into cleansed properties. The point of this strategy, led by ethno-national ideology, was to secure the territory in question by removing the prospect for opposition, whether purely political or violent.

Milošević's adversaries generally shared the objective of asserting the principle of sovereignty and rejecting the Serbian project and its atrocities. Slovenia, Croatia, and Bosnia and Hercegovina sought to protect and establish their formal constitutional sovereignty with recognition of full independent international personality as members of international society, while maintaining the principle of territorial integrity. Kosovo sought to transform its status from administrative province within Serbia to sovereign statehood with independent international personality. The various elements of international and Western engagement were all geared towards upholding and protecting the principles of sovereignty and territorial integrity, while also opposing gross abuses of human rights and the commission of atrocities, and Miloševićs's Serbian ambition. The partial exception to this was Serbia's sovereignty with regard to Kosovo, where completely coherent international opposition to Belgrade's ethnic cleansing was tempered by divisions about supporting the Kosovan quest for independence, with a majority, later, behind a notion of 'remedial self-determination', in which the victims of great abuse become entitled to self-determination at the level of sovereign statehood and full independent international personality.

Available Means

As the SFRY disintegrated and war loomed, it was necessary for Serbian president Slobodan Milošević to gain a military capability. It took Milošević nine years to have all armed forces properly and officially under his control. The change in the ethnic composition of the Yugoslav military, caused by the war, had effectively put the bulk of the JNA's capability at the disposal of his Serbian cause. However, to achieve this degree of control, it had been necessary for political and practical reasons to use paramilitary forces of a more purely Serbian orientation and a more vicious character to complement and compete with the regular army. Despite significant Serbianisation, however, Milošević still could not trust the regular army completely, as was seen with the sacking of General Momčilo Perišić, whom he had appointed, at the end of 1998. By the Kosovo campaign of 1999, all generals in charge had been appointed by Milošević. Even then, the prospect of adverse civil–military relations remained, as his final removal confirmed, when General Pavković made clear that the army would not protect him.

The armed forces of the SFRY comprised two elements. The first tier, the JNA, was a regular armed force, including ground, air and naval services, controlled at the federal level. The second tier, a Territorial Defence Force (TO, *Teritorialna Odbrana*), was an irregular force, derived from the tradition of the Partisans in guerrilla warfare, controlled at the republican level. The command structures of the JNA and the TOs were decentralised, because the maintenance of a command and control network across all SFRY territory would have been too difficult in the event of an invasion. Both tiers were intended to be components of a unified defence capability within the doctrine of General People's Defence (GPD).

In the course of the armed conflict, the character of the JNA changed substantially in ethnic and ethnopolitical terms. Prior to 1990–1991, the JNA was a mixed force of professional regulars, almost entirely officers and non-commissioned officers, and a conscript cadre. At the highest levels in the JNA, an 'ethnic key' principle operated to ensure proportional representation of all the major communities in the SFRY. The middle and junior ranks of the JNA were overwhelmingly dominated by Serbs. In May 1992, the JNA, by then over 90 per cent Serbian in composition, was formally disestablished and divided into two. Serbian domination was the combined effect of circumstance and active Serbianisation. There was also an active campaign by the Serbian Security Service and those 'in the know' – including General Mladić. Serb officers were recruited by members of Milošević's Security Service into a 'clandestine network'.[13] This web of Serbian officers was known as the *Vojna Linija* ('the military line').[14]

In May 1992, the JNA was divided into three separate forces: the OS RSK, later the VSK (the armed forces, or army, of Serbian Krajina) in Croatia attached to the putative Serb statelet there; the VRS – the Army of Republika Srpska in Bosnia and Hercegovina, the instrument of the Serb entity there; and the VJ – the Army of Yugoslavia, the part that remained directly under Belgrade's control. This division was a move carefully conceived and planned several months earlier to deal with fears that Belgrade's campaign against Bosnia would meet a hostile international response and accusations of aggression. Implementing the decision to divide the JNA greatly reduced Belgrade's open participation in the war in Bosnia. This was part of an attempt to deceive the outside world that Belgrade was not responsible for action there.

The OS RSK was the successor to a force initially locally raised and led by Milan Martić. This was based on elements of territorial defence units and elements of police units. The first signs of unrest had come around Knin in the Krajina area in August 1990 after the local police chief, Milan Martić, was removed from his post by the Croatian interior ministry. This was perceived as an act of anti-Serb persecution, and Martić immediately began to distribute firearms from police stores to local Serb volunteers. This was the beginning of what was essentially a form of a party-army in Krajina. This force was assisted and organised by the SDB. It was originally led by Martić and numbered up to 50,000 troops, although its real strength was mostly less. With the withdrawal of remaining JNA units and then the JNA's disestablishment, and the unification of Serb self-proclaimed autonomous regions into the self-declared state of Republic of Serbian Krajina, all armed elements became part of the VSK. The Krajina Serbs in Croatia had inherited capability, command and control structures from the JNA.

The VRS was the name given to Serbian forces in Bosnia. This was essentially the former JNA Second Military district command covering Bosnia turned into a formally separate army. The VRS and the VJ each gained

---

13 T. Judah, *The Serbs: History, Myth and the Destruction of Yugoslavia* (New Haven and London: Yale University Press, 1997), 170.
14 L. Bulatović, *General Mladić* (Belgrade: Biblioteka Svedočanstva, 1996), 188.

around 80,000 personnel.[15] For the most part, the units involved kept the equipment at their disposal.[16] While formally divided, the old chain of command did not change and the VRS continued under Belgrade's ultimate control,[17] albeit with broad operational authority given to the commander in Bosnia, General Ratko Mladić.

The most important element of the troika of Serbian armed forces remained the one formally attached to Belgrade's political leadership – the VJ. The VJ comprised all three services of land, air and sea. The VJ continued to support the VRS, regularly supplementing it with troops crossing the River Drina from Serbia. The level of these reinforcements varied, but ran up to 20,000 personnel and over 100 pieces of armour. The VJ also continued assistance to the VSK in Croatia, which also remained part of the Belgrade command structure.

In addition to the formal state and putative state-linked regular armed forces, Serbia nurtured two types of militarised alternative to the JNA and its successors: seemingly private, or independent, 'volunteer' paramilitary groups, albeit established and financed by the Serbian Security Service; and forces tied to official state structures, the Serbian Interior Ministry and the Serbian Security Service. The organisation of 'volunteer' paramilitary units served the purposes of strategic deception and ambiguity. This meant that supposedly independent forces could be blamed for atrocities and the appearance of chaos in the field. In operational terms, the paramilitary forces provided a cadre of infantry 'shock troops' that could carry out tasks which the regular army could not be counted on to perform. These included close combat and street-to-street fighting. Crucially, their role also included commission of the catalogue of acts that added up to ethnic cleansing: murder, mutilation, torture, rape and terrorisation. Some of the best-known paramilitary groups on the Serbian side were: the Serbian Guard (*Srpska Garda*, SG), the Serbian Volunteer Guard (*Srpska Dobrovolska Garda*, SDG), the Serbian Chetnik Movement (*Srpski Četnički Pokret*, SČP), and, lastly, *Dušan Silni* and the *Beli Orli*. Although each was attached to a particular political organisation, all but one owed their prominence to support from the SDB. Yet, all appeared to be separate actors in the chaos of conflict. All were eventually officially subordinated to regular military command.

---

15 M. Vego, 'Federal army deployments in Bosnia-Hercegovina', *Jane's Intelligence Review*, (October 1992), 445.
16 The VRS inherited, in fact, forty-three aircraft, of which the most important were Yugoslav-produced Galeb G-4 ground attack aircraft.
17 See Vego, 'Federal army deployments'.

The most prominent official paramilitary force was the Ministry of Internal Affairs (*Ministarstvo unutrašnjih poslova*, MUP), a highly organised large force, capable of action on a far greater scale than that of the various 'volunteer' paramilitary forces. First and foremost, the MUP offered Milošević a strong instrument of power and terror. A key purpose in building alternative sources of armed force was loyalty. In this context, the development of the MUP in Serbia was crucial. The MUP standing force strength was around 5,000 personnel, although it had large reserve contingents. These troops were organised into six detachments, each of which co-ordinated with larger local MUP units. Each of these detachments had a Specialist Anti-Terrorist Unit (SAJ). This was a separate part of the MUP structure comprising around 400 personnel, with 60–80 troops attached to each MUP detachment. They were equipped with armoured personnel carriers, mortars and heavy machine guns.

A further official force – though its official status was not acknowledged for many years, as part of the strategies of ambiguity and deception – was the security service special operations unit (*Specialna Jedinica za Operacije*, JSO), often referred to as simply 'the unit', or 'the Red Berets'. The JSO was also involved in a more extensive range of activities that included murder, both of individuals and groups. It had a total strength of 500 individuals. Organised under the operational arm of the SDB, the unit was in some sense a sibling of the paramilitary forces used in the field in Croatia and in Bosnia. Like the latter, the JSO was organised by the Head of Operations in the SDB, Frenki Simatović. Highly secretive, this specialist force was organised into squads of around twenty and used modern armoured vehicles. Trained to the highest standards, highly motivated and capable of acting as instant execution squads, they were, according to one British officer 'very dangerous'.[18] These same troops would be the ultimate line of protection for Milošević.

The MUP as a whole provided the assault troops for the Kosovo campaign and ethnic cleansing, but it was the JSO that supplied the lead 'shock troops' and murder squads. Better trained, equipped, fed and paid than Belgrade's regular army, one of the MUP and JSO's roles was to set the pace for the regular army and carry out tasks that the army might not. In Kosovo, for the first time, the regular army – the VJ – operated in formal conjunction with the MUP. Both the MUP and the VJ followed Milošević's orders and, even with his own men in command of the VJ for the first time, the MUP

18 Maj. J. Moir, Ministry of Defence Briefing, 1 April 1999. Moir's briefing is included in 'Briefing by The Foreign Secretary, Mr. Robin Cook, and The Deputy Chief of the Defence Staff, Air Marshal Sir John Day'.

continued to provide Milošević with the only force that was wholly and truly his. In the Kosovo campaign in 1999, Milošević finally controlled and commanded all the armed forces together, as he formally became commander-in-chief of all forces when the MUP was subordinated to the VJ on 24 March. This was the point at which the force, which Milošević had developed as his own in Serbia, the MUP, was placed under the authority of the VJ, the regular force of which he had always been distrustful. Milošević, for the first time, put himself in a position of indisputable formal and legal responsibility for the commission of crimes against humanity.

Serbian forces had overwhelming superiority in quantity and quality of weapons. The imbalance of armaments between Serbian forces and their enemies was one of the most striking aspects of the Yugoslav War. It was also one of the most emotive in international intellectual and political discourse. Arguments over this issue were focused on the UN arms embargo imposed early in the conflict. That embargo had the effect of consolidating Serbian superiority. This is because Serbian forces began the war with the vast arsenal developed in Tito's Yugoslavia at its disposal, including unthinkable amounts of weapons and munitions stored under the SFRY's many mountains. In addition, the VRS inherited an air capability but its use was restricted when the UNSC imposed an 'air exclusion zone'.

The various adversaries of the Serbian project were considerably weaker in all respects: although in principle international and Western forces could have been dominant, they were compromised by the nature of their engagement and mostly incoherent strategy. The adversaries' armed forces mostly operated separately and comprised: Slovenia's TO; the Croatian *Hrvatska Vojska* (HV) and Croatia's proxy force in Hercegovina and Bosnia, the *Hrvatska Vijeća Odbrana* (HVO); the Army of Bosnia and Hercegovina; the Kosovo Liberation Army (KLA); the UN forces in the region – UNPROFOR – and Western forces framed around NATO.

A key factor in the imbalance was the JNA's impounding about 40 per cent of Slovenia's territorial defence arsenal and virtually all of Croatia's in spring 1990. It later carried out a similar programme in Bosnia in 1991. Each country immediately sought to replenish their denuded stocks by making purchases outside Yugoslavia. The weaponry involved included artillery, anti-air and anti-tank rocket systems (and rockets). Croatia, for example, had 200 of each type of rocket system and 9,000–10,000 rockets for each.[19] Croatia captured around 230 tanks, including 65 T-55s in good working order at Varaždin, while

---

19 S. Letica and M. Nobilo, *Rat Protiv Hrvatske* (Zagreb: Globus, 1991), 72.

another 100 tanks, mostly M-84s, fell into Slovene hands during the conflict there. Even when, by 1993, the Army of Bosnia–Hercegovina (*Armija Bosna i Hercegovina*, ABiH) had built up its level of equipment, it remained weak. The ABiH had around forty T-34 and T-54/55 tanks and armoured personnel carriers at this point, as well as larger numbers of artillery pieces of 76 mm, 105 mm and perhaps even 155 mm calibre. The Bosnian Army did not have such a serious lack of light weaponry, although ammunition supplies presented problems. The Bosnian Army also had relatively significant quantities of 60 mm, 82 mm and 120 mm mortars, as well as good supplies of shoulder-launched anti-armour rocket systems. The Bosnian military had, in addition, fifty air force personnel, one Jastreb-2 aircraft (not in use) and four Mi-8 helicopters. Despite all of this, there was an enormous imbalance in terms of the heavy weapons categories. When it came to the weapons that secured battlefield dominance – tanks, guns and howitzers – the JNA and its successor the VRS usually had a ten-to-one, or greater, advantage. The Kosovo Liberation Army was a small insurgent force, relying on light armaments for the most part. None of the local adversaries had a significant strategic level capability, although Croatia developed one (with US support) in the latter stages of the conflict in Croatia, and Bosnia and Hercegovina, and worked jointly with the Army of Bosnia and Hercegovina in key operations towards the end of that part of the conflict.

The various international forces deployed different capabilities at different points in complex operations that inhibited coherent use of force much of the time, a factor entwined with mandates that initially focused on peacekeeping and the avoidance of a use of force. Although UNPROFOR had 60,000–70,000 authorised troops, it did not have full complements and its humanitarian mandate meant not only that use of force was limited, but also that the spider's web of small exposed and vulnerable positions meant that the force was hard to use. However, as the conflict developed, Western actors through NATO became more disposed to use armed force, and did so with decisive effect in Bosnia and Hercegovina, and again over Kosovo.

The basic imbalance established at the outset of the war was effectively cemented by well-meaning but often-questioned international efforts to prevent the import of weapons into the region. In September 1991, the United Nations Security Council passed resolution 713 banning all transfer of arms to the SFRY or any part of its territory. The Bosnian presidency and government persistently called for the arms embargo to be lifted in its favour, arguing that the state and its threatened people should have the right to defend themselves; a position supported by many outside, including, rhetorically, the US. This ran counter to the initiatives of European countries, under the auspices of the UN, using the limited military commitment of UNPROFOR to ameliorate suffering in Bosnia through operations to provide humanitarian relief.

Process of Prioritisation

Milošević's actions until the very late stages in the armed conflict were premised on the assumption that almost no other actor had his understanding or command of the situation, and that, while for some time he could not trust all pro-Serbian forces, those forces were superior to any immediate adversary. His objective was to create a set of ethnically pure, linked and contiguous Serbian territories built around ethnic Serb populations and from which Croats and Muslims to the west and ethnic Albanians to the south would be largely removed, whether by murder, expulsion or flight. To do this he used the Belgrade military, which was not controlled by him, as such, but became politically and culturally more aligned as the conflict emerged, and the Serbian Security Service.

Widely regarded as tactically adept but strategically limited, Milošević set in motion a strategy of ambiguity, where a mix of armed forces including paramilitary forces of differing types and proxy forces that could rarely be directly his formal responsibility conducted operations marked by atrocity. Because the dotted-line nature of leadership command, deliberately designed to obscure responsibility for atrocities, meant autonomy for proxies, while Milošević was always dominant, he did not have full control of all forces at all times. This meant that, in certain periods, it took months for his priorities to be met. However, until his eventual fall in 2001, his preferences prevailed on the Serbian side.

It was Milošević who translated strategy into operations via Stanišić, chief of the SDB, and Mladić, commander of Serb Bosnian forces from May 1992. The former orchestrated a range of paramilitary forces, some directly linked to the SDB, others to other organisations, which forces led the strategy known as 'ethnic cleansing'. This occurred in an interactive way, with some initiative emerging at lower levels and being harnessed. Stanišić not only oversaw the establishment of the 'military line' of officers in the JNA deemed to be loyal to the Serbian new state cause, but also the development of a range of paramilitary forces; some run directly by the SDB, others semi-detached. This included identification and management of leaders and groups, often around experienced criminals and individuals with special forces training, who were suitable for carrying out special roles in terrorising civilians in Croatia and Bosnia, performing tasks, such as murder and mutilation, that 'regular' troops would not. Stanišić orchestrated these groups, providing funding and weapons for them. He was also involved in command roles on the ground in Western Bosnia in 1994 and 1995. In addition, Stanišić was primarily responsible for establishing the leaders of the self-declared Serbian entities in Croatia and Bosnia, and was Milošević's messenger to these leaders and their military counterparts – including a disputed visit to Mladić just ahead of the notorious massacres at Srebrenica in July 1995. Crucially, as much as Stanišić was involved in rolling out Milošević's campaigns in Croatia, Bosnia and Kosovo, he was also vital in ending the war and his leader's rule. It later emerged, including in evidence during his initial trials for crimes against humanity at the ICTY, that in the latter years, when he disagreed with Marković about the plan to launch extensive ethnic cleansing in Kosovo and also lost Milošević's trust, he was co-operating with British and American secret intelligence, playing a pivotal strategic role in undoing that which he had helped to create.

Milošević and Stanišić evolved the strategy in Croatia and Bosnia with local figures: Milan Martić, Goran Hadžić and Radovan Karadžić. This became an iterative process of decision making, with the Belgrade leaders both guiding and responding to local initiatives. Martić, Hadžić and Karadžić were significant in the evolving situation prior to the collapse of the federation, at the onset of conflict and also in the course of it. Martić and Hadžić were important in the very earliest moments of violence in 1990 and 1991, before the war is generally judged to have started, as such, and before they became leaders of the RSK. The degree to which they were agents of Belgrade or autonomous actors in those earliest instances is not certain. So, there may be some ambiguity over who was setting priorities and making decisions. Clearly, these figures had some autonomy. Equally, they were supported, encouraged and directed by Belgrade – Milošević via Stanišić and others (and this is an issue that also has strong relevance in Bosnia with Karadžić). On balance, the evidence suggests that they were more agents carrying out provocations as part of the Belgrade strategy, but that this was not always straightforward. They were figures who had emerged and were then harnessed by Belgrade, rather than ones who were simply introduced by it; and, in the case of Karadžić, certainly, there were moments where he acted autonomously. This was a function of Belgrade's ambiguous approach – trying to ensure deniability while being able both to run events and to take credit for them. Thus, there was some flux regarding decision making and the setting of priorities, although, ultimately, Milošević in Belgrade was responsible.

The JNA and the Belgrade leadership's assessments incorporated two crucial miscalculations about the situation in Slovenia, initially. The first was that Slovenia's Territorial Defence Force would be neither able nor willing to respond to a show of force. This was a serious intelligence failure. This failure has to be explained in part by assumptions about Slovenia. Among those which have been suggested in various quarters are the following: first, that those responsible for defence and interior ministry forces were inexperienced, having come from the ranks of the anti-military opposition; second, that the Slovenes were not fighters; third, that the 'secessionist' leaders in Slovenia did not have the support of the people.[20]

For whatever reason, the military-political elite in Belgrade appears to have believed that a simply symbolic show of force would be enough. The JNA did not, it may be concluded, think that it was going into battle. Belgrade leaders also operated on the assumption that there would be no Western use of force, so long as actions were kept below certain thresholds, until significant force was used in 1995 – at which point, the NATO air action helped Milošević to reassert political control in order to pursue an end to armed hostilities, as VRS military commander Ratko Mladić's control of the situation on the ground was removed. By the time the Kosovo engagement came in 1999, the pattern of assumptions was opposite: while Western actors, notably US Secretary of State Madeleine Albright, assumed that the mere threat or show of force would make Milošević co-operate in international talks on Kosovo, Milošević assumed that he could provoke a use of force that would then be cover for extensive ethnic cleansing action in Kosovo to be blamed on NATO, and also that the NATO action would be no more than a show of force and not last a week. The assumptions about a show of force on both sides were misplaced.

Execution / Application of Strategy

The essence of the Serbian strategy was control of territory through removal of the population. This practice became known as 'ethnic cleansing'. Generally, the inhabitants of whole regions were not displaced as a contingency of war,

---

20 One of the most prominent JNA officers in Slovenia (at the time, a colonel) later recounted how he simply did not believe that who he regarded as his fellow countrymen would fire on the JNA. Rather, he and his colleagues assumed that their concern was with difficult political leaders who were out of touch with their own population. General M. Aksentijević in *Death of Yugoslavia* (aka *Yugoslavia: Death of a Nation*), Programme 3, Brian Lapping Associates for the BBC (1995).

seeking safety from the fighting. Although there were certainly some who fled the fighting, the overwhelming majority was subject to forced migration, directly or indirectly. Where this was indirect, it was as a function of the direct impact of ethnic cleansing elsewhere. The political aim was complete control of territory. The aim was to create the boundaries of a new state in which there would not be a hostile, or potentially hostile, population to mount opposition, or even guerrilla resistance, leaving only Serbs and those who accepted second-class status to inhabit the lands in question. The same understanding was applied to Kosovo, with the exception that the need was to consolidate the formal borders of the state and through ethnic cleansing to remove a problem that had come to involve armed insurgency, once and for all. In all cases the equation was simple: remove the people using purposeful and organised coercive violence; secure the territory for Serbian control. The strategy to accomplish this was use of largely unrestrained coercive violence to eliminate any potentially hostile population. These methods were used initially to attack and secure key communications and strategic locations, and extend control. The four elements to this pattern of attacks were preparation and provocation; takeover and the use of force; concentration camps; and, lastly, elimination through expulsion and execution.

Most elements of this scheme were evident in early actions in Croatia, prior to the onset of major armed hostilities in June 1991. The template for later action could be seen in events in August 1990 and spring 1991. In August 1990, Milan Martić, who had been removed as local police chief, led an insurrection in the Krajina region around Knin. Supported by then-Colonel Ratko Mladić from the JNA Knin garrison, he erected a series of log barriers to prevent Croatian police from entering or transiting the region. This was an exclusion zone into which the Croat authorities could not gain entry without risking bloodshed. A tense stand-off left Martić with de facto control of a self-declared Serbian Autonomous Region of Krajina, spurred by Mladić's local military, Stanišić's service and Milošević's political support. That *Srpska Autonmna Oblast* (SAO) was the precursor to two others in Croatia and six in Bosnia, which were consolidated into the statelets of the RSK and RS, respectively.

Martić and Mladić also combined to place Kijevo under siege at the end of April 1991. Kijevo was an almost purely ethnic Croat village in a sea of ethnic Serb villages within the self-declared Serb autonomous region. This operation, almost entirely overlooked at the time and by commentators since, became the template for Mladić's modus operandi and for Serbian operations in the war. The JNA surrounded the village and cut off all utilities and access, while Krajina paramilitaries engaged in skirmishes with local ethnic Croats. The siege of Kijevo lasted two weeks, during which time almost no one was allowed into the village and no one was allowed out and back in again. This 'dry-run' ended after two weeks, following mass protests surrounding the JNA naval headquarters in Split, where one JNA soldier was killed by gunfire, which led to a negotiated stand-down at Kijevo. While the water, fuel and food supplies were eventually allowed back in, it would only be a matter of months before Kijevo would again be encircled, after which the other elements of ethnic cleansing were applied. Mladić reapplied the siege on 17 August. That second phase of siege would finish on 26 August with an artillery bombardment targeting every house in the village, accompanied by close air support raids, followed by Martić's paramilitary units in concert with JNA armour and infantry entering and taking control of the village. As a result, no ethnic Croats remained, either fleeing from destroyed homes, or driven out – Serbian forces and JNA aircraft harassed those fleeing. The tactical model of army encirclement with heavy weapons, cutting off and paramilitary action against non-Serbs would return many times over the next four and a half years in Croatia, Bosnia and Hercegovina, and Kosovo.

Preparation and Provocation

Provocation was a common element in the transition from preparation to implementation of Serb takeovers. Other early acts of provocation also involved Martić. In spring 1991, around Easter, Serbian leaders held a political rally at the Plitvice Lakes in Croatia to demand that the Plitvice National Park should be incorporated into the territory of Martić's SAO, which already encircled Plitvice. Serb forces then took over the park headquarters, evicting those working there. In the days that followed, Croatian special police units attempted to remove Serb control of Plitvice in a series of armed actions which resulted in injuries on both sides, casualties being airlifted for treatment by a JNA helicopter at the request of the Zagreb interior minister. The Croatian authorities were able to establish a police station, at which point JNA units were deployed officially to create a buffer zone, although they de facto protected the Krajina Serb forces when they issued an ultimatum to the Croatian police to leave the area – which the special units did, but not those who had been based in the police station. Another early instance of provocation included Serbian Četnik Movement action resulting in the deaths of twelve Croatian government 'Specials' at Borovo Selo, over a month before fighting broke out in earnest at the end of June.

During the weeks preceding the war, across Bosnia, local Serb politicians increased the pressure on their municipal governments. The Bosnian Serbs were well prepared for the takeover, according to one centralised programme (even if local application inevitably varied). Plans for the takeover of each municipality (or *opština*) had been made. An SDS document, dated 19 December 1991, was circulated to relevant individuals in the party. The document concerned the organisation and activity of the 'organs of the Serb people' in Bosnia and 'emergency' circumstances. It indicated preparations for the creation of para-governmental structures through the establishment of crisis headquarters. The document, marked 'strictly confidential' set out instructions, 'For the organisation and activity of organs of the Serbian people in Bosnia–Herzegovina in extraordinary circumstances'.[21]

The document, prepared by the Serbian political leadership, provided two versions of the plan to take control and make ethnically pure territories: option A was for areas of Bosnia and Hercegovina in which there was an absolute Serbian majority; and option B was for areas in which there was not an absolute Serbian majority. In either case, the aim was to prepare the loyal Serbs in a particular area for the takeover, and to prepare for co-ordination with the JNA and the security apparatus. Some key elements of preparation involved contacts with public security service centres in certain areas and ensuring readiness to take over security service centres and also involvement. Another aspect of preparation was pre-mobilisation of active and reserve members of the police forces, the TO and civil defence units so that adequate numbers would be in place whenever they were needed. The document indicated the need and intention throughout to co-operate with units of the JNA. In particular, there was an instruction to begin equipping wartime units with personnel, military resources and livestock reserves according to JNA designations.

At least from the end of 1991, Serb leaders in conjunction with security service centres were making provision for shadow secret governments, which would take up their role when the plan was put into effect. This involved the creation of 'crisis headquarters',[22] which made preparations

---

21 This document was produced as prosecution Exhibit 70 in the case of *Prosecutor v. Dušan Tadić* IT-94-1 and prosecution Exhibit 206 in the case of *Prosecutor v. Delalić et al. (Čelebići)* IT-96-21 at the ICTY in The Hague.

22 'Crisis headquarters' is a translation of the Serbian '*Krizni Štab*', where 'headquarters' is used in preference to 'committee', sometimes used (including on early occasions by me) and 'staff', which is a more obvious literal translation (also used sometimes) yet has too strong a military connotation in English. The term 'staff' reflects the defence heritage of the concept, associated with the political dimensions of a liberation struggle under the old defence system.

primarily for the political but also some of the military aspects of the takeover. The crisis headquarters constituted a vital part of political preparations for taking control further to the declarations of the Serb autonomous regions. From the very outset, they had official letterhead paper, documents and stamps ready to administer the bureaucracy of ethnic cleansing. The crisis headquarters established curfews, restricted travel of local residents, dismissed non-Serbs from their jobs and positions of authority (in many cases) or allowed them to continue (in a few cases) under licence, and helped identify individuals for detention. For those whose ethnic community was being systematically destroyed – primarily the Slav Muslims of Bosnia and Hercegovina – there was a stark choice between summary murder or death after deprivation and torture in camps on the one hand, or paying to sign away their possessions, property and right to remain in their homeland on documents specially prepared by the new Serbian administration on the other.

Takeover and the Use of Force

Initial Serbian attacks followed similar patterns. The JNA, or one of its successor forces, positioned troops and equipment in strategic areas; for example, surrounding Vukovar in eastern Croatia; or, just before the Bosnian referendum on independence, deploying JNA tank, artillery and anti-aircraft units on the Serbian side of the Drina River, across from Zvornik, to assist the forces inside Bosnia. In Foča, the JNA placed artillery on the surrounding hills in positions to shell the city. In Brčko and Bosanski Šamac, the JNA activated reserve units, staffed them and then stationed them in Serbian neighbourhoods and at strategic points. Usually, artillery was used during the initial stages to shell non-Serb neighbourhoods into rubble. The shelling discouraged resistance, expelled non-Serbs from targeted areas and, where resistance occurred, crushed it with a greater-than-necessary show of force. Often, the shelling was co-ordinated with street fighting conducted by paramilitary squads.

The JNA supplied the paramilitary groups and Bosnian Serb volunteers with weapons and ammunition directly from its own inventories, and redistributed the weapons it took from the non-Serb TOs. Serb paramilitary groups conducted street fighting, rounded up non-Serb civilians and secured the area. Local Serb irregulars sometimes requested the intercession of paramilitary groups. Paramilitary units were vital to takeover operations. In Zvornik, Arkan, leader of the Serbian Volunteer Guard – 'The Tigers' – used and threatened violence to compel the town's Muslims to divide the city and give the industrial section to the Serbs, before the town was eventually more fully cleansed. In Brčko, several paramilitary groups were prepared to fight when hostilities erupted, following provocations. In Foča, the same happened, involving the White Eagles. Many people were simply killed on the spot.

As soon as Serb forces secured a location, the local Serbs immediately established a crisis headquarters in line with the December 1991 document to serve as a provisional government. Crisis headquarters worked closely with the military and usually had military representatives as members. Although on a few occasions members of the paramilitary squads participated in these provisional governments, ordinarily, the paramilitary forces departed for other areas of fighting.

In each location, police, broadcasting and civil administration functions were taken over by local crisis headquarters, composed entirely of Serbs. Local officials worked with paramilitary units to identify and interrogate non-Serb residents and evict them from their homes. Non-Serbs were ordered to display white flags from their homes as a sign of loyalty. Tanks and infantry then swept through areas identified by the flags, destroying homes and gathering non-Serb residents for transport to camps or for expulsion. Armed local Serbs and paramilitary bands terrorised non-Serb neighbourhoods, plundering homes. In the occupied areas, Serb forces destroyed the cultural and religious symbols of the non-Serb community. Serbs bombed and burned mosques and Roman Catholic churches and sometimes bulldozed the sites, removing all traces that a sacred building had once been there. Serb forces destroyed houses and businesses owned by non-Serbs.

Concentration Camps

The Serbs established a network of camps throughout Bosnia (and some prisons inside Serbia too) to serve as detention facilities for the huge numbers of non-Serbs they had collected. In these locations, non-Serb men of 'military age' and many non-Serb women were imprisoned in camps and detention centres. Some of the camps were set up in school gymnasiums and were apparently run by civil authorities, while others used regular army facilities and were run by military and police units. Women and children were often held in the camps until the Serbs transported or expelled them to non-occupied areas. In most camps where women were detained, the camp commanders organised, or at least condoned, repeated and systematic rape. According to witness reports, non-Serbs were systematically killed, beaten, raped and mutilated in all of these camps. The best-known camps were in north-western Bosnia. Some of these were among the most infernal. Beginning in late May 1992, thousands of non-Serbs from the Prijedor *opština* were rounded up and sent to camps at Omarska (a former mining complex), Keraterm (a former ceramics factory) and Trnopolje (a former school). The brutal conditions in all of these camps were apparently in furtherance of a campaign of terror designed to persuade the non-Serbs to abandon their homes and leave the area. By September 1992, this design had been largely accomplished. Most of the survivors in Bosnia were eventually deported to areas beyond Serb control.

Although the focus in the Kosovo campaign came to be principally on rapid expulsion and killing, detention facilities also operated there. When NATO troops entered Kosovo in June 1999, they found 60,000 ethnic Albanians in concentration camps near the town of Podujevo. Most of those incarcerated had been rounded up in brutal campaigns to take them from mountain camps and hideouts. These villages were surrounded by troops and tanks. Anyone trying to escape was shot. Inside the camp, the inmates, including all children, were given identity cards with name, number and the name of their 'prison village'. Serb snipers in the hills overlooking these concentration camps were reported to have randomly killed people in the camp.[23] Other reports of major detention centres included 20,000 Kosovans being held in a munitions factory at Srbica and reports concerning the Trepča mines.

Elimination

There were two methods by which the non-Serb population could be eliminated in pursuit of the strategic end of purely Serb territories. One was expulsion. This was often induced by demonstrative examples of the other – killing. The brutal administrative processes for expulsion of those who had not already fled in fear ensured the expulsion of millions of Muslims from Serb-controlled parts of Bosnia. The most acute case of expulsion was that of the ethnic Albanians from Kosovo in 1999.

Throughout the territories they controlled, the Serbs expelled the non-Serb population. Most of those released from prison were deported immediately. The few non-Serbs who were not imprisoned and remained in their homes were harassed and came under increasing pressure to leave. The non-Serbs often had to pay significant sums for 'permission' to leave. Mass

23 *The Daily Telegraph* (20 June 1999).

expulsion was promoted by cold-blooded killing. While most non-Serbs were expelled, tens of thousands were murdered – direct elimination, as well as a clear means to intimidate others to leave their homes. Notorious sites of killing include Prijedor, Foča, Višegrad and Zvornik. The most notorious of all is Srebrenica, where over 8,000 Muslim males were killed in an act of genocide.

Following a year-long programme of low-level ethnic cleansing – a village a day kept NATO away – in spring 1999, Serb forces in Kosovo initiated an overwhelming campaign of expulsion. MUP, JSO or paramilitary units would knock on the door to a Kosovan home. Those inside would be told immediately to leave. Where they were too slow, they would be shot immediately. The men would generally be separated from the women and children. The former would often be shot nearby, or taken away for questioning. The latter would either be scared into fleeing, or would be taken at gunpoint to pre-arranged buses or trains to be carried to the border.[24] With 300,000–400,000 Kosovan Albanians already refugees or deportees from Serbian campaigns during 1998, in a matter of days Serb forces were able to apply a turbo-charge to their ethnic cleansing. This scale of cleansing was always the ultimate goal of the Serb operations in Kosovo. However it was only when a commitment to force had been made by NATO that there was no longer any need to be restrained in order to prevent NATO action. Once that which it was hoped to avoid had happened, there was no need to pretend any more.

In the last week of March and the first weeks of April 1999, in the region of a million Kosovans were forced out of their homes and their land. This included 750,000 refugees and deportees given shelter primarily in the neighbouring lands of Macedonia, Albania and Montenegro. Estimates suggested that up to 700,000 Kosovans were also internally displaced in Kosovo itself, unable or afraid to remain in their homes but unable to escape the province.

One of the most dangerous moments in the process of expulsion from Kosovo was the decision to stop it on two occasions. The first of these was on 7 April 1999. Abruptly, Serbian forces closed the borders across which they had been forcing hundreds of thousands of people for two weeks. The same refugees that had been driven to the border at gunpoint were then turned back at gunpoint. There were two reasons for this. The first was the potential to use the Kosovan Albanians as human shields against NATO attacks. The second was to limit the impact that the images of deported and distraught Kosovans had made on public opinion around the world,

24 *The Daily Telegraph* (17 April 1999).

strengthening the resolve and commitment of the NATO countries seeking to stop the ethnic cleansing of Kosovo. An implication of this second reason was ominous.

The effects of ethnic cleansing strategy can be exemplified in the demographics of one town in Bosnia. Before the war, the population of Prijedor was almost evenly divided between Muslims and Serbs. According to the 1991 census, the *opština* had a total population of 112,470 people, of whom 44% were Muslims, 42.5% were Serbs, 5.6% Croats and 5.7% Yugoslavs and 2.2% others (Ukrainians, Russians and Italians). According to the report of the Commission of Experts established pursuant to Security Council Resolution 780 (1992), by June 1993 over 43,000 of nearly 50,000 Muslims in the *opština* had left Bosnia or been killed. By the end of that year, no more than 1,000 Muslims remained there.

Conclusion

The Serbian strategy of war crimes lay at the heart of the state project to forge new borders and new population arrangements. Their immediate neighbourhood adversaries responded in ways also characterised by war crimes and crimes against humanity, at times. The strategy was a way of reconciling the available means and the desired ends. The quest for new Serbian borders for the Serbs was to be achieved with the available means – limited manpower and considerable stocks of weaponry. Where there was insufficient manpower to achieve control of territory and to secure it, removing the population or subjecting civilian towns to siege and bombardment could be seen to make a curious kind of sense – albeit one where the skewed logic was an evident affront to humanity. That made it bad strategy, in the end – all the more so in that it mobilised forces against its proponents who might otherwise have shown little concern. It also meant the appearance for the first time of war crimes charges for military personnel ostensibly doing their jobs, not for actions outside the normal scope of war, such as mass murder of civilians. Soldiers were charged with crimes such as indiscriminate or excessive use of force in the context of siege and bombardment, raising questions for the conduct of operations and the gauging of strategy everywhere.

The Serbian strategy gave the term 'ethnic cleansing' to the world and provoked extraordinary and unprecedented international intervention – military and judicial. The international engagement fuelled by humanitarian concern and offence at the strategy of war crimes had to be shaped in a way that would both tackle the aims and the means of the Serbian project, and, also, at a subordinate level, the worst conduct of the other Yugoslav parties. In military terms, this meant shaping and conducting operations that were as far apart in character from those of the Serbian project – exercising maximum restraint and ensuring lawfulness – as could be, yet could stop it. In the end, while the Serbian strategy of war crimes was successful on some levels, by making clear that war with serious breaches of international humanitarian law at its core was not tolerated internationally and by provoking a significant response, ultimately, the strategy largely backfired. That response included the creation of the Yugoslavia Tribunal, and together the Tribunal and the Serbian strategy had the effect of significantly increasing attention to the boundaries of war and war crimes globally, and to the importance of international humanitarian law in strategy. After the Yugoslav War, armed campaigns everywhere became exponentially more scrutinised – and planned – in terms of their lawfulness and the avoidance of accusations of committing war crimes.

21

Terrorism and Insurgency

COLIN P. CLARKE

While there is usually a clear distinction between terrorism and insurgency – the former is a tactic while the latter is a movement with a strategy – this distinction is not always recognised in the academic literature. Insurgent groups can and almost always do rely on terrorism as a tactic, but terrorism itself is violence, or the threat of violence, used and directed in pursuit of, or in service of a political aim.[1] Insurgency, on the other hand, is 'an organised movement aimed at the overthrow of a constituted government through the use of subversion and armed conflict'.[2]

This chapter will explore the question of whether, and to what extent, terrorism is utilised by modern terrorist groups in a strategic manner. In other words, do terrorist attacks fit within a broader strategic framework, and if so, how? Many terrorist groups use terrorism as a tactic to achieve intermediate objectives, for example, demonstrating to the population that the government and its security forces are unable to protect civilians. But there is a debate over whether terrorism rises to the level of strategy, particularly in how it is used by groups such as Al-Qaeda and the so-called Islamic State, as well as their respective affiliates, regional branches and franchise groups around the globe.

Terrorism is a classic tool utilised by violent non-state actors and extremists that pits the weak against the strong. Indeed, this tactic has roots, among others, dating back to ancient Rome in places such as Gaul and Judea.[3] Only

---

[1] B. Hoffman, *Inside Terrorism*, 2nd ed. (New York: Columbia University Press, 2006), 3.
[2] Headquarters, US Department of the Army, and Headquarters, US Marine Corps, *Counterinsurgency Field Manual*, Field Manual 3–24/Marine Corps Warfighting Publication 3–33.5 (Chicago: University of Chicago Press, 2007).
[3] B. E. O'Neill, *Insurgency and Terrorism: Inside Modern Revolutionary Warfare* (McLean: Brassey, 1990), 1.

by tracing the evolution of terrorism can one begin to understand how it has been used, conceptualised and developed. Terrorism featured prominently as a tactic in nineteenth-century warfare, as discussed already by Beckett in Chapter 2. This pattern continued in the First and Second World Wars and the wars of liberation and decolonisation, which have been covered in Chapter 14 by von Bülow. Culture, emotion and psychology intersect with the impact of globalisation on conflict, while advances in technology and communications, and a resurgence of religiously inspired identity politics shape our current view of terrorism and terrorist organisations.

Terrorism scholar Max Abrahms has argued passionately that 'terrorism does not work', suggesting that 'there has been scant empirical research on whether terrorism is a winning coercive strategy'.[4] Yet, if Osama bin Laden's objective was to lure the United States into Afghanistan in an attempt to spill blood and treasure, the terrorist attacks of 11 September 2001 (9/11) should be considered an overwhelming success. Moreover, the Al-Qaeda bombings in March 2004 of three Spanish commuter trains killed 191 people and injured an additional 1,500.[5] They could be seen as successful because shortly after the attack, Spanish voters elected a new government, led by the Socialist Party, in large part because of the Party's campaign promise to withdraw Spanish troops from Iraq, which it ultimately did.[6]

Sources

The study of terrorism is blessed by an abundance of primary sources, where terrorists themselves, typically cloaked in the banner of 'freedom fighters', publish manuals and guides for how to effectively conduct military campaigns, thus providing unfettered access to their tactics and strategies. Sun Tzu, the ancient Chinese military strategist and author of *The Art of War*, laid out some of the basic principles of guerrilla warfare – deception, intelligence, hit-and-run manoeuvres – many of which are still relevant today.[7] One of the more prolific authors on terrorism insurgency in the modern era though, is another practitioner-philosopher of Chinese origin, Mao Zedong.[8] Mao's

---

4 M. Abrahms, 'Why terrorism does not work', *International Security*, 31 (2006), 42.
5 R. S. Chari, 'The 2004 Spanish election: terrorism as a catalyst for change?', *West European Politics*, 27 (2004), 954.
6 W. Rose, R. Murphy and M. Abrahms, 'Correspondence: does terrorism ever work? The 2004 Madrid train bombings', *International Security*, 32 (2007), 185–92.
7 See T. Sun, *The Art of War*, S. B. Griffith (trans.) (Oxford: Oxford University Press, 2005).
8 D. Porch, 'The dangerous myths and dubious promise of COIN', *Small Wars & Insurgencies*, 22 (2011), 245.

book *Guerrilla Warfare* (*Yu Chi Chan*) remains a standard text for militants today, and Mao was among the first strategists to realise the importance of focusing on the population during low-intensity conflict. His activities have been discussed above in Chapter 7 by Yung.

Insurgents, terrorists and self-styled revolutionaries have published numerous other prominent texts and publications, including Che Guevara's *Guerrilla Warfare*, Carlos Marighella's *Minimanual of the Urban Guerrilla*, and the Provisional Irish Republican Army's (IRA) *Green Book*. For Al-Qaeda and other transnational jihadist groups, to include the Islamic State, Abu Bakr Naji's *Management of Savagery* has served as a blueprint for how to approach a global insurgency with decentralised affiliates and branches operating throughout myriad regions of the globe.

Debates and Definitions

Too often, terrorism and insurgency are used interchangeably. With the proliferation of post-9/11 studies focusing on these issues, the problem became even more acute. The literature on civil wars also overlaps with insurgency literature, with distinctions between civil war, guerrilla warfare and insurgency occasionally hinging on a body-count threshold (per year or throughout the duration of the conflict), tactics employed (low intensity vs conventional military), the actors involved (state vs non-state, indigenous vs foreign), or other categorical variables which classify conflicts as coups, countercoups, mutinies, insurrections or other 'revolutionary' activities. There is also no clear agreement on what differentiates irregular warfare from asymmetric warfare, or unconventional warfare from hybrid warfare. The recent popularity of the term 'gray zone',[9] meant to connote 'competitive interactions among and within state and non-state actors that fall between the traditional war and peace duality',[10] has further muddled our conceptual understanding of these categories, where one begins and where another ends.

While some scholars focus on territorial size to discern between terrorist and insurgent groups, Byman et al. believe that the tactics used to gain and control territory are a more appropriate indication of typology, and suggest that the Liberation Tigers of Tamil Eelam (LTTE, aka Tamil Tigers) and Lebanese Hezbollah could be considered *both* terrorists and insurgents because of their relentless use of terrorism *in addition to* a host of other tactics

---

9 P. Kapusta, 'The gray zone', *Special Warfare; Fort Bragg*, 28:4 (Oct–Dec 2015), 18–25, www.proquest.com/docview/1750033789.
10 Kapusta, 'The gray zone'.

used to control territory. The authors go on to note that size can also be a useful distinguishing characteristic, commenting, 'terrorist groups often consist of a small number of individuals, sometimes no more than a handful. Insurgent organisations, like Hizballah or the LTTE, in contrast, number in the thousands'. In his research on proto-insurgencies, Byman notes that 'many of the most important "terrorist" groups in the world – including the Lebanese Hizballah, the Liberation Tigers of Tamil Eelam, and the Revolutionary Armed Forces of Colombia (FARC) – are better described as insurgencies that use terrorism than as typical terrorist movements'.[11] Groups including the Provisional IRA, Hezbollah, LTTE and the African National Congress (ANC) were each consistent practitioners of terrorism, but also used a range of other tactics in their effort to control territory.[12] O'Neill finds that terrorism is merely a form of warfare in which violence is used primarily against civilians, while insurgent terrorism has a purpose. Unlike the former, the latter is used in the pursuance of a range of objectives, from short-term goals to intermediate and long-term.[13] But when applying Kagan's definition of strategy – the setting of objectives and or priorities among those objectives in order to allocate resources and choose the best means to prosecute a war[14] – it becomes less clear that insurgent terrorism directed against civilians could serve any purpose other than inducing fear in the population.

Bard O'Neill admits that definitions can be somewhat arbitrary or ambiguous, and that terms such as *insurgency, terrorism, guerrilla warfare* and *revolutionary warfare* have often been used carelessly. He attempts to remedy this quandary by offering his own definition of insurgency, which he clearly states as 'a struggle between a non-ruling group and the ruling authorities in which the non-ruling group consciously uses *political resources* (e.g., organisational expertise, propaganda, and demonstrations) and *violence* to destroy, reformulate, or sustain the basis of legitimacy of one or more aspects of politics'.[15] Insurgencies are complex though, and rarely involve only one ruling group vs one non-ruling group. Typically, insurgents are split among several factions and counterinsurgents can be comprised of indigenous forces, external intervening nations ('occupiers') or international organisations (e.g. NATO),

---

11 D. Byman, *Understanding Proto-Insurgencies* (Santa Monica: RAND, 2007), 1.
12 D. Byman, P. Chalk and B. Hoffman, *Trends in Outside Support for Insurgent Movements* (Santa Monica, RAND, 2001), 5.
13 B. E. O'Neill, *Insurgency and Terrorism: Inside Modern Revolutionary Warfare* (Washington, DC: Brassey's Inc., 1990), 24.
14 K. Kagan, 'Redefining Roman grand strategy', *Journal of Military History*, 70:2 (2006), 333–62, 348.
15 O'Neill, *Insurgency and Terrorism*, 13.

'ferret forces', indigenous militias, and private military companies (PMCs) such as Executive Outcomes (EO) or Xe Services (formerly Blackwater USA). Steve Metz, a long-time scholar of insurgency and counterinsurgency, thoughtfully adds the following elements to the definition, noting that the essence of insurgency is 'protracted, asymmetric violence; political, legal, and ethical ambiguity', and that insurgency 'arises when a group decides that the gap between their political expectations and the opportunities afforded them is unacceptable and can only be remedied by force'.[16] Anthony James Joes argues that guerrilla insurgency is primarily a political problem. Insurgents wage guerrilla warfare because they are weaker than the state they are fighting to replace and are almost always at a disadvantage in terms of men and materiel. They seek to mitigate this disadvantage through employing asymmetric tactics such as ambushes and attacking enemy supply lines.[17] Improvised explosive devices (IEDs) are the new weapon of choice for modern-day insurgents, favoured because they are cheap, easy to construct and detonate, and are extremely lethal, as both Iraqi and Afghan insurgents have demonstrated. Joes believes that the preponderance of ethnic groups agitating for autonomy – Basques, Chechens, Kashmiris, Kurds, Moros, Uighurs – means that insurgency will persist as a form of warfare well into the twenty-first century.[18] Of course, these groups possess agency as well, and will have to decide whether terrorism is, or can be, an effective means of reaching their respective goals. A current snapshot of their case would suggest otherwise, although the Moros and Kurds have achieved varying degrees of autonomy over time, with success at least tangentially connected to their use of terrorist tactics.

Actors

The primary actors under examination are violent non-state actors (VNSAs). There have been myriad motivations propelling them. The key actors in an insurgency are the local/indigenous government (and domestic allies), insurgent groups (and domestic allies), external actors (both state and non-state) and of course, the population. In general, the courses of action adopted by insurgent groups are a product of its members consisting of the ideal types of: ideologues, radicals and politicos.[19]

---

16 S. Metz, *Rethinking Insurgency* (Carlisle: Strategic Studies Institute, 2007), 1.
17 A. J. Joes, *Resisting Rebellion: The History and Politics of Counterinsurgency* (Lexington: University of Kentucky Press, 2004), 1.
18 Joes, *Resisting Rebellion*, 5.
19 C. Irvin, *Militant Nationalism* (Minneapolis: University of Minnesota Press, 1999).

Ideologues are the 'hard' members of insurgent organisations that are drawn more to action than political discussion, and who believe that their goals can only be achieved through armed struggle, viewing non-violent struggle as futile. These individuals are unwilling to compromise the organisation's ideological principles even to secure concessions from the incumbent regime, and view the levers of control as the government and its bureaucracy, the educational system, the mass media and the economy. Ideologues believe that any participation by the movement in institutional politics legitimates the incumbent regime and thereby diminishes the legitimacy of armed struggle as a strategy for political change. In turn, participation in political institutions leads to reformism, diminishes the effectiveness of the military wing and diverts essential resources (both human and material) from the struggle. When faced with extreme repression or a lack of popular support, ideologues will withdraw from the political arena and retreat into isolation rather than compromise the organisation's principles or demands.

Radicals, like ideologues, prefer an active strategy to a passive one, but believe that armed struggle alone cannot achieve results. Still, radicals are both willing and able to call upon arms when they view it as necessary. These are no mere thugs – radicals are shrewd and calculating. They may have been ideologues at some point, but have altered their thinking because they subscribe to a dual strategy that values tangible concessions more than ideological/doctrinal purity. This agenda demonstrates that the sect is willing to compromise but not abandon the core tenets of the movement if those sacrifices appear aimed at achieving real concessions from the host nation government. They favour electoral politics and 'tactical participation in existing political institutions', and view their path as the surest way to gaining popular support. For radicals, alliance formation is opportunistic, and they are more likely than ideologues to see value in ideological diversity over strict dogmatic rigidity.[20]

Politicos see violence as both counterproductive and ostracising to the group's supporters (both domestic and international), roundly rejecting the notion that armed struggle can be used successfully to mobilise the masses. This subset supports a strategy of base-building and political education, believing that influence can be measured in terms of real political power, not ideological purity. The main area to focus on with politicos is elections.

20 J. Darby, 'Northern Ireland: the persistence and limitations of violence', in J. V. Montville (ed.), *Conflict and Peacemaking in Multiethnic Societies* (Lexington: Lexington Books, 1990), 154.

For them, elections are seen as an opportunity (1) to present the public with their image of an alternative political structure and society; (2) to develop the personnel capable of implementing those changes; and most importantly, (3) to demonstrate their capability to administer the new society. Of course, these roles are hardly ever static, and individuals can adopt different roles and postures over the course of a terrorist campaign.

Adversaries

The adversaries of terrorists are most commonly the state, but can also be external actors (both state and non-state) and other violent groups inside and outside the country. In the literature, the adversaries of insurgents are the counterinsurgents. Counterinsurgency (COIN) refers to military, paramilitary, political, economic, psychological and civic actions taken by a government to defeat insurgency.[21] Whether fighting insurgencies in Algeria, Northern Ireland, Tibet, Burma, Afghanistan, Angola or Vietnam, there is no magic formula that can be applied in order to achieve success in counterinsurgency. However, observing what has worked and what has not worked in the hundreds of small wars and insurgencies that have been fought throughout time does provide insight on various elements of counterinsurgency, and has led to a robust body of knowledge and writing on the subject.

Causes of the War(s)

'Root cause' is a contentious term in the literature, and surely conflicts as complex as terrorism and insurgencies have no single cause. Throughout history, numerous factors have contributed to the start of political violence, although at the core of these struggles are typically an array of grievances held by the population. Grievances can be related to land; inadequate distribution of resources; marginalisation of particular ethnic, religious or other (often minority) groups; government and/or elite corruption; a lack of political legitimacy; and an inability or unwillingness to protect certain populations in a country, to name just a few. David Rapoport's 'waves of terrorism' is a concept that the terrorism scholar developed to describe the ideologies that define the expansion and contraction of specific periods of time dominated by certain typologies of terrorism.[22]

21 US Army and Marine Corps Field Manual FM 3–24, 2.
22 David C. Rapoport, 'The four waves of rebel terror and September 11', *Anthropoetics*, 8:1 (Spring/Summer 2002).

Objectives (Ends)

The most important difference to keep in mind, though, is the role of politics. Insurgency is akin to an armed political campaign, while terrorism is a form of armed political communication, something of a strategy in and of itself. Insurgency uses mass mobilisation by sub-state actors of a counterstate to challenge a national government for political power. Terrorism, on the other hand, is characterised by the use of violence by sub-state actors to attack innocent civilians in order to garner attention for their cause and ultimately, create pressure in order to attain political ends. This 'propaganda by deed' was first popularised by Russian anarchists in the nineteenth century who hoped that their attacks would transform them from 'a small conspiratorial club into a massive revolutionary movement'.[23]

One of the most important strategic thinkers and a strategist who continues to influence thinking about warfare was Mao. Mao sought to cultivate positive relations with the peasants in rural China, and put forth his 'Six Main Points for Attention', which provided his troops with directions on how to treat the population as they marauded through the countryside. Among the tenets proffered by Mao were: replace straw bedding and wooden bed-boards after sleeping at peasant homes overnight; return whatever was borrowed; pay for any item damaged; remain courteous and humane; and be fair in any business dealings.[24] Commenting on Mao, T. X. Hammes observes, 'he understood that maintaining the goodwill of the peasants was not simply a propaganda slogan but essential to his army's survival. He knew that only the peasants could provide an unbeatable intelligence network, a constant source of manpower, and resources in the form of food and labor'.[25] For Mao, the population was the sea in which the insurgents, or fish, would swim. For these reasons, Mao is still studied by insurgent cadres as well as soldiers and military theorists in both eastern and western military academies to this day.

The other essential contribution Mao made to insurgency was to emphasise the importance of the political element. Mao, like Clausewitz, understood that war and politics were intimately intertwined. Maoist insurgency

---

23 G. Chaliand and A. Blin (eds), *The History of Terrorism: From Antiquity to Al-Qaeda* (Berkeley: University of California Press, 2007), 33. Also see P. Eltzbacher, *The Great Anarchists: Ideas and Teachings of Seven Major Thinkers* (Mineola: Dover, 2004).
24 P. Short, *Mao: A Life* (New York: Holt, 1999), 222; another great source on Mao is J. Chang, *Mao: The Unknown Story* (New York: Knopf, 2005).
25 T. X. Hammes, *The Sling and the Stone: On War in the 21st Century* (St Paul, MN: Zenith, 2004), 47.

doctrine underscores the notion that insurgency is about politics, specifically the relationship between the government and the population. By politics, Mao was referring to the process by which society decides and implements who receives certain rights, resources, privileges and obligations. Mao advocated violence to initiate structural change and favoured a bottom-up approach to mobilisation. Mao's framework for insurgency became so popular, largely due to its effectiveness, that insurgencies worldwide began to emulate the Maoist model of warfare, giving way to a whole spate of insurgencies that could aptly be characterised as Maoist.[26] In Vietnam, Ho Chi Minh and Vo Nguyen Giap waged Maoist insurgencies against France and then the United States, adding to Mao's model by targeting the national will of their adversaries' respective populations.[27]

During the era of decolonisation, Asian countries were not the only locales to experience extreme upheaval. On the contrary, insurgencies raged across the globe, from North Africa to South America. The *focoist* approach to insurgency is credited to Che Guevara, who developed and refined this theory based on his experiences of fighting alongside Fidel Castro in Cuba. Guevara believed that with a small group of politically organised armed guerrillas as its core, the insurgency would spark a popular uprising among the rural population that would then fan out and spread to the cities. In the final stage, the insurgents, now mobilised, would overthrow the existing regime.[28] The *focoist* approach, in stark contrast to Maoism, advocates mobilisation from the top down. Throughout history, Mao's approach has been far more successful than Che's in exploiting the grievances of the population to mobilise the masses.

Although their approaches to mobilisation were distinct, Guevara and Mao (along with Ho Chi Minh) both remained keenly aware of the importance of politics in revolutionary warfare. They each believed that it was not likely to wage a successful insurgency against a government that was democratic, or at least maintained a democratic facade.[29] The data on pseudo-democracies, or anocracies, appears to validate these beliefs.[30]

A contemporary of Che Guevara, the Brazilian Marxist Carlos Marighella attempted to develop a new strategy combining urban and rural guerrilla

---

26 T. A. Marks, *Maoist Insurgency Since Vietnam* (London: Routledge, 1996).
27 See also Chapter 14.   28 Hammes, *Sling and the Stone*, 77.
29 E. Guevara, *Guerilla Warfare* (New York: Vintage, 1960).
30 Fifteen of the eighty-nine case studies by Libicki and Connable were coded as anocracies and of those fifteen, only one case (Croatia) succeeded in countering the insurgency while fully democratising. B. Connable and M. Libicki, *How Insurgencies End* (Santa Monica: RAND, 2010), xiv.

combat. Marighella wanted to provoke the state and generate a heavy-handed response. The overreaction would then lead to draconian measures and severe repression, which would galvanise the support of the population behind his movement.[31] But a major shortcoming of Marighella's strategy was his inability to comprehend the complexity of popular support. In reference to his strategy of provocation leading to repression, Chaliand and Blin argue that Marighella 'had little understanding of the depth of the potential social base for such actions and failed to grasp that there is a big difference between sympathy and organized support'.[32] Furthermore, Marighella underestimated the strength of the Brazilian state, which in 1964 was still a dictatorship and as such, had the ability to marshal government resources effectively to swiftly quell dissent.

The Latin American flavour of insurgency has a rich lineage, beginning with Castro and Guevara, extending through Marighella and up to Abraham Guillen, Abimael Guzman (Sendero Luminoso/Shining Path), Humberto Ortega (FSLN/Sandinistas), Manuel Marulanda Velez (FARC/Revolutionary Armed Forces of Colombia) and Raul Sendic (MLN/Tupamaros). Guillen saw urban warfare as a necessary, though not sufficient, element of success in insurgency. In line with Guillen's vision, action in the cities was crucial but not decisive. The struggle would inevitably move from an urban to a rural setting.[33] This move from the cities to the countryside was predicated on the belief that widespread popular support was essential to defeat the government, and this support existed in far greater numbers in the rural parts of the country, where peasants viewed the central government with distrust.

The Sandinista strategic approach, or as Hammes has dubbed it, 'the Sandinista Refinement'[34] to evolutionary insurgency doctrine, sought to further emphasise the importance of political development. Overmatched and underequipped against the Nicaraguan state, the Sandinistas brought the mass appeal of a broad-front political organisation into the movement, utilised the clout of the Catholic Church to gain the moral high ground (through liberation theology), targeted US and world opinion through skilful use of the media, and established a strong public affairs/information office.[35] What was unique about the Sandinistas' approach was that it eschewed the push for a final conventional military offensive, instead relying upon the

---

31 Chaliand and Blin, *History of Terrorism*, 230–2.
32 Chaliand and Blin, *History of Terrorism*, 231.   33 O'Neill, *Insurgency and Terrorism*, 46.
34 Hammes, *Sling and the Stone*.
35 J. D. Waghelstein, 'A Latin American insurgency status report', *Military Review*, 67 (1987), 45.

political end game to bring about a change in the 'correlation of forces'.[36] The Sandinistas provided hope to other insurgents engaged in asymmetric conflict, demonstrating that even when outmatched militarily, a steadfast focus on the political dimension could lead to victory. The Sandinistas' victory inspired insurgents from Northern Ireland to South Africa. But their victory was short-lived. The insurgents would soon become the counterinsurgents, fighting the US-backed Contras throughout the 1980s and early 1990s.

Available Means

Warfare is constantly evolving. Technological advances, innovations in real-time communications and media, and the diffusion of weaponry are all elements of globalisation that differentiate insurgencies from each other over time. One of the defining characteristics of insurgency is the use of terrorism. Contemporary insurgency is linked directly to the phenomenon of transnational terrorism, spanning countries and continents.[37] In the past, terrorism was used in the operational sense. But today, terrorism has been elevated to a strategic threat, largely because of the emergence of Al-Qaeda and groups of its ilk, which use the narrative of 'global jihad' as a rallying cry against the United States in particular, and the West more generally.

Terrorism has strategic characteristics and the reach of terrorist groups such as Al-Qaeda has become global. If 'all politics is local', then in the modern era, 'all conflict is global'. Rarely do conflicts remain confined within the borders of where civil wars and insurgencies began. There is the constant threat of spillover violence. However, just because the use of terrorism may be ubiquitous in contemporary insurgency does not make it effective. In their analysis of eighty-nine insurgencies, Connable and Libicki found that 'those insurgent groups that were able to restrict their use of terrorism by minimising civilian – *vice* government – casualties were more likely to win than those that did not'.[38] The use of indiscriminate terror by insurgents can be perceived as a sign of weakness. In other words, terrorism often backfires.

Insurgencies have always been transnational and trans-dimensional, but this trend has accelerated in the modern era. In the classic context, insurgencies were hierarchical and often received funding from a state sponsor. This template held true to form for Cold War proxy conflicts in Angola and El Salvador and to a lesser extent, Vietnam and Afghanistan. The driving force

36 Hammes, *Sling and the Stone*, 88.   37 Metz, *Rethinking Insurgency*, 7.
38 Connable and Libicki, *How Insurgencies End*, xvii.

behind the evolution of insurgency is globalisation, although contemporary insurgents and terrorists alike have been something of a by-product of globalisation. Changes have occurred not only in areas such as organisational structure and threat finance, but also in urbanisation (terrain), the role of religion (ideology) and the information dimension (media/publicity), to name a few. Defined simply as the rapid cross-border movement of goods (weapons), services (training), people (recruits) and ideas (ideological beliefs and tactical adaptation) including the spread of Salafism, the diffusion of IEDs and the infiltration of suicide bombers, globalisation has altered the strategic context of the international security environment. Several effects and after-effects follow.

First, globalisation has ushered in a deluge of information that serves as something of a precondition for recruitment and intelligence. Populations previously isolated from external events are now inundated with real-time news from around the world. The follow-on effect is that disenfranchised populations now have the capacity to realise their disenfranchisement. A disconnect between society's expectations and the state's ability to meet them is magnified. If this disconnect becomes pronounced and firmly entrenched, society could move towards a state of anarchy and possibly even anomie.

Second, these feelings of alienation, isolation and marginalisation can then be exploited by 'identity entrepreneurs', whose goal is to exacerbate already simmering resentment and further ethnic, religious or racial cleavages to provoke groups and sub-groups into possible violent actions.[39]

Third, the proliferation of weapons of mass destruction has offered new opportunities to small groups seeking to make a big impact. In the mid-1990s, a Japanese apocalyptic cult named Aum Shinrikyo dispersed sarin gas through the Tokyo subway system. This terror attack caused the deaths of 13 people while leading another 6,000 to require medical attention.[40] Still, the threat of terrorists detonating a crude nuclear device, or 'dirty bomb' does not align with the hype such a possibility has created.[41] In short, globalisation makes states more vulnerable to the ideologies of violence, rampant disinformation and influence operations, and puts at-risk governments in the crosshairs of

---

39 T. S. Thomas, S. D. Kiser and W. D. Casebeer, *Warlords Rising: Confronting Violent Non-State Actors* (Lanham: Lexington Books, 2005).
40 R. Danzig, M. Sageman, T. Leighton et al., *Aum Shinrikyo: Insights Into How Terrorists Develop Biological and Chemical Weapons* (Washington, DC: Center for a New American Security, 2011).
41 B. Jenkins, *Will Terrorists Go Nuclear?* (Amherst: Prometheus Books, 2008), 58.

would-be extremists.[42] It also makes the job of governments, intelligence agencies and the 'forces of order' infinitely more complicated.

Global communications, the proliferation of cellular phones and the seeming ubiquity of the internet have also amplified pre-existing grievances. In 2007, 80 per cent of the world's population had mobile phone coverage and 25 per cent had a mobile phone.[43] 'The medium's benefits to the insurgent are obvious: it provides a remarkably effective, easy-to-use, largely anonymous global communications network at virtually no cost', remarks US Army Captain Chris Ford.[44] What were once parochial conflicts can be lumped together into a larger conflagration, much as various local Islamist insurgencies have done by swearing fealty to Al-Qaeda and asserting the place of the *umma* in the global jihad.

Undoubtedly, insurgencies have become less centralised and more networked operations, as insurgents from North Africa can conduct attacks in the Middle East with money wired from south-east Asia in an operation planned in the mountains of north-west Pakistan. Physical location aside, insurgents can now unite over the internet to voice displeasure with certain iniquities, real or perceived. Throughout history, technology has even impacted the command, control and organisational structures of insurgent groups, such as in Algeria, Vietnam, Northern Ireland and Iraq.[45] Insurgencies can now communicate from leader to leader, leader to fighter, fighter to fighter, as well as to civilians and the international community, in what might be considered a communication parallel to Jomini's lines of operation.[46] Mostly though, insurgents use the internet to rally supporters to their cause.[47]

While the internet is a valuable tool for terrorists and insurgents to share religious and ideological information, it is not a practical source of experiential or situational knowledge.[48] Scholars should remain wary of affording too much influence to the internet. While online chat forums and jihadist websites can be effective recruitment tools and vehicles for ideological

42 Metz, *Rethinking Insurgency*, 11.
43 C. M. Ford, 'Of shoes and sites: globalization and insurgency', *Military Review* (2007), 86.
44 Ford, 'Of shoes and sites', 86.
45 K. C. Leahy, 'The impact of technology on the command, control, and organizational structure of insurgent groups', thesis, Ft. Leavenworth, US Army Command and General Staff College (2005).
46 J. J. Clark, 'The effect of information technologies on insurgency conflict: framing future analysis', Master's thesis, Monterey, CA, Naval Postgraduate School (1998), 6–7.
47 Y. Tsfati and G. Weimann, 'www.terrorism.com: terror on the internet', *Studies in Conflict and Terrorism*, 25 (2002), 317–32.
48 M. Kenney, 'Beyond the internet: *Metis, Techne*, and the limitations of online artifacts for Islamist terrorists', *Terrorism and Political Violence*, 22 (2010), 177–97.

inculcation, cyberspace is not an ideal medium for training and real-world expertise. It is this experiential and situational knowledge that is needed in order to handle operations involving any degree of complexity.

Process of Prioritisation

What do we know about terrorists' and insurgents' strategy-making process, or at least, the process of the prioritisation of resources and objectives as an overall indication of strategy? The goals and objectives of an insurgency can be divided along strategic, operational and tactical lines, and can be physical or psychological. The strategic objective of an insurgency is its desired end state, be that the unification of two separate countries into one, the separation of one whole country into two (or more) distinct entities, or a host of other social, political, economic or religiously inspired goals. Operational objectives are those that insurgents pursue to erode the legitimacy of the ruling power while attempting to establish their desired end state. Tactical objectives are the immediate aims of insurgent acts.

At least in the classical rational actor model, group goals are closely tied to decision making in the sense that groups often make decisions with the belief that a particular action will advance the group's interests. Terrorism scholar Max Abrahms, however, posits that terrorists are often less interested in politics per se and more concerned with social solidarity.[49] Some millenarian groups, including Aum Shinrikyo, have defied the rational actor model and have made decisions that have baffled authorities and analysts. As discussed earlier, some religious groups, including Al-Qaeda, espouse quixotic and difficult-to-grasp goals – at least from the perspective of outsiders – such as establishing a global caliphate. But for the most part, insurgent groups seek concrete and realisable goals, such as independence, secession, expulsion of an occupying power or the redress of long-standing grievances resulting from ethnic discrimination. Some insurgents are more malleable in pursuit of their goals and objectives, and it is essential to examine how and why goals change over time.

Different disciplines approach decision making in insurgent groups in different ways. Economic perspectives focus on the choices a group makes which can be explained by their perceived utility, based on assumed costs and benefits.[50] An older but still relevant analysis from social psychology can be

49 M. Abrahms, 'What terrorists really want', *International Security*, 32 (2008), 94.
50 T. Sandler and W. Enders, 'An economic perspective on transnational terrorism', *European Journal of Political Economy*, 20 (2004), 301–16.

applied to insurgent group decisions through the lens of group polarisation, which examines the tendency of people to make decisions that are more 'extreme' when they are in a group, in contrast to a decision reached independently or in isolation.[51] Political scientists correctly consider the issue of context. Organisational theorists look at how differences in organisational design and functioning can affect decision making. For organisational theorists, factors such as intentions, understandings, risks, resources and information are key.[52] Alternatively, game theoretical approaches seek to explain decision making through the effects of competition and other dynamics on group choices.[53]

Execution / Application of Strategy

How successful have insurgents been, historically? Is it true, as the popular maxim goes, that insurgents win simply by not losing? In a 2013 study for the RAND Corporation, a total of seventy-one cases of resolved insurgencies were studied, spanning the period from the Second World War to 2010.[54] These cases were perfectly representative of the modern history of insurgency and represented geographic variation (mountains, jungles, deserts, cities), regional and cultural variation (Africa, Latin America, central Asia, the Balkans, the Far East) and variation in the military capabilities and tactics of both the insurgent and counterinsurgents. The seventy-one cases do contain a subset of cases that are unlike the others, however, and are therefore not appropriate comparisons for the larger set of cases. Specifically, their outcomes were not driven primarily by the effectiveness of the counterinsurgent force, but rather by exogenous factors related to broader historical currents: the end of colonialism and the end of apartheid. Those that were fought 'against the tide of history' (and one more case with an indeterminate outcome) were removed from the quantitative analyses,

---

51 S. Moscovici and M. Zavalloni, 'The group as a polarizer of attitudes', *Journal of Personality and Social Psychology*, 12 (1969), 125–35.
52 B. A. Jackson, 'Organizational decision-making by terrorist groups', in P. K. Davis and K. Cragin (eds), *Social Science for Counterterrorism: Putting the Pieces Together* (Santa Monica: RAND, 2009), 209–10.
53 See G. McCormick, 'Terrorist decision making', *Annual Review of Political Science*, 6 (2003), 473–507; S. Chai, 'An organizational economics theory of antigovernment violence', *Comparative Politics*, 26 (1993), 99–110; and T. Sandler and M. D. G. Arce, 'Terrorism & game theory', *Simulation & Gaming*, 34 (2003), 319–37.
54 C. Paul, C. P. Clarke, B. Grill et al., *Paths to Victory: Lessons From Modern Insurgencies* (Santa Monica: RAND, 2013), www.rand.org/pubs/research_reports/RR291z1.html.

leaving an analytic core of fifty-nine cases. In total, the insurgents won thirty-one of the conflicts and the counterinsurgents won twenty-eight.

Since the Al-Qaeda terrorist attacks of 9/11 and the advent of the so-called 'global War on Terror', there has been a fundamental shift in the conversation about terrorism and insurgency. Yet, if the dynamics of insurgency have changed, who are today's strategists, the contemporary equivalent of Mao, Che and Ho? Primarily, and almost exclusively, the bulk of guidance on global insurgency is manufactured by Salafist ideologues. And while Al-Qaeda founder and long-time leader Osama bin Laden, killed in Pakistan in May 2011 by US Special Operation Forces, is the best-known jihadist, Al-Qaeda boasted impressive strategists that crafted the organisation's approach. Veteran jihadists including Ayman al-Zawahiri, Abu Musab al Suri, Abu Yahya al-Libi and Abu Bakr Naji served as Al-Qaeda's main insurgent theorists, proffering advice on strategy, operations and tactics. These modern-day insurgency theorists are highly adept at propagating the narrative that the Muslim *umma* is being oppressed by an American–Israeli (or 'Crusader–Zionist') nexus that seeks to subjugate all Muslims worldwide while draining their natural resources, sullying their honour and besmirching their traditions.

Abu Musab al Suri was arguably Al-Qaeda's most prolific author on insurgent and terrorist strategy and tactics. Dubbed the 'architect of the New Al Qaeda', few individuals have done more to shape Al-Qaeda's strategy since 9/11.[55] Al Suri's 'The Call for Global Islamic Resistance' called for individual terrorism to replace Al-Qaeda's hierarchically structured design. He argued that a decentralised, looser network would be a more significant challenge for the West and called for cells to form spontaneously and autonomously. A former member of the Libyan Islamic Fighting Group (LIFG), Abu Yahya al-Libi was at one point believed to be in line as bin Laden's successor. Al-Libi was 'young, media-savvy, ideologically extreme, and masterful at justifying savage acts of terrorism with esoteric religious arguments'.[56]

In what has become one of the most important strategy documents in modern-day terrorism studies, Abu Bakr Naji's *The Management of Savagery* urges Al-Qaeda supporters to study Western works on management, military principles, political theory and sociology in order to better understand the strategies that Western governments employ and how to exploit American

55 P. Cruickshank and M. H. Ali, 'Abu Musab al-Suri: architect of the new Al Qaeda', *Studies in Conflict and Terrorism*, 30 (2006), 1.
56 J. Brachman, 'The next Osama', *Foreign Policy* (September 10, 2009).

and European vulnerabilities.[57] Bakr Naji advocates attacks on the American economic and financial infrastructure, including tourist sites and oil facilities. But any discussion of Al-Qaeda's strategy would be incomplete without mention of Ayman al-Zawahiri, Al-Qaeda's long-time operational planner who was killed in a US drone strike in Kabul in late July 2022.[58] In 'Knights Under the Prophet's Banner', Zawahiri lays out a two-phase strategy to instigate a global Islamic insurgency.[59] First, he proposes a focus on the 'near enemy', to include the corrupt and apostate regimes of the Middle East. Next, he argues, after an Islamic caliphate is restored in Egypt, it will be used as a staging ground to launch attacks against the West, and eventually usurp the United States and its allies to reclaim its rightful place as a global example of strength and wisdom.

Al-Qaeda and the Islamic State have led scholars, policy makers and practitioners to consider the concept of a global insurgency, united by a core ideology and spanning countries and entire regions. At its peak, Al-Qaeda maintained a permanent or semi-permanent presence in seventy-six countries, 'including those without discernible Muslim communities, but which are suitable for procurement, e.g. Japan, Bulgaria, Slovakia'.[60] Throughout the early to mid-2000s, Al-Qaeda expanded to Saudi Arabia (2003), Iraq (2004), Algeria (2006) and Yemen (2007). It formed franchises in Somalia (2010) and Syria (2012), and an affiliate in south Asia through Al-Qaeda in the Indian subcontinent (2014).[61] Al-Qaeda's expansion occurred in two specific ways – either implementing 'in-house' expansion through establishing an affiliate group on its own, as it did in Saudi Arabia and Yemen, or merging with existing jihadist groups in exchange for an official pledge of allegiance from the group to Al-Qaeda.

As with any organisation that has existed for more than three decades, Al-Qaeda's strategy has shifted over time, with adaptations implemented in response to macro-changes in the operating environment. In an effort to blunt Western counterterrorism efforts designed to disrupt and dismantle Al-Qaeda's command-and-control network, the organisation has periodically realigned its priorities and re-evaluated its objectives, thus necessitating

---

57 J. M. Brachman and W. F. McCants, *Stealing Al Qaeda's Playbook* (West Point: Combating Terrorism Center, 2006), 6.
58 See M. C. Dunn, 'The operations man: Ayman al-Zawahiri', *The Estimate*, 13 (2001).
59 D. Kilcullen, 'Countering global insurgency', *Small Wars Journal*, Version 2.2 (2004), 3–4.
60 R. Gunaratna, *Inside Al-Qaeda: Global Network of Terror* (New York: Columbia University Press, 2002), 105.
61 B. Mendelsohn, 'Al-Qaeda's franchising strategy', *Survival*, 53 (2011), 29–50.

adjustments to its strategy. Al-Qaeda's strategic vision has been a merger of global and local interests. The so-called 'near enemy' is represented by the regional 'apostate' regimes backed by the West. As such, expelling American influence in the region is a top-tier goal for Al-Qaeda and its branches.[62] By attacking the 'far enemy', the United States and the West more broadly, Al-Qaeda seeks to weaken the resolve of the American people to remain in the region and coerce elected officials to push for a reduced presence in the Middle East.[63] Various affiliates have assumed a more local agenda, but as a whole, Al-Qaeda continues to balance global and local priorities.

Al-Qaeda's decision making calculus is less about 'near versus far enemy' and more akin to a continuum. Al-Qaeda attacked the United States to achieve some of its most high priority objectives, including a strong desire to drive the US out of the Middle East and dislodge American support for governments in the Arab and Islamic world that vehemently opposed Al-Qaeda. While it may prefer large, dramatic attacks on hard targets such as the 1998 US Embassy bombings in East Africa or the 2000 USS *Cole* bombings, Al-Qaeda will support smaller attacks on Western or Jewish targets.[64] Al-Qaeda also sees value in striking symbolic or culturally significant targets, such as the 2015 Charlie Hebdo attack.

Initially, bin Laden sought to keep 'Al Qaeda's aims broad enough' so that he could 'create a somewhat cohesive organization'.[65] But by launching terrorist attacks against Western (particularly American) targets, the Al-Qaeda leader was trying to imbue a shared sense of purpose among jihadists. Accordingly, the attacks themselves served a strategic purpose. Bin Laden believed that launching highly symbolic spectacular attacks could forge unity among 'foreign militants' in the global jihadist movement. This would compel smaller groups to recognise Al-Qaeda as the 'strong horse' capable of expelling Western nations from Muslim lands and then turning to focus on what the jihadists considered apostate regimes in the Middle East and North Africa.[66]

---

62 M. C. Libicki, P. Chalk and M. Sisson, *What Drives al Qaeda's Choice of Target?* (Santa Monica: RAND, 2007).
63 A. H. Soufan, *Anatomy of Terror: From the Death of Bin Laden to the Rise of the Islamic State* (New York: W.W. Norton & Company, 2017).
64 D. L. Byman, 'Comparing Al Qaeda and ISIS: different goals, different targets', *Brookings* (April 29, 2015).
65 P. Bergen and P. Cruickshank, 'Revisiting the early Al Qaeda: an updated account of its formative years', *Studies in Conflict & Terrorism*, 35 (2012), 11.
66 L. Farrall, 'How Al Qaeda works: what the organization's subsidiaries say about its strength', *Foreign Affairs* (2011), 128.

In the immediate aftermath of the US invasion of Afghanistan in late 2001, Al-Qaeda still sought to remain the vanguard for change leading to a broader Islamist revolution. But deprived of its safe haven in Afghanistan, Al-Qaeda moved most of its surviving leadership to Pakistan, particularly the areas of Sindh and Punjab; other leaders would end up in Iran, forcing the group into clandestine operations across vast distances and uncertain communications. Ultimately, Al-Qaeda's strategy for most of the 2000s was plotting external operations against the West. Spectacular attacks were intended to garner widespread attention for the global jihadist cause, unite the *umma* under the banner of Al-Qaeda, and drive the United States and its allies from Muslim lands.[67]

To maintain pressure on the West, Al-Qaeda embarked upon a process of geographic expansion, developing a range of affiliates and franchise groups in different parts of the world. Expansion formed the cornerstone of a multipronged strategy that also included 'bleeding wars' of attrition in Afghanistan and Iraq, and devoting resources to cultivating loyal supporters and promising recruits from Western countries, especially in Europe.[68] One of the major strategic debates during the decade following the 9/11 attacks and US invasion of Afghanistan was between those in Al-Qaeda who advocated for a more decentralised approach vs those who believed that a centralised and hierarchical structure was a prerequisite to organisational success. Those in favour of the decentralised approach prevailed, but Al-Qaeda would look to alter its strategy yet again.

In the years since the Arab Spring and the rise of ISIS, Al-Qaeda has consistently attempted to portray itself throughout the Middle East as the moderate alternative to Islamic State.[69] At times, this approach has borne fruit, with Al-Qaeda-linked groups securing direct and indirect state support in both Yemen and Syria.[70] Al-Qaeda's approach in Syria has been compared to that of a 'lean startup model', wherein strategy is developed in both a bottom-up and top-down fashion.[71] For Al-Qaeda, this translates to

---

67 D. Malet, 'Why foreign fighters? Historical perspectives and solutions', *Orbis*, 54 (2010), 105.
68 B. Riedel, *The Search For Al Qaeda* (Washington, DC: Brookings Institution Press, 2008), 121–2.
69 C. Clarke, 'The moderate face of al-Qaeda: how the group rebranded itself', *Foreign Affairs* (2017), www.foreignaffairs.com/articles/syria/2017-10-24/moderate-face-al-qaeda.
70 D. Gartenstein-Ross and V. Koduvayur, 'How to win friends and wage jihad: understanding al Qaeda's pragmatism', *Foreign Affairs* (2019), available at: www.foreignaffairs.com/articles/middle-east/2019-07-01/how-win-friends-and-wage-jihad?.
71 D. Gartenstein-Ross, 'A strategic history of Hayat Tahrir al-Sham's formation', in A. Y. Zelin (ed.), 'How al-Qaeda survived drones, uprisings, and the Islamic State: the nature of the current threat', Washington Institute for Near East Policy, *Policy*

a strategy shaped primarily by its senior leadership, but with input from regional representatives. In both its propaganda and internal communications, Al-Qaeda has repeatedly warned about the danger in failing to heed valuable lessons from failed jihadist campaigns in countries such as Algeria and Iraq. In both of these cases, draconian measures alienated local populations. In an effort to remind Al-Qaeda's followers of the importance of its brand, Zawahiri released the *General Guidelines for Jihad* in 2013, imploring militants to eschew attacking civilians and deliberately juxtaposing the group's methodology to that of Islamic State.[72]

The relationship between Al-Qaeda and disparate jihadist groups can be mutually beneficial. Al-Qaeda is lionised as the vanguard of Islamic resistance (one of its stated aims), and each time an attack is executed somewhere in the world in its name, the Al-Qaeda 'brand' is strengthened and its image burnished among its followers. The group that carries out the attack, for its part, gains the credibility of association with the Al-Qaeda 'brand', and a successful operation can even result in 'follow up funding' to plan and execute future attacks.[73] Retracing the evolution of Al-Qaeda could be instructive for mapping the Islamic State's potential next moves.[74]

As its core group in the Levant has been decimated, ISIS has focused on expanding elsewhere. According to one tally, over the first six months of 2021, the Islamic State claimed 1,415 attacks worldwide, an average of just under 8 attacks per day.[75] When compared to data collected and analysed during the same period in previous years, the comparison suggests that based on figures from 2020, several affiliates have gained momentum – Islamic State West Africa Province (ISWAP), Islamic State Central Africa Province (ISCAP) and Islamic State Khorasan Province (ISK) in Afghanistan.

Focus, 153 (June 2017), 34–5, www.washingtoninstitute.org/policy-analysis/how-al-qaeda-survived-drones-uprisings-and-islamic-state.

72 T. R. Hamming, 'Jihadi competition and political preferences', *Perspectives on Terrorism (Lowell)*, 11 (2017), 63–88, www.jstor.org/stable/pdf/26295957.pdf.

73 J. Marret, 'Al-Qaeda in Islamic Maghreb: a "glocal" organization', *Studies in Conflict and Terrorism*, 31 (2008), 541–52.

74 C. P. Clarke, *What Does the Islamic State's Organisational Restructuring Tell Us?* (The Hague: International Centre for Counterterrorism (ICCT), 2019), https://icct.nl/pub lication/what-does-the-islamic-states-organisational-restructuring-tell-us/.

75 C. P. Clarke, 'Twenty years after 9/11: what is the future of the global jihadi movement?' *CTC Sentinel*, 14 (2021), 91–102, https://ctc.usma.edu/twenty-years-after-9-11-what-is-the-future-of-the-global-jihadi-movement/.

Meanwhile, Islamic State branches in Egypt's Sinai Peninsula and the Islamic State in East Asia (ISEA) have experienced a marked decrease in activity. There has also been a near complete drop-off in attacks by Islamic State franchise groups in both Yemen and Libya, although a claimed Islamic State attack in Zillah, southern Libya, in August 2021 could indicate the group's opening stages of a campaign to revive its organisation in that country.

Even with its physical 'caliphate' in Iraq and Syria in tatters, the Islamic State is still managing to wage a global insurgency, maintaining an operational presence in at least twenty separate countries.[76] The organisation's global diffusion recently led a group of leading terrorism experts to describe IS as an 'adhocracy', better understood as a group of 'structurally fluid organizations in which "interacting project teams" work towards a shared purpose and/or identity'.[77] By maintaining this structure, the group's leaders seek to harness the benefits of a transnational network spanning multiple regions and continents.

Conclusion

The blueprint for start-up success as a terrorist organisation – evidenced in Iraq and North Africa – is now widely known. After gaining a foothold in a failed state or ungoverned region, the group seeks to latch onto a marginalised ethnic or religious group, exploit local grievances, and lend guidance, resources, expertise and manpower to the fight. It is not difficult to imagine the Islamic State replicating this formula in any number of places, from Libya to Afghanistan and West Africa. Indeed, the group has already done so in Mozambique and Nigeria. These countries and regions are awash in weapons and plagued by poor security forces and a weak rule of law, making them the ideal candidates for splinter groups seeking to regenerate and exploit new bases of operations, if they choose to relocate abroad.

In conclusion, what this chapter demonstrates is that terrorists clearly use terrorism in a strategic manner, specifically in an effort to force governments and states to make political or policy changes. The litany of grievances can vary, but the methods of attempting to address these grievances are

---

76 H. J. Ingram, C. Whiteside and C. Winter, *The Islamic State's Global Insurgency and its Counterstrategy Implications* (The Hague: The International Centre for Counter-Terrorism, 2020), 21–46, https://icct.nl/app/uploads/2020/11/Special-Edition-2-2.pdf.
77 H. J. Ingram, C. Whiteside and C. Winter, 'The routinization of the Islamic State's global enterprise', *Hudson Institute* (April 5, 2021), www.hudson.org/node/43763.

frequently rooted in violence directed against civilians and symbols of the state. The most successful terrorist groups of the modern era, including Al-Qaeda and the Islamic State, develop strategies that depend on terrorism, and must co-ordinate attacks across large geographical distances as their branches, affiliates and franchise groups proliferate, posing a significant challenge to law enforcement, security services and intelligence agencies worldwide.

22

The Forty-Year War in Afghanistan

JAN ANGSTROM

Afghanistan has been ravaged by war since the late 1970s. It is highly unlikely that those involved in making strategic decisions at the time could ever have imagined that their actions would set the conditions for over forty years of strife and hardship in the poverty-stricken country. Lawrence Freedman's description of strategy as a starting point rather than an end state appears far more apt to describe the situation in this country.[1] The long war in Afghanistan should also serve as a reminder of too optimistic estimations of the utility of force. Furthermore, it raises pressing questions of conceptualisations of war, strategic practices, the limits of strategic agency, and the interconnectedness of the use and creation of military force. Hence, the war in Afghanistan has far greater reach and importance than has often been recognised.

Beside its longevity, the war in Afghanistan has also sprung plenty of other surprises on its participants, outside observers, intelligence officers and scholars. For example, and perhaps most stunning, despite being propped up by twenty years of modernisation efforts, Western training, new technology and equipment, Afghan government forces offered little resistance against advancing Taliban in 2021 as Kabul fell and the country was swept within weeks. Hardly anyone expected the Mujahideen to defeat the mighty Red Army in the 1980s either. Nor was it expected that loyalties in the conflict would be highly variable as constellations shifted so very quickly.

The war in Afghanistan also serves as an excellent case to illustrate the interconnectedness of different strategic practices. Strategic practice could very well be described as a juggling act of balancing the needs for creating new military capabilities while simultaneously and interdependently considering

[1] L. Freedman, *Strategy: A History* (Oxford: Oxford University Press, 2013), xi.

how best to use and control military force. Hence, the practical strategic challenge for the actors in the war in Afghanistan cannot be reduced merely to use of force. It also involves the dilemmas of simultaneously creating military force, such as whether to have your best commanders in the field fighting or in the barracks training new cadres of commanders. Moreover, to achieve decisive victories you often need to mass forces. However, concentration of force also makes you vulnerable since the larger the forces, the more complex command and control of the forces become. Negotiating these dilemmas while at the same time defeating an able enemy is at the core of every war and the Forty-Year War in Afghanistan is no exception.

Before entering the analysis of the practices of strategy in the Forty-Year War in Afghanistan, we need to address whether it is reasonable to treat the war as one or many. On the one hand, it may seem reasonable to understand the Afghan wars as individual wars and divide them into at least three different major wars: the Soviet War, the Civil War and the Western war against the Taliban. We could make and defend such a position since, for example, the actors involved in the wars and their aims partly differ. On the other hand, it is also reasonable to treat the wars as one long strategic interaction, where one sequence of action and reaction set the stage for the next. In other words, it is unlikely that we would have had a Taliban movement at all without the fertile recruitment grounds in Pakistani refugee camps, and had it not been for the Soviet invasion as well as a civil war between the former Mujahideen groups. From this perspective, over forty years of war in Afghanistan can be seen as one long strategic interaction, and as such can usefully be understood as a single unit of analysis.

Sources

There are numerous sources and available datasets on the war in Afghanistan. Perhaps most problematic, however, is that the sources are rather lopsided. There are plenty of written records as well as data on troop sizes for the Western side since 2001; files relating to the Soviet war effort are also reasonably accessible and the war is well documented. However, there is still a dearth of reliable sources of the Mujahideen, Taliban and other non-state organised armed groups involved throughout the war. There are, of course, numerous accounts made by journalists and scholars who have interviewed key Mujahideen leaders for example, but there is still an imbalance in favour of the state actors when it comes to written sources. Without key documents it is also more difficult to assess the strategic processes of the non-state actors, and how particular combinations of ends, means and ways were reached and later reviewed and modified. For the state actors, the situation is different since it is possible to recreate and analyse the strategic decision making processes in detail. The asymmetry in documentation was also apparent when practically every analyst of the war was surprised by the Taliban quickly regaining power in 2021 as the Western forces withdrew and the Afghan government forces collapsed within weeks. Intelligence services, scholars and journalists alike – clearly – have not had available data or assessed it properly.

The obvious asymmetry in sources taps into, among others, one key conceptual debate on strategy. Since there is a lack of traces of a formal, procedural strategic process and formal strategic documents among the non-state groups, one could claim that these actors do not have a strategy. Indeed, the side-swapping of some of the local warlords throughout the war could be interpreted as short-term, incremental opportunism, rather than a carefully laid out, long-term plan. However, understanding strategy as a formal document directed at one adversary underestimates the dynamic and multi-faceted nature of strategy, while at the same time overestimating the importance of formal decision-making procedures. Hence, when trying to understand the non-state actors' strategy, much is about attributing a particular strategy to the actors on the basis of their behaviour. One should not overestimate this difference, however, since state actors' strategies and behaviour also need to be coherent. After all, written strategies may just be paper products.

Actors, Adversaries and Sometimes Allies

The more than forty years of war in Afghanistan have witnessed a vast number of individual and collective actors. In such a long war, it is hardly surprising that some have endured over shorter or longer time periods. To keep matters in perspective, Barack Obama, former US president and commander-in-chief who led the US war effort in 2008–2016, had just graduated high school when the still leader of *Hezb-e-Islami* Gulbuddin Hekmatyar first led his forces against the invading Soviet Red Army in 1979. Sequencing the war as well as dividing the actors into primary or secondary status provides an accessible tool with which to analyse these actors. Yet, it should be made clear from the beginning that during different phases of the war, many actors including superpowers, regional great powers and various non-state actors have acted as primary actors, while in other phases they have been secondary actors, only supporting those primarily involved in the fighting. The Afghan government, furthermore, has changed hands and form many times during

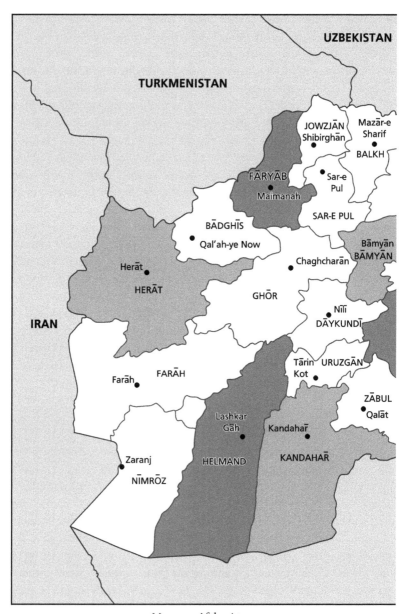

Map 22.1 Afghanistan.

The Forty-Year War in Afghanistan

Map 22.1 (cont.)

the conflict. Indeed, throughout the war the patterns of allegiance and adversity have shifted. A major difference between the various leaders involved in the war is that while outsiders have usually been replaced in elections, most of the Afghan leaders have met violent deaths.

During the Soviet phase of the Afghan War (1979–1989), the primary actors were the Soviet-backed Afghan then communist government led by Babrak Karmal and the intervening Soviet forces that fought against heterogeneous groups of locally organised Mujahideen that were supported to a varying degree by Pakistan and the United States. The Soviets intervened in an armed insurrection that had been ongoing since the communists seized power in 1973 and attempted to modernise the country. The communist programme included downplaying the role of religion and traditional society, which meant that an opposition consisting of a toxic mix of Islamist and conservative tribal values took shape. The resistance against the Soviets did not have a national-level unified chain of command, instead relying upon tried and tested local-level, small-unit ambush tactics. Naturally, the Mujahideen military strategy (even if we cannot talk of a homogenous, across-group, agreed-upon strategy) was a direct reflection of a quite sober military assessment that should they have tried to concentrate force, the overwhelming power of the invading Red Army would have been able to demolish the Afghan resistance. However, by relying upon local allegiances to recruit, create and sustain the ten-year war, an existing localised political order in Afghanistan was further reinforced.

In 1986, Karmal was replaced by Mohammed Najibullah, the former head of the Afghan secret service, in a Moscow-backed coup. The shift signified a turn towards hardliners in the war. To a greater extent than before, the Red Army started to act in larger size units. This reinforced the decentralisation on behalf of the Mujahideen, even if they were slowly acquiring more and more advanced weapons technology from Pakistan and the United States. While the major Mujahideen groups slowly became better at national-level loose co-ordination during the 1980s, it was primarily at the local level that their military forces gradually became organised hierarchically and sometimes even in regular, standing force structures. International support was not evenly distributed, which meant that the variation and lack of national level co-ordination was reinforced. For example, Pakistan primarily favoured the slightly more extreme Islamist Mujahideen groups such as *Hezb-e-Islami* led by Hekmatyar and mostly centred in the mountains and valleys of south-eastern Afghanistan, while Iran supported Ismail Khan whose organisation mostly acted around Herat in the south-west. Ahmad Shah Massoud's *Jamiat*, by comparison a moderate Islamist group, centred around the north-eastern valley of Panjshir, received the majority of Western support.

Despite facing a common enemy, the Mujahideen groups could not work out their differences and once the Soviets withdrew in 1989, fighting broke out between the six largest groups, which meant that the then incumbent government of Najibullah survived for longer than anyone had expected. The heterogenous, decentralised organisation of the Mujahideen that had been the key to success against the Soviets suddenly became its downfall.[2] During the Civil War (1989–2001), even some Afghan government senior military broke ranks and formed their own factions. Most notably, then General Abdul Rashid Dostum, expecting a swift demise of the government and fearing a complete Pashtun takeover, formed the *Jowzjani* mainly Uzbek militia in the north-west. Despite having recently been enemies, the *Jamiat* and the *Jowzjani* quickly agreed a ceasefire to be able to focus on the more immediate war objectives. After the fall of Najibullah in 1992 and during the uneasy, low-intensity infighting between the warlords that characterised the government of Burhanuddin Rabbani, international support dwindled, which added further importance to, and thus also continuous rivalry about, the revenues from the illegal trade of opium. Hekmatyar, who once turned down an invitation to visit the White House during Ronald Reagan's presidency, meanwhile, was occasionally left out of (or refused to be a part of – accounts differ) the major power-sharing arrangements during Rabbani's presidency, which meant that he continued to rely upon support from Pakistan. Hence, during the period of unrest and civil war, the Mujahideen groups continued as primary parts in the conflict, but the shifting sides and agreements upon ceasefires and collaboration in some areas of the country did not prevent them from fighting in others.

The continuous unrest and violence, first during the Soviet phase of the war and then second during the first part of the civil war phase, created a deeply held contempt for the regional warlords among the hundreds of thousands of Afghans that lived in refugee camps across the border in Pakistan. It was in these refugee camps and the Pashtun-dominated southern regions of Afghanistan in the early 1990s that the Taliban was formed. Beginning in earnest in 1995, the Taliban managed to switch from hit-and-run small units in the south to a nationwide campaign with larger size units, and as their campaign progressed, they acquired more weapons, including

---

2 A. Sinno, *Organizations at War in Afghanistan and Beyond* (Ithaca: Cornell University Press, 2008).

tanks and armoured combat vehicles, from the defeated opponents. Eventually, the extremist Islamist movement seized Kabul in 1996. The Taliban never controlled the entire country, though. Hekmatyar – pursuing the same extremist Islamic agenda – never fully collaborated with the Taliban, who mostly left *Hezb* to mind its own business in the south-east. More importantly, the former major warlords that had fought it out after the Soviet withdrawal – Dostum, Massoud, Khan and Rabbani – again united to form the Northern Alliance to repeatedly resist new Taliban advances. Like the Soviets, the Taliban never managed to completely control the north-east.

Among the many volunteers that had joined the Mujahideen during the Soviet phase of the war, there were even some with a more violent and ambitious agenda than the Taliban. Among them, Osama bin Laden started the terrorist network Al-Qaeda. The group found refuge in Taliban-led Afghanistan, and was able to plan and carry out a series of attacks against US targets in the greater Middle East. The attacks on US soil on 11 September 2001 (9/11), however, became a game changer. The remaining superpower, the United States, suddenly went from a rather passive onlooker on Taliban atrocities to a primary actor in the Afghan War. After refusing to extradite the leaders of Al-Qaeda, the Taliban were quickly ousted from power by a combination of US air power as well as ground offensives from the Northern Alliance supported by US special forces.[3] By December 2001, Afghan leaders gathered in Bonn to negotiate a new, democratic constitution. Eventually, it became led by Hamid Karzai. It was decided that Western forces would intervene to stabilise and rebuild Afghanistan after decades of war.

As in virtually all other attempts to centrally govern Afghanistan, however, the allied forces consisting of fifty-three contributing states of International Security Assistance Force (ISAF) soon realised that defeating the Taliban was one thing but rebuilding and modernising Afghanistan a completely different one. After a period of rebuilding, the Taliban renewed hit-and-run attacks mainly in Helmand and Kandahar provinces in the south. Soon, they were joined by new Islamist groups with their origins in the Pakistani tribal areas. Among them was the Haqqani Network, and in the ever-rebellious Kunar and Nuristan provinces, Western forces struggled – much like the Soviets and even the Taliban had done previously. In Kabul, Karzai was replaced as president by Ashraf Ghani, but this had little effect on the level of violence.

---

3 S. Biddle, 'Toppling the Taliban in Afghanistan', in Jan Angstrom and Isabelle Duyvesteyn (eds), *Understanding Victory and Defeat in Contemporary War* (London: Routledge, 2007).

From around 2009, the Taliban insurgency was in full flow. Pakistan's role in the conflict has been as central as it is multifaceted. Occasionally backed by the West and seen as a key partner in the 1980s, Pakistan has received fierce and somewhat unjustified criticism for not cracking down harder on the Taliban and Al-Qaeda when they fled Afghanistan in late 2001. The homegrown Islamist threat in Pakistan is still a problem there. Even the death of Osama bin Laden by US Special Forces in a raid in Abbottabad in Pakistan did not stop the Taliban, who grew in strength during the 2010s while the Afghan government forces gradually weakened, despite Western training and equipment.

Causes

Unpacking the causes of the Afghan Forty-Year War is challenging. Indeed, many standard theories of the causes of war are found wanting in the Afghan case. The war cannot, for example, be reduced to ethnicity, although there have been instances of tension between the majority Pashtun, regional-level majorities such as Tajiks and Uzbeks, and minorities such as the Hazaris. If ethnicity explained the conflict, however, we would not have seen collaboration between one partly Pashtun faction (*Jamiat*) with Uzbeks (e.g. *Jowzjani*) and Tajiks against other Pashtun movements (*Hezb* and the Taliban). Moreover, economic inequalities cannot quite explain the patterns of the war either, although there is a resource dimension to parts of the conflict. The revenue from the poppy trade is clearly important for the economy; not even during Taliban rule was poppy production significantly reduced. Even Western-supported schemes to incentivise farmers to change and grow grain instead were only partially successful, as poppy production increased despite ISAF presence.[4] However, had revenue been the driver in the conflict, we should have witnessed more fighting centred around the poppy fields or at important trade routes, which has not been the case.

More promising, already alluded to, as an explanation of the war and indeed one of the key incompatibilities of the conflict and one that has been present for a long time in Afghanistan is the role of the state.[5] It should be pointed out that the conflict has not primarily revolved around *who* the decision makers in Kabul are, but rather the relations between state and individual, and those between worldly and spiritual power. For the greater

---

4 S. G. Jones, *In the Graveyard of Empires: America's War in Afghanistan* (New York: W.W. Norton, 2010), 193.
5 B. R. Rubin, *The Fragmentation of Afghanistan* (New Haven: Yale University Press, 2002).

part of the country's history, Afghanistan has not been a unitary, modern state. It has not existed as a central power that has been able to permeate societal, economical and social structures in a way that Western states are accustomed to. Instead of enforcing centrally decided laws and decisions, Kabul – regardless of who has occupied the presidential palace – has rather had to strive for the creation of such laws through compromises and a complex web of balancing acts.

Efforts to change this traditional social and political order, in particular attempts to modernise, have been met with great suspicion by many of the traditional leaders in the country. Modernisation programmes, in particular those based on communist ideology, from the beginning suffered a huge image problem in a deeply religious country such as Afghanistan, since Marx famously described religion as the 'opium of the people', something that was 'illusory' and needed to be removed. Modernisation, however, also challenged the traditional, partly tribal, social structure in Afghanistan. Tellingly, and as Sebastian Junger has described, it was not aid, a new road, new schools or the new infirmary deep into the Kunar Valley that stopped the American reconstruction phase; it was the bus line that allowed individuals to travel to Jalalabad to earn their own living and gain more independence that crossed the line for the local, traditional leaders of the community.[6] Modernity, or the threat of modernisation programmes, has therefore been able to unite traditionalism and Islamism in a way that has created a brick wall against the idea of a strong central power. Indeed, not even the Taliban during their first run in power in 1996–2001 strictly enforced all central directives. It was only towards the end of their rule when they started to become more ambitious, something that also failed insofar as recruitment to the Northern Alliance – the former Mujahideen warlords – increased and new local insurrections occurred, even in the south-east Pashtun heartland. Which leader or faction that holds power centrally or controls the Afghan provinces – although not the most important cause of either the outbreak or the continuation of the war – still seems to matter. Neither Massoud, Hekmatyar, Rabbani nor Dostum aimed for constitutional changes during the civil war phase, but fighting between them was still fierce.

Even if it is clear that one central driver of the war can be found internally in Afghanistan, it is equally clear that the war would not have started or even developed the way it did during the 1980s without superpower rivalry during the Cold War. During the 1950s and 1960s, the Soviet Union initiated and

6 S. Junger, *War* (New York: Twelve, 2010).

funded an ambitious modernisation programme improving roads, airfields and hospitals. However, hardly any attempts to export Marxist ideology were initially made. It was assumed that as living standards improved, the Afghan people would be receptive to communist influence. At first, the plan seemed to work although an Islamist resistance started to take shape in the early 1970s, but the coup in 1978 by the Afghan Communist Party was not greeted with popular support. Instead, and as internal Afghan resistance spread, Moscow began to believe rumours that suggested the Central Intelligence Agency (CIA) was operating in Afghanistan and trying to thwart the communist takeover. We now know that these rumours were widely overstated, but at the time, Moscow started to plan a more active strategy. Roughly at the same time, Afghan resistance began to plan for and increase violent attacks against the rule in Kabul. Facing this seemingly double opposition, the Soviet Union responded with escalation and intervened in the conflict in 1979.

Furthermore, it is also obvious that the continued support of the warring parties from outside actors influenced the duration of the war. The 1980s Mujahideen, arguably, would not have been able to pursue the war in the way they did, and may even have had to terminate their war efforts, had it not been for the support from Pakistan and the United States. Besides offering safe havens for training, recuperation and logistics on the Pakistani side of the border for parts of the resistance, Pakistani intelligence services (ISI) also provided the Mujahideen with intelligence on Soviet and Afghan government troop movements, details about the units recycling and assessments of Moscow political developments. In the same way, during the Civil War, Hekmatyar and later on the Taliban received the lion's share of Pakistani support, thus sustaining their war efforts.

Objectives (Ends)

Not surprisingly for a war that has been fought over four decades, the parties' objectives have varied – both along the lines of new actors being formed or drawn into the war and established, long-term actors modifying their original objectives. Variation in objectives also raises more broader issues of the Afghan War. For example, how can we assess progress in the war if objectives shift and change?

The Afghan government in the mid- to late 1970s sought to modernise the underdeveloped country by continuing the large-scale, state-run infrastructure programmes that had already begun during the 1960s. It was thought that shifting the population from small-scale farming to industry would mean that the Afghan population would also realise improved living standards and then turn their backs on traditional leadership and religion. This way, the communist regime would succeed in sustaining its control of the country. As already alluded to, this backfired and resistance started to grow. Eventually, the Afghan government understood that it could not defeat the gradually forming Mujahideen, and requesting aid became important. Soviet intervention in the war was never intended to be an occupation or a territorial conquest. Instead, Moscow's objective was to stabilise and support the then Afghan government in its efforts. Besides the more immediate goals, the Soviets also intended to prevent what was perceived as an increase of US influence in the region. Moreover, and as the war gradually turned into a lengthy, costly campaign in which the religious and ethnic ties with other southern Soviet republics such as Uzbekistan and Tajikistan became more telling, Moscow gradually became concerned that the rebellion would spread into the Soviet Union proper. This was of course unacceptable, and achieving its ends also became a way of signalling to the population of the southern republics that resistance against the Red Army was futile.

One cannot, meanwhile, speak of any commonly formed, coherent objectives of the Mujahideen, besides removing the Afghan communist government and forcing the Red Army to leave Afghanistan. There was no consensus of what a post-war Afghanistan would look like, how it should be ruled or how its resources ought to be allocated. This did not significantly change during the war either, which set the stage for the subsequent civil war phase. Once the Soviets retreated in 1989, the unity of the Mujahideen quickly disappeared and they started to fight each other. Indeed, this even prolonged the Soviet puppet Najibullah's reign until 1992. The warlords fell out due to differing objectives along both ideological and ethnic lines. Dostum had perhaps the most outspoken ethnic agenda in attempting to protect the Uzbek minority in the north, but never ventured south to Kabul to seize government power on his own. In a similar way, Ishmail Khan was rather trying to protect the Herat province, but did not participate in the race for Kabul. Instead, Hekmatyar on the one side and Massoud and Rabbani on the other fought each other and Najibullah for central power, attempting to take over Kabul. Hekmatyar's objective was to introduce a strict Islamist society, while Massoud and Rabbani were slightly more moderate. As the Civil War progressed without any clear decisive victories, the Taliban – with similar (yet even harsher) Islamist political objectives to Hekmatyar – entered the fray. Upon defeating and partially assimilating Hezb in the south-east, the Taliban managed to defeat or strike deals with warlord after warlord, finally seizing Kabul in 1996. The remains of Massoud's and Rabbani's Mujahideen as well as Dostum quickly reverted to the old Afghan way of war, of hit-and-run tactics and ambushes. In the process, they also adapted their more immediate military strategic objectives into defending the north-east with the Panjshir Valley and its inaccessible mountain ranges at its centre.

While the more immediate goals of the Taliban when in power centred around the rule of Afghanistan, including introducing sharia, reinforcing its grip on the Pashtun ethnic group and defeating the Northern Alliance, its long-term objectives were more ambitious – among them, to encourage Taliban-inspired movements in Pakistan, seize control of its nuclear weapons and thus decrease the likelihood of Great Power interventions. One of the significant obstacles for this plan was the lack of legitimacy of the Taliban among the wider Pashtun ethnic group, since the Taliban was not broadly recruited from its traditional strong tribal families. The Karzai family, for example, was far more respected and had belonged to the Pashtun elites for hundreds of years. Still, attempting to instigate rebellion of the second largest ethnic group in Pakistan was tempting. Another major long-term goal of course was the defeat of the United States – long considered to be a cause of undermining traditional Muslim values in the world. For these purposes, the Taliban had no major problems with harbouring Al-Qaeda, which at the time had begun to target US military assets around the world, while planning 9/11.

The 9/11 attacks prompted the US to intervene directly in the war in Afghanistan. At first only requiring the Taliban government to extradite Al-Qaeda leadership, the Bush administration quickly raised its ambitions when the Taliban refused. The US's early objectives became to topple the Taliban regime and kill or capture Al-Qaeda leadership echelons. Relatively quickly, however, it was also realised that the US would have to oversee a regime change in the Afghan government. Massoud had been assassinated by Al-Qaeda just days before 9/11, but Rabbani took control of a provisory government when the Taliban were unceremoniously ousted, while negotiations in Bonn at the end of 2001 were intended to form a more stable constitution and democratic rule in Afghanistan. The failure to capture Osama bin Laden, however, set the stage for a prolonged US presence in Afghanistan, and in doing so the US also modified its objectives. Gradually, the US began to form its objectives around 'nation-building' and liberal values such as rule of law, market economy and democracy – and the rest of NATO followed suit.[7] Turning Afghanistan

---

7 S. Rynning, *NATO in Afghanistan: The Liberal Disconnect* (Stanford: Stanford University Press, 2012).

into a stable state showed a marked increase in ambition from the US and its allies, and it was further reinforced by a neoconservative agenda of turning the entire Middle East into democracies. While the US had relatively clear objectives in Afghanistan, the situation was far from similar for its allies. In many European capitals, political decision makers effectively abstained in forming objectives for their participation besides the too vague to shape military strategy 'support the US' or acting as a good NATO ally without further specification. By making partaking in war the objective of war, many Western capitals effectively confused the ends, means and ways of strategy.[8]

The prolonged and increased Western presence in Afghanistan also created the conditions for a resurgence of the Taliban. Able to tap into the same networks of support and political sentiments in western Pakistan that created the Taliban a mere ten years earlier, the Taliban slowly rebuilt their military capabilities and again started to operate in Afghanistan, first in the southern provinces and gradually nationwide. Yet, it was not as easy for the Taliban to organise for war against the West as it had been ten years earlier. This time, due to Western supremacy in surveillance, command and control, it was difficult to combine movement with geographical reach. Rather than organising hierarchically, the Taliban had to issue strategic-level directives, while giving local and provincial commanders leeway to strike deals whenever local or tribal interests were in line with the Taliban. This was effective since it 'allowed the Taliban to partner with individuals and organizations beyond the Pashtun south'.[9] As before, they were also supported on the Pakistani side of the border by the Haqqani network and a growing number of Pakistani Taliban. The objective, on both sides of the border, was to expel Western forces and seize control of the governments. After initial successes, Western forces started a strategy of rebuilding, equipping and training Afghan government forces.

Available Means

Even if the AK-47, the RPG and the stinger missile symbolised the Mujahideen struggle against the Hind MI-24 attack helicopter and main battle tanks of the Red Army during the 1980s, telling the story of the Afghanistan War through its weapons technology would miss key elements of the means of warfare. Most importantly, the force structure of the belligerents is

---

8 J. Angstrom, 'Contribution warfare: Sweden's lessons from the war in Afghanistan', *Parameters*, 50 (2020), 61–72.
9 R. Johnson, *The Afghan Way of War: How and Why they Fight* (Oxford: Oxford University Press, 2012), 279.

arguably more important. The Mujahideen faced the regular force posture of armoured regiments of the Soviets with much smaller units, rarely even fighting in company size in a concentrated manner. The smaller yet flexible organisation of the Mujahideen fitted their tactics like a glove. Ambushes occurred in which platoon-size units were dispersed but co-ordinated in a way that one squad attacked and stopped the front of an armoured convoy, another attacked the rear of the convoy where the softer targets often were, and the final squad protected the others' escape by pinning down the Soviets with fire from a third angle. This was often the modus operandi, a form of warfare which required little formal command or control hierarchy, little extended logistics or intelligence gathering, and little of the co-ordination sorely needed if fighting in larger units. It also meant that the units could quickly assemble and disperse before and after ambushes.

The Soviets, meanwhile, started out lightly equipped since their initial military strategy was to support the Afghan government in much the same way that ISAF and the US would try to implement its counterinsurgency strategy some twenty-five years later. The units were initially assembled from soldiers mainly from the southern Soviet republics, since it was thought that they would be culturally more attuned to the situation in Afghanistan. Gradually, however, as Ivan Arreguin-Toft has demonstrated, the Soviets became under pressure from two directions.[10] First, increasing levels of desertion due to the appalling conditions of the Red Army made Moscow nervous about the conflict spreading into the Soviet Union proper. Second, the losses gradually also took their toll, and many Soviet soldiers and officers informally complained about the lack of armoured protection from small arms fire. In the mid-1980s, this prompted a Soviet change of strategy, in which armoured units from Russia were sent to relieve the infantry regiments. At the same time, new artillery units and more attack helicopters were sent. This allowed the Soviets to change tactics and use a far more heavy-handed approach, with extensive bombardments up valleys and mountain sides before entering with armoured units. It should be pointed out that the Soviet Union never committed its full strength in Afghanistan. At the most, some 115,000 troops were stationed in Afghanistan out of a total armed forces of around 5,500,000 during the 1980s. For the Soviet Union the Afghan War was limited, while for the Mujahideen it was existential.

10 I. Arreguin-Toft, *How the Weak Win Wars: A Theory of Asymmetric War* (Cambridge: Cambridge University Press, 2005).

Once the Soviets retreated, and during the civil war phase, the warlords were able to obtain much abandoned materiel including tanks and artillery. During the battle for Kabul, regular equipped battalion-size units fought each other with heavy equipment, and the city was shelled repeatedly over the subsequent years, leading some 75 per cent of its inhabitants to flee the city. As the Civil War raged on, however, the Mujahideen groups struggled to recruit large enough numbers of soldiers to make a difference. Instead, the conflict froze at a point in which neither party could decisively defeat the other, but life was still unbearable for hundreds of thousands of civilians. Battle formations in the Taliban offensives in 1994 (seizing Kandahar), 1995 (seizing Herat) and 1996 (seizing both Jalalabad and Kabul) grew in size as the campaign progressed, with more soldiers turning coat on the way forward, and more equipment being seized. During the fighting for Herat, the Taliban acted in co-ordinated battalion-sized units supported by artillery for the first time, which continued during the battles of 1996 and 1997 when the Taliban conducted co-ordinated attacks involving 10,000 troops.[11]

Neither the Soviet Union nor the United States used all their military might in their respective attempts to subjugate resistance and stabilise Afghanistan. In this sense, the Afghan Forty-Year War has been both limited and existential at the same time. In a special kind of symmetry, the Western intervention in Afghanistan also peaked at around 120,000 soldiers, similar to the Soviet effort, but one should also remember that at most, an additional 100,000 private contractors also operated in Afghanistan during this period. Still, the United States began its Afghan campaign with smaller forces, mostly relying upon Special Forces and air power. The initial success of the so-called Afghan model together with the upcoming war in Iraq effectively put a cap on the US war effort at an early stage. Even if other Western states contributed with troops, it was not until the Iraq War slowly wound down in 2008–2009 that US troop sizes increased significantly. Concurrently, the nationwide Taliban insurgency started in earnest around the same time.

Process of Prioritisation

As alluded to in the introduction to this chapter, we know little of any formal strategic decision-making procedures on behalf of the Mujahideen and the Taliban. Clearly, such decision making occurred, but it is difficult to establish

---

11 A. Rashid, *Descent into Chaos: The US and the Disaster in Pakistan, Afghanistan and Central Asia* (London: Penguin, 2009), 17.

its deliberations in detail. A few things stand out, however, in the non-state actors' prioritisation. First, due to its military inferiority one can question the decision to fight, first the Soviets, then each other and then the West. Surely, at several points in time, suing for peace would have been a better option. However, the ever-available opportunity to garner external support also meant that the Mujahideen, like the Taliban later, never needed to strike compromises. It was always easier to gain external support than to bargain with either each other or intervening forces to broker a peace.[12] This is also evident in the shifting alliances and decentralised military organisations of the Mujahideen and later Taliban.

Second, the strategic skill of the Taliban should be stressed. Faced with a multitude of squabbling warlords, the early Taliban concentrated force and organised hierarchically and centralised. By not attacking Kabul directly, moreover, they could pick off the warlords one by one until only the Northern Alliance was left. They did not follow the same strategy when faced with Western military might. Instead, they fought a classic insurgency, allying with and tapping into local grievances, while still moving in from the south and then west as before.[13] They increased mobility this way, but did not possess the same degree of centralisation of political and military goals across provinces. With hindsight, the Western withdrawal and build-up of Afghan government forces in 2014–2021 was also a period in which the Taliban was able to centralise its organisation in preparation for the major offensive in 2021.

Third, the intervening forces, whether they be Soviets or the West, have never been able to become politically attuned to Afghan society. Both have attempted to modernise and centralise the country, and these attempts have been in conflict with religious and traditional local society. Even the early Taliban regime struggled with finding the balance between centralisation and decentralisation insofar as they never controlled society to the same degree in different provinces and districts. As Ahmed Rashid has reported, there were times when the Taliban's feared religious police came back in body bags and the Taliban pretended that nothing had happened.[14] Even the constitution resulting from the Bonn conference was more centralised than ever in Afghan history. Arguably, war in Afghanistan is not only about prioritising the means and ways to fight, but also about being more careful about selecting ends.

12 J. Angstrom, 'Inviting the leviathan: external forces, war and state-building in Afghanistan', *Small Wars and Insurgencies*, 19 (2008), 374–96.
13 C. Malkasian, *War Comes to Garmser: Thirty Years of Conflict on the Afghan Frontier* (London: Hurst, 2013).
14 A. Rashid, *Taliban*, 2nd ed. (London: IB Tauris, 2012).

Finally, the intervening forces – Soviets and Westerners alike – also had domestic agendas that influenced their prioritisation. Once Moscow started to fear that Red Army desertions could imply insurrections in the southern republics, it started to mobilise and deploy Russian-recruited units instead. Although this solved the desertion, casualties and returning veterans created new problems at home. An already growing discontent among civil society due to the crippled economy as well as the Chernobyl nuclear disaster was perfect tinder to fuel unrest in Russia. While Moscow had been able to deflect the consequences of war when it happened 'elsewhere', rumours flourished about vastly exaggerated losses (tenfold of the actual 12,000 killed Soviet soldiers), drug addictions and veterans spreading HIV in Russia. While never forming a unified anti-war movement, the growing and open unpopularity of the war made Moscow uncomfortable, eventually leading to Gorbachev's decision to withdraw.

In a similar way, it is difficult to ignore the influence of domestic politics in the West. During the early part of the post-9/11 Afghan War, the Bush administration – heavily influenced by the neoconservative doctrine of spreading democracy in the Middle East – launched a war against Iraq. This had little to do with actual connections to Al-Qaeda or Iraq acquiring weapons of mass destruction, and more to do with US domestic agendas. Unfortunately, it also meant that the Taliban was able to reorganise and re-establish themselves in Afghanistan in relative calm. Had the US instead deployed sizeable numbers of troops and begun rebuilding immediately after ousting the Taliban, it could have been a relatively quick gain of legitimacy among the population. The outcome, eventually, may not have changed, but it would have been more difficult for the Taliban to nestle in locally if grievances had already been addressed.

Execution of Strategy

Capturing the dynamics of the Afghan War and thus the execution of strategy is more than merely describing events as they unfolded. Drawing upon an analytical tool developed by Schelling, we can distinguish between the different ways of using force.[15] By differentiating between deterrence, coercion and brute force, we can also plot different ways that the actors in the Afghan War have escalated or de-escalated the conflict.[16]

---

15 T. C. Schelling, *Arms and Influence* (New Haven: Yale University Press, 1967).
16 For a recent treatment of escalation in modern warfare, see I. Duyvesteyn, *Rebels and Conflict Escalation: Explaining the Rise and Decline in Violence* (Cambridge: Cambridge University Press, 2021).

Beginning with the Karmal government in the mid- to late 1970s, the Afghan leadership introduced legal measures and strengthened the secret police, mainly to deter the resistance and gather intelligence about recruitments and organisational affiliation. Once it became clear that this strategy was insufficient and that the state of the Afghan Army was too weak, the Karmal government escalated the war by inviting the Soviets to intervene in the conflict. The Red Army, as was mentioned above, began operations with a near textbook counterinsurgency strategy, recruiting from culturally attuned Soviet republics, patrolling with light equipment, and co-ordinating the military effort with a substantial aid and reconstruction package. The Mujahideen, however, was able to tap into two major political grievances to their advantage. First, the communist political agenda created suspicion of the aid and economic and social modernisation attempts. Even if these were not explicitly directed against the traditional and religious communities, the Mujahideen could exploit those sentiments and worries to boost recruitment and support for their military operations. Second, the presence of Soviet forces made the Kabul government appear more illegitimate in the eyes of many Afghans. Sustaining a continuous, low-intensity campaign against the Soviets thus was not difficult in terms of local support. What was more challenging was finding modern weapons to replace the First World War rifles that many tribesmen would wield. Here, Pakistani and later US support proved important. Following these considerations, the Mujahideen could not militarily defeat the Red Army with concentrated, large-scale battles, but instead opted to convince Moscow that the resistance could not be defeated, and that remaining in Afghanistan would cost more than it benefited the Soviet Union.

As the war progressed and the Soviets gradually sustained increasing losses and desertions, Moscow changed its military strategy into a more suppressive style. The Mujahideen should be defeated militarily and once that was achieved, the Kabul government would be able to continue its modernisation policies. This new strategy implied that the Soviets started to actively seek out resistance strongholds along the valleys. Using suppressive fire from artillery and air power, ground was supposed to be cleared and held. The problem with this strategy, however, was that the Mujahideen were able to spot convoys from a distance and disperse before the artillery even opened fire. Those that were not able to flee were the civilian population that suffered heavily. This, of course, fed the resistance narrative of the Soviets and their Kabul puppets being illegitimate. Even the more precise hunt for resistance fighters using attack helicopters that did take a horrendous toll on the Mujahideen, failed once the portable surface-to-air missile Stinger was gifted to the resistance from the US. Soviet attempts to first coerce and then militarily defeat the elusive resistance thus failed, just like the Kabul government's initial attempts to deter them.

During the Civil War, patterns of conflict and co-operation were more similar to a short-term, opportunistic war of attrition. The various warlord armies (numbering six main opposing sides at times, but when semi-autonomous and sometimes local groups are also included, the real number was multiplied) were all too weak to defeat one another but too strong to be defeated. This set the stage for a drawn-out, low-intensity war that occasionally flared up to entail regular armoured battles and artillery duels. During this phase of the war, cycles of escalation and de-escalation were more short-lived than during the Soviet part of the Afghan War. Once the Taliban entered the war with a sustained offensive campaign that gradually became more conventional as military assets were seized by opponents, there was also a mixture of coercion and brute force in their fighting. Occasionally, the Taliban first opted to negotiate, with local militias offering to join the movement or suffer the consequences, instead of just attacking. Just as the Soviets had done, however, the Pashtun-dominated Taliban struggled to pacify the north-east, where other ethnic groups dominated, and the resistance was able to quickly disperse and assemble once the Taliban attempted to launch offensives.

US participation in Afghanistan has also displayed circles of escalation and de-escalation as well as various military strategies. To begin with, the Western footprint in Afghanistan was limited thanks to a combination of Special Forces and air power, but after the Taliban had been defeated, a reinforced guard unit to protect the provisory government in Kabul was established. In all, the forces numbered only a few thousand before gradually starting to grow and expand to all the provinces of Afghanistan, numbering 130,000 at its peak in 2012 in addition to some 100,000 private contractors with tasks ranging from auxiliary to combat. As this escalation progressed, the number of soldiers in the regular Afghan government armed forces also grew to over 350,000 by the early 2020s.

The brunt of the escalation occurred once it was clear that the Taliban had re-established itself in 2007 and was not only operating in the south. In 2007 the war in Iraq had wound down and Western forces were available to counter the deteriorating security situation in Afghanistan. Inspired by General David Petraeus's so-called 'surge' to defeat the insurgency in Iraq, the US increased troop numbers substantially and began a large-scale counterinsurgency campaign. Not too dissimilar to earlier Soviet efforts, the Western forces were supposed to 'clear, hold, and build'. In this way they would militarily defeat the Taliban in a region, hold the territory and then rebuild infrastructure, establishing schools and hospitals. Thus, ultimately, they would win the civilian Afghans' hearts and minds through improved security and improved living standards.

Although not too bad in theory, the Western counterinsurgency suffered from three major problems that ultimately made the war 'unwinnable'.[17] First, the strategic narrative of the Western intervention was to rebuild Afghanistan and make it into a stable democracy. This narrative, however, was constantly undermined by ongoing violence and, arguably, a mismatch of means and ends.[18] Second, Western efforts were conditioned upon the Afghan state earning the legitimacy of the people. Due to, among other factors, severe corruption, neither Karzai's nor Ghani's government were able to sustain effective government in many provinces. Third, the Taliban fighting together with local allies had home-turf advantage and proved difficult to defeat – even with the increased use of drones for targeted killings. Knowing the local terrain better than the West ever managed, the Taliban copied the Mujahideen playbook and fought the war in a way that was particularly unsuitable for their opponents.

After Osama bin Laden had been killed in 2011 by a Special Forces team operating deep into Pakistani territory, the US gradually started to withdraw the main bulk of its forces and increased their efforts to equip, train and prepare the Afghan National Army to take over responsibilities for security. In late 2014, ISAF was officially disbanded and with the exception of smaller forces that continued to prepare the Afghan security forces, Western forces started to withdraw. In August 2021, the last US troops started to leave the country. Rather than a general de-escalation, the Taliban surprised everyone and launched a major offensive that swept the country, and the Afghan national security forces quickly crumbled.

Conclusion

Famously dubbed 'the graveyard of empires' by Rudyard Kipling, Afghanistan has witnessed war and unrest for over forty years. Nearly two generations of Afghans can only relate to life as it is during war. Expressed

17 T. Farrell, *Unwinnable: Britain's War in Afghanistan, 2001–2014* (London: The Bodley Head, 2017).
18 E. Simpson, *War from the Ground Up: Twenty-First Century Combat as Politics* (Oxford: Oxford University Press, 2013).

differently, war is *normal* for more than 90 per cent of Afghans since available data on the age demographics suggest that an overwhelming majority of the population is below fifty. The idea that war is ever present is difficult to relate to for outsiders spending their entire life only indirectly affected by war. It also raises important methodological and historiographical issues. Can we expect to find or trust archival evidence at all in such a situation? How much of the actual strategic decision making can we expect to have a remaining archival track record when we at the same time can assume that decisions in wartime in Afghanistan are made under time pressure with incomplete administrative machinery and information?

The scholarly solution to the problem has at large so far been to carry out versions of ethnographical research. This has produced some magnificent pieces of research where the in-depth knowledge is extremely impressive, but it has also meant that we know a lot about local-level decision making and local-level consequences of decision making but less about strategic decisions. From this perspective, reading the scholarly literature on the Afghan War, one can be led to believe that war is about combat, rather than about how combat and politics are related to each other. As such, the Afghan War – or our knowledge about it – raises important questions of scholars' conceptualisation of war in general.

War as a normal state of affairs also forces us to rethink our assumptions on co-operation during wartime. The Afghan War demonstrates that allegiances shift within and among what appear to be the main 'sides' in the conflict. This more or less continuous renegotiation has also occurred at local level, which raises issues of strategic agency in war. What level should we observe in order to find out what modern war entails? Finally, war as a normal condition also invites us to reconsider how we separate war from peace in time and space. Clausewitz's old dictum that results are never final in war,[19] was always a reminder of the fact that politics never ends in or after war, but bearing in mind the Afghan Forty Year War, should we also read it as: wars are never final?

---

19 Carl von Clausewitz, *On War*, Michael Howard and Peter Paret (trans.) (Princeton: Princeton University Press, 1976).

23
The Three Gulf Wars and Iraq

AHMED S. HASHIM

Sources

This chapter addresses three wars that have taken place in the Persian Gulf within the last forty years. All of them involved Baathist Iraq under Saddam Hussein. The first Gulf War, more often known as the Iran–Iraq War (1980–1988) was an eight-year war between Iraq and the Islamic Republic of Iran (IRI). The second Gulf War (1990–1991) had two distinct phases: the Iraqi invasion and occupation of Kuwait in August 1990, and the American-led international coalition to evict Iraq from Kuwait in Operation Desert Storm in 1991. The third Gulf War (2003) was overwhelmingly an American war against Iraq.

At one point, sources for the Iran–Iraq War (1980–1988) were few and far between. Historians Williamson Murray and Kevin Woods, who wrote the definitive book in English on that war, stated that it was 'one of the least documented conventional conflicts in the twentieth century'.[1] The war was 'remote'; few in the West cared to address its causes, adopted strategies and military lessons. The poor military performance of both belligerents inspired little desire to study the Iran–Iraq War. The extensive use of chemical weapons and ballistic missiles barely caught the attention of outsiders, and when it did, it was only to lament the futility of the war and the 'callousness' of its 'irrational' leaders who would utilise such 'unethical' weapons. Few journalists showed much interest in venturing onto the battlefields of the Iran–Iraq War; the few who did were carefully 'minded' by their respective hosts. The war produced a few early studies that were short on primary

---

The views expressed here are solely those of Ahmed S. Hashim and not those of the institutions with which he is affiliated.

[1] W. Murray and K. Woods, *The Iran–Iraq War: A Military and Strategic History* (Cambridge: Cambridge University Press, 2014), xi.

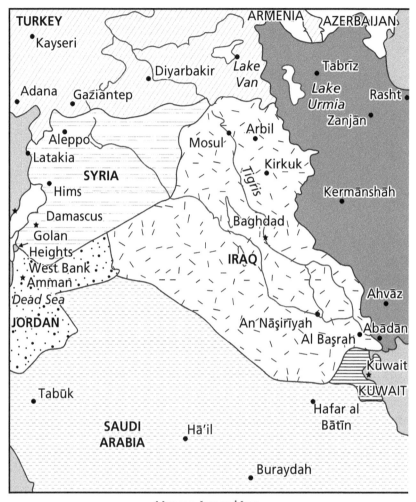

Map 23.1 Iraq and Iran.

sources and research in the field, but for many years these were the only available sources of information on that war. Later these were joined by a greater number of studies based on recently available primary sources and interviews of participants in the war.[2]

2 A. Cordesman and A. Wagner, *The Lessons of Modern War*, Volume II: *The Iran–Iraq War* (Boulder: Westview Press, 1990); S. Zabih, *The Iranian Military in Revolution and War* (London: Routledge, 1988); A. Tucker-Jones, *The Iran–Iraq War: The Lion of Babylon 1980–1988* (Barnsley: Pen and Sword, 2018); P. Razoux, *The Iran–Iraq War* (Cambridge, MA: Belknap Press of Harvard University Press, 2015); Murray and Woods, *Iran–Iraq War*.

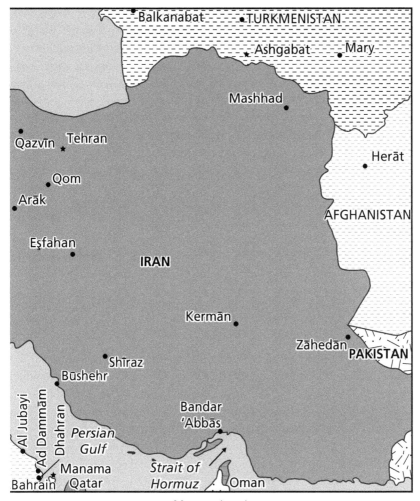

Map 23.1 (cont.)

Better knowledge of the workings of the Baathist regime following its downfall in 2003 provided greater insight into Iraqi strategy for war against the revolutionary regime in Iran.[3] Iran itself has produced an enormous amount of literature on the war, which it refers to as Holy Defence (*defa moqaddas*) or the 'imposed war' (*jang-e-tahmili*). While most of this is about military strategy and operational matters, as decisions at the highest levels

3 Murray and Woods, *Iran–Iraq War*.

have not been discussed in detail, we have enough to assess the Iranian leadership's decisions concerning the war. Until we have more access to Iranian deliberations on the war, a definitive study of that war is still distant.

The sources on Desert Storm (1991) and Operation Iraqi Liberation (2003) from both sides of the two wars are extensive. First, except for the still classified documents, there is considerable documentation on the US decision making and strategies for both operations. Second, despite the destruction of millions of records on the eve of war by the regime and during the war itself by looters, the overthrow of the Iraqi regime in 2003 allowed researchers to gain access to decades worth of documents of the Baathist regime's policies, allowing for the study of the decision making procedures and strategies of the Baathist regime across all three Gulf wars. Murray and Woods, with their collaborators, created a series of remarkable products on Iraqi strategic thinking and practice through their interviews with several senior Iraqi officers who had participated in every Gulf war. Hal Brands and David Palkki have also accessed Iraqi government documents to write a series of articles on Iraqi decision making on the Iran–Iraq War and bilateral Iraqi–US relations.[4]

Actors and Adversaries

The key countries involved in the three Gulf wars, namely Iraq, Iran and the United States, had vastly different political systems and that, of course, determined who were the main decision makers in each country. However, the three Gulf wars are associated with the names of Saddam Hussein, Ayatollah Khomeini, George H. W. Bush, and George W. Bush.

When the nationalist and secular Baathist regime took over in 1968, the young Saddam Hussein was already a key player. He gradually climbed up the ladder of power through the simple expedient of shooting his opponents dead. With Saddam Hussein's elevation to the presidency, which was consolidated by the public denunciation and then execution of twenty-one senior members of the Baath Party, all brakes on Saddam Hussein's future excesses in power were removed.

The formulation and implementation of Iraqi strategy in all three wars were dominated by one single individual at its apex: Saddam Hussein

[4] See H. Brands, 'Why did Saddam invade Iran? New evidence on motives, complexity, and the Israel factor', *Journal of Military History*, 75 (2011), 861–85; H. Brands, 'Saddam and Israel: what do the new records reveal?', *Diplomacy and Statecraft*, 22 (2011), 500–20; H. Brands, 'Saddam Hussein, the United States, and invasion of Iran: was there a green light?', *Cold War History*, 12 (2012), 319–43; H. Brands and D. Palkki, '"Conspiring Bastards": Saddam Hussein's strategic views of the United States', *Diplomatic History*, 36 (2012), 625–59.

al-Tikriti.[5] A Central Intelligence Agency (CIA) study on Baathist Iraq stated, 'Saddam totally dominated the Regime's strategic decision making'.[6] His world view – heavily skewed by conspiratorial thinking that affected strategic practice – was what mattered in Iraq.[7] In each of these Gulf wars that turned out to be disastrous for Iraq, Saddam Hussein was not aided by a group of policy or military advisers willing to suggest a wide range of strategic policy options for the dictator to consider. Saddam Hussein was the ultimate 'decider', although he would often make a pretence of inviting discussion of a decision he was about to take. Given the Iraqi leader's unbending belief in the rectitude and correctness of his goals and courses of action, few within the top echelon of the ruling elite were willing to challenge him; to do so could adversely affect their careers or their lives. The group that was closest to him, those at the highest levels of government, remained remarkably consistent in terms of its size, composition and values between the years 1979 and 2003.[8]

Iran's system was vastly different. With the overthrow of the Shah in 1979, Ayatollah Khomeini emerged as the paramount political and spiritual leader of a theocracy, the IRI, with a myriad set of convoluted institutions often working at cross purposes. Ayatollah Khomeini stood at the apex of the political system by virtue of having been the man who overthrew the powerful Pahlavi dynasty and by his position as supreme political and spiritual leader. While Khomeini undoubtedly dominated the new theocracy, there was none of the monumental personality cult that existed in Iraq. Even after it had consolidated power against its myriad internal enemies, the IRI was a highly factionalised system with the various Islamist circles competing over the contours of domestic, foreign and security policies.[9]

---

5 F. A. Jabbar, A. Shikara and K. Sakai, *From Storm to Thunder: Unfinished Showdown Between Iraq and U.S.* (Tokyo: Institute of Developing Economies, 1998), 1–28.
6 'Regime Strategic Intent', *Global Security*, www.globalsecurity.org/wmd/library/repo rt/2004/isg-report_key_findings_30sep04.pdf.
7 On Saddam Hussein's world view and strategic thinking, see A. Baram, 'Saddam Hussein: a political profile', *Jerusalem Quarterly* (1980), 115–44 and 'Saddam Husayn and Nasirism (1968–2000)', *Orient*, 41 (2000), 461–71; O. Bengio, *Saddam's Word: Political Discourse in Iraq* (Oxford: Oxford University Press, 2002); Murray and Woods, *Iran–Iraq War*, 33–7. For hagiographic biographies, see F. Matar, *Saddam Hussein: The Man, The Cause and the Future* (London: Third World Centre, 1981) and Ch. Saint-Prot, *Un Gaullisme Arabe?* (Paris: Albin Michel, 1987).
8 K. Woods and M. Stout, 'Saddam's perceptions and misperceptions: the case of 'Desert Storm', *Journal of Strategic Studies*, 33 (2010), 8; S. Hosmer, *Why the Iraqi Resistance to the Coalition Invasion Was So Weak* (Santa Monica: RAND, 2007), 7–29.
9 E. P. Rakel, *Power, Islam, and Political Elite in Iran: A Study on the Iranian Political Elite from Khomeini to Ahmadinejad* (Leiden: Brill, 2009).

These competing factions, however, needed the imprimatur of the supreme leader for their respective policies to be chosen and executed. This also extended to strategic decision making concerning the prosecution of the war, the *defining* event of the first decade of the IRI. For Khomeini, Baathist Iraq was an 'evil' entity and it had to be confronted. While he allowed the government to shape the contours of the war against Iraq and admonished clerics who interfered in military matters, he would step in when there was vicious sparring between competing views on how to prosecute the war. This happened in 1981, when he ousted the then president, Abol Hasan Bani-Sadr, who was immersed in a deep conflict with Khomeini acolytes in the government concerning military strategy and which element of the armed forces – the regular military or the newly created Islamic Revolutionary Guards Corps – would take the lead in formulating and conducting military operations.

Khomeini's views were also the deciding factor in Iran prosecuting the war into Iraqi territory after Iran's victories in mid-1982 resulted in the ejection of Iraqi forces from Iranian territory. In the summer of 1982, flush with victory, the senior leadership debated the merits of taking the war onto Iraqi territory. The debate ended when Khomeini came down on the side of those committed to prosecuting the war into Iraq to overthrow the Baathist regime. The euphoria evaporated when Iraq did not succumb, following the bloody failures of Iranian offensives from late 1982 to 1985. When it became obvious, even to the most committed, that Iran's war effort was faltering in early 1988, many senior Iranian decision makers became focused on an 'exit' strategy from the war.

Once Iran suffered major battlefield defeats in the spring and summer of 1988, officials told Ayatollah Khomeini that Iran could no longer prosecute the war effectively due to horrendous personnel and materiel losses. Iran's objective to oust the regime in Iraq could not be met: the ways and means available could no longer sustain that ambitious goal. Officials and military officers outlined what resources Iran would need to continue prosecuting the war and concluded that these resources were not within Iran's grasp. The list of requirements may have been overinflated to reinforce the view that Iran's objectives could not be achieved under the prevailing conditions. While senior officials, even those who had formerly supported the war, could recommend an end to it, only Khomeini had the authority and power to take this monumental decision, and did so reluctantly when he accepted United Nations Security Resolution 598, which put into effect a ceasefire on 20 August 1988.

In the second Gulf War (1990–1991), the main Iraqi actor, of course, remained Saddam Hussein, who had emerged unscathed from the ruinous first Gulf War. If anything, his 'success' in the first Gulf War by forcing Iran to accept a ceasefire seemed to confirm in him the soundness of his path and reinforced his belief in Iraq's military power. In the second Gulf War, Iraq found itself facing a country, the United States, that it understood even less than its neighbour, Iran. Saddam Hussein's views of the United States were marred by a thoroughly negative perception of the superpower. He saw the United States as an enemy of Iraq and of the Arabs; the Americans were 'conspiring bastards', engaged in all sorts of policies designed to hold back Iraq and the Arab world.[10] Saddam Hussein became his own analyst of Iraq's most formidable foe, a country whose power he failed to comprehend and whose resilience in war he underestimated, even as he simultaneously pointed admiringly to its technological and scientific achievements.[11]

Iraq faced the world's strongest military power but also an implacable foe in the administration of George H. W. Bush, which had come into office in 1989. Bush was an accomplished politician who had served in Congress and as vice president under Ronald Reagan. He had solid foreign policy credentials gained from service as US ambassador at the UN, which was also compounded by considerable knowledge of the Middle East. Furthermore, a stint at the CIA as director had given him an ability to read intelligence effectively and to understand its relevance to decision making at the strategic level.

Bush was ably served by a robust group of pragmatic national security experts and officials, including Brent Scowcroft, the national security adviser, James Baker, the secretary of state, Richard Cheney, the secretary of defense, and General Colin Powell, the chairman of the Joint Chiefs of Staff. Below them were the second and third echelon of policy makers, diplomats, military officers and intelligence personnel who provided them with information and formulated the possible courses of action. That they were not all necessarily on the same sheet of music was to be expected. Despite concerns about potentially heavy casualties at the hands of what proved to be an overrated Iraqi military, the administration got the Congress and the American public on board.

President Bush was the decision maker and actively participated in the proceedings concerning the Kuwait crisis once he had made up his mind that the Iraqi occupation of Kuwait would not stand. Furthermore, once the decision was made to use offensive force to eject the Iraqis from Kuwait in late October 1990, he saw to it that the US military was provided with the requisite forces to do the job. Bush also proved adept at international diplomacy: he

10 Brands and Palkki, 'Conspiring Bastards'.   11 Brands and Palkki, 'Conspiring Bastards'.

persuaded first the United Nations to unequivocally condemn the Iraqi action, and second a skittish and conservative Saudi Arabia to do the unthinkable and accept tens of thousands of US troops, though there was no sign of an impending Iraqi invasion. Saudi Arabia thought it was best to move forwards based on a worst-case scenario that was ably assisted by alarmist US reports about the allegedly offensive disposition of Iraqi troops on the Saudi border.

In the third Gulf War (2003), Iraq under Saddam Hussein again faced the US, but this time it was a US administration headed by one of George H. Bush's sons, George W. Bush. Saddam Hussein's views had remained essentially unaffected over the years; the tight vice on Iraq in the shape of sanctions and military attacks by Western forces reinforced his conspiratorial stance even as he tried to seek compromise with his enemies so that he could remain in power.

Throughout the 1990s, Iraq continued to be a thorny problem for the US. Despite vociferous calls in the waning days of the Clinton administration for 'regime change' in Iraq, the incoming Bush administration began by maintaining the previous administration's robust containment of Iraq. While the Bush administration was in favour of ending the Iraqi regime, no active plan for regime change was envisioned. Contrary to popular perceptions, the administration was not decidedly ideological when it came into office in January 2001, although it contained many ideologues who preached the virtues of American military might and extolled the country as a 'force for good' around the globe. Given the military preponderance of America in its unipolar moment, the administration was very optimistic about what the US could accomplish with this might. They were waiting for the opportunity to unleash that instrument.

The Al-Qaeda terrorist attack on American soil on 11 September 2001 (9/11) changed everything. The views of the realists, such as Colin Powell, now secretary of state, who advocated caution and co-ordination with the international community, receded and the views of those who advocated regime change in Iraq and more far-reaching changes in the Middle East came to the fore. They believed that the finely honed US military was the way to do it. By some convoluted logic, Saddam Hussein's Iraq went from being an irritating problem in the region to an existential threat that had to be removed. Most accounts of the decision-making process leading up to the invasion and occupation of Iraq in March 2003 have stressed the importance of key administration officials such as Dick Cheney, the vice president – who had now moved from a believer in containment of Iraq to a fervent advocate of regime change – Donald Rumsfeld, the secretary of defense, and Paul Wolfowitz, the deputy secretary of defense.

In many mainstream accounts, George W. Bush did not seem to figure prominently as a decision maker but as someone who followed the proposed policy advice of his key administration personnel. This has been challenged in Robert Draper's massive bestseller, *To Start a War: How the Bush Administration Took America into Iraq*. George W. Bush was indeed the 'decider' and even those pushing for a more belligerent policy towards Iraq after 9/11 have acknowledged this.[12] George 'Dubya' Bush had little foreign policy experience, unlike his father, but his education into foreign policy began *before* taking office and under the aegis of the accomplished but ideologically conservative transition team he had brought together. However, it was only after 9/11 that it became evident that he had imbibed much of their world view that the US was involved in a battle against evil, and that this battle could not be limited to just one set of 'evil-doers' in Afghanistan. George W. Bush readily bought into the narrative that Baathist Iraq was a dire threat to the United States.

Causes

Each of the Gulf wars had specific underlying and immediate/proximate causes.

The *underlying* causes of the first Gulf War (1980–1988) lie in territorial, ideological and geopolitical differences between the two neighbours. The two countries had serious conflicts over boundary demarcation along their extensive borders, including ownership of the Shatt al-Arab river, over which Iraq demanded complete control because of its limited access to the Persian Gulf. For close to three centuries, their predecessor, the Ottoman Empire, which controlled Iraq and various Iranian dynasties, had unsuccessfully negotiated these matters. Geopolitically, the Ottoman–Iranian contest was between two empires over control of the strategically located buffer known as Mesopotamia, that is, modern Iraq. The Ottoman Empire and the various Iranian dynasties from the sixteenth century onwards had serious religious differences, which complicated the situation immensely: the Ottomans viewed themselves as the defenders of Sunni orthodoxy against an Iran, which had gone 'rogue' and adopted the heterodox Shia branch of Islam as its official ideology and religion of the state in the early sixteenth century.

In contemporary times, ideological and geopolitical rivalries between republican Iraq and monarchical Iran under the Pahlavi dynasty poisoned their

---

12 R. Draper, *To Start A War: How the Bush Administration Took America Into Iraq* (New York: Penguin Press, 2020).

bilateral relations. In 1958, much to the consternation of the Iranian monarchy, the army overthrew and murdered Iraq's own monarchy; bilateral relations between the two neighbours were never the same again. Between 1968 and 1975, Baathist Iraq, a socialist and Arab nationalist anti-status power, and Imperial Iran, a conservative status quo power, sparred verbally in diplomatic fora and clashed along their mutual border. Baghdad's propensity for disturbing the regional order, the continued existence of unresolved territorial and maritime disputes, and the tendency of both countries to exploit each other's domestic vulnerabilities constituted the primary sources of poor relations. Iraq was threatened by Iran's ambitions and its close relations with the United States and Israel, whom the Iraqi leadership viewed as the biggest enemies of the Arab world. Iraq tried to take on the mantle of Arab leadership in the Persian Gulf to oppose Iran, but Iraq's efforts to counter Iranian ambitions ran into problems due to Iraq's domestic weaknesses, lack of resources at the time and the suspicion with which its Arab neighbours viewed it.

In 1975, the Shah and Saddam Hussein resolved their differences with the signing of the Algiers Accords. Saddam Hussein acceded to Iran's demand that the Shatt al-Arab be shared in return for Iran ceasing its support for Kurdish separatists in northern Iraq, who were waging a tough fight under their leader Mullah Masoud Barzani. Iranian military preponderance in bringing about Iraq's accession to the accord was undeniable.[13] Saddam Hussein told the German news weekly *Der Spiegel* in a revealing interview that Iraq entered into the 1975 agreement because it was militarily under pressure at that time.[14] After the agreement, Saddam Hussein then focused his attention on the undisputed leadership of Iraq, building up his country's military power and ensuring Iraq's emergence as a force to be reckoned with in inter-Arab affairs.

The *immediate/proximate* causes of the first Gulf War stem primarily from the unfolding of regional events and their profound implications. Dramatic events changed regional dynamics beginning in 1978–1979. In 1978, Egypt opted out of the Arab–Israeli conflict and made peace with Israel. Saddam Hussein believed that it was Iraq's destiny to play the decisive role in regional Arab politics. This is what he was gearing to do from 1979 on; his ambitions were lubricated by the 'exit' of Egypt from the conflict with Israel and by the massive

13 E .R. Hooten, T. Cooper and F. Nadimi, *The Iran–Iraq War: The Battle for Khuzestan* (Warwick: Helion and Company, 2017), vol. 1, 3–4.
14 'Jawohl, wir sind eindeutig die Sieger: Der irakische Staatspräsident Saddam Hussein über den irakisch-iranischen Krieg', *Der Spiegel* (1981), 133 ('we entered this agreement unwillingly and under duress . . . we were at that time under military pressure').

and rapid growth of the Iraqi military machine into a hi-tech conventional military designed to project power into the Arab–Israeli conflict.

Iraq's regional emergence was derailed in 1979. The most powerful monarch in the Middle East, Mohammad Reza Shah of Iran, was overthrown in the Iranian Revolution, which was led by a fragile coalition of revolutionaries running the gamut from middle class liberal nationalists to leftists and Islamists. When the Shah fell, the Iraqis, by their own admission, were pleased. In the early days of the Iranian revolution, Iraq sought to work with the provisional government of lay nationalist revolutionaries in Tehran. Iraq preferred to have a stable relationship with the new Iran as it wished to focus on development and on the Arab arena, where the strategic position of the perennial enemy, Israel, had improved greatly with Egypt's defection from Arab ranks. The Iranians recognised the dangers of provoking Iraq at that juncture. They realised that the tables had turned and that given Iran's political instability, economic disarray, disorganised military and ethnic discontent, it was not wise to entertain conflict with Iraq.[15]

But it was precisely because Iran was seriously weakened that Saddam Hussein felt emboldened to test his neighbour. On 31 October 1979, Saddam Hussein publicly called for the abrogation of the Algiers Treaty; he specifically demanded full Iraqi control of the Shatt al-Arab waterway, surrender of the three islands in the Persian Gulf that both Iran and the United Arab Emirates (UAE) claimed, and ironically, given Iraq's own separatist problems, autonomy for Iranian Kurds in northern Iran and for the Arab minority in Khuzestan.

The seizure of the US embassy in Tehran in November 1979 by 'radicals' with Khomeini's blessing brought about the collapse of the provisional government, and the consolidation of power by Islamist radicals within the ranks of the government in Tehran led Iraq to conclude that Iran was not going to be a 'normal' neighbour with whom issues could be tackled by negotiations. Instead, Iraq saw a revolutionary power dedicated to fomenting subversion and instability in the Arab world. More specifically, Iran's growing interference in Iraqi domestic politics, by allegedly fomenting religious dissidence, a major red line for Iraq, constituted the key reason for Saddam Hussein's decision for war. Iraq was worried most of all about the demonstration effect of Iran's revolution on Iraqi society, where 57–60 per cent of the population was Shia, many of whom were thrilled by the success of the revolution next door. This was too much for Iraq. On 22 September 1980,

---

15 Central Intelligence Agency – National Foreign Assessment Center, 'Iran–Iraq; Deteriorating Relations' (TOP SECRET, SC 00518/1979; declassified 11 November 2006), 2.

after days of border clashes, Saddam Hussein ordered his military to launch an invasion of Iran. In retrospect, Iran provoked a fight with a paranoid regime while they themselves were unprepared to deal with Baghdad's mounting frustrations and failed to discern its decision to transfer their differences to the battlefield.

The second Gulf War (1990–1991) began on 2 August 1990, when Saddam Hussein invaded his tiny oil-rich neighbour to the south, Kuwait. The invasion and occupation of Kuwait by its more powerful neighbour was the culmination of a crisis between the two countries that had been going on for some time. The Kuwait war had both *underlying* and *proximate* causes. Iraq had irredentist designs over Kuwait going back decades, based on the claim that Kuwait had been a part of the Ottoman Empire together with Iraq.[16] Iraq challenged Kuwait's sovereign status on several occasions, following the emergence of both entities as independent states. Iraq had a narrow coast on the Persian Gulf, and its lack of unhindered access to the open sea had been a constant source of frustration and conflict with Kuwait (and Iran). The lack of ready access to the Persian Gulf was demonstrated during the Iran–Iraq War when the Iranian Navy managed to destroy Iraq's offshore oil terminals and bottle up Iraq's tiny navy in its sole naval port of Umm Qasr.

Saddam Hussein's ambitions to ensure the re-entry of Iraq into the regional Arab arena as the most powerful country, following its 'defeat' of Iran, was a proximate cause of the war with Kuwait.[17] The eight-year war had derailed Iraq's inter-Arab ambitions. In the two years between the end of the Iran–Iraq War in August 1988 and Iraq's invasion of Kuwait in August 1990, Saddam Hussein manoeuvred Iraq to take the dominant role in inter-Arab affairs. But there was a monumental problem. The first Gulf War had dissipated Iraq's financial reserves, put a halt to development and modernisation, and left it with a massive army that could not be demobilised since there was no cash to invest in the civilian economy. Iraq needed massive financial resources to recover, ensure domestic stability and implement its regional ambitions. Kuwait's refusal to forgive the enormous debt Iraq owed to it infuriated Iraq, which also accused the sheikhdom of 'deliberate' over-production of oil to keep oil prices depressed. In Saddam Hussein's mind there was, thus, no solution but to take over the world's 'biggest bank', Kuwait, by force.

16 P. Sluglett, 'The resilience of a frontier: Ottoman and Iraqi claims to Kuwait, 1871–1990', *International History Review*, 24 (2002), 783–816.
17 For the Iraqi perspective, see for example, 'Article analyzes Iraq's pan-Arab priorities', *Joint Publications Research Service – Near East and Asia*, 90046 (27 August 1990), 11; translation of Hamida Na'na, 'Historic dilemma', *al-Thawrah* (25 June 1990), 1, 15.

There are no ambiguities about the causes of the latter phase of the second Gulf War. For most of the international community, Saddam Hussein's action was a flagrant violation of international law and a threat to regional and international order. In this context, the illegal Iraqi occupation of a sovereign state was the cause of the war. For the West to allow Iraq's absorption of Kuwait to stand unchallenged would mean accepting the emergence of a mercurial regional 'superpower' with vast financial and oil reserves, and the wherewithal to further its ambitions at the expense of other regional powers, particularly those allied with the West.

The underlying cause of the third Gulf War (2003) was simple enough: the continued existence of the Saddam Hussein regime constituted 'unfinished business' from the second Gulf War. While his overthrow was not an explicit goal of the US-led coalition in 1991, the allies fervently hoped it would happen. That Saddam Hussein was not overthrown was a vexatious and troublesome issue as far as the US and its allies were concerned. Though calls for Saddam Hussein's overthrow were articulated during the presidency of Bill Clinton, it was not until the events of 9/11 that the Baathist regime came squarely into the US sights. The attacks on 9/11, the 'constructed' links between the incumbent Baathist regime and Al-Qaeda, and the belief that Saddam Hussein was still hiding residual weapons of mass destruction from United Nations inspectors constituted the proximate causes of the third Gulf War.

Objectives

Iraq's stated and unstated objectives in the Iran–Iraq War have been extensively discussed. The stated objectives included: (1) force Iran to stop instigating sedition in Iraq and engaging in subversion; (2) stop its calls for the overthrow of the Baathist regime; (3) force Iran to provide autonomy to its ethnic minorities; and (4) return three islands in the Persian Gulf seized by the Shah from the newly independent UAE. The first two objectives were the key objectives.

Some academics believe that Iraq wished to seize control of Iran's oil-producing region of Khuzestan, which is a low-lying extension of the Mesopotamian plains and Arab-populated. That this province was an Iraqi political objective cannot be conclusively proven; it would have been difficult to hold and would have poisoned any effort to improve bilateral relations in the future. Similarly, it is not clear whether another unstated objective was overthrow of the revolutionary regime in Tehran. Iraq may have fervently wished that its military operation could have contributed to this ambition, but the military strategy was not directly designed to achieve that objective.

Iran's objectives in the early years of the war were simple: (1) thwart Iraq's objectives; (2) refuse point-blank any negotiation with Iraq while the latter's forces were ensconced on Iranian territory; and (3) defend itself against internal enemies seeking to take advantage of the seeming weakness of the regime. As the tide turned in favour of Iran in 1982, with significant Iranian military victories in spring and summer, which pushed the Iraqi forces back onto Iraqi territory, Iranian objectives became more expansive and ambitious. Those Iranian policy makers advocating a continuation of the war argued that Iraq was on the run and that Saddam Hussein's regime was tottering and faced considerable opposition. But Iraqi resolve stiffened; and the Baathist regime managed to convince most of the Iraqi people that they were fighting an existential war of national survival and not just for the regime's survival. Iraq's original objectives were long gone.

For the second Gulf War (1990–1991), we need to address the political objectives of the two distinct phases – the Iraqi invasion and occupation of Kuwait, and Operation Desert Storm – separately for the sake of clarity.

Iraq's invasion of Kuwait specifically sought to achieve four goals: (1) to resolve its immense financial and socio-economic problems occasioned by the eight-year war with Iran; (2) to further Iraq's regional ambitions and continue a massive arms build-up by invading oil-rich neighbour, Kuwait; (3) to 'wipe out' the vestiges of colonialism by 'returning' Kuwait to the motherland from which it had been detached by British imperialist machinations during the time of Ottoman control over Iraq; and (4) to provide Iraq with a permanent window onto the waters of the Persian Gulf by annexing the best natural harbour on that waterway.[18] Once Iraq's invasion of Kuwait was completed, Saddam Hussein installed a provisional 'government' headed by a puppet. The puppet did not last long before the Iraqi leader annexed the city state and declared it to be Iraq's nineteenth province. This step was undoubtedly his ultimate objective.

The objectives of the international coalition assembled by the United States were designed to: (1) show Iraq that naked force does not pay and nor does disruption of international stability. For the United States, the looming end of the Cold War was an opportunity to promote the emergence of a more stable world order, one with the US naturally at the helm. An action such as Iraq's flagrant violation of the sovereignty of a member state of the international community did not accord with that vision; (2) defend Saudi Arabia from a possible Iraqi invasion; (3) overturn the Iraqi invasion of

---

18 See D. Hiro, *Desert Shield to Desert Storm: The Second Gulf War* (London: Paladin, 1992), 9–97; L. Freedman and E. Karsh, *The Gulf Conflict, 1990–1991* (London: Faber and Faber, 1993), 42–64.

The Three Gulf Wars and Iraq

Kuwait; and (4) extensively degrade Iraqi economic and military power, which would also severely curtail its regional ambitions.

Removing Saddam Hussein was not an explicit objective. The US and its closest allies did not believe that Saddam Hussein could survive such a humiliating defeat of his military and such colossal damage to his prestige. They had no intention of helping the massive Shia uprising that erupted in the south and central provinces in the wake of Iraq's disastrous defeat in Desert Storm. The Americans hoped for a military coup by a thoroughly disgruntled officer corps to overthrow Saddam Hussein. As George H. W. Bush and Brent Scowcroft related in 1998 when they wrote their overview of Desert Storm, elimination of Saddam Hussein was not one of the defined objectives of the international coalition as it would have created a serious headache.[19] The political objective of regime change would have expanded the military mission and forced the coalition to march into Baghdad; the painstakingly built coalition would have collapsed. Bush and Scowcroft concluded that the United States would conceivably have had to occupy Iraq well into 1998. Desert Storm had been a masterfully crafted but unstable coalition, and bringing it into existence had been one of the solid achievements of the war, the other being the impressive military victory. The conservative Sunni Arab states feared that the one thing that might be worse than Saddam Hussein would be the unstable situation that might follow his removal from power, which Arab leaders believed could be exploited by Iran and its Iraqi Shia allies, both of whom they viewed with unalloyed suspicion. The ultimate post-war objective, for the George H. W. Bush administration and the Arab allies alike was to restore order and stability, and not to impose a radically new order on the region. If the humiliating defeat led to Saddam Hussein's downfall, all the better.

When the administration of George W. Bush took over in January 2001, it looked as if policy towards Iraq was going to remain the same: containment. With 9/11, the 'threat' posed by Iraq became front and centre, to the delight of those who had advocated more robust measures against the Baathist regime. Though determined now to eliminate the Baathist regime, the Bush administration knew it would be a hard sell and thus set about trying to convince the international community of the utter perfidiousness and irredeemable nature of the Iraqi regime. Throughout 2002, the official position of the administration was to aggressively seek Iraqi compliance with UN Security Council Resolutions concerning the inspections regime,

---

19 G. H. W. Bush and B. Scowcroft, *A World Transformed* (New York: Knopf, 1998), 489.

while holding out the possibility of UN Chapter VII action if Iraq failed to comply.[20] President Bush articulated a list of conditions that Iraq must meet if it wanted to avoid military action: give up or destroy all WMD and long-range missiles; end all alleged support to terrorist groups; cease persecution of its civilian population; account for all missing Gulf War personnel and accept liability for losses; and end all illicit trade outside the oil-for-food programme.[21]

These were stringent demands that the Bush administration did not expect Iraq to meet and hoped it would not, as that would derail the goal of removing the regime. On 8 November 2002, following negotiations among the 'Permanent 5' members, the UN Security Council issued Resolution 1441. The resolution declared that Iraq remained in 'material breach' of its obligations to disarm and that the Security Council would afford Iraq 'a final opportunity to comply', stressing further that failure to comply would 'constitute a further material breach', and that in that case, Iraq would 'face serious consequences'.[22] However, most UN members did not consider it to imply 'automaticity' – that is, Iraqi non-compliance would automatically trigger a UN-authorised response under Chapter VII – much to the chagrin of the US.

The Bush administration was determined to take military action and in retrospect, all the diplomatic manoeuvrings were designed to provide a fig leaf to legitimise the march to war. This was evident in the document, 'Iraq: Goals, Objectives and Strategy', which set out the administration's objectives. The first objective was not just intended to topple a dictator but supposedly to build a democratic post-Baathist Iraq, although little effort was put into planning for the post-war period.[23] The second objective was to disarm Iraq of its dangerous weapons once and for all, so that they would not constitute an instrument of Iraqi ambitions and threat to its neighbours and US interests in the region. On 17 March 2003, President Bush issued an ultimatum to Saddam Hussein and his sons to leave Iraq within forty-eight hours. 'Their refusal to do so', he said,

20 Chapter VII of the Charter of the United Nations authorises the UN Security Council to 'determine the existence of any threat to the peace, breach of the peace, or act of aggression' (Article 39), and should the Council consider other specified measures inadequate, to 'take such action by air, sea, or land forces as may be necessary to maintain or restore international peace and security' (Article 42); Charter of the United Nations; www.un.org/aboutun/charter/.
21 'President Bush's address to the United Nations General Assembly' (12 September 2002), https://georgewbush-whitehouse.archives.gov/news/releases/2002/09/20020912-1.html.
22 United Nations Security Council Resolution 1441, 8 November 2002, paragraphs 1, 2, 4, and 13.
23 See M. R. Gordon, 'The conflict in Iraq: road to war; the strategy to secure Iraq did not foresee a 2nd war', *New York Times* (19 October 2004), www.nytimes.com/2004/10/19/washington/the-conflict-in-iraq-road-to-war-the-strategy-to-secure-iraq-did.html.

would 'result in military conflict'.[24] In that speech, the US president once again strongly reiterated the American objective of regime removal and building 'a new Iraq that is prosperous and free'.[25]

Available Means

The states involved in the three Gulf wars had a wide range of means available to them. During the first Gulf War (1980–1988), despite the view of Saddam Hussein as a bully whose first impulse was to use violence to attain his goals, the fact is that he initially sought to resolve his problems with Iran by means of diplomacy with the government of 'lay' revolutionaries under Prime Minister Mehdi Bazargan. As the chances for diplomacy receded, both Iran and Iraq reverted to the use of subversion to undermine each other's governments.

Once Iraq had decided on using the military instrument, Saddam Hussein and his senior circle, including civilian officials, generals and those in charge of the intelligence services, believed that the Iraqi military could take on and defeat Iran. The reasons for their optimism were clear: their army was in better shape than that of Iran, which had suffered terribly following the revolutionary purges and decline in operational readiness.[26] The material imbalance in military power contributed to the Iraqi leader's view that Iran could be 'punished'.

The Iraqis overestimated the readiness of their military and its operational ability to fight a conventional war. The weaknesses of the Iraqi military were deep-seated and structural. The offensive started with an air attack on Iranian air bases, but the Iraqi Air Force proved unable to carry out an air offensive of any complexity. The ground forces fared marginally better but they were not supremely effective, and the Iranians were not suitably impressed or sufficiently chastened to surrender. The Iraqis proved unable to conduct integrated and combined arms operations in which the combat arms – armour, mechanised infantry, artillery and engineers – worked together to achieve military goals. The lack of initiative and flair on the Iraqi side was palpable: commanders were afraid to take decisions without reference to their superiors and the latter without referring to headquarters in Baghdad, which naturally involved informing and seeking orders from Saddam Hussein, the

---

24 'Full text: Bush speech', *The Guardian* (18 March 2003), www.theguardian.com/world/2003/mar/18/usa.iraq.
25 'Full text', *The Guardian* (18 March 2003).
26 'General Military Intelligence Directorate Report assessing political, military, and economic conditions in Iran', Conflict Records Research Center, SH-GMID-D-000-842.

'military genius'.[27] Almost as quickly as he initiated the war, Saddam Hussein began looking for an exit when he realised that his military pressure on Iran was not working. He was baffled by the fact that Iran's revolutionary leaders did not act 'rationally' and 'logically', and decide to negotiate.

The Imperial Iranian military had once been, on paper, one of the most advanced militaries in the world.[28] Now in the aftermath of revolutionary purges, desertions and executions, the Iranian armed forces were in a state of utter shambles. They were distrusted by the new revolutionary government, which nonetheless recognised the need for a military under its tight control. Khomeini realised he needed the former military establishment once it had been purged of the Pahlavi imprimatur and weened away from its dependence on the United States. However, to ensure the security of the IRI he ordered the formation of the Islamic Revolutionary Guards Corps (IRGC), which would recruit those motivated by religion and serve to protect the regime from its domestic enemies of all stripes.[29]

Relations between the regular military and the IRGC were off to a bad start from the beginning of the revolution when they tried to co-operate in fighting the new government's internal enemies. However, matters between them deteriorated when Iraq invaded Iran in September 1980. The initial forces facing the Iraqi invaders were militia, members of the IRGC and a few regular units. All of them fought with considerable fervour and panache against the Iraqis, making it hard for the Iraqis to seize the city of Khorramshahr. Many within the IRI sought to promote a people's war against the Iraqis and to downgrade the role of the regular military. As units of the latter appeared on the front, they fought well and Iranian president Abol Hassan Bani-Sadr extolled their role, much to the suspicion and chagrin of the clerics. The upshot was that Iranian defensive military operations lacked any co-ordination or effective command and control.

In the run-up to the Iraqi invasion of Kuwait, the Iraqi leader sought to bully or coerce the Kuwaitis to give him what he wanted. Negotiations, in which the Iraqis sought this coercion, went nowhere. Saddam Hussein then

---

27 Several sources address the weaknesses of the Iraqi military: Murray and Woods, *Iran–Iraq War*, 52–72 provides one of the most concise and succinct analyses. On Iraq and Iran, see C. Talmadge, *The Dictator's Army: Battlefield Effectiveness in Authoritarian Armies* (Ithaca: Cornell University Press, 2015), 139–232; M. Heller, 'Iraq's army: military weakness, political utility', in A. Baram and B. Rubin (eds), *Iraq's Road to War* (New York: St Martin's Press, 1993), 38–50.
28 On the Iranian military during the imperial era and then the Iran–Iraq War, see Murray and Woods, *Iran–Iraq War*, 72–84.
29 A. S. Hashim, *Iranian Ways of War: From Cyrus the Great to Qassem Soleimani* (London: Hurst, forthcoming).

defaulted to military threats by steadily moving forces south. The Iraqi invasion and occupation of Kuwait was undertaken by the elite Republican Guards divisions, which had been given operational guidance concerning the objective only weeks before. Nonetheless, the operation was impressively executed on 2 August 1990 at 2 a.m., and by the afternoon, the tiny state was in Iraqi hands. The Kuwaiti military was no match for the Iraqi divisions, but the latter failed to capture the Kuwaiti royal family, which seemed to have been a military objective. If the Iraqis had succeeded in this coup, it would have been difficult for the US-built coalition to have made restoration of the royal family an achievable objective.

The international coalition's available means proved to be more formidable than those at Iraq's disposal. Intensive diplomacy resulted in the building of an effective if somewhat unwieldy coalition. Even the tottering Soviet Union, despite its misgivings and warnings about military action against Iraq, was brought around by James Baker to condemn the Iraqi action and cease providing Iraq with arms. International sanctions shut off Iraqi oil exports and access to Kuwait's financial reserves, and cut off imports into Iraq.

However, it was military power that was the most formidable means available to the coalition. Early in the crisis, there was little in the way of hardware available to oppose the Iraqi military threat. Colin Powell ordered General Norman Schwarzkopf, head of CENTCOM – the unified combatant command dedicated to the south-west Asia area of operations – to draw up operational plans for a defence of Saudi Arabia *initially* and then to formulate operational plans for taking the offensive to throw Iraq out of Kuwait and degrade its forces. By October 1990, there were sufficient forces in place to thwart a move by Iraq into Saudi Arabia; the military mission after that was to build up forces for an offensive to take the war to Iraqi forces in Kuwait. The early offensive plans were unimaginative and rigid, which required CENTCOM to come up with a plan to bypass the entrenched Iraqi forces in Kuwait and deliver a blow on the western flank of Iraqi forces – the 'left-hook' – across the desert into Iraq. This plan required more forces, which Bush readily consented to provide in November. By the end of December 1990, the coalition was ready for offensive military operations.

The Iraqi regime fell victim to the belief that it could take on the coalition's military might, even though many Iraqi professional officers must have thought otherwise before Desert Storm. Saddam Hussein thought he could bloody the coalition in an extended war of attrition, similar to what happened during the Iran–Iraq War. In his single-minded focus on the human element of warfare, Saddam Hussein thought that his country and military had greater morale, will and resilience than that of the coalition, which he saw as a group of countries brought together with the promise of material rewards. This was a decidedly odd conclusion to reach for a leader whose recognition of the dire state of his country and its morale led him to invade Kuwait as a way out of his domestic problems. Finally, Saddam Hussein, who had never served in the Iraqi military, had little inkling of the impact of technology on contemporary warfare or knowledge of the enormous changes in the United States military in the 1980s, which had led to the creation of a finely honed all-volunteer and well-trained force.

Early in the morning of 17 January 1991, the US-led coalition launched air attacks against Iraqi targets, which devastated Iraqi infrastructure and eroded the combat capabilities of the Iraqi ground forces. Iraqi air defence proved incapable of dealing with the coalition air offensive, and a significant portion of the massive Iraqi Air Force took to the air for Iran, thinking that that would be a haven from the punishing air assault. On 24 February, coalition ground forces began their attack but not where the Iraqis had expected them. Furthermore, the Iraqi units had been devastated by the air campaign and failed to put up effective resistance. On 27 February Kuwait City was declared liberated, and with allied forces having driven well into Iraq, the coalition halted the war.

The Iraqi military in the run-up to Operation Iraqi Freedom was a shadow of its former self. Its weaknesses were numerous and insurmountable. It had lost vast stores of supplies, ammunition and weapons systems in 1991, which had not been replenished. Its officer corps was disgruntled and there were numerous abortive coup attempts in the 1990s; this magnified Saddam Hussein's paranoia, and he redoubled his efforts to keep tight control over the military, curtailing its field-training exercises. He gave greater powers to fiercely loyal paramilitary units, which could not conduct force-on-force operations against an enemy in a conventional encounter. He interfered in the war plans of his most professional units, the Republican Guards, and then startled his senior officer corps when he told them that Iraq no longer had weapons of mass destruction with which to deter or even fight enemy forces in a coming war. By way of contrast, the US marched into war with a military that had learned solid lessons from Desert Storm, was more technologically advanced and had amassed considerable operational experience from post-Desert Storm operations, both inside and outside the Middle East.

Execution and Application of Strategy

The three wars involved one common belligerent, Iraq under its leader Saddam Hussein. In all three wars, Saddam Hussein miscalculated badly and made monumental mistakes. His co-belligerents in these wars also had their visions and their share of miscalculations. Iran miscalculated badly when it thought its provocations of Iraq in 1979–1980 would have no consequence, and when it prosecuted the war into Iraq in 1982; its belief that it would win was not an irrational one. Iraq, because of Saddam Hussein's belief that the Americans were bluffing about coming to Baghdad and then because he thought they could be conventionally stopped, did not plan an effective asymmetric response. Nonetheless, the US was briefly stymied by a form of fighting for which it had not planned. But it was only later, after the regime was overthrown and the country occupied, that the US witnessed a fully fledged violent insurgency and controversies about whether it had been adequately prepared for what was called phase IV post-war reconstruction.

When Saddam Hussein decided to go to war with Iran in September 1980, he believed that all the stars were aligned in his favour. Iran was in turmoil and friendless; the consensus was that its massive and hi-tech military was in disarray. The Iraqi intelligence service wrote a long report on the state of the Iranian military, which echoed the views of Western observers. Saddam Hussein hoped for a short war in which his objectives would be met. Instead, the Baathist regime had to mobilise the entire society for total war, and had to fight for its very existence.

In 1982 it was the turn of the Iranians to miscalculate when they invaded Iraq after an intensive debate within the government concerning the pros and cons of prosecuting the war further, following Iran's decisive battlefield victories in the spring and summer of 1982. Iran had made a supreme effort to mobilise and co-ordinate forces for these victories, which crushed Iraqi occupation forces in Iran and sent them reeling back across the border. It proved difficult to produce this effort for cross-border offensive operations after 1982. Iranian forces began to suffer chronic shortfalls and weaknesses in logistics, effective mobilisation, and command, control and co-ordination of the various forces on the front lines. By 1985, low morale and questioning the rationale behind the war compounded operational problems.[30] In 1987, the Iranian war machine was close to breaking: the human losses in front of the Iraqi city of Basra, which was bristling with defences, were horrendous; furthermore, the stock of weaponry and ammunition had declined precipitously.

30 Hashim, *Iranian Ways of War*, chapter 9.

For the invasion of Kuwait, it was Saddam Hussein and a very small group of civilian advisers and military officers of the elite Republican Guards Corps that were involved in the goal setting and decision making of seizing Kuwait and then of incorporating it as part of Iraq. Once again, Saddam Hussein gave his senior commanders very little time to set in motion the invasion of Kuwait; this, however, was offset by the fact that the invasion was placed in the hands of the most professional and ready Iraqi forces: the elite Republican Guards. Few dissenting voices were raised within Iraqi decision-making circles prior to the operation and after Iraq's incorporation of Kuwait had elicited considered international opposition. Once Iraq was faced with the presence of a large US-led military coalition geared for offensive action after December 1990, it continued to negotiate for some modicum of 'reward' for its misadventure. The coalition was having none of it, so why did Saddam Hussein not withdraw and avoid a debacle? He thought that he could mire the coalition in a costly and protracted war of attrition, which he hoped would unravel it and possibly cause domestic dissension within coalition members. That would be a victory for him. Finally, it is possible that for him the domestic consequences of a humiliating withdrawal under coercion would be far worse than a courageous stance against an enemy, which he would regard a *moral* victory.

The response of the United States to the Iraqi occupation of Kuwait was masterful and carefully co-ordinated with several key allies, a fact aided by the universal condemnation of and abhorrence for the blatantly illegal Iraqi act of annexation. The US built a global coalition which included key regional states, and transported massive forces to the Persian Gulf, first to defend Saudi Arabia from invasion by Iraqi forces, and then, by December 1990, to take the offensive should the 'green light' be given. Colin Powell believed that if force were to be used, it must be for definite political objectives with the application of force overwhelming, decisive and of short duration.[31] As soon as the objectives were attained in a war, American forces must be speedily withdrawn. Furthermore, the military should maximise the chances of victory as much as possible because of the fear that the US public could turn against a military endeavour if the objectives were vague, and the application of force protracted. The ghost of Vietnam must be laid to rest.

In the lead-up to Operation Iraqi Freedom, there was a contentious debate within the US Department of Defense over the military strategy and forces

---

31 M. Gordon and B. Trainor, *The Generals' War: The Inside Story of the Conflict in the Gulf* (Boston, Little, Brown and Company, 1995), viii.

needed to overthrow the Baathist regime. Donald Rumsfeld was adamant that Operation Iraqi Freedom was not going to be consciously modelled on Desert Storm, in which direct political objectives had been more modest than regime change. The Pentagon's plan to invade and occupy Iraq was in striking contrast to the doctrine for using military power which was developed by Powell. Instead of assembling a giant invasion force over six months, as Powell did in the Persian Gulf War in 1991, the administration in 2003 intended to attack with a much smaller force. This was consistent with Rumsfeld's determination to transform the military so that it would rely less on heavy ground troops and more on technology, intelligence and special operations forces. The increasingly dominant view was that if the Iraqi military mounted a tougher fight than anticipated, which most defence planners thought unlikely, the US could continue to 'feed' in more forces. If the resistance were light, as was expected by many within the administration, the flow of troops would stop. The main concern was to deter and deal with the possibility of the use of weapons of mass destruction by the Iraqis, which most believed Iraq still had.

Many officials worried that the smaller force numbers would be insufficient. They were not really concerned that the US forces would be inadequate for the conventional phase of the war; there was none of the pre-Desert Storm 'fear' or 'awe' of the Iraqi Army. Instead, they were concerned about the Phase IV post-conflict period, warning that Iraq could descend into chaos after Saddam Hussein was deposed. They voiced concerns that the United States would not have sufficient troops immediately after the dictator was ousted.

As the operation unfolded, instead of a major force-on-force clash of arms, however mismatched, the American forces found themselves harassed by small-sized paramilitary units and even occasional suicide bombers. Thousands of Saddam Fedayeen paramilitary troops were using cities as bases from which to attack American convoys and supply lines. The fact that they were not effective was not the primary concern; their very emergence seemed to presage the beginnings of a much more protracted and dirtier war, which did happen and would cause the US considerable problems in the succeeding years after the invasion, making it very difficult to establish a stable Iraq.

In Washington, however, the complete collapse of the Iraqi forces on the battlefield led US government officials to believe that the worst was over. Iraqi forces and the police went home (they did *not* disband themselves, as claimed by some US officials). The Bush administration convinced itself that the burden of occupation could be shifted to multinational forces. Things did not work out that way, but the history of the occupation and the messy insurgency is another story.

Conclusion

Did any of the belligerents meet their formulated objectives?

Beginning with the first Gulf War between Iran and Iraq, Saddam Hussein's initial objectives were quite modest, but he was unable to achieve them as there was a significant mismatch between goals or objectives and ways and means. His military was simply unable to achieve the political objectives. In the early days of the first Gulf War, Iran's objectives were to resist the Iraqi invasion and consolidate the revolution against its enemies. As the tide of the war turned in 1982, Iran formulated ambitious objectives: invade Iraq and overthrow the Baathist regime. It believed that Saddam Hussein was ripe for overthrow and that it would be aided by elements of the Iraqi population. That did not happen, and Iran wasted its resources and manpower trying to achieve an objective that receded into the distance year by year. By 1988, Iran's objective was to extricate itself from the war with the least possible humiliation and cost to the revolution and national security.

In the second Gulf War (1990–1991), Saddam Hussein's objectives were reversed by the US-led international coalition, which achieved its stated objectives: defend Saudi Arabia, free Kuwait and degrade Iraq's military power. As argued above, overthrow of Saddam Hussein was not an objective, so the George H. W. Bush administration cannot be faulted for failure to achieve an 'objective' that was not articulated. To be sure, the failure to eject Saddam Hussein in 1991 set the stage for military confrontation in the future, namely in 2003, but that was not foreordained.

The third Gulf War (2003) was a result of decisions taken by the administration of George W. Bush after 9/11. The US achieved one of its explicitly stated objectives: the elimination of the Baathist regime; and there were no weapons of mass destruction to eliminate as this had been done by the United Nations weapons inspectors. Saddam Hussein wanted to maintain the fiction that he possessed them to deter his regional enemies, namely Iran and Israel. At the same time, he was trying to prove to his major nemesis, the US, that he no longer had them. It proved difficult to square that circle. The third objective, building a democratic society and state in Iraq, was never wholeheartedly endorsed by the US administration, which did not pay much attention to planning for it or providing this phase of 'nation-building' with the requisite resources. Indeed, one wonders whether it was a genuine objective at all, since the George W. Bush administration contained policy makers who wanted to foist a disparate group of Iraqi exiles – whose only common link with each other was a pronounced antipathy towards the Baathist regime – on a shattered nation.

24

China's Wars, 1950–2021

CHRISTOPHER YUNG

This chapter, the second of two discussing modern Chinese strategy, covers the period from the founding of the People's Republic of China (PRC) to the present.[1] A history of Chinese strategy since the mid-twentieth century must inevitably be presented within a larger Chinese foreign policy framework. China wrestling with its role as Communist power and ally of the Soviet Union, its turning to an independent foreign policy, its opening up to the West and then it becoming a strategic competitor of the United States all shaped Chinese strategy. The main actors in the management and formulation of strategy were Mao Zedong as China's paramount leader followed by Deng Xiaoping and then subsequent general secretaries (Hu Yaobang, Zhao Ziyang, Jiang Zemin, Hu Jintao and Xi Jinping) in the post-Mao and post-Deng periods. The Chinese have referred to the post-Mao period as New China, and this chapter will follow a similar naming convention.

The Chinese Communist Party's (CCP) system of strategic formulation has remained remarkably consistent since the founding of the PRC. The Central Military Commission (CMC), and until the 2015 Joint Reforms, the General Headquarters of the People's Liberation Army (PLA) have all consistently been central to the process, involving: the general secretary of the Party providing guidance on the perceived security environment (the Guiding Strategic Thought); the CMC and the General Headquarters identifying the primary threat (the Main Strategic Direction); the CMC and the General Headquarters characterising the nature and type of war to be expected (Guiding Operational Thought); and the military's assessment of the types of weapon systems it will need to develop over time (Guidance to Army Building). China's adversaries have shifted over time, beginning with

[1] Please see Chapter 7 for a discussion about the sources.

the United States and its allies during the early part of the Cold War, the Soviet Union during the Sino-Soviet split, shifting to a period of tension with the United States following the Tiananmen Square massacre, and then settling on the US as China's most formidable competitor and possible adversary from the early 1990s to the present. In between these shifts, China became embroiled in conflicts along its periphery, erupting in some cases out of events related to the larger geopolitical struggles of the Cold War or resulting from particular tensions between China and its neighbours. Of these, the most notable are Korea, India, South Vietnam, North Vietnam and then the maritime conflicts with rival east Asian nations. Throughout this modern history, China's strategic priorities consistently centred on defence and security of its territorial integrity.

This chapter opens with the Chinese involvement in the Korean War and concludes with China's strategic competition with the United States at the beginning of the third decade of the twenty-first century. The chapter is divided into two sections, the first focusing on China's use of force and its military campaigns between 1950 and 1988. Since China shifted strategy in the 1980s and focused on accomplishing its strategic objectives short of large-scale conflict, the second section focuses on that strategic formulation process and the activities that the PLA has engaged in to accomplish those strategic objectives short of war.

Chinese External Military Strategy (1950–1988)

Korea (1950–1953)

Following the Nationalist defeat and retreat to Taiwan in 1949, the Chinese Communists formed the PRC and set out to both consolidate their power and rebuild the nation.[2] At the same time, because the Nationalists had fled to Taiwan, the Chinese Civil War remained unfinished, and Mao Zedong and his military advisers began planning for the invasion of Taiwan. The outbreak of the Korean War and US deployment of the Seventh Fleet in the Taiwan Strait prevented the PLA from militarily resolving the Civil War in the CCP's favour. Before the North Korean attack on South Korea, Mao and Stalin had been approached by Kim Il-Sung, who asked for their tacit approval. Since the United States appeared to have excluded Korea from its stated defence perimeter, both Stalin and Mao agreed. When the United States unexpectedly intervened in the conflict, Stalin asked Mao to dispatch Chinese forces to

2 See also Chapter 17.

assist North Korea. Mao convened a meeting of the Politburo to discuss the possibility of intervention. At that meeting, the PLA high command was close to unanimous that China should not intervene in the conflict. Mao's military advisers noted the imbalance of military capability between the United States and China, the vulnerability of China's economic and international position, and China's status as a new country which had not completely consolidated power. Mao, however, believed that the Sino-Soviet Treaty, which was a mutual defence treaty – and China's position within the larger international communist movement, which, alongside with the Soviet Union, represented the source and inspiration for post-Second World War liberation and communist movements – obliged China to intervene.[3] The late arrival to the meeting of Marshal Peng Dehuai, perhaps the most aggressive of China's military leadership during the Chinese Civil War and a leading candidate to command Chinese forces in Korea, and his endorsement of PLA intervention sealed the decision in favour of intervention.[4]

Mao's objectives were to demonstrate to Stalin that Communist China was a vital ally in the ideological struggle with the United States; a second objective was to ensure the survival of the North Korean regime as a buffer state to a dangerous American military presence likely to exert strong strategic pressure on China's periphery. His strategy was to stabilise the situation in North Korea, giving the North Korean regime breathing space by pushing UN forces south and then eventually off the Korean Peninsula. Although the military operations designed to attain these objectives varied, Mao's strategic objectives remained largely consistent throughout the course of the war.

Most historians of the Chinese participation in the conflict note that the PLA suffered from some command and control difficulties in the conduct of the war. The primary difficulty lay in the difference of opinion between military commanders on the ground (Peng and his subordinates) and Mao in Beijing: the former preaching for a realistic assessment of the situation and then tailoring strategies to reflect that reality; the latter consistently looking for large-scale decisive victories over the allies in order to force a political decision to withdraw UN forces.[5] The five offensives launched by the Chinese

---

3 X. B. Li, *A History of the Modern Chinese Army* (Lexington: University Press of Kentucky, 2007), 82–3.
4 D. H. Peng, *Memoirs of a Chinese Marshal: the Autobiographical Notes of Peng Dehuai (1898–1974)* (Beijing: Foreign Language Press, 1984), 472–4.
5 Li, *A History*, 84, 96–101.

CHRISTOPHER YUNG

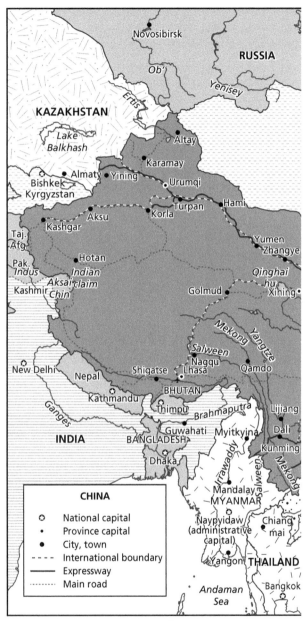

Map 24.1 China.

China's Wars, 1950–2021

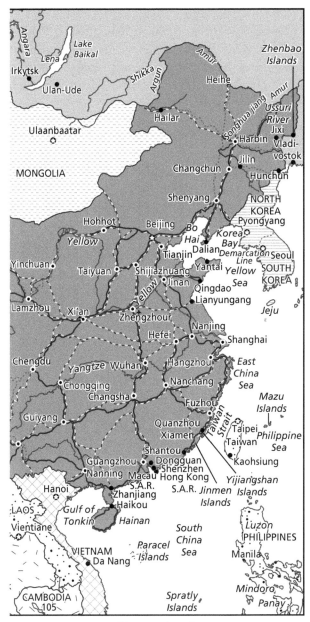

Map 24.1 (cont.)

People's Volunteers (CPV) over the course of the war repeat this pattern. Peng Dehuai largely advocated for stabilising the military situation, building up military capability through enhanced supply and the influx of better trained troops, and only then launching a well-timed counteroffensive. After absorbing attacks from the enemy, China and North Korea should shift to the offensive, and at some point UN forces were expected to reach a culminating point, at which time the CPV and North Korean Army would launch a counteroffensive. With the exception of the surprise attack on MacArthur's forces as they approached the Yalu, this is not how the CPV fought in Korea. Mao repeatedly ordered Peng to engage in large offensive campaigns in battles of positional warfare. None of these had the effect that Mao had hoped they would have.[6] After these offensives ended in 1951, the PLA found itself in a two-year stalemate with the United States and UN forces, forcing a negotiated end to the Korean conflict in 1953.

The PLA subsequently underwent a process of re-evaluation of its warfighting requirements, based largely on its experience in the Korean War. In 1956, the CMC issued a release of its first revised Military Strategic Guidelines since 1949. The new guidelines emphasised the development of conventional warfighting capabilities, combined arms operations and defending fixed geographic positions in cases of an invasion of China by the United States or Taiwan.[7]

Yijiangshan, and Jinmen and Mazu (1954–1958)

By the mid-1950s, China's leadership confronted a number of strategic challenges involving Taiwan. First, the challenge posed by Taiwan's military stationed on the offshore islands in the Taiwan Strait continued to be a thorn in the PRC leadership's side by continually attacking mainland targets. Additionally, the United States had increased its support for the government of the Republic of China (ROC), and Mao feared that recent international diplomatic efforts to stabilise the tensions between East and West would permanently freeze the division between mainland China and Taiwan. These concerns led to a series of military actions between 1954 and 1958. To address the former concern, Mao and the PLA decided to enhance the defensive posture of the PLA without drawing in the United States. General Zhang

---

6 S. G. Zhuang, 'Command, control and the PLA's offensive campaigns in Korea, 1950–1', in M. Ryan, D. Finkelstein and M. McDevitt (eds), *Chinese Warfighting: The PLA Experience Since 1949* (Armonk: M.E. Sharpe, 2003), 112–13.

7 M. T. Fravel, *Active Defense: China's Military Strategy Since 1949* (Princeton: Princeton University Press, 2019), 72–106.

Aiping, commander of the Zhejiang Front, drew up plans for a piecemeal seizure of offshore islands, starting with the smallest and moving from north to south, the initial operations hundreds of miles from the Taiwan Strait and Seventh Fleet units.[8] These were successfully executed, starting with seizure of the Dongji Islands in 1954 with negligible resistance from *Guomindang* (GMD) forces, and then concluding with the large-scale amphibious assault of the Yijiangshan islands in 1955. Owing to significantly improved air and naval co-operation with ground forces, the use of pre-invasion naval bombardment and simply outnumbering the defenders, the assault on Yijiangshan was an unquestionable PLA success. The entire GMD defence force of over 1,000 troops was lost, while the PLA suffered about 1,600 casualties (approximately 600 dead and 1,000 wounded).[9]

To address the equally concerning problem of US involvement and protection of the Nationalists on Taiwan, Mao and his generals introduced the use of long-range shelling of the offshore islands as a means of strategic communication. The first shelling campaign against Jinmen and Mazu took place in 1954 for the purposes of signalling to both Taipei and Washington that the Communist leaders still considered Taiwan an internal affair, and that Washington should not assume that the PLA was unwilling to utilise lethal force to prevent Taiwan from achieving de facto independence. The islands were hit by several thousand rounds, and two American military officers were killed in the barrage.[10] Shelling became a favourite method for Beijing to strategically communicate with Washington on issues pertaining to Taiwan, up until the normalisation of relations between the two in the 1970s.

This form of strategic communication would re-emerge in 1958 when Mao decided to shell Jinmen and Mazu with an even larger artillery attack. Between 1956 and 1958, the GMD had increased military activities against the mainland. In 1958 the United States and its allies were preoccupied with the US intervention in Lebanon, and Mao decided at a CCP Central Committee meeting in July to punish the GMD Army's harassing actions against Fujian from Jinmen and Mazu. In August the CCP authorised the shelling of Jinmen and Mazu for the purposes of blockading the islands: 30,000 shells were fired onto the islands in the first 85 minutes of the bombardment, killing 600 GMD troops.[11] Although initially successful at preventing the supply of these offshore islands, this was not to last. Despite persistent shelling into October, the ROC military figured out how to continue

---

8 X. B. Li, 'PLA attacks and amphibious operations during the Taiwan Strait Crises of 1954–5 and 1958', in Ryan et al. (eds), *Chinese Warfighting*, 145–6.
9 Li, 'PLA attacks', 151–5.   10 Li, 'PLA attacks', 148–51.   11 Li, 'PLA attacks', 158–67.

supplying the islands and the US Navy continued to escort its Taiwanese counterparts. Seeing the futility of this effort, Mao announced a new 'noose' strategy in which the CCP would allow Chiang to retain control over Jinmen and Mazu as a continued noose around America's neck.

The Sino-Indian Border Conflict (1962)

Chinese historians agree that a root cause of the Sino-Indian border conflict of 1962 was the CCP leadership's belief that India was attempting to undermine Chinese rule in Tibet. They have pointed to leadership notes leading up to the conflict which highlight the following themes: Prime Minister Nehru was practising similar policies and intrigues to those of the British; India was lending aid to the exiled Dalai Lama; the Indian government was coordinating actions with the American Central Intelligence Agency (CIA) to erode and undermine Chinese rule there; and India harboured hegemonic ambitions in south Asia.[12] In 1958–1959, both India and China began to expand their military presence into previously uninhabited areas along their border. To demonstrate Indian resolve in the face of Chinese encroachment, the Nehru government announced a 'Forward Policy' and the Indian Army was ordered to execute it.[13]

By early October 1962, Mao directed the CMC to come up with plans to push Indian forces in the eastern sector from the area north of what traditionally had been seen as the boundary. During one of these planning sessions, CMC planners came up with the idea of a unilateral withdrawal after the PLA had accomplished these objectives.[14] In the midst of this planning it is clear that the CCP leadership understood the international effects of a large conflict with India: Nehru had a positive international image and therefore was very likely to be perceived as a sympathetic figure; and international perceptions of PLA superiority to the Indian military was sure to elicit the belief that China was the aggressor. To counter this narrative, China launched official diplomatic protests for almost a year, along with authoritative *People's Daily* commentaries denouncing India's aggressive policies.[15]

12 *Zhong Yin Bian Jiang Ziwei Fanji Zuozhanshe* [*History of the Sino-Indian Self-Defense Border War*] (Beijing: Military Science Publishing House, 1994), 37–40; Y. Xu, *Zhong Yin Bian Jiezhezhan Lishi Zhenxiang* [*True History of the Sino-Indian Border War*] (Hong Kong: Cosmos Books, 1993), 28, 29–30, 50, 53 as noted by J. Garver, 'China's decision for war with India in 1962', in A. I. Johnston and R. Ross (eds), *New Directions in the Study of China's Foreign Policy* (Stanford: Stanford University Press, 2006), 86–130, 125–6.
13 Garver, 'China's decision', 99–106.   14 Garver, 'China's decision', 106–17.
15 P. Godwin and A. Miller, *China's Forbearance has Limits: Chinese Threat and Retaliation Signaling and Its Implications for a Sino-American Military Confrontation*, China Strategic Perspectives, 6 (Washington, DC: National Defense University Press, 2013), 37.

Following receipt of Mao's approval, the PLA moved several divisions from the Chengdu and Lanzhou Military Regions (MRs) into Tibet. PLA operational doctrine typically called for concentration of forces at the point of attack for the purposes of a lightning attack and rapid decision. To do this, the PLA would have to build up the logistical network and support forces in order to move more materiel, military capability and numbers of forces into a local area where it could overwhelm Indian forces in one or a few sharp blows.[16] PLA planners anticipated that the pattern of PLA counterencirclement of Indian positions would elicit an Indian attack on PLA forces. The Chinese strategy called for absorbing this attack and then counterpunching with unexpected force from a different direction.[17]

The PLA had expected India to launch an offensive at Thagla Ridge, and on 9 October that is what happened. Hundreds of Indian soldiers crossed the base of Thagla and engaged with the Chinese there. Unbeknown to the Indians, the PLA had a full battalion waiting to counterattack and it did so with devastating effect. Subsequently, the Indians launched another offensive in late November which the PLA also anticipated and counterattacked with a large-scale, overwhelming counteroffensive on 18 November overrunning and destroying Indian opposition, whose defences were shattered. PLA forces then moved forward to the Bhrampatra River, at which point they withdrew back to pre-war positions.[18]

In 1964 the CMC again revised its Military Strategic Guidelines to reflect the reality of a Sino-Soviet split and the potential grave danger posed by Soviet forces to China's national security. The 1964 Military Strategic Guidelines altered the expected main strategic direction from the north-east coast and Shandong Peninsula to an expected invasion 'from all directions', but especially one from the north to account for the possibility of a Soviet invasion of the PRC. The operational guideline issued by the CMC was 'luring the enemy in deep'.[19] Underlying these changes to the PLA's military strategy was the growing radicalisation of Chinese politics as Mao was pushing the country into the chaos of the Great Proletarian Cultural Revolution; the post-Stalinist Soviet leadership was very hostile to Mao's ideas of 'continuous revolution'.[20]

---

16 Garver, 'China's decision', 118. 17 Garver, 'China's decision', 119.
18 Garver, 'China's decision', 119–24. 19 Fravel, *Active Defense*, 107–38.
20 Mao put forward the idea that Socialist states despite having achieved power and placing the means of production in the hands of the Communist Party were still in an early stage of socialist development. This meant that it was the responsibility of the Communist Party to sponsor and support 'continuous revolution' or continued struggle of the masses against the established Socialist Party until the masses had attained a certain degree of socialist consciousness which would prevent the likelihood of socialist revisionism. The Soviet leadership saw this idea as a recipe for anarchy.

The Sino-Soviet Border Clash (1969)

Two major border clashes took place between the Communist giants in 1969. The first at Damansky/Zhenbao island on the Usurri River took place on 2 March 1969 and was initiated by the Chinese; the second also at Damansky/Zhenbao on 15 March involved Russian retaliation. There are at least four origins at the heart of these conflicts. First, Russian–Chinese broader international relations had been on a downward slide since the late 1950s and were especially poor by the mid-1960s. In part this deterioration was related to some of the post-Stalin efforts by the Soviet Politburo to demystify the cult of Stalin; this had the unexpected effect of offending the CCP who were in the process of building up the cult of Mao's personality. Second, Chinese insecurity and fear of Russian socialist imperialist intentions heightened after the 1968 Soviet invasion of Czechoslovakia and the declaration of the Brezhnev Doctrine which advocated intervention in 'wayward' non-Soviet socialist states. Third, Mao's ideas on 'continuous revolution' led Red Guards during the Cultural Revolution to direct verbal and physical attacks on the Soviet Embassy, Soviet citizens and the Russia–China border. Finally, both countries had begun a steady military build-up along the border. The Soviet build-up followed the signing of a mutual defence treaty with Outer Mongolia, allowing for a substantial Soviet military presence within striking distance of Beijing.[21]

Scholarship demonstrates that the PLA ambushed Soviet forces on 2 March, leading to a handful of casualties on both sides but more so on the Russian side. On 15 March, the Russians retaliated with overwhelming force. After nine hours of combat, the battle was over, with the Russians reporting that they had lost 60 soldiers and that the PLA had lost 800. We have no reliable Chinese casualty reporting.[22]

Subsequent border clashes between the two Communist powers resulted in large Chinese casualties, and the Russian margin of victory in these clashes eventually led the Chinese to the negotiating table with the Russians. That historical point would suggest that the Chinese objective at Damansky/Zhenbao failed; however, there is increasing historical scholarship which suggests that Mao used the initial Damansky/Zhenbao clash as an opening

---

21 US State Department, Bureau of Intelligence and Research, 'USSR/China: Soviet and Chinese Forces Clash on the Ussuri River', Intelligence Note (4 March 1969), Secret/No Foreign Dissemination/Controlled, nsaarchive2.gwu.edu/NSAEBB/NSAEBB49/Index2.html; and T. Robinson, 'The Sino-Soviet border conflicts of 1969: new evidence three decades later', in Ryan et al. (eds), *Chinese Warfighting*, 203–5.
22 Ryan et al. (eds), *Chinese Warfighting*, 199–201.

bid for closer ties with the United States.[23] Mao wanted to demonstrate to the US that China was not afraid to directly confront the Soviet Union militarily and therefore could play a significant part in the balance of power between the Soviet Union and the US. The 1969 border clashes then should, as Thomas Robinson has observed, be seen as the opening bid for improving ties between Communist China and the Nixon administration.[24]

Paracel Islands (1974)

Ironically the Chinese decision to seize some of the islets of the Paracels in the South China Sea arose not out of enmity to the South Vietnamese regime which controlled these islands in 1974; rather the PLA feared a close alignment between North Vietnam and the Soviet Union, and believed that China needed to seize the islands before Soviet naval presence in the South China Sea posed a direct threat to China's southern coast. Tensions between Hanoi and Beijing had been increasing since the latter had improved relations with Washington since the late 1960s and early 1970s. This, coupled with American bombardment of Hanoi while Beijing was engaging in direct talks with Washington, rankled the North Vietnamese leadership. In the meantime, Chinese leaders were suspiciously eyeing the improved relations between Hanoi and Moscow.[25] By 1973, PLA assessments indicated that as Saigon grew weaker, the PLA could probably seize several islets in the Paracels. This opportunity would slip away, the assessments concluded, if/when Saigon fell and Hanoi came to power. At this point, the close ties between Hanoi and Moscow posed the possibility of Soviet naval presence being introduced right onto the Chinese doorstep. It was opportune to seize some of the Paracel islands because Saigon was weak, the United States was inclined to not interfere, and Hanoi and the USSR were in no position to stop the Chinese move.[26]

Mao, in January 1974, tasked Marshal Ye Jianying, the vice chair of the CMC, to plan for the operation to seize some of the Paracels.[27] From all appearances, this operation, like those in previous territorial clashes, involved a period of logistics build-up, moving PLA forces into place, diplomatic signalling and sabre rattling, and a wait-and-see period during which the PLA anticipated being attacked by the rival claimant. Clashes between the

23 Y. Kuisong, 'The Sino-Soviet border clash of 1969: from Zhenbao Island to Sino-American rapprochement', *Cold War History*, 1 (2000), 21–52.
24 Robinson, 'Sino-Soviet border', 203.
25 Q. Zhai, *China and the Vietnam Wars, 1950–75* (Chapel Hill: University of North Carolina Press, 2000), 157–75.
26 J. Garver, 'China's push through the South China Sea: the interaction of bureaucratic and national interests', *The China Quarterly*, 132 (1992), 1001.
27 Garver, 'China's push', 1003.

naval forces led to the sinking of Vietnamese naval vessels, the killing of over a hundred Vietnamese military personnel, and Chinese forces landing and occupying three of the islands of the Paracels.[28]

Chairman Mao died on 9 September 1976, ending the ten-year radical period of the Cultural Revolution. In 1979 Deng managed to fully consolidate power and place his key allies in the CMC before it could issue its views on a new military strategy. The Military Strategic Guidelines of 1980 reversed the strategy issued in 1964, and returned to the 1956 guidelines calling for a focus on conventional military capability, combined arms operations and defending fixed geographic positions in China. The guidelines maintained the conclusion of the 1964 assessment that the main strategic direction came from the north in a Soviet threat, but it no longer advocated 'luring the enemy deep into Chinese territory'.[29]

The Sino-Vietnamese Border Clash (1979)

The Chinese perception that North Vietnam was increasingly becoming aligned with the Soviet Union exacerbated tensions between Hanoi and Beijing that had grown since the end of the Second Indochina War. Vietnam additionally was assuming an aggressive posture in south-east Asia. Furthermore, the CCP leadership strongly believed that the Vietnamese communist leadership was showing ingratitude for all of the assistance China had offered during Vietnam's two Indochina wars.[30] Nonetheless, several military historians have observed that the Chinese motivation to launch a punitive attack against Vietnam came down to: (1) an effort to teach Vietnam a lesson and compel it to withdraw from Cambodia; (2) a warning against Soviet encroachment in China's backyard; and (3) a warning to Vietnam that the Soviet Union would not be an effective protector of Vietnam's interests in south-east Asia.[31]

In early December 1978 at a meeting convened by the CMC, the PLA leadership made the decision to engage in a limited conflict along the Sino-Vietnam border for the purpose of teaching Vietnam a lesson. The CMC

---

28 Garver, 'China's push', 1004; T. Yoshihara, 'The 1974 Paracels sea battle: a campaign appraisal', *Naval War College Review*, 69 (2016), 50.
29 Fravel, *Active Defense*, 139–81.
30 X. M. Zhang, 'China's 1979 war with Vietnam: a reassessment', *The China Quarterly*, 184 (2005), 853–5.
31 H. Kenny, 'Vietnamese perceptions of the 1979 war with China', in Ryan et al. (eds), *Chinese Warfighting*, 218–23; K. Chen, *China's War with Vietnam, 1979: Issues, Decisions and Implications* (Stanford: Hoover Institution Press, 1987); A. Gilks, *The Breakdown of the Sino-Vietnamese Alliance, 1970–1979* (Berkeley: Institute of East Asian Studies, University of California, 1992).

guidance explicitly stated that the conflict would be limited and geographically restricted to 50 kilometres from the border, and its duration was not to exceed two weeks. The guidance followed traditional PLA doctrine which called for the concentration of forces to ensure superiority, to engage in a classic tactic of envelopment, and to isolate Vietnamese border units and defeat them in battles of annihilation. After accomplishing these objectives, the PLA forces were to quickly withdraw.[32]

While the PLA leadership was worried about a potential Soviet response, they assessed that Soviet intervention was unlikely. First, Soviet forces along the border were insufficient for a large-scale attack into China proper. Second, the speed of the operation and the predetermined decision to withdraw after teaching Vietnam a lesson would make the Soviets disinclined to intervene. Additional international factors involved Deng Xiaoping's anticipated tour of the United States to dissuade American opposition to the operation, and his diplomatic visits to some of the countries of south-east Asia to drum up opposition to Vietnam's aggressive policies in the region.[33]

The success of the operation depended heavily on the PLA's ability to penetrate and flank the provincial capitals of Cao Bang and Lao Cai. However, difficulties with terrain, a poor road network and in some cases no roads at all, plus fierce resistance by Vietnamese regular forces and militia slowed PLA advances and led to missed timetables. Additionally, PLA forces started to suffer a high number of casualties as they became bogged down and Vietnamese forces still hardened from years of war with the US started to mount successful attacks on the invaders.[34]

In the face of these setbacks, local commanders on the scene asked for an extended timetable and received permission from the CMC to extend the operation until PLA forces had captured at least part of Lang Son. This they did and the CMC declared a withdrawal on 5 March. Initial PLA estimates of casualties were about 20,000 troops KIA or WIA. Subsequent studies of the campaign show that the PLA casualty figures are closer to 25,000 killed and an additional 37,000 wounded. PLA studies claim that close to 60,000 Vietnamese soldiers were killed in the operation, and regular divisions and several regiments were also damaged.[35]

Subsequent PLA and Chinese historical assessments of the Vietnam operation conclude that the PLA attained its larger strategic objectives. PLA assessments of military performance repeatedly refer to evaluating the

---

32 Zhang, 'China's 1979 war', 857. 33 Zhang, 'China's 1979 war', 859.
34 Zhang, 'China's 1979 war', 863–4. 35 Zhang, 'China's 1979 war', 865–8.

'overall situation' as a key measure.[36] In this case, the end result of the PLA operation demonstrated Soviet reluctance to come to Vietnam's aid in a south-east Asia conflict and the PLA's ability to continue to exert military pressure on Vietnam, did not produce a significant international reaction to the operation and had no impact on improved US–China relations.[37]

By the mid-1980s, Deng Xiaoping had issued a new Guiding Strategic Thought to the military. In 1985 Deng Xiaoping concluded that China was entering into a 'Period of Strategic Opportunity'. During this period China had an opportunity to focus on economic development, and the military could engage in a period of peacetime restructuring and modernisation.[38] China faced a number of security threats around its periphery. These threats were largely centred on local conflicts, particularly smaller countries attempting to encroach upon China's territories and its sovereignty.[39]

Spratly Islands (1988)

In his memoirs, Admiral Liu Huaqing, then vice chairman of the CMC, notes that Vietnam had been encroaching upon Chinese maritime territorial rights and had, through increased military occupation, increased patrolling and harassment of Chinese fishermen, been nibbling away at China's sovereign position of the Nansha Islands (Spratlys). Liu advised Zhao Ziyang to engage in a multipronged 'struggle' with Vietnam to include military force, but also employing other instruments of power (e.g. the diplomatic, economic and ideological). Zhao agreed, and directed Liu to begin planning for an operation in the Spratlys.[40]

In a scene reminiscent of the Paracels conflict, Vietnamese naval vessels and amphibious landing ships dispatched approximately forty personnel on Johnson Reef in mid-March 1988. China had already dispatched an 'investigation' team there, but had also, in a repeat of the 1974 operation, dispatched naval forces to the area. When Vietnamese military personnel confronted the

---

36 R. Christman, 'How Beijing evaluates military campaigns: an initial assessment', in L. Burkitt, L. Wortzel and A. Scobell (eds), *The Chinese People's Liberation Army at 75* (Carlisle: US Army War College, 2003), 260.
37 Zhang, 'China's 1979 war', 867–8.
38 G. Q. Peng, 'Deng Xiaoping's strategic thought', in M. Pillsbury (ed.), *Chinese Views of Future Warfare* (Washington, DC: NDU Press, 1997), 3–9.
39 H. Bin, 'Deng Xiaoping's perspective on national interest', in Pillsbury, *Chinese Views*, 27–36.
40 H. Q. Liu, *Memoirs of Liu Huaqing* (Beijing: PRC, Liberation Army Press, 2004), as cited by C. Yung, 'The PLA Navy lobby and its influence over China's maritime sovereignty policies', in P. Saunders and A. Scobell (eds), *PLA Influence On China's National Security Policy Making* (Stanford: Stanford University Press, 2015), 277–9.

Chinese on Johnson Reef, they opened fire, wounding one of the Chinese personnel. Ships then attacked the Vietnamese vessels, damaging two Vietnamese ships and sinking one of them. The Vietnamese reported that three Vietnamese had been killed, but seventy-four were reported missing at the time. We now know that sixty-four Vietnamese were killed in action.[41] At this point, the PLA occupied seven of the twenty-one naturally occurring Spratly features, and Hanoi attempted to enter negotiations with Beijing which subsequently refused, declaring their sovereignty rights 'inviolable and indisputable'.[42]

Military Strategy and New China (1989 to the Present)

Tiananmen Square, Desert Storm and the 1993 Military Strategic Guidelines

China's security situation by the late 1980s dramatically changed with the dissolution of the Soviet Union and the fall of several communist governments. By the summer of 1989, the CCP felt itself under siege, with massive student protests in Beijing and across the country. The Party's decision to break up the protest through violent force brought the Party back in firm control over its political situation, but the sheer violence of the event and the willingness of the Party to ruthlessly take the lives of its own citizens created a de facto break in China's alignment with the Western powers – especially the United States. This strategic realignment, coupled with the results of Operation Desert Storm in which the United States military systematically destroyed the Iraqi Republican Guard, pushed the CMC to think through the strategic implications of this new security environment for the PLA.

In 1993, the CMC revised its Military Strategic Guidelines. The new guidelines concluded that China could be embroiled in a local war around its periphery, most likely Taiwan, with the United States intervening in the conflict. Under such a circumstance the conflict would be under 'modern, especially high tech conditions'. The CMC called for a force structure development process which focused on the naval and air domains, strategic rocket forces and information as a warfighting domain.[43] Subsequent revisions to the Military Strategic Guidelines in 2004 and 2014 elevated the information element of war to include changing the expected character of

---

41 'The day Vietnam lost a Spratly Reef to China', *VN Express International* (14 March 2017).
42 Garver, 'China's push', 1013.   43 Fravel, *Active Defense*, 182–216.

war to include the term 'local war under conditions of informatization' and then subsequently called for the PLA to be prepared to fight 'informatized war';[44] however, the foundation of the PLA's force structure development for close to three decades originated from the 1993 Military Strategic Guidelines.

PLA's Operations Short of War

Over three decades, the PLA has evolved from the largest military on the planet with 1950s and 1960s era weapons systems and platforms to the largest military on the planet with pockets of very modern military equipment. The PLA now has a 'blue water' navy capable of circumnavigating the globe, and has conducted out-of-area operations. The PLA Air Force has been gradually developing, and is now the second largest modern air force in the world after the US Air Force, with the latest fighter aircraft. The PLA strategic rocket forces are still outnumbered by the nuclear arsenals of the US and Russia, but China has enough intercontinental ballistic missile (ICBMs) to ensure that it can launch a devastating second strike against any nuclear power which attacks it first. The PLA has also taken up Xi Jinping's call to be prepared for an 'informatized war' by developing alternative domain warfare capabilities (e.g. cyber, space, psyops, political warfare) and a force (the Strategic Support Force) dedicated to the co-ordinated prosecution of such types of conflicts.[45]

The modernisation programme just described was undertaken in a peaceful environment as Deng had correctly assessed. At the same time Deng warned that a number of threats to China's national security still existed. These were mainly threats to China's sovereignty and territory, and involved: the possibility of Taiwan declaring independence and breaking out of the Chinese political orbit; loss of maritime territory to rival east Asian countries; and China's long-standing border dispute with India.

The PLA was left to create a solution to the seeming contradiction of fostering an environment of stability and peace while at the same time deterring or addressing specific perceived threats to Chinese sovereignty and territory. Such strategic policies are discussed and co-ordinated through a forum known as Leading Small Groups, which includes members of the military and other key members of the Party and government. In 1995 and

44 Fravel, *Active Defense*, 217–35.
45 J. Costello and J. McReynolds, 'China's strategic support force: a force for a new era', in P. Saunders, A. Ding, A. Scobell et al. (eds), *Chairman Xi Remakes the PLA: Assessing Chinese Military Reforms* (Washington, DC: NDU Press, 2019), 437–515.

1996, this contradictory challenge came to the fore when the Taiwan population appeared to be about to elect a pro-independence candidate to the Presidency. The end of 1995 and the beginning of 1996 saw the PLA launching short-range ballistic missiles in impact areas around the island and raising tensions in the region, until the United States responded with two aircraft carrier battle groups. Since that time the PLA has not undertaken anything so brazen, but has sought to manage Taiwan actions through pressure from PLA aircraft, surface ships, and submarines and cyber intrusions. The PRC has also employed such blunt diplomatic instruments as stripping Taiwan from membership of international organisations, encouraging countries to switch recognition from Taiwan to the PRC through generous economic packages and offering Taiwan ships 'protection' from pirates in waters far from Taiwan.[46]

Maritime sovereignty tensions also re-emerged in the mid-1990s as southeast Asian countries occupied islets in the South China Sea, and in some cases increased their military presence on these features. Tensions came to a head when the PLA ejected Philippine military personnel from Mischief Reef in 1995. A similar confrontation took place in 2012 when China and the Philippines confronted one another again, this time over Scarborough Shoal. The strategic importance of China's maritime territorial disputes was illustrated by the creation in 2012 of CCP Leading Small Group on maritime sovereignty protection and Xi Jinping, the then expected next general secretary, to lead it. The Scarborough Shoal confrontation had similar results to the Mischief Reef incident: the Philippines withdrew from the features while China retains a paramilitary presence there. China has managed this contradictory balancing act over the past twenty years by utilising maritime law enforcement vessels as the instrument of its power, engaging in coercive economic diplomacy, engaging in a competition of narratives through social media and the press, and activist diplomacy in ASEAN regional dialogues.[47]

In 2010, China's maritime territorial dispute in the East China Sea with Japan reignited when, first, the Japanese government announced that it would be nationalising or formally taking ownership of the Senkakus (*Diaoyus* in Chinese) islands; and, second, when the Japanese Coast Guard sought to arrest a Chinese fisherman fishing within the Japanese territorial

---

46 R. Cliff, P. Saunders and S. Harold (eds), *New Opportunities and Challenges for Taiwan Security* (Santa Monica: RAND, 2011).
47 C. Yung and P. McNulty, 'An empirical analysis of claimant tactics in the South China Sea', *Strategic Forum* (Washington, DC: NDU Press, 2015), vol. 289, 8–9.

waters and to bring him to Japan to stand trial. What occurred next was a multiyear military, economic and diplomatic stand-off between the two countries. Included in these actions were China's cutting off the sale of rare earth materials to Japan; the dispatch of Chinese coast guard and PLA aircraft into Japan's exclusive economic zone (EEZ) with Japan responding with coast guard cutters and aircraft of its own; disinviting the Japan Maritime Self-Defense Force ships from the PLA Navy military to military events; and a cessation of high-level dialogues between the two militaries. The tension was reduced only in 2018 when the two sides implemented the Japan–China maritime and air communication mechanism to avoid an accidental clash, and subsequent high-level meetings between Xi Jinping and Shinzo Abe and Suga Yoshihide, his successor, to reinforce the agreements.[48]

The PLA's most serious confrontations over territory took place along the Chinese–Indian borders, particularly in the Aksai-Chin corridor. Since the Sino-Indian border clash of the early 1960s, the PLA and the Indian military have skirmished numerous times.[49] In May 2020, after years of tension, minor altercations and provocations on both sides (including the construction of roads and troops setting up camps near disputed areas), both militaries found themselves in a major skirmish in which they reported loss of life. In the case of India, twenty Indian soldiers lost their lives.[50] We have no accurate reporting on the number of PLA casualties. Remarkably, these clashes have not led to wider conflicts between the PLA and the Indian military, which may reflect the fact that the PLA is still operating under the guidance that they must manage territorial disputes and deter countries from infringing upon Chinese sovereignty without destabilising China's immediate security environment.

The PLA Goes Global

With growing Chinese global economic interests, the PLA found itself in the position of having to design missions to meet the demand to protect China's growing out-of-area interests. In 2009 the PLA Navy embarked on its first out-of-area operational mission when it deployed three surface combatants to the Gulf of Aden for a UN-mandated counterpiracy mission. These

---

48 S. Smith, *Japan Rearmed: the Politics of Military Power* (Cambridge, MA: Harvard University Press, 2019), 118–22.
49 S. Singh, 'India-China border dispute: what happened in Nathu La in 1967?', *The Indian Express* (June 2020), https://bit.ly/44dJ918.
50 E. Anbarasan, 'China–India clashes: no change a year after Ladakh stand-off', BBC News (1 June 2021), www.bbc.co.uk/news/world-asia-57234024.

deployments, involving six-month rotations of two surface combatants and a replenishment ship, were in response to a problem faced by civilian ships from pirates operating out of the Gulf of Aden. Twelve years later, the PLA Navy has now undertaken over thirty-five of these deployments. The Chinese government announced that it was taking up the UN charge to help address this international crisis, but an underlying rationale for the 'far seas' deployment was that the PLA would obtain out-of-area operational experience. The PLA is on the hook to defend these economic interests. In 2011 the PLA was called to conduct a non-combatant evacuation operation (NEO) of over 30,000 of its citizens from the rapidly deteriorating situation in Libya, and it was called again in 2014 to do another NEO in Yemen. To ease the logistical burdens of operating out of area, in 2017 the PLA established its first overseas base in Djibouti, and is currently in the process of negotiating additional access sites in the Indian Ocean. Finally, China continues to contribute to the UN peacekeeping force, which deploys to such volatile locales as South Sudan and northern Mali.

Conclusion

There is a notable contrast between Chinese military strategy of the early to mid-twentieth century and the strategy marking the latter half of the twentieth century and early part of the twenty-first. Military strategy within China, marking the time period from the Northern Expedition to the Communist victory in 1949, is notably more violent and bloody. Casualties from the earlier period, described in Chapter 7 about Chinese pre-Revolutionary strategy, number in the tens of millions, while those in the latter period are much lower. While a whole of government approach to strategy applies to both the earlier and later time periods, the early time period is not marked by several decades in which no large-scale military force is employed, whereas the latter is marked by such a phenomenon. The PRC has not been engaged in large-scale conventional combat since 1979. The whole of government approach to accomplishing China's strategic objectives is particularly pronounced in the later period. The invasion of Vietnam in 1979 was preceded by a leadership public relations tour to diplomatically pave the way towards acceptance of China's use of force. The 1962 Sino-Indian border conflict was preceded by a Chinese diplomatic and media blitz criticising the Indian government for its aggressive policy.

Because strategy in the latter part of the twentieth century and the early part of the twenty-first centres around the newly formed PRC, military strategy described in this chapter is tightly entangled with how the CCP perceives threats, makes strategy and co-ordinates that strategy with other instruments of power, especially its diplomacy/foreign policy. Because the CCP was aligned with the Soviet Union in the opening phases of the Cold War, Mao's foreign policy of 'leaning to one side' (e.g. allying with the Soviet Union) put China directly into those geopolitical struggles. Thus the PLA found itself embroiled in the Korean War only a year after the founding of the People's Republic; however, when relations between the USSR and PRC turned sour in the 1960s, the PLA found itself in a direct military confrontation with the Soviet Union in 1969, and with a perceived proxy in 1974 and 1979. The direct relationship of China's perceptions of threat with its geopolitical situation is also linked to its use of force against Taiwan and the US throughout the 1950s and 1960s.

In most cases, the Chinese decision to use force around its periphery appears to be a corrective measure to something that has disrupted Chinese security. In these cases, the Chinese seem to have been motivated by the following: to address an injustice; to punish a neighbouring state; to fix a problem which put China into a strategically disadvantageous position; and to deter a threat. In each of these cases, China attempted to bring the strategic situation back to a status quo or some kind of political equilibrium. This applies to the Korean conflict, the Sino-Indian border dispute, the Sino-Soviet border clash, PLA operations and attacks on the offshore islands in the Taiwan Strait, the Sino-Vietnamese border clash, and clashes in the South China Sea with both North and South Vietnam.

The use of force appears to follow a distinct pattern of building up a support network and logistics for a military operation, placing PLA forces in harm's way, initially holding the PLA personnel under strict rules of engagement, anticipating the rival military attacking PLA forces, and then suddenly and surprisingly retaliating with overwhelming force. This pattern applies to military force in Korea, India, Russia, the Paracels and the Spratlys. Although historically there are exceptions to this rule, the degree of meticulous planning and preparation in the run-up to these military operations suggests that the modern PLA is comparatively risk-averse and unwilling to engage in large-scale military force unless its military commanders have attained a certain degree of assurance that factors are in place for victory.[51]

---

[51] This pattern of strategic behaviour appears to be consistent with today's PLA as well. See D. Blasko, 'The Chinese military speaks to itself, revealing doubts', War on the Rocks (19 February 2019), https://warontherocks.com/2019/02/the-chinese-military-speaks-to-itself-revealing-doubts/.

There appears to be an element of opportunism in the Chinese decision to use force. During the Sino-Indian crises, both the Soviet Union and the US were entangled in the Cuban Missile Crisis and so were distracted by superpower confrontation. The bombardment of Jinmen and Mazu took place during the US intervention in Lebanon in 1958. The PLA Navy seizure of islets in the Paracels took place just prior to Saigon's fall and before Hanoi could occupy the territory itself.

One major observation of Chinese military strategy in the New Period is that it is wholly integrated into a larger grand strategy and consistently subordinate to it. It is highly unusual for a military to conclude that it is in a period of relative peace and stability, and can afford to be considered last in a list of government priorities. It is even more remarkable that that military can hold to that restriction for a prolonged period of time. While the CCP and PLA began to perceive threats to national security following the West's break from alignment with it following the events at Tiananmen Square, the PLA still professes that it is in a 'period of strategic opportunity' and is still considered to be in an era of peacetime military building.

A final word on the PLA becoming a 'World Class military': it is entirely related to the strategic objectives and perceived desired end states of the CCP. If the Party's vision is that it seeks complete modernisation, a stable periphery, access to global markets, energy and raw materials, a peaceful resolution of its territorial disputes within Asia – including with Taiwan – and an international system conducive to supporting the governance efforts of authoritarian states, the CCP can accomplish these objectives with a PLA that is designed to specifically address the narrow military components of these objectives. The PLA can establish a military presence abroad, co-operative military partnerships with nations around its periphery, a defensive posture designed to coax Taiwan back into a peaceful reintegration into the CCP system and prevent other major powers from coercing China, and a force structure designed to balance an American presence in the Western Pacific. On the other hand, if CCP objectives insist on China being central to an emerging international system, this will obviously entail a greater degree of competition and friction with the West, especially the United States. China would therefore require a much more powerful and activist PLA, a more extensive military presence abroad and a more dominant military presence and capability in the Asia–Pacific; and there would be a greater likelihood of conflict with the established global military power – the United States.

Conclusion

ISABELLE DUYVESTEYN AND SAMUEL ZILINCIK

Previously, scholars of the study of the practice of strategy have claimed that strategy is indeed a universally consistent phenomenon:

> By surveying the history of warfare, examining the Greek wars of Epaminondas, Philip, and Alexander, the Roman wars of Hannibal, Scipio, and Caesar, and the Byzantine wars of Belisarius and Narses, and comparing them with the wars of the nineteenth and twentieth centuries, we recognize that strategic reasoning has very strong elements of constancy and continuity.[1]

While universal templates have been claimed before,[2] divergence has also been noted. In a study of global strategy, culture was identified as the most important observable variation.[3] These earlier studies are based on a smaller number of case studies. Moreover, they risked being influenced by teleology; if you think there is a pattern in strategy, you will find one. In this series, we have tried to use a more inductive approach. We have selected what we think are the most important case studies that offer an interesting story about strategy. This larger number of cases derive from different parts of the world, represent a larger set of polities and offer a longer time frame than existing studies. We applied a very broad conceptualisation of strategy in the hope that it would capture the phenomenon in its widest sense.

---

[1] J. A. Olsen, 'Introduction', in Olsen and C. S. Gray (eds), *The Practice of Strategy; From Alexander the Great to the Present* (Oxford: Oxford University Press, 2011), 1–11, 10.

[2] M. I. Handel, *Masters of War: Classical Strategic Thought*, 3rd ed. (London: Routledge, 2001); C. S. Gray, *The Strategy Bridge: Theory for Practice* (Oxford: Oxford University Press, 2012).

[3] J. Black, *Military Strategy; A Global History* (New Haven: Yale University Press, 2020), in particular the conclusion.

Conclusion

In the contributions above detailing the rich historical diversity of practices, we have been confronted with the time- and location-specific nature of what we tend to consider as the parameters of the discussion. What is legal or illegal, what is extortion and what is taxation, who are soldiers or mercenaries, what is war and peace, what is victory and defeat – these are all binary questions to which the historical record tends to give a far more nuanced answer.

Problematic Concepts

We observe that our implicit normative framework is based on nineteenth-century conceptualisations, which do not neatly fit the diverse historical praxis we encountered. Not only is our normative framework a product of nineteenth-century history, it is also a product of the West. In politics and in our thinking about war and international relations in particular, we are unduly marked and blinkered by concepts that crystallised in the nineteenth century; we see the world through a nineteenth-century lens, one quite inappropriate for the understanding of most of earlier and later history. As one historian put it, conceptually, in many ways, 'we are [still] living in the 19th century'.[4] We tend to operate based on binaries, which we need to engage with more fundamentally. The most prominent and problematic binaries we highlight here are the distinction between what is war and what is peace, the distinction between rationality and emotion, and the preoccupation with the territorial nation state. We discuss these briefly in turn.

War/Peace

War is understood to be the opposite of peace: when there is war, there cannot be peace, and vice versa. For long periods of history, however, war was endemic and in some civilisations considered cyclical, depending for instance on the rise and decline of dynasties. Alternatively, war was a way of life, with the existence of a warrior class in society and, therefore, war also possessed perennial features. Even today, in many parts of the world violence is a fact of daily life.[5] The fuzzy boundaries between war and peace, and the

---

4 H. Schulze, 'Wir leben im 19. Jahrhundert', in *Wir sind, was wir geworden sind: vom Nutzen der Geschichte für die deutsche Gegenwart* (Munich: Piper, 1987).
5 T. Barkawi, 'Decolonising war', *European Journal of International Security*, 1:2 (2016), 199–214.

many instances of conflict-affected regions where daily life also continued, invite us to think differently about this binary.

A case in point in the above chapters has been the Israeli experience where what the authors called the 'between wars' warfare could be seen as part of a century-long struggle for security. In Afghanistan, a whole generation has now grown up in the Forty-Year War experienced by the country. What does this mean for their perception of war? Moreover, wars in more recent times tend not to be formally declared for various reasons, and the phenomenon of 'forever wars' and 'neverending wars' reinforce this claim.[6] Moreover, the long history of economic blockades, as well as the phenomenon of cyber war, add to the blurring of the division between war and non-war.

The war/peace binary is influenced by the development of international law and legal categorisation; international law operates on the basis of a clear distinction between a state of war and a state of peace. It cannot deal with neither war nor peace or peace and war at the same time. The consequences for thinking about strategic practice are obviously significant. Is the practice of strategy stulted, extended, perennial, impossible or nonexistent?

Rationality/Emotion

A second binary that hampers our understanding of the practice of strategy is the presumption of rationality being in contradiction with emotion. There is a long tradition in Western philosophy of distinguishing between emotion and reason, between mind and body. The distinction in strategic studies can be traced back to specific interpretations of Carl von Clausewitz. His *On War* claimed that war consisted of fear, courage, honour and ambition, pointing also clearly to the role of emotions. These factors have generally been seen as difficult or even immeasurable.[7] Most interpretations of Clausewitz's trinity of passion, reason and chance have predominantly focused on the assumed rationality of politicians in contrast to the passions of the population. This distinction was exacerbated during the Cold War, with deterrence

---

6 D. Filkins, *The Forever War* (New York: Alfred A. Knopf, 2008). A. Hironaka, *Neverending Wars: The International Community, Weak States, and the Perpetuation of Civil War* (Cambridge, MA: Harvard University Press, 2005). S. Rynning, O. Schmitt and A. Theussen (eds), *War Time: Temporality and the Decline of Western Military Power* (Washington, DC: Brookings Institution Press, 2021).

7 See also discussion in: J. Angstrom and J.J. Widen, *Contemporary Military Theory; The Dynamics of War* (London: Routledge, 2015), 87.

scholarship, for instance, assuming that emotions can only ever be a burden to rational calculation.[8]

There was plentiful evidence in our case studies, despite the challenges with sources, that the Roman emperors were in the business for glory. Individual social and political standing were also intimately tied up with the culture of Roman society. Importantly, we have seen how emotions in recent times influenced the process of prioritisation, often leading to what could be described as quite reasonable, if not perfectly rational, decisions. For example, fear motivated the Truman administration to allocate resources to the conduct of the Korean war rather than to solving domestic issues in the early 1950s. During the Russia–Turkey war in the late nineteenth century, fears of a more complex war with new adversaries motivated the Russians to prepare for such eventuality and make peace with Turkey. Judging decisions like these as either emotional or rational does not add much to the discussion.

All strategically meaningful decisions are likely to be emotional because emotions are the key mechanism which people possess in order to cope with the uncertainties inherent in strategic affairs.[9] Indeed, research from neuroscience and psychology shows that the distinction between rational and emotional decision making is illusory.[10] Strategic studies need to incorporate these insights in a more structured manner.

State/Non-State

A third important binary is the state versus the non-state actor. We are excessively focused on states as actors, and by extension on their regular armies distinct from a body politic. We operate based on the nineteenth-century ideal of each state containing one entire (and each only one) ethnic nation. We are conned into thinking that this exists in reality, speaking about 'nation states'. However, wherever we look, no such ethnically pure nations exist. Moreover, we think in terms of 'national interests' (i.e. what state governments suggest to their populations as being their interests); of the rule

---

8 For a more detailed discussion about the dichotomy in strategic studies, see S. Zilincik, 'Emotional and rational decision-making in strategic studies: moving beyond the false dichotomy', *Journal of Strategic Security*, 15:1 (2022), 4–6. For more in-depth treatment of the dichotomy between the two different strategic studies traditions, see N. Gardner, 'An object suspended between three magnets? A closer look at Clausewitz's trinity', *Military Strategy Magazine*, 7:3 (2021), 26–31; and F. Sauer, *Atomic Anxiety: Deterrence, Taboo and the Non-use of U.S. Nuclear Weapons* (New York: Palgrave Macmillan, 2015).
9 Zilincik, 'Emotional and rational decision-making in strategic studies', 6–7.
10 E. A. Phelps, K. M. Lempert and P. Sokol-Hessner, 'Emotion and decision making: multiple modulatory neural circuits', *Annual Review of Neuroscience*, 37 (July 2014), 263–87; A. Damasio, *Descartes' Error: Emotion, Reason, and the Human Brain* (New York: Penguin Books, 2005).

of territory, or clearly drawn albeit perhaps disputed state borders; and of media that operate within one country only, reflecting 'public opinion' rather than influencing it and very selectively representing views from outside the state apparatus.

In fact, the very notion of a clearly bounded territorial state that can be depicted on maps with sharply drawn borders is not universal. Buffer states or regions have existed throughout history. In Europe, territories referred to as 'marches' constituting a no-man's land, perhaps fought over, perhaps tolerated as zones best to be left alone, can be found from the Anglo-Scottish and Anglo-Welsh borders to the *Mark* Brandenburg or the *Kraina* or *Militärgrenze* or military frontier area between the Habsburg and the Ottoman empires. Arguably Belgium was always such a borderland where Germanic and Francophone cultures met. This does not stop the populations of such areas from developing their own collective identity, but nor has it stopped expansionist neighbouring powers from fighting over them for centuries, as the histories of Belgium or indeed Ukraine illustrate. The idea of thinking about territory in terms of precisely drawn borders captured on maps only crystallised in the late seventeenth to eighteenth centuries, when an obsession with measuring things extended itself to geography.[11] Louis XIV operated on the idea that France acquired borders based on natural frontiers such as the River Rhine. This is not a universal pattern that is visible across time and place. The south-east Asian conceptualising of rule in terms of a *mandala* was another alternative, based on circles of influence. This also applies to pre-colonial Africa or America where firm territorial demarcations were absent. A clear political centre embracing a territory, a population and a claim to authority, echoing Max Weber, is a conceptualisation that is very much a product of a distinct historical trajectory.

A corollary of this focus on the territorial state is the central idea that wars between sovereign states culminate in battles which are limited in time and space. This idea is central to our perception of war, with Austerlitz, Waterloo, Sadowa and Sedan emblematic of this, admittedly with precedents of battle-centric behaviour that can be found in many eras, especially of European history. Alexander the Great of Macedon, Caesar, Louis XIV, Louis XV and Napoleon were keen on bringing about decisive battles. However, for most parts of history and in most parts of the world, battle was just one of several key tools of war. Even in the nineteenth century, these included

---

11 J. Black, *Maps and History: Constructing Images of the Past* (New Haven: Yale University Press, 1997).

sieges, asymmetric wars between state forces and insurgents, and many massacres of civilians especially in colonies, from the Balkans (colonies of the Ottoman Empire) to Algeria or the Philippines.

Other corollaries of this state/non-state binary are, among others, the distinction between what is legal and what is illegal, what is legitimate and what illegitimate. Moreover, judgements as to who is military and who is civilian follow from this binary, informing the core of international humanitarian law. Yet reality has seen many degrees of involvement, from the entirely 'in-nocent' – those doing no harm, as the Latin word suggests – to active sympathies or auxiliaries to the combatants, whether marked as such by distinctive dress or not. For legal reasons – to give civilians and combatants the respective forms of protection that international law has gradually constructed for them – the distinction needs to be upheld. But in order to understand what is going on and to devise appropriate strategies for each case, one needs to transcend this conceptual binary.[12]

It is clear from our case material that both state and non-state actors can behave strategically, and the distinction might be useful for legal purposes, not for strategic ones. Indeed, the recent research by Stephen Biddle finds no clear pattern of strategic behaviour associated with non-state actors. Instead of the state/non-state status, factors such as domestic politics seem to dictate strategic choices.[13] This dominant binary is tied to the general problem of intrusion of legal and international relations into the strategic realm.[14] In short, we are confronted with shortcomings of our concepts. Our first conclusion is that our basic conceptual framework is found wanting and we need to rethink these core concepts. Below, we suggest ways in which we can reconceptualise the practice of strategy.

Practising Strategy

It would seem that Kimberly Kagan's definition we adopted for this study has met this goal: strategy making requires the leader to identify 'objectives, establish priorities among them, and allocate resources to them, whether or

---

12 B. Heuser, *War: A Genealogy of Western Ideas and Practices* (Oxford: Oxford University Press, 2022), 218–306. J. Angstrom, 'The changing norms of civil and military and civil-military relations theory', *Small Wars & Insurgencies*, 24:2 (2013), 224–36.
13 S. Biddle, *Nonstate Warfare: The Military Methods of Guerillas, Warlords, and Militias* (Princeton: Princeton University Press, 2021).
14 See also discussion in F. Doeser and F. Frantzen, 'The strategic and realist perspectives: an ambiguous relationship', *Journal of Strategic Studies* (2020), https://doi.org/10.1080/01402390.2020.1833860.

not they develop or keep to long-range systematic plans'. Strategy is thus 'the setting of a state's [ruler's, oligarchy's, etc.] objectives and of priorities among those objectives' in order to allocate resources and choose the best means to prosecute a conflictual engagement.[15] The evidence we have amassed in these two volumes suggests that, according to this definition, there was indeed strategy before the word. Moreover, the strategies studied have produced repeated patterns, some of them common to all parts of the world and to most periods of history. This observation has an important caveat, that strategy in practice diverges substantially from the ideal, and this is our second main conclusion: instead of being neatly conceptualised, linear and premeditated, the practice shows a messy, reactive and often incoherent reality. The logics of strategic practice we have found include not only the dominant utilitarian logic: a performative logic, opportunism and what we shall call here an ordering/disordering practice are also visible. These practices can be found across time and space, and are not always mutually exclusive.

Before we discuss these in more detail, it is necessary to make an important preliminary remark. In some cases, authors have noted that it is difficult to assess specific strategic logics given the absence, dearth or poverty of the available sources. Without transcripts or other recordings of actual discussions (a gap we still find in government decision making in many states, even in the early twenty-first century), we must often make do with accounts stemming from only one participant whose record might be biased and selective, and who may well have filled in what remained unsaid, embellished on what little was articulated, or omitted what they found of little interest. Such accounts cannot aspire to capture the entirety of a decision-making process. In the case of ancient Greece for example, strategic logic is open for interpretation in the case of the city states because of the nature of the available sources. For the Umayyad Caliphate, it has been argued that it is difficult to find a pattern other than the overriding concern not to be defeated. The nature of the sources also plays a role in this assessment. Therefore, there remain limitations to some of the claims that can be made regarding praxis. Still, the authors agreed that the definition provided was useful to study the case material.

Practising Strategy: The Utilitarian Perspective

We find consistent evidence for the tenability of the dominant framework for strategic practice, which is utility. In the practising of strategy, the ends are

---

15 See our Introduction to Volume I.

formulated and the means, methods and prioritisation are, in one way or another, visible. Writing about strategy is dominated by the notion that it is problem-driven, that it sets a 'strategic' (i.e. overall) objective and then pursues this objective with available means, employed in most suitable ways. We first find this basic idea reflected in Sunzi's premise that war is a rational pursuit of the polity's political interest. This utilitarian practice is, however, far more diverse than might hitherto have been realised. We will discuss the most notable utilitarian practices of controlling territory and populations. These exercises of prioritising required different processes of calibration.

Over the course of history, a whole series of motivations and justifications have accompanied the utilitarian notion of controlling territories and populations. The redress of grievances is a prominent factor, as well as grander ideas of universal religious and dynastic rights and ideologies such as the powerful ideas of nationalism, democracy and Marxism. A series of classic causes and objectives surface in the case material. In preliterate societies (in which we included pre-Columbian North America), the objectives have been argued to be the reclaiming of land after aggression, protecting the population and avenging the dead. In Republican Rome we also find a main cause of war to be redress for injury or lost property. This is a very powerful and prevalent mechanism. A variation is the defensive posture to prevent the occurrence of loss and injury; in regards to the Dutch naval strategy in early modern Europe, a defensive posture was adopted to defend what had been achieved earlier and in the process fortify the position. Protection of lines of communication on land or at sea informs another recurrent defensive exercise. For the case of the Mughals, it has been argued that the main objective was to control communication routes, both over land and via river routes. Fortifications were built on these routes to exercise control. Also in the case of the Habsburg king Charles V, maintenance of communication between the elements of the composite empire was of prime concern. A notable example of a polity which was very apt at this exercise was the Byzantine Empire, which engaged in an elaborate calibration by using its versatile set of instruments to appease, counterbalance and defend both in depth and reactively. In exerting these claims, the main focus tended to be on territory and/ or the population inhabiting the territory.

Territory

This is a dominant and very visible practice of strategy in which the prioritisation and calibration of objectives and means have a distinct territorial focus. Examples of the aim of territorial conquest range from Ancient China and Persia to the Macedonian rulers, Indian rulers before the arrival of Muslim invaders, European rulers of the Middle Ages, the Rashidun, Umayyad and Abbasid caliphates that controlled the early Muslim world, the Selçuk and Ottoman Turks, various Muslim rulers of India (under the guise of promoting the spread of Islam) and, well into the nineteenth century, south-east Asian rulers. The colonial expansion of the various European powers either into neighbouring areas or onto other continents, or both, are also examples of this practice.

In more recent times, we see the continuation of this territorial aim, for example: the confrontation between Israel and the Palestinian Arabs; unresolved issues between India and Pakistan; at the core of the first two Gulf wars; at the heart of many of China's past and present relationships; India and the border in the Himalayas; Vietnam, the Philippines and Japan when it comes to borders in the South China Sea and the East China Sea.

Still, the control of territory often extended beyond the mere claims on the physical space. Territory can hold symbolic weight and the control over tracts of land can be tied up with questions of identity and ideology. The ideologically driven yearning for the domination of certain territories – mythical homelands or 'cradles' of one's civilisation or special historical sites – can be such that a strategy of conquering them is pursued despite enormous costs. Examples include the competing Jewish, Christian and Muslim desires to dominate Jerusalem; the Serb obsession with Kosovo, where Serbs suffered a heroic defeat at the hands of the Ottomans; and the Russian obsession with the ownership of Kyiv, where Vikings are said to have created the first urban settlement associated with Russians. Outsiders may agree that fighting for such territory makes no economic or even political sense, but such a preoccupation can be driven by culture and tradition.

Territorial expansion can also be linked to economic exploitation. Territorial expansion has included the despoiling of the conquered territories, and the movement of populations as slaves or their exploitation as cheap labour. There is the utilitarian notion of turning populations into permanent sources of income without actually integrating them into one's own territory, by turning them into client states who must pay tribute regularly and furnish soldiers for the hegemon's wars. Examples of this abound from ancient Greece, Rome and Persia to medieval Europe and the many Indian polities in pre-Islamic times. European overseas colonies largely fit this pattern. Notable examples are the early Persian kings, who saw the control of territory and populations as additional income that could facilitate the functioning of their empire. The early Umayyad Caliphate as well as the

Conclusion

Byzantine Empire had the common practice of resettling populations to control them and prevent them from being conquered by others. Evidence from the Gupta Empire similarly brings forward economics as the only justified motivation for foreign conquest. This was elevated to such an extent that instructions were given that the production structures should not be destroyed so that the invaders could come back for more. For the south-east Asian kingdoms, conquered populations were considered mobile wealth, that is, labour force, and formed a core strategic practice. In pre-colonial Africa, Dahomey's wars aimed to control the slave trade, cutting off rivals and using skilled armed forces to serve this purpose.

War as an economic or even purely pecuniary undertaking has been recently linked to the resource curse, that is, the statistical correlation between the presence of natural resources and the risk of war breaking out. This debate, which played out in the 1990s and the first years of the twenty-first century, looked at explanations for strategic behaviour and warfare informed by confrontations over access to product, control, trade and export of resources.[16] These form longer standing patterns, as the case studies attest.

Population

Across the chapters, a notable version of utilitarian practice has been strikingly evident: the control over populations rather than territory, perhaps not hitherto clearly explored.[17] We are specifically hindered here by outdated beliefs that possession of land is what matters most and the noble ideal that civilians should be spared in war, a concept diametrically opposed to nationalism let alone racism. In many instances in the past, the population itself was seen as a specific target of war. Populations were not only a resource to be used for exploitation, in the shape of labour force or as slaves; they were also specifically captured to weaken or eradicate the opponent, to prevent a resurgence of their power and to demonstrate control. This practice can be identified across time and place, and is also linked to instances of mass killing of enemy soldiers or even civilians. This type of killing might have occurred to deny them to the enemy as an asset, for example: in the case of Ancient China there is evidence for this practice under the Qin dynasty; there was extreme destruction in the wars between the Greek city states, with the

---

16 P. Collier, *The Bottom Billion; Why the Poorest Countries are Failing and What Can Be Done about It* (Oxford: Oxford University Press, 2007). D. Keen, *The Economic Functions of Violence in Civil Wars* (Oxford: Oxford University Press, 1998).
17 This echoes long-standing debates about biopolitics: M. Foucault, *Security, Territory, Population: Lectures at the Collège de France, 1977–1978* (New York: Palgrave, 2004).

practice of razing cities to the ground; when populations were not willing to submit to their rule, the Mongols resorted to mass killing and exceeded their capacity to force those people into slavery. We see similar instances of strategic annihilation aimed at destroying the *mandala* claims of an adversary in the south-east Asian kingdoms.

This practice ties in with recent discussions about the logic of civil war, which gained a notable impetus from the work of Stathis Kalyvas on the Greek Civil War who showed that the targeting of civilians is subject to a logic of control.[18] When there is contested control, indiscriminate violence against populations occurs. When control is uncontested, this violence is absent. Moreover, the evidence from our cases shows that population-centric warfare has a long lineage. It invites us to reconsider the arguably barbaric practices that some conflicts exhibit. We see chopping off hands and limbs as a notable feature of warfare in and around Muslim lands for centuries. In Europe, Christians also engaged in this practice only until the late Middle Ages as punishment for individual criminals, rather than as a practice in war. By contrast, blinding was a measure that was applied by Christians in warfare.[19] Some civil wars in the 1990s, notably the Sierra Leonean Civil War, exhibited mutilation and the chopping off of hands in particular.[20] Also, the practices of wartime rape can be considered in this context.[21] All of these actions exhibit features that fit within the utilitarian logic and align with the notion of control.

The preoccupation with geography and people displays strong continuity. The role of these two factors in utilitarian notions is still evident today. The Islamic State, with their declaration of the Caliphate in June 2014, exemplified a recent group seeking a territorial stronghold and control over populations. Their territorial defeat in 2017 did not signal their demise, and they still claim to represent the interests of the believers. These developments might indicate new trajectories of strategic practice in which the emphasis might be more on control of people rather than territories. Moreover, the outbreak of the Ukrainian war on 24 February 2022 also signalled the return of war focused on territory and people in Europe, a continent which had long

---

18 S. Kalyvas, *The Logic of Violence in Civil War* (New York: Cambridge University Press, 2006).
19 Heuser, *War: A Genealogy*, 338.
20 P. Richards, *Fighting for the Rainforest; War, Youth and Resources in Sierra Leone* (Oxford: James Currey, 1996).
21 D. K. Cohen, 'Explaining rape during civil war; cross-national evidence (1980–2009)', *American Political Science Review*, 107:3 (2013), 461–77.

treasured the belief that these kinds of preoccupations would be a thing of the past.

The utilitarian perspective on practising strategy is specifically goal-orientated with a focus on attaining a defined end or end state. This has been the dominant way of looking at conflictual engagement since the nineteenth century; distractions and sideshows might emerge but the overall direction remains consistent. We find, in contrast, several approaches to practising strategy which are far more process-orientated. The focus is on the doing rather than getting. We will now discuss the three most important process-focused sets of practices.

Practising Strategy: Performative

In several of the case studies, we encountered instances in which the practice of strategy was part of a way of life, based on a militarised society. A performative logic of strategy as a practice is focused on outward display, in contrast to the other logics which are mostly polity-inward looking. It also challenges part of the definition of strategy, as the prioritisation process is least linked to larger or systematic plans or change but rather to social and societal structures and concerns.

Some societies were stratified so as to put a warrior class at the top of the social pyramid, along with glorifying a military lifestyle. Early discoveries of the links between the different branches of the Indo-European languages and the cultural heritage they transported led to a theory that they also shared a perception of populations as divided into the three categories of priest, warrior and peasant. The theory was put forward by the French scholar Georges Dumézil in the 1920s that the emphasis on the rule of the warrior in this society was a particular Indo-European phenomenon, and it enjoyed considerable popularity.[22] One would thus not be surprised to find this theory confirmed in ancient Greece, where Alexander the Great hankered for personal glory akin to that achieved by his hero Achilles, or ancient Rome with its bellicose culture that valued military prowess and glory; this ambition also motivated the early Persian kings who strove for heroism to outshine their predecessors. We find it in the medieval European culture of chivalry, with formulaic warfare according to codes and conventions also influencing lifestyle in general, focusing on courage and loyalty instead of

---

22 J. Gonda, 'Dumézil's tripartite ideology: some critical observations', *Journal of Asian Studies*, 34:1 (Nov. 1974), 139–49.

discipline. In the historiography of medieval war, violent interactions had not been ascribed a greater logic beyond an exercise in social ordering.

We find that this pattern applies beyond the narrow Eurasian sphere, where it is initially found. Practising strategy was, in different societies, an important performative act. In Ancient China, war was a societal and cultural phenomenon practised by the aristocracy, who engaged in warfare based on formulaic, cultural codes and expectations. Specifically, cultural codes were objects of organised violence and were engaged in as cultural practices among the elite. It involved their status and position at court. The warrior also held prime place in society among the Turkic tribes, the Mongols, the Japanese, pre-colonial African societies as well as societies of the south-east Asian islands. Glory and ambition were allegedly the drivers for Shaka Zulu in the early nineteenth century.

The practice was not only informed by social status; religion and spirituality also contributed to the picture offered in the case studies about strategic praxis. The metaphysical dimension of culture appears in many variations and degrees of intensity. In some societies, such as ancient Rome, religious rituals were used to assuage superstitions, and were at best accessories to warfare. In ancient Greece oracles were used to divine the most opportune timing of battle and engagements. For Sasanian Iran, the Zoroastrian religion influenced the practice of strategy, the symbol of 'victorious fire' burning in the temple considered especially important.

In other societies such as the Islamic world and medieval and early modern Europe, religion was central to much warfare. In China, the mandate of Heaven was first formulated in the eleventh century BC. Political legitimacy was based on the personal virtue of the rulers and there was an organised use of shamans to motivate troops by communicating signs from spirits. For the European Middle Ages, deeply felt religious motivations informed the practice of crusading, which was accompanied by a chivalric culture infusing all aspects of these military undertakings. Also, the central place of the Church in warfare led to war being infused with spiritual meaning; fasting, praying, processions and repentance were key elements in the repertoire of actions. Strategy as performative practice involves direct societal engagement and ritualised behaviour.

Practising Strategy: Opportunity

A second set of practices can be grouped around the notion of opportunism. We find that a dominant pattern of strategic practice is not so much geared towards attaining a premeditated goal or carried out in the shape of ritualised practices but forms a practice that seizes upon opportunities pragmatically. These opportunities occur, are capitalised on in a developing situation and allow the polity to improve its position. This practice can, of course overlap with utilitarianism, performative practice and ordering/disordering as described below. Such opportunism is often found on an operational level in military commanders whom Clausewitz would admire for their *coup d'oeil*, their intuitive ability to take advantage of new situations that lend themselves to such exploitation. Strategic studies scholar Colin Gray noted that '[i]n warfare, as in other human behaviours, one should not do things for no better reason other than that they can be done'.[23] However, this is exactly what we see happening across time and place, which fits better with the conceptualisation by Lawrence Freedman who has offered this idea as 'the art of creating power', where the situation is exploited to make more of it than the initial disposition of resources would predict.[24] This goes a long way to explain the growing ambitions of an Alexander III of Macedon, a Chinggis Khan, a Napoleon, a Hitler and indeed a Vladimir Putin. In fact, most empires expanded by exploiting opportunities as they presented themselves. Other than a vague ideal of a 'universal monarchy' that was amazingly widespread even when the term 'universal' could only refer to known parts of the world, we find few if any systematic blueprints for conquest. The one exception was perhaps that of Ottoman emperor Mehmet II's ambition not only to capture Constantinople, but to make himself the master of all the lands controlled by the caesars of old. The strategic aims of the unplanned seizure of opportunities as they arise are based on several logics: lack of control, raiding, the unfolding of events and distractions.

Lack of Control

Until the nineteenth century if not later, political leaders were based far away from the theatre of war and even supreme military commanders could exercise limited control over their forces. The general rule that one needed to defend oneself, protect friends and harm enemies, at whichever opportunity and juncture, fed in practice opportunism. In the case of Alexander the Great, it has been argued that his armies led him rather than his carrying out a premeditated plan or strategy. For the case of Republican Rome, the fact that the expansion process was patchy and haphazard underlines the idea that most of the activities did not follow a master plan but were part of an organic

---

23 C. Gray, 'Conclusion', in Olsen and Gray (eds), *Practice of Strategy*, 287–300, 294.
24 B. Wilkinson and J. Gow, *The Art of Creating Power: Freedman on Strategy* (Oxford: Oxford University Press, 2017).

process. In late Imperial China, strategy unfolded as a response to events rather than wilful and premeditated purposive action. Also half a world away and two millennia later, Frederick II of Prussia has been argued to be skilful at capitalising on unfolding events and favourable circumstances rather than possessing statesmanship and foresight. In more recent times, the lack of control of the Belgrade leadership during significant periods of the war in Bosnia in the 1990s allowed local commanders to grab opportunities as they arose and act as they saw fit.

Raiding

Apart from the nature of decision making and control, raiding is also an important opportunistic strategic template. Interestingly, this has been linked to geographic differentials.[25] In China in the first millennium AD, neighbouring nomadic populations took advantage of the sedentary Han populations to seize resources such as grain or luxury goods such as silk which were produced in the agricultural empire. The fact that the neighbours stored grain made them very attractive targets for nomads living off the land. Evidence from the Gupta Empire similarly brings forward raiding as the only justified motivation for foreign conquest. In pre-colonial Africa, we also find the geographic differential. Raiding occurred frequently on the border zone between the Sahara Desert occupied by nomadic populations and the Sahel, where sedentary agriculture started.

Even beyond these parameters of geography, raiding constitutes an important practice across the ages. For early medieval European warfare, looting was a strategic purpose, as war between kings was a common condition and the exploitation of opportunities was a specific skill. The acquiring of plunder had important strategic effects as it benefited the legitimacy and support for the king. Moreover, strategy could be seen as a 'protection racket' of opportunistic and entrepreneurial leaders. These advanced protection rackets formed the first kernels of the European state-building process.[26]

Our case studies confirm Jeremy Black's argument that raiding is not simply a tactical activity, as has often been argued in earlier literature. Instead, '[r]aiding was a key strategy, one that in practice collapsed into the

---

25 P. Turchin, 'A theory for formation of large empires', *Journal of Global History*, 4 (2000), 191–217.
26 C. Tilly, *Coercion, Capital and European States, 900–1900* (Cambridge, MA: Blackwell, 1990). Tilly, 'War-making and state-making as organized crime', in P. Evans, D. Rueschemeyer and T. Skocpol (eds), *Bringing the State Back In* (Cambridge: Cambridge University Press, 1985).

Conclusion

more common distinctions of strategic, operational and tactical moves. Raiding is also an aspect of what has been referred to as "little war", a form of conflict that lacks systematic study, and especially so at the strategic level'.[27] Our findings are also in accord with the work of Archer Jones, who elevated raiding to the status of mainstream strategic mode, a counterpart to what he calls persisting strategy.[28] Raiding ends up with important strategic repercussions and forms a primary motivation to practise strategy.

Unfolding Events

A third set of opportunistic practices is informed by responding to unfolding events. In the case of late Imperial China, we read that what was perceived as strategy was simply a response to unfolding events. For the largest contiguous land empire in world history, the empire of the Mongols, there is no evidence that Chinggis Khan set out with an ambition to rule the world. Rather, feuding, providing security and addressing threats on the frontiers informed violent activities. The empire arrived by accident. After the death of Chinggis Khan, based on the prophecy of a shaman, his successors started to subscribe to the idea of world domination, of Heaven's Will. Also for Frederick II of Prussia, skill and good judgement were the main ingredients of success in advantageous circumstances rather than deeper thought and planning. Napoleon's invasion of Russia in 1812 was based on vengeance rather than pure political calculation. It turned out to be a huge strategic blunder with great human and material costs. No thoughts had been devoted prior to the invasion to whether or not Russia should be part of the French Empire. Opportunism to punish Russia was the main driver for this action.

In more recent times we find evidence for this opportunism in the case study of Israel and the capture of territory in the 1973 war. While the primary objective was to destroy the Syrian and Egyptian military forces, occupying territory could be used as a lever in subsequent negotiations. In the 1982 war, the initial aim to push back the PLO further into Lebanon beyond the range of their rockets turned into the ambition to expel the PLO from Lebanon altogether.

Distraction

A last instalment of strategic practice as opportunism is the transition to action when international attention is distracted elsewhere. This is particularly notable in the case of China. In the chapters devoted to Chinese strategic

---

27 Black, *Military Strategy*, 22.
28 A. Jones, *Elements of Military Strategy: An Historical Approach* (London: Praeger, 1996).

practices, at three points we encountered the Chinese capitalising on distractions elsewhere; first, while the world was preoccupied by the Cuban Missile Crisis in 1962, the Sino-Indian border crisis played out; second, when the United States intervened in Lebanon in 1958, the Chinese bombarded Jinmen and Mazu; third, the Chinese Navy captured the Paracel islands while the world was watching the fall of Saigon in 1975.

This type of opportunistic ad hockery in strategic practice seems to confirm the pattern identified by Robert Chia and Robin Holt, namely that strategy as practised is more often a response occurring spontaneously and reactively rather than the result of a premeditated plan and thought-out plan of action.[29] This line of inquiry should be pursued in more depth by strategic studies scholarship.

Practising Strategy: Ordering and Disordering

A fourth pattern of practising strategy is what we call here ordering and disordering.[30] This is distinct from the utilitarian perspective because this shaping exercise lacks a concrete end goal, focusing instead on a process. (Dis)ordering is analogous to mowing the grass. When the grass becomes too high, action becomes necessary. We find two variations: one aiming at creating a more favourable order for the polity; the other creating more disorder for the opponent, which it is hoped would be beneficial.

Ordering

Strategy can be practised in a process of creating order. The narrative of Rome's imperial expansion was that Rome always reacted defensively to attacks, but then integrated defeated adversaries in its sphere of power in order to pacify them. This logic of imperial pacification can be found in many other areas of the world,[31] such as the early caliphates, where the ideology of jihadism informed a practice of security maximisation based on expansionism. The conduct of jihad to shape the world in a specific image led to a perennial state of war without an endpoint, short of extending the Dar al Islam to encompass the entire globe.

---

29 R. Chia and R. Holt, *Strategy Without Design; The Silent Efficacy of Indirect Action* (Cambridge: Cambridge University Press, 2009).
30 Also I. Duyvesteyn and H. Drop, 'Alternative imaginings: order and disorder in early Chinese military theory', unpublished manuscript.
31 I. Morris, *War: What Is It Good For? The Role of Conflict in Civilisation, from Primates to Robots* (New York: Profile Books, 2014).

Conclusion

The practice can also be found in 'imperial policing',[32] with the aim of repressing insurgencies or organised crime, and has been a key element of peacekeeping. General Rupert Smith noted that the peacekeepers being charged with creating a safe and secure environment are useless when politicians do not capitalise on this condition.[33] We can equally identify it in interstate relations when a rules-based order is upheld and 'rogue states' transgressing these rules are punished in a joint effort by several states who claim to be acting for the international community, in the interest of international peace and 'the security' and 'the tranquillity' of all, as is said in the treaties of Utrecht, for example.[34] A safe and secure environment in itself is a condition rather than an outcome.

Disordering

The flipside of this ambition can be found in the strategic aim of creating disorder and chaos as a desirable condition for the opponent. The attainment of clearly defined ends may not be necessary, or possibly not feasible, in the given circumstances. We can already find this idea in Sunzi's *The Art of War* as a major premise for operating successfully, preserving our own order and disordering our opponent.[35] A recent variation of the disordering practice could be observed in disinformation campaigns, election meddling and grey zone operations, which have preoccupied a host of scholars focused on activities of the Russian Federation.[36]

In the case studies we see this kind of activity in ancient Greece in the feuding between the city states. In the case of the Byzantines, disordering and incapacitating opponents by violent means and sowing death and destruction was an important practice. Medieval European warfare was substantially aimed at destruction, and disordering would also aptly describe the activities of the Ottoman *Ghazi* soldiers. For the Persian Achaemenid Empire, punitive action, putting down rebellions and executing enemy leaders would act as

---

32 J. Bartelson, *War in International Thought* (Cambridge: Cambridge University Press, 2018).
33 R. Smith, *The Utility of Force; The Art of War in the Modern World* (London: Allen Lane, 2005).
34 G. Chalmers (ed.), *A Collection of Treaties Between Great Britain and other Powers* (London: J. Stockdale, 1790), vol. 1, 390; F. I. Israel (ed.), *Major Peace Treaties of Modern History, 1648–1967* (New York: Chelsea House, 1967), vol. 1, 183.
35 V. H. Mair, *The Art of War: Sun Zi's Military Methods* (New York: Columbia University Press, 2007). E. O'Dowd and A. Waldron, 'Sun Tzu for strategists', *Comparative Strategy*, 10:1 (1991), 25–36.
36 See for instance a special journal issue, 'Contentious narratives: digital technology and the attack on liberal democratic norms', *Journal of International Affairs*, 71 (2018), 1–5.

deterrents to further opposition. The Mongols devastated lands beyond any area they wished to rule in order to create a buffer zone that the other side would have to cross to seek revenge or recover their enslaved fellows. In the Spanish wars of King Louis XIV of France, armies were ordered to destroy enemy lands not only to prevent the population from feeding itself and their state from raising taxes but also to prevent the re-emergence of the opponent at a later stage. Scorched-earth tactics contributed to an overall strategy of denying assets to adversaries in the medium or longer term.

In more recent times, the practice of strategy as disordering is also visible in the Israeli strategy in dealing with the occupied territories. In the case of Israel, the 'mowing of the grass' has been a continual feature of confrontations with adversaries, both near and further away.[37] The shaping of the environment to temporarily create more safety for the population has repeatedly carried the Israel Defence Forces (IDF) into the occupied territories and the border zones. The 'mowing of the grass' strategy can also be used to degrade the capabilities and opportunities for Israeli adversaries to engage in future strikes. These are always temporary solutions and never attain a permanent character.

A related argument about disordering has been made for the many civil wars in Africa since the 1990s, and the emergence of war systems in which warlords tend to thrive. These wars are not focused on an outcome but on the maintenance of disorder and chaos in order to continue systems of predation and financial benefit.[38] In the twenty-first century, the Islamic State subscribed to a disordering approach; in *The Management of Savagery*, a key document detailing the approach to their strategic agenda, the creation of chaos and disorder features prominently.[39] This disordering approach has been focused on undermining, among others, Western societies and discourses.

We see interesting ambiguities also in siege warfare, in itself a perennial component of warfare until today, with recent examples in the sieges of the Syrian Civil War and the current war in Ukraine with sieges of Ilovaisk,

---

37 E. Inbar and E. Shamir, '"Mowing the grass": Israel's strategy for protracted intractable conflict', *Journal of Strategic Studies*, 37:1 (2014), 65–90.
38 D. Keen, *Useful Enemies; When Waging Wars Is More Important than Winning Them* (New Haven: Yale University Press, 2012).
39 Abu Bakr Naji, 'The management of savagery; the most critical stage through which the Islamic nation will pass 2004', https://web.archive.org/web/20170110084554/https://azelin.files.wordpress.com/2010/08/abu-bakr-naji-the-management-of-savagery-the-most-critical-stage-through-which-the-umma-will-pass.pdf.

Donetsk, Debaltseve and Mariupol.[40] It seems that the capture of a besieged city did not always have as its aim the long-term occupation by the conqueror. Especially in antiquity, there are many examples of cities being destroyed but not resettled, indicating that the strategic aim was to disperse the adversary rather than formal occupation. Disordering thus forms a significant strategic practice.

Practising Strategy: Problems and Challenges

While the text above has tried to outline the predominant patterns of strategic practices, we do not want to suggest that practising strategy is a neat and focused phenomenon in the real world in the different times and places which we have studied. Rather the opposite, and this is our third conclusion. The definitional lens we applied, viewing the practice of strategy as the aligning of objectives in an order of priority and marrying them to appropriate resources and methods to attain them, highlighted significant recurring problems. Practising strategy is challenging and, as already noted in the Introduction to this second volume, there are few examples where the practices actually followed the premises that have been formulated in theory. Even when the lens of strategy applies and we see the different elements in action, they hardly feature as the clear-cut guidance they supposedly promise. We now discuss the most notable and challenging aspects, to wit: seeing strategic practice as a one-sided exercise; the instability of objectives; and the faulty alignment of objectives and resources.

Strategy as Interaction

There are many instances over the course of history in which we can see the exercise of strategy as an inward-looking affair. Actors are often preoccupied with their own aims and considerations about what they want to gain from a particular situation, rather than concerning themselves with what the opponent desires. Neglecting to consider or pre-empt the opponent's response in the calculations and calibrations occurs often. We saw this, for instance, in the case of the Russo-Japanese War, where the dominant perception on the part of the Russian decision makers was that the Japanese were weaker. This was based not only on prejudice but also involved a serious miscalculation of how Japan would use nationalism and a patriotic spirit to

---

40 A. Fox, 'On sieges', *Rusi Journal*, 166:2 (2021), 18–28, https://doi.org/10.1080/03071847.2021.1924077.

motivate the troops. We can also see this in the case of the First World War, where coalition decision making was heavily preoccupied by internal processes among allies rather than a common understanding of a shared idea of how to prosecute the war using all the available means. A last example of one-sided strategic practice comes from Iraq's Saddam Hussein. Not only did Hussein underestimate the capability and willingness of the Iranians to resist in the early 1980s, he also had little grasp of the American commitment as well as technological abilities that proved his defeat in 2003. This phenomenon has also been visible in the Ukraine war, where it appears that serious strategic miscalculations occurred on the side of the Kremlin regarding the level of resistance of the Ukrainian population and their preparedness for war.

Instability of Objectives

In strategic theory, the formulation of a feasible objective is an important premise for the successful execution of a strategy. In our case material, however, we encounter time and again the absence, late formulation or change of a central objective. Most of the contributions offered a reasoning or rationale for the events that were witnessed. Still, the centrality of a formulated goal seems overstated. Several variations are offered. First, ad hoc decision making was prevalent. Decisions did not include long-term visions for a desired future, but were dominated by responding to unfolding events. Second, causes of war were very often produced by war rather than preceding it. This is, in fact, a central premise in revolutionary people's war, where the state by its own actions demonstrates itself to be illegitimate and acting against the interests of its own people by killing. This was visible after the 2001 invasion of Afghanistan: the initial aim was to capture Osama bin Laden, but developed to toppling the Taliban-led regime, then building and modernising the Afghan state. This does not mean that we argue against the phenomenon of what is also called 'mission creep'. Changes in the objectives do not inherently form a problem. The consequences, however, namely a realistic reassessment of the ends of the conflict, would need to lead to a reprioritisation. This is where problems emerge: reprioritising requires a realignment of the means and methods to calibrate them with the (attainable) ends.

Mismatching Objectives and Resources

This misalignment of ends and means forms a notable and perennial problem in the practising of strategy: mismatches or lacking calibration between the objectives set and the means and methods to achieve them is pervasive. The chapters abound with examples of this problem. In the case of the United States and the First World War, there is a clear mismatch between the lofty Fourteen Points plan developed by President Woodrow Wilson to end the war and the lack of appropriate means, among others caused by political circumstances in the US itself. We also saw a mismatch between means and ends in Afghanistan, where many of the International Security Assistance Force (ISAF) allies supported the mission to be seen as good allies. They mistook participation in the mission for the objective of the war, which displayed a painful lack of strategic understanding.[41]

Ways Forward

The ambition with which we started was to move beyond the present limits of the field of strategic studies and shift the parameters of hodiecentrism or presentism, of Western and state centrism, as well as of the theory and utilitarian focus. Looking back at our journey of discovery, we hope the insights offered here will have brought us further. The long historical lens we have applied did open up and broaden the perspective on strategy. Selecting significant case material from outside the usual Western case studies helped to shed light on the issue of universality of the strategic experience. Questioning the means-ends instrumentalism, so dominant in strategic studies, helped us to trace alternatives.

The findings we would like to highlight are threefold. First, our conceptual framework to study the practice of strategy is in need of rethinking. Taking the nation state as a benchmark for understanding strategic practice has overshadowed other significant and valid practices, which deserve further attention and research effort. Second, the diversity of strategic practices invites us to decidedly move beyond the dominant utilitarian focus and take on board other logics of praxis. We have found in particular performative practice, as well as opportunism and ordering/disordering logics, as worthy of further study. Third, the practice is messy and subject to perennial change, so what appears in strategic theory, and is discussed as strategic thought of universal application, forms in practice a rather different picture. This observation leads to a new question: should we consider therefore the existence of multiple strategic theories, one for each logic of strategic practice? Or does mainstream strategic theory, predominantly rooted in the

---

41 Research in the cases of the Netherlands, Sweden and Norway have highlighted this logic, e.g., M. Berdal and A. Surkhe, 'A good ally; Norway and international statebuilding in Afghanistan (2001–2014)', *Journal of Strategic Studies*, 42:1-2 (2018), 61–88.

utilitarian perspective, exhibit sufficiently flexible characteristics to accommodate all the distinct logics? This would be an interesting avenue for further research.

At this point we must insert a caveat. To what extent are similarities that we have identified in human societies the product of largely similar social configurations and contexts? Are we finding similar weapons due to similar (quite basic) technology inventing the same thing independently from one another? Or is it due to diffusion (cultural transfer) of means and ways of doing things? Or is it that the interpretational framework that we have imposed leads us to categorise as 'similar' things that should not be seen as such, being too crude to allow sufficiently for cultural variety or even uniqueness? It may be that there are variations which it does not capture, but which are not sufficiently significant to be mentioned or even dwelt upon, given the word limits of these volumes. From the paucity of sources, it is not clear whether the commonalities are the result of diffusion or reflect a natural proclivity among human societies to configure in a certain way; this would be a good subject for further research. Other avenues for future work, apart from the obvious broadening of the pool of case material, could be a more fundamental rethink of strategic theory. The diversity in practices is larger than the scholarship has hitherto recognised. Moreover, ad hockery appears to be a core component of these practices. Academics thus might exhibit a proclivity to over-rationalise decision making, including the practice of strategy. This might form an important new line of inquiry.

If there is one thing that the material above demonstrates, it is that despite attempts at categorisation, practising strategy is messy and very often reactive, rather than rational, linear and neatly conceptualised. This appears to be a truism across time and place. Still, there is more we can say about the diversity of strategic practices. We find that the utilitarian conception of linking ends with means is a straitjacket that captures only part of the story. We appear to be hostages to the nineteenth-century conceptualisation of strategic practice as the systematic pursuit of political goals and territory, and the preoccupation with victory. Instead, the case studies have offered us food for thought in light of common patterns of practising strategy to create disorder, to capture people instead of territory and to seek a condition rather than a clear political outcome based on military victory.

Further Reading

Strategic History of the Napoleonic Wars

Bell, D. A., *The First Total War: Napoleon's Europe and the Birth of Modern Warfare* (London: Bloomsbury, 2007).
Colson, B. (ed.), *Napoleon on War* (Oxford: Oxford University Press, 2015).
Esdaile, C., 'Deconstructing the French wars: Napoleon as anti-strategist', *Journal of Strategic Studies*, 31 (2008), 515–52.
Heuser, B., *Strategy Before Clausewitz. Linking Warfare and Statecraft, 1400–1830* (London: Routledge, 2018).
Luvaas, J. (ed.), *Napoleon on the Art of War* (New York: The Free Press, 1999).
Mikaberidze, A., *The Napoleonic Wars: A Global History* (New York: Oxford University Press, 2020).
Riley, J., *Napoleon as a General: Command from the Battlefield to Grand Strategy* (London: Continuum, 2007).
Robbe, É. and F. Lagrange (eds), *Napoléon Stratège* (Paris: Liénart / Musée de l'Armée, 2018).

Strategic History of The First World War

Afflerbach, H. (ed.), *The Purpose of the First World War: War Aims and Military Strategies* (Berlin: De Gruyter Oldenbourg, 2015).
Beckett, I., *The Great War, 1914–1918* (London: Routledge, 2007).
Broadberry, S. and M. Harrison (eds), *The Economics of World War I* (Cambridge: Cambridge University Press, 2005).
Chickering, R. and S. Förster (eds), *Great War, Total War: Combat and Mobilization on the Western Front, 1914–1918* (Cambridge: Cambridge University Press, 2000).
Greenhalgh, E., *Victory Through Coalition: Britain and France During the First World War* (Cambridge: Cambridge University Press, 2005).
Howard, M., *The First World War* (Oxford: Oxford University Press, 2007).
Nieberg, M. S., *Fighting the Great War: A Global History* (Cambridge, MA: Harvard University Press, 2005).
Stevenson, D., *The History of the First World War: 1914–1918* (London: Allen Lane, 2004).
Strachan, H., *The First World War: A New History* (London: Simon & Schuster, 2014).

Further Reading

Strategic History of the Second World War

Aglan, A. and R. Frank (eds), *1937–1947. La guerre-monde*, 2 vols. (Paris: Gallimard Folio, 2015).
Burgwyn, H. J., *Mussolini Warlord: Failed Dreams of Empire 1940–1943* (New York: Enigma, 2012).
Dear, I. C. B. (ed.), *The Oxford Companion to World War II* (Oxford: Oxford University Press, 2005).
Dower, J. W., *War without Mercy: Race and Power in the Pacific War* (New York: W.W. Norton & Company, 1986).
Ferris, J. and E. Mawdsley (eds), *The Cambridge History of the Second World War*, 3 vols. (Cambridge: Cambridge University Press, 2015).
Frieser, K.-H. with J. T. Greenwood, *The Blitzkrieg Legend: The 1940 Campaign in the West* (Annapolis: Naval Institute Press, 2005).
Gailey, H., *The War in the Pacific: From Pearl Harbor to Tokyo Bay* (Novata: Presidio, 1995).
Gildea, R. and I. Tames (eds), *Fighters Across Frontiers. Transnational Resistance in Europe, 1936–48* (Manchester: Manchester University Press, 2020).
Glanz, D. M. and J. House, *When Titans Clashed: How the Red Army Stopped Hitler* (Lawrence: University Press of Kansas, 1995).
Ienaga, S., *The Pacific War: World War II and the Japanese, 1931–1945* (New York: Pantheon, 1978).
Militärgeschichtliches Forschungsamt (ed.), *Germany and the Second World War* (Oxford: Clarendon Press, 1990).
Muracciole, J.-F. and G. Piketty (eds), *Encyclopédie de la Seconde Guerre mondiale* (Paris: Robert Laffont, 2015).
Overy, R., *The Bombing War: Europe, 1939–1945* (London: Penguin, 2015 / Allen Lane, 2013).
Roberts, G., *Stalin's Wars: From World War to Cold War, 1939–1953* (New Haven: Yale University Press, 2006).
Roberts, A., *The Storm of War: A New History of the Second World War* (New York: HarperCollins, 2011).
Sarantakes, N. E., *Allies Against the Rising Sun: The United States, the British Nations, and the Defeat of Imperial Japan* (Lawrence: University Press of Kansas, 2009).
Spector, R., *Eagle Against the Sun: The American War with Japan* (New York: The Free Press, 1985).
Symonds, C. L., *World War II at Sea: A Global History* (Oxford: Oxford University Press, 2018).
Thorne, C., *Allies of a Kind: The United States, Britain and the War against Japan, 1941–1945* (New York: Oxford University Press, 1978).
Willmott, H. P., *The Second World War in the East* (London: Cassell, 1999).

Strategic History of the Korean War

Chen, J., *China's Road to the Korean War: The Making of the Sino-American Confrontation* (New York: Columbia University Press, 1994).
Cummings, B., *The Origins of the Korean War* (Lawrence: University Press of Kansas, 1981 and 1990).
Goncharov, S. N., J. W. Lewis and L. Xue, *Uncertain Partners: Stalin, Mao, and the Korean War* (Stanford: Stanford University Press, 1993).

Halberstam, D., *The Coldest Winter: America and the Korean War* (New York: Hyperion, 2007).
Li, X., *China's War in Korea: Strategic Culture and Geopolitics* (London: Palgrave Macmillan, 2019).
Millett, A. R., *The War for Korea, 1950–1951: They Came from the North* (Lawrence: University Press of Kansas, 2010).
Stueck, W. W., Jr, *Rethinking the Korean War: A New Diplomatic and Strategic History* (Princeton: Princeton University Press, 2004).
Zhang, S. G., *Deterrence and Strategic Culture: Chinese-American Confrontations, 1949–1958* (Ithaca: Cornell University Press, 1992).

Strategic History of the Arab–Israeli Wars

Gabriel, R. A., *Operation Peace for Galilee: The Israeli–PLO War in Lebanon* (New York: Hill and Wang, 1984).
Harel, A. and A. Issacharoff, *34 Days: Israel, Hezbollah and the War in Lebanon* (New York: St Martin's Press, 2008).
Hecht, E., 'Israeli strategy in the First Lebanon War, 1982–1985', *Infinity Journal*, Special Edition: *Strategic Misfortunes* (2012).
IDF General Staff, *IDF Strategy 2015*, Belfer Center for Science and International Affairs (trans.) (August 2016), www.belfercenter.org/sites/default/files/legacy/files/IDFDoctrineTranslation.pdf.
Kober, A., 'From blitzkrieg to attrition: Israel's attrition strategy and staying power', *Small Wars and Insurgencies*, 16 (2005), 216–40.
Luttwak, E. and D. Horowitz, *The Israeli Army* (London: Allen Lane, 1975).
Rabinovich, A., *The Yom Kippur War: The Epic Encounter that Transformed the Middle East* (New York: Schocken, 2007).
Shamir, E. and E. Hecht, 'Gaza 2014: Israel's attrition vs Hamas' exhaustion', *Parameters*, 44 (2014–15), 81–90.
Tal, D., *War in Palestine, 1948: Israeli and Arab Strategy and Diplomacy* (Abingdon: Routledge, 2004).
Tal, I., *National Security: The Israeli Experience* (Westport: Greenwood Publishers, 2000).

Strategic History of the Afghan War

Egnell, R. and D. Ucko, *Counterinsurgency in Crisis: Britain and the Challenges of Modern Warfare* (New York: Columbia University Press, 2013).
Farrell, T., *Unwinnable: Britain's War in Afghanistan, 2001–2014* (London: The Bodley Head, 2017).
Grau, L. W., *The Bear Went Over the Mountain* (Washington, DC: National Defence University Press, 1998).
Guistozzi, A., *Empires of Mud* (New York: Columbia University Press, 2008).

Johnson, R., *The Afghan Way of War: How and Why they Fight* (Oxford: Oxford University Press, 2014).
Jones, S. G., *In the Graveyard of Empires: America's War in Afghanistan* (New York: W.W. Norton, 2010).
Malkasian, C., *War Comes to Garmster* (Oxford: Oxford University Press, 2013).
Rashid, A., *Descent into Chaos: The US and the Disaster in Pakistan, Afghanistan and Central Asia* (New York: Penguin, 2009).
Rubin, B. R., *The Fragmentation of Afghanistan* (New Haven:Yale University Press, 2002).
Rynning, S., *NATO in Afghanistan: The Liberal Disconnect* (Stanford: Stanford University Press, 2012).
Tanner, A., *Afghanistan: A Military History from Alexander the Great to the Taliban* (Cambridge: Perseus, 2009).

Strategic History of the Gulf Wars

Abdulghani, J., *Iraq and Iran: The Years of Crisis* (Baltimore: Johns Hopkins University Press, 1984).
Cramer, J. K. and A. T. Thrall (eds), *Why Did the United States Invade Iraq?* (London: Routledge, 2012).
Devlin, J., 'Iraqi military policy: from assertiveness to defense', in Thomas Naff (ed.), *Gulf Security and the Iran-Iraq War* (Washington, DC: National Defense University Press, 1985), 129–56.
Freedman, L. and E. Karsh, *The Gulf Conflict, 1990–1991* (London: Faber and Faber, 1993).
Gordon, M. and B. Trainor, *COBRA II: The Inside Story of the Invasion and Occupation of Iraq* (London: Atlantic Books, 2006).
The Generals' War: The Inside Story of the Conflict in the Gulf (Boston: Little, Brown and Company, 1995).
Harkavy, R. and S. Neuman (eds), *The Lessons of Recent Wars in the Third World, Volume 1, Approaches and Case Studies* (Lexington: Heath and Company, 1985).
Hashim, A. S., *Iranian Ways of War: From Cyrus the Great to Qassem Soleimani* (London: Hurst, forthcoming).
Hiro, D., *Desert Shield to Desert Storm: The Second Gulf War* (London: Paladin, 1992).
The Longest War: The Iran–Iraq Military Conflict (London and Glasgow: Paladin, 1990).
Hurst, S., *The United States and Iraq since 1979: Hegemony, Oil and War* (Edinburgh: Edinburgh University Press, 2009).
Murray, W. and K. Woods, *The Iran–Iraq War: A Military and Strategic History* (Cambridge: Cambridge University Press, 2014).
Nelson, Ch. E., 'Revolution and war: Saddam's decision to invade Iran', *Middle East Journal*, 72 (2018), 246–66.
Ricks, T., *Fiasco: The American Military Adventure in Iraq* (London: Penguin Books, 2006).
Woods, K., *The Mother of All Battles: Saddam Hussein's Strategic Plan for the Persian Gulf War* (Annapolis: Naval Institute Press, 2008).
Woods, K., J. Lacey and W. Murray, 'Saddam's delusions: the view from the inside', *Foreign Affairs*, 85 (2006), 2–26.

Woods, K., W. Murray and T. Holaday, *Saddam's War: An Iraqi Perspective of the Iran–Iraq War* (Washington, DC: Institute for National Strategic Studies, National Defense University, 2009).

Strategic History of the Wars of Decolonisation

Alexander, J., J. McGregor and B.-M. Tendi (eds), *Transnational Histories of Southern Africa's Liberation Movements* (Abingdon: Routledge, 2020).
Beckett, I. F. W., *Modern Insurgencies and Counter-Insurgencies: Guerrillas and Their Opponents since 1750* (London: Routledge, 2001).
Chabal, P., *Amilcar Cabral: Revolutionary Leadership and People's War*, 2nd ed. (London: Hurst, 2002).
Dhada, M., *Warriors at Work: How Guinea Was Really Set Free* (Niwot: University of Colorado Press, 1993).
Kriger, Norma J., *Zimbabwe's Guerrilla War: Peasant Voices* (Cambridge: Cambridge University Press, 1992).
Macmaster, Neil, *War in the Mountains. Peasant Society and Counterinsurgency in Algeria, 1918–1958* (Oxford: Oxford University Press, 2020).
Marcum, J. A., *Conceiving Mozambique*, Edmund Burke III and Michael W. Clough (eds), (Cham: Springer, 2018).
Ranger, T., *Peasant Consciousness and Guerrilla War in Zimbabwe* (London: James Currey, 1985).
Reid, R. J., *Warfare in African History* (Cambridge: Cambridge University Press, 2012).
Sapire, H. and C. Saunders (eds), *Southern African Liberation Struggles: New Local, Regional and Global Perspectives* (Claremont: University of Cape Town Press, 2013).
Saul, J. S. and S. Brown, *Namibia's Liberation Struggle: The Two-Edged Sword* (London: James Currey, 1995).
Simpson, T., *Umkhonto we Sizwe: The ANC's Armed Struggle* (Cape Town: Penguin Books, 2016).
Stapleton, T., *Africa: War and Conflict in the Twentieth Century* (London: Routledge, 2018).
Thomas, M., 'Violence, insurgency, and the end of empires', in M. Thomas and A. S. Thompson (eds), *The Oxford Handbook of the Ends of Empire* (Oxford: Oxford University Press, 2018), 497–518.
Vince, N., *The Algerian War, the Algerian Revolution* (Cham: Palgrave Macmillan, 2020).
Weigert, S. L., *Angola: A Modern Military History, 1961–2002* (New York: Palgrave Macmillan, 2011).

Strategic History of the India–Pakistan Wars

Bass, G. J., *The Blood Telegram: Nixon, Kissinger and a Forgotten Genocide* (New York: Penguin Random House, 2014).
Brines, R., *The Indo-Pakistani Conflict* (New York: Pall Mall, 1968).

Cohen, S. P., *The Indian Army: Its Contribution to the Development of a Nation* (Berkeley: University of California Press, 1971).
The Pakistan Army (Berkeley: University of California Press, 1984).
Ganguly, S., *The Crisis in Kashmir: Portents of War, Hopes of Peace* (Washington, DC: Woodrow Wilson Center Press and New York: Cambridge University Press, 1997).
Kapur, S. P., *Jihad as Grand Strategy: Islamist Militancy, National Security and the Pakistani State* (New York: Oxford University Press, 2016).
Kavic, L., *India's Quest for Security: Defense Policies, 1947–1965* (Berkeley: University of California Press, 1967).
Shah, A. M., *The Army and Democracy: Military Politics in Pakistan* (Cambridge, MA: Harvard University Press, 2014).

Strategic History of the Yugoslav War

CIA, *Balkan Battlegrounds: A Military History of the Yugoslav Conflict, Volumes 1 and 2* (Washington, DC: CIA Office of Russian and European Analysis, 2002 and 2003).
Gow, J., *The Serbian Project and Its Adversaries: A Strategy of War Crimes* (London: Hurst, 2003).
Vukušić, I., *Serbian Paramilitaries in the Breakup of Yugoslavia* (New York: Routledge, 2022).

Modern Chinese Strategic History

Fravel, T., *Active Defense: China's Military Strategy since 1949* (Princeton: Princeton University Press, 2019).
Jordan, D., *The Northern Expedition: China's National Revolution of 1926–8* (Honolulu: University Press of Hawaii, 1976).
Meisner, M., *Mao's China, A History of the People's Republic* (New York: The Free Press, 1977).
Mitter, R., *China's War with Japan, 1937–45: The Struggle for Survival* (London: Penguin Books, 2013).
Ryan, A. M., D. M. Finkelstein and M. A. McDevitt (eds), *Chinese Warfighting: The PLA Experience since 1949* (Armonk: M.E. Sharpe, 2003).
Saunders, P., A. Ding, A. Scobell, A. Yang and J. Wuthnow (eds), *Chairman Xi Remakes the PLA: Assessing Chinese Military Reforms* (Washington, DC: NDU Press, 2019).
Saunders, P. and A. Scobell (eds), *PLA Influence on China's National Security Policymaking* (Stanford: Stanford University Press, 2015).
Shambaugh, D., *Modernizing China's Military: Progress, Problems and Prospects* (Berkeley: University of California Press, 2003).
Yung, Ch., R. Rustici, S. Devary and J. Lin, '*Not an Idea We Have to Shun*': *Chinese Overseas Basing Requirements for the Twenty-First Century, China Strategic Perspectives # 7* (Washington, DC: NDU Press, 2014).
Zhu, D., *Selected Works of Zhu De* (Beijing: Foreign Language Press, PRC, 1986).

Further Reading

US Strategic History

Biddle, S., 'The new way of war? Debating the Kosovo model', *Foreign Affairs*, 3 (2002), 138–44.
Boot, M., *Savage Wars of Peace: Small Wars and the Rise of American Power* (New York: Basic Books, 2002).
'The new American way of war', *Foreign Affairs*, 4 (2003), 41–58.
Brigety II, R. E., *Ethics, Technology and the American Way of War: Cruise Missiles and US Security Policy* (London: Routledge, 2007).
Buley, B., *The New American Way of War: Military Culture and the Political Utility of Force* (London: Routledge, 2008).
Cebrowski, A., 'The new American way of war', Speech to the Heritage Foundation delivered 13 May 2003, quoted in *Transformation Trends* (27 May 2003).
Cohen, E. A., *Conquered into Liberty: Two Centuries of Battles Along the Great War Path That Made the American Way of War* (New York: Free Press, 2011).
'Kosovo and the new American way of war', in A. J. Bacevich and E. A. Cohen (eds), *War Over Kosovo: Politics and Strategy in a Global Age* (New York: Columbia University Press, 2001), 38–62.
Echevarria II, A. J., *Toward an American Way of War* (Carlisle, PA: US Army War College, Strategic Studies Institute, 2004).
War's Logic: Strategic Thought and the American Way of War (Cambridge: Cambridge University Press, 2021).
Grant, U. S., *Memoirs and Selected Letters: Personal Memoirs of U. S. Grant. Selected Letters, 1839–1865* (New York: Literary Classics, 1990).
Gray, C. S., *Irregular Enemies and the Essence of Strategy: Can the American Way of War Adapt?* (Carlisle, PA: US Army War College, Strategic Studies Institute, 2006).
Grimsley, M., *The Hard Hand of War: Union Military Policy Toward Southern Civilians, 1861–1865* (Cambridge: Cambridge University Press, 2008).
Hanson, V. D., 'The American way of war', *National Review* (1 April 2003), www.nationalreview.com/2003/04/american-way-war-victor-davis-hanson/.
Hattaway, H. and A. Jones, *How the North Won: A Military History of the Civil War* (Urbana: University of Illinois Press, 1991).
Hoffman, F. G., *Decisive Force: The New American Way of War* (Westport: Praeger, 1996).
Jarecki, E., *The American Way of War: Guided Missiles, Misguided Men, and a Republic in Peril* (New York: Free Press, 2008).
Kaplan, F., *The Insurgents: David Petraeus and the Plot to Change the American Way of War* (New York: Simon & Schuster, 2013).
Lewis, A. R., *The American Culture of War: The History of U.S. Military Force from World War II to Operation Iraqi Freedom* (New York: Routledge, 2007).
Lind, M., *The American Way of Strategy: US Foreign Policy and the American Way of Life* (Oxford: Oxford University Press, 2006).
Linn, B. M. and R. F. Weigley, 'The American way of war revisited', *Journal of Military History*, 2 (2002), 501–30.
Luraghi, R., *A History of the Confederate Navy*, P. E. Coletta (trans.) (Annapolis: Naval Institute Press, 1996).

Mahnken, T., *Technology and the American Way of War since 1945* (New York: Columbia University Press, 2008).
Muehlbauer, M. S. and D. J. Ulbrich, *Ways of War: American Military History from the Colonial Era to the Twenty-First Century* (London: Routledge, 2014).
Record, J., 'Collapsed countries, casualty dread, and the new American way of war', *Parameters*, 2 (2002), 4–23.
The American Way of War: Cultural Barriers to Successful Counterinsurgency (Washington, DC: The CATO Institute, 2006).
Rockoff, H., *America's Economic Way of War: War and the US Economy from the Spanish-American War to the Persian Gulf War* (Cambridge: Cambridge University Press, 2012).
Shannon, T., 'The Native American way of war in the age of revolutions, 1754–1814', in R. Chickering and S. Förster (eds), *War in an Age of Revolution* (Cambridge: Cambridge University Press, 2010), pp. 139–43.
Stoker, D., *Purpose and Power: US Grand Strategy from the Revolutionary Era to the Present* (Cambridge: Cambridge University Press, 2024).
The Grand Design: Strategy and the U.S. Civil War (Oxford: Oxford University Press, 2010).
'There was no offensive-defensive Confederate strategy', *Journal of Military History*, 73 (2009), 177–208.
Symonds, C. L., *Lincoln and His Admirals* (Oxford: Oxford University Press, 2010).
Tierney, D., *How We Fight: Crusades, Quagmires, and the American Way of War* (New York: Little, Brown, 2010).
Warren, J. W. (ed.), *Drawdown: The American Way of Postwar* (New York: New York University Press, 2016).
Weddle, K. J., 'The blockade board of 1861 and Union naval strategy', *Civil War History*, 48 (2002), 123–42.
Weigley, R. F., *A Great Civil War: A Military and Political History, 1861–1865* (Bloomington: Indiana University Press, 2000).
Wilson, I., *Thinking beyond War: Civil–Military Relations and Why America Fails to Win the Peace* (New York: Palgrave Macmillan, 2007).
Woodworth, S. E., *Jefferson Davis and His Generals: The Failure of Confederate Command in the West* (Lawrence: University Press of Kansas, 1990).

Modern British Naval Strategic History

Corbett, J. S., *Some Principles of Maritime Strategy* (London: Longmans, 1911).
Lambert, A. D., *Seapower States: Maritime Culture, Continental Empires, and the Conflict that Made the Modern World* (London: Yale University Press, 2018).
The British Way of War: Julian Corbett and the Battle for a National Strategy (London: Yale University Press, 2021).
Mahan, A. T., *The Influence of Sea Power upon History 1660–1782* (Boston: Little, Brown, 1890).
Neilson, K. and G. Kennedy (eds), *The British Way in Warfare: Power and the International System, 1856–1956: Essays in Honour of David French* (Farnham: Ashgate, 2010).

Further Reading

Modern Russian Strategic History

Bailer, S. (ed.), *Stalin and His Generals. Soviet Military Memoirs of World War II* (New York: Pegasus, 1969).
Barry, Q., *War in the East: A Military History of the Russo-Turkish War 1877–78* (Warwick: Helion and Company, 2012).
Cimbala, S. J., 'The Cold War and Soviet military strategy', *Journal of Slavic Military Studies*, 10 (1997), 25–55.
Connaughton, R. M., *The War of the Rising Sun and Tumbling Bear: Russia's War with Japan*, rev. ed. (London: Cassell, 2003).
Douglass, J. D., Jr, *Soviet Military Strategy in Europe* (New York: Pergamon Press, 1980).
Erikson, J., 'The Great Patriotic War: Barbarossa to Stalingrad', in R. Higham and F. Kagan (eds), *The Military History of the Soviet Union* (New York: Palgrave, 2002), 109–36.
Frank, W. C., Jr, and P. S. Gillette (eds), *Soviet Military Doctrine from Lenin to Gorbachev, 1915–1991* (Westport and London: Greenwood Press, 1992).
Friedman, N., *The Fifty Year War: Conflict and Strategy in the Cold War* (Annapolis: Naval Institute Press, 2000).
Glantz, D. M., 'Developing offensive success: the Soviet conduct of operational maneuver', in W. C. Frank Jr and P. S. Gillette (eds), *Soviet Military Doctrine from Lenin to Gorbachev, 1915–1991* (Westport and London: Greenwood Press, 1992), pp. 133–174.
Hagen, M. von, 'From the First World War to Civil War, 1914-1923', in A. Gleason (ed.), *A Companion to Russian History* (Oxford and Hoboken: Wiley Blackwell, 2014), pp. 337–52.
Hamby, J. E., 'Striking the balance: strategy and force in the Russo-Japanese War', *Armed Forces & Society*, 30 (2004), 325–56.
Holquist, P., *Making War, Forging Revolution* (Cambridge, MA: Harvard University Press, 2002).
Kowner, R., *Historical Dictionary of the Russo-Japanese War*, 2nd ed. (Lanham: Rowman & Littlefield, 2017).
 (ed.), *Rethinking the Russo-Japanese War, 1904–05: Centennial Perspectives* (Folkestone: Global Oriental, 2007).
 (ed.), *The Impact of the Russo-Japanese War* (London: Routledge, 2007).
Tsushima (Oxford: Oxford University Press, 2022).
Lensen, G. A., *Balance of Intrigue: International Rivalry in Korea and Manchuria, 1884–1899*, 2 vols. (Tallahassee: Diplomatic Press, 1982).
Lomagin, N. A., 'The Soviet Union in the Second World War', in A. Gleason (ed.), *A Companion to Russian History* (Oxford and Hoboken: Wiley Blackwell, 2014), 386–413.
McMeekin, S., *The Russian Origins of the First World War* (Cambridge, MA: Harvard University Press, 2011).
Menning, B. W., *Bayonets Before Bullets: The Imperial Russian Army, 1861–1914* (Bloomington: Indiana University Press, 2000).
Novikova, I. N. and N. Vlasov (eds), *Rossia v strategii Pervoj mirovoj vojny, Rossija v strategii Tsentralnykh derzhav* (St Petersburg: RHGA, 2014), vol. 2.

Overy, R., *Russia's War. The History of the Soviet War Effort: 1941–1945* (New York: Penguin Books, 1997).
Pavlov, A. (ed.), *Rossia v strategii Pervoj mirovoj vojny, Volume 1, Rossija v strategii Antanty* (St Petersburg: RHGA, 2014).
Reese, R. R., 'Red Army professionalism and the Communist Party, 1918–1941', *Journal of Military History*, 66:1 (2002), 71–102.
  The Imperial Russian Army in Peace, War, and Revolution, 1856–1917 (Lawrence: University Press of Kansas, 2019).
Reynolds, D. and V. Pechatnov, *The Kremlin Letters. Stalin's Wartime Correspondence with Churchill and Roosevelt* (New Haven and London: Yale University Press, 2018).
Schimmelpenninck van der Oye, D. and B. W. Menning (eds), *Reforming the Tsar's Army: Military Innovation in Imperial Russia from Peter the Great to the Revolution* (Cambridge: Cambridge University Press, 2004).
Scott, H. F. and W. F. Scott, *The Soviet Art of War: Doctrine, Strategy and Tactics* (Boulder: Westview Press, 1981).
Snel, G., *From the Atlantic to the Urals: The Reorientation of Soviet Military Strategy, 1981–1990* (Amsterdam: VU University Press, 1996).
Sokolovskii, V., *Soviet Military Strategy* (Santa Monica: RAND, 1963).
Steinberg, J. W., B. W. Menning, D. Schimmelpenninck van der Oye, D. Wolff and S. Yokote (eds), *The Russo-Japanese War in Global Perspective: World War Zero* (Leiden and Boston: Brill, 2005).
Stone, D., *The Russian Army in the Great War: The Eastern Front, 1914–1917* (Lawrence: University Press of Kansas, 2015).

Guerrilla Warfare

Beckett, I. F. W., *Modern Insurgencies and Counter-Insurgencies: Guerrillas and their Opponents since 1750* (London: Routledge, 2001).
  'The campaign of the lost footsteps: the pacification of Burma, 1885–95', *Small Wars and Insurgencies*, 30 (2019), 994–1019.
Beilein, J. and M. Hulbert (eds), *The Civil War Guerrilla: Unfolding the Black Flag in History, Memory, and Myth* (Lexington: University Press of Kentucky, 2015).
Esdaile, C., *Fighting Napoleon: Guerrillas, Bandits and Adventurers in Spain, 1808–1814* (New Haven: Yale University Press, 2004).
  The Peninsular War. A New History (London: Allen Lane, 2002).
Heuser, B., 'Exploring the jungle of terminology', *Small Wars and Insurgencies*, 25 (2014), 741–53.
  'Lessons learnt? Cultural transfer and revolutionary wars, 1775–1831', *Small Wars and Insurgencies*, 25 (2014), 858–76.
Pretorius, F., *Life on Commando during the Anglo-Boer War, 1899–1902* (Cape Town: Human & Rousseau, 1999).
Sutherland, D., *A Savage Conflict: The Decisive Role of Guerrillas in the American Civil War* (Chapel Hill: University of North Carolina Press, 2009).
Tone, J., *The Fatal Knot: The Guerrilla War in Navarre and the Defeat of Napoleon* (Chapel Hill: University of North Carolina Press, 1994).

Terrorism

Abrahms, M., 'Why terrorism does not work', *International Security*, 31 (2006), 42–78.
Chaliand, G. and A. Blin (eds), *The History of Terrorism: From Antiquity to Al-Qaeda* (Berkeley: University of California Press, 2007).
Clarke, C. P., *After the Caliphate* (London: Polity Press, 2019).
Hammes, T. X., *The Sling and the Stone: On War in the 21st Century* (St Paul, MN: Zenith, 2004).
Hoffman, B., *Inside Terrorism*, 2nd ed. (New York: Columbia University Press, 2006).
Jackson, B., 'Organizational decision-making by terrorist groups', in P. K. Davis and K. Cragin (eds), *Social Science for Counterterrorism: Putting the Pieces Together* (Santa Monica: RAND, 2009), 209–55.
Libicki, M. C., P. Chalk, and M. Sisson, *What Drives al Qaeda's Choice of Target?* (Santa Monica: RAND, 2007).
McCormick, G., 'Terrorist decision making', *Annual Review of Political Science*, 6 (2003), 473–507.
Soufan, A. H., *Anatomy of Terror: From the Death of Bin Laden to the Rise of the Islamic State* (New York: W.W. Norton & Company, 2017).
Zelin, A. Y. (ed.), 'How al-Qaeda survived drones, uprisings, and the Islamic State: the nature of the current threat', Washington Institute for Near East Policy, *Policy Focus*, 153 (June 2017), www.washingtoninstitute.org/policy-analysis/how-al-qaeda-survived-drones-uprisings-and-islamic-state.

Air Power

Fedorchak, V., *Understanding Contemporary Air Power* (London: Routledge, 2020).
Hippler, T., *Governing from the Skies, A Global History of Aerial Bombing* (London: Verso, 2017).
Olsen, J. (ed.), *A History of Air Warfare* (Washington, DC: Potomac Books, 2010).
(ed.), *Airpower Applied: US, NATO, and Israeli Combat Experience* (Annapolis: Naval Institute Press, 2017).
(ed.), *Routledge Handbook of Air Power* (London: Routledge, 2018).

Nuclear Power

Ellsberg, D., *The Doomsday Machine: Confessions of a Nuclear War Planner* (London: Bloomsbury, 2017).
Freedman, L. and J. Michaels, *The Evolution of Nuclear Strategy*, 4th ed. (London: Palgrave, 2019).
Fuhrmann, M. and T. S. Sechser, *Nuclear Weapons and Coercive Diplomacy* (New York: Cambridge University Press, 2017).
Gavin, F. J., *Nuclear Weapons and American Grand Strategy* (Washington, DC: Brookings Institution Press, 2020).

Further Reading

Heuser, B., *NATO, Britain, France and the FRG: Nuclear Strategies and Forces for Europe* (London: Macmillan, 1997).

Kaplan, F., *The Bomb: Presidents, Generals, and the Secret History of Nuclear War* (New York: Simon & Schuster, 2020).

Kissinger, H., *Nuclear Weapons and Foreign Policy* (New York: Harper, 1957).

Narang, V., *Nuclear Strategy in the Modern Era: Regional Powers and International Conflict* (Princeton: Princeton University Press, 2014).

Rhodes, R., *The Making of the Atomic Bomb* (New York: Simon & Schuster, 1987).

Tannenwald, N., *The Nuclear Taboo: The United States and the Non-Use of Nuclear Weapons Since 1945* (New York: Cambridge University Press, 2008).

Index

A Strategic Sketch of the War of 1914–1918 (Red Army Military History Commission), 59
ABC-1 strategy, 256
Abd el-Kader, 41
ABDA (American-British-Dutch-Australian) command, 260
Abrahms, Max, 436, 448
Achaemenid Empire, 541
Acheson, Dean, 350
actors, agents and adversaries, 5–6
Afghan Communist Party, 467
Afghan National Army, 477
Afghanistan, war in, 445, 457–8, 477–8, 526
  actors, adversaries and allies, 459–65
  air-land integration, 223
  Al-Qaeda's war of attrition, 453
  available means, 470–2
  causes, 465–7
  execution of strategy, 474–7
  instability of objectives, 544
  objectives, 7, 467–70
  process of prioritisation, 472–4
  Russian plans for, 52, 61, 116
  sources, 458–9
  Soviet intervention, 270, 289–90, 343, 397, 400
  US war aims, 345
afrancesados (Spanish collaborators), 42
African civil wars, maintenance of disorder, 542
African National Congress (ANC), 294, 296, 297, 298, 300, 301, 303–5, 306–7, 438
African wars of decolonisation, 308–9
  causes and objectives, 297–9
  means, 299–304
  priorities and outcomes, 304–8
  sources, 294–7

Afro-Asian People's Solidarity Organisation, 307
Aguinaldo, Emilio, 338
Aideed, Muhammed Farah, 345
Air Corps Tactical School (ACTS), 207, 208
air power, 204
  air-land school, 209–12
  Asia–Pacific War, 259, 267–8
  Chinese, 361, 518
  engagement of non-state actors in the twenty-first century, 222–4
  First World War, 168, 210–11
  France, 231
  Indo-Pakistani wars, 404, 405
  Israeli, 384
  Second World War, 212–16, 241–2
  Soviet, 241
  strategic attack school, 205–9
  strategy during the Cold War, 216–18
  technological advancements, 219
  technological developments during the Cold War, 216
  theoretical innovation, 1990–2000, 219–20
  theory development, 205
  Western Interventions 1990–2000, 219–22
Air War Plans Division-1, 208
air-to-air refuelling aircraft, 216
Alabama, 46, 92, 94
Albania, Italian invasion, 233
Alekseyev, Mikhail Vasilyevich, 76–7
Alekseyev, Yevgeni Ivanovich, 72
Alexander I, Emperor of Russia, 26, 29, 35
Alexander II, Emperor of Russia, 60, 68, 69
Alexander III, Emperor of Russia, 60, 61
Alexander the Great, 528, 535, 537
Alexander, Edward, 47
Alexander, Jocelyn, 296
Algeria, 529
  activity of Al-Qaeda in, 451, 454

Index

Algeria (cont.)
  Anglo-American landing, 244
  provision of training to African insurgents, 302
Algerian War of Independence, 294, 304–6
  Challe offensive, 303–4
  defensive lines isolating insurgents, 13, 303
  guerrilla warfare, 41
  means, 300
  Sétif and Guelma massacres, 298
  sources, 296
Algiers Treaty, Hussein's withdrawal from, 489
alliances, alliance politics, 8
Almond, Edward 'Ned', 351
Al-Qaeda, 17, 435, 447, 456, 464–5, 474
  11 September 2001 attacks, US response to, 222, 469, 486
  air strikes against, 224
  global reach, 445
  goals, 448
  sources, 437
  Spanish train bombings (2004), 436
  strategy, 450–4
American Civil War, 7, 14
  actors, 83
  adversaries, 83
  British attitudes to, 105
  causes, 83–4
  guerrilla warfare, 40, 45–7
  sources, 46
  means, 85–6
  military strengths, 85
  objectives, 335
  political objectives, 84
  practice and execution of strategy, 335–6
    Confederate cordon strategy, 87, 91, 95
    Confederate invasion of Kentucky, 89–90
    Confederate offensives, 94–5
    Confederate strategy of concentration, 92
    eastern theatre, 92–3
    Grant's plan for ending the war, 97–8
    initial mistakes of the Confederacy, 87–7
    McClellan's grand plan, 88–9
    Scott's Anaconda plan, 88, 335
    Vicksburg, Battle of, 95–7
    western theatre, 90–92
    appointment of Halleck, 93–4
  process of prioritisation, 86
  sources, 79–82
  Union and Confederate population and infrastructure, 85

American Expeditionary Force (AEF), 168, 340
American War of Independence, 20, 110, 114, 330–2
Anaconda plan, 88, 335
  variant of, 336
ancient China, 531, 533, 536, 538
ancient Greece, 530, 532, 535–6, 541
Andalusia, 43
Anderson, Robert, 87
Andropov, Yurii, 274, 289
Anglo-Boer War, 51–4, 299
Anglo-Burmese War. *See* Burma
Anglo-Dutch wars (1652–1674), 112
Anglo-French wars (1688–1815), 99, 109, 113–14
Anglo-Japanese Alliance, 159, 162
  ending of, 250
Anglo-Japanese Treaty (1902), 128
Anglo-Russian War (1807–1812), 114
Anglo-Transvaal War (1881), 51
Angola
  as a refuge for the SWAPO, 301
  attendance at the Conference of Nationalist Organisations of the Portuguese Colonies, 300
  sources, 296
Angolan War of Independence, 294, 301, 304, 308, 441, 445
  suppression of the Baixa de Cassanje revolt, 298
annihilation, 12–13, 244, 329, 330, 346, 534
  campaigns in the First Nationalist-Communist Civil War, 148
Anson, Admiral Lord, 102
Anti-Apartheid Movement, 307
Anti-Ballistic Missile Treaty, 318
Anti-Comintern Pact (1936), 230, 251
Antietam, Battle of, 94
Anti-Imperialist League, 338
Arab League, 300
Arab Spring, 453
Arab–Israeli wars. *See* Israeli wars
Arakan offensive, 266
Arcadia Conference (1942), 260
Archive of Foreign Policy of the Russian Empire (AVPRI), 59
Archives of the President (APRF), 349
Argentina, 3
Arkansas, 46, 97
armed force
  coercive action, 11–12
  decapitation, retaliation and escalation, 12
  deterrent action, 10–11
  generation and size, 9–10

Index

used for occupation and control, 13–14
used for oppression and annihilation, 12–13
used to pre-empt and surprise, 11
Armée de libération nationale (ALN, National Liberation Army), 301, 303–5
Armistice of Cassibile, 245
arms control, 327
Army of Bosnia–Hercegovina (ABiH, Armija Bosna i Hercegovina), 422
Army of Italy, 33
Army of Northern Virginia, 45, 336
Army of Tennessee, 98
Army of Yugoslavia (VJ), 418–19, 420
Arnold, Hap, 207
Arranz, Gregorio González, 42
Asia-Pacific War, 341–2
  Allied counteroffensive strategies, 264–6
  Allied strategy, 269
  conclusive campaigns and bombing of Japan, 266–9
  Japan's successful military strategy, 259
  Japanese actors, 250–2
  Japanese conflict with China and steps to war, 252–3
  Japanese objectives, 257–9
  Japanese strategy, 269
  pre-war tensions between Japan and the West and Allied war plans, 254–5
  proximate causes of, 255–7
  setting of Allied priorities, 260–1
  sources, 247–9
  underlying causes, 249–50
  US control and execution of Allied strategy, 261–3
  use of the atomic bomb, 268, 312–16
Asprey, Robert, 295
Atlanta campaign, 85, 98, 336
Atlantic Charter, 16, 238
atomic bomb, 312–16
attrition, 12–13, 97, 171–3, 236, 329, 330, 341–2, 346, 392, 408, 453, 497, 500
Aum Shinrikyo, 446, 448
Aung-Thwin, Michael, 49
Australia, 269
  American troops in, 261
  approach to extended nuclear deterrence, 325
  declaration of war on Germany, 233
  involvement in Allied strategy, 254, 256, 262
  Japanese plans to invade, 261, 263
  Papuan campaign, 263, 264
  supply of troops in the Korean War, 358
Austria, 187

Austria-Hungary, 62, 169, 173
  break-up of, 178
  First World War
    assertion of independence, 170
    influence of propaganda, 175
    objectives, 165
    political situation prior to, 159–60, 162–4
    struggle to replace manpower losses, 176
    perceived threat to Russia, 63–4, 65
    relationship with Russia, 61
    Russian plans to counter threat from, 66–7, 70, 75–6
Austro-Prussian War, 40
Avelan, Fedor, 124
Awami League (AL), 395

Baath Party, 482
Baathist regime, 491–2
Baixa de Cassanje revolt, 298
Baker, James, 485, 497
Balkan wars, 58, 165
Balkans, 61, 67, 68–70, 73, 76, 170, 230, 235, 243
Banana Wars, 338–9
Bandung Conference (1955), 364
Bangladesh, 396
Bani-Sadr, Abol Hasan, 484, 496
Banks, Nathanial, 95
Barbary Wars, 333
Barfleur, Battle of, 112
Barzani, Mullah Masoud, 488
Basques, 439
Basra, 499
Battlefield Air Interdiction, 218
Bazargan, Mehdi, 495
Beat Hitler First strategy, 16, 256, 260, 262
Beilein, Joseph, 46
Belarus, 192, 193, 200, 203
Belgium, 105, 232, 243, 245, 528
  coercion of population into service, 167
  German offensive, 236, 238, 240
  German plans to annex, 165
  Napoleonic Wars, 112–14, 117
  pursuit of policy of independence, 237
  supply of troops in the Korean War, 358
Beli Orli, 419
Bell, David, 28
Benes, Edvard, 281
Bengalis, 401
Ben-Gurion, David, 372, 380
Bennigsen, Levin, 29
Bentobal, Lakhdar, 296
Beria, Lavrentii, 273

561

Index

Berlin
 declaration of martial law, 284
 uprisings of 1953, 276–8
Berlin Conference (1885), 5
Berlin Wall, collapse of, 272, 290
Berlin, Battle of, 201
Berthier, Louis-Alexandre, 18, 23
 Mémoire sur l'organisation du service d'état-major, 33
Bertrand, Henri Gatien, 21
Bessarabia, 26
Bezobrazov Circle, 129
Bharatiya Janata Party (BJP), 409
Bhutto, Zulfiquar Ali, 393, 396
Bianco, Carlo, 40
bin Laden, Osama, 436, 450, 452, 464, 465, 469, 477, 544
Black, Jeremy, 31, 538
Blaze, Elzéar, 42
Blin, A., 444
Bo Hla U, 50
Boers, guerrilla warfare, 41, 51–4
Boh Swe, 50
Bohlen, Charles, 364
Bolsheviks, 8, 77, 186–8, 203
Bombay–Burma Trading Corporation, 48
Bonaparte, Jerome, 23
Bonaparte, Joseph, 23, 41
Bonaparte, Louis, 23
Bonaparte, Lucien, 23
Bonaparte, Napoleon, 8, 9, 14, 110, 528, 537
 Continental System, 114
 defeat in Russia, 57
 evidence of strategic objectives, 21
 execution of strategy, 34–6
 grand tactics (*la grande tactique*), 20
 imperial ambitions, 7, 27, 29–31
 influences and advisors, 22–3
 invasion of Russia, 13, 539
 military mobilisation, 31–3
 prioritisation of the army, 33–4
 strategic reputation, 21–2
Borneo, 254, 258, 260, 268
Bosnia and Hercegovina, Bosnian War, 414, 426
 air campaign, 221
 armed forces, 418–19, 421–3
 concentration camps, 430–1
 effects of ethnic cleansing, 433
 expulsion of Muslims, 431
 lack of control, 538
 leadership, 413–14
 Milošević and Stanišić's strategy, 423–4

 objectives, 416
 preparation and provocation, 428–9
 shelling of populated areas, 12
 takeover and the use of force, 429–30
 US intervention, 344
Bosnia and Hercegovina, uprising (1875), 67
Boxer Uprising, 128
Boyne, Battle of the, 112
Bradley, Omar N., 350
Bragança, Aquino de and Wallerstein, Immanuel, *African Liberation Reader*, 297
Bragg, Braxton, 82, 92, 93–4
Branche, Raphaëlle, *L'embuscade de Palestro*, 295
Brands, Hal, 482
Brandt, Heinrich von, 42
Bratislava, Warsaw Pact meeting, 276
Brazil, 176
 Marighella's insurgency strategy, 443
 US intervention, 343
Breytenbach, J. H., 51
Brezhnev Doctrine, 283, 289, 512
Brezhnev, Leonid, 275–6, 278, 289, 291
Briand, Aristide, 170
Britain. *See also* British naval strategy
 aftermath of First World War, 228
 and the American War of Independence, 330–2
 civilian authority, 160
 conflict with Napoleon in India, 31
 control and conflict in Burma, 48–51
 domestic political tensions, 160
 First World War
  conscription, 167
  development of tanks, 168
  execution of strategy, 172–4
  objectives achieved, 179
  prelude and objectives, 162–5
 influence of the airpower theory of strategic attack, 205–9
 involvement in the Yugoslav War, 414
 Napoleon's plan to invade, 29–30
 Napoleon's threat to the economy, 34
 nuclear strategy, 319, 326
 pre-Second World War strategy, 231
 recognition of the Soviet Union, 187
 relationship with Russia, 61–2
 restraint of Russian expansion, 116–17
 sale of weapons to Israel, 374
 Second World War in Europe
  attempts to avoid, 232–3
  co-operative relationship with US, 239

562

Index

execution of strategy, 243–4
military means, 241
objectives and prioritisation, 236–7
Second World War in the Pacific, 253, 269
offer of additional support, 267
preparations for, 254, 256
Suez crisis, 370, 382
support for the Confederacy, 335
War of 1812, 333
British Expeditionary Force (BEF), 167
British Guiana, US intervention, 343
British naval strategy
actors, 102–3
adversaries, 103–4
available means, 107–9
causes of wars, 104–5
execution, 111–20
First World War, 173
historiographic debates, 120–1
Napoleonic Wars, 31–3
alliances, 24, 25
objectives, 26–7
recruitment of manpower, 28
objectives, 105–7
process of prioritisation, 110–11
Second World War, 231, 236, 241, 243
Singapore strategy, 254, 269
sources, 101
Broers, Michael, 29
Brusilov, Aleksey Alekseyevich, 77, 172
Buchanan, James, 84
Buell, Don Carlos, 90, 92, 93, 94
Bugeaud, Thomas Robert, 42
Bulgaria, 76
activity and influence within the Soviet bloc, 275, 278, 280, 281, 283, 288
Al-Qaeda in, 451
First World War
alliance with the Central Powers, 160
collapse, 176–8
dependence on German industry, 169
initial objective, 165
struggle with manpower losses, 176
joining of the Axis alliance, 234
Russian plans to occupy in the Russo-Turkish War, 68
uprising (1875), 67
Bulge, Battle of the, 246
Bull Run, Battle of, 88
Bulletins de la Grande Armée, 21
Burma, 441
guerrilla warfare, 41, 48–51
sources, 48–9

Burma campaign, 260, 261
counteroffensive strategy, 264, 266, 268
Japanese invasion, 258
Bush, George H. W., 398, 482, 485–6, 493, 502
Bush, George W., 482, 486–7, 493–4, 502
decision to abandon the Anti-Ballistic Missile Treaty, 318
Byman, D., 437
Byzantine Empire, 531, 533, 541

Cabral, Amílcar, 296, 305–6, 307, 309
Caesar, 528
Callwell, Charles, 41
Cambacérès, Jean-Jacques-Régis de, 23
Cambon, Paul, 226
Campagne de France (French Campaign), 35
Canada, 102, 113, 118
entry to the Second World War, 233
involvement in Allied strategy, 260, 262
US incursions, 333
Cape Frontier Wars, 41
Carlyle, Thomas, 52
Carnation Revolution, 304
Carpathians, 171
Carthaginians, 100
Casablanca Conference (1943), 239, 264, 341
Castlereagh, Lord, British Foreign Secretary, 115
Castro, Fidel, 299, 443, 444
Caucasus
campaign in the Russo-Turkish War, 69
First World War campaign, 171
German operations in, 197, 198, 244
guerrilla resistance against the Russians, 41
Caulaincourt, Armand de, 22
causes and objectives of wars, 6–8
central Asia (formerly Turkestan), 187
Central European University Press, 272
Central Intelligence Agency (CIA), 400, 510
Central Military Commission (China), 143, 145, 349, 358, 361, 503, 510, 511, 513–14, 515, 517
Četnik Movement, 427
Chabal, Patrick, 296
Chaliand, G., 444
Chaliand, Gérard, 294
Chamberlain, Neville, 231
Champagne, Battle of the, 171
Charles II, King of England, 111
Charles IV, King of Spain, 41
Charles V, Holy Roman Emperor, 111, 531
Charney, Michael, 49
Chattanooga, 92–3

Index

Chechens, 439
Chen Jian, 142
Cheney, Richard (Dick), 485, 486
Chengdu and Lanzhou Military Regions (MRs), 511
Chernobyl disaster, 474
Chiang Kai-shek, 142, 144–5, 146–7, 148, 154, 155, 239, 252, 260, 266, 510
   'block house' strategy, 149
   strategy in the Second Sino-Japanese War, 150–3
Chile, 5
China, Chinese military strategy. *See also* Korean War
   actors and adversaries, 144–6, 503–4
   and the Tiananmen Square protests, 517
   Boxer Uprising, 128
   despatch of forces to Korea, 347
   entry to First World War, 176
   evolution of, 521–3
   First Nationalist-Communist Civil War (1927–37), 148–9
   global missions, 520–1
   guerrilla opposition to the Qing dynasty, 40
   Indian border conflict (1962), 510–11, 521–3
   Indian border dispute (2020), 520
   late Imperial strategy, 538, 539
   management of the situation in Taiwan, 518–19
   mandate of Heaven, 536
   maritime territorial dispute with Japan (2010), 519–20
   modernisation programme, 518
   Northern Expedition (1926–1928), 146–8
   nuclear strategy, 318, 320
   Paracel Islands, 513–14, 522, 540
   recognition of the Soviet Union, 187
   relations with India and Pakistan, 407–8
   relations with Russia, 70, 128
   revision to the Military Strategic Guidelines, 517–18
   Second Nationalist–Communist Civil War (1946–1949), 153–4
   self-determination, 165
   sources, 142–3
   Soviet border clash, 512–13
   Spratly Islands, 516–17, 522
   strategies to deter American nuclear use, 324
   support for wars of decolonisation, 8, 303
   tensions with the Philippines, 519
   territorial issues, 532
   US missions to (1912–1938), 341
   Vietnamese border clash, 514–16
   war of resistance against Japan (1937–1945), 150–3
   Yijiangshan, and Jinmen and Mazu, 508–10
Chinese Communist Party (CCP), 142, 504
   alliance with the *Guomindang*, 146, 150
   alliance with the Soviet Union, 522
   and the Korean War, 360
   and the Sino-Indian border conflict, 510
   and the Sino-Soviet border conflict, 512
   and the Sino-Vietnamese border conflict, 514
   First Nationalist–Communist Civil War, 149
   histories of the Second World War, 152
   initial objectives in the civil war, 145–6
   Leading Small Group on maritime sovereignty protection, 519
   perception of threat from the West and vision for modernisation, 523
   response to the student protests, 517
   system of strategic formulation, 503
Chinese Eastern (North Manchuria) Railway, 70
Chinese People's Volunteer Force (CPVF), 347, 357–8, 359–60, 505–8
   logistics and transportation, 361
   strategy, 361–3
Chinggis Khan, 537, 539
Chins, 48
Chrzanowski, Wojciech, 40
Churchill, Winston, 201, 241, 247
   plan to invade Sumatra, 267
   Second World War objectives, 236, 238–9, 341
   strategy in the Asia–Pacific War, 260, 262, 264
civil wars, targeting of civilians, 534
Clausewitz, Carl von, 6, 21–2, 118, 121, 148, 343, 415, 442, 478, 537
   On War, 526
Clinton, Bill, 400, 414, 486
close air support (CAS), 210–12, 214, 217, 218, 223, 427
Cold War. *See also* Korean War; Soviet Union: interventions within the Soviet bloc
   air power, 216–18
   'massive retaliation' and 'flexible response' nuclear strategy, 320–1
Cold War International History Project (CWIHP), *Bulletin*, 349
Collective Armies (CA, China), 148

Index

Colombia
　supply of troops in the Korean War, 358
　US intervention, 344
Colson, Bruno, 22
Commonwealth and Dominion Navies, 111
concentration camps, 13, 426, 430–1
Concord, Battle of, 330
Congress of Vienna (1815), 105, 115
Connable, B., 445
Connelly, Matthew, 307
Connelly, Owen, 36
conscription, 9
　American Civil War, 86
　First World War, 108, 167
　Napoleonic Wars, 32, 42
　Peninsular War, 28
　Russia, 63, 67
　Third Reich, 230
Copenhagen, Battle of, 25
Coral Sea, Battle of the, 263
Corbett, Julian, 101, 106, 120
　England in the Mediterranean, 112
　Some Principles of Maritime Strategy, 104
cordon strategy ('cordon defense'), 87
Cornwallis, Charles, 331
Corregidor, 261
corsa terrestre (land corsairs), 43
Cortes of Cadiz, 43
Corvey, Jean Le Mière de, 42
Cot, Pierre, 210
Council of People's Commissars
　(*Sovnarkom*), 185
counterinsurgency, 295, 438, 441, 445, 449
　African wars of decolonisation, 301, 303, 304
　Indian strategy, 398, 401
　sources, 295
　Soviet strategy in Afghanistan, 475
　theory, 297
　US campaign in Afghanistan, 471, 476
　US operations in the Philippines, 338
　use of airpower, 222
Crimea, 200
　Russian annexation (1783), 26, 57
　Russian annexation (2014), 11
　Soviet attempts to drive German forces
　　from, 196
Crimean War, 36, 57, 62, 64, 67–8, 111, 116,
　136, 164
Cripps, Stafford, 195
Croatia, 413, 414
　armed forces, 418–19, 420
　Plitvice Lakes incident, 427
　Serbian strategy in, 423–4, 426

shelling of populated areas, 12
siege of Vukovar, 429
weaponry, 421–2
Cromwell, Oliver, 111
Cronje, Piet, 52
Crosthwaite, Charles, 48
Cuba
　support for wars of decolonisation, 8, 302
　US intervention (1909), 338
　US intervention (1961), 343
Cuban Missile Crisis, 523, 540
Cuban Revolution, 294, 443
Cuban War of Independence, 337–8
Curtin, John, 262
Czechoslovakia, 277
　carving up of, 236
　founding of, 178
　German occupation, 188, 233
　removal of Soviet and American
　　troops, 281
　Soviet invasion, 11, 270, 287–9, 512
　　compared with Putin's invasion of
　　　Ukraine, 290–1
　　justification, 283–4
　　Soviet objectives, 280
　　Soviet response to the programme of
　　　liberalisation, 275–6, 278–9

dacoits (Burmese bandits), 41, 48, 50–1
Dahomey, 533
Dalai Lama, 510
Damansky/Zhenbao, battles of, 512–13
Danilov, Yuri Nikiforovich, 76
Daudet, Léon, 14
Davidov, Denis, 40
Davidson, Basil, 294
Davis, Jefferson, 47, 83, 98, 336
　appeal for guerrilla resistance, 45
　correspondence, 79
　execution of strategy, 86–7, 90, 92, 94,
　　95
　objectives, 335
Davis, Stephen, 296
Dayan, Moshe, 378, 379
de Gaulle, Charles, 237
de Graaf, Beatrice, 36
de Wet, Christian, 51–3
Debray, Régis, 294
Decapitation and Incapacitation strategy, 221
Declaration of Paris (1856), 106
decolonisation, 5, 292
　wars of, 292–4. *See also* African wars of
　　decolonisation

Index

Delaware, 85
Deng Xiaoping, 503, 514, 515, 518
  issue of a Guiding Strategic Thought, 516
Denial strategy, 221
Denmark, 174
  recognition of the Soviet Union, 187
Diaz, Juan Martín, 41, 45
Điện Biên Phủ, Battle of, 12, 299, 316
diplomacy, 8, 35, 495, 497
  activist, 519
  campaigns of the African liberation movements, 307–8
  coercive, 337, 406, 519
  militarisation of, 163
disarmament initiatives, 327
Dnepr River, 200
Dominican Republic, US intervention, 338, 343
Domino theory, 343
Donbas Operation (1941), 195, 198
Dostum, Abdul Rashid, 463–4, 466, 468–9
Douhet, Julio, 206, 209–11
  Command of the Air, 206
Draper, Robert, *To Start a War: How the Bush Administration Took America into Iraq*, 487
Dresden, 13
drones. *See* Unmanned Aerial Vehicles
Dubcek, Alexander, 275, 277, 278, 280, 288, 289
Dulles, John Foster, 351
Dumézil, Georges, 535
Dunkirk, 241
Dušan Silni, 419
Dutch East Indies, 257
  defensive plans, 256
  destruction of the US Asiatic Fleet, 261
  Japanese invasions, 258, 260
Dutch Republic, 100
Dyle–Breda manoeuvre, 237
Dyle River, 237
Dzur, Martin, 288, 289

Eaker, Ira, 207
East Germany
  collapse of, 290
  discussions relating to Czechoslovakian intervention, 275–6
  participation in the invasion of Czechoslovakia, 288
  Soviet invasion, 270
    available means, 281
    causes, 277–8
    compared to Putin's invasion of Ukraine, 290–1

execution of strategy, 284–5
legitimisation, 282–3
objectives, 279–80
workers' protests, 273, 276
Eastern Crisis (1875), 67
economic warfare, 8, 102, 106, 114, 117, 119, 120
  American Civil War, 336
  First World War, 174
  Napoleonic Wars, 34
Egypt
  assumption of Israeli nuclear capability, 324
  conflict with Israel, 11, 368–9, 370, 375–6, 379, 382–3
  Israeli objectives, 384, 539
  withdrawal from, 373, 488
  Islamic State branches in, 455
  Israeli decision to return Sinai to, 371
  Italian invasion, 243
  Napoleon's campaign in, 31
  resistance to Rommel's Italo-German units, 244
  Soviet supply of military equipment, 374
  support for anti-colonial nationalism, 300, 302
Egypt–Israel Peace Treaty (1979), 368
Eisenhower, Dwight D., 15, 229, 239, 320, 351, 364
  offer of military assistance to India, 404
El Salvador, 445
  US intervention, 344
El-Alamein, second battle of, 244
electronic warfare (EW), 217
Ellis, Stephen, 296
Emmert, Thomas, 413
Esdaile, Charles, 42
Espoz y Mina, Francisco, 42, 43
Estonia, 233
Ethiopia, 358
  Italian operations in, 210, 231, 243
ethnic cleansing, 13, 344, 416, 419, 420, 423–4, 425–7, 429, 432–3
Executive Outcomes (EO), 439
extended nuclear deterrence, 325

F-117 Stealth aircraft, 219
Fair, C. Christine, 388
Fairbairn, Geoffrey, 295
Falkenhayn, Erich von, 172–3
Fanon, Franz, *The Wretched of the Earth*, 299
Farragut, David, 94
Fellman, Michael, 46
Feng Yuxiang, 147
Ferdinand VII, King of Spain, 41, 43

Index

Fiji, 261, 263
Finland, 187, 188, 196, 203, 233. *See also* Finnish War; Soviet–Finnish War
  alliance with the Nazis in the Continuation War with Soviet Union, 192
Finnish War, 26
First Carlist War, 40
First Moroccan Crisis, 117
First Sino-Japanese War, 127, 135
First World War, 14, 156, 178–80, 544
  actors, 157–61
  aftermath, 226–8
  air power, 204, 205, 209
  collapse of the Central Powers, 177–8
  execution of strategy, 171–8
    attrition, 171–3
    economic warfare, 174
    naval warfare, 173–5
    offensives, 173
    Western Front offensive, 177
  means, 166–9
    aircraft, 168
    comparative populations of the Central and Entente Powers, 166
    competition for manpower, 166–8
    navies, 169
    weapons, 168
  objectives, 163–5
  origins, 162–3
    militarisation of diplomacy, 163
    pre-war alliances and agreements, 162–3
  prioritisation, 170–1
  role of United States, 340
  Russian collapse, 175–6
  Russian strategy, 73–7
  sources, 156–7
  Soviet and Russian historiography, 58–9
  US entry, 175–6
Fisher, John, 117
Fisher, Noel, 46
Fiume, 228
Foch, Ferdinand, 118, 177
Foote, Andrew H., 91
Ford, Chris, 447
Fort Sumter, Battle of, 87
Fouché, Joseph, 22
Fourth Romanian Army, 244
France. *See also* Anglo-French wars; Napoleonic Wars
  air power, 210, 212, 241
  Algerian insurgency. *See* Algerian War of Independence
  alignment with Britain, 117
  alliance with Russia, 61–2, 65–6, 115, 127, 162, 164
  civilian authority, 161
  entry to the American War of Independence, 110, 331
  First World War
    economic consequences, 227
    execution of strategy, 172
    means, 166
    objectives, 164
    territories gained and lost, 179
  involvement in the Yugoslav War, 414
  naval power, 32–3, 103
  nuclear strategy, 319, 326
  recognition of the Soviet Union, 187
  sale of weapons to Israel, 374
  Second World War
    allied landings, 239
    events leading up to, 232–4
    German invasion, 253, 255
    military means, 240–1
    Normandy landings, 245
    objectives and prioritisation, 237–8
    preparations, 231
    resistance operations, 244
  Suez crisis, 370, 382
  supply of troops in the Korean War, 358
  undeclared war with the United States, 333
  Vietnamese insurgencies against, 443
Franco, Francisco, 8
Franco-Austrian War, 40
Franco-Prussian War, 40
Franz Ferdinand, Archduke of Austria, 164
Franz Joseph, Kaiser, 160, 170
Frederick II, King of Prussia (Frederick the Great), 20, 22, 52, 538, 539
Frederick William III, King of Prussia, 24
Freedman, Lawrence, 28, 457, 537
French–American alliance (1778), 333
Frente de Libertação de Moçambique (FRELIMO, Mozambique Liberation Front), 296, 300, 301, 303, 306
Frente Nacional de Libertação de Angola (FNLA, National Front for the Liberation of Angola), 297, 301, 306
Front de libération nationale (FLN, National Liberation Front), 296, 299, 300–1, 302, 305–7
Fu Zuoyi, 153

Gallipoli campaign, 171
Galula, David, 294
game theory, 449

567

Index

Gamelin, Maurice, 237
Gandhi, Indira, 395–6
Garibaldi, Giuseppe, 40
Gates, Robert, 398
Gaza, 224, 376, 380, 383, 384
General People's Defence (GPD), 417
Geneva Conference (1954), 364
Geneva Protocol (1925), 312
genocide, 13, 432
George III, King of Great Britain, 331
Georgia (country), 26, 31
Georgia (US), 46, 95, 97–8
German Imperial Navy, 173
Germany, 119. *See also* East Germany; West Germany
  air power, 211, 241
  alliance with Austria–Hungary and threat to Russia, 61, 63
  Anti-Comintern Pact, 251
  Continuation War against Soviet Union, 192
  effects of economic warfare, 117
  First World War, 160
    alliance with Austria–Hungary, 162
    armistice, 178
    attack on the Western Front, 176–7
    consequences, 226
    effects of Entente propaganda, 175
    manpower, 166–7
    naval warfare, 173–5
    objectives, 73, 164–5
    prioritisation, 170
    Russian offensive against, 75–6
    strategic failures and consequences, 179–80
    weaponry, 168–9
  imperial ambitions, 7
  loss of possessions to Japan, 250
  naval power, 103, 117, 230
  Russian plans to counter threat from, 65–7
  sale of weapons to Israel, 374
  Second World War, 253
    air offensive against, 206, 207
    alliance with Italy and Japan, 256
    Allied objectives and prioritisation, 236–9
    allied plans for war, 230–2
    available means, 240–1
    declaration of war on the US, 260
    defeat in Africa, 111
    invasion of the Soviet Union, 11
    Italian dependence on, 235
    Japan's failure to consult on the Pearl Harbor attack, 259
    military technology, 240
    objectives, 15
    objectives and prioritisation, 230–2
    offensives and counteroffensives, 242–6
    path to war, 232–4
    relations with Soviet Union in the lead up to, 186–9
    Soviet strategy, 181–4, 185–6, 191–202, 235–6
    the air war, 212–16
    US strategy, 341–2
  support for Russia against Japan, 127
Gettysburg, Battle of, 96–7
Ghani, Ashraf, 464, 477
Ghormley, Robert, 263
Gibraltar, 113
Gilbert Islands, 265
global interconnection, 9
Goa, 390
Goltz, Colmar von der, 12
Gorbachev, Mikhail, 290, 321
  decision to withdraw from Afghanistan, 474
Gorchakov, Alexander Mikhailovich, Prince, 67
Gorlice-Tarnow offensive, 171
Gourgaud, Gaspard, 21
Govorov, Leonid, 284
Grant, Ulysses S., 83, 91, 94, 95–8, 336
Gray, Colin, 537
Grechko, Andrei, 273, 276, 289
Greece. *See also* ancient Greece
  German forces sent to, 245
  guerrilla forces, Second World War, 244
  Italian invasion, 243
  recognition of the Soviet Union, 187
  supply of troops in the Korean War, 358
Greek Civil War, 534
Greeley, Thomas, 335
Grenada, US intervention, 344
Gribeauval, Jean-Baptiste Vaquette de, 20
Grimsley, Mark, *The Hard Hand of War: Union Military Policy Toward Southern Civilians*, 81
Grivas, George, 38
group polarisation, 449
Grundlingh, Albert, *In Different Times*, 296
Grundy, Kenneth, 294
Guadalcanal campaign, 263–4
Guam, 254, 257, 258, 259
  granted to the United States, 338

Index

Guatemala, US intervention, 343
Guelma massacre, 298
guerrilla warfare, 14, 38–41, 293, 324, 438–9
  African decolonisation wars, 299, 302, 304–5, 308–9
  Burma, 48–51
  definition, 38
  First Nationalist–Communist Civil War, 148
  in the Confederacy, 45–7
  Israeli wars, 376
  Second Sino-Japanese War, 152
  Second World War, 195, 244
  sources, 436–7
  South Africa, 51–4
  Spain, 40, 41–5
Guevara, Che, 38, 293, 299, 443–4
  Guerilla Warfare, 437
Guibert, Comte de, 20
Guillen, Abraham, 444
Guinea-Bissau, 294, 298, 304, 306, 308
Guinea-Cape Verde, 300
Gulf War, 16, 325, 532
  actors and adversaries, 484–6
  available means, 496–8
  Iraqi invasion and occupation of Kuwait, 11, 13, 479
  causes, 490–1
  execution of strategy, 500
  objectives, 492
  objectives achieved and failed, 502
  Operation Desert Storm, 13, 220–1, 344, 479
  causes, 491
  execution of strategy, 500
  influence on Chinese strategy, 517
  lessons learned from, 498
  objectives, 492–3, 501
  sources, 482
gunboat diplomacy, 333, 339
Guomindang (GMD, Nationalist Party), 154, 155
  alliance with the Chinese Communist Party, 146
  conflict in Yijiangshan, and Jinmen and Mazu, 509
  negative assessment of, 142
  offensives in the First Nationalist–Communist Civil War, 148–9
  seizure of Beiping, 148
  war of resistance against Japan, 150–2
Gupta Empire, 533, 538
Gustav IV, King of Sweden, 25
Guzman, Abimael, 444

Habsburgs, 24
Hadžić, Goran, 413, 424
Hague Conferences (1899 and 1907), 106
Haiti, US intervention, 338
Halberstam, David, 351
Halleck, Henry W., 83, 90, 91, 93–4, 97
  Elements of Military Art and Science, 82
Halsey, William, 263–4, 267
Hamas, 4, 222, 369, 376, 381
Hamas Charter, 370
Hammes, T. X., 442
Hannibal, 100
Haqqani Network, 464, 470
Hardwicke, Lord Chancellor, 102
Hari Singh, Marharaja, 390
Harris, Arthur, 207
Hattaway, Herman and Jones, Archer, *How the North Won: A Military History of the Civil War*, 81
Hawaii, 259
Hazaris, 465
Hekmatyar, Gulbuddin, 459–64, 466, 467, 468
Helsinki Final Act (1975), 290
Henriksen, Thomas, 294
Hertling, Georg Graf von, 178
Hertzog, Barry, 52
Hezb-e-Islami, 459, 462, 464, 465, 468
Hezbollah, 4, 222, 369, 376, 379, 381, 383, 385, 437
High Altitude Precision Daylight Bombing, 207
Hindenburg Programme, 166
Hindenburg, Paul von, 161, 166, 170, 175
Hindu nationalism, 410
Hirohito, Emperor of Japan, 250, 252
Hiroshima, bombing of, 202, 268, 312–13, 315
Hitler, Adolf, 9, 183, 197, 227, 351, 537
  declaration of war on the United States, 238
  domination of Axis strategic decisions, 239
  invasion of Soviet Union, 197
  objectives, 230
  path to war, 232–3
  plan to invade Britain, 243
  salami tactics, 240
  Stalin's appeasement of, 185
  strategy, 234, 244–6
  territorial ambitions, 13
  threat to the Soviet Union, 188, 191
Hồ Chí Minh, 293, 443
Hohenzollerns, 24
Holbrooke, Richard, 414
Hong Kong, 258, 259
Howard, Michael, 20, 101, 317

569

Index

Hu Jintao, 503
Hu Yaobang, 503
Huai-Hai campaign, 153
Hugo, Joseph Léopold, 42
Hulbert, Matthew, 46
humanitarian assistance operations, 344–5, 422–3
humanitarian concerns, 208, 395, 433
Humbaraci, Arslan, 294
Hundred Days, 35
Hungarian Communist Party, 279
Hungary, 188
  joining of the Axis alliance, 234
  named as adversary to the Soviet Union, 188
  Soviet invasion, 270, 272
    available means, 281
    compared to Putin's invasion of Ukraine, 290–1
    execution of strategy, 285–7
    objectives, 279–80
    prioritisation, 282, 283
    student revolts, 277
  Soviet concern over, 274–5, 278
Huns, 14
Hussein, Saddam, 6, 479, 502
  annexation of Kuwait, 492
  belief in Iraqi military power, 495–8
  domination of Iraqi strategy, 482–3
  invasion of Kuwait, 490–1
  execution of strategy, 500
  Iran–Iraq War
    execution of strategy, 499
    precursors, 488–90
  issued ultimatum by Bush to leave Iraq, 494
  rise to power, 482
  strategic miscalculation, 544
  US plan to overthrow, 491, 492–3
  views of the United States, 484, 486
  warnings of the effects of his deposition, 501

ideologues, 439–40, 486
Iguchi Shōgo, 134
Immigration Act (1924), 250
Imperial Japanese Army (IJA), 129, 134, 136, 140
Imperial Japanese Navy (IJN), 124, 134, 137–7, 138–9
Imperial Russian Army (IRA), 134, 135–6, 139
Imperial Russian Navy (IRN), 124, 136–7, 140
Imphal, Battle of, 266
improvised explosive devices (IEDs), 439, 446
India, 102, 105. *See also* Indo-Pakistani wars

border conflict with China (1962), 510–11, 521
border conflict with China (2020), 520
British return of French possessions, 114
defeat of the Japanese offensive, 266
Japanese plans for, 261
Napoleon's expeditions to, 31
naval routes to, 115
nuclear strategy, 322, 326
Russian expansion towards, 116
Indian Army, 392, 396, 510
indigenous Americans, 333
Indochina
  Việt Minh, 303
  Japanese occupation, 255, 257
Indochina wars, 12, 293, 294, 299, 514
Indo-Pakistani wars, 11, 532
  available means, 403–6
  causes, 392–3
  execution of strategies, 408–9
  India's strategy and practice, 389–90
  insurgency in Jammu and Kashmir (1989), 397
  Kargil War, 316, 391, 398–401
  Kashmir crisis of 1990, 398
  objectives, 7, 401–3
  Pakistan's strategy and practice, 391–2
  period of peace, 397–8
  post-war relations, 409–10
  process of prioritisation, 406–8
  Second Kashmir War, 393–4
  Sikh insurgency in the Punjab, 397
  sources, 387–8
  war of 1971
    causes, 394–6
    onset, 396
Indo-Soviet Treaty of Peace, Friendship and Cooperation (1971), 396
Ingrao, Charles, 413
insurgency. *See* African wars of decolonisation; terrorism and insurgency
Inter-Allied Independent Air Force, 169
international humanitarian law, 434, 529
International Stabilisation Assistance Force (ISAF), 222–3, 464, 465, 471, 477
Iran. *See also* Iran–Iraq War
  Al-Qaeda in, 453
  development of bases for operations against Israel, 376
  involvement in conflicts against Israel, 368–9, 376, 381
  Israeli measures to prevent acquisition of nuclear capability, 322

Index

nuclear strategy, 327
support for Ismail Khan, 462
Iranian Revolution, 489
Iran–Iraq War, 479, 532
  actors and adversaries, 483–4
  available means, 495–6
  causes, 487–90
  execution and application of strategy, 499
  failure to achieve objectives, 502
  objectives, 491–2
  sources, 479
Iraq. *See also* Gulf War; Iran–Iraq War; Iraq War
  Al-Qaeda activity, 451, 453–4
  Baathist regime, 481–4, 487, 491, 493, 499, 501, 502
  conflict with Israel, 368, 375–6, 382
  deterrence of nuclear attack, 325
  in the Arab–Israeli conflict of 1948, 370
  Israeli measures to prevent acquisition of nuclear capability, 322
  Operation Inherent Resolve, 223–4
Iraq War, 16, 479
  actors and adversaries, 486–7
  available means, 498
  causes, 491
  execution and application of strategy, 500–1
  objectives, 493–95
  objectives achieved, 502
  sources, 481
  US objectives, 345
Iraqi Air Force, 498
Irgun, 299
Iroquois Confederacy, 331
Islamic Revolutionary Guards Corps (IRGC), 484, 496
Islamic State (ISIS), 222, 223, 435, 437, 451, 453–6, 534
  air strikes against, 224
  disordering approach, 542
Islamic State Central Africa Province (ISCAP), 454
Islamic State in East Asia (ISEA), 455
Islamic State Khorasan Province (ISK), 454
Islamic State West Africa Province (ISWAP), 454
Isonzo, battles of the, 171
Israel
  'mowing of the grass' strategy, 542
  nuclear strategy, 322
  peace treaties with Arab states, 368
  policy of retaliation, 12

Israeli Defence Force (IDF), 367, 372–5, 376, 378–9, 380, 382, 383, 384
Israeli wars, 11, 526, 532
  adversaries, 368–9
  air power operation, 224
  available means, 372–5
  causes, 369–71
  deterrence, 380–1
  doctrine, 378–81
  military objectives and methods, 383–5
  objectives, 371–2
  opportunism, 539
  periods of military practice, 381
  principle of pre-emption, 381–3
  prioritisation, 375–6
  strategies for Routine Threats and Fundamental Threats, 378–80
Italy, 111, 119, 170, 188
  air power strategy, 209
  Anti-Comintern Pact, 251
  civilian authority, 161
  contribution of manpower in First World War, 166
  expansionist aims, 230
  membership of the Triple Alliance (1882), 162
  neutrality in the First World War, 164
  recognition of the Soviet Union, 187
  risk of nuclear attack, 325
  Second World War
    air raids against, 214
    alliance with Germany and Japan, 233–4, 256
    Allied objectives, 236, 237, 238
    armistice of Cassibile, 245
    entry, 243
    military capability and increasing dependence on Germany, 240
    objectives and prioritisation, 234–5
    territories gained following First World War, 179, 228
Iwo Jima, 267, 268
Izetbegović, Alija, 414

James II, King of England, 111, 112
Jamiat, 462, 465
Jammu and Kashmir, 387, 390, 391, 397, 401, 409
Janvier, Bernard, 414
Japan, 11, 13. *See also* Asia–Pacific War; First Sino-Japanese War; Russo-Japanese War; Second Sino-Japanese War
  Al-Qaeda in, 451

Japan (cont.)
  annexation of the Korean Peninsular, 140, 250
  Anti-Comintern Pact with Germany, 230
  maritime dispute with China (2010), 519–20
  naval power, 257–8
  pre-Second World War threat from, 232
  relations with Soviet Union, 187–8
  Siberian expedition, 140
  terrorist attacks, 446
  US exertion of economic pressure, 8
  war with Soviet Union, 201–3
Japanese–Soviet Neutrality Pact (1941), 257
Jaruzelski, Wojciech, 290
Jashari, Adem, 414
Jews, 188
  threat from Hitler, 230
Jiang Zemin, 503
jihadism, 540
Jinmen, 509–10, 523, 540
Jinnah, Mohammed Ali, 391
Joes, Anthony James, 439
Joffre, Joseph, 172
Johnson, Andrew, 336
Johnson, Chalmers, 295
Johnson, Joseph, 83
Johnson, Louis, 350
Johnston, Albert Sidney, 91–2
Johnston, Joseph, 91–2, 95
Joint Forces Air Component Commander, 219
Jomini, Antoine-Henri, 42, 82, 148, 336, 447
  Précis de l'art de la guerre, 21
Jordan, 368, 371
  as an entry point for Iraqi forces to the Israeli border, 375–6, 382
  in the Arab–Israeli conflict of 1948, 370
  peace agreement with Israel, 368
  relations with Israel, 375
  withdrawal from conflict with Israel, 373
Jowzjani, 463, 465
Jundanian, Brenda, 294
Junger, Sebastian, 466
juramentado (anti-guerrilla units), 44
Jutland, Battle of, 13, 173

Kachins, 48
Kádár, Janos, 275, 287
Kagan, Kimberly, definition of strategy, 298, 438, 529
Kalyvas, Stathis, 534
Kansas, 45, 88
Kapur, S. Paul, 388

Karadžić, Radovan, 413, 424
Karelia, 189, 190, 193
Karens, 48
Kargil War, 316, 391, 398–401, 405
Karmal, Babrak, 462, 475
Karzai family, 469
Karzai, Hamid, 464, 477
Kashmir. *See* Indo-Pakistani wars
Kashmiris, 439
Katsura Tarō, 125, 128
Keitel, Wilhelm, 234
Kennan, George, 343
Kentucky, 46, 85, 88, 89–90, 91, 94
Kenya Emergency (1952–1960), 294
Kenya Land and Freedom Army (KLFA), 304, 308
Keraterm concentration camp, 431
KGB, 288
Khalkhin Gol, battles of, 233
Khan, Ismail, 462, 464, 468
Khan, Mohammed Ayub, 393
Khe Sahn, Battle of, 316
Khomeini, Ayatollah, 482–4, 489, 496
Khrushchev, Nikita, 273–5, 276, 278, 290–1
Khuzestan, 489, 491
Kim Il-sung, 362, 504
  preparations for war, 354–5
  pursuit of national self-reliance, 353–4
  war objectives, 356
Kim, Jinwung, 352
King, Ernest J., 239, 247, 260, 261–2, 264
Kingdom of Holland, 23
Kingdom of Westphalia, 23, 25
Kipling, Rudyard, 477
Kirby Smith, Edmund, 94
Kissinger, Henry, 395
Kitchener, Herbert, 172
Kitson, Frank, 294
Koiso Kuniaki, 265
Kojong, King of Korea, 127
Komura Jutarō, 125
Konev, Ivan, 201, 287
Konoe Fumimaro, 253, 258
Koos de la Rey, 52
Korea, 111, 126–9
  annexed by Japan, 250
  Japanese objectives, 133
Korean War, 16, 347
  actors, 350–2
  adversaries, 352–4
  air power strategy, 216–17
  causes and intentions, 354–6
  Chinese strategy, 504–8

Index

executions and modifications of strategy, 361–4
fear of the use of nuclear weapons, 317
mobilisation and available means, 358–9
objectives and changes, 356–8
process of prioritisation, 360–1
role of fear in decision making, 527
sources, 347–50
Soviet involvement, 270
US strategy, 342–3
Kosovo Insurgency, 414
adversaries, 414
Kosovo Liberation Army (KLA), 222, 414, 421–2
Kosovo War, 424, 425
application of strategy, 426
armed forces, 420–2
campaign of expulsion, 431–3
concentration camps, 431
objectives, 416
US intervention, 344
Western air power intervention, 221–2
Kotkin, Stephen, 186
Kronstadt, 116
Kruger, Paul, 52
Kučan, Milan, 414
Kurds, 439, 488, 489
Kurile Islands, 126, 201–3, 258
Kuropatkin, Aleksey Nikolayevich, 15, 65, 72, 124
Kursk, Battle of, 199, 236, 245
Kuwait, Iraqi invasion and occupation. *See* Gulf War
Kwantung Army, 150, 251, 253, 258
Kyiv, 532
Kyushu, 268

La Hougue, 112
Lagos, 114
Lamsdorf, Vladimir, 124
Lapchinsky, Alexander, 210
Laqueur, Walter, 295
Las Cases, Emmanuel de, *Mémorial de Sainte-Hélène*, 21
Lashkar-e-Taiba (LeT), 401
Latvia, 233
Lawrence, T. E., 38
Le May, Curtis, 267
League of Nations, 228, 340
Germany's withdrawal from, 230
Italy's withdrawal from, 231
Japanese withdrawal from, 251
Soviet Union membership, 232

Leahy, William, 262
Lebanon
conquered by Allied forces, 243
Hezbollah in, 369
in the Arab–Israeli conflict of 1948, 370
threat to Israel, 368, 376
US intervention of 1958, 509, 523, 540
Lebanon War (1982), 379, 381, 383, 384–5, 539
Lebanon War (2006), 378, 379, 384, 385
Leclerc, Charles, 30
Lee, Robert E., 45, 47, 51, 83, 94–7, 98, 336
Lend-Lease Bill (1941), 238
Leningrad, 186, 190, 191, 195–6, 232
Lexington, 330
Leyte Gulf, Battle of, 13, 267
Li Xiaobing, 142
Liao-Shen campaign, 153
Liaoyang, Battle of, 139
Liberation Tigers of Tamil Eelam (LTTE, Tamil Tigers), 437–8
Libi, Abu Yahya al-, 450
Libicki, M., 445
Libya, 17, 368
Chinese involvement in evacuation of citizens, 521
decrease in Islamic State attacks, 455
German intervention, 243
NATO operation, 223
resistance to Rommel's Italo-German units, 244
support for anti-colonial resistance, 302
Libyan Islamic Fighting Group (LIFG), 450
Liddell Hart, Basil, 101, 206
Ligonier, General Lord, 102
Li–Lobanov Agreement (1896), 128
Lincoln, Abraham, 83, 84, 335–6
correspondence, 79
effectiveness as a strategist, 86
execution of strategy, 88–94, 96–8
issue of the Preliminary Emancipation Proclamation, 95
Lissoni, Arianna, 296
Lithuania, 233
Liu Huaqing, 143, 516
Liu Shaoqi, 350, 358
Lloyd George, David, 161, 167, 170
Locarno Treaties (1925), 232
Louis XIV, King of France, 112, 528, 542
Louis XV, King of France, 528
Louisiana, 95
guerrilla warfare, 46
sale of to the Americans, 31
Louverture, Toussaint, 30

Ludendorff, Erich, 161, 166, 170, 175
Luftwaffe, 211, 215, 241, 243
Lukashenko, Aleksandr, 291
Lushais, 48
Luxembourg, 358

MacArthur, Douglas, 247
  Asia–Pacific War
    appointed commander of the US army in the Far East, 257
    Battle of Leyte Gulf, 267
    counteroffensive strategy, 264–5
    offensive strategy, 262–3
    ordered to prepare for invasion of Japan, 268
    withdrawn to Australia, 261
  Korean War, 351, 352, 508
    appointed UNF command, 347
    execution and modification of strategy, 361–3
    objectives, 356–8
    relieved from command, 343, 362
Macedonia, 432
Macedonians, 100, 532
MacKey, Robert, 46
Macmaster, Neil, *War in the Mountains*, 295
Macmillan, Hugh, 296
Mahan, Alfred Thayer, 83, 103, 257, 333
  The Influence of Sea Power upon History, 249
Main Military Council of the Red Army (GVS RKKA), 185
Major, John, 414
Malaya, 254, 257, 258
  Allied troops in, 256
  Japanese invasion, 259, 260
Malenkov, Georgii, 273
Malinin, Mikhail, 285
Manchuria, 123, 150, 154, 253, 257, 266, 269, 355. See also Russo-Japanese War
  Japanese invasion (1931), 188
  Liao-Shen campaign, 153
  Soviet invasion, 201–3, 268
Manchurian Incident, 251
Mandela, Nelson, 297, 299, 300, 305
Manhattan Project, 312
Manstein, Erich von, 243
Mao Zedong, 16, 145, 150, 293, 299, 351, 503
  death, 514
  documents of, 350
  Guerrilla Warfare, 436
  insurgency doctrine, 442–3
  'leaning to one side' foreign policy, 522
  plans for operations in the Paracels, 513
  purchase of arms from Russia, 361
  and the Sino-Indian border conflict, 510–11
  and the Sino-Soviet border clash, 512–13
  strategy in the First Nationalist–Communist Civil War, 148–9
  strategy in the Korean War, 352–6, 504–8
    legitimisation of China's involvement, 360
    mobilisation of troops, 358–9
    modification, 362–3
    objectives and changes, 357–8
  strategy in Yijiangshan, and Jinmen and Mazu, 508–10
Maori, 41
Marcum, John, 294
Marianas operations, 265
Marighella, Carlos, 294, 443–4
  Minimanual of the Urban Guerrilla, 437
Marković, Mirjana, 414, 424
Marlborough, Duke of, 102, 110, 113
Marshall Islands, 265
Marshall, George C., 238, 239, 262, 313, 350
Martić, Milan, 413, 418, 424, 426–7
Marx, Karl, 466
Marxism–Leninism, 186, 270, 276, 282
Maryland, 85, 94
Maspero, François, 299
mass killings and atrocities, 533–4
Massoud, Ahmad Shah, 462, 464, 466, 468–9
Matsuoka Yosuke, 252
Mau Mau. *See* Kenya Land and Freedom Army (KLFA)
Maurice, Frederick, *British Strategy: A Study of the Application of the Principles of War*, 118
Maximilian, Prince of Baden, 178
Mazarire, Gerald Chikozho, 296
Mazu, 509–10, 523, 540
McClellan, George B., 82, 88–95
McGregor, JoAnn, 296
McKinley, William, 337–8
McNamara, Robert, 343
means of strategy, 8–14
Mecozzi, Amedeo, 209
medieval warfare, 532, 536, 538, 541
Mediterranean, British naval dominance, 112–13
Mehemet Ali, Pasha of Egypt, 115
Mehmet II, Ottoman emperor, 537
Meiji Restoration, 125, 126
Meiji, Emperor of Japan, 125
Mendietta, Jean de, 42, 45
Meretskov, Kirill, 190–1

Index

Mesopotamia, 171, 487
Metz, Steve, 439
Mexican–American War, 334
Mexico, 5, 88
   US interventions, 11, 339, 345
Midway, Battle of, 262–3
Mikoyan, Anastas, 285
Millett, Allan R., 362
Milne, George, 118
Milošević, Slobodan, 221, 413–14, 415, 416,
   417–18, 420–1, 423–5, 426
Milyutin, Dmitry Alekseyevich, 63, 64, 68
Mindanao, Battle of, 267
Mindon, King of Burma, 48
Ministry of Internal Affairs forces (MUP,
   Ministarstvo unutrašnjih poslova),
   420–1, 432
Minorca, 113
miqueletes (Spanish home guards), 43
Mischief Reef, 519
Missouri, 85, 88, 90
   guerrilla warfare, 45–7
Mitchel, Ormsby, 92
Mitchell, Billy, 206, 207
Mitter, Rana, 142
Mladić, Ratko, 413–14, 418, 419, 423–4, 425,
   426–7
Mohammad Reza Shah, 483, 488, 491
Mohammed, Prophet, 393
Mokhtefi, Mokhtar, 296
Moldova, 26, 200, 203
Moloto, Vyacheslav, 273
Mondlane, Eduardo, 296, 300, 309
Mongolia, 202–3, 233, 253, 512
Mongols, 14, 534, 539, 542
Mons, 48
Montenegro, 67, 432
Montholon, Charles Tristan de, 21
Morice Line, 13, 303
Morillon, Philippe, 414
Morocco, 303
   Anglo-American landing (Second World
      War), 244
   Conference of Nationalist Organisations of
      the Portuguese Colonies, 300
   support for the *Front de Libération Nationale*
      (FLN, National Liberation Front),
      301, 302
Moros, 439
Moscow criterion, 319
Moscow Peace Treaty (1940), 191
Moscow, Battle of, 183, 186, 195–7, 243
Mountbatten, Louis, 266, 392

Movimento Popular de Libertação de Angola –
   Partido do Trabalho (MPLA,
   People's Movement for the
   Liberation of Angola – Labour
   Party), 297, 301, 303, 306
Mozambique, 294, 455
   as a base for insurgents, 301
   attendance at the Conference of
      Nationalist Organisations of the
      Portuguese Colonies, 300
   war of independence, 300, 308
Mugabe, Robert, 297
Mughals, 531
Mujahideen, 457–8, 462–4, 477
   equipment and recruitment, 470–2
   execution of strategy, 475–6
   objectives, 468–9
   Pakistani and US support for, 467
   sources, 458
   strategic decision making, 472–3
Mujuru, Solomon, 297
Mukden, 72, 135, 139, 203
Mukti Bahini (anti-Pakistani guerrilla
   movement), 396
Multilateral Force (MLF), 326
Munich crisis, 236
Münnich, Ferenc, 287
Murat, Charles Louis Napoleon Achille, 23
Murray, Williamson, 479, 482
Musharraf, Pervez, 398, 399
Muslim League, 391
   resolution of 1940, 399
Mussolini, Benito, 9, 214, 228, 230, 233,
   234, 243
Myint, Ni Mi, 49
Myinzaing Prince, 49

Nagasaki, bombing of, 268, 312–13, 315–16
Nagy, Imre, 277, 279, 282, 286–7, 288
Naji, Abu Bakr, 450
   Management of Savagery, 437, 450, 542
Najibullah, Mohammed, 462–3, 468
Namibia, 294, 296, 301, 306, 308
Nanchang uprising (1927), 148
Napoleon III, 97
Napoleonic Wars, 18–21, 114–15
   actors, 22–3
   adversaries, 23–7
   American neutrality, 333
   available means, 31–3
   causes, 27–8
   execution of strategy, 34–6
   means, 8

Index

Napoleonic Wars (cont.)
  objectives, 29–31
  prioritisation, 33–4
  sources, 21–2
  Spanish resistance, 40, 41–5
Nasser, Gamal Abdel, 300, 382
National Archives and Records
  Administration (NARA), 348
National Institute of Defence Studies
  (Japan), 249
National Revolutionary Army (NRA), 147, 155
National Security Archive, 272
National Security Council (NSC), 367
National-Socialism, 188
National-Socialist ('Nazi') party, 226
Native Americans, US wars against, 337
NATO (North Atlantic Treaty Organisation),
  414, 422
  air power strategy, 218, 221–2
  American leadership, 344
  Atlantic treaty, 273
  nuclear strategy, 320–2, 325–6
  objectives in Afghanistan, 469
  operations in Afghanistan and Libya, 223
  West German entry, 273
naval power, naval operations, 99–100. *See also* British naval strategy
  Asia–Pacific War, 256–8, 504–5
  failure of the British Singapore
    strategy, 269
  Guadalcanal, 263
  Japanese losses, 266
  US plans, 254–5
  China
    dispute with Japan, 519–20
    global missions, 520–1
  First World War, 169, 173–5
  Napoleonic wars, 32–3
  Russo-Japanese War, 124, 134, 137,
    138–41
  Second World War, 230–2, 240–2
    blockade of Germany, 233, 236
Navarre, 42
Nazi–Soviet Pact (1939), 253
Nehru, Jawaharlal, 389, 390, 392, 394, 404, 510
Nelson, Horatio, 32, 109
Netherlands, 23, 27, 174, 176, 254, 260, 262, 358
Neto, Agostinho, 296
New Britain, 260, 263, 264
New Caledonia, 261, 263
New Georgia, 264
New Guinea, 258, 260, 262, 263, 264–5, 268
New Zealand, 260, 269

entry to the Second World War, 233
involvement in Allied strategy, 254, 262
supply of troops in the Korean War, 358
New Zealand Wars, 41
Nicaragua, US intervention, 338, 341
Nicholas I, Emperor of Russia, 57, 62, 124
Nicholas II, Emperor of Russia, 60, 64, 72, 76,
  124, 160
Nie Rongzhen, 143
Nigeria, 455
Nikolaevich, Nikolai, Grand Duke, Jr, 75
Nikolaevich, Nikolai, Grand Duke, Sr, 69
Nile, Battle of the, 109
Nimitz, Chester, 259, 262, 263, 265, 267, 268
Nine Years' War, 112–13
Nishi–Rosen Agreement (1898), 128
Nitze, Paul, 350
Nixon, Richard, 351, 395
Nkomo, Joshua, 297
Nomonhan, 253
Non-Aligned Movement, 307
North Carolina, 46
North Korea, 203. *See also* Korean War
  nuclear strategy, 322, 326
North Korean People's Army (NKPA), 354,
  356–7, 362–3, 366
North Vietnam, 217–18, 504, 513
Northeast Border Defense Army
  (NEBDA), 358
Norway, 26, 174, 234
  German invasion, 242
  recognition of the Soviet Union, 187
Novikov, Alexandr, 210
nuclear strategy, 216, 310–12, 327–8
  Indo-Pakistani wars, 398, 405, 406
  of non-nuclear states confronting nuclear
    states, 323–7
  of nuclear states, 316–23
  sources, 311
  Soviet, 270
  use of the atomic bomb, 268, 312–16

O'Ballance, Edgar, 294
O'Brien, Sean Michael, 46
O'Neill, Bard, 295, 438
Obama, Barack, 459
Obruchev, Nikolai Nikolayevich, 61,
  63–4, 68–9
Okinawa, Battle of, 267–8
Omarska concentration camp, 13, 431
Operation Blau, 244
Operation Allied Force, 221
Operation Bagration, 245

576

Index

Operation Barbarossa, 11, 195
Operation Brasstacks, 397
Operation Cast Lead, 224
Operation Chengiz Khan, 396
Operation Citadel, 245
Operation Defensive Shield, 383
Operation Deliberate Force, 221
Operation Deny Flight, 221
Operation Desert Shield, 344
Operation Desert Storm. *See* Gulf War
Operation Enduring Freedom, 222
Operation Gibraltar, 394
Operation Inherent Resolve, 222, 223–4
Operation Iraqi Freedom, 222, 482, 498, 500
Operation Iraqi Liberation, 482
Operation Koltso, 198
Operation Kutuzov, 245
Operation Linebacker (I and II), 218
Operation Market Garden, 245
Operation Overlord, 214
Operation Pillar of Defence, 224
Operation Protective Edge, 224
Operation Rolling Thunder, 218
Operation Rumiantsev, 245
Operation Saturn, 198
Operation Sea Lion, 243
Operation Torch, 244
Operation Unified Protector, 223
Operation Uranus, 197–8, 244
ordenança (Spanish home guards), 43
Organisation of African Unity (OAU), 300, 302, 307
Organisation Spéciale (Special Organisation), 300
Ortega, Humberto, 444
OS RSK, 418
Oslo Accords, 370
Ottoman Empire, 104, 487, 490, 492, 529
 and Russian affairs, 57
 relationship with Russia, 60–1. *See also* Russo-Turkish War
Overy, Richard, 185, 197

Pahlavi dynasty, 483, 487
Pakistan. *See also* Indo-Pakistani wars
 Al-Qaeda's move to, 453
 death of Osama bin Laden, 450, 465, 477
 involvement in removing Soviets from Afghanistan, 400
 nuclear strategy, 322, 327
 refusal to allow US invasion of Afghanistan from, 222
 role in the war in Afghanistan, 464–5
 support for the Mujahideen, 462, 467, 475
 Taliban objective to inspire Islamic movements in, 469
 Taliban recruitment from, 458, 463, 470
Pakistan Army, 399, 403, 407
 Inter-Services Intelligence Directorate (ISI-D), 400
Pakistan People's Party (PPP), 395
Palarea, Juan, 41
Palestine Liberation Organization (PLO), 4, 370, 375, 381, 383, 384–5, 539
Palestine, Irgun guerrilla tactics, 299
Palestinian Authority, 373
Palestinian Islamic Jihad, 369
Palestinians, 368, 370, 375, 379–80, 381, 383, 385, 386
Palkki, David, 482
Pan-African Freedom Movement for East, Central and Southern Africa, 300
Panama, 255
 US interventions, 338, 341, 344
Panzer tanks, 240
Papua campaign, 263–4
Paracel Islands, 513–14, 522–3, 540
Parallel History Project on Cooperative Security, 272
Paret, Peter, 22, 294
partidas (partisans), 43–4
Partido Africano para a Independência da Guiné e Cabo Verde (PAIGC, African Party for the Independence of Guinea and Cape Verde), 296, 301, 304, 305–6, 307
Partisan Ranger Act (1862), 46, 47
partisan warfare, 38–40, 293
Pashtun, 463, 465, 466, 469, 470, 476
Passchendaele, Battle of, 171
Patel, Sardar Vallabhai, 389
Pavković, Nebojša, 417
Pavlovskii, Ivan, 287
Peace of Amiens (1801), 30
Pearl Harbor, 11, 238, 247, 254, 255, 314
 Japanese attack on, 257–9, 341
 US Pacific Fleet, 256
Pedron Line, 303
Peloponnesian War, 100
Peng Dehuai, 143, 353, 357, 364, 505–8
Peninsular War, 28
People's Liberation Army (PLA), 145–6, 152, 504
 and 'informatized war', 518
 assault on the Yijiangshan, Jinmen and Mazu, 508–9

Index

People's Liberation Army (PLA) (cont.)
  evolution of, 518, 522–3
  Indian border conflict (1962), 510–11
  Indian border conflict (2020), 520
  Korean War, 354, 365, 504–8
    prioritisation, 360
    troop rotation, 359
  management of the situation in Taiwan, 518–19
  modernisation programme, 518
  Second Nationalist–Communist Civil War strategy, 153–4
  seizure of the Paracel Islands, 513–14
  Sino-Soviet border clash, 512
  Sino-Vietnamese border clash, 514–16
People's Liberation Army Airforce (PLAAF), 361, 518
People's Liberation Army Navy
  dispute with Japan, 519–20
  global deployments, 520–1
people's war, 17, 292–4, 308–9. *See also* African wars of decolonisation
  instability of objectives, 544
  Maoist model, 298, 442
People's Commissariat for Defence, 185
People's Commissariat for Military and Naval Affairs (*Narkomvoenmor*), 185
Pericles, 100
Perišić, Momčilo, 417
Pershing, John J., 339
Persia
  alliance with Napoleon, 31
  British–Russian agreements, 62
  Russian influence, 52
Pétain, Philippe, 237
Peter I, Tsar of Russia, 55
Petraeus, David, 476
Petropavlovsk, Russian battleship, 139
Philip II, King of Spain, 111
Philippine–American War, 338
Philippines, 529, 532
  Allied forces in, 260–1, 262
  Allied plans for, 264
  American landing at Mindanao, 267
  concern over the security of, 254, 255, 256–7
  conclusive campaigns, 268
  confrontations with China, 519
  granted to the United States, 338
  Japanese attack on, 259
  Japanese plans for the seizure of, 257–8
  supply of troops in the Korean War, 358
Phoney War, 240
Pidjiguiti massacre, 298

Pierpaoli, Paul G., Jr, 360
Pillow, Gideon J., 90
Pilsudski, Jozef, 187
Ping-Jin campaign, 153
Pitt, William, the Elder, 102
Pitt, William, the Younger, 107
Plan Dog memorandum, 238, 256
Plehve, Viacheslav, 124
Plevna, seige of, 69–70
Poland, 187, 193, 212
  First World War, 167, 173
  German invasion, 233, 242, 253
  German objectives, 188, 234
  non-agression pact with Soviet Union, 187
  Russian control, 26
  signing of the Treaty of Riga, 228
  Soviet invasion, 233
  Soviet operations against the Germans, 200–1
  Soviet reaction to the crisis of 1980–1981, 289–90
  Soviet war plans for, 232, 235
  support for Czechoslovakia, 278
  threat from Germany and Austria–Hungary, 63
  war with Ukraine and the Soviet Union, 187
Polish–Lithuanian Union, 55
Politburo (Chinese), 357, 358, 505
Politburo (Soviet), 184–5, 191, 273, 276, 279, 289, 512
Political Administration of the Workers' and Peasants' Red Army (PURKKA), 184
Political Consultative Committee (PCC), 273
politicos, 440
Polk, James K., 334
Polk, Leonidas K., 90, 91
Porlier, Juan Diaz, 41, 45
Port Arthur, 13, 70–3, 124, 128, 133, 134–5, 137, 138–9, 203
Port Moresby, 261, 263
Portugal, 24, 27, 31, 41, 106, 302, 390
Potsdam Conference (1945), 202
Potsdam Declaration (1945), 268
Powell, Colin, 485, 486, 497, 500–1
Prague Spring, 275, 277, 278, 280, 288
Precision Guided Munitions (PGMs), 219–20
Presidential Libraries of Truman and Eisenhower, 347
Pretorius, Fransjohan, 51
Price, Stirling, 46
Princeton, Battle of, 331
private military companies (PMCs), 439

Index

propaganda, 9
 African liberation movements, 297, 307
 Al-Qaeda, 454
 Chinese Communist Party, 360
 First World War, 174–5
 Putin's, 291
 Second World War, 184, 236, 240
 Soviet, 286
Provisional IRA, 438
 Green Book, 437
Puerto Rico, 338
Punic Wars, 99
Punishment strategy, 221
Putin, Vladimir, 272, 290–1, 537

Qiang Zhai, 142
Qin dynasty, 533
Qing dynasty, 40
Quadrant Conference (1943), 239
Quiberon, 114

Rabaul, 263–5
Rabbani, Burhānuddīn, 463–4, 466, 468–9
racism, 533
Radford, Arthur, 351
radicals, 440
Rakosí, Mátyás, 281
Ramet, Sabrina, 413
Ranger, Terence, 294
Rapoport, David, 441
Rashid, Ahmed, 473
Reagan, Ronald, 397, 463, 485
 Strategic Defense Initiative, 318
Red Army (Chinese)
 engagement in the First Nationalist–Communist Civil War and the Long March retreat, 148–9
 recruitment, 145
Red Army (Soviet), 181–4, 187, 188
 armaments and equipment, 241–2
 counteroffensives and operations against the Germans, 191–201, 235, 243–4, 245–6
 Finnish campaign, 189–91, 242
 Hungarian intervention, 287
 liberation and occupation of East Germany, 280
 Military History Commission, 58
 war in Afghanistan, 457, 459–62, 468, 475
 desertion, 471, 474
 equipment, 470
 war with Japan, 201–3
Reitern, Michael Graf von, 67

Reitz, Deneys, 51
Republican Guards (Iraqi), 497, 498, 500
Republika Srpska (RS, Republic of Serbia), 413, 426
Republika Srpska Krajina (RSK, Republic of Serbian Krajina), 413, 426
Revolution Settlement (1688), 112
Revolutionary Armed Forces of Colombia (FARC), 438
Rhee, Syngman, 352, 356
Richmond, Herbert, 101
Ridgway, Matthew B., 351, 362, 363
Roberto, Holden, 297, 301, 303
Roberts, Frederick (Field Marshal Lord), 51
Robinson, Thomas, 513
Rocca, Albert de, 42
Romania, 166, 188, 232, 285
 entry to the First World War, 74
 excluded from Warsaw Pact meeting, 275
 involvement in the Russo-Turkish War, 69
 joining of the Axis alliance, 234
 neutrality in the First World War, 164
 Operation Blau, 244
 relations with the Soviet Union, 282
 Second World War offensive, 200
Romanov, Aleksei Aleksandrovich, 124
Romanov, Sergei Aleksandrovich, 124
Rome, 100, 103, 435, 531, 536, 537, 540
Rommel, Erwin, 213, 244
Roosevelt, Franklin D., 238–9, 247
 and the development of the atomic bomb, 312
 condemnation of Japanese aggression, 252
 despatch of troops to Australia, 261
 discussions with Stalin, 201
 'Germany first' strategy, 341
 Pacific strategy, 257, 262, 264, 267
 prioritisation, 260
Roosevelt, Theodore, 338
Rose, Michael, 414
Rosecrans, William S., 95
Royal Air Force (RAF), 169, 213–14, 231, 236, 241, 243
Royal Navy, 111, 115, 116
 Battle of Jutland, 173
 domination of the Mediterranean, 112
 Napoleonic Wars, 25, 31, 109
 Second World War operations, 231, 236, 241, 243
Rozhestvensky, Zinovy Petrovich, 73
Rumsfeld, Donald, 486, 501
Rushdie, Salman, 391

579

Index

Russia. *See also* Russian Civil War; Russo-Japanese War; Russo-Turkish wars
actors in strategic decisions, 60
adversaries and allies, 60–2
annexation of Crimea, 11
causes and objectives of war, 62
conflicts from Ivan III to the nineteenth century, 55–8
defeat of Napoleon, 57
exit from the First World War, 175–6
French invasion of, 29–30, 35–6
historiography of strategy, 58–9
invasion of Ukraine, 7, 11, 290–1
military mobilisation, reform and preparation for war, 62–5
naval power, 116–17
nuclear strategy, 321–2
partisan warfare, 40
process of prioritisation, 65–7
strategic plans for the Far East, 70–3
strategy in the First World War, 73–7
Russian Civil War, 186–7, 250
Russian Revolution, 8
Russian State Archive of Military History (RGVIA), 59
Russian State Naval Archive (RGAVMF), 59
Russo-Japanese War, 7, 13, 15, 57, 65, 203, 250
adversaries and actors, 123–5
application of strategy, 138–41
available means, 136–8
causes, 62, 126–9
premises underlying and the prioritisation of strategic objectives, 129–35
Russian miscalculation of Japanese strategy, 543
Russian strategic plans, 70–3
sources, 122–3
Russo-Turkish wars, 57
1805–1812, 26
1877–1878, 57, 527
causes, 62
execution of strategy, 67–70
preparations, 64
Ryan, Mike, 414
Rybachenok, I. S., 59
Ryukyu Islands, 268

Saint-Domingue, 25, 30, 32
Saipan, Battle of, 265
Sakhalin, 126, 201–3
Salafism, 446
Salazar, António de Oliveira, 390
Samoa, 261, 263

sanctions, 8
Sandinistas, 444–5
Saratoga, Battle of, 331
Sasanians, 536
Saudi Arabia, 220, 368, 502
expansion of Al-Qaeda to, 451
placement of US forces in, 11, 486, 497, 500
threat to develop nuclear weapons, 327
withdrawal of US troops from, 17
Savimbi, Jonas, 297, 303
Saw Yan Paing, 50
Saxe, Maurice de, 20
Scarborough Shoal confrontation, 519
Schelling, Thomas C., 474
distinction between brute force and and coercive force, 337
theory of exerting 'graduated pressure', 334
Schroeder, Paul, 36
Scott, Winfield, 83, 88, 335
Scowcroft, Brent, 485, 493
Scud ballistic missiles, 220
Scud launchers, 222
Second Manassas, Battle of, 94
Second Sino-Japanese War, 144–5, 150–3, 252–3, 293
Second World War, 111, 341–2
actors, objectives and prioritisation, 234–9
adversaries, 230–2
application of strategy, 242–6
available means, 239–42
Chinese strategy, 145
development of strategic plans and practice, 15–16
German war plans, 188–9
path to war, 232–4
sources, 228–30
Soviet strategy, 181–4, 185–6, 191–202
the air war, 212–16
war in the Pacific. *See* Asia–Pacific War
Seeckt, Hans von, 211
self-determination, 165
Semyonov, Vladimir, 273
Sendic, Raul, 444
Serb Bosnian Army (VRS, *Vojska Republika Srpska*), 413, 419, 421, 422, 425
Serbia, 67, 160, 164, 414. *See also* Yugoslav War
Russian defence of, 73, 76, 164
Serbian Chetnik Movement (SČP, *Srpski Četnički Pokret*), 419
Serbian Guard (SG, *Srpska Garda*), 419
Serbian Security Service (SDB, *Služba Državna Bezbednost*), 413, 418, 420, 423

Index

Serbian Volunteer Guard (SDG, *Srpska Dobrovolska Garda*), 419
Serov, Ivan, 285, 287
Sétif massacre, 298
Seven Years' War, 9, 102
Shah of Iran. *See* Mohammad Reza Shah
Sha-ho, Battle of, 139
Shaka Zulu, 536
Shamil (Shamyl), 41
Shans, 48
Shaposhnikov, Boris, 188, 190, 192, 194
Sharif, Nawaz, 399–400
Sharpeville massacre, 298
Shastri, Lal Bahadur, 394, 404
Shatt al-Arab river, 487, 488, 489
Shays' Rebellion, 332
Shelepin, Alexander, 276
Sherman, William Tecumseh, 85, 95, 97–8, 336
Shia, 489, 493
Shia Islam, 487
Shinzo Abe, 520
Shunroku Hata, 144
Sibanda, Eliakim, 296
Siberia, 187
  Japanese expedition, 140
  US expedition, 340
Sicily, 100, 239, 245
siege warfare, 542
Sierra Leonean Civil War, 534
Silvester, Jeremy, *Re-Viewing Resistance in Namibian History*, 296
Simatović, Frenki, 420
Simpson, Thula, 296
Sinai War, 384
Singapore
  Allied troops in, 256
  Britain's naval strategy, 254, 269
  Japanese capture of, 260
Sino-Indian border conflict (1962), 404, 510–11, 521–3, 540
Sino-Indian border conflict (2020), 520
Sino-Soviet border conflict, 512–13
Sino-Soviet Treaty of Friendship, Alliance, and Mutual Assistance (1950), 353, 505
Siping Offensive, 153
Six Day War, 11, 371, 378, 382
slavery, 83
Slessor, John, 206
Slovakia, 234, 451
Slovenia, 414, 416, 425
Slovenian Territorial Defence (TO), 421
Smith, Rupert, 414, 541

Social Darwinism, 12
Socialist Federative Republic of Yugoslavia (SFRY), 415, 417, 421, 422
Sokolovskii Vasilii, 273, 284
Solidarnosc (Polish trade union), 289
Solomon Islands, 258, 261, 263–4, 268
Somalia
  Al-Qaeda franchises in, 451
  US intervention, 344
somatenes (Catalan home guards), 43
Somme, Battle of the, 171
Sone Arasuke, 125
sources, 3–4
South Africa, 294
  abandonment of its nuclear capability, 327
  entry to the Second World War, 233
  liberation movements, 304, 308. *See also* African National Congress
South Korea, 342. *See also* Korean War
  American nuclear presence in, 326
  approach to extended nuclear deterrence, 325
South Vietnam, 217–18, 504, 513
South West Africa People's Organisation (SWAPO), 296, 301, 306
Southern Rhodesia, 298
Soviet Union, Soviet military strategy
1917–1945
  actors, 184–6
  adversaries, 186–9
  sources, 181–4
  aftermath of First World War, 228
  air power theory, 210
  border clash with China, 512–13
  border clashes with Japan, 253
  Cold War strategy, 270
  East Prussian offensive, 200–1
  Eastern Front offensive, 200
  First World War historiography, 58–9
  interventions within the Soviet bloc
    actors, 272–6
    adversaries, 276–7
    available means, 280–1
    causes, 277–9
    execution of strategy, 284–9
    objectives, 279–80
    process of prioritisation, 282–4
    sources, 270–2
  invasion of Afghanistan, 343
    execution of strategy, 475–6
    influences on prioritisation, 474
    objectives, 468
    troops deployed, 472

Index

Soviet Union, Soviet military strategy (cont.)
  weapons technology, 471
  involvement in conflicts against Israel, 368–9, 371, 374, 382
  Manchurian operation (1945), 268
  modernisation of combat technology, 199
  nuclear strategy, 318, 321–2, 325–6
  relations with India, 396
  Second World War
    military means, 241–2
    objectives and prioritisation, 235–6
    operations and offensives, 194–203
    plans in the lead up to, 191–4, 232
    strategies to deter American nuclear use, 323–4
  support for wars of decolonisation, 8, 302
  ties with China, 146, 505
  ties with Pakistan, 404
  war with Japan (1945), 201–3
Soviet–Finnish War, 181, 185, 241
  causes, 189–90
  execution of strategy, 190–1
Soviet–Japanese Neutrality Pact (1941), 257
Soviet–Ukrainian–Polish War, 187
Spain, 110, 112
  acquisition of Louisiana, 30
  entry to the American War of Independence, 331
  guerrilla warfare, 40, 41–5
  Napoleonic Wars, 24–5, 30, 33, 114
  naval power, 103
  political influence of the train bombings of 2004, 436
Spanish Armada, 111
Spanish Civil War, 8, 210, 211, 233
  strategic bombing, 209
Spanish Socialist Workers Party, 436
Spanish–American War, 337–8
Specialist Anti-Terrorist Unit (SAJ), 420
Specialna Jedinica za Operacije (JSO), 420, 432
Spratly Islands, 516–17, 522
Spruance, Raymond, 265
Srebrenica massacre, 13, 221, 424, 432
Srinagar, 393
Stalin, Joseph, 185–6, 188, 214, 235, 239, 272, 351, 362
  and the Korean War, 352–3, 354–5, 504–5
  attack on Finland, 189–90
  death, 364
  excommunication of Tito, 274
  non-aggression pact with Nazi Germany, 233
  operation in Manchuria, 201–2
  strategy during the German invasion, 193–7
  views of his plans before and during the Second World War, 183–4
  vision for Soviet expansion, 16
Stalingrad, Battle of, 197–8, 244
Stalinism
  Putin's reversion to, 291
  Soviet shift from, 273–4, 289, 512
Stanišić, Jovica, 413–14, 423–4, 426
Stanton, Edwin, 93
Stark, Harold, 238, 256, 260, 261
Stavka, 185, 197, 235
Stein, Baron von, 24
Stevens, Simon, 296
Steyn, Martinus, 52
Stoker, Donald, *The Grand Design: Strategy and the U.S. Civil War*, 80
Strachan, Hew, 22
Stranka Demokratska Akcija (SDA), 414
strategy, definition, 1–2, 529
strategy, practice of, 529–30
  aim of creating disorder, 541–3
  opportunism, 536–7
  distraction, 539–40
  lack of control, 537–8
  raiding, 538–9
  responding to unfolding effects, 539
  performative logic, 535–6
  problematic concepts
    emotion/rationality binary, 526–7
    state/non-state binary, 527–9
    war/peace binary, 525–6
  problems and challenges, 543
    instability of objectives, 544
    mismatching objectives and resources, 544
  strategy as interaction, 543–4
  process of creating order, 540–1
  utilitarian perspective, 530–1
    control of populations, 533–5
    control of territories, 531–3
submarines, submarine warfare
  Asia–Pacific, 264, 266, 268
  First World War, 104, 169, 174–5
  Second World War, 240
Suchet, Louis, 42
Sudan, 368
Suez Canal
  attack during the 1973 Arab–Israeli War, 367
  crisis (1956), 284, 290, 370, 382
  raid (1915), 171, 173
Suga Yoshihide, 520
suicide bombers, 446, 501

Index

Sumatra, 267
Sumava Exercises, 281
Sun Chuanfang, 144, 146–8
Sungari River campaign, 153
Sunni Islam, 487
Sunzi, 148, 531
  The Art of War, 436, 541
Suppression of Enemy Air Defenses (SEAD), 216, 217, 218
surface-to-air missile (SAM) systems, 192, 217, 218, 222, 476
Suri, Abu Musab al-, 450
Suslov, Mihail, 285
Sutherland, Daniel, 46
Suvorov, Viktor, 183
Svoboda, Ludvík, 288
Sweden, 116, 123
  arms control and disarmament initiatives, 327
  convinced to reduce trade with the Central Powers, 174, 176
  and the Napoleonic Wars, 25–6
  recognition of the Soviet Union, 187
  war with Russia (1700–1721), 57
Switzerland, 174
  arms control and disarmament initiatives, 327
Syria, 17, 455
  Al-Qaeda in, 451, 453
  assumption of Israeli nuclear capability, 324
  conflict with Israel, 367, 368, 370, 375–6, 379, 382–3, 385, 539
  Soviet assistance, 368–9, 374
  conquered by Allied forces, 243
  establishment of Iranian military base in, 369, 376
  Israeli decision to return Golan Heights to, 371
  Israeli measures to prevent acquisition of nuclear capability, 322
Syrian Civil War, 542
Syrian Crisis (1840), 115

Taiping rebellion, 146
Taiwan, 353, 354–5, 358, 365, 504, 508–10, 517
  Chinese management of, 518–19, 523
  evacuated by Chiang Kai-shek, 154
  perceived threat to China, 522
  secured by Japan, 249
Taj Hotel attack, 401
Tajikistan, 468
Tajiks, 465

Taliban, 457–8, 463–5, 466, 544
  air strikes against, 222–3, 224
  execution of strategy, 476–7
  means, 472
  objectives, 468–70
  Pakistani support for, 407, 467
  poppy production during the rule of, 465
  prioritisation, 472–4
  sources, 458–9
Talleyrand, 22
Tambo, Oliver, 297
Tampico Affair, 339
Tannenberg, Battle of, 171
Tanzania, 300–1
Tariff War (1893–1894), 61
Taylor, William A., 349
technological innovation, 10
Tehran, US embassy seizure, 489
Tendi, Blessing-Miles, 296
Tennessee, 88, 90–92, 93–4, 97
  guerrilla warfare, 46–7
Terauchi Masatake, 125
terrorism and insurgency. *See also* African wars of decolonisation
  actors, 439–41
  adversaries, 441
  available means, 445–8
  causes, 441
  definitions and distinctions, 435–6, 442
  debates surrounding, 437–9
  execution of strategy, 449–56
  focoist approach, 443
  Maoist approach, 442–3
  objectives, 442–5
  process of prioritisation, 448–9
  sources, 436–7
terrorist attacks
  11 September 2001, 222, 346, 436, 450, 464, 469, 486
  Bombay (Mumbai), 401
  Indian parliament, 406
  Pulwama attack, 409
  Spanish train bombings, 436
  Tokyo subway, 446
  USS *Cole* bombings, 452
Thaçi, Hashim, 414
Thailand, 259, 358
The War of the Rebellion: A Compilation of the Official Records of the Union and Confederate Armies, 79
Thibaw, King of Burma, 48, 49
Tibet, 62, 441, 510, 511
Tilsit, 24, 26, 29, 31

583

Index

Timoshenko, Semyon, 185, 191
Tinian, 265, 267
Tirpitz Plan, 104, 117
Tito, Josip Brod, 274, 421
Todorov, Nicola, 30
Tōgō Heihachirō, 135
Tojo Hideki, 258, 265
Tokyo
   considered for atomic bombing, 312, 314
   firebombing of, 13, 267, 313
   terrorist subway attack, 446
Tomás, António, 296
Tone, John, 42
Toshizo Nishio, 144
Trafalgar, Battle of, 32, 109
Transcaucasia, 187
Trans-Siberian Railway project, 70, 127–9, 132, 133
Treaty of Brest-Litovsk (1918), 176
Treaty of Commerce and Navigation (1911), 253
Treaty of Finkenstein (1807), 31
Treaty of Ghent (1814), 333
Treaty of Guadalupe Hidalgo (1848), 334
Treaty of London (1915), 179
Treaty of Paris (1783), 331, 333
Treaty of Paris (1814), 105
Treaty of Paris (1856), 116
Treaty of Paris (1898), 338
Treaty of Portsmouth (1905), 140
Treaty of Rapallo (1922), 187
Treaty of Riga (1921), 187, 228
Treaty of Tilsit (1807), 29
Treaty of Utrecht (1713), 104, 113
Treaty of Versailles (1919), 226, 228, 232
   Hitler's disregard of, 230
Treaty on the Non-Proliferation of Nuclear Weapons (1968), 275, 327
Trenchard, Hugh, 206, 207
Trenton, Battle of, 331
Trident Conference (1943), 239
Tripartite Pact (1940), 256
Triple Alliance (1882), 162
Triple Entente, 62, 141, 164
Trnopolje concentration camp, 13, 431
Trotter, William, 46
Truman, Harry S., 202, 239
   appointment of MacArthur to head UNF in Korea, 347
   Korean strategy, 342, 350–1, 355, 356, 358, 362
   prioritisation, 360
   orders halt to further atomic bombing, 315
Tudjman, Franjo, 414

Tukhachevskii, Mikhail, 188, 210
Tunisia, 231, 244, 301, 303
   support for anti-colonial resistance, 302
Turkey, 188, 230. *See also* Russo-Turkish wars
   deterrence of Russian aggression towards, 116
   entry to the First World War, 74
   provision of troops in the Korean War, 358
   risk of nuclear attack, 325
   status of during Second World War, 234
Turner, J. M. W., 114
'Two Thousand Words' manifesto, 278

U Ottama, 49
Uighurs, 439
Ukraine, 528
   abandonment of nuclear capability, 327
   expansion of Soviet borders towards the Western region of, 192
   German intentions to divide with Poland, 188
   rejection of nuclear weapons, 327
   Soviet fears of German advancement on, 193
   Soviet operations to drive Germany out of, 200
   war with Poland and the Soviet Union, 187
Ukraine War, 11, 14, 290–1, 534
   Russian miscalculation of Ukrainian resistance, 544
   Russian objectives, 7
   siege warfare, 542
Ulbricht, Walter, 277, 279
Ulm, Battle of, 18
Umayyad Caliphate, 530, 532
uMkhonto we Sizwe (MK), 297, 299, 300, 301, 304–5
União das Populações de Angola (UPA, National Front for the Liberation of Angola), 297
União Nacional para a Independência Total de Angola (UNITA, National Union for the Total Independence of Angola), 297, 301, 303, 306
United Fruit Company, 339
United Nations
   Assembly, 355
   International Criminal Tribunal for the former Yugoslavia (ICTY), 411, 424
   International Residual Mechanism for the International Criminal Tribunals (IRMICT), 411
   involvement in the Indo-Pakistani conflicts, 392–3, 404

Index

involvement in the Yugoslav War, 414, 421
involvement with African insurgency movements, 307
operations in Korea (UN Command, UNC, UN Forces, UNF), 347, 359
   composition of the forces, 358
   crossing of the 38th Parallel, 354
   military leadership, 351
   objectives, 356–8
   sources, 349
   strategy, 360, 361–3
Security Council Resolution 1441, 494
Security Council Resolution 598, 484
United States. *See also* American Civil War; Asia–Pacific War; Gulf War; Iraq War; Korean War
   civilian authority, 161
   Cold War conflicts, 342–4
   deterrence of Iraqi invasion of Saudi Arabia, 11
   exertion of economic pressure on Japan, 8, 256
   First World War, 340
   economic influence, 174
   humanitarian assistance, 344–5
   imperial wars, 337–9
   influence of the air power theory of strategic attack, 205–9
   interventions in Mexico, 339
   involvement in the Indo-Pakistani wars, 395, 398, 400
   involvement in the Yugoslav War, 414
   military pact with Pakistan (1954), 404
   naval power. *See* US Navy
   nuclear strategy, 318–19
   objection to granting Japan exclusive rights in Korea, 127
   overseas missions (1912–1938), 340–1
   post-Cold War conflicts, 344–5
   provision of assistance to Israel, 374
   provision of economic and military assistance to Pakistan, 397
   Second World War, 341–2
   military means, 242
   plans for, 231, 238–9, 254–5
   strength of following First World War, 228
   threat to British economic and naval dominance, 118–19
   war in Afghanistan
   execution of strategy, 476–7
   objectives, 469
   prioritisation, 474
   troops deployed, 472
   wars of consolidation, 332–3
   wars of expansion, 333–4
   wars on the northern and southern plains, 337
Unmanned Aerial Vehicles (UAVs, drones), 224
UNPROFOR, 421, 422
Unsan, Battle of, 357
US Air Corps Tactical School, 206
US Air Force, 217, 518
US Army, 213, 242
   counterinsurgency operations in the Philippines, 338
   treatment of Native Americans, 337
US Army Air Corps (US Army Air Forces, USAAF), 242
US Constitution, 332
US Department of Defense, 344, 345
US Embassy bombings (East Africa, 1998), 452
US Joint Army and Navy Board, 238, 254
US Marine Corps, 255
US Marine Corps Air Wing, 217
US Navy
   Asia–Pacific War
   counteroffensives, 504–5
   deployment to Pearl Harbor, 255
   Japanese attack at Pearl Harbor, 341
   Japanese kamikaze attacks, 268
   Japanese objectives, 257–8
   losses at Guadalcanal, 263
   plans, 254–5
   Korean War, 217
   operations in North Korea and Taiwan, 355
   operations in the Great Lakes regions, 333
   Pacific Fleet, 242, 254, 255, 256
US State Department, Foreign Relations of the United States (FRUS), 349
USS *Cole*, 452
USS *Maine*, 337
USS *Missouri*, 269
Ustinov, Dmitrii, 289
Uzbekistan, 468
Uzbeks, 463, 465, 468

Vajpaye, Atal Bihari, 399
Valencia, 42
Van Dorn, Earl, 94
Van Evera, Steven, 408
Van Fleet, James A., 351, 363
Vandiver, Frank E., 82
Vatutin, Nikolai, 198
Velez, Manuel Marulanda, 444
Vicksburg, Battle of, 95–7

Index

Vietnam
  border clash with China (1979), 514–16
  clash with China over the Paracel Islands, 513–14
  conflict with China over the Spratly Islands, 516
  territorial issues, 532
Vietnam War, 16, 111, 294, 343, 445
  air power strategy, 217–18
  fear of the use of nuclear weapons, 317
  influence on Soviet intervention in Czechoslovakia, 284
Vikings, 532
Villa, Francisco 'Pancho', 11, 339
Vimy Ridge, Battle of, 171
violent non-state actors (VNSAs), 439
Virginia Peninsula Campaign, 92, 93, 95
Vladivostok, 70–2, 124, 127, 128, 133, 134–5, 139, 340
Võ Nguyên Giáp, 293, 443
Volkogonov, D. A., 181
Voroshilov, Kliment, 189, 190

Waag, Ian van der, 296
Wake Island, 258, 259, 351
Walachia, 26
Wang Jingwei, 145
war crimes, 386, 411, 433–4
War of 1812, 334
War of Attrition, 378, 382
War of the Austrian Succession, 20
War of the Spanish Succession, 113
War on Terror, 17, 295
War Plan Orange, 232, 254–5
War Plan Rainbow 5, 238
War Plan Red-Orange, 232
Warden, John, 219, 221
Warsaw, 171
Warsaw Pact, 272–6, 280, 349
  air power capability, 218
  collapse, 16, 290
  deployment of Soviet troops within the countries of, 281
  Hungarian withdrawal from, 278
  sources, 272
  Soviet prioritisation of socialism over sovereignty within, 283
  support for Soviet interventions, 287–9, 291
  war plan, 270
Washington City, 333
Washington Navy Conference (1921–1922), 254

Washington, George
  defusion of the Whiskey Rebellion, 332
  military strategy in the American War of Independence, 331–2
Wavell, Archibald, 260
Weapons of Mass Destruction (WMD), 220, 446
Weber, Max, 528
Wehrmacht, 15, 192, 195–7, 200–1, 232–3, 234, 240, 243–6, 341
Weigert, Stephen, 296
Weigley, Russell, *The American Way of War*, 82
  A History of United States Military Strategy and Policy, 329–30
Weimar Republic, 226
Wellington, Duke of, 42, 44
Wells, H. G., 206
Wessels, André, 51
West Germany, 288
  entry to NATO, 273
  nuclear threat from the Soviet bloc, 325
Western Front, 170, 171, 173, 176–7
Wever, Walther, 211
Whiskey Rebellion, 332
Wilberg, Helmut, 211
Wilhelm II, Kaiser, 160, 178
William III, King of England, 101, 110, 112, 113
Williams, Christian, 296
Wilson Center Digital Archive, 272
Wilson International Center, 349
Wilson, Woodrow, 107, 178
  commitment to Russian and Siberian expeditions, 340
  First World War strategy, 340–1
  Fourteen Points, 165, 178, 340, 545
  interventions in Mexico, 339
Witte, Sergei, 124
Wolfowitz, Paul, 486
Woods, Kevin, 479, 482
Wu Peifu, 144, 146–7

Xe Services, 439
Xhosa, 41
Xi Jinping, 364, 503, 518–20
Xi'an Incident, 150
Xu Xiangqian, 361

Yafeng Xia, 354
Yakubovskii, Ivan, 275, 287
Yamamoto Gonnohyōe, 125
Yamamoto Isoruku, 258, 261, 262–3
Yan Xishan, 147

Yasuji Okamura, 144
Ye Jianying, 143
Yemen, 453
    Chinese involvement in evacuation of
        citizens, 521
    decrease in Islamic State attacks, 455
    expansion of Al-Qaeda to, 451
Yijiangshan, 508–10
Yom Kippur War, 11, 324
Young, Benjamin, 354
Ypres, Battle of, 171
Yuan Shikai, 146
Yugoslav People's Army (JNA, *Jugoslovenska Narodna Armja*), 413, 417–19, 421–2, 423, 425, 426–7, 428, 429
Yugoslav War, 11
    actors, 413–14
    adversaries, 414
    atrocities, 13
    available means, 417–23
    causes, 415
    execution of strategy, 425–7
    concentration camps, 13, 430–1
    elimination, 431–3
    preparation and provocation, 427–9
    takeover and the use of force, 429–30
    NATO air campaign, 221–2
    objectives, 416–17
    process of prioritisation, 423–5
    sources, 221–2
Yugoslavia, 5, 273
    acquisition of Fiume, 228
    consultations with Soviet Union, 274, 278
    German forces sent to, 245

guerrilla forces, Second World War, 244
Yugoslavian Territorial Defence Force (TO, *Teritorialna Odbrana*), 417, 428

Zakharov, M. V., 181
Zawahiri, Ayman al-, 450–1
    General Guidelines for Jihad, 454
Zayonchkovsky, A. M., 59
Zhang Aiping, 509
Zhang Shuguang, 142
Zhang Xueliang, 148, 150
Zhang Zhen, 143
Zhang Zongchang, 147–8
Zhang Zuolin, 144, 146, 148
Zhao Ziyang, 503, 516
Zhdanov, Andrei, 190
Zhihua Shen, 354
Zhilinsky, Yakov Grigoryevich, 66
Zhou Enlai, 150, 350, 359
Zhou Shizhao, 355
Zhu De, 143, 148
Zhukov, Georgy, 190, 193, 195, 196, 201, 285
Zia-ul-Haq, Muhammad, 397, 400–1
Zimbabwe African National Liberation Army (ZANLA), 301
Zimbabwe African National Union (ZANU), 297, 299, 301, 303, 306
Zimbabwe African People's Union (ZAPU), 297, 299, 301, 303, 306
Zimbabwe, war of liberation, 294, 296, 299, 301, 303, 306, 308
Zoroastrianism, 536
Zulu, 53